HISTORY OF ANCIENT GEOGRAPHY

BY

J. OLIVER THOMSON

Professor of Latin in the University of Birmingham

CAMBRIDGE
AT THE UNIVERSITY PRESS
1948

Printed in Great Britain at the University Press, Cambridge
(Brooke Crutchley, University Printer)
and published by the Cambridge University Press
(Cambridge, and Bentley House, London)
Agents for U.S.A., Canada, and India: Macmillan

HISTORY OF
ANCIENT GEOGRAPHY

VXORVM CARISSIMAE
ET PIAE MEMORIAE
MATRIS

CONTENTS

Illustrations   *page* ix

Preface   xi

Introduction   1

Chapter I. EARLY HORIZONS   4
§1. The Phantom Peoples. §2. Egypt. §3. Babylonia and the Hittites. §4. The Aegean World and Homer. §5. Assyrians, Phoenicians and Hebrews. §6. The Chinese. §7. Early Theory.

Chapter II. THE GREEK HORIZON TO HERODOTUS   44
§1. The Colonial Movement. §2. The Western Line. §3. The North-Eastern Line. §4. The South. §5. The East. *Appendix:* Between Herodotus and Alexander.

Chapter III. GREEK THEORY TO ARISTOTLE   94
§1. The Earth-Disk. §2. The Earth as a Globe.

Chapter IV. FROM ALEXANDER TO ERATOSTHENES   123
§1. The East. §2. Africa. §3. Europe.

Chapter V. THEORY IN THE SAME PERIOD   154

Chapter VI. THE ROMAN REPUBLIC   169
§1. The East. *Appendix:* The Chinese Horizon. §2. Africa. §3. Europe.

Chapter VII. THEORY IN THE SAME PERIOD   202

Chapter VIII. THE GREAT DAYS OF THE ROMAN EMPIRE   222
§1. Times and Writers. §2. Europe.

Chapter IX. THE SAME: AFRICA   256

Chapter X. THE SAME: ASIA   282

CONTENTS

Chapter XI. THEORY IN THE SAME PERIOD *page* 320

Chapter XII. THE DECLINE 351

Note on Books and Abbreviations 392

Addenda 395

Index 414

ILLUSTRATIONS

PLATE I *facing page* 38
    A. Babylonian map of the world
    B. Coin of Panticapaeum
    C. Coin of Cyrene
    D. Arabian coin with owl of Athens

PLATE II *facing page* 174
A, B. Coins of Graeco-Bactrian invaders of India
    C. Coin of Augustus with Capricorn and globe
    D. Athena on a seal-impression found in Chinese Turkestan
    E. Britannia welcomes Carausius

TEXT-FIGURES

1.	Egyptian ships at Punt	*page* 8
2.	Egyptian map of roads to the gold mines	38
3.	Western Greek colonies	50
4.	Black Sea colonies	58
5.	Scythian trade-route	61
6.	The same	63
7.	Cup of Arcesilas II	67
8.	Hanno's voyage	75
9.	The Near East	83
10.	Frame of the Ionian map	97
11.	Map of Hecataeus	99
12.	Map of Herodotus	99
13.	Zones	116
14.	Alexander's march	125
15.	Eratosthenes: map of the East	135
16.	Eratosthenes: map of the West	142
17.	Dicaearchus: zones	154
18.	Eratosthenes: measurement of the earth	159
19.	Eratosthenes: zones	163
20.	Eratosthenes: latitudes	164
21.	Eratosthenes: length-line	165
22.	The same	165
23.	Silk routes	179
24.	Spain	187

ILLUSTRATIONS

25.	Gaul	page 191
26.	Strabo's Europe	194
27.	Orb of Crates	203
28.	Latitudes of Hipparchus	206
29.	Spain and Gaul (Ptolemy)	232
30.	Ptolemy's Britain	236
31.	German tribes	243
32.	Germany (Ptolemy)	245
33.	Danube frontier	247
34.	Danube (Ptolemy)	250
35.	Ptolemy's Sarmatia in Europe	251
36.	Ptolemy's Sarmatia Asiatica and vicinity	253
37.	N. W. Africa	257
38-9.	Ptolemy: N. W. Africa (*a*) and (*b*)	260
40.	Libya	263
41.	Ptolemy's Cyrenaica-Egypt	264
42.	Africa	265
43.	Juba's Nile theory	268
44.	Africa (Ptolemy)	269
45.	E. Africa (Ptolemy)	276
46.	Porro's map (from Ortelius), 1598	279
47.	Asia Minor and eastern frontier	283
48.	Ptolemy: Near East	287
49.	Iran (Ptolemy)	292
50.	East of Caspian (Ptolemy)	293
51.	Arabia (Ptolemy)	296
52.	Arabia (modern)	297
53.	India	303
54.	Ceylon (Ptolemy's and real)	304
55.	Ptolemy's India	305
56.	Silk-roads over the Roof of Asia	308
57.	Ptolemy's Serica and vicinity	310
58.	Far East (Ptolemy's and real)	314
59.	Ptolemy: length-line	338
60.	Ptolemy: latitudes	341
61.	Suggested projection of Marinus	344
62.	Ptolemy's first projection	344
63.	Ptolemy's second projection	345
64.	Peutinger map: west section of Europe and N. Africa	380
65.	The same: east section of Asia	380
66.	Notions of Cosmas	387

PREFACE

For various reasons (about to be mentioned) this subject is seldom well understood. It deserves to be treated in its full scope, as here conceived, and only so can it be given its due, no more but no less, in the story of geographical discovery and science as a whole. There is no doubt that a comprehensive and critical survey is needed. With the difficulties of the evidence and the mass of detail to be controlled, it is a hard enterprise. If the present effort seems ambitious, it has cost the writer more years than he foresaw or than he sometimes cares to look back upon.

The afterthoughts come crowding in a subject of such scope and complexity. By its very nature it leads in every direction to the borders of the unknown, and few subjects are therefore better worth research. The task here undertaken involves the whole range of ancient history and literature, and needs doing in their interest, while it is important, of course, for the intelligent study of geography itself, and for the general history of science, which is now receiving very marked attention.

Such a book is vastly the better of having abundant references, as the original sources are of every kind and value and still variously interpreted in many important matters. There is added at the end a general note on bibliography and on abbreviations used.

It is only fair to this book to state that it was sent to press in Sept. 1943. Advantage has been taken of the delay in publication to add a good deal, mainly to the notes; but one cannot help having missed something of value in recent foreign work which is still not easily accessible under present conditions. Some recent writings have been noticed in final Addenda: the untidiness could not be avoided, and it has been freely used to make amends for various omissions.

To the staff of the University Library I am indebted for much trouble and some valuable references. The City Library has often been useful. Among many libraries elsewhere, special thanks are due to that of the University of Glasgow for rich browsing in several vacations.

J. O. T.

BIRMINGHAM

AUGUST 1947

INTRODUCTION

THE achievement of ancient times in some kinds of science has been adequately described. But in at least one it still needs a thorough restatement and revaluation. Somehow the ancient contribution to geography, as regards both theory and practical discovery, is seldom studied intelligently and as a whole. Very few seem to understand just how good and how bad it was, on the sum total of the evidence: geographers are not familiar with the original sources, while classical scholars pass by some of the most valuable as being of no great literary merit, if not quite unreadable like Ptolemy (of his mapping, and any that led up to his, they rarely attempt serious discussion). The lack of systematic knowledge of the subject is obvious, even in good historians and other scholars, who, when they find occasion to deal with such matters, are often strangely uncritical and superficial.

How much of the world became known to the Greeks and Romans at various periods? If this refers only to the range of war and colonization, such things are usually prominent in record, and the question is easily answered by a survey of the history, with the limelight focused on the outposts. But how much farther did trade and exploration go, and what hearsay was picked up about regions beyond the farthest to be visited? On all this the information is rather meagre and leaves plenty of gaps and ragged edges. Ancient historians were not interested in trade, so that its scale and enterprise are uncertain: there have been some too modernistic estimates, and it is tempting to be over-picturesque, but prudent scholars are chary of sending argosies and caravans over the map without reasonably good data. (Some such there are, indeed, as for the silk-route across the heart of Asia and the monsoon sailings to India and at least one excursion far beyond to the sea-gates of China.) Of exploration for its own sake, for pure adventure or the pleasure of adding to knowledge, fairly sure instances are hard to find: the clearest is the northern voyage of Pytheas of Marseilles, with his observations of the sun and the lengthening day, important for the new mapping on the basis of a spherical earth. There was little, it seems, of the itch of moderns for penetrating to wild and unsafe places. One reason is obvious: the means of transport and the equipment in weapons and instruments and medicines were poor and not to be compared, of course, with those of recent times. But plainly there was some want of will or energy to explore parts quite within reach, or the exploration was very spasmodic: so the west coast of Africa was never well mapped, though the

Romans were established in Morocco and Hanno of Carthage had sailed far down centuries before. Some questions remained unsolved after being debated for ages and more than once arousing official interest: so no one really approached the sources of the Nile (yet Nero's scouts went quite far up, and a skipper heard from Zanzibar of the great lakes). The advance of discovery was irregular and slow, and it was not even sure: there were bad relapses. Thus the Caspian lake was made a gulf of the outer Ocean, strangely enough just when Greek conquerors reached its southern coast and sent out explorers; by Ptolemy's time it was again a lake, but the old error was to revive, to the great damage of the whole map of Asia.

The ancient writings more or less directly concerned will be described in their proper places. They are of very various scope and quality. There is a shortage of a kind of travel report which we like and expect, full of colour and personal interest and the exhilaration of difficulty and danger overcome and new things seen. We are ill served especially for some of the more notable journeys. Hanno's own document is tantalizingly brief. We miss the accounts of India by Alexander's companions and a later envoy at Patna, though they are fairly well known through many who used them. For the agents of the silk-merchant Maes and for the skipper named as going beyond Malaya there are only dry notices at third hand. Pytheas is represented by scraps, mostly from writers who thought him a liar. For an alleged voyage all round Africa there is a paragraph of Herodotus. The feat, which makes the long Portuguese effort before Vasco da Gama look rather silly, is now commonly accepted, too lightly, if one considers how very little the ancients ever learnt of the continent; at best it must remain doubtful, and the doubt is grave indeed, affecting our whole sense of proportion about these matters. Unfortunately, much else is questionable in the knowledge shown of distant parts, and one must often stop to deal with such obscurities. It is a pity, and does not make for ease of writing or of reading, but the evidence should be honestly stated as no better than it is.

This is a subject which crosses many frontiers, and it is desirable to bring in what other peoples than the Greeks and Romans have to say, like the remarkable Chinese information derived from the contacts maintained by the silk-trade. Also, by way of introduction, one must give some idea of what was known to the earlier civilizations. The task is obviously risky for any but specialists; nevertheless, for the sake of completeness and perspective, it should be attempted. Most of the written sources are accessible in books like Breasted's *Ancient Records of Egypt*. Archaeology helps by checking and sometimes supplementing: its data may be enough to prove direct trade and so a geographical horizon, but often they are hard to interpret in this sense; elsewhere it may have a negative value, by failing to support an uncritical reading of meagre and doubtful record, like the exaggerated statements long made about the Phoenicians.

When all is said, the service of the ancients to discovery was not highly distinguished, though their known world was not a mere *orbis terrarum* round the Mediterranean lake. Far more important is the other half of the matter, which receives far less attention, their contribution to theory. At first, and by some people long afterwards, the earth was supposed a flat (or nearly flat) disk, as it appears to be, and there were various efforts to map the 'inhabited earth' and also—a hopeless business—to account for climates and such phenomena on this assumption. It is a serious question just how and when the earth-globe was accepted and applied to geography. Eratosthenes made a very clever calculation of its size, one of the best things in ancient science (it is incredible, by the way, that some general handbooks to the classics do not even try to explain his method!). Many good authorities think his result almost exactly right, but only by making him give a special value to the stade (a doubt about this unit unhappily pervades the rest of the subject too). Henceforth some had the will to produce a scientific map, but none had the necessary data: there was no good means of observing longitudes, and the prescribed work of collecting a mass of latitudes was never carried out, so that too much depended on dead reckonings of voyages and other inaccurate measurements. With Ptolemy comes the final effort of mapping, surprisingly good and bad in many ways. Its chief features are its worst mistakes: he, and still more Marinus, overstretched the Old World round the globe, and thus encouraged Columbus to sail west to seek Asia, and, as Columbus himself thought, to find it; there was also the fancy of a great southern unknown land, which was to cost centuries of exploring to disprove completely. After Ptolemy there was a long decline, until nearly everybody again thought the earth flat and some had notions about it queerer than any held a thousand years before: all this could happen because the Romans had not the minds even to keep science at the level already reached, and because Christians believed themselves bound by a few phrases of antique Jews.

CHAPTER I

EARLY HORIZONS

§ 1. THE PHANTOM PEOPLES

FAR the longer stretch of the past of mankind was over before writing was invented, and has therefore been lost beyond recall, except for such an outline, shadowy at best, as can be inferred from tools and other mute relics. By then men of modern type, to say nothing of their human or not quite human predecessors, had lived and died for perhaps 30,000 years, anyhow some span beside which the whole of recorded history since is quite brief. The earliest such men, those of the latter part of the Old Stone Age, are best known from evidence found in western Europe, though they had come in from elsewhere: possibly they had evolved in the north Sahara, then a wide grassland, and had crossed by the land-bridges which still connected Africa with Spain and Italy. Besides their tools of flint and bone they have left wonderful drawings and paintings of the animals—reindeer and wild horse, bison and mammoth—which roamed in a sub-arctic climate as far south as the Pyrenees; the art is so vivid because it was a form of magic to ensure good hunting. They remained hunters, living in small hordes and sometimes straying far in pursuit of their prey. Then conditions changed: the climate softened with the dwindling of the ice-sheets, and forest spread. The northern fauna retreated, and so, it seems, did many of the hunters, while those who stayed were reduced to a miserable food-gathering. After an obscure transition there appeared groups of men with new arts, making pots and grinding and polishing stone for tools and weapons. What is more important, they had discovered new ways of life, how to produce a regular supply of food. Somewhere a remnant of the hunters had learnt to tame animals and live on their herds; somewhere too they had begun to sow seeds of wild grain (perhaps in nearer Asia, with a secondary centre in north-east Africa?). It was probably from the south and south-east that the Neolithic men entered Europe, and a chief line of invasion seems to have been up the Danube. Many other drifts of population are guessed for these long ages to account for the differentiation and distribution of races dark-white and white, black and yellow. (Man had begun in a temperate region, probably, and black skin and kinky hair, for instance, were special adaptations to a torrid climate.) There was also some movement of wares, very little among the hunters but more with comparatively settled peoples: thus a fine flint of Touraine found its way to the Swiss lake-dwellers, as did northern amber and Indian

Ocean shells. It is likely that these things were handed slowly along by 'dumb barter' or some such primitive form of exchange at tribal frontiers, and they do not prove the activity of far-travelling traders. (Yet there are remarkable things to account for, like the blue stones of Stonehenge brought apparently by sea and river all the way from the hills of Pembrokeshire.) What any prehistoric people called itself or its neighbours is not ascertainable, of course: the archaeologist can merely apply his own clumsy labels, Magdalenians or First Danubians or this battle-axe or bell-beaker folk or that painted pottery 'culture'. He detects various interrelations, invasions or slow spreads of peoples or radiations of 'influences' (the very direction may be uncertain). A good deal of all this is highly speculative. The data are hardly enough, and the time-table is too large and vague, to enable safe guessing of the outlook of any particular group. Much of the world remains in this dim twilight long after history has begun in a few more favoured lands. It is to these earliest civilizations that we turn for the first information of geographical horizons, and in general we find that this is full enough on near neighbours but seldom goes far afield. From the same sources we hear the kind of notions first conceived about the earth as a whole and the workings of the universe which affect it, many of them easy to see, like the apparent movements of the sun, but desperately hard to explain and long explained only by myths.

§ 2. EGYPT

The Egyptian civilization emerged from an already long 'pre-dynastic' development into history at a time now generally put not before 3500 B.C. Three main periods are relatively well known from their own written records. There are the Old Kingdom of the pyramid-building dynasties IV–VI, and the Middle Kingdom of dynasties XI–XII, neither absolutely datable owing to the uncertain length of the dark age of barbarian invasion which followed: the short chronology usually makes them 2850–2360 and 2160–1788 B.C.[1] Lastly there is the New Kingdom or Empire of dynasties XVIII–XX, far the best documented and certainly dated as 1580–1100 B.C.

Many of the records scattered down this whole great stretch of time concern relations of war, diplomacy and trade, and they seem numerous and consistent enough to give a fair notion of the geographical horizon, which at its widest is very limited. (The argument from silence is sometimes risky, but less so when the silence lasts a score of centuries, and serious historians cannot ignore it so cavalierly as a few writers who imagine

---

1 Hall, *C.A.H.* I, 170, eases them back to 3100–2600 and 2375–2000 B.C.: Kees, *Aegypten*, 1933, has 2684–2270 and 2060–1788 B.C.: Sewell, *Legacy of Egypt*, 1942, has 2690–2294 and 2085–1777 B.C. Records translated in Breasted, *Anc. Records of Egypt*, 5 vols. 1906–7.

'prospectors' or emigrants spreading 'civilization' far and wide from the Old Kingdom.)¹ Of exploration for its own sake, a thing rare throughout ancient times, there is hardly a trace. This people did not even think of finding the sources of the river to which they owed everything, the most wonderful of rivers, carrying the far southern rains through a desert to lay out a ribbon and fan of fertile mud; they had occasion to go some way upstream, but were content to leave the question almost unasked or answered only by childish myths.

They ventured early enough on the sea. The Delta coast was harbourless and difficult, with its dunes and swamps, and the native timber very poor for ship-building, but they had the advantage of long practice with river-boats: the Nile was their natural highway, and a handy wind blowing upstream much of the year encouraged the art of sailing. Snefru, a king just before the builder of the Great Pyramid, sent forty ships to bring wood, probably fir rather than the famous cedar of Lebanon. These are the first sea-going ships mentioned, though others had no doubt prepared the way for so big an expedition. Probably they were built of imported wood themselves and were, like those shown on a slightly later relief, modified river-boats. They had oars and sail and a tripod mast which could be lowered; with their high stem and stern they were apt to hog or rise amidships, but this was corrected by a strong truss. Gradually ships were improved until they carried thirty rowers and a very broad sail on curved yards. They were hardly so slender or low in the water as the artists drew them; yet at best they remained small oared galleys with very little cargo-room, the sail was used only with the wind straight behind, and the steering-gear was primitive. How regularly the sea was used at various periods it seems hard to judge: the accounts leave an impression that long voyages were intermittent, made only on royal service, and beyond the means of private merchants. It is notable that these last are seldom mentioned in any kind of text.²

The most commendable voyages were on the Red Sea (the name does not

---

1 Against 'diffusionist' fallacies, Toynbee, *Study of History*, 1934, I, 222, 428: Wheeler in *Eur. Civ.* ed. Eyre, 1935, II, 186. Limited, Ralph Turner, *The Great Cultural Traditions*, 1941, I, 213.

2 Erman-Ranke, *Aeg. und aeg. Leben im Altertum*, 1923, pp. 494, 587: Glanville, *Egyptians*, 1933, pp. 47–9: Petrie, *Social Life in Anc. Eg.* 1923, p. 20 (little trade): Breasted, *C.A.H.* II, 97 (some private): Kees, op. cit. p. 103: E. Meyer, *Gesch. des Altertums*, I, 1⁵, 282 (not private): intermittent, Hornell, *Antiquity*, 1941, pp. 233, 241–2: Turner, op. cit. pp. 181, 293, citing Dykmans, *Hist. écon. et soc. de l'anc. Egypte*, 1936. Ships, Köster, *Ant. Seewesen*, 1923, pp. 19, 42 (praises Red Sea voyages): Kees, p. 116: J. H. Rose, *Man and the Sea*, 1935, pp. 21, 51: Clowes, *Sailing Ships*, 1930, I, 17–25: Van Loon, *Ships*, 1925, pp. 40–2 (not over 60 tons): Boumphrey, *Story of the Ship*, 1933, pp. 16–22. Fir, C. D. Forde, *Ancient Mariners*, 1927, p. 29.

seem so old, and later the Greeks had no clear notion how they came by it). The gulf of Suez was soon disliked for persistent north winds, besides rocks and currents, and as making the sea-way too long; so the starting-point was shifted down towards Kosseir. (The head of the sea has always been disliked by sailing ships, and a British force sent from India against Napoleon landed at Kosseir.) The approach was from the Nile, five days' march over a rocky desert, the 'red land'; it was otherwise useful only for granite and patches of quartz-gold and gems (emeralds are mentioned later by the Romans). Beyond, for a thousand miles and more, was a barren coast with few safe roadsteads and fringed with coral reefs, but convenient north-west winds prevailed in summer, and south-east winds helped the return to about Suakin, after which oars were needed. The goal is more or less vaguely 'the divine land', where the sun-god rises, Punt, or 'the frankincense terraces'. It is generally understood as the African shore from about Massawa to Somaliland, and more especially the latter, though south Arabia, later equally noted for incense, may also have been visited.

Already the old kings got from Punt incense, gold, fine woods, and a dwarf; whether such things came always direct and by sea is not quite clear, but one man boasts of having been there eleven times. In the Middle Kingdom Henu, after providing the desert road with wells and military posts, built and sent off a ship for incense; another officer thanks his gods for his safe return to port. Such a man is the hero of a popular story: he is blown away to be wrecked on an island of Punt ruled by a bearded serpent, and this strange person, when another ship comes along, lets him go with incense and ivory and other treasure, and then vanishes with the island into the sea (there is something eerie about the place, which may be partly a mythical island of the dead).[1]

About 1500 B.C., apparently after a long interruption in the voyages, Hatshepsut sent for incense-trees to adorn her beautiful temple, wishing to 'make for Amon a second Punt in his garden'. Coloured reliefs depict her five ships with their stately sails; her captains barter at the incense terraces with the native chief, who wears rings on his legs and has a wife of a monstrous fatness (these people are not negroes but seem backward kinsmen of the Hamite stock). There is a village of round huts on piles.

---

1 So Maspero, *Contes populaires*³, 1906, p. 84, approved by Reitzenstein, *Hellenist. Wundererzählungen*, 1906, p. 115: Erman, *Lit. der Aegypter*, 1923, pp. 56–61: Budge, *Lit. of Eg.* 1914, pp. 207–13: Hall, *C.A.H.* I, 348. Old Kingdom, Hall, ibid. pp. 289, 295: Breasted, *A.R.E.* I, 70, 162. M.K., ibid. pp. 208–10, 275. Punt includes S. Arabia, Hitti, *Hist. of Arabs*², 1940, p. 34. Somali, Drower, *L.E.* p. 28. Rose, op. cit. after Budge moves Punt on to Jubaland or even Mombasa. Punt or Pwene(t) not beyond Massawa, Wainwright in *Man*, 1947, p. 143. Name Red, see p. 81, n. 2, p. 133, n. 1. Old Kingdom travellers, also Newberry, *J.E.A.* 1938, pp. 182–4. Emeralds, Plin. xxxvii, 66.

8

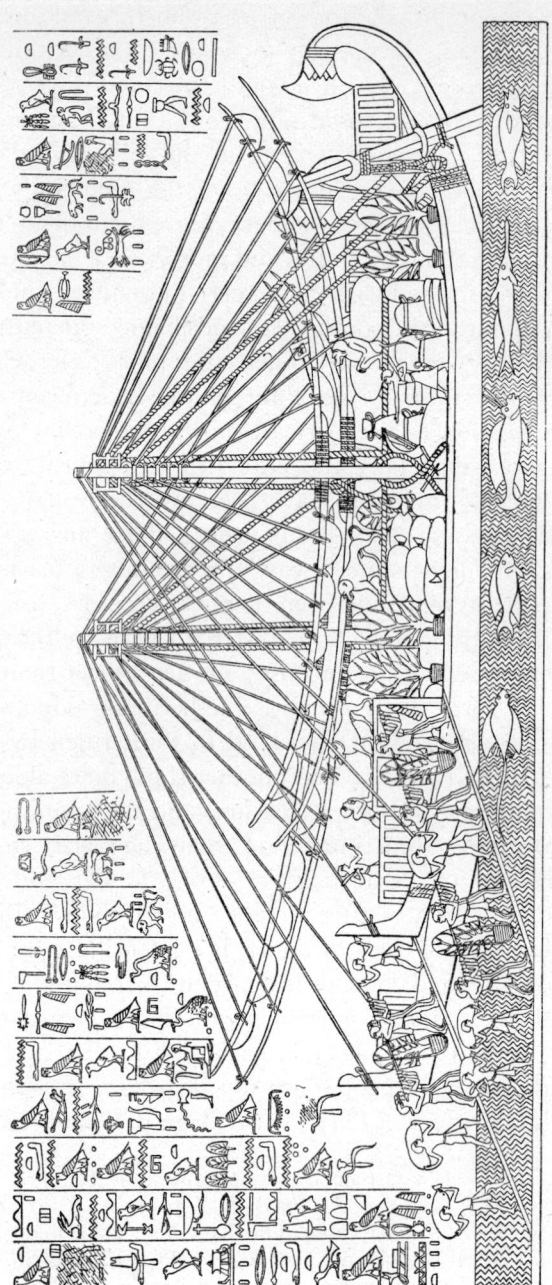

Fig. 1. Egyptian ships being loaded with the wares of Punt.

Thirty incense saplings are being carried aboard in tubs, and, while baboons play about on deck, the ships are loaded with 'wonders of Punt, the like of which was never brought for other kings', incense, fine woods, ivory and gold, slaves and other wares, some no doubt traded down from inland. Later the Queen dedicates this 'tribute', along with that of Kush or Nubia, to her god. Most understand the ships as passing out from the Nile by a Delta–Red Sea canal, and returning the same way.[1]

Tribute lists name many places on the route to Punt, but few seem safely identified. The 'tribute' of Punt still came to enrich the temples of Rameses II and III. A memory of this royal trade may have helped to form the Greek notion of a conqueror Sesostris, who attempted a canal from Nile to Red Sea, ruled Ethiopia, and 'was the first, the priests said, to take a war-fleet along the shores of the outer sea, stopping only when it could no longer be sailed for shoals' (some took this as meaning no farther than Somaliland). One name has been referred to islands off southeast Arabia, but there seems no good evidence that ships went all the way round to the Euphrates, though that river was well enough known (it was called the 'reversed water', because it was so odd as to flow southwards, unlike the Nile).[2] Whether India was even heard of is quite obscure: possibly some Arabian middlemen brought its wares, and thus Henu's desert road was already, what it was again to become long afterwards, an avenue for eastern trade.

Above Egypt is Nubia, barren except for patches in the narrow valley; rapids due to outcrops of rock hinder boats at several points, and the river makes a big loop, which can be avoided by a short cut across the desert. Beyond the first tributary, the Atbara, the country is little better (Greek writers were to overpraise it as Meroe). Only at the Blue Nile junction, 1100 miles from Aswan, is the gateway of the rain-watered lands, Sennar and Kordofan, and of the true Sudan or 'land of the blacks'; the first pure negro tribes are on the White Nile, where the equatorial Africa of marsh and forest begins.

The push up this dismal corridor started at once, but never quite reached the end. The Nubians were backward kinsmen with at first little negro

---

1 Doubted by Hennig, *Terrae Incognitae*, 1936, I, 11, against Breasted, *A.R.E.* II, 102–22, Kees, op. cit. p. 121, Hornell, op. cit. p. 242. Naville, Deir el Bahari, *Eg. Expl. Fund*, 7 vols., work of 1892–1907. Canal left unfinished by 'Sesostris', Arist. *Met.* I, 14, 352*b*, Plin. VI, 165 (wrongly): Diod. I, 33 ignores him (see p. 71, n. 2, p. 81, n. 2).

2 Kees, op. cit. p. 125. Islands, Hommel, *Ethnogr. u. Geogr. des alten Orients*, 1926, p. 648: Sesostris, Herodotus, II, 102, 104: Som., Str. 790, Plin. *N.H.* VI, 174: canal, ibid. 165, Arist. *Met.* I, 14, 20. (He is also partly a notion of Senusret III of the M.K.) Punt names, Schiaparelli, *Geogr. dell'Africa orientale*, 1916, e.g. pp. 117, 205 Auhul= Aualite gulf of Greeks?

infiltration; they are described by various tribal names and presently as 'wretched Kush', when the Middle Kingdom subjected them to Wadi Halfa. They supplied slave-troops and especially gold, worked by forced labour in the eastern desert. In the Old Kingdom Harkhuf had made four journeys from Aswan, one seven months long, and brought back on his donkeys 'tribute' of ivory, ebony, and incense, and a dancing dwarf as a present for the boy king. He need not have gone very far, as many wares could drift to hand by downstream trade, and so certainly the dwarf, if this was a genuine Akka pygmy from the Nile-Congo forests. Some take the traveller only to Dongola and the western oases, another on to Kordofan (and he thinks of a negrillo from south Abyssinia).[1]

Finally the corridor was annexed up to Napata, short of the Atbara, with raids some way beyond; only now was there much contact with pure negroes. Tombs of southern governors have scenes of negroes with gold and ivory, gums, ebony, hides, ostrich feathers and giraffes. Tribute lists give rigmaroles of barbarous names, and boast vaguely of rule to the marshlands, the borders of the darkness, and the southern pillar of heaven. Later independent Kings arose at the frontier capital, whom the Greeks call 'Ethiopians'; they had viceroys in Meroe and warred perhaps to the sudd swamps which barred access to the great lakes. But even these did not control what is now called Ethiopia, the Abyssinian plateau, and it hardly appears in the records except in so far as it may be vaguely included in 'Punt'.[2] Ethnologists trace much Hamitic blood and culture as filtering from early times into the negro world of Africa, but it does not seem contended that all this came from Egypt itself or that it proves a wide horizon in this direction.

Far more important for Egypt were its relations with Asia. It belongs, indeed, as the Greeks were at first inclined to think, more properly to Asia than to Africa. It has been mentioned (p. 6) how coasting began to the cedar-port later known as Byblos of the Phoenicians, which long remained under Egyptian influence (these people, on a narrow shelf of coast and much dependent on trade, were to gain great fame by their own doings

---

1 Schiaparelli, op. cit. pp. 241, 296. Breasted, *A.R.E.* I, 150–4, 159–61 (Akka?). Griffith in *Enc. Brit.* ed. 14, Nubia and Libyan oases. This a real pygmy, W. R. Dawson, *J.E.A.*, 1938, pp. 185–9, though some dwarfs were not. Pygmies once farther north?, Quatrefages, *Pygmies*, 1895, 17.

2 Hommel, op. cit. p. 741. Marsh-lands, Breasted, *A.R.E.* III, 206. Tribute, ibid. II, 283–90: J. G. Wilkinson (rev. Birch), *Manners and Customs of Anc. Eg.* 1878, I, plate 2: Budge, *Eg. Sudan*, 1907, II, 326: gold-mining, ibid. ch. 17, with echo in Agatharchides ap. Diod. III, 12: Rickard, *Man and Metals*, 1932, I, 204–20. Hamitic, Seligman, *Races of Africa*, 1930, pp. 19, 96, *Egypt and Negro Africa*, 1934, pp. 3, 60: C. K. Meek in *Europe and West Africa*, 1940, p. 7. A few beads drifted by barter to Kenya c. 850 B.C., Leakey, *Stone Age Africa*, 1936, pp. 70, 194.

EARLY HORIZONS

on the sea, and even to be reputed the earliest sailors). The desert isthmus helped to make Egypt unusually self-contained, but it could not prevent the passage to and fro of traders and sometimes armies. Early raids to Palestine seem to have been defensive, and fears of invasion from there were justified more than once, and especially when the Hyksos came with their novel horses and chariots (ultimately from the fringe of Asia Minor, where they learnt the chariot from northern immigrants?). These hated conquerors were at last expelled; in the effort Egypt became aggressive, and vengeful kings of dynasty XVIII easily overran all Syria. They found it rich in booty and exploited it freely until Ikhnaton, absorbed with his new religion, let his empire fall to pieces (1360 B.C.). The abundant records fill the map with names like Tyre, Jerusalem, and Damascus, and many less lasting and familiar. Egypt is now in close touch with the great powers beyond, exchanging princesses and royal presents; Babylon reproves it for dealing with her Assyrian vassal; Mitanni is uneasy between Assyria and the Hittites; the last are encroaching far into north Syria, while the south is troubled by desert nomads, Habiru, who may be Hebrews, even perhaps in name (Israel is first mentioned only in 1231 B.C., as settled already and ravaged by a Pharaoh, and the connection of the Exodus story is still obscure). The next dynasty could recover only a part of the lost ground and make a treaty with the Hittites (1272 B.C.); it has occasion to name various allies of theirs in Asia Minor to near Troy.[1] The war had strained both sides, and by 1200 B.C. the Hittite empire was overwhelmed by great migrations. The backwash swept southwards, leaving deposits of Philistines and other displaced peoples on the Syrian coast. Egypt was thrown on the defensive. About 1100 B.C. its envoy was flouted even in Byblos, and the sea-trade of the Delta itself was largely in Phoenician hands. Even in the great age of international relations the Egyptians were curiously hazy in their geography, as when they made the Euphrates rise vaguely in 'the marshes'. An ancient notion about the semi-fabulous Sesostris, that he reached the far end of the Black Sea, has no substance.[2] Equally wild are other statements about eastern conquests by him or a Rameses as far as India.

1 Discussed by several writers in *C.A.H.* II, 8, 141, 281, 487: Garstang, *Hittite Empire*, 1929, pp. 171–8. Exodus, Oesterley in *L.E.* p. 223: Hyksos, ibid. pp. 33, 220. On the Syrian place-names Jirku, *Klio* Beiheft, 1937. An exile of M.K. in Palestine, Budge, *Lit. of Eg.* 1914, pp. 155–69: *A.R.E.* I, 233–9: *L.E.* pp. 74, 219. 'Prima ratem ventis credere docta Tyros', Tib. I, 7, 20, etc. On geogr. of Phoenicia Newbigin, *Med. Lands*, 1924, ch. 5. R. Weill, *Phoenicia and W. Asia*, 1940.

2 Hdt. II, 104, naïvely repeated by Dion. Per. 588, Amm. Marc. XXII, 8, 24. India, Diod. I, 55, Str. 769 but cp. Megasthenes ap. Str. 687. Rameses, Tac. *Ann.* II, 60, Str. 816: see p. 271, n. 1 (Ses. also far west! Lucan, x, 276). Envoy Wen-Amon, Budge, op. cit. pp. 185–95: *L.E.* p. 76: Burn, *Minoans, Philistines and Greeks*, 1930, pp. 173–81: Ormerod, *Piracy in the Anc. World*, 1924, pp. 74–5.

West of Egypt was desert and little else. Along the coast there were reprisals on tribes which encroached on the Delta whenever their strip of grassland got less than its usual short allowance of winter rains. They are sometimes depicted as of the blond Berber type. Among the names is Libu, which the Greeks were to adopt as Libya and extend to the whole continent; another is Meshwesh, usually thought the same as their Maxyes in Tunisia (the Berbers call themselves Amazigh). There is no report of trade or exploration going far along, though there may have been indirect radiations of influence.[1]

The older records have only slight references to northerners of the great sea. Yet there was certainly frequent exchange of wares with Crete, and it has served to date the various phases of the 'Minoan' civilization there, the earliest on European soil. The Aegean with its many stepping-stones was an easy school for sailors, and produced little ships of its own quite unlike the adapted Nile boats. It seems that they did most of the traffic, cutting south across the open with the steady etesian winds to Libya and so to Egypt, and returning with the northward current up Syria; probably some Egyptian ships too did the round trip, 'the great circle of the lands'. The Empire at least has a good deal to say. It claims 'tribute' from 'Keftiu and the Isles' and shows their men, red-skinned and dressed much like those of the Cretan frescoes, bringing metal ingots and vessels. The phrase covers Crete and sundry islands and coasts affected by its culture along Asia Minor to past the Syrian corner, where recent finds show a long-flourishing colony at Ras Shamra, among the Phoenicians, before these became conspicuous as sea-traders. The Keftiu are now sometimes placed about this bend, rather than in Crete itself; so too are Asy and Alashia, which sends 'tribute' of copper and is worried by Lycian pirates, but both are generally taken as Cyprus.[2]

Presently, about 1400 B.C., Crete was ruined, and its power passed to

1 Ashby in *C.A.H.* II, 578: Gsell, *Hist. d'Algérie*, 1927, p. 8 and *Hist. anc. de l'Afrique du Nord*, 1913, I, 206, 231: apparently to Spain before 2500 B.C., C. F. C. Hawkes, *Prehist. Foundations of Europe*, 1940, pp. 83, 161, 199. M. not = Maxyes, Gsell, p. 354, but are, O. Bates, *Eastern Libyans*, 1914, p. 42 cited by Worrell, *A Study of Races in the Anc. Near East*, 1927, p. 82 and Honigmann, *R.E.* XIII, 151 s.v. Libye, 1926. Ptol. IV, 2, 5 has Mazices. Also Asbet, Breasted, op. cit. IV, 405, cp. Asbystae, Hdt. IV, 169. Rendel Harris, *Voyage of Hanno*, 1928, argues fancifully for old Eg. colonies down the Moroccan coast.

2 As by Sir G. Hill, *Hist. of Cyprus*, 1940, I, 36–49, despite Hall, *C.A.H.* II, 281. K. in corner, Wainwright, *J.H.S.* 1931, p. 1: Schaeffer, *Cuneiform Texts of Ras Shamra-Ugarit*, 1939, p. 21: Drower in *L.E.* p. 34. Circle, Myres in *Eur. Civ.* I, 139. Aeg. ships, ibid. p. 158: Sir A. Evans, *Palace of Minos*, 1921–36, II, 239–45: Köster, op. cit. pp. 56–68: Glotz, *Civ. égéenne*, 1923, pp. 217–20: Pendlebury, *Archaeology of Crete*, 1939, p. 271 (K. = Cretans, p. 223): Wace, *C.A.H.* II, 462: Marinatos in *Bull. Corr. Hell.* 1933, pp. 170–235. Egypt and Crete, Glotz, op. cit. pp. 233–46. Keftiu, *C.A.H.* Plates I, 155, cp. Cretan of 156a.

Greece, as its culture had already. In the epic tradition the king of Mycenae there led the Achaeans against Troy, about 1200 B.C.; after the war many of them wandered to settle in Cyprus or elsewhere, or raided Egypt from Crete. From the Egyptian side we hear that 'the north lands in their isles were restless' and several 'sea-peoples' began to attack the Delta (1225 B.C.), including one sounding like 'Achaeans'. Most of the tribes seem to have come from Asia Minor way, the Tursha being generally equated with the Tyrseni. These went west from Lydia, said Herodotus and nearly all ancients after him, to settle in Italy as the Etruscans, and the great majority of recent writers agree, though they date the movement only 800 B.C. or thereabouts. The Sherden are supposed to have wandered to Sardinia after the repulse, or even to have been there before.[1] Soon there was a stronger attack (1194 B.C.): a host of migrants came down Syria by land and sea, no doubt propelled by the invasion which broke the Hittite empire. Among them were the Philistines, who now settled in Palestine and gave it their name.

As for the western Mediterranean, there is no written proof that the Egyptians sailed there or had an inkling that their great sea was a lake with an outlet to the Ocean. (What proof is there of the statement in the *Legacy of Egypt* that their traders carried products of industrial art throughout the Mediterranean basin?) In their records the whole mass of mainland Europe is a blank, unless some of the sea-raiders came from there. If any wares drifted far, like a little amber from the north, such traffic apparently brought no knowledge. Some things may have reached Spain through Aegean carriers, and perhaps a few beads passed on to Britain at third hand. The outer sea had very ancient mariners of its own, who spread the fashion of megaliths along the islands and coasts to Jutland, and traded in Irish gold and Cornish tin. (A statement that Cretans themselves sailed to Britain and Norway is as little warranted as the other quoted above.) The beginnings of bronze are still quite obscure, but it seems most likely that it was invented in the Near East, and the tin may have been got at first locally, perhaps in Iran and even, it has been suggested, in Syria.[2] Rays

---

1 So C. Dawson, *Age of the Gods*, 1934, pp. 300, 357. Perhaps to Sard., Drower in *L.E.* p. 41: Weill, op. cit. p. 153. Schulten, *Klio*, 1930, p. 414 fancies the Tursha as flying west to found Tartessus in Spain about 1150 B.C.! Not Tyrseni but from Tarsus, Wainwright, *J.E.A.* 1939, p. 148. Lydia, Hdt. I, 94, etc. (but not some ap. Dion. Hal. I, 28–30): most, as Conway, *C.A.H.* IV, ch. 12 (but not Last, ibid. VII, 379): MacIver, *Etruscans*, 1928: Ducati, *Le Problème étr.* 1938: Gomme in *Eur. Civ.* II, 20, 27: Piganiol, *Hist. de Rome*, 1939, pp. 7–9: Whatmough, *Foundations of Roman Italy*, 1937, pp. 213–32 (about 850 B.C., others rather eighth cent.). Survey of theories, Renard in *L'Ant. classique*, 1940, pp. 77–111.

2 Wainwright, *J.E.A.* 1934, pp. 29–32: A. Lucas, *Anc. Eg. Materials and Industries*, 1934, pp. 175–6. Iran, Str. 724: Crawford, *Antiquity*, 1938, p. 79: Lucas, loc. cit. Spain, Leeds, *C.A.H.* II, 590 denies even this, cp. p. 12, n. 1. Beads, Evans, op. cit. I, 23, 492–4:

of influence are more or less safely traced as filtering from civilization (rather the Aegean than Egypt itself) into the outer darkness. Objects of copper and bronze pass along and are imitated in stone and presently in metal, as local deposits are found and worked in various parts: so the upper Danube, with some tin handy in Bohemia, develops its own flourishing bronze culture and communicates the impulse as far as Scandinavia. But such data do not prove direct trade from the original focus, or a wide geographical horizon.

There is another kind of clue to what may have happened in this dim twilight. For many languages now spread from Ireland to India there must be postulated a common ancestor, Indo-European (less correctly 'Aryan'). As far back as it can be followed, it had already dialects and was spoken over a considerable region. The speakers were not of one 'race', but probably a mixture of the three racial stocks generally recognized as contributing in various measures to form the peoples of Europe, namely the dark Alpine broad-heads, the dark Mediterranean long-heads, and the Nordic. They were mainly herdsmen, counting wealth by cattle, but also had ploughs and some kind of grain; apparently they were in a late Neolithic phase with metal beginning to reach them as an import. It has not been possible to peg them down quite safely to any one of the barbaric cultures known to archaeology. Reams have been written on an 'original home', which will probably never be found. The first assumption was for Asia, and some have now revived it since the discovery of 'Tocharic' and other extinct languages of this type in Chinese Turkestan. Most agree on Europe, but choose different parts in the area between Jutland and Hungary and the Urals. An argument from the kindred words φηγός—fagus—beech for beech-country west of a line Königsberg-Odessa is not decisive, as the first means 'oak' and the distribution of trees need not have been the same as now. A thesis of a Herrenvolk spreading culture from north Germany or Scandinavia has had an influence of which the results are only too well known. Much has lately been said in favour of south Russia. Anyhow swarms went off in several directions; some indication of the time is the fact that Aryans (the Indo-Iranian branch) were already in Iran about 2000 B.C. How soon the ancestors of the Greeks came in is still doubtful, but there is evidence for a similar date, though the epic can trace the

Hawkes, op. cit. pp. 348–9. Atlantic route, *C.A.H.* I, 98–9, II, 598: Dixon, *Iberians of Spain*, 1940, p. 19: Hencken, *Archaeology of Cornwall*, 1932, pp. 64, 78. Conspectus of arch. data in Childe, *Dawn of Eur. Civ.*^{2} 1927 (^{3} 1939), *Bronze Age*, 1930: Peake and Fleure, *Corridors of Time*, VI–VII, 1930–1: Hawkes, op. cit. 1940. On the west, esp. Wheeler in *Eur. Civ.* ed. Eyre, 1935, II, 177–218. Basin, Capart in *Legacy of Egypt*, 1942, p. 115. Norway, Sewell, ibid. p. 24. Cretans perhaps to Brittany and Britain(?), Grenier in Frank's *Econ. Survey*, III, 389 (1937): Cary, *J.H.S.* 1924, p. 168.

Achaeans only two or three generations back to gods. By 1500 B.C. 'Italic' invaders from the north or north-east are prominent in their new country, and others may have come well before. The Celts seem not clearly discernible till after 1000 B.C., in or near south Germany (the names Rhine and Danube and many others are theirs).[1] Teutons had long occupied Scandinavia and the near-by Baltic coast, getting metals for their amber and developing a notable bronze culture; only later were they to reach the lower Rhine or push south against the Celts.

Such are the kinds of things we conjecture about a nebulous prehistoric Europe, but the Egyptians say not a word about these remote parts.

§ 3. BABYLONIA AND THE HITTITES

The other primary civilization, which entered history about as early, was in the plain of the lower Euphrates and Tigris. The rivers then flowed separately into a long lagoon well behind the present coast-line. Only hard work on irrigation had redeemed the land from fen and desert, and made and kept it very fertile. Two peoples were early in contact, the mysterious Sumerians, perhaps from somewhere in the eastern highlands, and Semitic-speakers probably from Syria (it is not correct to speak of a Semite 'race', and the theory of successive swarms from Arabia is now little favoured). There arose a number of small city-states, each round its temple, and several in turn held a sort of headship. The most famous of the old kings was Sargon of Akkad (2870 B.C.?). Babylon first became prominent with a dynasty including the lawgiver Hammurabi (now reduced from about 2100 B.C. to some centuries later), but soon it fell to alien Kassites from the eastern hills. Under their long rule (18th to 12th centuries B.C.) Babylonia declined till it began to be secondary to Assyria, the poorer country of the middle Tigris, which had early borrowed its civilization.

The chief resources were cattle-raising and land-produce, corn and oil and dates. But industry and commerce were lively. There was a kind of money-economy more highly developed than in Egypt; the temples played a large part by lending their capital, and caravan-trade was active, as appears from the attention of the code to its conditions, while 'contract tablets' about more or less petty business turn up without number. For

---

1 Hubert, *Celtes*, 1932, pp. 178–95: Wheeler, op. cit. II, 220, 243, 266. Teutons, ibid. pp. 256–8. Italics, Gomme, ibid. pp. 6–10. Greeks, Wace and Blegen, *Klio*, 1939, pp. 139–40 (Minyan ware, etc.): Hawkes, op. cit. p. 240. S. Russia, Schrader, *Indogermanen*, 1910: Childe, *Aryans*, 1926: Dawson, op. cit. p. 278: Wheeler, op. cit. II, 192: Myres, *C.A.H.* I, 82–5 (but Hungary, Giles, ibid. pp. 68–70). Warrior cultures of C. Europe (from S. Russia?), Hawkes, p. 233. C. Asia, E. Meyer, *Gesch. des Alt.* I, 2, 889 (1926). A discussion in Grousset, *Hist. de l'extrême Orient*, 1929, I, 6–9: *Hirt-Festschrift*, 1936: H. M. Chadwick, *Nationalities of Europe*, 1945, pp. 157–64. J. Fraser, *Ling. Evidence and Arch. and Ethn. Facts*, Rhys Lecture, 1927 is very sceptical.

canal and river transport there were round ferry-boats or coracles, and large rafts made of logs and inflated skins, used only for downstream traffic and then broken up (Herodotus was to describe both and they are to be seen to-day). The rivers were not nearly so regular and useful as the Nile, nor a good school for sea-shipping. The things chiefly needed from outside were metals, wood, and stone.

Westwards between desert and hills was what has been called the 'fertile crescent' of Mesopotamia, though at best it is a grassland only in winter and spring and has always mattered rather as a passage. Along it trade and sometimes even armies early reached Syria. Marble and cedar were got in the mountains there and rafted down the Euphrates when it had water enough. North-west off the high-road trading colonies were pushed well out to work the copper and silver of the Taurus; they transmitted some culture to the Hittite kingdom, which emerged there after 2000 B.C. and grew strong enough to make a transient raid on Babylon itself. A few early seals found in Cyprus and Crete seem to imply no more than indirect trade, though a late text credits Sargon with raids across the upper or sunset sea to these islands (some accept this for Cyprus at least, and Sayce even detected a mention of Spain as a 'tin-land' dependent on Crete, but it has since been read as a lead-land and meaning Greece).[1] Babylonian influence contributed to the civilization which the Egyptians found when they overran Syria; the relations of the powers at that time have already been sketched.

Eastwards a broad mass of parallel ranges, the Zagros, walls off the plain. From early days there was fighting with the nearest hill-men. The Kassites were pushed down by the Aryans, who were occupying Iran and giving it their name. Babylonian wares seem to have found their way far into the plateau in return for things like lapis lazuli, and also northwards, where copper and axes and the words for them may have reached the Aryans before these people had crossed the Caucasus. Metal vessels resembling early Sumerian appear there and at Astrabad, east of the Caspian. Lapis coming indirectly from Badakshan occurs already among the wealth of imported gold and silver in the early 'royal graves' at Ur.[2]

---

[1] Sayce in *Anc. Egypt*, 1924, p. 1: cp. Albright, *J. Amer. Or. Soc.* 1925, cited by Rickard, op. cit. 1, 342. Accept, Meyer, op. cit. p. 520, Langdon, *C.A.H.* 1, 520 (but cp. ibid. pp. 143, 587); insufficiently attested, Hill, op. cit. 1, 28–9. Colonies in Cappadocia, Götze, *Kleinasien*, 1933, pp. 64–76: Delaporte, *Hittites*, 1936, pp. 44–54: *C.A.H.* 1, 191, 467. On difficulties of Bab. chronology Cook, ibid. p. 156: Hamm. reduced, ibid. Plates I, 66: Carleton, *Buried Empires*, 1939, pp. 95, 281 (and see Addenda).

[2] Woolley, *Sumerians*, 1928, p. 46. Caucasus, Childe, *Aryans*, p. 87: Dawson, op. cit. p. 133. Metal, Rostovtzeff, *Iranians and Greeks in S. Russia*, 1922, pp. 22–32 and (Astrabad) *J.E.A.* 1920, pp. 4–27.

EARLY HORIZONS

The Persian Gulf is described as the 'lower sea'. Across the lagoons at its head attacks were made on Elam, which had a very early culture of its own. Southwards we hear of the early conquest of the 'ship-land' Magan with its copper and wood and stone, and the two last and gold were got by trade from Melukhkha somewhere beyond: both names mean, it seems, the east Arabian coast as far as Oman, and were only later misunderstood by Assyrian scribes and moved on to the Red Sea.[1] No record speaks of sailing along the inhospitable shore to India. Yet very early (for most of the third millennium) there was touch with the remarkable pre-Aryan city-civilization which has recently been discovered in the Indus valley: some seals must have come from there, including one with an elephant and rhinoceros design, though certain affinities are ascribed to a common parent culture rather than to intercourse.[2] Whether the contact was by sea or overland or both is not known. The Aryans, who entered the valley from Kabul way at some vague date, probably by 1500 B.C.?, appear in their oldest hymns as an aristocracy of horse-riding warriors and cattle-breeders and having little to do with the sea.

The Hittites are becoming better known from the gradual decipherment of their own records, nothing less than a royal library of the fourteenth and thirteenth centuries found at their capital east of Ankara. The official language turned out to contain Indo-European elements, and these of a surprising kind, different from the Aryan discovered just before in Mitanni and more like the European branches: it seems to belong to conquerors invading from Europe who had merged in a native mass. The tablets reveal the existence of several other languages and peoples, and name various neighbouring kingdoms, independent or loosely vassal, which are not all safely identified.[3] In their great days the over-kings directed their ambitions mainly southwards to Cilicia and on to Syria, where they clashed with Egypt in the way already described. It is not clear how much they

---

[1] *C.A.H.* I, 172, 416, 431 (but cp. Hall, ibid. p. 583): Hommel, op. cit. pp. 557, 634: Meissner, *Bab. und Assyrien*, 1920–5, I, 345, II, 375: Hitti, *Hist. of Arabs*[2], 1940, p. 36: Hornell, *Antiquity*, 1941, pp. 336–9: Carleton, op. cit. pp. 129–30, 171. Magan=Oman, Peake, *Antiquity*, 1928, p. 452. Albright, *Archaeology and the Religion of Israel*, 1942, p. 134 makes Mel. S.W. Arabia, possibly including Somaliland.

[2] Sir J. Marshall, *Mohenjo-Daro and the Indus Civ.* 1931: E. Mackay, *Indus Civ.* 1935: Childe, *Antiquity*, 1939, pp. 5–15 (close intercourse): Carleton, op. cit. pp. 137–66 (overland): Myres in *Eur. Civ.* I, 140 (perhaps sailing to Indus): H. G. Rawlinson, *India*, 1937, pp. 13–18: Casson, *Discovery of Man*, 1939, pp. 306–9: Sir P. Sykes, *Hist. of Afghanistan*, 1940, I, 28: J. Murphy, *Lamps of Anthropology*, 1943, ch. 10. Indian shell in early Ur, etc., Hornell, op. cit. p. 239. The seals prove active intercourse by land, Mookerji, *Hindu Civilization*, 1936, pp. 25–8 (but he also assumes Indian wares via Punt, p. 45, and Aryan sea-ships, p. 76).

[3] Götze, op. cit. pp. 48–60: Garstang, *Hittite Empire*, 1929: Hrozný, *Enc. Brit.* 14th ed., Hittites, 1929: Delaporte, *Hittites*, 1936 (on languages, pp. 302–11).

had to do with the Aegean coast. Here a large part was played by Troy, a much rebuilt fortress near the Dardanelles. The second town on the site was remarkable for its wealth in metals, and its influence reached down to Cyprus and far up the Danube, where it gave the impulse to metalworking and a barbaric culture. It also got amber from the north and a piece of jade from Central Asia, though these must have drifted along through many hands and it is absurd to talk of 'trade relations'.[1] This place was burnt by invaders not long after 2000 B.C., it was thought (the date is now pushed back some centuries). A much later town, the sixth, was drawn into the circle of the Aegean culture, which had hitherto won little foothold on the coast. According to the Greek epic Troy was attacked by the Achaeans under Agamemnon, king of Mycenae (about 1200 B.C. was the popular date). Well before that the tablets mention certain Ahhiyawa encroaching on the south coast and Cyprus, and Forrer saw in the names not only Achaeans but important kings of Greece including Agamemnon's father, but all this has been denied. Much else is obscure regarding the horizon of the Hittites, for instance northwards across the Black Sea (they were not seafarers).[2] About 1200 B.C. the empire collapsed, with repercussions felt all the way to Egypt, as already indicated. The Greeks knew of Phrygians invading over the straits from Thrace, but of the power thus overthrown they had hardly the ghost of a memory, even of the name: perhaps it survives as Keteioi, once in Homer. They mention an 'Assyria' or (White) Syrians hereabouts, possibly an echo of the old mining colonies in the Taurus. Also they ascribed the discovery of iron-working to a Black Sea tribe, the Chalybes, and it seems that iron may have spread from these to the Hittites and so outwards (an Egyptian king asks a Hittite for some, though iron was not generally used in Egypt till long after).[3] Small Hittite or half-Hittite states continued for a time in north Syria, until

1 As does Leaf, *Homer and History*, 1915, p. 354. Danube, *C.A.H.* I, 105, 614: Childe, *Danube in Prehistory*, 1929, pp. 33, 414–15. For Troy 2, Götze, op. cit. pp. 27–34: Childe, *Dawn*, pp. 53–64: Dawson, op. cit. pp. 184, 316.

2 Garstang, op. cit. p. 41. Denied, Götze, op. cit. p. 172 and others against F. (1924): see *Bulletin...Budé*, Suppl. Crit. 1935, p. 16: Weill, *Phoen. and W. Asia*, 1940, pp. 131–4. Some slight Hittite hold on Cyprus, Hill, op. cit. pp. 45, 47. Much controversy on Hypachaei of Cilicia in Hdt. VII, 61. Troy 2 is now dated 2500–2300 B.C., Troy 6 is 1900–1350 B.C. and the Homeric is Troy 7a, Hawkes, op. cit. pp. 107, 358.

3 *L.E.* p. 135: Rameses II asks, Garstang, op. cit. p. 295: Wainwright, *J.E.A.* 1936, pp. 5–24: Dawson, op. cit. p. 303: Heichelheim, *Wirtschaftsgesch. des Alt.* 1938, pp. 200–1. Cp. Vernadsky, *Anc. Russia*, 1943, p. 43, ironworking from Armenia to Caucasus by 1000 B.C. (as copper by 2000 B.C., ibid. p. 29). Chalybes, Aesch. *P.V.* p. 709, Strabo, 544–50, etc. Keteioi, *Od.* XI, 521: Garstang, pp. 17, 172. Syrians, Hec. fr. 200–1, Hdt. I, 76: Ass., Ps.-Scyl. 72: echo?, Honigmann, *R.E.* Syria. Phrygians, Hdt. VI, 45, VII, 73: already in *Il.* III, 187, XVI, 719, if not an anachronism there, Garstang, pp. 10, 15. Nose, Hertz, *Race and Civ.* 1928, p. 133, after P. von Luschan.

destroyed by the Assyrians, who knew that district as Hatti-land. It is suggested that the Jewish nose, common also in Armenia, is due to a strain of Hittite blood. As mentioned above, the Etruscans are thought to have been in Lydia, and under Hittite influence, before they wandered to Italy.

§4. THE AEGEAN WORLD AND HOMER

Europe has made but a slight appearance within the horizons hitherto considered. The first civilization on its own soil was the Cretan. It has its written records, many tablets, which seem to be tallies of stores and tribute, in a language no doubt pre-Greek, but they have not been deciphered. The island, rocky and hilly, had only modest resources, olive and wine, corn in a few plains, and timber (plenty then) for ship-building; it must have prospered rather by sea-enterprise, and a love of the sea is obvious in its bright art. The good harbours looked towards the Aegean, where the cluster of islands made sailing easy, but from the first there were also constant relations with Syria and Egypt. The most brilliant period was 1600–1400 B.C., when the kings lived secure in luxurious palaces and ruled the Aegean: 'Minos' was the first in Greek memory to be lord of the sea. Just before this the culture was transmitted to Mycenae and other places in Greece, and it may have been their men who sacked Crete; anyhow they took over its headship and spread the culture, in their own version, even more widely. The Greek epic remembers these places as held by Greek-speaking Achaeans, who ruled as far afield as Rhodes and were summoned by an overlord of Mycenae to the Trojan war (about 1200 B.C.).

Westwards and northwards Aegean influence is traced as working very early in various barbaric cultures. Some seems to have filtered (only indirectly?) to the head of the Adriatic, where amber came down from the north. In Italy the influence is oddly very slight. In Sicily the evidence suggests an entrepôt or even a colony, and there is a legend that 'Minos' perished in an attempt at conquest there. Some stamped ingots of copper reached Sardinia. Beyond that the data are less clear for direct contact, but it seems likely that there were some Minoan explorers in the western basin, as far as Spain and quite early (before 2000 B.C.—indeed more then than in the main period, when the Spanish culture appears to stagnate).[1]

---

[1] Wheeler in *Eur. Civ.* II, 212–15. Before Middle Minoan, Hawkes, op. cit. pp. 199, 304. Spain denied by Leeds, *C.A.H.* II, 590: indirect, Dixon, op. cit. p. 20: contacts negligible, Bosch-Gimpera, *Etnologia de la Pen. Iberica*, 1932, p. 242. Cp. Evans, *Scripta Minoa*, 1909, I, 98: *Palace*, I, 22; II, 180: Schulten, *Tartessos*, 1922, p. 9. In west early, Myres, *C.A.H.* I, 105: Dawson, op. cit. p. 186. Ingots, *C.A.H.* II, 583. Legend, Hdt. VII, 170, Tim. ap. Diod. IV, 76–9, Str. 273, 282: Burn, op. cit. p. 96. Colony, Evans, *S.M.* p. 95, *Palace*, II, 626, IV, 959: but hardly from Crete?, Wace and Blegen, *Klio*, 1939, p. 136. Amber, *Palace*, II, 174, but not from head as *S.M.* p. 95?: Hawkes, op. cit. pp. 305, 353: and see p. 27, n. 1. Italy, Gomme in *Eur. Civ.* I, 906, II, 6.

Was there a good idea of the Mediterranean lake, and was the later Greek knowledge only a rediscovery?

From Troy there were disastrous 'returns', the tradition says: some heroes wandered abroad, as to Cyprus; others came back, but soon their little kingdoms went down before the Dorians, ruder Greeks invading from the north. Swarms of displaced people crossed to Asia Minor, settling much of the west coast as Aeolis and Ionia, while the invaders themselves overflowed to the south part of the same coast and the southern islands. On the homeland there came an age of comparative barbarism, from which historic Greece began to emerge only in the eighth century B.C. But the memory of the heroic age had lived on, and it was embodied in two glorious poems, the *Iliad* and the *Odyssey*.

These give the earliest picture of the world as seen through European eyes. But there is always the 'Homeric question': how and when were they composed and written, and how far do they represent the conditions of any one time? After over a century of ruthless dissection it has again become fashionable to suppose that both, much as they stand, are by a great poet, who lived in Ionia and, as Herodotus seems to think, about 850 B.C. (anyhow not earlier, he says). But even so the picture is a composite: generations of bards had gone before, as the highly developed art and language show, and they and he may well have added their own colours. Also some allowance must be made for later interpolations before the text became fixed. One view is that the poems reflect in the main the economic conditions of the ninth to eighth centuries B.C., slightly archaized.[1] The subject is a real war which had already passed into saga.

Some moderns suggest that the war was not fought for Helen or loot but to force the passage to the Black Sea. Bérard thinks that, as it was hard to enter the strait against the prevailing north-east wind and the swift outward current, goods had to be landed south of Troy and carried past that fortress, which could exact heavy tolls. Leaf thinks rather that it blocked a sea-passage and forced an annual fair under its walls. But it has been roundly denied that any form of the trade theory is true for a heroic age.[2]

The rival alliances are recounted in formal catalogues (*Il.* II, ll. 494–700, the ships of the Achaeans, and ll. 816–79, the Trojans). Both were later vastly discussed: Apollodorus wrote twelve books on the longer, and

---

[1] Heichelheim, op. cit. p. 226 (how far usable for Myc.? p. 942). H. not later than 9th cent., Bury, *C.A.H.* II, 517: *c.* 850 B.C. and tells of a sub-Myc. age 1250–1000 B.C. of wider horizons, Burn, *World of Hesiod*, 1936, pp. 17, 27. 8th cent., Bowra, *Tradition and Design in the Iliad*, 1930, p. 265. Herodotus, II, 53.

[2] Bury, *C.A.H.* II, 490. Bérard, *Phéniciens et l'Odyssée*, 1902, I, 79–82: G. Murray, *Rise of Greek Epic*², 1911, p. 59. Leaf, *Troy*, 1912, pp. 257, 314: similar Sartiaux, *Guerre de Troie*, 1915. Denied, Bowra, op. cit. pp. 180–1.

EARLY HORIZONS

Demetrius a book for every two lines of the shorter, and Strabo, while drily remarking on this excess of commentary, encumbers his own geography with such antiquarian details. Leaf and others have attacked the Achaean list, but it is now defended as a well-preserved piece of early chronicle coinciding well with the area of Mycenaean finds.[1] Among the minor questions raised is one about Ithaca. If it is the island now so called, the poet is wrong once in describing it as close offshore and west and north of the other islands of Odysseus, though some will not have Homer nodding and insist that it is Leucas; the Greeks themselves bothered only about another place assigned to the same hero (and in the catalogue to somebody else).[2]

Roughly the Achaeans hold the west and south Aegean, their enemies the east and north. Homer has no idea of the war as a clash of Europe and Asia, as it was later conceived. He uses neither name as a geographical term, unless his local Asian meadow by the streams of Cayster is the humble beginning of a continent. 'Europe' appears a little after him and at first means only the north Aegean coast. For Hesiod both are merely daughters of Ocean, and Herodotus is puzzled to explain how two mythical ladies had by his time become continents (the oldest extant mention of both names and Libya in this sense is only just before him, in Pindar). Later ancients make worthless guesses. A modern derivation from Semitic words for sunrise and sunset is not quite convincing, and others from Indo-European seem to fail, so that the origins remain obscure.[3] Are they to be sought in Crete? After all Europa was carried there from Phoenicia to become the mother of Minos.

Among Troy's allies is Thrace. The poet has heard of its mountains, whence blows the northern blast (*rhipé*). Vaguely behind are Mysians and mare-milking nomads, who are 'noble' and 'just'. It is the first case of a persistent Greek weakness for idealizing the simple life of wild tribes at the outer edges of the known, a fancy for the 'noble savage' which was to be shown by many later times and peoples. Here too are the first hints of 'Rhipaean' mountains and of happy Hyperboreans. If the latter had

---

1 T. W. Allen, *Homeric Catalogue of Ships*, 1921, p. 174: Bury, *C.A.H.* II, 499, 514: Gomme in *Eur. Civ.* I, 993. Attacked by Beloch, *Griech. Gesch.* 12², 133 (1913) and Leaf, op. cit. though in *Troy*, 1912, he respects the Trojan list. Drily, Str. 603, on Demetrius.

2 Dulichion. For L. are Leaf, op. cit., Dörpfeld, *Alt-Ithaka*, 1927: H. L. Jones in Loeb *Strabo*, 1928, V, 523–30. Hennig, *Geogr. des hom. Epos*, 1934, is for Corfu.

3 *R.E.* II, 1533, VI, 1298 and Berger, *Erdkunde*², p. 77. E. first in *Hom. Hymns*, III, 251, 291, ed. Allen, Halliday and Sikes, 1936. Sem., they accept as Kiepert, *Lehrbuch der alten Geogr.* 1878, p. 1, and cite Hesychius 'land of sunset or dark': Eust. ad Dion. Per. 270. Meadow, *Il.* II, 460. Hes. *Theog.* pp. 357–9. Hdt. IV, 45: guesses Str. 627, Dion. Hal. I, 17. Pindar, *Pyth.* IX. 8. Homer no idea of continents, Str. 553. On their boundaries, see p. 59, n. 2, p. 66, n. 1.

originally been something else ('bearers' of offerings to Apollo?), they were already misunderstood as 'beyond the north wind'. They were to have a long and disreputable history (it is a queer notion that there should be a mild climate in such parts). As knowledge expanded, both range and people were gradually to recede into the northern distance. The nomads are a rumour of the Scythians, who are presently named, as is the Ister or Danube.[1]

There are rightly barbarous-speaking Carians in what was to become Ionia only after the war. Eastwards Troy has allies to near the Bosporus; a group of names on the Black Sea coast was not in the text of some ancient readers and is suspect as interpolated. On a more inland line are Paphlagonians as far as Eneti, where are wild asses, and in the vague background Halizones of the silver-land Alybe. The latter were often to be connected with the Chalybes, though these were ironworkers (Strabo discusses the matter at great length). Homer has no very serious use for the fabulous Amazons, unless once as attacking the Phrygians and their Trojan allies from quite close behind. Presently, though sometimes brought from Thrace to help Troy, they are usually housed half-way along the Black Sea coast. When they were not found there by colonists, it was explained that they had withdrawn northwards to become a people ruled by women beyond the Don. The origin of the whole notion of these warrior women is still obscure, and why they were localized where they were.[2]

On the renowned ship Argo, which sailed a generation before the war, Homer is brief and has nothing but fairy-tale beyond Lemnos: it went to the land of Aeetes, offspring of the Sun, and on its way back (presumably with the Golden Fleece) it escaped the Clashing Rocks. These were later generally put at the Bosporus. But, as the fleece is a magical treasure, so 'the land' (Aea) is at first a mythical Far East, as it still is for a lyric poet. Strabo perversely insists that Homer already knew of Colchis, at the east

1 By Hes. ap. Str. 300. Mysians=Moesians. Rhipé, *Il.* xv, 171, from Thrace, ibid. ix, 5. Just, ibid. xiii, 5: Rohde, *Griech. Roman*², 1900, pp. 216–18: Lovejoy and Boas, *Primitivism and Related Ideas in Antiquity*, 1935: Myres in *Anthropology and the Classics*, 1908, p. 161. Bearers (of Hdt. iv, 33), as Ahrens, 1862, Farnell, *Cults of Greek States*, iv, 102. On Rhip. esp. Kiessling, *R.E.* I A (1920), pp. 846–916: E. Wikén in ΔΡΑΓΜΑ *Nilsson dedicatum*, 1939, pp. 540–52. Nansen, *In Northern Mists*, 1911, i, 13–20. See also p. 61, n. 1. Fairchild, *Noble Savage*, 1928: Dampier-Whetham, *History of Science*, 1929, pp. 205–6: Mowat, *Age of Reason*, 1934, pp. 284–5: Preserved Smith, *Hist. of Modern Culture*, 1930–4, i, 118–21, ii, 149–57.

2 Toepffer, *R.E.* i, 1754–71. *Iliad*, iii, 185-9, vi, 186. Housed on Thermodon, Hdt. ix, 27, Diod. iv, 16, Ap. Rhod. ii, 987. Don, Hdt. iv, 110, Str. 504, etc. Chalybes, p. 18, n. 3. Suspect, even to Allen, op. cit. p. 158, as not read by Erat. and Apoll. ap. Str. 298, 533. Amazon legend from matriarchy of Azov tribes, thinks Vernadsky, op. cit. p. 54: from Hittites apparently dressed like women, Leonhard, *Hittiter u. Amazonen*, 1911 (fanciful, says *C.A.H.* ii, 647).

end of the Black Sea, where a river washed down gold nuggets and the natives caught them in fleeces, a piece of silly rationalism which should not have deceived anybody. Others were more sensible and thought the fleece a myth localized there only when Ionian colonists reached these distant parts. It proves nothing that late poetic versions set the chief scenes in Colchis and bring the heroes back up the Danube and by other devious routes. (There are, however, faint hints of early Aegeans in this sea, and some believe in a thirteenth century B.C. voyage all the way.)[1]

The *Odyssey*, the most famous of the 'returns' from Troy, is naturally full of seafaring. (Yet it may be doubted if its hero or any Greek after him was a Viking or at heart a traveller, like Tennyson's romanticized Ulysses.) The ships are mainly open war-boats, with half-decks fore and aft and twenty oars; only a magic ship has fifty, and another in a doubtful passage. A mast and sail can be put up. We hear of 'freighters', vaguely 'broad', but they seem little different—one has expressly twenty oars too—except perhaps those of non-Greeks. There is hardly a word for professional traders, trade being only an occasional sideline of pirates. The small ships do not willingly cross the open, and are usually beached at night, as steering by the stars is a desperate business (mentioned only once).[2] Ships may be blown any distance by storms, or detained for weeks by contrary winds. Yet such conditions do not deter many a hard-bitten gentleman who needs to mend his fortunes by raiding overseas (it is no offence to ask a stranger if he is a pirate).

A favourite line of enterprise is southwards. Cretan lords 'easily' cut across to 'the river Egypt' (the name Nile occurs only later). Menelaus himself roams lucratively for seven years to Cyprus, Phoenicia, Egypt, the Ethiopians, Sidonians, Erembi, and Libya teeming with sheep—an odd series of names. Some ancients saw in these apparently detached Sidonians a second lot of Phoenicians on the Persian Gulf, and took the hero by a canal or even round Africa to visit them: a notion of their original home being

---

1 Miss J. R. Bacon, *Voyage of the Argonauts*, 1925, p. 161. Aegeans, before Troy blocked the way, Minns, *Scythians and Greeks*, 1913, p. 436: Carians (cp. names like Odessus), Hogarth, *C.A.H.* II, 556: but Leaf can find little evidence, Bowra, op. cit. p. 181. Sensible, Erat. and Dem. ap. Str. 45, 48, as cp. Strabo himself, 21, 499, who deceives Hennig, *T.I.* I, 17: 'silly', Halliday, *Indo-Eur. Folk-Tales and Greek Legend*, 1933, p. 63. Magical, H. J. Rose, *Handbook of Greek Mythology*[2], 1933, p. 196. Some Aegean things reached the Kuban very early, by 2500 B.C., Hawkes, op. cit. pp. 222, 225 (how directly?).

2 *Od.* v, 271–7: not willingly, ibid. 100, 174. Heichelheim, op. cit. pp. 227, 241: Knorringa, *Emporos*, 1926, p. 7: Hasebroek, *Trade and Politics in Anc. Greece*, 1933, pp. 67–9. Fifty, *Od.* VIII, 39, and *Il.* XVI, 70, doubted by Torr, *Anc. Ships*, 1895, p. 3 and J. H. Rose, *Man and the Sea*, 1935, p. 16. Freighter, *Od.* IX, 322. Pirate, *Od.* III, 72, IX, 252, noted by Thuc. I, 5, 2. Ulysses, Oakeshott, *Commerce and Society*, 1936, p. 14.

thereabouts may rest largely on this bad guess.[1] There were many guesses for the Erembi. What the poet says of Egypt is vague enough, even the wealth of hundred-gated Thebes (a later writer notes it as odd that he knows of ivory but not of elephants). The Ethiopians, linked above with real lands, are otherwise quite fabulous for him: they are a blameless people, whose pious sacrifices are often attended by gods, and they are the farthest of men, dwelling by the Ocean-stream in two parts, some at the sunrise, others at the sunset. Soon they are more explicitly dark folk and 'burntfaces' nearest the sun, especially at its rise (yet their king Memnon, the handsome son of the Dawn who comes to help Troy, is never represented as black). Hesiod seems to extend them all along the south of the known earth. Some wrongly credited Homer with knowing already of Indians as well as Africans. His vague Ethiopians were to continue as a poetic tradition long after blacks were familiar and the name was specially applied to those above Egypt.[2] Very remarkable is his mention of Pygmies or 'cubit-men', far on the Ocean-stream, repelling the cranes which fly south from the Mediterranean winter: as 'that small infantry, warred on by cranes' they were still a commonplace of poetry in Milton's time, when Browne thought them a 'pleasant figment'. The flight is real, and the rest is now usually thought a rumour of the real pygmies at the Nile sources, who may have provided a pet or two for old Pharaohs.[3]

Much is said of cunning Phoenicians—also called men of Sidon but never of Tyre—who are rather traders than pirates. They bring skilled metalwork, such as Greece can no longer make, purple cloth, and other luxuries, like an amber necklace (there is no hint where the amber came from, and tin is mentioned but not in connection with them). They sail to Egypt and past Crete to Libya; they stay long bartering in Aegean islands and on occasion kidnap the natives and sell them as far afield as Ithaca. This account, once ascribed to 'younger layers' of the seventh century B.C., is now thought credible for the ninth or even earlier. Homer says nothing of Phoenicians in the west and has no tangible name beyond Sicily. Strabo conceived that he used their reports for western waters, and Bérard still

---

1 Though in Hdt. I, 1, VII, 89, Str. 784, scorned by Meyer op. cit. I. 2, 424. (Phoen. legends now point Sinai way, Schaeffer, op. cit. p. 58, but denied by Albright, op. cit. p. 59.) Menelaus, *Od.* IV, 83–5, Str. 35, 38: Erembi, ibid. pp. 41–2, 784. Thebes, *Od.* IV, 126 (suspect as added in *Il.* IX, 352–4). 'Nile', Hes. *Theog.* 338. Pharos island later silted, Str. 30.

2 Beardsley, *Negro in Greek and Roman Civ.* 1929. Indians, Pos. ap. Str. 103. Dark, Hes. *Op.* 527 and fr. 55 (ap. Str. 300): in east, *Od.* V, 282, Mimnermus fr. 10, Aesch. and Eur. ap. Str. 33, cp. 38. Two parts, *Od.* I, 23, echoed in Hdt. VII, 70, etc. Originally fabulous, Beloch, op. cit. p. 61. Elephants, Paus. I, 12, 4.

3 As Hennig, *Rhein. Mus.* 1923, pp. 23, etc. *Il.* III, 3–6. Migration often later, as Arist. *H.A.* VIII, 12, Lucan, V, 711–16. Sir D'Arcy Thompson, *Glossary of Greek Birds*, 1936, pp. 72–3.

proceeds on this theory to find him accurate for every place and wind and current. Yet evidently, as some ancient critics said, these were for Homer unknown seas, to be filled with marvellous fictions: to learn where his hero went one must find the cobbler who sewed the bag of the winds.[1]

The wanderings, with the few statements of direction and distance, read as follows, starting from the dreaded south cape of Greece (it would not be worth while to labour all this if many Greeks had not taken it so seriously). South nine days to the Lotus-eaters, who ought to be in Africa, where the ancients put them, Cyrene or often Tunisia way; over a night to the Cyclopes or Round-eyes, cannibal giants living like savage shepherds and quite unlike the mythical forgers of lightning except for having one round eye (even Strabo dismisses them, but Bérard sees a rumour of the craters near the bay of Naples). Then to the floating isle of Aeolus, lord of the winds; east nine days to sight Ithaca; back, after the men rashly open the bag and loose the wrong winds, to the isle, which had presumably floated some way; six days' hard rowing to the Laestrygones, cannibal giants in an almost nightless land; somehow to the isle of the witch Circe, daughter of the Sun and sister of the Aeetes visited by the Argonauts (here are the dancing-places of the Dawn and the rising of the sun, but by now the hero and his men 'know not where is west or where east', *Od.* x, 190, cp. xii, 3). Then at her bidding south one day from the sea to the bounds of the Oceanstream and the Cimmerians ('them the sun never looks upon, but baneful night is over men, and land and city are shrouded in mist and cloud'); near-by is Hades—usually in the far west but not necessarily at that edge of the world?—where the hero summons the dead and learns his fate. So back to Circe; quickly past the isle of the Sirens and the surf-beaten Planctae (often thought the same as the Clashing Rocks) and a strait between a monster Scylla and a whirlpool Charybdis; south one night to Thrinacie, a small uninhabited island, where the hungry mariners kill the Sun's cattle; starting south, the ship is blasted by lightning; the hero, left alone clinging to the keel, barely escapes the whirlpool and drifts nine days to the Ogygian isle of Calypso, daughter of the wizard Atlas, who keeps the depths of the sea and the pillars supporting the heavens. After years of detention he builds a big raft and sails east seventeen days and nights to be wrecked by the sea-god, who espies him from the Lycian mountains; he drifts ashore on Scheria of the Phaeacians, a luxurious people, near to

---

1 Erat. and Apoll. ap. Str. 24, 298 as cp. Strabo himself, 149–51 and Bérard, op. cit. and *Navigations d'Ulysse*, III, 1929, partly approved by J. H. Rose, op. cit. 1. 7th cent. B.C., Beloch, op. cit. p. 67. 9th cent., Gomme in *Eur. Civ.* I, 995: earlier, Cary-Warmington, *Anc. Explorers*, 1929, p. 16. Stories in *Od.* xv, 403–84, etc: amber, ibid. 460, xviii, 296. Tin, *Il.* xviii, 564, 574. For Erat. on Homer, Berger, *Fragm. des Erat.* 1880, pp. 19–40. Speciosa miracula, Hor. *A.P.* 144: Juv. xv, 13–26.

the gods and living apart from men, yet giving all men hurtless convoy in ships of magic swiftness, one of which brings him in a night to his own home.

When Greek colonists settled in the west, they began to place these adventures. There was barely a tangible name to help them out, only Temese, perhaps in Italy, though some thought of Cyprus, while Sicily appeared as Sicanie and Sicels (in parts of the poem now often thought late). Yet the giant shepherds, Thrinacie (supposed to mean 'three-cornered'), and the nightless land were all found in Sicily! The whirlpool seemed the Messina eddy, a poor affair, as a critical historian admitted, though moderns incline to accept it as adequate. Circe was strangely housed on the Latin coast, and what passes as Hesiod has the Etruscans in 'isles' under her sons Latinus and 'Wildman'. The nightless giants were often put near, with the Sirens at the bay of Naples. The lord of the winds was in the Lipari islands, where the smoke puffs of a volcano foretold coming winds (Stromboli is called the 'fisherman's weather-glass' to-day). And so on; some ancient writers explain every detail with perverse ingenuity. Bérard defends much, even about Circe, and shifts the nightless giants only to Sardinia. As for the uncanny Phaeacians, most placed them humdrumly in Corfu, and he agrees. But Strabo, as a magic ship can do anything, removed them to the outer sea (Hennig thinks of south Spain, which was also Atlantis, he supposes). Strabo found Calypso too outside, and some moderns put her in Madeira, near her sky-bearing father, the Peak of Teneriffe, but Bérard at Gibraltar with the Atlas mountains opposite.[1] One name stands out: real Cimmerians lived in and near the Crimea until, driven out by Scythians about 700 B.C., they invaded Asia Minor. The description is quite unrecognizable, but Strabo explains that the poet used the licence of his art to transfer them to the west. Hennig thinks of Kymry of foggy Britain! Others suggest a hearsay of the Cimbri of Jutland, where amber came from. An ancient scholar, Crates, took the hero far into outer seas to find both dayless and nightless peoples in high latitudes. Many moderns plausibly detect rumours of long winter and short summer nights and even of the midnight sun, drifting down with tin and amber, while a sailors' tale of icebergs has been supposed to underlie the notion of a floating island (and of Clashing Rocks). It is argued too that the poet transfers a set of Black Sea adventures to the west and so makes nonsense of the Cim-

---

[1] Outside, Str. 157. Madeira, Wilamowitz, *Ilias u. Homer*, 1916, p. 497, Hennig, *T.I.* p. 40. Ph.=Atlantis, ibid. and *Von rätselhaften Ländern*, 1935, pp. 7–64. Corfu, Thuc. I, 25, etc. Critical, Thuc. IV, 24, cp. VI, 1–2: eddy, Bunbury, *Anc. Geogr.* I, 61. Temese, *Od.* I, 184, Str. 255. Latinus, Hes. *Theog.* 1013. Laestr. at Formiae, Ovid, *F.* IV, 69, etc. Perverse, Polybius ap. Str. 20–5: volcano, Pol. ap. Str. 275–6, Plin. III, 94. Cyclopes and craters, approved by J. H. Rose, op. cit. p. 12: fable, Str. 21. Malten, *Kyrene*, 1911, p. 209 argues for early (pre-Dorian) colonists in Cyrenaica.

merian darkness and much else, ill-understood hearsay from the once wider Minoan knowledge.[1] And from all the discussion nothing seems very clear except that he does what he pleases with a blank. There may be echoes of forgotten voyages, but they are faint, and oddly mixed with elements of folk-tale and also of sheer fiction. If some Aegeans long before could have told real things of the west, it had faded into a haze of fable. If Odysseus had 'seen the towns of many men and learnt their minds', here he sees almost only giants and the like, from popular yarns which seem to have ousted more sober adventures. Of the Mediterranean as a lake Homer has no idea, and his Ocean-stream seems to have nothing to do with the real Ocean or its tides, despite some ancients: he distinguishes it from the sea, but not as a known outer from an inner sea, as Strabo conceives. Some moderns hint that, though at first purely mythical, it was already being affected by Phoenician knowledge of a real outer sea. An oceanographer fails to understand how mythical the stream was, and thinks it was suggested by the strong northern tides, while Hennig wrongly refers 'back-flowing' to the contrary currents at Gibraltar, and Charybdis also to the tides there, as exaggerated by 'Phoenician lies'. The order of ideas to which the river Ocean belongs will be discussed presently; it is no more a tidal sea than 'Leviathan that crooked serpent' or the Worm that winds itself for ever round the earth-disk in Teutonic mythology.[2]

§ 5. ASSYRIANS, PHOENICIANS AND HEBREWS

The Assyrians had sometimes been aggressive before and now had their great days as the dominant power in the Near East (900–612 B.C.). They ruined the kingdoms of Damascus and Israel, and blackmailed and bullied the Phoenician trading cities (the name Syria itself seems a memory of their power). They wrung homage from the 'Aribi' of north-west Arabia, and towards the end even mastered Egypt for a short while. They attacked

1 Burn, *World of Hesiod*, 1936, pp. 20–2. Licence, Str. 20, 149. Rumours, Müllenhoff, *Deutsche Alt.*[2] 1890, I, 5–8: Hübner, *R.E.* Britanni (1899), 858: from Scand., T. R. Holmes, *Anc. Britain*, 1907, pp. 218, 513. Cimbri, Bury, *Klio*, 1906, pp. 79–88: Ridgeway, *Early Age of Greece*, 1901, I, 359, 368. Amber, ibid., *C.A.H.* II, 452, Glotz, op. cit. p. 257, Déchelette, *Arch. préhist. celt. et gallo-rom.* 1908, I, 623–6, and see p. 19, n. 1. Northern nights, but Laestr. misplaced by redactor, who put wanderings in Black Sea (not yet known as closed), Wilamowitz, *Hom. Untersuch.* 1884, p. 167 (his Circe in N.E. and Hades in far north). Icebergs, Kellett, *Story of Myths*, 1928, pp. 39, 86.

2 Kellett, op. cit. pp. 89, 124: despite Krappe, *Science of Folk-lore*, 1930, p. 319. Hennig, *Geogr. des hom. Epos*, 1934. J. Johnstone, *A Study of the Oceans*, 1926, pp. 29–31. Hint, Gisinger, *R.E.* Okeanos, 1937, citing *Od.* I, 52. Distinguishes, *Od.* XI, 1, XII, 2, Str. 3–7: tides, Pos. ap. Str. 7 and Str. himself. See also p. 35, n. 2. Ousted, Woodhouse, *Comp. of Homer's 'Odyssey'*, 1932. Faded, C. Hardie, *Antiquity*, 1942, pp. 273–4. A curious map 'ad mentem Homeri' in Spruner-Menke's *Atlas Antiquus*, 1865. Forgotten, Chadwick, *Heroic Age*, 1926, pp. 261, 303.

a strong kingdom in Armenia, and raided the 'silver mountains' of the Taurus, where they held up northern invaders, the Cimmerians, who broke the Phrygian kingdom and worried its Lydian successor and the Ionian cities. There was direct contact with Greeks when they checked some 'Javan' attempting to colonize in Cilicia and received tribute from princes of Cyprus. Evidence has now been found of another early Greek settlement, tapping the trade of north Syria.[1]

These events give the setting for the appearance of Gomer, Javan, and others in the chapters of the Bible which represent the Jewish outlook at the end of this period. The table of nations in Genesis is a much revised document, a composite of older and newer horizons, so that it is not easy to reconstruct the map implied. There is a highly coloured picture of the commerce of Tyre in Ezekiel (just after 600 B.C., with some slightly later interpolations). Two names, those of Gog and Magog, who shall 'come out of the uttermost parts of the north...riding upon horses', were to have countless strange echoes down the centuries. A recent attempt to extract an old Phoenician and Jewish map from the late Book of Jubilees is quite unconvincing.[2]

Eastwards the Assyrians destroyed a kingdom of Elam, and early penetrated the mountains to attack the Medes towards the Caspian, now first mentioned as the 'great eastern sea' (836 B.C.). But the later story of a queen (Semiramis) marching to the Indus is a fable. A form of the name Parthia already appears. The Medes could not be prevented from growing strong, and at last, with the help of Babylonian rebels, they overthrew the hated empire, turning Nineveh 'into a mound and a ruin', to the immense relief of many oppressed peoples (612 B.C.). They occupied the northern part to the borders of Lydia; their allies took the southern to the borders of Egypt, and followed a bad example by deporting Judah. By 538 B.C. both the new empires and also Lydia were absorbed by the Persian Cyrus, once a Mede vassal.

Little is heard of sea doings. One king makes a fuss of an expedition across the head of the Persian Gulf, and depicts the queer biremes built for it by his Phoenician subjects. There is still no report of eastward voyaging, though some wares came from India, which borrowed an alphabet in return (or so it was thought before recent finds of the very early civilization

---

[1] Probably = Poseideion of Hdt. III, 91, S. Smith, *Antiq. Journ.* 1942, pp. 87–112 after Sir L. Woolley, ibid. XVII and *J.H.S.* LVII. Javan, L. W. King, *J.H.S.* 1910, pp. 327–35: Berossus ap. Eus. Chron. 1. Arabs, Hitti, op. cit. pp. 37–9, Worrell, op. cit. p. 14. Name, Honigmann, *R.E.* Syria. Assyrian records translated by Luckenbill, 1926-7.

[2] Herrmann, *Erdkarte der Urbibel*, 1931. Table, Gen. ix. 18–x. Tyre, Ezek. xxvi–xxvii. Gog, Ezek. xxxviii (not his and re-editing Jeremiah iii–vii), cp. Gen. x. 2, Rev. xx. 8: Marinelli, *Scritti Minori*, 1908, pp. 387–438: A. K. Anderson, *Alexander's Gate, Gog and Magog, and the Inclosed Nations*, 1932: J. K. Wright, *Geogr. Lore of...the Crusades*, 1925, pp. 72–3.

there). The literature of north India says nothing of merchants to 'Baberu' till probably a good deal later, but it is very monkish in its interests. When they are mentioned, strangely enough they carry peacocks.[1]

Otherwise there is only the tale of Solomon's enterprise (about 970 B.C.). Like other glories of that national hero it was much edited and embellished, and the texts are more or less late and full of obscurities. With his ally Hiram of Tyre he manned ships (or a ship?) at Ezion-geber at the head of the Red Sea. 'And they came to Ophir and fetched from thence gold.... And the navy also of Hiram, that brought gold from Ophir, brought in from Ophir great plenty of almug trees and precious stones....And all King Solomon's drinking vessels were of gold....For the king had at sea a navy of Tarshish with the navy of Hiram: once in three years came the navy of Tarshish, bringing gold, and silver, ivory, and apes, and peacocks.' (The last word, *tukkiyim*, is from a south Indian one, *togai*, but it may be an interpolation; Josephus read 'black slaves' and the Greek texts have some gibberish about stone—incidentally they spell Sophir etc. in eight ways). 'And when the queen of Sheba heard of the fame of Solomon...she came...with camels that bare spices, and very much gold, and precious stones.' About a century later 'Jehoshaphat made ships of Tarshish to go to Ophir for gold: but they went not, for the ships were broken at Eziongeber'. Presumably ships are meant of the same kind as went to Tarshish. Josephus thought this Tarsus, as being among the sons of Javan, but it is usually taken as Tartessus in Spain; even so it may well be an anachronism for this time. 'Once in three years' is variously understood and discounted. Very possibly there was already in south-west Arabia a trading kingdom, if not Sheba, which is said to have succeeded Ma'an only later, so that the queen is fabulous. The table of the nations puts Ophir near, and most agree to find it hereabouts, or perhaps a little on, in Oman; the Indian wares, if authentic at all, might be picked up here.[2] But many take the ships up

---

1 About 4th cent. B.C., *C.H.I.* 1922, I, 203, 291 (but 7th cent. *R.E.* Pfau and see p. 81, n. 2). Alphabet, *C.H.I.* I, 62, but denied in Mookerji, *Hindu Civ.* 1936, p. 38. Meissner, *Bab. u. Ass.* I, 351, II, 304: L. D. Barnett, *Antiquities of India*, 1913, p. 14. Partakka in 7th cent. B.C., Debevoise, *Pol. Hist. of Parthia*, 1938, p. 2. Herzfeld, *Iran in the Anc. East*, 1941, pp. 192–3: name Caspian connected with Kassites, ibid. p. 182.

2 Most, as Kittel, *Hist. of Hebrews*, 1895, II, 189: Lods, *Israel*, 1930, p. 429: (S. Arabia?) Cook, *C.A.H.* III, 357: Kiernan, *Unveiling of Arabia*, 1937, p. 20: Bertram Thomas, *Arabia Felix*, 1932 introd. (Dhufar): Tarn, *Hell. Civ.* 1927, p. 196: J. A. Montgomery, *Arabia and the Bible*, 1934, pp. 38–9. Even A. short of strait, Moritz, *Arabien*, 1923, II, 59. Oman, Hitti, op. cit. p. 41: H. G. Rawlinson, *Intercourse between India and Western World*, 1916, pp. 10–13. Texts, I Kings ix–x, cp. II Chron. viii–ix (a late version, about 300 B.C.). Broken, I Kings xxii. 48. Table, Gen. x. 29 (of J., *c.* 850 B.C.), but cp. x. 7. Arabian inscriptions not safely put so early, Huart, *Hist. des Arabes*, 1912, I, 144, Albright, *Arch. and the Religion of Israel*, 1942, p. 56, against Hommel, etc. Queen fable, Worrell, op. cit. p. 118. Tarsus, Jos. *Ant.* I, 127, Wainwright, *J.E.A.* 1936, p. 16. But to Spain for tin of Tin Islands, *L.E.* p. 44. (For Jerome Tarshish was Indiae regio!) A.V. spells Tharshish.

the Persian Gulf or on to India itself, either at the Indus mouth, where Ptolemy has an Abiria, or Bombay way—the Sovira coast of Buddhist writings, and some compare the same geographer's Supara thereabouts— or down to Malabar. Josephus even thought of the Malay 'gold-land', and Columbus agreed, and the Spaniards discovered Solomon Islands still farther afield. Few moderns are so imaginative, but one thinks of Indo-China and another talks wildly of expeditions which seem to have taken three years and 'certainly went as far as India, if not to Australasia'.[1] A few besides the author of *King Solomon's Mines* have tried to make a case for east Africa, or south-east, the gold-land of 'Sofala thought Ophir' (so Milton already), but it is a poor case, and a supposed connection of the Zimbabwe ruins in Rhodesia with the Phoenicians has been exploded. Some argue more reasonably for Somaliland, or for the Afar coast within the strait, as an outlet for the gold of Sennar behind.[2] Possibly, of course, African wares as well as Indian were picked up in Arabia, which can hardly have ever had much gold of its own. Altogether this royal traffic sounds like an imitation of the old Punt voyaging, and it was apparently short-lived: the texts do not justify speaking of regular Phoenician trade in these seas.

What showing the Phoenicians make in Homer has been told above. Somehow the Greeks later got an exaggerated idea of them, and on this cue moderns saw them busy early and everywhere as colonists and pioneers of civilization. It is now clear that much ascribed to them was really due to the forgotten Minoans: for Greece they played only a minor part as middlemen in the dark age, except that they did bring its alphabet. How soon they appeared in western waters is very doubtful. Cadiz and a colony in Africa were dated 1100 B.C. or 'soon after the Trojan war', but the greatest, Carthage, more plausibly 813 B.C. In Sicily they may have somewhat preceded the Greeks and, when these came, retired into the western corner. The texts on Tarshish, if it is in Spain, need not be older than the eighth century B.C. Archaeological evidence for Phoenicians in

---

1 Garstang, *Heritage of Solomon*, 1934, p. 373. Cambodia, Pavie ap. H. Clifford, *Further India*, 1904, p. 12. Chryse, Jos. *Ant.* VIII, 164. W. India, *C.H.I.* I, 212, 329, 391, 594 more or less hesitatingly: Hall, *Anc. Hist. of Near East*[4], 1919, p. 434: Hornell in *Ant.* 1941, p. 244. Abhira, Lassen, *Ind. Alt.* 1847, I. 538. P. G., Hommel, op. cit. p. 552 and 'most' ap. T. H. Robinson, *Hist. of Israel*, 1932, I, 256: Glaser, *Gesch. u. Geogr. Arabiens*, 1890, II, 345–83, cited by Rickard, *Man and Metals*, 1932, I, 255–68 and Guthe in Schaff-Herzog, *Enc. of Rel. Knowledge*, 1910, s.v. Ophir.

2 Hennig, *T.I.* I, 32, earlier for Sofala, *V.R.L.* pp. 65–81, as is Gsell, *Hérodote*, 1916, p. 232. Exploded, Caton-Thompson, *The Z. Culture*, 1931 (confirming D. R. MacIver, *Medieval Rhodesia*, 1906): discussed by Rickard, op. cit. pp. 242–55. For Punt=Som. Albright, op. cit. pp. 133–5, J. H. Rose, op. cit. p. 23 (that or Jubaland). For beads to Kenya see p. 10, n. 2.

the west is lacking before then.¹ (Many dismiss this objection, however, on the plea that tiny trading factories on capes or inshore islets could have existed without leaving any trace.) Carthage comes into real history only in the sixth century B.C., though already as important, protecting old settlements and sending out new. The mother-cities at home suffered from Assyrians and Babylonians, Sidon being destroyed and Tyre twice in danger. It was during the second siege that Ezekiel gloated prematurely over the 'renowned city' and her coming fall. 'All the ships of the sea with their mariners were in thee to occupy thy merchandise....Tarshish was thy merchant...with silver, iron, tin, and lead they traded in thy fairs. Javan, Tubal, and Meshech, they were thy merchants: they traded the persons of men and vessels of brass in thy market....The merchants of Sheba and Raamah, they...occupied in thy fairs with chief of all spices, and with all precious stones, and gold.' Just before this, we hear elsewhere, some Phoenician seamen in the service of Egypt had gone all round Africa, but of this tale more presently. Little enough is known of the ships. An early one shown on the Nile is high at both ends, with a square sail. They were roomier and better built for the sea than the Nile boats, from which they cannot be derived. They were round freighters and mainly sailers, with oars only to help them out in calms. No doubt they remained small and inclined to coasting. But there is a hint of bolder cuts: they used the Little Bear, called Phoenice, having learnt to do so perhaps early along the north-south coast of Syria (it gives a better course than the Great Bear, being nearer the pole, but is less easy to find). An Athenian later, who saw one of their vessels in his port, could not help admiring how neatly the gear was stowed, and how the first mate was walking round to see that everything was shipshape. Quite as late probably is the edifying story telling how Jonah chartered a ship going to Tarshish (bidden go east on an unwelcome mission, he tries to flee as far west as possible). When the tempest came and the mariners cast forth the wares, he was gone down into the sides of the ship and asleep, and the men rowed hard to bring it to land, but they could not. About then, too, coins of Sidon show a galley with a square sail furled, while those of Tyre have Melkart riding on a sea-horse.²

1 *C.A.H.* II, 578, III, 642 (yet IV, 367 accepts early dates): Bosch-Gimpera, *Klio*, 1929, pp. 345–68: Heichelheim, op. cit. p. 232: Dixon, *Iberians of Spain*, 1940, p. 23 (Gades 8th): Contenau, *Civ. phén.* 1928, pp. 91, 93 (9th or 8th): so Weill, op. cit. p. 180. Albright, op. cit. p. 132 ascribes the great expansion to Hiram *c.* 950. Texts, Beloch, op. cit. p. 252. 'Soon after', Str. 48: *c.* 1100, Vell. Pat. I, 2, 4, defended by Gsell, *Afr. du. Nord*, I, 359, Burn, *World of Hesiod*, pp. 243–7, etc. Name Phoenice once wide = Keftiu, Weill, op. cit. p. 16.

2 Head, *Hist. Numorum*, 1911, figs. 348, 352. Admiring, Xen. *Oec.* 8. Ezek. xxvii (9–25 is early, if not his, ed. G. A. Cooke, 1936). Bear, Aratus, 36–44, Callimachus ap. Diog. Laert. I, 23, Ovid, *F.* III, 107, Val. Flaccus, I, 17, Manilius, I, 304–8: *R.E.* Kynosura: Sir D'Arcy Thompson, *Science and the Classics*, 1940, p. 93, and see pp. 24–5. Ships, Köster, op. cit.

§6. THE CHINESE

Utterly beyond the horizon of any of these civilizations was another, in China. The earliest centre is indicated as in the north, near the last sharp elbow of the Yellow River and the opening of its fertile lower plain. Attempts have been made to trace the origin of the people or main elements of its culture back to Babylonia, but historians like Cordier deny any evidence of immigration. The highly artificial native tradition begins with two mythical persons who taught their people to live in families, keep flocks, and plough; the third, Hwang-ti, the 'Yellow Emperor', is credited with inventing many arts, about 2700 B.C., a date admittedly quite fictitious. Various antique rulers are held up as models in the classics edited by Confucius, who died in 479 B.C., and by his school, but little fact can be found behind this moralizing lore. Yü (supposed 2200 B.C.) drained the land after a great flood, and a chapter in the Book of History gives his tribute from nine provinces; it has been called the oldest geographical document in the world, but seems to represent much later conditions (even so the horizon is narrow, with a vague desert westwards). Some fine bronze vessels are referred to the Shang dynasty, said to end in 1122 B.C. There followed the Chou, whose feudal empire became more and more nominal, while the vassal kingdoms fought each other. It is only now, from 841 B.C., that the records are taken seriously by the first great native historian, and probably the genuine texts preserved in the classics are no older.[1] The excellent writer referred to is Szu-ma Ch'ien (otherwise spelt Se-ma Ts'ien), who flourished about 90 B.C., and there will be more occasion to use him about times nearer his own.

From very early times the enemies chiefly in view are the nomads of north and west, the 'dog barbarians', ancestors of the later Hiung-nu and thus ultimately, as most hold, of the Huns. Certain westward advances ascribed to old rulers sound very fabulous, and not very far was something hardly better than Utopia, where a queen or ogress lived in a jade tower near the mount of sunset and the western sea. A ware already available for export was silk, said to have been discovered by Hwang-ti's wife, and it was

pp. 45–9 and Taf. 11: Contenau, op. cit. pp. 291–7 and *Manuel d'Arch. Or.* 1927, I, 73–8: Gsell, op. cit. I, 34, II, 452, IV, 111: Février, *Rev. de l'Hist. de la Phil.* 1935, p. 97: Dussaud in *Syria*, 1936, pp. 60, 93: Hornell in *Ant.* 1941, p. 245. Night sailing, Str. 757.

[1] H. Maspero, *La Chine antique*, 1937, XII: Chavannes, *Mém. Hist. de Se-ma Ts'ien*, 1895, I, XLV: E. H. Parker, *China*², 1917, p. 16. Oldest, De Groot, *Chin. Urkunden zur Gesch. Asiens*, 1926, II, 25, 172: Wilhelm, *Short Hist. of Chin. Civ.* 1929, pp. 89–92 (end of Shang), but cp. Maspero, pp. 100, 610, Hirth, *Anc. Hist. of China*, 1908, pp. 35, 122, Chavannes, CXLI, Granet, *Civ. chinoise*, 1929, pp. 80–1. No immigration, Hirth, op. cit. p. 14, Cordier, *Hist. gén. de la Chine*, 1920, I, 31, etc. (but cp. Ungnad in Ebeling-Meissner, *Reallex. der Assyriologie*, 1938, II, 91).

to establish trade-routes across the fearsome deserts and mountains of Central Asia and cause an overlap of the horizons of east and west. But as yet it does not appear to have got through even indirectly, and one can hardly talk of silk-roads. Nobody now sees China in Isaiah's land of Sinim, and Ezekiel's 'silk' was not Chinese or probably silk at all, any more than the 'Mede dress', which only a very late writer assumes to have been silk.[1] It seems, however, that a few pieces of jade found their way along, one to turn up surprisingly in early Troy.

The original China was inland. South China, cut off by wooded ranges, was only slowly to be taken over from aboriginal peoples. A story of a 'south-pointing chariot' being given to some early envoys returning to Tongking is dismissed as a fable.

§ 7. EARLY THEORY

Primitive tribes are said to know their own environment very well, a little of people in direct contact, and nothing accurate of anybody beyond. They are shrewd observers in their way of many things which concern them, like their country and climate and food-supply, while their attempts at reasoning are peculiar, full of wishful thinking and assumptions which they never try to verify. All can see the more obvious movements of the heavenly bodies, however far they may be from understanding them.

The Old Stone men were busy with their hunting and the magic meant to ensure its success, but already they must have seen the Great Bear wheeling round and associated certain stars with changes of season and weather. Cattle-breeding and agriculture brought more dependence on the seasons and need of a calendar read from sun and stars. Apart from these practical uses men must have wondered how it all came about, where the sun went at night, and so on. But they boggled at these hard questions, and for long, finding it easier to imagine than to reason, answered only with myths or stories. The Greeks, who were the first really to shake off this kind of thinking, noted that 'the early historians and philosophers of nature', including their own, 'were writers of myths'.

'And darkness was upon the face of the deep: and the Spirit of God moved upon the face of the waters.... And God made the firmament, and divided the waters which were under the firmament from the waters which were above the firmament.... And God said... "Let the dry land appear...."'

---

[1] Proc. *B.P.* 1, 20, 9 on Hdt. 1, 135. Ezek. xvi. 10: Is. xlix. 12: Yule-Cordier, *Cathay and the Way Thither*, 1915, 1, 3. Roads, despite De Groot, II, 42, Maspero, pp. 87, 383, 607. Utopia, H. A. Giles, *Chin. Lit.* 1901, p. 49, Cordier, op. cit. I, 122, Hirth, op. cit. p. 148, Granet, p. 357, though De Groot, I, 21, II, 7, 172 treats more seriously. Barbarians, ibid. I, 5–8, Hirth, p. 67, Cordier, pp. 67, 127. Chariot fable, Cordier, p. 117, Hirth, p. 127.

This account of Genesis is not in fact very early, having been often revised down to the 'Priestly' editors, and it is far less crudely mythical in expression than many others. Yet it is like enough, even keeping a hint of a very primitive notion of brooding and a world-egg hatching into heaven and earth, which is more explicit elsewhere, in Egyptian, Phoenician, Greek and other myths. In the Babylonian story, with which the Hebrew had some distant contact, a god vanquished Tiamat, the older power of the chaos, and cut her up 'like a shell-fish' into two halves, heaven and earth. The 'deep' of the Bible has a kindred name, Tehom, and various other texts preserve more or less distinct traces of a conflict between Jehovah and a monster of chaos, Rahab or Leviathan, or a dragon or serpent, sometimes called simply the sea. In Egypt the Sun-god arose out of the formless waters, Ocean, origin of all things, and created Shu to force heaven off earth (he is depicted between them, supporting with his hands the star-spangled body). An Aryan god pushed up the sky and spread out the earth and held them apart. Homer has a casual phrase about Ocean being 'the origin of all', not merely of rivers and springs and seas: otherwise he seems deliberately to ignore the crude mythology of this matter. It is found in Hesiod, who makes a 'theogony' or pedigree of the business. First there came into being Chaos, the yawning gap, then somehow Earth and Tartarus 'in the depths of the earth' and Night and others; Earth of herself produced Heaven and by him the Titans, including Ocean, who rose and parted their parents; in the next generation were the Sun, Atlas the sky-bearer, and Zeus, and so on. It is a strange medley of gross old myths and a kind of early philosophizing. Elsewhere in Greek it is more simply stated that earth and heaven were mingled in a chaos before being parted; one writer explained that Hesiod's Chaos was 'waters' from which the earth was deposited.[1] Parallels could be cited from the cosmogonies of many lowlier peoples: so the Polynesians say that Earth and Sky were parted by their children. In general, such myths have the conception of an original form-

[1] Zeno, *Schol. Ap. Rhod.* I, 498. Mingled, Eur. fr. 484 N.: Orphic cosmogony, Cornford, *From Religion to Philosophy*, 1912, pp. 66, 178. Egg, ibid.: Aristophanes, *Birds*, 693: Plato, *Tim.* 40d: Rey, *Jeunesse de la Science grecque*, 1933, p. 61: A. Lang, *Myth, Ritual and Religion*, 1906, I, 298–9: Nilsson, *Hist. of Greek Religion*, 1925, pp. 73, 215–16: Petrie, *Rel. of Anc. Eg.* 1908, p. 68: Phoen. ap Eus. *P.E.* I, 10, Contenau, *Manuel*, I, 317–19, Hooke, *Myth and Ritual*, 1933, p. 82: Macdonell, *Vedic Mythology*, 1897, p. 14: L. D. Barnett, *Antiquities of India*, 1913, p. 197. Pedigree, Hes. *Theog.* pp. 116f.: H. J. Rose, *Greek Mythology*, ch. 2. Casual, *Il.* XIV, 246. Ocean, Kees, *Aegypten*, p. 297. Hommel, op. cit. p. 86. On Gen. comm. of Skinner², 1930, pp. 17–22, 41–50: Driver¹², 1926, pp. 19–33. Eg. myths, Budge, *Lit. of Eg.* pp. 67–70. Parting, Frazer, *Worship of Nature*, 1926, I, 26, 71. Many authorities in Hastings, *Enc. of Rel. and Ethics*, s.v. Cosmogony and Cosmology, IV, 125–79 (1911). 'Writers of Myths', Str. 20, cp. Arist. *Metaph.* I, 2, 982b. Kellett, *Story of Myths*, 1928, pp. 116–25. Rahab, Isaiah li. 9: T. H. Robinson in Hooke, op. cit. pp. 176–8. Best comparison of Greek and primitive cosmogonies still A. Lang, op. cit. chs. 6 and 10.

EARLY HORIZONS

lessness, often called 'the waters', which are then divided into upper and lower. Often the earth 'appears' from the lower, like an island. (The idea was specially natural in Babylonia, which was made by draining a swamp, but it is far too widespread to have any such single origin.) The question of the earth's foundations is hardly raised at this stage: it rests like a plate on the primal Ocean, though there may be a dim idea of a sort of lower vault, a counterpart of the sky: so there is perhaps in Homer, and the Hebrews seem to have a lower vault holding in 'the waters under the earth'.[2]

The earth itself looked flat (or at best slightly concave), and there is nothing to show that anyone had yet dreamt of doubting that it was so in fact. The horizon seems naturally to suggest a round plate, though the Egyptians in their valley groove thought rather of an oblong, extended north-south, like the bottom (flat or concave) of a long box. The heaven was stretched overhead 'as a tent to dwell in'. How was it kept up? By God's will or his appointed sky-bearer like Shu, who might be helped out by pillars or mountains at the horizon. (In Homer Atlas merely guards the pillars, presently he holds the broad heaven at the ends of the earth before the Hesperides, or he stands towards the west supporting with his shoulders the pillar of heaven and earth; only very late is a fancy that he supports both heaven and earth themselves.) The horizon becomes a 'back-flowing' or circular stream, a thing mythical in origin and often badly misunderstood later as referring to known outer seas, though Aristotle at least tries to explain 'the secret meaning of Ocean in early writers'.[2] It seemed natural to many peoples that the earth should be encircled by the waters, out of which it had arisen, and should rest on 'the waters under the earth', which supplied all its springs and rivers and seas (there is presumably some idea of subterranean connections). The Sun's cattle eaten by the hungry comrades of Odysseus were akin to those pastured by the Babylonian Sungod beyond the Ocean-stream.

What happens to the sun at night? An Australian tribe thinks that he

1 J. Y. Simpson, *Landmarks in the Struggle between Science and Religion*, 1925, pp. 40, 43. Gen. xlix. 25, Exod. xx. 4, Amos vii. 4. *Il.* VIII, 16: Hes. *Theog.* 720–5. Gilbert, *Meteor. Theorien des Griech. Alt.* 1907, p. 276: Kees, loc. cit.: Hommel, p. 124. For earth resting on water, Jensen, *Kosmologie der Bab.* 1890, pp. 153, 254: G. Maspero, *Dawn of Civ.*[4] 1901, p. 542: many refs. in A. B. Cook, *Zeus*, III, pt. i, 18 (1940).

2 *Met.* I, 9, 347 a; cp. *Metaph.* I, 3, 983b: Geminus, 16, 28 (horizon): Gilbert, op. cit. p. 394. Berger, *Erdkunde*[2], 35, and in Roscher's *Lex. der Myth.* Suppl. 1904: Gisinger, *R.E.* Okeanos (but originally?). Waters, Exod. xx. 4, etc.: Driver, op. cit. p. 8. Pillars or Atlas, poets ap. Plut. *de Facie*, 6, cp. Job xxvi. 11, Psalm civ. 32. Atlas, *Od.* I, 52, cp. Hes. *Theog.* pp. 746–8, Aesch. *P.V.* pp. 348–50: late, Paus. v, 11. Tent, Is. xl. 22, xlv. 12, Ps. civ. 2. Oblong, Schaefer in *Die Antike*, 1927, p. 93: J. Ball, *Egypt in the Classical Geographers*, 1942, pp. 1–2 (after G. Maspero): Dreyer, *Hist. of the Planetary Systems*, 1906, p. 3: Dampier-Whetham, *Hist. of Science*, 1929, p. 7. Long oval, Cebrian, *Gesch. der Kartographie*, 1923, p. 19.

sinks into a hole near Lake Eyre and travels underground to the east. For the Egyptians he passes through the rim mountains, changes to a night boat, and floats along a sort of Nile answering to the heavenly stream or sky, while demons seek vainly to stop him and the dead are cheered by his visit. For Homer, despite one phrase about going 'under' the earth, he does not light up Tartarus, but somehow returns to the east without leaving the upper vault. Presently various poets explain that he floats along the Ocean-stream from the Hesperides to the eastern Ethiopians, where his chariot awaits him: evidently he passes round the rim of the earth-disk and is hidden by its high northern part, and Aristotle understands them as meaning this. The Babylonians had fancies of the earth as an overturned boat or a pyramidal temple in seven stages or a great boss or hollow mountain rising from the deep, and of the sun being hidden at night in the north behind a mountain (this last was to crop up again very strangely in late antiquity in the monk Cosmas). The old Indian hymns do not say that the sun passes below or explain why it is darkened; later texts have a mount Meru at the centre of the earth-disk and the sun moving behind it at night. Here again we find an idea of happy Hyperboreans (their native name was to reach the ears of the Greeks and they were to figure even on Ptolemy's map).[1] 'Around Meru are four quadrants (like the petals of a lotus) of which India is the southern one. Around this central continent are seven concentric oceans and continents'—but we need not go into these fanciful embellishments.

Crude notions of the earth did not prevent much practical knowledge of the stars, which had their uses for the seasons and the calendar. The Babylonians watched them mainly for a supposed influence on mankind, and under this obsession gave each country and city a heavenly counterpart in which its fortunes could be studied. They were interested less in the fixed stars than the 'interpreter' planets and 'the way of the sun'. The amount of their early astronomy is much in question. Latterly at least they gathered a good deal, recording eclipses, for instance, and noting their periods, and they were long to be the teachers of others in the subject. Yet they did not try to explain eclipses or the whole system of movements, as the Greeks

---

1 See p. 131, n. 2: Lassen, op. cit. I, 846: Barnett, op. cit. pp. 196–202: W. E. Clark in *Legacy of India*, ed. Garratt, 1937, pp. 346–8: hymns, Macdonell, op. cit. p. 10, H. W. Wallis, *Cosmology of the Rigveda*, 1887, pp. 115–17. Boat, (Berossus ap.) Diod. II, 31, 7. Boss, Rey, *Science Or. avant les Grecs*, 1930, p. 187: Dreyer, op. cit. p. 2: Handcock, *Mesop. Archaeology*, 1912, p. 399: Hommel, loc. cit.: Meissner, *Klio*, 1923, pp. 97–100: Sayce in Hastings, op. cit. pp. 128–9: temple, W. F. Warren, *J.R.A.S.* 1908, pp. 977–83. Cp. Isaiah xiv. 13. 'Under', *Od.* X, 191: Tartarus, *Il.* VIII, 13, 480, Hes. *Theog.* 119. Poets, Mimnermus etc. ap. Athen. XI, 466d, 469d–470d, Arist. *Met.* II, 1, 354a: Gilbert, op. cit. p. 671: see p. 22, n. 1. Eg., Dreyer, op. cit. p. 4: on sun Roeder in Ebert's *Reallex.* XII, 307. Australians, Fallaize in Hastings, op. cit. XII, 63.

EARLY HORIZONS 37

were to do. (The latter sometimes credited them with too much early science, as on the moon being eclipsed by the shadow of the earth, though the earth is 'boat-shaped and hollow'!) The Egyptians had from the first a very accurate year, since the dog-star Sothis appeared just before sunrise on 19 July in close association with the Nile flood; thus they had a good solar calendar from 4241 B.C., which has been called the earliest fixed date in history. But they, too, hardly felt the need of any theory of the heavenly bodies. The early Greeks had no superstition of astrology, and used the stars merely to fix the right times for farming and sailing, the Bear also to give the right direction. They knew the risings and settings of certain constellations, the solstices or turnings of the sun, and the Bear which never bathes in Ocean. Such observations were too elementary to be applied then, or even much later, as the basis of maps: 'the fact that the Bear does not set, being regarded simply as a fact, did not even suggest an Arctic circle.'[1]

Very primitive men, especially roaming hunters and seamen, have been known to draw rough local sketch-maps; occasionally they have been of service to explorers like Parry and Captain Cook, who began to doubt, however, if his Tahitian knew as much as he appeared to do. The Melanesian islanders are said to make diagrams to plan expeditions, though samples seem little better than mnemonics. Some praise the useful coast-charts of the Eskimo and the bark maps of the Labrador Indians. Among higher barbarians the Mexicans had fairly elaborate maps before the Spaniards came, and one of the Gulf coast painted on cloth was presented to Cortes; the Peruvians are credited even with maps in relief.[2] It seems

1 Heidel, *Frame of the Anc. Greek Maps*, 1937, p. 9: *Heroic Age of Science*, 1933, pp. 124–5. Hes. *Op.* 479, 525, 564, 663. Bear, etc., *Il.* XVIII, 483–9, *Od.* v, 271–7: Syrie where the sun turns, ibid. xv, 403, Heidel, *Frame*, 18, 58, Rey, *Jeunesse de la Science grecque*, 1933, pp. 406–10: Sir D'Arcy Thompson, *Proc. Class. Assoc.* 1929, p. 28. Bab., E. Meyer, op. cit. I, 1, 591–5 (more science from 8th): L. W. King, *Hist. of Babylon*, 1915, p. 312 (late): Thorndike, *Hist. of Magic and Experim. Science*, 1929, I, 15–17: Boll-Bezold[3] (Gundel), *Sternglaube u. Sterndeutung*, 1926, pp. 1–15: Tannery, *Mém. Scient.* 1925, III, 335–7. 'Interpreters', Diod. II, 29–31: a ref. to their astral geography in Deut. iv. 19. Counterpart, Meissner, *Bab. u. Ass.* 1925, II, 107–10. Opitz in Ebert, op. cit. XII, 422–35(1928). Shadow, Diod. II, 31, cp. Berossus ap. Aet. II, 25, 29, Cleom. II, 4: Boll, *R.E.* Finsternisse. Eg., Breasted, *Hist. of Eg.* 1912, p. 100: Moret, *Le Nil et la Civ. ég.* 1924, pp. 528–30: Sloley in *L.E.* pp. 161–5. Movements, Rey, *Sc. Or.* pp. 173, 181: Burnet, *Early Greek Philosophy*, 1924, p. 5. On primitive time-reckoning, Nilsson, *Acta Soc. hum. Litt.*, Lund, 1920: Hogben, *Science for the Citizen*, 1938, ch. 1: Sloley in *J.E.A.* 1931, pp. 166–78 (Eg. dials).

2 *Enc. Brit.* ed. 14, Map. *Enc. Ital.* s.v. Cartografia. Hind, *Labrador*, 1863: C. F. Hall, *Life with the Esquimaux*, 1864, I, 127, II, 332: Flaherty, *Geogr. Rev.* 1918, p. 440. Diagrams, Malinowski in *Science, Religion and Reality*, ed. Needham, 1925, p. 35. Lowie, *Introd. to Cultural Anthropology*, 1934, p. 334. E. C. Semple, *Influences of Geogr. Environment*, 1911, p. 299. Cook, J. H. Rose, *Man and the Sea*, 1935, p. 196. Mnemonics, Johnstone, *Study of Oceans*, 1926, p. 32. Van Loon, *Home of Mankind*, 1935, pp. 63–4. See also Boas, *General Anthropology*, 1938, p. 275: Raisz, *General Cartography*, 1938, pp. 7–10: W. W. Jervis, *The World in Maps*[2], 1938, pp. 12–13.

unlikely, therefore, that the Egyptians had nothing better than the very few rough plans which happen to survive. Herewith is a sketch (omitting the explanatory writing) from a papyrus fragment of about 1300 B.C. It represents a mining region in the eastern desert with the 'roads leading to the sea' past 'mountains where gold is washed', shown in a childish perspective. Maps must have begun everywhere with this sort of picture of things seen along a road, and this has been called the oldest 'map' in the world.[1] There is a second plan of a mining 'mountain'. Another of the

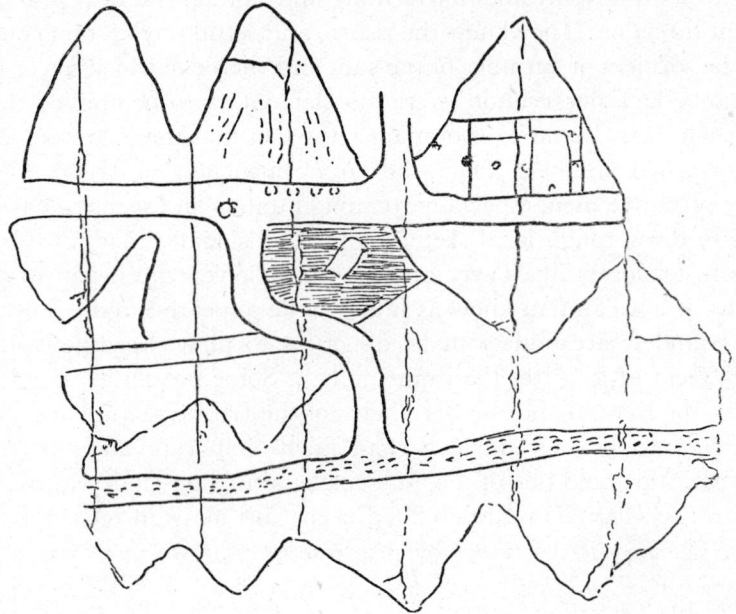

Fig. 2. Egyptian map of roads to the gold mines.

same time shows the isthmus road and a lake and canal with fish and crocodiles. The Egyptians had for taxation purposes constantly to survey the amount of land reached and fertilized by the Nile flood and to recover the landmarks which it wiped out. So they became reputed for their 'geometry', though it did not go much beyond rule-of-thumb. The local field-plans may have been strung into larger ones, and perhaps the lists of tributary peoples were thrown into some sort of map form, but there is no evidence (a director of modern survey work in the same country denies that any general or even district maps could have been constructed from

[1] Erman-Ranke, op. cit. p. 466, Budge, *Eg. Sudan*, 1907, II, 335–6. Cebrian, op. cit. p. 29. Originally in Lepsius, *Urkunden*, 1842, pl. XXII (from Turin papyrus). Hardly a 'map', *Enc. Brit.* loc. cit. *L.E.* pl. 33. Rickard, *Man and Metals*, 1932, I, 219–20. G. W. Murray in Ball, op. cit. pp. 180–2, gives two coloured plates and identifies the mine near the Wadi Hammamat.

PLATE I

A. Babylonian map of the world (see p. 39).

B. Coin of Panticapaeum (Crimea) with Griffin (see p. 64).

C. Coin of Cyrene with silphium plant (see p. 67).

D. Arabian coin copying the owl of Athens (see p. 133).

LIBRARY
STATE TEACHERS COLLEGE
WAYNE, NEBRASKA

the field measurements). For anything like a map of the world there is only a late statement that 'Sesostris' left in Colchis—where he never was—maps graven on pillars, from which the Argonauts learnt of another possible way home, up the Danube: this is a grotesque invention, but the poet had lived in Egypt and may have seen native maps of some kind.[1] One kind interested a superstitious people far more than any other, namely guide-maps of the other world, which they placed in tombs, with all the spells necessary to avoid its many dangers.

Babylonia has quite a few plans of towns and districts. A recently found clay-tablet of Sargon's time shows canals or rivers (the Tigris and a tributary?) between mountains, apparently in the Kirkuk region: it has now been claimed as probably the oldest map. There is even a general map, though one almost unbelievably queer (see Plate I A). It is not very old (sixth century B.C.?), but seems to reproduce an extremely antique type, with a text perhaps referring to Sargon. The Euphrates runs south from the mountains past Babylon to the swamps, and within circles are given some names of countries and cities like Assur; close around flows the Bitter River or Ocean, and in triangles beyond there is a dangerous horned bull or 'semi-darkness reigns' or 'the sun is not seen'. The text and the whole conception are desperately obscure. One writer explains that the 'seven islands' are regions supposed to lie between the earthly Ocean and the heavenly, which is described with its zodiacal signs, while the round earth with Babylon as its hub is only roughly sketched in. Another takes the circle as a notion of Persian Gulf–Caspian–Black–Mediterranean, which seems very doubtful. Another wonders if the whole has anything but a decorative purpose. It has also been suggested that the underlying idea was brought from an older home between the Caspian and the Black Seas, but this carries little conviction.[2] Elsewhere various rulers boast of dominating 'the four quarters', from Elam north to Assyria and west to Syria, though this hardly covers all their known world.

The Hebrews had a method, not without value, of casting their information into a table of the nations descended from the sons of Noah, 31 from Ham, 27 from Shem, and 13 from Japhet. There are hints of mapping: Joshua, before allotting shares of the promised land, sent men who 'passed

1 Apoll. Rhod. IV, 272–81. Lists, as Schiaparelli, op. cit. p. 121, Cebrian, op. cit. p. 19. Survey, Ball, op. cit. p. 7.

2 Carleton, *Buried Empires*, p. 71. Decorative, Cebrian, pp. 42, 50. Circle, Thompson in *C.A.H.* I, 494, and Sayce, loc. cit. (perhaps). Explains, Unger in *Antiquity*, 1935, p. 314. Also Meissner, op. cit. II, 378: Delaporte, *Mesopotamie*, 1923, p. 261: Budge, *Bab. Life and History*[2], 1925, pp. 213–15: *Cuneiform Texts from Bab. Tablets in Brit. Mus.* 1906, XXII, pl. 48. Other plans, Unger, op. cit. pp. 311–22. Kirkuk, Meek, *Excavations at Nuzi*, 1935, III, no. 1 and *Ann. Amer. Sch. Or. Research*, 1933, pp. 1–13. Raisz, op. cit. p. 10. Photo in *Nat. Geogr. Mag.* 1932, p. 762.

through the land, and described it by cities into seven parts in a book'. There is the usual notion of 'the circle of the earth', 'a circle upon the face of the deep', with themselves of course in the centre. They had also their Utopia, Eden with its four rivers, the Euphrates and Tigris and two others which were to give headaches to Christian commentators. Most thought them the Indus (or Ganges) and Nile, and put Eden far east in or beyond the Ocean, under which its rivers flowed to emerge in the known world. Some, however, explained the business away as an allegory of the four cardinal virtues. All are obviously wrong, whatever the original conception was: somebody now thinks of two wadis in east Arabia, while another supplies two rivers from the geography of Babylonian astrology.[1] (The rivers seem an interpolation, and various other Biblical passages cited above are not really early, but may be taken as reflecting mythical views which were not outgrown.)

One can only guess about the Minoans. Homer has a hint of rough maps from the 'measures of the route', and of a world-map or earth-disk with a surrounding Ocean-stream, as in the design of the shield. The name Ocean does not seem Greek, and both name and conception may be a legacy from the Minoans. As for the stars, their religion was apparently little concerned with them. It has been argued that certain designs in Cretan and other prehistoric art represent early cosmological notions like the Babylonian earth-mountain or the navel of the earth, but they do not seem quite convincing in this sense. Very ancient, no doubt, was the temple of Delphi and a round marble stone, perhaps a fetish of the Earth-goddess, said to be the navel of the earth; alongside were two eagles of gold, and it was explained that two eagles sent by Zeus from far east and far west had met there (the legends were invented, Rohde thinks, about a stone which was called the navel at first merely because of its shape). Homer makes a few favoured heroes retire to an Elysian plain at the ends of the earth, with soft zephyrs blowing from Ocean; this is unlike usual Greek ideas of the other world, including his own, and may well come from the Minoans, for whom it would be natural to think of such happy isles. (Strabo foolishly guesses that the poet had heard enough of the wealth of south Spain to locate his paradise there.) Sea-traders like the Phoenicians must have gathered reports of voyages and made maps, but nothing is said of

[1] Lutz, *Amer. Anthropologist*, 1924, pp. 160–74. Wadis, Hommel, op. cit. p. 561: Montgomery, *Arabia and the Bible*, 1934, p. 93. Paradise and rivers, J. K. Wright, *Geogr. Lore of...Crusades*, 1925, pp. 71–2. A strange map 'ad mentem Hebraeorum', showing rivers, Spruner-Menke's *Atlas Antiquus*, 1865. Joshua xviii. 6 (writing now known as early in Palestine, Sir F. Kenyon, *The Bible and Archaeology*, 1940, pp. 158–9): cp. Ezek. xlvii–xlviii. Circle, Is. xl. 22: Prov. viii. 27: centre, Ezek. v. 5, xxxviii. 12. Table, see p. 28, n. 2. Numbers in Aug. *C.D.* xvi, 3, Jerome (Migne, III, 317), and cp. Jos. *Ant.* i, 6, 1.

EARLY HORIZONS 41

these. Some after Diodorus have guessed 'Ocean' to be derived from them. There are now known some writings of theirs as old as the fourteenth century B.C.; a mention of western 'fields of El' has seemed suggestive for the origin of Elysium; a text connects this Sun-god, often symbolized as a bull, with Crete, which recalls the myth of Zeus as a bull carrying off Europa to that island.[1]

A rational theory of Nature was beyond the older peoples: they could not break the habit of myth hardened into priestly tradition. But already in Homer the gods have become very human, and there is a new and brighter air, which heralds the dawn of philosophy in his native Ionia and is the beginning of the European spirit.[2] Hesiod is darker, with his peasant superstitions, but he is too hard-headed to be enslaved by them. Many, indeed, and not only poets, were to continue mythical ways of thought and expression long after. There is an Earth-shaker, it is said, the same who causes tidal waves; an eclipse is due to an angry god; a plain by the Rhône is covered with stones thrown by Hercules at his enemies; a volcano is a smithy of the Fire-god or the prison of a vanquished giant, or a rather unhappy combination of both. Yet the Greeks were set on the road to science. They were struck by the lack of intelligent curiosity in others. When a temple scribe said that the Nile rose at Aswan from bottomless caverns and flowed half north, half south, the tourist looked hard at the poor man, who was in fact glibly repeating an antique notion stereotyped in religious art. The priests also said that the Nile came from the Ocean, and some of the visitors did not grasp how mythical this was.[3] (Later we

1 Kenyon, op. cit. pp. 158–9. Elysium, Schaeffer, *Ras Shamra*, 1939, p. 61. 'Ocean', Diod.v, 20: Tozer, *Anc. Geogr.* p. 21, as Kiepert, p. 30: not Greek, Rose, *Greek Myth.* p. 21: Minoan, V. Burr, *Nostrum Mare*, 1932, p. 96, ap. *R.E.* Okeanos. Spain, Str. 150. Elysium Minoan, Nilsson, *Minoan-Myc. Religion and its Survival in Greek Religion*, 1927, pp. 541–5 (ultimately from Egypt): Malten, *Arch. Jahrb.* 1913, p. 35 (even name). Navel, see esp. Frazer's note on Paus. x, 16, 3: Pindar, *Pyth.* IV, 74, Bacchylides, 4, 4, Aesch. *Eum.* 40, 166, Eur. *Ion*, 223, Plato, *Rep.* 427c, Str. 419. Rohde, *Psyche*[8], Engl. tr. 1925, p. 97. Designs, Gaerte, *Anthropos*, 1914, pp. 956–79. Shield, *Il.* XVIII, 483, cp. Hes. *Scut. Herc.* 139–317. Route, *Od.* IV, 389, cp. Hes. *Op.* 689: Heidel, *Heroic Age of Science*, 1933, p. 123.

2 H. A. L. Fisher, *Hist. of Europe*[2], 1938, I, 17: Farrington, *Science in Antiquity*, 1936, p. 65. Heiberg, *Maths. and Phys. Science in Class. Ant.* 1922, pp. 7, 17: cp. Hesiod, Burn, *World of Hesiod*, 1936, pp. 44–7, 72–3.

3 Diod. I, 19 and 37, cp. Hdt. II, 23: scribe, ibid. 21: tears, ap. Paus. x, 32, 18. Eclipse, Pindar, *Hyporch.* fr. 107. Wave, Eph. ap. Diod. xv, 48–9, Str. 385, Paus. VII, 24, 6. Stones, Aesch. ap. Str. 183 (cp. Arist. and Pos. ibid. 182). Smithy, Eur. *Cycl.* 20, popular opinion ap. Thuc. III, 86: Virg. *Aen.* VIII, 416–32, *Georg.* IV, 170–5. Giant, *Il.* II, 782, Hes. *Theog.* 820–80, Pindar, *Pyth.* I, 30–55 (and ap. Str. 266–7), Virg. *Aen.* III, 578–82, IX, 715, Ovid, *Met.* v, 346–58, etc. Combined, Aesch. *P.V.* 351–72. Myths discussed, Str. 243, 249, 626. G. W. Tyrrell, *Volcanoes*, 1931, pp. 10, 131. On Poseidon as Earth-shaker, esp. A. B. Cook, *Zeus*, III, pt. i, 1–20. Greeks have curiosity, Plat. *Rep.* 435E, as cp. money-making Egyptians and Phoenicians.

hear of another myth that the rise of the river is due to the tears of the goddess Isis for her husband.) In general, the Greeks could not be fobbed off with such things. They were the first to ask causes and answer with theories which were not myths, if often over-bold or wrong. It is their supreme importance in history.

Long afterwards Christians were to get into a false position towards science by not dealing sensibly with the Old Testament on these matters. There the earth is obviously flat under a tent-like heaven; it has vague 'foundations' or is 'stretched out above the waters'; the firmament is 'strong as a molten mirror' and has waters above it, and at the Flood 'the windows of heaven were opened'. (Once in a late book 'He hangeth the earth upon nothing', which sounds bold but need not be taken very seriously in view of the rest.) These notions were treated in every way but the right one of frankly dismissing them as only the myths of antique Jews, for whom Nature was a witness to the power of God rather than an object of rational inquiry. Entangled in the texts, many Fathers hesitated to assert the earth-globe, or denied it, though it had long since been proved and even reasonably well measured. They debated whether the firmament was fixed or merely firm, and what was above it, ice or vapour or really water, suspended somehow and perhaps cooling the axle of the universe. A few gave it up and took to allegory. Augustine gently rallies these naïve speculations and concludes that we must not be led into doubt anyhow, while others detest all arguing about revelation on things beyond our understanding.[1] The texts are often magnificent poetry, but they do imply primitive ideas, and it was a queer accident that they were long upheld against the best results of ancient science, and even of modern.

The Chinese have kindred myths, the world-egg, the parting of Heaven and Earth, and the rim-Ocean. But they fancy the earth as a square rather than a round plate; the Tribute of Yü implies a naïve map of concentric squares, and the idea of a square or oblong continues much later, with some very random guesses at its size. There is a wild legend that under Yü two men measured the earth: they walked from north to south and then from east to west and both times got the same result, said to mean 84,000 miles! The native tradition ascribes a calendar and a lot of astronomy to a very early time, but it seems very dubious. The Book of History mentions two sages as put to death for failing to predict an eclipse (in 2158 B.C.!);

---

[1] Aug. *Civ. Dei*, XI, 34, *Conf.* V, 5, etc. Axle, Ambrose, *Hex.* II, 3–9. Basil, *Hex.* III, 2–9. Duhem, *Système du Monde*, 1913, II, 487–94. Kimble, *Geogr. in the Middle Ages*, 1938, p. 150: see p. 387, n. 1. Hangeth, Job xxvi. 7 (Singer in Needham, op. cit. p. 108 sees Greek influence). Cp. foundations, Job xxxviii. 4, Ps. civ. 5, cxxxvi. 6, Zech. xii. 1. Windows, Gen. vii. 11. Tent, see p. 35, n. 2. A. D. White, *History of the Warfare of Science with Theology*, 1896, I, chs. 2 and 11, is still of value.

EARLY HORIZONS

another, about 1100 B.C., apparently determined the obliquity of the ecliptic well, but the sun's distance badly as he assumed a flat earth.[1]

The Greeks were to be rather slow in thinking of the earth-globe and slower in really applying it to geography. That it ever occurred to anybody before them there is no evidence. Ancient mariners may have seen southern stars disappear below the horizon, while the Bear rose higher. The Egyptians had a special regard for the stars round the pole as 'the never vanishing ones'. But, as said above, such things could be observed for ages without suggesting the true shape of the earth.

It may seem rather heavy-handed to deal thus with poetic fancies like the pillars. Often indeed they were vague enough, and phrases about the four corners of the earth need not always imply a denial of the usual disk.[2] (Recently it has been insisted that the square, with the corners at the cardinal points, is at least as early as the disk and more widespread than has been generally supposed.) But anyhow such primitive notions were really held, and they cannot be ignored: they had an influence long after, even among the Greeks, who went on quoting their Homer, while many Christians gave up the globe of pagan science and reverted to the old disk, or took the four corners literally and drew an oblong, like Cosmas.

Even in the mythical stage there were shrewd anticipations of science. Thus the widespread story of a great Flood was probably due, at least in some cases, to observing shells far inland and up hills: the sea, it was inferred, must once have risen to these high levels (it was not suspected that the shell-bearing strata might have been lifted by earth-movements). The usual Greek myth seems an inference from another fact of physical geography, the plain of Thessaly, where a lake must have risen high till it was drained by a remarkable ravine torn through the mountains. Samothrace, an island off the Dardanelles, had its own version, that the Black Sea was once a lake, until it was swollen by many rivers and burst out through the straits, an early guess which was to be repeated later as a serious theory.[3]

---

[1] Clerk, *Enc. Brit.* ed. 14, 'Astronomy', II, 582. Needs criticism, Tannery, *Mém. Sci.* 1925, III, 335–6. T. Fu defends in Hastings, op. cit. XII, pp. 74–80. Unreal, Whewell, *Hist. of Inductive Sciences*[3], 1857, I, 120. Ocean, Fung Yu-lan, *Hist. of Chin. Phil.* 1937, pp. 160–1. Egg, Granet, *Pensée Chinoise*, 1934, p. 349. Map, Rey, *Sc. Or.* p. 396. Square, Fu, loc. cit., Granet, pp. 350, 358: guesses, Forke, *The World Conception of the Chinese*, 1925, pp. 59–60. Map in 3rd cent. A.D. oblong, Herrmann, *Land der Seide*, 1938, p. 5, Soothill in *Geogr. J.* 1927, I, 532. Legend, Tsui Chi, *Short Hist. of Chin. Civ.* 1942, p. 20.

[2] Macdonell, op. cit. p. 9, Wallis, op. cit. p. 112, cp. Warren, loc. cit. Aryan square as Chinese. Eg., Sloley in *L.E.* p. 168. Corners, Isaiah xi. 12. Square, Menon, *Early Astronomy and Cosmology*, 1932, e.g. Indian, p. 68, Babylonian 'mountain-house', p. 130, citing Jensen, etc., Chinese, p. 111.

[3] See p. 156, n. 1. Samothrace, Diod. v, 47, 3–4: Frazer, *Folk-lore in the Old Testament*, 1919, I, 167–71, 360. Thessaly, p. 105, n. 2: Frazer, op. cit. pp. 171–4.

CHAPTER II

THE GREEK HORIZON TO HERODOTUS

§ 1. THE COLONIAL MOVEMENT

HISTORIC GREECE emerged as a number of small city-states. Small units were natural enough in a country broken up by sea and mountains, but just why were they cities? Anyhow Greeks cared to live only in independent 'poleis'—

> Better a little town perched on a hill,
> Well-governed, than the pride of Nineveh,

as an early poet said. In many they proceeded to run through the gamut of 'political' experiment ending in 'democracy'. They were the first people free and lively enough to try such adventures, and we owe to them a great deal of the vocabulary in this kind. But they did not achieve a wider patriotism worthy of their talents. They were to pay the price of failure to foreign conquerors, if one can speak of failure when they did so much for civilization.

Greece is a poor land, thin-soiled and with few considerable plains. Poverty is own sister to her, as her first great historian admits. The climate is the typical 'Mediterranean': grain-crops are restricted to the rainy season of winter, and may fail if the rain is insufficient, while in the hot summer little pasture is left but rough herbage on the hills for sheep and goats, and the drought is resisted only by olive, vine and fig, and evergreen trees. The import of corn was often a vital need.

The coast of Asia Minor was more fertile, and the emigrant cities there developed sooner. They had some good river-plains, and by handy valleys tapped the trade of flourishing kingdoms behind, first Phrygia and then Lydia. The latter subjected them, but did little harm, being attracted by their culture and also teaching them some things, including apparently coinage. It seemed very strong and rich, and obscured their view of greater powers beyond, though soldiers of fortune like the brother of Alcaeus went as far as Babylon. It was a shock when Croesus suddenly collapsed before Cyrus (546 B.C.), and they found themselves annexed to a huge Persian empire. Rather than submit some like the Phocaeans chose to sail away.

Many had gone long since because of political and economic troubles. The homeland cities had similar discontents, and several joined in the process by which the coasts from Spain to the Caucasus were dotted with colonies (eighth to sixth centuries). The colonists wanted land and elbow-room rather than trade: so the Megarians at first preferred Chalcedon to the splendid port of Byzantium opposite, and it was only later that they seemed 'blind' in their choice. Trade grew, however, and it tended to follow the lines of connection with the various 'mother-cities'. Of these Corinth was jealous of her western line, while Miletus, 'mother of over ninety cities in all seas', was specially active in the Black. Some cities played little or no part in colonizing. Sparta conquered her neighbours instead, and turned herself into barracks, 'not a city but a camp'. Athens developed rather slowly and then moved towards full democracy. Latterly she began to show an interest in the route to the Black Sea, and her pottery won many markets opened by others, as in Italy. In the great days of her sea-power which followed she could boast of drawing the produce of 'every land', that is from Sicily and Cyrene to the Crimea.

The scale of trade and industry is very much in question. A recent writer insists that there were no big merchants or manufacturers demanding outlets for mass wares, and that even in democratic cities the citizen was really an aristocrat engaged in politics and leaving trade and industry to resident aliens and slaves, while the state, existing for his benefit, took no interest in trade except to tax it and to ensure the supply of some necessities like corn and ship-timber. It can be shown against this that in pottery at least the export was considerable, and others rate more highly the rise of trade with the introduction of coinage and the colonial expansion. But the citizen was largely an economic failure, and Hasebroek's case is sound against too modernistic views. It is not easy to remember how small these city-states were: Athens with her home territory, hardly bigger than the Isle of Wight, may have had something like 300,000 people, about a third slaves. Technical progress was slight because of slavery and a snobbish idea that there was something rather ignoble in the practical application of science.[1]

The sea, almost fogless and tideless and with many islands, was inviting. Hesiod's farmer might resent being driven to 'stressful seafaring' in order 'to avoid need and cheerless hunger'. But others took to it readily and

[1] Sir R. W. Livingstone, *Greek Ideals and Modern Life*, 1935, pp. 64, 104. Population, W. S. Ferguson, *Greek Imperialism*, 1913, p. 42: similar Tod, *C.A.H.* v, 11: Gomme, *Pop. of Athens*, 1933 (citizens under 50,000, slaves 120,000). Case, Hasebroek, *Trade and Politics in Anc. Greece*, 1933, modified by Heichelheim, *Wirtschaftsgesch. des Altertums*, 1935, pp. 323, 370 and Michell, *Economics of Anc. Greece*, 1940, pp. 222–30. An attack by Gomme, *Essays in Greek Hist. and Lit.* 1937, pp. 42–66: Glover, *Challenge of the Greek*, 1942, pp. 73–4. Trade little part, Oakeshott, *Commerce and Society*, 1936, pp. 10–14 (in Hellenistic much greater, pp. 18–23). Meg. blind, Hdt. IV, 144, Str. 320. 90 cities, Plin. v, 112. Wanted land, Burn, *World of Hesiod*, 1936, pp. 232–3. A.'s brother, Str. 617. Poverty, Hdt. VI, 102. Thin-soiled, Thuc. I, 2, II, 36, Str. 333. Verses by Phocylides. On Med. region, Philippson, *Mittelmeergebiet*[4], 1922: Newbigin, *Med. Lands*, 1924, *Southern Europe*, 1927: E. C. Semple, *Geogr. of Med. Region, its Relation to Anc. History*, 1932: G. East, *Med. Problems*, 1940, pp. 14–21: E. Ludwig, *The Med.* 1943: Kendrew, *Climates of the Continents*[3], 1941, ch. 30: see also p. 254, n. 2. Drawing produce, Thuc. II, 38, Ps.-Xen. Ath. Const. 2, 6–12.

went far on the supposed tracks of the Argonauts and Odysseus. Ships were still small. Some were open war-boats like the 'fifty-oars' of the piratical Phocaeans. (They grew into big triremes, uncomfortable vessels packed with 200 men and hugging the coast for water and provisions, but these were built solely for speed and power in battle.) There were also 'round' sailing ships for trade, long barely separable from piracy. We hear of a range from a dozen to some 360 tons (7000 bushels of wheat), but probably most were nearer the lower figure. Sailing technique was imperfect, and the steering-gear bad: indeed ships were to remain dangerous throughout ancient times for lack of a properly fixed rudder. There was no compass, of course, and little means of storing food and water. The season was short, if hardly confined to the fifty days after the summer solstice, as in the landlubber poet's timid advice (some venture also in spring, but he thinks this risky). Ships usually coasted or cut over from one headland to another visible in the clear air. They seldom sailed at night or faced the open, where it was hard to keep a course except with a reliable wind like the etesians blowing across to Egypt; yet trading ships were not quite so bound to coasting as the trireme.[1] A day's sail varied a lot, from 500 stades (so the usual, it seems) to 700; it was a week from Carthage to Gibraltar, implying a rate of 600 stades, and from Athens slightly more to Egypt, ten days to the Crimea, and a fortnight to Syracuse—at the best.[2] Voyagers were still terribly at the mercy of storms. Colaeus the Samian was blown west against his will, it is said, along most of North Africa and out past the Pillars of Hercules (Gibraltar, before 631 B.C.). But he duly returned with a dazzling profit, second only to that made somewhere by a skipper of Aegina, a barren island so active in piracy and trade that it needed no colonies. Soon others found a less risky way to the western Eldorado, especially the Phocaeans, though they were hardly 'the first to make long voyages and explore the Adriatic, Etruria, and Spain'.[3]

1 Gomme, *J.H.S.* 1933, p. 16. Hes. *Op.* 618–91. Conditions, Hasebroek, op. cit. pp. 67–9, 81: Burn, op. cit. pp. 79–81, ships, pp. 240–3. Rudder, Commandant Lefebvre des Noettes, *Mém. Soc. Antiquaires*, 1934, pp. 24–44. Tonnage, Thuc. IV, 118, VII, 25: Knorringa, *Emporos*, 1926, p. 61: Tod, *C.A.H.* V, 19: Köster, *Ant. Seewesen*, p. 161: Heichelheim, op. cit. p. 365: Glover, op. cit. p. 94 as Glotz, *Anc. Greece at Work*, 1926, p. 293 (360 tons). Strictly coasting, Clowes, *Geogr. J.* 1927, I, 216, *Sailing Ships*, 1930, I, 32–8 (and small, until Roman corn-ships of 250 tons).

2 Heichelheim, loc. cit. 500 stades, Ap. Rhod. I, 603: Cary-Warmington, *Anc. Explorers*, 1929, p. 4: Hennig, *Terrae Incognitae*, I, 77 (500–600 stades). Carthage, Ps.-Scyl. 111 (=rate of 107 km. and data in Tim. ap. Diod. V, 16 give 100–135, Gsell, *Afrique du Nord*, IV², 112). 700 stades, Hdt. IV, 86. 500 stades, Ps.-Scyl. 69.

3 Hdt. I, 163. Phoc. in Spain, ibid. 150. Burn, *J.H.S.* 1927, p. 176. Beaumont, ibid. 1936, p. 171. Colaeus, Hdt. IV, 152. Hasebroek, op. cit. p. 69 doubts the story unjustifiably, Heichelheim, p. 247: so does Michell, op. cit. p. 301: C. lied about his route, Beaumont, *J.R.S.* 1939, p. 80. Aegina, Eph. ap. Str. 376: Pindar, *Nem.* VI, 33.

THE GREEK HORIZON TO HERODOTUS

There were long gaps in the fringe of colonies. Certain coasts were avoided as harbourless, it seems, or otherwise unsuitable. Settlement was rarely forced against civilized powers, though there was a brush with the Assyrians in Cilicia; the one colony in Egypt was rather a treaty-port. Yet the western ventures were enough to rouse Carthage and the Etruscans. Not that Greeks admitted any but themselves to be really civilized: one result of the expansion was a growing consciousness of their superiority to all 'barbarians', meaning 'anything who is not our sort of chaps', as the British sailor said of Dagoes.

For geography the main effect was the realization of the inner sea: with its Black Sea alcove it was a lake, except for a strait to 'the sea outside the Pillars called the Atlantic'. Not all parts of the great basin were accurately known, but there was a fair idea of its size and outlines. The colonies also learnt something of their hinterlands, though less than might be expected. The total gain in knowledge may best be judged by following the overseas movement in the various directions and seeing how much each group of colonies contributed.

Details are unfortunately scanty. Much of the exploring was done before prose writing had begun. When the work was nearly over, it was at Miletus, which had taken so large a part, that the data were gathered up. About 550 B.C. Anaximander, the second 'wise man' of its brilliant series, 'first ventured to draw a map of the inhabited world'. Presently (about 500 B.C.) came the historian Hecataeus, 'much-travelled' we are told, though no journey is specified except to Egypt; he 'improved the map with such detail that it was greatly admired'. Apparently he published his along with a description of the earth in two books entitled *Europe* and *Asia*, the latter including Libya. We have only fragments, over 300 but nearly all very short, most as quoted in a late dictionary of geographical names on the formula 'Dandarians, a people above the Caucasus, Hecataeus in his Europe'. They have been attacked as an Alexandrian forgery or partly interpolated from Herodotus, but that they are in the main genuine is now strongly upheld. The original has been disparaged as a mere coastal description, but it seems to have added peoples inland to the limits of knowledge, including Pygmies, and there are hints of intelligent curiosity about climate and customs, flora and fauna, so that it deserves to be called a general geography, the first of which anything is known.[1] Apart from

---

[1] Now best in Jacoby, *Fr. griech. Hist.* (*F.G.H.*), I, 1–47 and commentary, pp. 317–75, and L. Pearson, *Early Ionian Historians*, 1939, pp. 25–108. Forgery, Wells, *J.H.S.* 1909, pp. 41–52: mere coastal, Caspari, ibid. 1910, pp. 234–48. Diels, *Hermes*, 1887, pp. 411–44 and Jacoby, op. cit. and *R.E.* VII, pp. 2667–750 rate the debt of Hdt. very high: customs, ibid. p. 2697: Gsell, *Hérodote*, 1916, p. 57. Improved map (Erat. ap.) Agathem. I, 1 (*G.G.M.* II, 471). Very full on Hdt. is *R.E.* Suppl. 2, 206–519 (also by Jacoby, 1913).

these snippets most of our best matter comes from the history of Herodotus, written about 450–425 B.C., on the epic conflict of Greece and Persia. He goes far back to explain everything leading up to it, and generous digressions display the information gathered in his own travels. It detracts little from his delightful book to admit that in geography he borrowed much, and in the ancient manner without acknowledgement. Besides these two some others wrote of 'foundings of cities' and the Persian wars and 'barbarian customs', like Hellanicus, though their fragments add few things important for geography.

§ 2. THE WESTERN LINE

The Adriatic was at first called the Iŏnian (not Iōnian) gulf or sea, a name later limited to the southern end. Legends of no serious value sent various old heroes all over these waters. Regular colonies reached only a little past the entrance, to Durazzo; beyond, after some experiments, the whole eastern side was avoided. The long tangle of inshore islands gave plenty of shelter from the squally winds, and had a Mediterranean climate and some soil good for vine and olive, but were mostly stony and barren; the coast, closely backed by forbidding limestone mountains, gave little foothold, and the hinterland was both inaccessible and poor (it has never been easily penetrated by civilization). That the Illyrians were already formidable pirates, as later, is often assumed and is likely enough. Various tribes along the stretch are named. There is no evidence that traders went far up country, though a few wares found their way in.[1]

Near the head a sinking in the mountain barrier gives access to a tributary of the Danube, or Ister, as then called. Was this tributary, the Save, at first mistaken for the main stream, as Gibbon suggested? The name of the Istrian peninsula may already have started a wild notion— first mentioned only a good deal later—that the Argonauts, returning up the Ister, emerged by a branch of it into this sea. An argument that the idea of a branch river arose from a land-portage of boats is not very convincing.[2]

---

1 Beaumont, *J.H.S.* 1936, pp. 159–204. Assumed, as by Str. 317: Ormerod, *Piracy in the Anc. World*, 1924, p. 167. Experiments, Str. 315, Ps.-Scymnus, 451 (Curzola). Name, Hec. fr. 91, 106, Hdt. VI, 127, Thuc. I, 24, Str. 317: V. Burr, *Nostrum Mare*, 1932, pp. 59–64 (and 'Adriatic', pp. 64–8). Tribes, Hec. fr. 92–8. Heroes, Str. 75–6, 283, Plin. III, 120. E. C. Semple, *Influences of Geogr. Environment*, 1911, p. 258.

2 Hennig's, *Rhein. Mus.* 1932, p. 204: already, Ridgeway, *Early Age of Greece*, 1901, I, 367. Branch, Theopompus ap. Str. 317, Eph. ap. Ps.-Scymn. 193, Arist. *Hist. Anim.* VIII, 13, Ap. Rhod. IV, 289, 325, Ps.-Arist. *Mir. Ausc.* 105: still in Mela, III, 63, rejected by Plin. III, 127. Notion early, Berger, *Erdkunde*², p. 235: Heidel, *Frame*, p. 35: Berthelot, *Rev. Arch.* 1934, p. 107. See p. 88, n. 1, p. 141, n. 1, and p. 197, n. 3. Gibbon, ch. 1 (note).

The neighbouring Veneti were rightly thought of Illyrian origin (some connected them with the Eneti who were allies of Troy, but this is plainly a reckless guess from a mere similarity of name). Two rivers are said to flow north to the Danube and named Carpis and Alpis, though there is strangely no word of the Alps. There were some Greek traders among natives at Spina (once described as a 'Greek city') and at Adria, which gave its name first to the head of the sea and later to the whole. These markets tapped the rich plain of the Po, to which the Etruscans had extended from the west side of Italy. They were also the outlet of an amber route from the dim north, by which amber had drifted down already in Mycenaean times. Some saw in the Po the fabulous Eridanus, where Phaethon fell from the Sun's chariot, and his sisters, turned into poplars, wept amber tears for him.[1] The swampy and rapidly silting coast was unattractive, and the great plain was really quite outside the Mediterranean climate.

The Italian flank of the sea was almost ignored, rather surprisingly. It was nearly harbourless, indeed, and with mountains often close behind; yet it had some good land, and the winds were not very dangerous in summer. The sea was overestimated in length and, to judge from some later statements, ill-mapped as running north or even north-east. So the Balkan peninsula was absurdly narrowed, and there was a queer fancy that both this sea and the Black were visible from a certain mountain, variously placed near the former or in the Haemus (Balkan range); but these vagaries may partly belong to a later writer.[2]

The instep and toe of Italy were so covered with colonies as to become a 'Great Greece'. Sybaris, dated 721 B.C., is said to have controlled some twenty-five towns and four native tribes. But in 510 B.C. she was destroyed by her kinsfolk of Croton, and such conflicts weakened the cities in their resistance to barbarian neighbours. Herodotus came to settle in a colony built to replace Sybaris, and could have told more about these parts if he had had occasion. Hecataeus has some curious matter with obscure names

---

1 Myth in Hes. *Theog.* 338 and fr. 199. Po, Pherecydes ap. Hyg. *Fab.* 154: Eur. *Hipp.* 737 and ap. Plin. XXXVII, 32. No real river, Str. 215. See p. 56, n. 1. The name Erid. is Greek in the first instance, Kretschmer in *Mélanges...offerts à J. van Ginneken*, 1937, pp. 207–10. Hyperborean route to Eneti, some ap. Str. 212, 543 and Plin. III, 30, VI, 5. Adr., Hdt. IV, 33 (see p. 22, n. 1). Amber, see p. 19, n. 1, p. 27, n. 1: Déchelette, op. cit. II, 19–21, 872–5: G. C. Williamson, *Book of Amber*, 1932: Berthelot, *Rev. Arch.* 1934, pp. 245, 251. Rivers, Hdt. IV, 49. Veneti, ibid. I, 196, V, 9, Hec. fr. 199. Spina, Str. 214, Plin. III, 120, Beaumont, op. cit. p. 179. Adria, Hec. fr. 90, Livy, V, 33. 'Adriatic' at head, Hdt. I, 163, V, 9. 'Amber Islands' there, Ps.-Scymn. 392, seem a fable, see p. 88, n. 1.

2 Theopompus ap. Ps.-Scymn. 371, Str. 317, and Mela, II, 17. Mapped, Jacoby, *F.G.H.* I, 338, Heidel, op. cit. p. 36. Mountain, Ps.-Arist. *M.A.* 104: Haemus, Polybius ap. Str. 313, Livy, XL, 21–2, see p. 220, n. 3. Narrowed, even Erat. ap. Str. 92.

of native towns. It was known that the name Italy meant 'calf-land' and at first belonged only to the toe.[1]

In Sicily Syracuse (from Corinth, 734 B.C.) was only the most notable of many colonies. The western corner was Phoenician and under the protection of Carthage: two attempts at settling here were repulsed. Most of the

Fig. 3. Western Greek colonies.

interior was left to the natives; of these the Sicels were thought to have come from Italy, no doubt rightly, and the Sicans from eastern Spain, where there was a river Sicanus to suggest this guess.[2]

A very old colony was Cumae, the mother-city of Naples; latterly she had to repel an attack by the expanding Etruscans (524 B.C.). The fragments of Hecataeus have a tribe of Ausones and three places hereabouts. Beyond, along the domain of the Etruscans, no colony was possible, and the fragments have only Elba (as an Etruscan island). The first known Greek mentions of Rome are by writers a little younger than Herodotus, like Antiochus of Syracuse. The site was well chosen as commanding the

[1] Antiochus ap. Str. 254: name, ibid., Hell. ap. Dion. Hal. I, 35, Thuc. VII, 33, Arist. *Pol.* 1329*b*, Pearson, op. cit. p. 168: Whatmough, *Foundations of Roman Italy*, 1937, p. 109. Sybaris, Str. 263. Hec. fr. 80–5 and nine Oenotrian towns, 64–71, Pearson, op. cit. p. 42, B. Schulze, 1912. On Greek reports of Italy to 300 B.C. E. Wikén, Lund, 1937.

[2] (Ant. ap.) Thuc. VI, 2, D.H. I, 22. Cp. Timaeus ap. Diod. v, 6 (native), Jacoby, op. cit. I, 457, Pearson, op. cit. p. 228.

only permanent crossing of the lower Tiber and a plain which was early not unfertile or unhealthy, when kept drained by peasant owners (the advantage of a central position in Italy was to matter more afterwards, as Rome's ambition grew). By her own tradition she fell under Etruscan kings, and expelled them in 509 B.C., after which she was long struggling with her close neighbours. According to one statement she had mattered enough at the end of the kingdom for Carthage to make a treaty with her. Far more important as yet were the Etruscans themselves. As mentioned before, they are generally thought to have come by sea from Asia Minor round about 800 B.C. They had soon prospered by trade and piracy on the sea called after them, and they had conquered southwards and also in the Po valley. They paid the Greeks the compliment of much imitation, and took any amount of their pottery from the seventh century on (they also borrowed the alphabet and conveyed it to others in Italy). But they made a bargain with Carthage to check any further colonizing in western waters. They drove off the Phocaeans trying to make a base in Corsica (536 B.C.). Their allies had landed in Sardinia and were ramming every ship approaching, so that various projects of settlement there had no chance of success.[1] But presently a strong invasion of Sicily was repelled by Syracuse, which also badly damaged Etruscan sea-power (480, 474 B.C.).

Past the long gap the Phocaeans had founded Massalia (Marseilles, about 600 B.C.); they chose a fine site, sheltered by a ridge from the mistral and well away from the silt and floods of the Rhône, yet handy for the valley, the only easy passage northwards from the whole western basin of the inner sea, one easier indeed than any from the other basin. This city threw out some (very minor) sub-colonies on either side, how soon is not told. The coast was truly Mediterranean, with winters hardly colder than Athens, which is much farther south, and the olive throve, as did the vine now introduced (it was to take a long time to spread far inland, while the olive does not go north of Avignon). The neighbours were Ligurians, a name liked by poets as representing the western barbarians. But the Celts, expanding from their centre in south Germany, had overrun most of their future home and perhaps the whole already: they are named in fragments of Hecataeus, which may be genuine enough, even if a story of an early

---

[1] Hdt. I, 170, v, 124: rammed, Str. 225: Carth. occupied Sard. and Balearics in 654 B.C., Tim. ap. Diod. v, 16. Phocaeans, Hdt. I, 163–7. Rome in Ant., Hell. and Damastes ap. D.H. I, 72–3, Pearson, op. cit. p. 189. Hec. fr. 61–3 Capri, Capua, Nola: Pearson, p. 39, and fr. 59 Elba. Treaty of 508 B.C., Polybius, III, 22, accepted by Gsell (see p. 69, n. 1), Last in *C.A.H.* VII, 405, 859–62, Schulten, ibid. 177, Beaumont, *J.R.S.* 1939, pp. 74–86, C. H. V. Sutherland, *Romans in Spain*, 1939, p. 15: but Piganiol, *Hist. de Rome*, 1939, p. 68 puts the first in 348 B.C. (cp. Livy, VII, 27). Origin of Etruscans, see p. 13, n. 1. Site, Whatmough, op. cit. pp. 272–3: G. East, *Hist. Geogr. of Europe*, 1935, pp. 6–9.

movement into Italy is not reliable.[1] Amber among other things came down the Rhône, which also claimed to be the famous amber-river. In return the wares of Massalia, and others from Italy, found their way to the upper Rhine, contributing to the development of the Celtic culture known from a chief find-place as La Tène (from 500 B.C.). It is not so clear that the colony's own traders went very far, and more likely they used Ligurian middlemen. The overland trade in tin later described may not have begun yet. Anyhow the little said of northern parts is startling in its ignorance. Herodotus has heard that the Danube rises among the Celts; really it did, among those of south Germany. But, apparently confusing with their outlying swarms, he adds 'at Pyrene'. He also describes some Celts as beyond the Pillars (meaning beyond their meridian?) and the westernmost people in Europe except the Cynetes, who are mentioned later as about Cape St Vincent but also near the eastern Pyrenees (a recent writer thinks that he perverts Hecataeus who meant this last group). It is almost incredible that Aristotle repeats the assertion about the Danube, merely correcting Pyrene into a range.[2] All this seems too bad to be true: some people at Massalia must have known better. (A poet put the source of the Danube in a vague northern forest, where Hercules sought the hind with the golden horns; this animal was not so incorrect after all, Ridgeway suggested, if it was a reindeer, lingering in Germany as still in Caesar's time.)

The Iberians are put from the Rhône westwards as well as in Spain. A few dubious statements extend Ligurians to Spain, and some argue that they were once widespread there, until driven into odd corners by the Iberians, and that they survive to-day as the Basques.[3] It is often accepted,

1 Livy, v, 34–5 (cp. Umbrians to Alps, Hdt. IV, 49): much too early, Whatmough, op. cit. p. 147. Hec. fr. 54–6 genuine, Jacoby, I, 333, Pearson, p. 37: Hubert, *Celtes*, 1932, p. 5: de Navarro, *C.A.H.* VII, 59, but cp. Cary, *J.H.S.* 1924, p. 173 (still Ligurians in Ps.-Scyl. 3), Berthelot, *Rev. Arch.* 1934, p. 77, Jullian, *Hist. de la Gaule*, I³, 1914, p. 247 (non-Celtic names in Avienus south of Lyons, and so on upper Rhône, Kaeppel, *Off the Beaten Track in the Classics*, 1936, p. 117). All by 600 B.C., R. L. G. Ritchie, *France*, 1937, p. 5. Poets, Hes. ap. Str. 300, Aesch. ap. Str. 183. Sub-colonies, Str. 151–3, 168, Plin. III, 38, 47. Site, Str. 182–3.

2 Arist. *Met.* I, 13, 350*b*. Hdt. II, 33, IV, 49. Perverts, Pearson, *Class. Phil.* 1934, p. 328: two lots in Avienus 201 and 556. Confusing, say Déchelette, Wheeler in *Eur. Civ.* 1935, II, 166. Celts in S.W. Spain, Dixon, *Iberians of Spain*, 1940, p. 4: Hubert, op. cit. pp. 6–7: but cp. Jullian, op. cit. pp. 305–8. Middlemen, De Navarro, *Antiquity*, 1928, p. 430, as Piroutet. Wares, Wheeler, op. cit. pp. 233–7, Gomme, ibid. p. 16: traders reticent, Kaeppel, op. cit. p. 118. Tin, Cary, *J.H.S.* 1924, pp. 172–3 despite Müllenhoff, I, 223, Jullian, I, 410, Schulten, *Tart.* 49: no Mass. coins of 5th cent. north of Durance, Cary, ibid. p. 174. Rhône (Rhodanus) = Erid., Aesch. ap. Plin. XXXVII, 32.

3 Jullian, op. cit. I, ch. 4 and Schulten, *R.E.* Hispania, attacked by Berthelot, *Rev. Arch.* 1934, pp. 72–120, 245–303. Scraps, Avienus, 196, 284, 612: Spanish L. of Thuc. VI, 2 probably interpolated, Berthelot, p. 81 (B.'s own theory from Av. 138–45 of L. from Jutland is very risky). Reindeer, Ridgeway, op. cit. I, 362 on Pindar, *Ol.* III, 31.

THE GREEK HORIZON TO HERODOTUS

from the statement cited above, that there were some Celts already near the south-west corner of the peninsula.

Colaeus, when blown out through the strait, got a rich cargo at Tartessus. It was a 'virgin mart', which sounds odd, as the Phoenicians had been at Cadiz presumably for some time and got so much silver that they are said to have made anchors of it. Soon Phocaeans came, at first apparently crossing direct by the islands. They were well liked by the local king, but made no settlement except perhaps a calling-station on the east coast and another, Mainace, on the south. Their kinsmen of Massalia had subcolonies at the end of the Pyrenees and perhaps two others down at and near Alicante. Presently Carthage began to make a preserve of the south, destroying Mainace and strengthening Gades and barring the strait.[1] Some detailed information dates from before the blockade. Antique matter is embedded in a versified description of the coasts by a very late Latin writer, Avienus, who boasts of using old sources, though the exact age and value of his statements are often in question. Part seems to come from a Massaliot skipper who sailed to Tartessus about 530 B.C. The fragments of Hecataeus show a praiseworthy knowledge of tribes and places (often not otherwise mentioned) as far as Tartessus. This name means for him a district, for others also a river (the Guadalquivir), early described as 'silver-rooted'; indications of a town are obscure enough, and it has been vainly sought at the mouth. Soon after him Spain recedes from view, and poets speak of sailing beyond the strait as an impossibility.[2]

'Whether sea girds Europe round on the north none can tell', says Herodotus: while admitting that tin and amber come from that way, he will not have Tin Islands or an amber-river Eridanus flowing north to the north sea. Clearly he was wrong in being so sceptical, and there was substance in the reports. For what these were in detail we have only what may have been said by early seamen of Tartessus and Gades, as dimly reflected in Avienus. After a few obscure points on the outer coast he reaches a high

---

[1] Dixon, op. cit. pp. 28–47. Phocaeans, Hdt. I, 163. Str. 156, 159–60. Stations, Str. 131–2, Eph. and Tim. ap. Ps.-Scymn. 202–6 (and Gallic colonies, 207–16): Rhode not probably Rhodian as said: Emporiae, *c.* 550 B.C. Anchors, Pos. ap. Diod. v, 34. Colaeus, see p. 46, n. 3. Colonies, Ure, *C.A.H.* IV, 118: M. Clerc, *Massalia*, 1927, I, 264–79. On Greeks in Spain, Rhys Carpenter, 1925: Schulten, *Rh. Mus.* 1936, pp. 289–346 (preceded by Etruscans!): Bosch-Gimpera in *Class. Quart.* 1944, pp. 53–9: Sutherland, op. cit. pp. 11–16.

[2] Pindar, *Nem.* IV, 69, *Ol.* III, 44: Eur. *Hipp.* 3, 1053, fr. 145 N. Hec. fr. 38–52, Pearson, op. cit. pp. 35–6: praised by Atenstädt, *Leipz. Stud.* 1893, pp. 1–172, Heidel, *Frame*, p. 38. Tart. river, Stesichorus ap. Str. 148. Town?, Avien. 284, Ps.-Scymn. 164 (two days W. of Gades), some ap. Str. loc. cit.: a town not proven, Berthelot, *Avienus*, 1934, p. 81. Schulten, *Avienus*, 1922 (and *Tartessos*, 1922, *R.E.* Tartessos, 1932, and in *C.A.H.* VII, ch. 24) is often speculative. Müllenhoff, *Deutsche Alt.* 1870, I, 181 thought of a Phoen. periplus of 8th cent. translated by a Mass. of 5th cent.

headland, of old called Oestrymnis, apparently Brittany. It faces south on a gulf with wide-scattered islands rich in tin and lead (those off Brittany, though they probably never had much tin and few accept them as deserving to be the famous Tin Islands). Its bold traders often cross the stormy sea in hide boats. Two days away is the large island of the Hierni (Ireland), and near by stretches the island of the Albiones. This last is not expressly mentioned for tin or as visited by any other foreigners.[1] (The name Albion was only occasionally to be repeated later alongside 'Britain', perhaps by Pytheas and curiously as late as Ptolemy; it is of unknown origin and has not probably any kinship with albus or reference to the white cliffs of Dover.)

The same Latin writer gives, professedly from 'remote Punic annals' but really at third hand, some statements of Himilco, a man elsewhere named only once and briefly as sent 'in the heyday of Carthage' to explore the outer parts of Europe, while Hanno explored those of Africa. 'These waters', we hear, 'in terminos Oestrymnidum', can hardly be crossed in four months (presumably there and back, and he took his time to establish relations for trade?). They are sluggish, windless, foggy, sometimes very shoaly and clogged with weed, and infested by formidable sea-monsters. Some lines have quite a flavour of the *Ancient Mariner*, whose author may well have known them: so

> navigia lente et languide repentia
> internatare beluas...
> multusque terror ex feris habitat freta...
> sic remis humor aequoris pigri stupet.

This vaguely alarming stuff, unreal and unlike the other matter from Tartessian seamen, can hardly do justice to Himilco, if he handed in anything like Hanno's detailed report. Perhaps only garbled versions were allowed to become current, with the dangers exaggerated to scare off competitors, though rather too much has been made of such 'Phoenician lies'. Already Plato heard of the alleged shoals, and accounted for them by sinking his Atlantis. We hear later of some offshore clumps of weed, and of one swarming with big tunny and visited by fishermen four days out from Cadiz; but even this can hardly refer to what Columbus was to call

[1] Avienus, 90–112. Name Albion, (Pytheas? ap.) Ps.-Arist. *de Mundo*, 3, Isid. ap. Plin. IV, 102, Ptol. II, 3, 1, VII, 5, 11, Hübner *R.E.* Britanni (1899), 860. A. and Hierni pre-Celtic (Iberian?), Hubert, p. 247. Name O. unknown elsewhere, though Pytheas has Ostimii (or something like) and Caesar Osismii in Brittany. Hdt.'s remarks III, 115, IV, 45. Berger, op. cit. p. 233 supposes that some connected O. and Ister. Berthelot strangely finds Alb. in Scotland. Breton islands = Tin, Mela, III, 47 (in Celticis): Siret in *Anthropologie*, 1908, pp. 129–312: Nansen, op. cit. pp. 29, 39: Schulten, *Tart.* 54: Philipp, *Tac. Germania*, 1926, pp. 37–8: Breton tin worked *c.* 500 B.C. but derelict soon after, Cary, *J.H.S.* 1924, p. 167: Ushant as Sieglin, but its tin from Cornwall, Gsell, *Hist. anc. de l'Afrique du Nord*, 1913, I, 468–71. Scillies, Jullian, op. cit. p. 387 as E. Meyer.

the Sargasso or Weed Sea beyond 35° W. (it is hardly possible that any one can have been driven there and got back to tell of it).[1] And what did Himilco do? Perhaps he was sent to find out more about the tin route. The text seems to indicate that, like the Tartessians, he reached the Bretons, who were trading with Britain. It does not prove, what is often assumed, that he himself went on to Cornwall and that others followed in his wake. A recent writer takes him even to Ireland and supposes regular voyages after him to a market at Ushant, if not to Cornwall. There is an odd notice of one Midacritus, who 'first brought tin from the Tin Island': long presumed a Phoenician, he is now thought a Greek, who merely picked up tin at Tartessus or perhaps made an isolated dash to Cornwall. Such are the data for direct Phoenician trade early to Britain, and archaeology does not support it, but it has its stout defenders, who insist that barter need have left no trace.[2] It is a pity to have to doubt Leighton's picture of hook-nosed traders spreading their bales before the Cornish chief and his too elegant women.

The Romans were to get tin in the north-west corner of Spain. Also in their time the Tin Islands are described as well out from that corner, with curious details and often so that they are plainly distinguished from Britain: no real group answers to these accounts. Some think that the early tin was already got from Spain, and that the original 'Tin Islands' were some offshore islets there, if not a fable.[3] No doubt the name represents a first very dim and floating conception of all the western sources of tin, later variously identified with real things heard about Britain and Spain. But it is tempting to suppose that the rich Cornish deposit was always the main reality lying behind the reports, which were so vague because they came through Gallic traders.

1 So Hennig, *T.I.* I, 19, Cary-Warmington, p. 32, Gsell, loc. cit., against Gaffarel, *Mer des Sargasses*, 1872, Elton, *Career of Columbus*, 1892, pp. 89, etc. and see p. 78, n. 1. Tunny, Timaeus ap. Ps.-Arist. *M.A.* 136. Himilco, Avienus, 117–29, 382–9, 406–15. Heyday, Plin. II, 169. Partly lies, Hennig, op. cit. pp. 79–91 (who dates *c.* 525 B.C.): Bunbury, *Anc. Geogr.* II, 688, cp. I, 403: written up, Dixon, op. cit. p. 38. See also Nansen, *In Northern Mists*, 1911, I, 36–42: Blasquez, *El Periplo de H.* Madrid, 1909.

2 Like Rice Holmes, *Anc. Britain and the Invasions of Julius Caesar*, 1907, pp. 511–14. Denied by Hencken, *Arch. of Cornwall*, 1932, p. 168 (trade via Bretons), followed by Collingwood in Frank's *Econ. Survey*, 1937, III, 46: J. H. Rose, *Med. and Anc. World*, 1933, pp. 44–5. Midacritus, Plin. VII, 197: dash, Cary-Warmington, op. cit. p. 31, Cary in *J.H.S.* 1924, p. 170, Kaeppel, op. cit. p. 120, as cp. Schulten, *Tart.* 24, Hennig, op. cit. p. 43, Hencken, p. 169 (not Britain): to Breton islands, Bosch-Gimpera, *C.Q.* 1944, p. 54. Him. to Ireland, Hennig, pp. 79–91. No evidence before H., and only to Brittany for long after, Kaeppel, p. 114. H. to Brittany but others possibly to Cornwall, Gsell, op. cit. IV[2], 143 (and Tin Islands = Oestrymnides). See also Rickard, *Man and Metals*, 1932, I, ch. 6.

3 So O. Davies, *Roman Mines in Europe*, 1935, pp. 104, 141, 144: similar Haverfield, *R.E.* x, 2328. By Tartessians from islands there and Spain, Ridgeway, *Early Age of Greece*, 1901, I, 609. Britain, Müllenhoff, *Deutsche Alt.* I, 91–2: Holmes, op. cit. pp. 483–98.

Britain had been heard of, but not yet by that name. Just when the Celts came remains obscure, and a linguistic theory of early waves of Goidels using qu where the later Brythons used p is now sometimes dismissed; but it seems that Celts were there by the beginning of iron in the sixth century B.C.

As for the Eridanus, there had come (perhaps overland and very early) hearsay of some German river; later it was to be known that the sea washed up amber on an island off the Elbe and the coast beyond the Vistula.[1] Otherwise the north of Europe was nebulous; the Greeks were to be surprisingly slow in learning about it, and it was to be late in coming into the foreground of history.

§3. THE NORTH-EASTERN LINE

The coast round to the Black Sea entrance was early studded with colonies. The series was crowned with Byzantium, on one of the world's great sites, but not playing a commanding part early because not quite secure on the land side against barbarian neighbours. Down the straits came the shoals of tunny, and the fish figures on the coins of Cyzicus. The northern hinterland was useful for ship-timber, gold and silver, corn and slaves. The Macedonians were still rude and struggling with ruder neighbours, Illyrians and others; the kings at least were recognized as Greeks of a sort, but gave small promise of the brilliant future. Further along was Thrace, a warlike kingdom reaching back to the Getae of the Danube: it had two ranges which were a serious hindrance to penetration northwards, but colonies were pushed (after 650 B.C.) along the east coast to Istros, near the river of the same name, later to be called the Danube. (In an islet off the mouth there was now strangely located what had been a purely mythical island of the dead, Leuce.) Hecataeus has many details, several otherwise unknown, and perhaps to him is due much of what Herodotus says on Thracian customs, some so unpleasant that it is odd to find the people described as noble and just, after the fashion of Homer's vague nomads thereabouts.[2] The size of the country is vastly exaggerated, because the

1 Floating, Cary, *J.H.S.* 1924, p. 166: Bremer in Ebert's *Reallex. der Vorgesch.* IV, 545 (1926): Tozer, *Anc. Geogr.* pp. 37–9. See p. 195, n. 1. Celts by 6th cent., Collingwood and Myres, *Roman Britain and the English Settlements*, 1937, pp. 18–19. Erid. Elbe or Vistula, Déchelette, I, 618: Rhine or another, Müllenhoff, I, 222: Philipp, op. cit. p. 25: originally northern, Nansen, op. cit. pp. 31–4: there Choerilus ap. Serv. ad Virg. *G.* I, 482. Paus. I, 30, 3 means Rhine, and this old, Wikén in ΔΡΑΓΜΑ *Nilsson dedicatum*, 1939, p. 546.

2 Hdt. v, 3–8: Getae, ibid. IV, 94–6. Hec. fr. 146–83, Pearson, op. cit. pp. 56–61, Jacoby, I, 346. Thuc. II, 95–101 has much topographical detail. Kings, Hdt. v, 20. Timber, Thuc. IV, 108, Xen. *Hell.* v, 2, 16, VI, 1, 11, Theophr. *H.P.* I, 9, 2: Hasebroek, op. cit. p. 143. Thracian timber, Hdt. v, 23. On site of Byzantium, F. Harrison, *Meaning of History*, 1895, ch. 11: the Horn, Str. 320. Coins, Head, op. cit. pp. 523–7: *C.A.H.* Plates II, 3e. Black Sea colonies, Pârvan, *Dacia*, 1928, ch. 3.

Danube, for reasons to be explained later, is pushed back so as to have a final southward bend. Direct trade may not have gone far, though there was a Greek settlement at the Sereth junction and coins are found 200 miles up, while a bronze jar found a way to Slovakia and other bronzes even to the Celts. (It has been suggested that one lot of 'Hyperboreans', those said to have sent offerings to the sanctuary of Delos, were Graeco-Getic half-breeds on the Danube.) Several southern tributaries are mentioned, including the Morava, and half a dozen northern as far as the Theiss; but the account is badly muddled from vague hearsay, some being transferred to the wrong side. Towards the Theiss are Agathyrsi, said to have plenty of gold and to hold their women in common, in order that the whole people may be brothers, an assertion made about many peoples elsewhere but probably quite fantastic. Hearsay ends with a vast cold desert and Sigynnae (apparently in Bohemia) who have swift shaggy ponies and reach almost to the Veneti.[1]

Many were familiar with
> the Pontic sea,
> Whose icy current and compulsive course
> Ne'er feels retiring ebb, but keeps due on
> To the Propontic and the Hellespont,

and there were already some attempts to explain it, leading up to a notable theory (Strato's, in the next period). The sea was never called Black in ancient times. For a moment, we hear, it was Axine or Inhospitable—after a native name which sounded like this?—and was changed for luck to the reverse, Euxine, just as the Romans dropped Epidamnus 'quia velut in damnum ituris id omen visum est', and Eric thought of 'Greenland' to attract people with a good name. In fact, the sea was stormy and foggy and cold, and even at times ice-bound in the north, while some of its peoples had an evil repute for savagery. But the south coast at least was quite habitable, though often backed by high wooded mountains and without good access inland. About half-way along Miletus planted her first and chief colony, Sinope, exporting salt-fish and timber and pitch; it was a good centre for coasting traffic, and one could also cut over the open to the Crimea, sometimes even, as it is stated, without losing sight of land. Colonies or sub-colonies were soon pushed east as far as Trapezus (Trebizond). In the forest-clad hills close behind were more or less primitive tribes with queer

---

1 Hdt. v. 9: Agathyrsi, ibid. IV, 104: Danube, ibid. II, 33, 49, tributaries, IV, 48–9. Muddled, Pârvan, op. cit. pp. 80–1. Jar, Alföldi in *C.A.H.* XI, 87: trade, Beaumont, *J.H.S.* 1936, p. 200. Celts, Wheeler in *Eur. Civ.* II, 231. Hyperboreans, Seltman, *C.Q.* 1928, pp. 155–9. Women, E. E. Sikes, *Anthropology of the Greeks*, 1914, pp. 13–14, Westermarck, *Origin and Dev. of the Moral Ideas*, 1908, II, 364, Penniman, *Hundred Years of Anthropology*, 1935, pp. 152–61.

customs, Tibareni, Mossynoeci so called from living in high wooden towers, the iron-working and therefore rather uncanny Chalybes, and others: the whole series is already given, to be constantly repeated later with minor variations.[1] Beyond near the Caucasus there were two outlying settlements, Phasis and Dioscurias, exporting timber and pitch and wax. The second

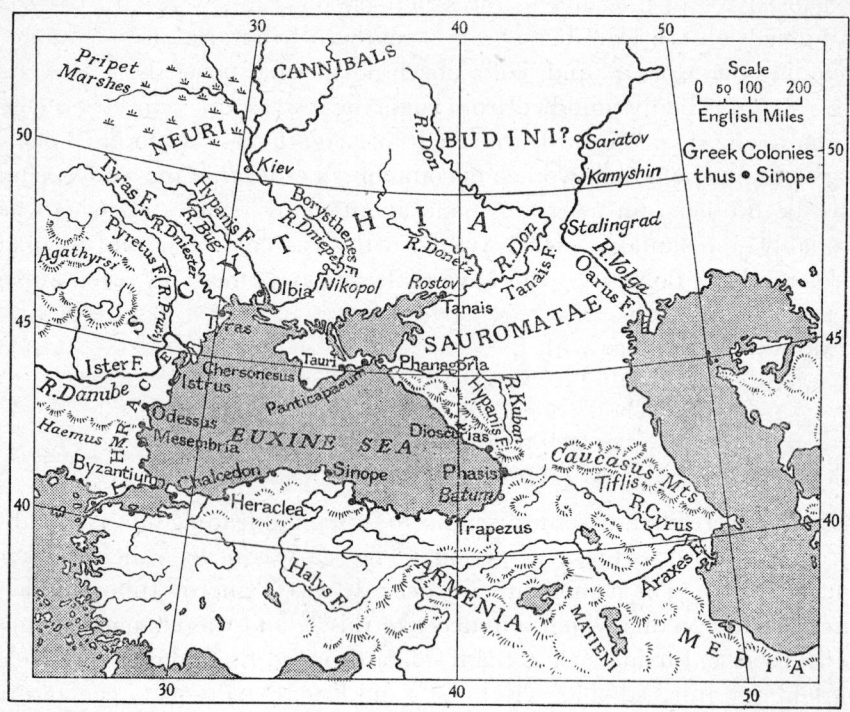

Fig. 4. Black Sea colonies.

was wrongly thought at the easternmost point of the sea. Tribes near-by were wildly explained as degraded 'Achaeans' and Heniochi or Charioteers descended from the Argonauts. Something was learnt of the polyglot hillmen coming down to barter, though later statements about 70 or even 300 languages are absurd. Strange and divergent things are said of the Colchians: they are dark, woolly-haired, and so like Egyptians in language

1 Long-heads of Hipp. *on Airs*, 14 here? Series, Hec. fr. 202–7, 288, Pearson, pp. 67–9, Jacoby, I, 356: Hdt. III, 94, VII, 78–9 (I, 28 is an interpolation): Xen. *Anab.* v, 4–5, Ps.-Scyl. 81 f. Ap. Rhod. II, 369–97, 1000–29, Str. 548–9, Plin. VI, 8, Dion. Per. 761. Sinope, Leaf, *J.H.S.* 1906, p. 1: Str. 545–6, sight, ibid. 309. 'Euxine', Pindar, *Pyth.* IV, 361, cp. *Nem.* IV, 80, Erat. and Apoll. ap. Str. 298, Ps.-Scymn. 754, Diod. IV, 40, Ov. *Trist.* IV, 4, 55, Mela, I, 102, Plin. IV, 76, VI, 1: from native (Iranian) name, Burr, *Nostrum Mare*, 1932, pp. 31–3, after Boisacq. Epid. (Durazzo), Mela, II, 3. Current, Hdt. VII, 35, Diog. of Apoll. ap. Sen. *N.Q.* IV, 2, 29, Plato, *Phaedo*, 90 c, etc.: Strato, see p. 156, n. 1. For Chalybes cp. p. 18, n. 3.

and customs that they must descend from them, or they are yellow, fat, and lazy from living in a sultry and marshy valley and drinking the stagnant water of the Phasis.¹ (It is sometimes inferred that Herodotus came all the way, but this seems very dubious.) The range was far the highest yet known; early maps seem to have drawn it too far north and running almost due east. For a moment the Phasis seemed a suitable line between Europe and Asia, and later there were suggestions of the Caucasus isthmus as such, like the present boundary there, but other ideas prevailed.²

Northward the sea penetrates to a climatic region quite alien from the Mediterranean: here is the wide Russian plain with its summer rainfall for ample pastures on the steppe and for wheat on the 'black earth'. Greeks missed the olive and vine, though vineyards were possible on the Crimean coast, sheltered by hills from the cold northern winds. They thought the winter long and bleak, but could manage by 'importing everything necessary for civilized life', and there were attractions, like the fine fisheries. Of the colonies the best placed were Olbia 'the rich', at the mouth of two rivers, which was flourishing by 600 B.C., and Panticapaeum (Kerch), commanding the strait into the shallow sea of Azov (Lake Maeotis). The farthest was Tanais on the river of the same name (the Don) and at the head of this 'lake', where the fish were hatched which later shoaled slowly along past Sinope westwards. All the towns exported hides and other produce got from the native nomads, and also slaves, but especially salt-fish and corn; the control of this corn supply had already become vital for Athens when Herodotus visited Olbia. His personal acquaintance does not prevent some very bad blunders in geography: he almost doubles the length of the sea, mistakes its axes both of length and breadth, and puts Sinope due south of the Danube mouths: he misconceives the shape and size of the Crimea, and bends the Azov northwards and even thinks it not very much smaller than the main sea, a queer error which was to persist long. A good comparison of the outline to a Scythian bow is probably only later. The Tanais was early chosen as the continental boundary, and later most favoured as such, being sometimes helped out by a vague line from it northwards (no one thought of the present line along the Urals). The poet Aeschylus takes the wildest liberties with

1 Hipp. *on Airs*, 18, as cp. Hdt. II, 104. Cauc. tribes, Hec. fr. 191–2, 209–10: Hdt. I, 203. D. easternmost still, Str. 497. Languages, ibid. 498, Timosthenes ap. Plin. VI, 15. Achaeans, Arist. *Pol.* VIII, 4, Str. 416, 495, 839: Heniochi, Plin. VI, 16, etc. Hdt. came, J. E. Powell, *Hist. of H.* 1939, p. 25.

2 Phasis, Pindar, *Isthm.* II, 41, Aesch. *Prom. Sol.* fr. ap. Arr. *Eux.* 19, Eur. *Andr.* 650, some ap. Hdt. IV, 45, at least considered by Pos. ap. Str. 492, Proc. *B.G.* IV, 2, 29, IV, 61 prefers: *R.E.* Phasis 1938, Diehl. Berger, *Erdkunde*², pp. 91–2. Range, Heidel, *Frame*, pp. 15, 31: Ionian maps in Arist. *Met.* I, 13, 305a. Isthmus, some ap. Str. 35, 66: some ap. Dion. Per. 19–22: Ps.-Arist. *de Mundo*, 5.

geography, even putting the Chalybes and the Caucasus vaguely northwest of the Kerch strait.[1]

The Scythians had invaded recently from the eastern steppes and expelled or subjected the Cimmerians (about 700 B.C.). They were Iranian in language, and appear in art as handsome and bearded, though there is an odd notice of a fat and beardless (Mongol?) type. They were nomads, except some who took to corn-growing under the influence of the 'black earth' and the Greek demand. For their wares they got wine and various things made to suit their artistic taste. Herodotus describes them well, far better than many then and long after who used the name loosely and repeated the old sentimentalities about noble savages (Aeschylus had recently spoken of 'just' Scythians who live on mare's-milk cheese). At close quarters they seemed far from 'just': they hung scalps on their reins, made cups of skulls, and buried their kings in a ring of slaughtered horses and human victims. He defines Scythia clearly as lying between Danube and Don, an almost treeless steppe extending twenty days inland (some 440 miles). In three separate passages he gives the rivers (IV, 47–58), the peoples up their courses (ibid. 17–20), and a supposed invasion of Darius all the way to the Don and beyond, with most of the rivers conveniently removed from his path (ibid. 99–117—later writers think of a raid only to the Dniester, and the story is generally admitted to be wild). No consistent map can be drawn from the three accounts, and the geography is a mess, because he makes all the rivers run due south: two are not to be identified, and the Gerrhus as described is an impossibility. How much he owes to Hecataeus is not clear: the fragments have little here, including some tribes and towns which he does not mention.[2]

1 Aesch. *P.V.* 707–29. Don-Ocean, Pos. ap. Str. 491: Ptol. II, 1, 6, VII, 5, 6. Don, Aesch. *P.V.* 734, 790, Hippocr. op. cit. p. 13, probably Hec. (ap. Hdt. IV, 45), Myres, *Geogr. J.* 1896, p. 625, Macan, Pearson, op. cit. p. 65 (despite Jacoby, I, 352): Ps.-Scyl. 68, Polyb. III, 59, Str. 490. Blunders, Hdt. IV, 85–6, 99: Bunbury, *Anc. Geogr.* I, 176. Corn, Plut. *Pericles*, 20: Hdt. VII, 147: Hasebroek, loc. cit. p. 143. Fisheries, Hdt. IV, 53, Arist. *H.A.* VI, 16: shoaled, Str. 320, cp. Plin. IX, 47–51, Juv. 4, 41–4, etc. Exports, Polybius, IV, 38, 51: importing, Str. 493. Climate, Hdt. IV, 28: Hipp. *on Airs*, 19: but sometimes hot, Str. 307. In general Minns, *Scythians and Greeks*, 1913: M. Ebert, *Südrussland im Alt.* 1921: Rostovtzeff, *Iranians and Greeks in South Russia*, 1922: Vernadsky, *Ancient Russia*, Yale, 1943. Bow, see p. 141, n. 1. Date, Ure, *C.A.H.* IV, 105.

2 Hec. fr. 186–90, Pearson, p. 63, but Jacoby, I, 349, ascribes also Eph. ap. Ps.-Scymn. 841 f. Wild, Macan's ed. of Hdt. IV–VI, 1895, II, App. 3: Cary in *C.A.H.* IV, 212. Dniester, Ctesias and Str. 368. Casson, *B.S.A.* 1918–19, pp. 175–93 argues unconvincingly that H. conflated two expeditions (from Danube and from Caspian). On the geography Macan, op. cit. App. 2 with the possible maps: Myres, *G.J.* 1896, p. 607: Minns, op. cit. ch. 3: monographs by Windberg, 1913, etc.: Ebert, op. cit. with map of Hdt. p. 84. Day= 200 stades, Hdt. IV, 101. Just, Aesch. *P.S.* fr. 8 ap. Str. 390. Wares to Scythian taste, *C.A.H.* Plates III, 79–113. Beardless, Hipp. *on Airs*, 22. Vernadsky, op. cit. p. 53. Gerrhus= Konka: Darius east to Budini, strangely put on the middle Donetz, ibid. pp. 62, 69–70.

THE GREEK HORIZON TO HERODOTUS

Along the north of the Scythian square and racially not belonging to it, as he insists against somebody, probably Hecataeus, are Neuri (perhaps Slavs?), who believe in were-wolves, and then Cannibals and Black-coats (perhaps Finnish tribes?). There is no word of a change from the prairie and the black earth to thick forests (on a line roughly from Kiev north-east to Kazan). Beyond are a snowy desert and some hypothetical lakes, needed

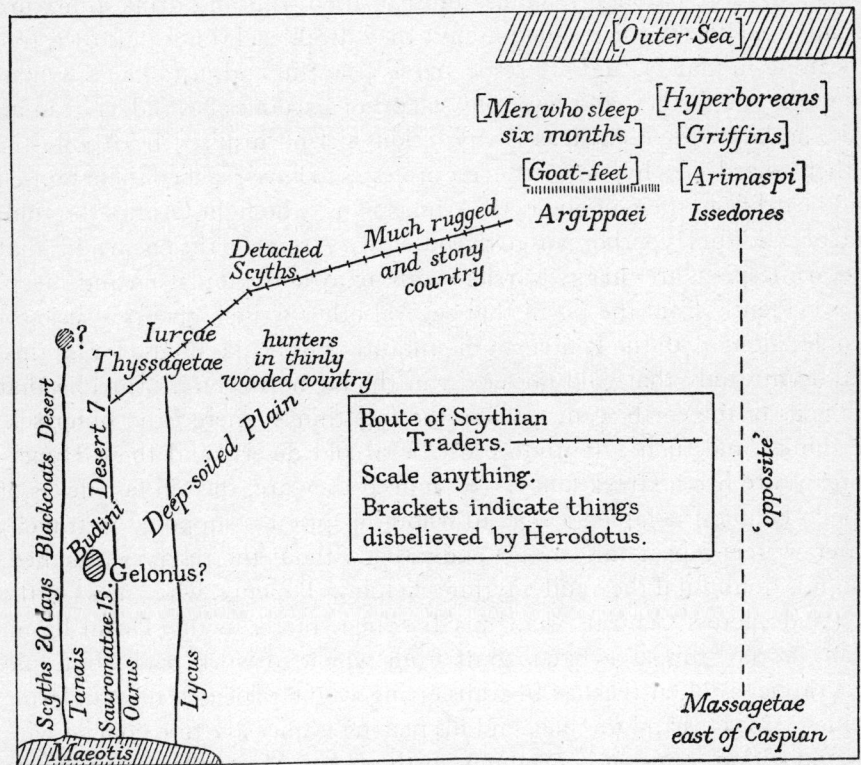

Fig. 5.

as sources of the big rivers, because he will not have the popular Rhipaean range, which others found useful to explain their surprising size and volume. From such faulty knowledge it does not appear that the colonists themselves travelled far inland, though their wares drifted all the way to Prussia.[1] Actually even the Volga, 2400 miles long, rises in a very modest watershed, the Valdai Hills, only 1000 feet high; the fact, surprising enough, was never suspected by ancient writers, who went on repeating vague suggestions of lofty mountains (see for instance what happens about these in Ptolemy).

[1] *C.A.H.* Plates III, 81 *b*. Rhip. still Arist. (see p. 87, n. 2). Danube from vague north, Pindar, *Ol.* III, 14. Aesch. fr. 66, 183, Berger, pp. 106, 124. See p. 22, n. 1. For Ptolemy's map see p. 251.

Eastwards Herodotus has some remarkable information, which may be sketched as on p. 61, very roughly and doubtfully, as no distances are given except the few stated. Gelonus is a wooden town with half-breed traders; a lake near it, amid woods, is broad and deep and reedy, and has otters and beavers and something else. The Budini are nomads and eat lice (not pine-cones, as some translate). The Argippaei are bald from birth, have flat noses and large (Mongol?) chins, and eat dried fruit and drink a mixture of milk and cherry-juice called aschy; they dwell each under his own tree (meaning in tents?), and are respected as peaceful and just. The Scythian traders go no farther, and have only heard of Issedones beyond. But in an epic, he knows, one Aristeas, a mysterious person inspired by Apollo (or rather 'seized' in a hypnotic trance), professes to have reached them himself and heard from them of one-eyed Arimaspians, who fight Griffins for gold, and of peaceful Hyperboreans to the outer sea. A scrap of the poem adds that the Arimaspians are shaggy warriors with many horses and oxen and sheep. It is evidently from the poem that several other writers give this series of peoples along with the Rhipaean mountains. But he has no use for all this, and admits only that gold does exist in the far north, on a principle that the ends of the earth seem to have the fine things; there is no outer sea, he thinks, and such a latitude must be a cold desert, and these Hyperboreans are just a Greek fancy. (So indeed they are, the old favourites of Apollo behind the fabled range, to whom his priest is supposed to travel.) Later writers repeat this matter endlessly, without the reserves attached, and it is doubtful if they add anything helpful. Ptolemy, who knows of the silk-trade across Central Asia, puts Issedones there, in the Tarim basin. Many accept this as a fixed point from which to work back; but that geographer is often reckless in transferring vaguely located or wandering names, Amazons and the like, and his placing is not easy to reconcile with the indication 'opposite' (meaning north of) the Massagetae, who are no farther east than the Aral region.[1]

The rivers are all wrong: the Don should bend east to approach the Oarus (Volga), which should flow to the Caspian. Thus there is a false start. Some find the wooden town at Saratov, Minns and others make it

[1] Hdt. I, 201, IV, 21–7, 32, 108–9, 123–4: (Aristeas) ibid. 13, 16, 48: fine things, III, 116. Ptolemy strangely transfers, Bunbury, I, 598: Herrmann, *Land der Seide*, 1938, p. 10. From the epic, Hec. fr. 193, Aesch. *P.V.* 805–8, Hellanicus, fr. 187*b*, Damastes, fr. 1 (Jacoby, *F.G.H.* I, 352), and Alcman's Essedones? (not same and Aristeas is *c*. 550 B.C., Norden, *Germ. Urgesch. in Tac. Germ.*³ 1923, pp. 19–21). Aristeas real, though story affected by cult stories of Apollo, How and Wells, *Comm. on Herodotus*, 1912 (²1928). Ar. early hearsay of road as due north, corrected by Hdt., Junge, *Klio* Beiheft, 1939, pp. 15, 20. Cones, Ebert, op. cit. p. 86. Trance, Nilsson, *Hist. of Greek Religion*, 1925, p. 202: ecstasy, Rohde, *Psyche*⁸, 1925, p. 300 (yet real person). 'Opposite' meant (in Hdt.'s source) divided by Caspian gulf, thinks Wikén in ΔΡΑΓΜΑ *Nilsson dedicatum*, 1939, p. 549.

THE GREEK HORIZON TO HERODOTUS

Kazan (they also compare the Thyssagetae in name with a river Chussovaya, Perm way, and the Iurcae with Ugrians on the Ob). The trade-route should strike the Urals somewhere, and people thereabouts are said to have the cherry-drink and even its name. The only mountains mentioned are 'high and impassable' and run west-east, but are perhaps misconceived Urals. The Issedones should not be far beyond, and some place them on a river Isset (route 1 of the sketch-map, see below). Others make the traders

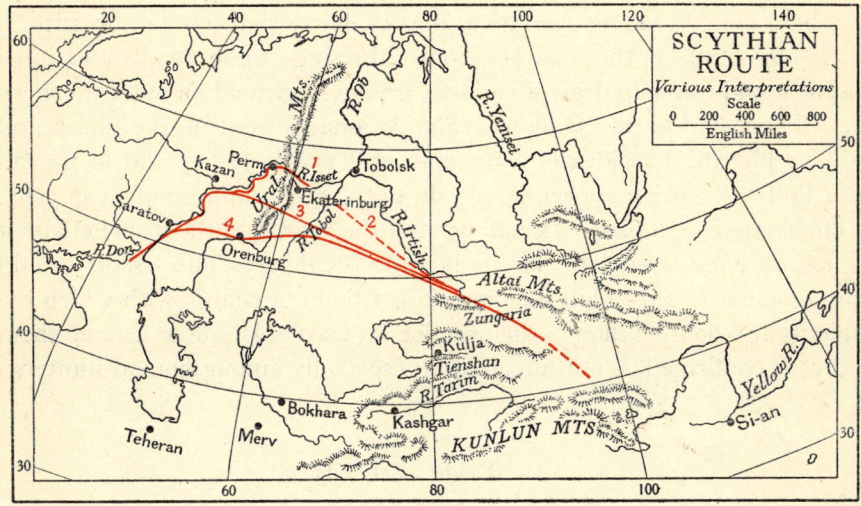

Fig. 6.

cross this low range here or farther south without noticing it at all and go a long way on (routes 2 and 3). Hudson, insisting on a drastic correction of the false start, takes them through the desert south of the range (route 4). All these reach the Issedones where Ptolemy has them, or rather a little east of that, on the edge of China.[1] They reach the Altai mountains, too, which run as described and are also noted for gold. Some suggest that the shaggy gold-hunters are Huns, and even that these Hyperboreans are a notion of the peaceful Chinese. A Russian study of Siberia in the accounts of foreign travellers concludes that there is some real, if distorted, informa-

---

[1] Minns, op. cit. pp. 101–14 (route 2) as Tomaschek, *Sitzb. Akad. Wien*, 1888–9 and *R.E.* Budini, E. Meyer, *Gesch. des Alt.* III, 106, Ebert, op. cit. pp. 188–90, Teggart, *Rome and China*, 1939, p. 209. Route 3, Berthelot, *Asie centr. et sud-or. d'après Ptolémée*, 1930, pp. 34–51. Route 4, G. F. Hudson, *Europe and China*, 1931, pp. 27–52 (followed by Sir P. Sykes, *Quest for Cathay*, 1936, pp. 16–20). Route 1, Westberg, *Klio*, 1906, pp. 182–92, How and Wells, op. cit., Herrmann, loc. cit. and *R.E.* IX, 2235 (Isset after Müllenhoff, III, 11). Iss. there invented Griffins, Hennig, *Rh. Mus.* 1930, p. 326, and these Hyp. are Samoyedes of Ob mouth, *Klio*, 1932, p. 1. Isset, Vernadsky, op. cit. p. 66 and Arg. probably Zungaria.

tion as far as the Argippaei, and everything beyond is legend and imagination, except that some Siberian gold may have passed along. Whether from Altai or Urals or both, there was plenty of gold at Panticapaeum, and the Griffin appears on its coins, with an ear of corn or a sturgeon, (see Plate I B) and on many gold ornaments made there.[1]

Except that the Issedones are 'opposite' the Massagetae, there is no hint how the trade-route is conceived in relation to the Caspian. For this Herodotus has a good report from another (Persian?) quarter. He knows it to be a closed sea; he even gives figures, fairly right for the breadth, if much too small for the length. (Some disparage these details and insist that he could not help drawing a lake here, as he denied an outer northern sea.) There had been a fancy that the Argonauts went up the Phasis and into the Ocean. The idea of a Caspian gulf was to revive and to prevail until Ptolemy and often even later still, to the great damage of geography.

The rumour of a people 'sleeping' half the year, and the disbelief about it, will be considered later for its bearing on theory. The Issedones and Massagetae are said to kill the old and eat them, a charge with which the ancients are too free, though the practice (at least of killing or leaving them to die) is confirmed as not uncommon, especially among nomad hunters.[2]

§4. THE SOUTH

Certain Ionians and Carians landed in the Delta about 650 B.C., we hear, and as the 'bronze men from the sea', foretold by an oracle, enabled a local prince to master the kingdom. His successors continued to use such mercenaries, and a few cut their names on the legs of a rock-statue in Nubia. Egypt did not love foreigners, but allowed a sort of treaty-port at Naucratis, up one arm of the Nile (just when and how it began has been much discussed). There had been traders perhaps as early as 750 B.C. Besides soldiers and traders there were some who came only 'to see', among them the old philosophers Thales and Pythagoras, who are supposed to have learnt a lot of practical science here (their visit is credible enough, though many

---

[1] Head, *Hist. Numorum*, 1911, fig. 168 (and Abdera, fig. 159 from cult of Hyperborean Apollo). *C.A.H.* Plates III, 21, 91, 93c. Study, Alexeiev, Irkutsk, 1932 (kindly translated by Prof. Konovalov). Macan, op. cit. II, 22 and *C.A.H.* V, 14, is very reserved. Griffin from Siberian art?, Hennig, *Klio*, 1935, p. 249. Seltman, *Greek Coins*, 1933, p. 180. Chinese, Sykes, op. cit. p. 20, S. Casson, *C.R.* 1920, pp. 1–3, as Gladisch and Tomaschek.

[2] Westermarck, op. cit. I, 387: Carr-Saunders, *Population Problem*, 1922, p. 154. Hdt. I, 216, IV, 26: Mass., Str. 513: Irish, ibid. p. 201, Diod. V, 32, etc. (see p. 110, n. 1). Sleep, Hdt. IV, 24: see p. 100, n. 1, p. 113, n. 3. Closed, Hdt. I, 202. Argonauts, Hes. and Hec. in Schol. Ap. Rhod. IV, 259, 284, Pearson, op. cit. p. 101, Jacoby, I, 364: Pindar, *Pyth.* IV, 44–7. Disparage, M. Dubois, *Examen de la Géogr. de Strabon*, 1893, pp. 200–1.

statements about such travellers are inventions of a later time inclined to ascribe Greek wisdom to eastern sources). The Persians conquered the country in 525 B.C., but this did not hinder tourists. Hecataeus came to Thebes and was abashed when shown proof of a past immensely longer than his own pedigree of sixteen generations from a god. It seems that he dwelt rather fully on this land of marvels and that Herodotus owes him a good deal more than appears.[1] The latter stayed a few months during the flood season, going up as far as Aswan, and his long digression on Egypt (Book II) is the best of ancient descriptions of travel.

The visitors were puzzled by the topsy-turvy customs, and the religion was a nightmare with its beast-headed gods and mummifying of sacred cats. Greeks could hardly doubt their own superiority; yet the huge temples and pyramids awed them, and the sheer antiquity of this civilization, so that they wrongly traced to it many of their own institutions. Herodotus picked up from guides some very mixed notions of history, even putting the pyramid-builders of dynasty IV after dynasty XIX (a blunder strangely repeated for long afterwards—was it due to some displacement in his notes?). But he was a lively observer of men and manners. There were wonders of nature too, queer animals like the 'river-horse' and an enormous lizard, the crocodile, which allowed a little bird to pick its teeth. But the greatest wonder was the Nile. Every summer it overflowed and laid its fertile mud to produce rich harvests in an almost rainless land. It had made the very land, and anyone could see that the Delta, if not more, was 'the gift of the river'. Where did it come from, and why, unlike all other rivers, was it highest in the dry season? The priests had no sensible answer, but Greeks could not do without theories. Some already got very near the truth, Thrasyalces, 'an old natural philosopher' (*physikos*), and presently Democritus: the flushing came, they said, from the heavy rains dropped by the etesian winds on the Ethiopian mountains (these had just been heard of and were still vaguely placed). Others like Anaxagoras thought of the melting of snows on the same mountains. Herodotus cannot accept snow in a country where men are burnt black, and he has his reasons against rains; his own odd explanation is that the sun moves farther away in summer and so evaporates the river less at that time (we must return later to his crude astronomy). He dismisses a theory, ascribed elsewhere to Thales, that the etesian winds blowing up the mouths dam back the

---

1 Hec. named only in Hdt. II, 143 but cp. 'the Ionians say', ibid. 15, etc. Hec. fr. 303–23, Pearson, pp. 81–3, 90, Jacoby, I, 366. Naucratis, Hdt. II, 152–4, 178–9, cp. Str. 801. Date and circumstances, Hasebroek, op. cit. pp. 60–6: *C.A.H.* III, 291, IV, 107: Kees, *R.E.* Naukratis, 1935: R. M. Cook, *J.H.S.* 1937, p. 227 (proposes 615–610 B.C.): J. G. Milne, *J.E.A.* 1939, pp. 177–83; Gjerstad, *Liv. Annals*, 1934, pp. 67–84 (earliest finds about 570 B.C.). J. E. Powell, *History of Herodotus*, 1939, pp. 25–9 argues for two visits of H.

current. He scorns a fancy of the priests that the river flows from the Ocean-stream, which belongs, he insists, to myth. Strangely Hecataeus seems to have made the Argonauts pass from a dim Caspian gulf round to the south side of 'Libya' and enter the Nile there, while others said they carried their ship overland from there to the river. Besides there was an idea of a western Nile, which must be discussed presently. A minor question about the Nile was whether to make it the boundary between 'Libya' and Asia: Herodotus finds this awkward and seems to prefer the isthmus. Before him 'Libya' was often not regarded as a separate continent but included in Asia, while some thought of three more or less equal continents; he rejects this, and makes Europe extend the whole length of the other two.[1]

Something was now known of Ethiopians as real blacks above Egypt, though the poetic tradition of them lingered on (Aeschylus has them far along the south of the world, on a 'red sea' and also on 'lakes by Ocean' where the sun rests his horses). From Aswan, Herodotus learnt, it was 56 days to a big town Meroe, 40 of them across the desert to avoid the Nile rapids. A first invasion by the Persians had failed disastrously, it was said (it seems that they took Napata but lost heavily in the desert short-cut on the way back). Yet soon they were getting tribute of gold and ivory and ebony, and negro boys, and a contingent of archers painted red and white and wearing beast-skins. Fable still clings to certain other Ethiopians far south and south-west along the outer sea, the tallest and handsomest of men and long-lived from bathing in a marvellous fountain. Beyond Meroe, 56 days again, we hear, was a people sprung from Egyptian deserters, apparently in Sennar, though that is only half the distance. 'There the river flows from west to east: above none has any sure knowledge of its course, as the country is uninhabited from excessive heat'. (Yet he believes that the upper course has been struck in the far west, how must be explained presently.) The distance mentioned would lead to the swamps where the Bahr el Ghazal does come in from the west, and the statement has been taken to represent a genuine rumour of the fact. Hecataeus has pygmies, with some curious details, how they stalk the cranes or scare them with

[1] IV, 42: Macan ad loc. (division Phasis–Caspian–Araxes). Three, Pindar, *Pyth.* IX, 8. Isthmus, Hdt. II, 16–17, cp. IV, 36, 45. Berger, op. cit. pp. 78, 82. Argonauts, Hec. in Schol. Ap. Rhod. IV, 259, 284 (overland, Hes. ibid. and Pindar, *Pyth.* IV): Pearson, p. 87, Jacoby, I, 323, 368. Theories, Hdt. II, 19–26, Diod. I, 37–9: rains, ibid. 39, Str. 790: snow, Anax. ap. Sen. *N.Q.* IV, 2, 17, Aesch. Suppl. 560, Eur. *Hel.* 3: Aet. IV, 1 (Diels, *Doxographi Graeci*, pp. 384–6): Berger, *Fragm. des Erat.* pp. 306–7 and *Erdkunde*[2], pp. 130–45, corrected by Capelle, *N. Jahrb.* 1914, 317–61: Heidel, *Heroic Age of Science*, 1933, p. 160 (Hdt. does not understand all that he rejects): now esp. *R.E.* Nil, Honigmann, and Nilsschwelle, Rehm, 1936. Hdt.'s bad dating still in Diod. I, 63–5: displaced notes, Kenyon, *Bible and Arch.* 1940, p. 58.

rattles.[1] A frieze of pygmies and cranes appears round the foot of the great François vase (about 550 B.C.).

The coast which we now call Libya became well known. Colonists were guided by a Cretan purple-fisher, and, after some fumbling with barren sites, pushed a few miles inland to found Cyrene (about 631 B.C.). Here was a strip of Mediterranean climate, sheltered by higher ground from

Fig. 7. Cup of Arcesilas II, about 550 B.C.

the scorching desert winds; vine and olive were possible, and the plateau terraces usually caught enough winter rains for good pastures. A speciality for export was silphium, a medicinal plant growing wild on the inner steppe; it is shown on many coins (see Plate I C) and a vase, where the king surveys the weighing and packing on a ship, while overhead a crane flies south to fight the pygmies. Among several sub-colonies was one at Benghazi. Various troubles brought about a Persian invasion from Egypt, and this gives Herodotus his cue for a general account of the Libyans and their

[1] Hec. fr. 338a, Pearson, p. 96. Rumour, Honigmann, *R.E.* Libye, 158. Deserters, Hdt. II, 30–1, Meroe, ibid. p. 29. Invasion of Cambyses, ibid. III, 17–25, 97, Str. 820, *C.A.H.* III, 313, IV, 21: J. v. Prašek, *Gesch. der Meder u. Perser*, 1906, I, 258–60. Long-lived, Hdt. III, 17, 114. Tribute, III, 97, VII, 69. Aesch. fr. 178: Myres in *Anthropology and the Classics*, 1908, pp. 132–3. Vase, *C.A.H.* Plates I, 380a.

customs. He implies that he had visited Cyrene and asked questions there, but he was not the first to write about these parts. Hecataeus had given more detail of the coast here, including the deep inlet of the Psyllic gulf (or Great Syrtis, to-day the Gulf of Sidra) and farther along. He may perhaps be credited also with the curiously definite and map-like arrangement of the inner zones. The younger writer's borrowing from him seems large, if not quite the wholesale pillage sometimes ascribed.[1]

Westwards the coast was mostly utter desert, with exposed roadsteads, to the other or Little Syrtis, apparently not at once so called. The only patch at all attractive, though its fertility was exaggerated, was one (Tripoli way) with wells and some rain; here there was a short-lived colonial venture, which the natives ended with the help of Carthage. The coast is described as low and sandy and inhabited only by nomads to a river Triton, to which nothing really answers; a shoaly lake Tritonis, enveloped in a mist of fable, seems to be the Little Syrtis itself (the Gulf of Gabes). But there may be confusion, as the name Tritonis was earlier and often given to a lagoon near Benghazi. Lotus-eaters were sometimes placed that way too, but frequently at the base of the same gulf and especially the island of Meninx or Jerba. Here the tides were less feeble than anywhere else in the inner sea, while the Great Syrtis also was feared for its shoals and its breakers driven by north winds.[2]

Round the corner was the domain of Carthage. She had subjected some Libyans for their corn-lands, but looked rather to sea-power and trade: no doubt she had a string of factories along the coast to the straits. The Persians thought of conquering her from Egypt, but the Phoenicians in their fleet refused to serve against their own kin. What Herodotus says of these parts is rather odd. Beyond the Triton are not nomads but settled Libyan tribes, which he places vaguely and badly, as he does not realize the marked

---

[1] By Diels, loc. cit. and Jacoby, *R.E.* VI, 2686, *F.G.H.* I, 371: less, Gsell, *Hérodote*, 1916, p. 61. Hec. fr. 329–333: Psyllic, 332, cp. Hdt. IV, 173. Libyans, Hdt. IV, 168–98. Cyrene, ibid. 150–9, Barca, 160, Euhesperides, 171: invasion, 164, 200–4: climate, 19. Visit, II, 32, 96 (though Macan doubts). Silphium, Str. 837, 839, Plin. V, 33, Arr. *Ind.* 43, 13, Ptol. *Geogr.* IV, 4, 6. Droop, *J.H.S.* 1932, p. 303 dates the cup as Arc. I, *c.* 575, cp. Lane, *B.S.A.* 1933–4, p. 161: *C.A.H.* Plates I, 378*b*. Seltman, *Greek Coins*, pp. 81, 182. Ure, *C.A.H.* IV, 109–12.

[2] Syrtes...aestuosas, Hor. *Odes*, I, 22, 5: Mela, I, 35; Plin. II, 218, V, 26: two first in Ps.-Scyl. 92 as cp. Hdt. II, 52, 150. Coast, Hdt. IV, 186–90: Cinyps patch, 198 and venture of Dorieus in 513, ibid. V, 42, *C.A.H.* IV, 112. Lake Tritonis, Hdt. IV, 178–80: Gsell, op. cit. p. 79 (not Shott Jerid as Perroud, *de Syrticis Emporiis*, 1881, p. 19). Lagoon, Pindar, *Pyth.* IV, 20, Str. 836, Plin. V, 28: Ptol. IV, 5, 21, 30: confusion, Strenger, *Strabos Erdkunde von Libyen*, 1913, p. 124: Honigmann, *R.E.* Libye, 1926, pp. 156–7: see p. 263, n. 1. Herrmann, *Rh. Mus.* 1937, pp. 67–93 is wildly fanciful. Lotus-eaters that way, Mela, I, 37, Plin. V, 28, but west of Cinyps, Hdt. IV, 177, Erat. ap. Polyb. I, 39, Str. 25, 834, Plin. V, 41.

northward projection of the Tunisian coast. He has much on coiffures and customs. The Gyzantes paint themselves red, like the Maxyes, and eat monkeys, and make a honey from flowers. One island has Lotus-eaters; in another, the Carthaginians say, gold nuggets are fished from a lake. Somewhere near are wooded mountains with many beasts, including elephants (they are often mentioned later as still existing here). There are rumours of 'wild men', if the text is genuine, and Dog-heads and No-heads, but these he prudently rejects. Otherwise he mentions nothing till the straits. Hecataeus had had some names identical or similar, Zaueces, a town Zygantis, Mazyes, though the last are nomads and the settled country begins with a town Megasa. Possibly from him a poet borrows Dog-heads and Breast-eyes (it is not said where these are). Near Carthage he has Libyphoenices, half-breeds or natives under her influence. He gives quite a series of coast places with names which seem to indicate calling-stations used by Greeks on the way to the straits, before Carthage became so jealous.[1]

Behind the whole coast Herodotus conceives two zones, a wild-beast country and then an utter desert. The former seems quite unreal except in the western part with the wooded mountains. The line between the two, all the way from Egypt to the Atlantic, is a 'sand-ridge'. Along it at intervals of ten days (say 220 miles) are places queerly described as salt-hills with sweet springs; really they are basin oases (the word is Egyptian, and he uses it, but only for 'the city Oasis' on the outskirts of Egypt at Kharga). The first is Ammon (Siwa) with a famous oracle and a spring said to be coldest at noon and to boil at midnight, a notion derived apparently from the bubbling up of dissolved gas. It is placed ten days from upper instead of lower Egypt. (There is a wild tale of a Persian expedition from the former against it, which reached Kharga in seven days, but was thereafter lost, presumably overwhelmed by sand-storms.) The false start throws the whole series too far south, though the mistake is partly neutralized by another: the Garamantes should be 16 days south-west of Augila and occupy not one oasis but a large area, Fezzan. This tribe, according to one of two inconsistent accounts, raid 'Ethiopian' cave-dwellers, who eat reptiles and have a language like the screeching of bats (probably in Tibesti). The next people have no personal names and curse the blazing sun. The next, dreamless vegetarians, live under a round

---

[1] Gsell, op. cit. p. 55: Cary-Warmington, *Anc. Explorers*, p. 23: Pearson, op. cit. p. 92. Hec. fr. 338–53. Hdt. IV, 191–6. Breast-eyes, Aesch. ap. Str. 43, 299, from Hec.?, Gsell, p. 60 doubts. On Libyan geography Macan's ed. II, 270–9: diss. by R. Neumann, 1892, Windberg, 1913, etc. Persians, Hdt. III, 19. Tribes, Gsell, *Hist. de l'Afrique du Nord*, v, 81–4. Romans early forbidden here, ibid. I, 450, IV, 118: see p. 51, n. 1. Elephants, Plin. VIII, 2, 32, etc.

cloud-capped mountain, Atlas, which they regard as holding up the sky. He cannot name the other oases 'to (? the meridian of) the Pillars and the Atlantic sea'. This desert Atlas, if it is anywhere, seems in mid-Sahara— some think of Ahaggar—and has nothing to do with the wooded mountains mentioned above. These were presently—by whom first?—named Atlas, as of course they are called to-day. Bérard thinks they are meant already and even in Homer. Rather it should be said that Homer's vague placing in the far west helped to fix the name here, especially the part of the range along the outer sea.[1]

A wild adventure is reported of five braves of the Nasamones, a coast tribe which used to visit Augila for dates and locusts, both good eating. They crossed the beast-zone to the desert, and travelled west (or southwest?) many days to a wooded plain; here they were seized by dwarfish blacks, and taken over great marshes to a town on a big river which had crocodiles and flowed eastwards. Somehow they got back to tell the chief of Ammon, who told men of Cyrene, and they all guessed the river to be the Nile, and Herodotus agrees. The Nile seems to him to flow eastwards a long way through the middle of Libya before turning north at the point in Ethiopia already mentioned. (So the Danube flows eastwards through the middle of Europe before turning south: there is a curious preconception of a necessary symmetry between the two rivers.) The ancients have queer things to say of Saharan water-courses, partly underground, and we shall find a Moorish king making the Nile flow from his own country, with crocodiles again as a main argument. Yet the story of the native explorers was seldom quoted, even by those disposed to believe in a western Nile. What did they really find? Very likely the Niger about Timbuctoo, most say, and its connection with the Nile was seriously discussed as a fact as late as 1822. But it is reasonably doubted if such a journey was feasible for five ill-equipped natives without camels (perhaps there was slightly more rain then, it is allowed, but only very slightly more, so that the journey was almost as foolhardy as it would be now). One writer takes them only to an east-flowing wadi in Fezzan. Others think of some oasis not too far south of the Atlas region, though in that case Cyrenaica is a curious starting-point, as indeed also for the Niger. Whatever river is meant in the story, the

---

[1] Hdt.'s not the ordinary Atlas, Gsell, *Hérodote*, p. 107, against Bérard, *Phéniciens et l'Odyssée*, I, 244: it is nowhere, Strenger, op. cit. pp. 21, 62: Ahaggar (Hoggar), Berthelot, *Afrique sahar. et soudanaise*, 1927, p. 162, Borchardt in *Pet. Mitt.* 1924, p. 221, Hennig, ibid. 1927, p. 80. Hdt. is echoed in Plin. v, 6, cp. 44. Series, Hdt. IV, 181–5, II, 32: city Oasis, III, 26, Hec. fr. 326. Gar. of Hdt. IV, 174, inconsistent with those of 183, were read by Mela, I, 47, Plin. v, 45 as Gamphasantes, and Gsell, *Hérodote*, p. 102 approves, and so Honigmann, op. cit. p. 156 after O. Bates, *Eastern Libyans*, 1914, p. 33, but Strenger, op. cit. p. 137, rejects, as Macan. Gas, J. Ball, *Egypt in the Classical Geographers*, 1942, p. 20.

historian may have no other basis for his previous statement that the Nile, where last known from Egypt, flows from the west. (Or is this a rumour of the Bahr el Ghazal?) He has plainly little notion of the width of the Sahara. There is poor evidence for trade from Carthage far inland: if negro slaves were sold there, some were to be had nearer than the Sudan. Not much can be made of one Mago, of uncertain date, who is vaguely said to have crossed 'the desert' thrice, eating only dry barley and drinking nothing![1]

That the continent is an island, except for the narrow isthmus, was first proved, we hear, by the Egyptian king Necho, about 600 B.C. He had tried vainly to open communication from the Red Sea by cutting a canal to the Nile Delta, a work which an oracle warned him to abandon. Then he ordered his Phoenicians to sail round. They passed into the southern sea, and in autumn they landed wherever they were and sowed corn, and waited to reap it. So in the third year they reached home through the straits. Of what they saw Herodotus can give only one detail: they declared that when rounding Libya (from east to west) they had the sun on their right. This he will not accept, and it seems that, even if he did, he could hardly see any significance in the fact, with his crude ideas of the sun. But he does not question the voyage itself. 'Thus was the extent of Libya first discovered', and of that he has so little conception that he makes the coast turn abruptly west just beyond the Red Sea, denying any inhabited land south of Arabia![2]

Later the story was hardly ever thought worth mentioning. Though most ancients were inclined to believe in a continuous Ocean, only two are known to have even considered the voyage as evidence.[3] Some implicitly rejected it by doubting or denying the theory, till in the end Ptolemy made the Indian Ocean a closed basin. The original absurd underestimate of the continent was never more than partially corrected, and to the last there was no serious knowledge far beyond Zanzibar, and even the Arabs did not go on with the strong Mozambique current southwards, for fear they might

---

1 Athenaeus, II, 44*e*. Carthage, Gsell, *Afr. du Nord*, I, 302, IV, 140, but cp, Bovill, *Caravans of the Old Sahara*, 1933, pp. 16–17. No other basis, Gsell, *Hérodote*, p. 208. Niger, Gisinger, *R.E.* Geogr. p. 570 (but Honigmann, ibid. Libye, p. 159 is very doubtful): least improbable, Bovill, p. 13; out of question, J. A. K. Thomson, *Art of the Logos*, 1935, pp. 39–41: dwarfs of Senegambia once on Niger?, Quatrefages, *Pygmies*, 1895, pp. 13–16. Fezzan, Hennig, *T.I.* p. 103. Ouargla, Vivien de St Martin, *Hist. de la Géogr.* 1873, p. 18: rather Saura, Gsell, loc. cit. Story in Hdt. II, 32–3. Rain, Gsell, I, 99, Bovill, *Antiquity*, 1929, pp. 414–23. Symmetry, see p. 100, n. 1: not from Hec., Honigmann, op. cit. p. 160.

2 Hdt. III, 107. Story, IV, 42. Ideas of sun, II, 24–6: significance, Heidel, op. cit. pp. 21, 57. Canal, see p. 81, n. 2 (Darius): some ignore Necho's work on it (Arist. and Plin.): Siegfried, *Suez and Panama*, 1940, pp. 38–41.

3 Posidonius ap. Str. 98 (Strabo carelessly says Darius for Necho). Ocean doubted, some ap. Ps.-Scyl. 112 (see p. 90, n. 2), Pol. III, 38, etc.

not return against it. Could Necho's men have really done so much, and said so little, and had so very slight an effect on geography? If Phoenicians were sometimes secretive, was there here any trade-route to conceal? It has been urged that Icelandic discoveries of America about A.D. 1000 were long forgotten, but the fact is rather that they were never really known to civilized Europe at the time. The motive suggested for the king's order is ridiculous: even if he thought Africa much smaller than it is, he can hardly have supposed that the round voyage would be a reasonable means of communication, and nothing but a zeal for exploration could account for such an effort. (Grote talked of an 'experimental voyage', which showed the route practicable but not useful and was therefore not repeated; but on second thoughts he had doubts.) Could ancient ships and seamen have done it? Herodotus thought so, but he had no idea of the real distance, something like 16,000 miles. Small ships were good for coasting a long way, no doubt, and this coast is unusually smooth and safe, and the winds and currents far easier for going round from east to west than in the reverse direction, though not without serious difficulties, especially in the western stretches. The time allowed is sufficient, even with long stops for the corn-sowing, for which some try to fix more or less suitable regions, Angola and Senegal, or Delagoa Bay and the Gold Coast, or South Africa and Morocco. Defenders pin their faith especially to the detail about the sun, which would be on the right at the Cape, though also long before that point. But are we dealing with a genuine observation and not a piece of story-telling, ben trovato and only accidentally true? Why are many so sure that it could not have been invented? Were not places well south of the tropic, like Meroe, already known? (Long ago Lewis in his *Astronomy of the Ancients* showed how lively was ancient imagination about the sun and how easily such an 'observation' could have been inferred.) There is no need to impugn the historian's honesty, but he did pick up some fables in Egypt and elsewhere. Was the real voyage something like the old ones to Punt, and exaggerated by his informants? Altogether it seems rash to accept so huge a feat on evidence so slender. Not proved false, says Gsell, and not improbable. Say rather very improbable and not proved true. Will the question ever be settled? Of those whose opinions matter, because they consider the history of geography, many have been hostile or at least sceptical. Many also have accepted, often too casually, and of late there has been a surprising tendency to belief.[1]

[1] As Cary-Warmington, pp. 87–95, Berthelot, op. cit. p. 169, Hennig, op. cit. pp. 49–53 and *Geogr. Zt.* 1934, pp. 62–5: apparently Macan, ad loc.: 'most', says Godley, Herodotus (Loeb, 1921–4): Pieper, *R.E.* Necho, 1935. Possible, Hornell, *Antiquity*, 1911, p. 245: J. N. L. Baker, *Hist. of Geogr. Explor.* 1931, p. 23: J. H. Rose, *Man and the Sea*, 1935, pp. 21–36, 244–6. Gsell, *Hérodote*, pp. 225–37. Sowing places, J. T. Wheeler, *Geogr. of*

Another round voyage was ordered, we hear, this time the reverse way and by the Persian king Xerxes, who reigned 485–465 B.C. He set the task on pain of death to an erring cousin, one Sataspes. This man started with a crew from Egypt, and doubled Cape Soloeis (in Morocco), very wrongly described as the westernmost point of the continent. Proceeding south for many months, he reached some dwarfish people, who fled from their 'towns' to the hills whenever he landed. Weary of the endless coast, he put about, and came back to report that his ship had 'stuck', literally, it seems, in a sea 'unsailable' for shoals, such as the writer mentions elsewhere (presumably the stoppage was due to winds and currents). He was disbelieved and duly impaled. A strange story from a strange source, a man who robbed another who had robbed the dead voyager. It has been doubted, not quite without reason, but there is little to be said for a guess that he stayed in the inner sea and concocted a tale with some local colour from Carthaginian informants. It seems likely that he passed the desert to a populous coast, at nearest the Senegal, or Sierra Leone with its hills(?), and in the time stated he might have gone much farther, to be stopped, some explain, by the northward current off lower Guinea.[1] It is worth noticing that in A.D. 1460 Diogo Gomez said that no anchor could hold in the strong currents beyond the Rio Grande and so he was prevented going farther. (In general the currents seem favourable—for the outward voyage —to past the Niger, and the winds too at least to Sierra Leone, but then comes a belt of 'doldrums' and along Guinea the winds blow north, sucked inwards by the Sahara.)

Already, Herodotus knows, the Carthaginians had sailed down that coast, where they did a dumb barter for gold, and they claimed to have been second to Necho, he says rather loosely, in 'proving that Libya is surrounded by sea'. He does not appear to have heard of Hanno and his exploring and colonizing work in detail, and he gives only one place, the cape abovementioned, probably the same as in Hanno and later writers (Cape Cantin),

---

H. 1854 (after Rennell): Rose, op. cit. p. 34: W. Müller, *Umseglung Afrikas*, 1891. Sceptical, Mannert, Forbiger, C. Müller, *G.G.M.* I, xxxv, St Martin, *Hist. de la Géogr.* 1873, p. 30: Bunbury, I, 289–96: Tozer, pp. 99–102: Berger, pp. 62–71: Sieglin, *Arch. Anz.* 1910, p. 523: Webb, *Engl. Hist. Rev.* 1907, pp. 1–14. Sun inference by analogy from N. hemisphere, Blakesley (cited by Macan). Meroe, H. E. Burton, *Discovery of Anc. World*, 1932, p. 36 (if true, exploration for own sake). Sun, Sir G. C. Lewis, op. cit. 1862, p. 513 (and the voyage too improbable, ibid. pp. 508–15, after W. Vincent, *Commerce and Navigation of Ancients in Indian Ocean*, 1807). For sun, cp. p. 134, n. 2.

1 Klotz, *Klio*, 1937, p. 343: Cary-Warmington, pp. 95–7: hills, Gsell, op. cit. p. 237: past desert, Bunbury, I, 298. Sceptical, Berger, op. cit. p. 75: concocted, Hennig, op. cit. p. 107. Story in Hdt. IV, 43, cape also, II, 32: shoals, II, 102 (and cp. Ps.-Scyl. 109). Gomez, Beazley, *Prince Henry the Navigator*, 1895, p. 289: Prestage, *Portuguese Pioneers*, 1933, pp. 130, 167, 207. S. perhaps to C. Palmas, Hyde, *Anc. Greek Mariners*, 1947, p. 241.

though he exaggerates it badly and has no real idea of its position. Yet his statements sound like a vague rumour of the result of Hanno's work. From them too it seems likely, as Gsell reads them, that the voyage should be put before rather than after Sataspes, though not necessarily before all sailing or barter in these parts. It is now often dated early, before 500 B.C., which suits the coupling with Himilco. The scraps of Hecataeus already name some places on the Moroccan coast, including one colony or its site, though his river Lizas is not Hanno's Lixus but much nearer (some, of course, dismiss the names as interpolated). There survives in a single manuscript (and a copy of the same) a Greek version of an inscription which Hanno himself dedicated in his native city, apparently a shortened form of his official report. The translation was made only quite late, it has been argued, for the historian Polybius, who saw the destruction of Carthage in 146 B.C.; but this is not proven, and much of the substance was current in Greek two centuries before.[1] Hanno tells how he was sent out with 60 ships and 30,000 colonists—the number is surely exaggerated—and planted seven colonies as far as Cerne, and then made two exploring voyages beyond. It is a peculiar document, with many omissions of directions and distances. The distances given are in terms of a day's sail, a variable unit more than usually uncertain in such strange waters. The diagram in Fig. 8 places the information, with its many blanks, alongside the modern map, according to two kinds of reconstruction. The one, Fischer's, is little favoured; the other is followed by many, with minor variations, and seems more plausible, though it has to amend one figure (just after the Lixus) from 2 to 9 or more days.[2] This river is described as flowing from high mountains (unnamed) through a country of wild beasts, savage Ethiopians, and nimble cave-dwellers to the nomad herdsmen of the coast (all accept it as the Draa and the mountains as the Atlas or rather the Anti-Atlas). The farthest colony Cerne is on a tiny island. The first reconnaissance beyond was to a big river Chretes and an island-strewn lake a day's sail long under high mountains; here wild men in beast-skins stoned the explorers off, and they went on to

---

[1] Eph. and Theophr.? ap. Ps.-Arist. *M.A.* 37 and cp. Ps.-Scyl. (see p. 90, n. 2). Polybius, Aly, *Hermes*, 1927, p. 319. Hec. fr. 354–7, Pearson, p. 95, Jacoby, I, 372–4 (interpolation, Strenger, op. cit. p. 22). Gsell, op. cit. p. 239. Cape, Macan, ad loc. Work known in some form to Hec. and result to Hdt., Honigmann, *R.E.* Libye, pp. 154–5.

[2] So in general Müller, *G.G.M.* I, xviii–xxxiii, text 1–14 and maps: Vivien de St Martin, *Nord de l'Afrique dans l'Antiquité*, 1863, pp. 326–425: Meltzer, *Gesch. der Karthager*, 1879, I, 237–45: Bunbury, I, 318–35: Tozer, pp. 104–9: Cary-Warmington, pp. 47–52: Berthelot, op. cit. pp. 181–204: Kaeppel, *Off the Beaten Track in the Classics*, 1936, pp. 27–61. Otherwise C. T. Fischer, *De Hannonis Carth. Periplo*, 1893, preferred by Strenger, op. cit. p. 26. Also Daebritz, *R.E.* VII, 2360. Many monographs: I have not seen Blasquez, 1909, Schoff, 1913, H. R. Palmer (Bathurst, 1911, cited by Bovill, op. cit.).

another big river with crocodiles and hippopotami (the sketching is a mere guess and not seriously meant). On the second effort it was at the 'immense opening' that they began to see by night fires flaring up at intervals. In the great gulf which the interpreters called Western Horn was a large island with a salt lagoon containing an islet; here by day they saw only forest, but by night many fires, and heard pipes and cymbals, tom-toms and yells. They sailed on, and for four more nights the coast was ablaze with torrents of fire pouring to the sea. In the middle was a towering fire seeming to

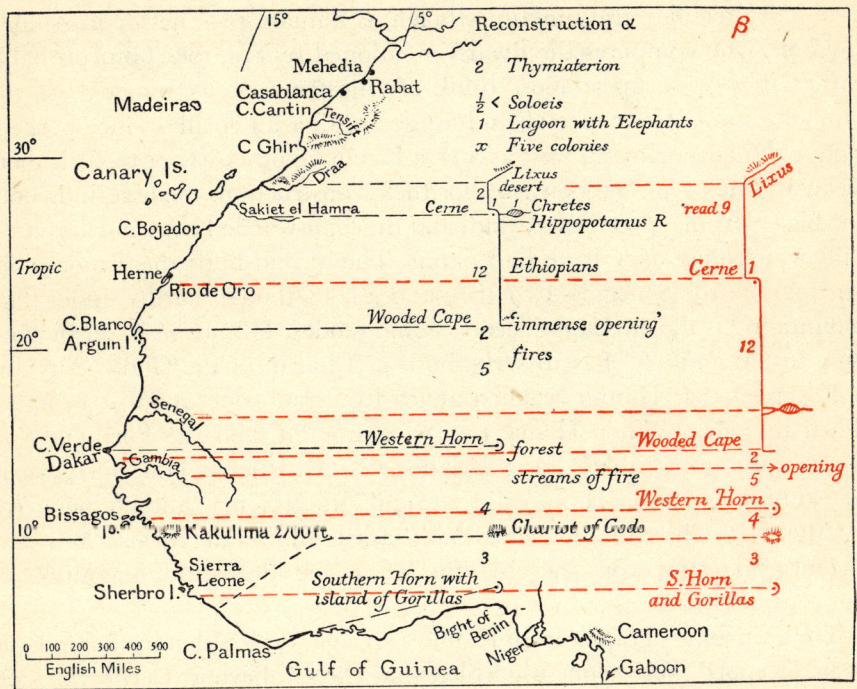

Fig. 8. Hanno's voyage.

reach the stars: by day it appeared as a very high mountain, Chariot of the Gods. After more streams of fire they came to the gulf Southern Horn, with an island shaped as before. The inner islet had wild men whom the interpreters called Gorillas; the males kept nimbly out of reach and defended themselves with stones (text? found refuge in the heights?), but three hairy females were taken, biting and scratching, and were flayed for the skins to be brought home. Here Hanno turned back, as provisions were short. The figures total $32\frac{1}{2}+x$, or with the emendation $39\frac{1}{2}+x$ days. But other accounts were current: unexplained is one which seems to mean that he sailed 35 days before turning east and again south to meet with difficulties from blazing heat, streams of fire, and shortage of water. Some press this to take him round very far, to Cameroon and even Gaboon.[1]

Mistranslations may be suspected, as well as omissions. The fires seem extravagant: no wonder Pliny and others thought of a non-stop volcano ('aeternis ardet ignibus'), and some suppose now that Hanno saw an eruption of the Cameroon, the only really high mountain on the whole coast, as first suggested by Richard Burton in 1863. But it is generally held that the fires were widespread bush-burnings such as are described by many travellers like Mungo Park (perhaps also native signal fires?). The hairy females are sometimes taken as human, pygmies or negrilloes; so Gsell, who compares the dwarfs mentioned by Sataspes. But probably rather they were apes: most think of chimpanzees or 'pongos', as did Gibbon, but a recent special study suggests after all gorillas, once perhaps ranging as far north and west as Sierra Leone (another writer regards them as an argument for Gaboon). As for the reconstructions the first finds both the big rivers in a poor desert wadi and the high-wooded cape in bare sand-hills which may once have had palms. The second finds them more convincingly in the Senegal—two arms and a lake, though hardly under high mountains?—and in Cape Verde. Some modest hill, at best conspicuous only in flat country, has to serve both as Chariot of the Gods. Anyhow it is agreed that Hanno reached at least Sierra Leone about 2300 miles down the coast. When Henry the Navigator inspired the Portuguese to round the 'impassable' Cape Bojador, it took them about forty years to venture as far as Hanno did straight off. (Henry himself believed, by the way, that the ancients had sailed all round Africa, and was encouraged in his work thereby, but he had no idea of the magnitude of the continent.)

The gain for geography from Hanno's voyage was less than it should have been. Reports were soon so garbled that the sea beyond Cerne was said to be unsailable for shoals and weeds. Even the general run of the coast, southward in the few indications given and really south-west, was hopelessly misread as south-east. Some misunderstood Cerne as on a meridian with Carthage, when the text meant only that both were equidistant from the straits, it seems. (Oddly enough the Portuguese on reaching Sierra Leone 'all thought that the line of Tunis...had been long passed'.) But anyhow there was a preconception that the coast must run south-east to the limit known from the side of the Red Sea. The later third-hand reports of Hanno are so bad and careless that one makes him sail all the way 'ad finem Arabiae'; this garbling of Pliny's became better known than

[1] Gsell, *Hist. anc. de l'Afrique du Nord*, 1913, 1, 502–3 (on H. at length, pp. 472–519): Klotz, loc. cit. Erat. ap. Arr. *Ind.* 43 (garbled).

THE GREEK HORIZON TO HERODOTUS

the original and was repeated in Henry's time and after him, as by Hakluyt.[1]

As a sample of the wild fables possible in very early days, when outer parts were unknown, some astounding statements are credited to one Euthymenes of Massalia. The Atlantic is sweet, he said, and has creatures like the Nile's; in fact the Nile flows from there, and floods because the winds drive the sea into it. The notions thus scrappily reported are barely credible in a man who claimed to have sailed in that sea. One is a curious variant of the theory of Thales that upstream winds dam back the Nile. The rest is very puzzling. A belated relic of the fresh-water Ocean, think some, but how could he keep such an idea if he knew the real Atlantic? Fresh water at the mouth of a river? Some take him seriously as having discovered a crocodile river, perhaps the same as Hanno's, the Senegal, and before him, about 530 B.C.; others think of a river nearer Morocco. Anyhow, just because his river had crocodiles, it is implied, he could wildly reverse its direction and identify it with the upper Nile. It is not proven that he had any influence on Hecataeus, who appears to bring his Nile from the southern Ocean, or on Herodotus, who brings his from the west but not right from the western sea. Presently Aristotle brings his from a watershed range, the Silver Mountains, from which the Chremetes (Hanno's Chretes?) descends on the western side; elsewhere, if the text is genuine, he derives the Nile flood from snow melting on mountains thereabouts, and cites a certain Promathos of Samos, who sounds antique. (Euthymenes used to be treated as much later, because he is described merely as older than his fellow-townsman Pytheas, who was about 320 B.C.)[2]

The nearest Canary Islands must have been sighted, and probably they

---

[1] Everyman ed. I, 21. Plin. II, 169, cp. v, 7–8, VI, 197–200: Mela, III, 90, 93–5, 99. Meridian as Erat. ap. Str. 825–6, Nepos ap. Plin. VI, 199: Berger, *Fragm. des Erat.* p. 208, denied by Strenger, op. cit. p. 25 (only similar arc). Unsailable, Ps.-Scyl. 112. Volcano, Plin. VI, 197, Mela, III, 94, Ps.-Arist. *M.A.* 37. Erupting Cameroon, Mer, 1885, Hennig, *T.I.* p. 78 and in *Geogr. Zt.* 1927, pp. 378–92: possibly, Aly, op. cit. p. 303: Bovill, op. cit. pp. 14–16: Daebritz, op. cit. after Illing, 1899. The two last deny apes, as do Gsell, op. cit. p. 505, Sarton, *Introd. to Hist. of Science*, 1927, I, 83, 103. Gorillas, McDermott, *Ape in Antiquity*, 1938, pp. 51–5: at Gaboon, Hennig, op. cit. p. 391. To Bight of Benin, Dickinson and Howarth, *Making of Geography*, 1933, p. 6: perhaps, Cana, *Enc. Brit.* ed. 14, Africa (and perhaps gorillas). At least 5° N., Honigmann, loc. cit. Probably not beyond Sierra Leone, Prestage, *Portuguese Pioneers*, 1933, p. 34. Signal fires are mentioned in Hakluyt, IV, 75, Prestage, op. cit. p. 183.

[2] So Kiepert, *Lehrbuch*, p. 4, and still Berthelot, op. cit. p. 219. Not proven, Heidel, *Frame*, p. 28, and Gsell, *Hérodote*, p. 210, against Diels and Jacoby, *R.E.* VI, 1510. E. in Sen. *N.Q.* IV, 2, 22, (Eph. ap.) Aristid. *Or.* 36, 85–96, Aet. IV, 1, 2, Athen. II, 87. Senegal, Cary-Warmington, p. 46: perhaps, Gsell, *Afrique*, IV, 117: or Gambia, Aly, op. cit. p. 306: nearer, Hennig, *T.I.* p. 67. Relic, Gilbert, *Meteorol. Theorien*, p. 399. See also Berger, pp. 132–4. Silver Mts., Arist. *Met.* I, 13, 350*b*: snow, Ps.-Arist. *Inund. Nili*: *R.E.* XIII, 160 (Libye), Honigmann, who doubts if Euth. was before Hdt.

were visited, though not mentioned for this time. To it, however, may refer two stories, or variants of one, about a short-lived settlement of Carthaginians in a large island several days off, which looks like an exaggerated Madeira. On the strength of a very dubious coin-find it has been suggested that a few of them were driven to the Azores. There had long been a mythical notion of an Elysium, which some began foolishly to localize in Spain, and of western Isles of the Blest, a name which was to be pegged down to the Canaries. By now (if not much earlier, as has been supposed) the idea of such isles was acquiring a new reality from Phoenician discovery.[1] It is from these southern latitudes that ships might have been most readily driven west to the Sargasso Sea, but that any really got there and back is not proved, as mentioned above, by ancient talk of weed and sluggish waters. There were patches of weed much nearer home.

§ 5. THE EAST

A huge Persian empire had come to fill the whole eastern horizon. Hecataeus knew its imposing array of subject peoples and warned the Ionians against rising, but in vain. His probably, or something like his, was a bronze map 'whereon was engraved the whole circuit of the earth, with all its seas and rivers' and with Persia bulking large; the rebel leader took it to the homeland in an appeal for help, but at Sparta, when he admitted that the march to the capital Susa was three months, he was bluntly dismissed. The revolt was easily beaten down, and Miletus was sacked. But Athens and others had sent a little help, and so they drew invasion on Greece; finally Xerxes came in person with a great host and was gloriously repelled (480–479 B.C.). The victors set about freeing Ionia, and even made strong efforts to rescue Cyprus and Egypt. In the process the leadership of Athens hardened into a naval empire, and the jealousy of Sparta and others caused a disastrous war (431–404 B.C.); at last they humbled her, though not without accepting Persian subsidies. It was early in this suicidal conflict that her admirer Herodotus completed his work. He records the Persian war as the supreme event in history, the heroic defence of that freedom which was the peculiar discovery of Greece. For lack of it the Persians are barbarians, though in many ways to be highly respected. Their empire had gathered up several older civilizations, and his generous scheme

---

[1] Perhaps earlier, Fischer, *R.E.* VII, 42. Blest, Hes. *Op.* 171: Elys., Hom. *Od.* IV, 563, in Tartessus, Str. 2, 150. Azores, Hennig, *T.I.* pp. 109–18: but Gsell, *Afrique*, IV, 142, distrusts, and J. H. Rose, op. cit. p. 84. Stories probably Timaeus (indirectly) ap. Ps.-Arist. *M.A.* 24 and Diod. V, 19–20. Bunbury, I, 605. Madeira, Gsell, IV, 116, I, 519–23 (but how early and how much true?). Rohde, *Griech. Roman*, 1900, p. 231. Sargasso, see p. 55, n. 1. Winsor, *Chr. Columbus*, 1891, p. 127 is wild. Patch near Arguin, Kimble, *Geogr. in Middle Ages*, 1938, p. 106.

allows long vistas into the past and over many lands. He had himself travelled to Babylon, apparently by way of Syria. He displays his eastern geography especially in long catalogues of the satrapies (or provinces) and of the 61 peoples represented in the army, also a brief account of the Royal Road, 90 days or 450 parasangs (13,500 stades) from Ephesus to Susa. It is not clear how much he owes to Hecataeus, who may well have travelled before him and certainly knew much about the great empire, as his warning shows, but the fragments are very meagre here.[1] (Philosophers like Pythagoras and presently Democritus are said to have visited Chaldees and Mages to learn from them, but such journeys are very suspect as forgeries of later periods with an exaggerated respect for eastern wisdom; yet there were other early travellers, witness the remarkable adventures of the doctor Democedes.)

The geography is often defective enough even for the nearer parts. Herodotus can hardly have gone by the Road, of which he makes a bad mess. The total distance from Sardis to the Euphrates is rightly 738 miles, from his authority, but the course as described would amount to 956. He pulls the road north of the central desert to make it cross the Halys, an absurd detour which ought not to be defended as a legacy from a distant past when the main road went round by the Hittite capital. He has a second crossing of the same river on the way to the Cilician Gates, and he makes it flow from Armenia through a vaguely large Cilicia. The whole peninsula was not yet given a single name like Asia Minor. The neck is queerly narrowed, by more than half (as five days for a light traveller or say 115 miles), a mistake which was to persist long or to be only gradually modified. He knows the Armenian Aras as flowing to the Caspian, but gives it many other mouths in marshes containing seals, apparently a confused rumour of the delta of some other river, the Oxus, it has been thought, or even the Volga, which seems to be the Araxes of another passage. In the eastern parts he seems hazy on the Matieni, about the upper Tigris, and 116 parasangs are missing of these or of Assyria. He has much to say of what he saw at and near Babylon, and his notions of Assyrian history are at least better than some which prevailed later. The fragments of Hecataeus have the Matieni and some obscure names of 'Persian cities'.[2]

1 The arrangement of Asia in Hdt. IV, 37–41 not likely from Hec., Pearson, p. 76, against Jacoby. Warning, Hdt. V, 36, map, ibid. 49. Road, ibid. 52–3: catalogues, III, 89–97, VII, 61–87. Map, Berger, pp. 101, 108: Anaximander's, Diels, *Rh. Mus.* 1933, p. 74 (see p. 97, n. 1). Mages, e.g. Plin. xxv, 13, xxx, 9, Hippol. *Ref.* I, 2 and 11. Democedes, Hdt. III, 129–37.

2 Hec. fr. 282–5, Pearson, p. 79. Matieni, Hdt. V, 5. Bab., ibid. I, 178–200. Araxes, ibid. I, 202: Volga in IV, 11: Aral delta, Herrmann, *R.E.* x, 2217. Neck, Hdt. I, 72, II, 34: see p. 87, n. 1, p. 288, n. 4. Road, Macan's ed. II, App. 13: pulls, Calder, *Class. Rev.* 1925, pp. 7–11 against Kiepert and Ramsay, *Hist. Geogr. of A.M.* 1890, pp. 27–43.

For Iran he can name a remarkable series of peoples as far as the Sacae beyond Bactria, and it has been found to agree very well with the famous inscriptions of Darius. But he would have been hard pressed to map some of them. No river answers to the Aces as described, though most take it as the Heri-rud. The north-east he knows only vaguely as conquered by Cyrus, who was killed by the Massagetae nomads beyond the 'Araxes', which must here be the Oxus or Jaxartes (more likely the former), though oddly said to flow eastward from the Caspian. Hecataeus has some curious details on the high wooded mountains near that sea. A remarkable description of the same tribe of nomads may go back to some source of this period. As mentioned in connection with the Scythian trade-route, Herodotus is right about the closed sea, and even gives figures (a writer concerned to prove pulsations of climate seems rash in inferring from them that the sea was then much bigger and nearly joined the Aral).[1]

'India', only the Indus valley, was annexed about 515 B.C. by Darius, who sent Scylax, an officer from an Asiatic Greek province, all the way down the river. Yet it is wrongly described as flowing east, or at best south-east, and remained so drawn on Ionian maps (a suggestion that the mistake was due to a sort of false start from the Kabul tributary is not very convincing). Like other ends of the earth India seems to be specially favoured with wonderful things. It has large beasts and birds and unusual plants, a wool-tree and a huge reed. It is the most populous of lands and pays a fabulous tribute in gold-dust. A northern tribe gets most of the gold in a desert from the sand-heaps of great 'ants', burrowing creatures more like foxes. (Presently Alexander's companions saw their skins, whereupon the sober Arrian gives them up, but it seems that the whole business started from an Indian fairy-tale of 'ant-gold', heard through the Persians, and that the gold really came down from Siberia, though not in any such quantity.) There are many tribes settled and nomad, lowly marshmen on the river, and east of them and far south cannibal Padaei and a people who have no houses and touch no animal food but live on a wild grain. All these are nearly as black as Ethiopians, though not so woolly-haired, and some close by (in Baluchistan) are expressly 'eastern Ethiopians'— many must have understood this as confirming Homer's two sections of that people. Beyond 'India' there is only desert, or 'none can say what it is like'; an eastern Ocean is not proven. Already Hecataeus has several of the same names, and two others, no doubt from Scylax and apparently

[1] Source, Hellanicus? ap. Str. 513, Aly, *Philologus*, 1930, p. 42. Hec. fr. 290–3, Pearson, p. 80. Cyrus, Hdt. I, 202. Aces, Bunbury, I, 247. Figures, see p. 64, n. 1. E. Huntington, *Pulse of Asia*², 1919, pp. 330–2, and see p. 128, n. 2.

from a written account of his, which is later sometimes quoted as if at first hand.[1]

From the Indus Scylax, we hear, sailed in thirty months to the head of the Arabian gulf, thus proving the existence all along of 'the southern sea called the Red', that is the Indian Ocean including the gulf to which we confine the name Red Sea. The king proceeded to use these waters, it is added, and finished the canal from the Nile. Later writers say he left this incomplete like Necho, though not because of an oracle but because the Red Sea, being higher, would overflow into the Nile and spoil the water (the ghost of this fear was to reappear more than once, as for Haroun al Rashid and even just before De Lesseps began his great enterprise). Inscriptions found during the making of the Suez canal confirm the work of Darius and its purpose. Yet the historian has no idea of a Persian gulf, and the mention of it in a scrap of Hecataeus seems interpolated. The idea of the Arabian gulf is poor: the length, 40 days, is fairly good, but the width half a day at most, is absurd, except for the very head. The voyage has not escaped suspicion for these reasons and because Nearchus later, when starting from the Indus, professed to doubt whether the sea was 'sailable' at all; but Alexander and his officers had some startling ignorances in geography. Scylax was not probably alone in these seas: there seems some evidence of Indian wares and perhaps ships to Babylonia in the same century. How the name 'Red' was come by is obscure, and later writers can only make bad guesses about reddish water or mountains or a fabulous king Erythras or Red; was it perhaps the sea of the red sunrise, as there was a mythical 'red' island, Erytheia, at the sunset?[2]

Of Arabia, except for some camel-riders in the army, little is told but fables. Winged snakes infest the incense trees, and bat-like creatures the marsh where cassia grows; the natives rob the sticks called cinnamon from large birds which carry them from the east to make their nests (a story which was to have echoes down to Sindbad); the tails of the sheep are so

---

1 As Arist. *Pol.* vii, 14. Hec. fr. 294–9. Hdt. iii, 98–106: iv, 44 (Scylax). Eth., ibid. vii, 70. Ants, Tarn, *Greeks in Bactria and India*, 1938, pp. 45–8, 107–8: among Dards, Plin. xi, 111: skins, Nearchus ap. Str. 705, Arr. *Ind.* p. 15 (marmots, Hennig, *Rh. Mus.* 1931, p. 331: probably, Kaeppel, op. cit. pp. 105–6 after Bunbury). A queer mixture of gold-ants and Griffins in Ctes. ap. Aelian, *N.A.* iv, 27. Greek notices of India before Alex. collected by W. Reese, 1914.

2 Guesses, Str. 766, 779 (Ctesias), Mela, iii, 72, Plin. vi, 107. Sailable, N. ap. Arr. *Ind.* 6, 8: 20, 2. Voyage doubted by C. Müller, *G.G.M.* i, xxxv (after W. Vincent, 1807); Bolchert, *Arist. Erdkunde von Asien u. Libyen*, 1908, p. 7: but cp. Tarn, *C.A.H.* vi, 402. P.G. missing in Hdt. i, 180, iii, 80, 90: interpolated in Hec. fr. 281, Jacoby, i, 362. Arabian gulf, Hdt. ii, 11. Canal, ibid. 158, cp. Arist. *Met.* i, 14, 352*b*, Diod. i, 33, Str. 804, Plin. vi, 165 (see p. 71, n. 2). Inscriptions, *C.A.H.* iv, 183, 200. Indian ships, Kennedy, *J.R.A.S.* 1898, p. 267, Hornell in *Antiquity*, 1941, pp. 247–8: cp. p. 29, n. 1.

long that they have to be supported on little trucks; from here comes the phoenix. Well might a comic poet place one Utopian city by the 'Red Sea'. The fragments of Hecataeus have nothing but some islands. Damastes is dubiously credited with an idea of a closed lake instead of a gulf (if he had this, it is very unlikely that he got it from Hecataeus). Some were very hazy or reckless about these distant parts, and could fancy that the Indus, having crocodiles, might be the upper Nile; this underlies the delirious poetic geography of Aeschylus, and Herodotus may allude slily to the notion in saying that the Indus is the only river with crocodiles save one. It is almost incredible, yet seriously attested, that Alexander, before going down the Indus, could still imagine that it might flow through vast deserts to Ethiopia, and the same theory of a land-bridge is ascribed to a Persian king Ochus a little before.[1]

APPENDIX: BETWEEN HERODOTUS AND ALEXANDER

Many Greeks were now taking service abroad, and thousands had a great adventure with Cyrus, the young Persian viceroy of Asia Minor 401 B.C., (see Fig. 9). Xenophon tells the story with much plain detail of days' marches and things seen. Starting as if he meant only to deal with some troublesome hillmen of the Taurus, the prince led on and on through the Cilician and Syrian Gates, till at last he had to admit his real purpose, nothing less than to overthrow his reigning brother. Somehow the men were wheedled over the Euphrates. They moved down the river, at first through pleasant country to the Khabur, then through the 'Arabian' desert, where ostriches and gazelles and wild asses gave good hunting, and so into Babylonia. In the battle they did what was expected of them, but the prince's death left them quite in the air. Refusing to surrender, they were shepherded up the Tigris; at the Zab their generals were treacherously seized, but they elected new ones, including their future historian. They went on beyond the ruins of Nineveh, of which he can tell nothing but fables. They came to where the road started west for Syria, but this too was now barred, and they plunged into wild hill country northwards. The Tigris whose sources they passed can mean only the little tributary near Lake Van. Thenceforth days' marches and parasangs, variable according to the ground, are hard to check in the snowy maze of mountains, and the track has been drawn in many ways, none entirely convincing. They needed six days to

[1] Ps.-Arist. *Inund. Nili*, 44. Alex. in Arr. *Anab.* vi, 1, 2, *Ind.* loc. cit., Str. 696: Tarn, loc. cit. Aesch. *P.V.* 809. Dam. ap. Str. 47, doubted by Jacoby, *F.G.H.* 1, 362 and Berger, *Erat.* p. 44: from Hec. (with Indus–Nile), think Sieglin, *Schulatlas* (map) and Breasted, *Anc. Times*, 1916, p. 319: oldest Ionians, *R.E.* Arabia, II, 347. Arabia, Hdt. III, 107–13: phoenix, II, 73. Camel-riders, VII, 82. Comic, Aristophanes, *Birds*, 145. Islands, Hec. fr. 271.

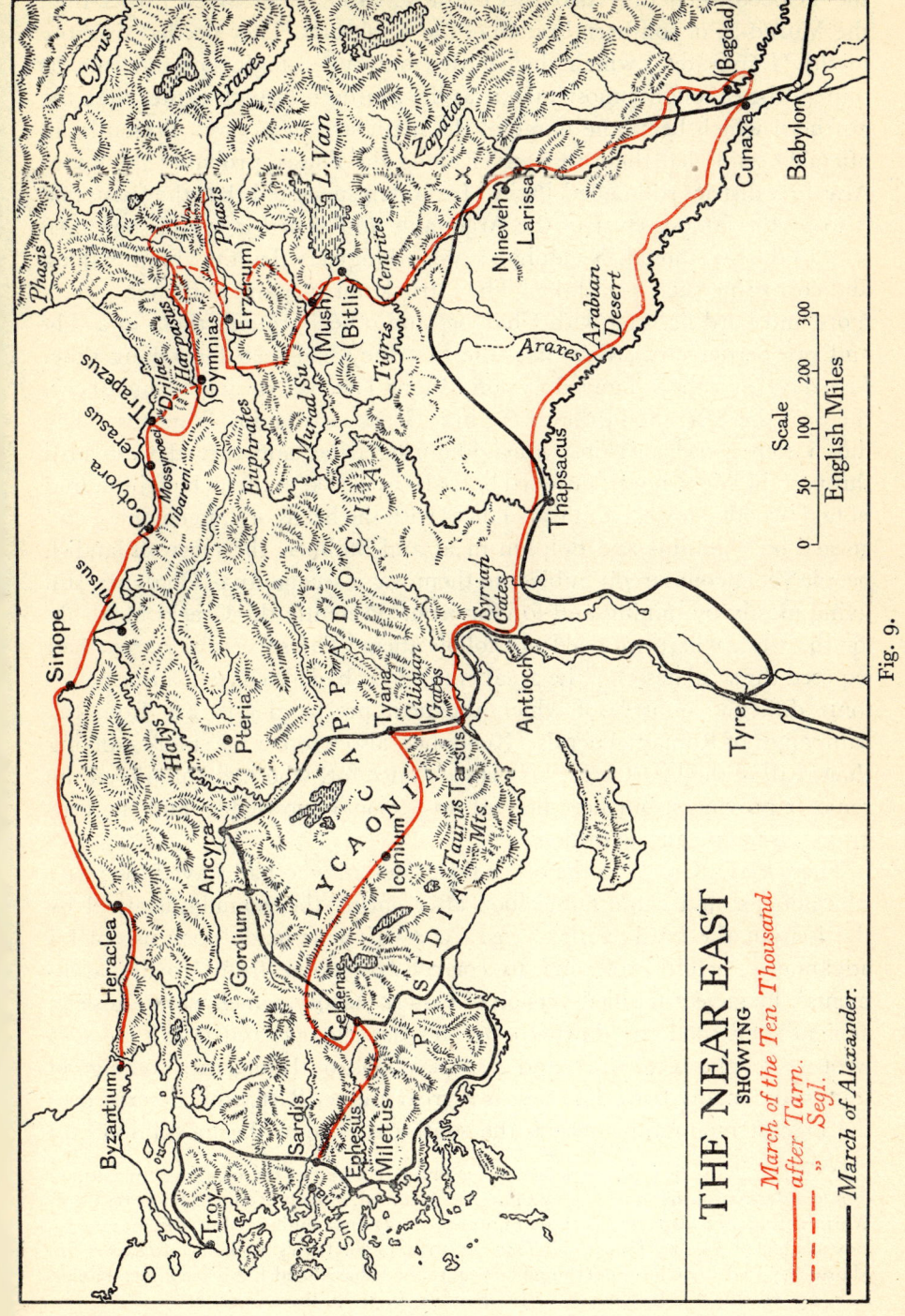

Fig. 9.

the Teleboas, generally taken as the little tributary of Mush rather than the Murad-su or southern branch of the Euphrates. They needed six more to the 'Euphrates', which they forded only waist-high, not far from its source, they thought; most take it as the southern branch rather than the northern which bears the name of the main stream to-day. Presently an offended guide left them to wander along the Phasis, probably the upper Aras in a district still called Pasin. It is often suggested that they assumed it to be the famous river of the Argonauts and hoped it would soon turn west to the sea, though Xenophon says nothing very definite about making and correcting such a mistake.[1] They struck north again, and twenty days more and hard fighting with Chalybes and others brought them to a 'big and prosperous city', Gymnias, the first they had seen for a long time. Five days later the vanguard was on Mount Theches, raising a general cry, the Sea, the Sea! Soon they were in a Greek city again, Trapezus. They did it some service against a neighbouring tribe, and turned westwards through the Mossynoeci, tattooed barbarians who kept their chiefs immured in high wooden towers, did war-dances with the heads of slain enemies, and gorged on chestnuts and dolphin meat and blubber, the most outlandish people yet encountered. Subject to them was a second lot of Chalybes, still living mostly by mining and forging iron. Presently the Greeks took ship for the west, where we need not follow them. The successful retreat had exposed the weaknesses of the great empire. It had also drawn a line across some difficult country, of which the next precise details are from the campaigns of Roman generals. Xenophon also wrote a life, more edifying than real, of the first Cyrus, his prince's ancestor, who had conquered the remoter provinces, but here he had no personal knowledge, and the geography is vague and worthless.

There was a Greek on the other side, Ctesias, who had stayed long as a court doctor and came home soon after curing the wound sustained by the king in the battle with Cyrus. As a writer he made poor use of his advantages; while professing to correct Herodotus from 'royal parchments', he gave a falsified version of eastern history, which was to mislead ancients and moderns down to Byron's *Sardanapalus* and later. He also wrote a geographical work and a special book on India, with some good things and many bad. The best is a great range, Parnassus, described as the highest mountains towards the south-east and as the most important

---

[1] Xen. *Anab.* IV, 6, 3 (seven stages along Phasis): a hint of the confusion in V, 7, 1? (Some as Dakyns misread as 'to' the Phasis). Assumed, already Rennell, Kiepert: Cary-Warmington, *Anc. Explorers*, p. 140: Bunbury, I, 355 (not unlikely, but the many days inexplicable): Segl, *Vom Kentrites bis Trapezus*, 1925, p. 36. Tarn's track in *C.A.H.* VI, 4–19. Masqueray's ed. 1930 has something like Segl to the 'Phasis' and like Tarn after. Fables, Xen. op. cit. III, 4. Mossynoeci, V, 4: Chalybes, V, 5, cp. those of IV, 7.

of known watersheds, with the head-streams of Indus and Araxes. It is the Paropanisus or Hindu Kush, and conceived as quite near the outer sea. The Araxes is the Oxus, with its general direction rightly given for the first time, but it is supposed to send off a branch to pass round the Caspian lake and end as the Tanais or Don; this branch seems an early and very wrong notion of the Jaxartes, and the same notion was shared by some of Alexander's companions when they reached that river. (One writer explains otherwise, however: he thinks that the branch was the present course of the Oxus to the Aral, as compared with the old arm which is supposed to have run to the Caspian.)[1] The size of India is grossly exaggerated. A river flowing to the eastern Ocean may be charitably thought a rumour of the Ganges, though Aristotle knows none bigger than the Indus and the amber near its mouth is fantastic, like a spring where nothing can sink. The onyx from the hills has some reality, as it is mentioned later in the western Ghats. The 'just' Indians are in an old Utopian vein, and he has a taste for monstrous peoples of eastern or Greek fancy, which others were to repeat and add to: in the mountains are Dog-heads with tails, just and long-lived, and in the middle Pygmies ugly and bearded, at most two cubits tall, and with tiny cattle: here men sleep wrapped in their long ears, there each has only one leg and holds up his foot as an umbrella (it is odd that Hecataeus already has Shadow-feet—but in Ethiopia). There is much on plants and animals including unicorns and others still more dubious like the martichora (Persian for man-eater), too kindly explained in one passage as a tiger, though he shoots prickles from his tail like the fabulous porcupine. Later writers on these matters used Ctesias, often with justifiable qualms, and he has been given some credit as 'in a sense the founder of plant and animal geography'.[2] Certainly to him, through Pliny, who 'rehearseth these wonders and many other mo', are due a lot of fables which were echoed right through the Middle Ages. 'And others there be in Ethiopia, and each of them have only one foot, so great and so large that they beshadow themselves with the foot when they lie gasping on the ground in strong heat of the sun....Also some have the soles of their feet turned backward behind the legs, and in each foot eight toes', and so on: poor

[1] Herrmann, *R.E.* x, 2278. Companions, Str. 509: Arr. III, 30, 7 (really not the same as Don, he adds): Tarn, *C.A.H.* VI, 394. Range and Araxes (Ctes. ap.) Arist. *Met.* I, 13, 350a. Parchments, Diod. II, 32. C. on India, McCrindle, 1882 (*Ind. Antiquary*, 1881).

[2] Bolchert, *Arist. Erdkunde von Asien u. Libyen*, 1908, p. 40. 'Not reliable', Arist. *Hist. Anim.* VIII, 28. Indus, Arist. loc. cit. Shadow-feet, Hec. fr. 327: Plin. VII, 23: Philostr. *Vit. Apoll.* III, 47. Eastern fancy, Rohde, *Griech. Roman*[2], 1900, p. 189. Tiger, Paus. IX, 21, cp. Plin. VIII, 75: unicorn, ibid. 76, XI, 44. Spring, Str. 703, Plin. XXXI, 21, Meg. ap. Arr. *Ind.* 6, 2. River, ap. Plin. XXXVII, 39 (and amber cp. Soph. ibid. 31). Onyx, ibid. 90. Snakes, Meg. ap. Plin. VIII, 36, etc.

Bartholomew the Englishman about A.D. 1250 still has no idea what to make of such things.

The conviction grew that Persia could be overthrown, if only the Greeks could stop quarrelling and find a suitable leader. In the end it was an invader who imposed the necessary union, Philip of Macedon. He was ready to start when he was murdered, leaving the task to his son Alexander, who was to perform it so brilliantly. Aristotle, the young man's tutor, was quite out of sympathy: he thought the conquest possible, but good neither for the Greeks, who could be free only in small city-states, nor for the barbarians, slaves by nature and incapable of real civilization, views soon to appear very narrow and obsolete. His geographical matter belongs to the stage just before: about the east it depends largely on Ctesias, as for the watershed range. The Caspian still rightly remains a lake, though he has a blundering mention of 'the Hyrcanian and Caspian seas', as if two (some have misread this to credit him with knowing of the Aral as well). Further the 'lake under the Caucasus' (the Caspian) is supposed to have an underground outlet to the Black Sea, and his royal pupil seems to have had a fancy of some joining between them.[1] It is strange that he has still no knowledge of a Persian gulf. One passage is often queerly misconceived to mean that Chinese silk was already arriving. A big worm with what looks like horns, it says, forms a cocoon, which is unwound (or rather carded) and spun, an industry begun in the island of Cos by one Pamphila; no suggestion here that the cocoons were imported. A longish silence follows till Roman poets talk of the light and transparent Coan fabrics worn by their less respectable lady friends. Then Pliny expressly adds that the worm was in the island, and associates it, though in a mistaken way, with the cypress and other trees. From all this there has been clearly recognized a wild silk-worm native to Asia Minor and its neighbourhood. The Seres or Silk-men had not yet been heard of: a supposed reference of Ctesias to them (as very tall and long-lived) is rightly dismissed as not genuine.[2]

---

1 Plut. *Alex.* 44: Tarn, loc. cit. (p. 85, n. 1). Aral, Ideler on Arist. *Met.* II, 1, 354*a*, cp. Webster's transl. Oxf. 1923. Outlet, *Met.* I, 13, 351*a*.

2 As by Müller, fr. 87: Yule-Cordier, *Cathay and the Way Thither*, 1915, I, 14: Herrmann, *R.E.* Seres: Hudson, *Eur. and China*, p. 59. Worm, Arist. *H.A.* V, 19, repeated with additions by Plin. XI, 76, ap. VI, 54, Yule-Cordier, pp. 196–200. Hirth, *China and Roman Orient*, 1885, p. 258 misreads Coan silk as Chinese and ignores Arist.: misconceived also by *Enc. Brit.* ed. 14, Silk, Forbiger, *Alte Geogr.* II, 493, Dalton, *Byz. Art and Arch.* p. 584, etc. Poets, Prop. I, 1, 5, 1, 2, 2, Tib. II, 3, 53, Ovid, *Am.* II, 298, Hor. *Odes*, IV, 13, 13. The worm is *Lasiocampa otus*, Keller, *Ant. Tierwelt*, 1909, I, 443, Sir D'Arcy Thompson, *Science and the Classics*, 1940, pp. 63–4, or a mixture of two others, W. T. M. Forbes in *Class. Phil.* 1930, pp. 22–6. Rostovtzeff, *Soc. and Econ. Hist. of Hell. World*, 1941, II, 1167. Not imported Indian silk as Tarn, *Hell. Civ.* p. 206.

Ephorus in a history of the Greeks, later much used, gave two books to a formal account of the known world, following the coastal method of description. The geography is of an old-fashioned cast, and the fragments are not remarkable. For the east they mostly concern Asia Minor, and he strangely repeats, like several others, the old error about its narrow neck.[1]

Knowledge of the Scythian hinterland had not seriously improved, despite the long and close relations of Athens with the Crimean corn-ports. So Ephorus talks of the people as 'just', except some cannibals, and ascribes a 'Platonic' communism of women (Plato himself had praised the warlike women of the Sauromatae, a tribe said to be descended from fugitive Amazons). The Pseudo-Scylax is much less good on this coast than the opposite, and still vastly overrates the Azov appendage as having half the circuit of the Black Sea, though this idea is distinctly better than before. Aristotle has heard of marked silting in sixty years, and predicts that this shallow lake will in time silt up completely. Not far north the country is said to become uninhabitably cold. Even he cannot quite dismiss the old Rhipaean range as the source of the big rivers, though 'stories of its size are altogether too fabulous'. He exaggerates the Caucasus and the number and importance of its rivers, of which only the Phasis is named, and he seems to push the range north-east like the old Ionian map. He assumes a northern Ocean, partly because he has heard of many nameless rivers flowing north from certain Arkynian mountains, 'the greatest and highest in these parts'. The term was derived from the word for oak, akin to the Latin quercus, in the Celtic language still dominant then in south Germany; as 'Hercynian Forest' it was later extended to cover all the wooded mountains from the Rhine to the Carpathians.[2]

Westwards Athens had made a disastrous attack on Sicily, partly because her citizens had a startling ignorance of its size and strength: she overstrained her own power and weakened the Greeks there in face of Carthage, which made large gains in the eastern half of the island. The colonial ambitions of Dionysius of Syracuse drew more attention to the Adriatic.

---

1 Eph. ap. Ps.-Scymn. 921, Diod. XIV, 20. So Ps.-Scyl. 102: Hell. Oxyrh. *F.G.H.* II, p. 35. Fragments of Eph. in *F.G.H.* II, 37–109: Dopp, *Geogr. Studien des E.* 1900–9. Forderer, *Eph. und Strabon*, 1913. G. L. Barber, *The Historian E.* 1935, pp. 175–6. Coast A.M.–Libya in Ps.-Scyl. 99–108 (Syria mutilated).

2 Oak, Hubert, *Celtes*, 1932, p. 184. *Met.* I, 13, 350*b*. Rhipaean, ibid. Azov, ibid. I, 14, 353*a*: its size, Ps.-Scyl. 79. Scythia in Eph. fr. 158–60, 161*b* (=Ps.-Scymnus, 835–85, 900–10): 'just', Eph. ap. Str. 302: see p. 110, n. 1. Plato, *Laws*, 804–6 (cp. Hdt. IV, 110). Ps.-Scylax, Bunbury, I, 389: for east part Müller, *G.G.M.* Tabulae, v. Cauc. N.E., Berger, p. 325, Gisinger, *R.E.* Geogr. 586 as Eudoxus. Corn, Demosthenes, *in Lept.* 31, *de Corona*, 87–9, etc.

Some Greeks came to help the cities of south Italy against barbarian neighbours. Celtic invaders had occupied the Po valley, and a vanguard had sacked Rome in 390 B.C. but had soon withdrawn. The Celts came into notice also as supplying mercenaries to Dionysius and sending a boastful embassy to Alexander, when he was fighting the tribes on his northern frontier. Of about 350 B.C. is a periplus or coastal description of the inner sea, the first of its kind which happens to survive fairly complete. It is a compilation often clumsily repeating obsolete matter from older sources. It passes as by Scylax, possibly another real person of the name, but usually dubbed Pseudo-Scylax to distinguish from the old Indian voyager. It gives the Adriatic in some detail, though not without bad mistakes and fables, the Eridanus-Po and amber islands off it (defended by some as having been overtaken since by silting) and the Danube branch to that sea. It names and places a good many peoples of Italy, and speaks of some Celts 'left behind' in the north after the foray against Rome. The historian Theopompus heard of that event; he exaggerated the Illyrian coast and had some queer geography in his showy digressions, including the same Danube branch and a fancy mountain from which the Adriatic and Black Seas were both visible.[1] We should like to have the work of Philistus, who wrote on the Sicilian wars and probably had some good information on Carthage and her possessions.

There were no great events to draw limelight on Spain. Her mercenaries fought on both sides in Sicily, and some were seen even in Greece. The few colonies continued, under the shield of Massalia, and their wares still had a strong influence on the native art. But the west was rather out of the picture, and the blockade at the straits was apparently effective. Little is said of western geography, and it betrays a surprising ignorance. The western basin of the inner sea seems to have been ill-conceived and seriously underestimated in proportion to the eastern, as by Eudoxus. The periplus thinks Sardinia bigger than Sicily, and as extant is meagre on Gaul and Spain. Beyond the strait it has, apart from Gades, vaguely 'many Carthaginian trading-stations and mud and high tides and open seas'. One writer, Euctemon (about 415 B.C.), knows of the submarine reef outside Gibraltar. Aristotle is very bad, making the Danube rise from the Pyrenees, as also a river Tartessus (the Guadalquivir)! He repeats

---

[1] See p. 49, n. 2. Branch, p. 48, n. 2. Illyria, ap. Str. 317. Rome, ap. Plin. III, 57. Silted, Ridgeway, *Early Age of Greece*, 1901, I, 364. Adr. coast, Ps.-Scyl. 20–30. Ps.-Scylax, *G.G.M.* I, xxxiii–l and 15–96 and Tabulae, III–V: Fabricius², 1878: Bunbury, I, 384–94: Tozer, pp. 118–21: Kaeppel, *Off the Beaten Track*, pp. 143–8: Gisinger, *R.E.* IIIa, 635–46 (1927). Mercenaries, Xen. *Hell.* VII, 1, 20, 31, Diod. XV, 70. Alex., Arr. I, 4, 6, Str. 301–2. Ignorance of Sicily, Thuc. VI, 1. Dionysius and Adr., Ormerod, *Piracy in Anc. World*, 1924, p. 168.

a statement that the sea outside the strait is shallow and muddy and windless: it is astonishing that neither he nor Plato knows anything of Ocean tides. Ephorus said strange things about the tin of Tartessus, which some supposed local, and was 'unreliable' on Celtic customs. He has a rumour of some 'Celts' on the North Sea, who literally take up arms against the sea encroaching on their land. He, too, brings the Danube from the far west, from Celts near a mysterious north-western 'pillar' or headland.[1]

On Africa there is some interesting discussion. Aristotle explains the Libyan depression with the Ammon oasis as once covered by sea-lakes, which dried up when cut off by a barrier of silt (the coastal escarpment—it has recently been proposed that this should be tunnelled and the sea let through). There are theories of the Nile and its summer flood, new or refining on old. Several are rather silly ones about underground water, which is supposed to be less consumed by internal heat in summer (Oenopides) or drawn up 'along secret channels' by the heated earth (Diogenes of Apollonia) or 'sweated' through the sun-cracked surface (Ephorus). Democritus rightly thinks of heavy rains, and says that they 'fill the lakes and the Nile', a remarkable suggestion of source-lakes. He even tries to account for the rains: clouds arise in the north, when the snow thaws there, and are blown to the mountains by the etesian winds. (This is not correct, as the north-east monsoon over the Red Sea reaches the mountains nearly dry, and the precipitation is by south-west winds from a very different area.) Aristotle accepts the rains and the reasons for them. He brings two tributaries, with names otherwise unknown, from the said mountains. But the main stream comes from the west, from a mysterious watershed, the Silver Mountains, whence the Chremetes (Hanno's Chretes?) flows to the western sea; what suggested this is obscure, but apparently the notion is old and the name refers to snow, though the position is quite unlike Ptolemy's snowy Mountains of the Moon. Not easy to square with all this are various passages crediting Aristotle with 'stagna per quae Nilus fluit', like those of Democritus, or with marshes above Egypt 'from which the Nile flows', and odd details of pygmies who fight cranes there and live in caves and have, 'as is said', pygmy horses to match. A statement that he urged Alexander to explore the Nile and ascertain the causes of its flood is

---

[1] Eph. ap. Ps.-Scymn. 188–95 (Oestrymnis?, Berger, p. 233): Ushant, Hennig, *Pet. Mitt.* 1927, p. 84. Arms, Eph. ap. Str. 293, cp. Arist. *Eth. Nic.* II, 7, 7, *Eth. Eud.* III, 1, 23: see p. 189, n. 2. Tin of river T., Eph. ap. Ps.-Scymn. 164–6, Str. 147: local, Avienus, 259–61, 291–300. Pyrenees, Arist. *Met.* I, 13, 350*b*, also Eph. ap. Ps.-Scymn. 170–85. Windless, Arist. *Met.* II, 1, 354*a*. Mud, Ps.-Scyl. 1. Reef, Euct. ap. Avien. 350. Eud. ap. Str. 290 (if the Eud. of this time). Mercenaries, Dixon, *Iberians of Spain*, 55: art, ibid. pp. 62, 71.

very likely valueless.[1] He has much about animals, and in this connection the saying, cited by him as if already familiar, that Africa always produces something new: he explains that various animals always crowd to the few water-holes and interbreed there to produce new species. For the outer coast there are now only garblings of Hanno, and perhaps deliberate 'Phoenician lies'. Cerne still flourished, it seems, and traded for ivory and skins and wine with 'Ethiopians', described in the old fabulous fashion as tall and handsome. If Hanno meant it to be the same distance from the strait as is Carthage, it is not so now. And the sea beyond is supposed to be 'unsailable' for shoals and mud and weed! Obscure are certain 'pillars' said to be the limit of sailing in the reverse direction, from the Red Sea, but they do not seem merely the strait at its exit. Aristotle assumes a 'southern sea outside Libya' without even mentioning Necho. With his earth-globe he knows that there must be a south temperate zone, habitable like the north one and presumably inhabited, and he is strangely confident that it 'will correspond in the ordering of its winds as in other things'. A story about an unnamed man, who sailed round the continent and turned up in Sicily, was an obvious invention by Heraclides, a writer who liked to make science readable, and no one took it seriously. A statement in the Pseudo-Scylax, that some believed in this sea all round, seems to imply that already others did not.[2]

The blank of western waters had room for a new and extravagantly large Utopia. Atlantis is a fiction with a purpose, which Plato frankly explains. In the *Republic* he had thought out an ideal state, and had claimed that, if realized, it would be strong enough to repel any state of the existing kind, 'inflamed with humours'. Later he has a fancy to show that once it was indeed realized and proved its strength in action.[3] The setting is as follows. When the old statesman Solon visited Egypt and aired the antique

---

1 Tarn, *C.A.H.* VI, 378. Ps.-Arist. *de Inund. Nili* (Arist. *Fragm.* Rose, 246–8): the stagna really Dem., Bolchert, op. cit. p. 54. Marshes, Arist. *H.A.* VIII, 12, 3: pygmies, ibid. Tributaries Aegon and Nysis, *Met.* I, 13, 350*b*: rains, ibid. 12, 349*a*, II, 5, 362*a*, Dem. ap. Diod. I, 39. Honigmann, *R.E.* Libye, 161 compares the Eth. Nysa of Hdt. III, 146, and the Nisitae, Plin. VI, 194. Sweats, Eph. and Theop. ap. Diod. I, 37: Oen. ibid. 41 and Sen. *N.Q.* VI, 8: Diog. ibid. III, 26. Silver Mts, see p. 77, n. 2. Ammon, *Met.* I, 14, 352*b*: proposed, Ball cited by Bagnold, *Libyan Sands*, 1942, p. 79.

2 Ps.-Scyl. 112. Cerne, ibid.: lies, Gsell, *Afrique*, IV², 117. Hanno's report still unknown to Greeks, Honigmann, *R.E.* Libye, 160. Xion seems Lixus = Draa. Story of Heraclides ap. Str. 98. Winds, Arist. *Met.* II, 5, 363*a*. New species, Arist. *H.A.* VIII, 28, 11, *Anim. Gen.* II, 7: Plin. VIII, 42: Bolchert, op. cit. p. 62. Pillars, Ephorus ap. Plin. VI, 199: not strait as Partsch, says Hennig, *Pet. Mitt.* 1927, p. 84.

3 Plato, *Rep.* 472*c*, 422*a*. Story in Plato, *Timaeus*, 21*a*–25*d*, sequel *Critias*. Freest fiction, Bunbury, I, 402: Rohde, *Griech. Roman*², 1900, pp. 211–13 and most as below. A fiction giving the keynote for the main (cosmogonic) myth, Hackforth, *C.R.* 1944, pp. 7–9. A. Delatte, *Musée Belge*, 1922, pp. 77–93.

Greek legend of the Flood, a priest smilingly answered that his records knew of far earlier catastrophes; one had befallen an Athens now quite forgotten by her own citizens. She was once, 9000 years before(!), everything that the *Republic* describes, and easily repelled a great western island-power, which threatened both her and Egypt. Thereafter in a day and night this glorious Athens perished by earthquake, while her enemy sank into the sea, leaving the shoals which have made the Atlantic 'impassable and unsearchable' ever since. Obviously the date is fantastic, and the whole is a 'noble lie': Atlantis is a bad Utopia, called from the vasty deep to test a good one, and consigned there again as plausibly as possible. Of course, as not even Utopias are created in a vacuum, some local colour is used. Atlantis is the great Barbarian, with a huge army and fleet shadowing forth the Persian to come; the elaborate port and mercantile luxury, and the neighbouring landscape, with 'mountains remarkable for size and beauty', seem to add suggestions of Carthage, and there are touches of Homer's Phaeacians.[1] In short, this Utopia is a composite like others of its kind. There was no trouble about placing it: 'the real sea of which ours is only a bay' could hold an immense island—actually it is made larger than Africa and Asia together (as then known)—and many lesser islands beyond, over which it had extended its power to parts of a Transatlantic continent. There was no trouble either about sinking it, which would help to explain the supposed shoals of the outer sea; the theory of enormous subsidences was quite familiar, and a famous earthquake and tidal wave had recently happened, destroying two places on the gulf of Corinth (373 B.C.). It is the continent which is the most striking feature for geography. On the globe, as the earth was now thought to be, the known world round 'our sea' was beginning to look small, and there was ample space for another 'inhabited world'. In a sense Plato may be said to have invented America. Later there were some other guesses at a New World, but the prevalent view was that, if one could sail west from Spain, one would strike not an unknown continent but the eastward prolongation of Asia. This was the fixed idea of Columbus, who never grasped that he had discovered America. Presently, when it was recognized for what it was, some like Gomara in his history of the Indies (A.D. 1552) and even Bacon were more or less seriously inclined to give Plato a little of the credit. Gilbert, arguing for a north-west passage to Cathay, said that 'Atlantis now called America was ever knowen to be an island', even before part of it sank beneath the waves: the geographer Dee

---

[1] Rivaud's ed. 1935, pp. 249–51: A. E. Taylor, *Plato*, 1926, p. 440 (Persians) and *Comm. on P.'s Timaeus*, 1928, pp. 50–6: C. Ritter, *Platon*, 1923, II, 860–6: J. A. Stewart, *Myths of P.* 1905, pp. 465–9: Frutiger, *Mythes de Platon*, 1930, pp. 192–5: Jowett, *Dialogues of P.*³ 1892, III, 429–33, 524–6: Delatte, op. cit. (traits from Persia and Carthage).

preferred the name Atlantis to America or West Indies, and Hakluyt himself thought that Plato 'plainly described the West Indies' and that antiquity had 'some kinde of dimme glimse and unperfect notice' of a New World. And indeed his fiction, read in a Latin version, had helped to keep the idea of a western world alive through the Middle Ages, though also to strew the Ocean with elusive islands.[1]

The ancients were more to be forgiven than we if bamboozled by Utopias. Yet many of them took this one at its exact value, or were very sceptical, and few seem to have mentioned it without serious questioning. Some, impressed by known cases of destructive earthquakes and disappearing islands, thought that the story might contain a tradition of a remote catastrophe. One of Plato's school took it as 'literal fact' and as referring to fairly recent history, apparently the Libyan attack on Egypt about 1200 B.C.[2] Quite lately there has been a strange eruption of theories on similar lines. The priest, it is argued, meant Minoan Crete overthrown by the Athenian Theseus. Or he meant by his 'bay' only Lake Tritonis, and Atlantis was Tunis, where lived the Phaeacians too. Or they were both Tartessus, which vanished from view after Carthage blocked the strait (the lesser islands are off Brittany and the continent is Britain!). Or the landscape suits the district round Bath, heard of from some Celt arriving in Sicily in a Carthaginian ship. There are scores of older guesses, including Sweden, the home of the sons of Japhet or Europeans (Rudbeck in 1677) and even Spitsbergen (Bailly in 1779) and the Niger delta (Frobenius in 1926). These things are of interest only as curiosities in the long tale of geographical mares' nests.[3] A cranky person has seen here the source of the Biblical tradition of the Flood, and the lost civilization from which Egypt and Mexico were both colonies. Something has been said for the islands off Africa like Madeira being the relics of a land which vanished comparatively recently; but, even if this can be proved, it is irrelevant, as the land did not vanish suddenly or within human memory, and anyhow

[1] Babcock, *Legendary Islands of the Atlantic*, 1922. Version, Chalcidius, see p. 383, n. 1. Hakluyt, *Princ. Navigations...of the English Nation*, Everyman ed. I, 21, 47: sank, ibid. p. 95. Dee, E. G. R. Taylor, *Tudor Geography*, 1930, p. 99.

[2] Crantor in Proclus, *in Plat. Tim.* p. 76, Diehl: Proclus himself. Tradition, Pos. ap. Str. 102. 'Si Platoni credimus', Plin. II, 205. More naïve, Tert. Apol. 32, Amm. Marc. XVII, 7, 13, Arnobius, I, 5. But even Theophrastus (?) in Ps.-Philo, *de Aet. Mundi*, 141. Fiction, Arist. ap. Str. 598 and others in Proclus, loc. cit.

[3] Collected by T. H. Martin, *Études sur le Timée*, 1841, pp. 257–332. Also Bessmertny, *Atlantisrätsel*, 1932: Bramwell, *Lost Atlantis*, 1937 (both much too patient of occultist and other rubbish). Crete, Frost, *J.H.S.* 1913, p. 189. Tunis, Borchardt, *Pet. Mitt.* 1927, p. 19, approved by Herrmann, ibid. p. 145. Tartessus, Hennig, *Von rätselhaften Ländern*, 1935, p. 7, and Schulten. Tunisia and Spain both absurd, Herter, *Bonner Jahrb.* 1928. Atlas region, Berlioux, *Les Atlantides*, 1885. Bath, Prof. V. Calestani cited in *Times* leader (date mislaid). For theories also H. Berger in *R.E.* Atlantis, 1896.

THE GREEK HORIZON TO HERODOTUS

Plato left no relics but shoals.[1] (It seems doubtful if volcanic Ocean islands can be explained as relics, and there is nothing nearer a 'shoal' than a long mid-Atlantic ridge at about a mile deep. That a vast connecting land-mass once existed has often been assumed to account for the distribution of kindred animals and plants on both sides. An alternative is a startling theory that the Americas were close up against the Old World, Brazil fitting snugly into Guinea, until they drifted apart! But whatever may have happened in remote geological times hardly comes into question for judging an event supposed to be within human tradition.)[2]

Bacon's application of the story in 1624 is worth study. He finds his New Atlantis somewhere in the vast and mostly still unexplored South Sea beyond Peru and Mexico. About 3000 years before, he says, there had been flourishing kingdoms in both these countries, part of 'the great Atlantis that you call America'. But soon they had been destroyed, not indeed by earthquake but by a flooding of the big rivers, only a remnant of the people surviving on the higher ground (hence the thin population of degraded Indians). As for his own Utopia, his whole interest is in its college for the advancement of useful science and 'the enlarging of the bounds of human empire, to the effecting of all things possible', a conception of science which is, by the way, quite unlike Plato's. Montaigne before him has a New Atlantis beyond America, which is itself beyond the vanished Atlantis.

Altogether Plato's story was a remarkable invention, liable to suggest various perverse theories but also containing ideas not without value for the progress of geography. It will be discussed presently how he had come to think of the earth as a globe, and how in an earlier 'myth' he had conceived it as of inordinate size; the notion implied in the new 'myth' was quite inconsistent with that, and a great improvement, though the globe was still much too large.[3]

---

1 Relics, already Kircher, 1678, Cadet, 1785, etc. J. Johnstone, *A Study of the Oceans*, 1926, pp. 144–8. Sinking comparatively recent, but P.'s details imaginary, T. Moreux, *L'Atlantide*, 1924. Colonies, Donnelly, *Antediluvian World*, 1882, and cp. L. Spence, *Problem of A.* 1924.

2 Drifted, Wegener, *Origin of Continents and Oceans*, 1924: discussed in R. A. Daly, *Our Mobile Earth*, 1926, pp. 260–3, 279–80: Van der Gracht, etc., *Theory of Continental Drift*, 1928 (many of the writers hostile): J. A. Steers, *The Unstable Earth*, 1932, pp. 159–79: S. J. Shand, *Earth-Lore*^{2}, 1937, pp. 135–44: Wooldridge and Morgan, *Physical Basis of Geography*, 1939, pp. 40–51: A. E. Trueman, *This Strange World*, 1941, pp. 201–15: A. Holmes, *Principles of Physical Geology*, 1944, pp. 487–509: A. A. Miller, *Climatology*^{3}, 1944, pp. 292–3: O. D. von Engeln, *Geomorphology*, 1942, pp. 29–31.

3 See pp. 113–15: P. Friedländer, *Jahrb. D. Arch. Inst.* 1914, p. 101. For theories add Hyde, *Anc. Greek Mariners*, 1947, pp. 155–9. A. Schulten, *Rh. Mus.* 1939, pp. 326–46 supposes that the E. part of Atlantis is a poetic picture of rich Tartessus, and the rest is Plato's invention. Montaigne, Payne, *Cambr. Mod. Hist.* 1907, I, 63.

CHAPTER III

GREEK THEORY TO ARISTOTLE

§ 1. THE EARTH-DISK

ABOUT 600 B.C. there arose in Ionia a 'wisdom' which was new in the world and contained the germ of modern science. A series of 'wise men' shook off the habit of thinking in myths and divine pedigrees, and they asked the boldest questions, even what the heavenly bodies are made of. They assumed the universe as explainable—it was soon, if not from the first, named as 'kosmos' or order—and each tried to explain it all at once on the scheme that there is an ultimate 'nature' or substance, which can change somehow into everything else. These large speculations were built on an absurdly small basis of ascertained facts, but it seems that science could start with nothing less ambitious than such theories from supposed first principles. Some observation there was already, perhaps more than appears from our fragmentary information, and a good deal of patient work was to come, at least in some fields like medicine. Yet the Greeks were nearly always too ready to theorize, and had little of the modern will to collect and sift facts, or of the instruments and techniques necessary for this purpose: they tried to explain things without first studying and describing them properly, preferring instead to analyse their own words and notions. So they initiated science but failed to sustain it, and never disengaged 'physics' from the general philosophy in which it began. There was a fatal neglect of detail and experiment and practical application, partly because most craftsmanship was left to slaves. Thus modern science, which rests on experiment, is in a sense not really continuous with ancient. In fact the Greeks observed too little and argued far too much, and never grasped the importance of method and training.[1] One reason may be, as Cornford says, that their philosophy continued (at least till Plato) to use a certain manner inherited from the cosmogonic myth; also the model

---

[1] Platt in *Science and Civ.* ed. Marvin, 1926, p. 78. Not continuous, MacMurray, *The Clue to History*, 1938, p. 24. Failed, Whitehead, *Science and the Modern World*, 1932, pp. 7, 19: Singer, *Short Hist. of Science*, 1941, p. 33: Heidel, *Heroic Age of Science*, 1933, pp. 79, 93: so already Whewell, *Hist. of the Inductive Sciences*³, 1857, 1, 26–8, 59. Cornford in *Background to Modern Science*, ed. Needham and Pagel, 1938, pp. 6, 12. Westaway, *The Golden Quest*, 1934, p. 78. Dampier-Whetham, *Hist. of Science*, 1929, pp. 20, 45 (deductive geometry suited Greek genius). Greeks did observe, De Burgh, *Legacy of Anc. World*, 1924, pp. 98–9, but not enough, Friend and Feibleman, *What Science Really Means*, 1937, pp. 27–9. For science, Rehm and Vogel in Gercke-Norden, *Einleitung in die Altertumswissenschaft*, II, 2, § 5, 1933.

science for them was geometry, which has no need of observation and experiment.

Part of the slender stock of knowledge was borrowed, no doubt, from the older civilizations, and the Greeks themselves rather exaggerated the debt. Thales is said to have 'brought geometry from Egypt', such as it was. Also, if he 'forewarned the Ionians of an eclipse of the sun, fixing the very year', he did this only by a lucky use of periods as recorded by the Babylonians. The same people had watched the apparent movement of the sun and several planets among the fixed stars, the signs of the zodiac, the more closely because eclipses occur here, about the 'ecliptic' or 'middle circle of the signs', which is the 'oblique circle', as being inclined to the equator. There was an early borrowing of the signs, it seems, and gradually a relearning of things which the East had known before, but astronomy remained very crude: there was no idea of the sizes and distances of the heavenly bodies, which were thought small as compared with the earth, and Anaximander put the fixed stars nearer than moon and sun (here the Babylonians themselves were wrong).[1] Among the questions raised was that of the shape of the earth, but it was not at first doubted that its surface was what it seemed to be, a flat (or at best a tilted or concave) disk; presently, when the Pythagoreans came to conceive the globe, it was by abstract reasoning rather than observation, according to the account, and even then there was a time-lag before the new idea was seriously applied to the task of geography. The sun-dial or gnomon, perhaps in the polos or bowl form (an inverted sky), is variously said to have been 'invented' by an early philosopher, Anaximander or Anaximenes, or introduced from Babylon, but for yet awhile this old instrument was little better than a time-reckoner: before the globe came in, men could not understand the length of the gnomon shadow (as significant for latitude) or the curve plotted on the dial by the sun between its risings and settings.[2]

The early systems are not quite unhaunted by memories of the myths which they replaced. So the water chosen by Thales as the primal substance recalls Ocean, the parent of all things, and the widespread idea that the earth 'appeared' from 'the waters'. So, too, Anaximander's something

---

[1] Aet. II, 15, 6: Boll-Bezold-Gundel, *Sternglaube u. Sterndeutung*, 1926, pp. 17, 88. Crude, Rey, *Jeunesse de la Science grecque*, 1933, pp. 403, 412–13: small, Farrington, *Greek Science*, 1944, p. 91. Signs, Cleostratus, *c.* 520 B.C., Plin. II, 31: Rey, p. 437: Rehm-Vogel, op. cit. p. 15 (partly C.'s own): from east, Fotheringham, *J.H.S.* 1919, pp. 164–84, 1925, pp. 78–83, criticized by Webb, ibid. 1921, pp. 70–85, 1928, pp. 55–63.

[2] Heidel, op. cit. pp. 124–5, *Frame of Anc. Greek Maps*, 1937, pp. 57–9, and see p. 37, n. 1. Invented, Diog. Laert. II, 1, Plin. II, 187: Babylon, Hdt. II, 109: Rey, op. cit. p. 82: J. E. Powell seeks to discredit Hdt. loc. cit. as an Alex. interpolation, *C.R.* 1940, p. 69, but wrongly, as D. S. Robertson shows, ibid. p. 180.

undefined and infinite, which is defined into everything else, seems a kind of Chaos. Thales conceives the earth as made from the water and floating on it like a round slab of wood; he has at least got it afloat and loosed from the heaven-lid. Anaximander boldly imagines it as hanging free and needing no support in the middle of the universe: in shape it is like a pillar-drum, its diameter being thrice its depth (the surface seems concave rather than flat). Round it turns a ring of fire, broken into hollow wheels of dark cloud filled with fire, which shows through at certain openings as the heavenly bodies: this sounds naïve enough, but the general conception is very daring. Anaximenes, who follows, takes a bad step back. For him the earth is a broad thin slab 'like a table', supported on the primal air, and the sun does not pass under but laterally round it. Why does the sun disappear at night? Because it moves farther away from us and is screened by the northern parts of the earth, which are higher. This was an old popular notion, and it was shared, Aristotle says, by many of the early 'meteorologists' or 'students of things above'.[1] It is also said that the earth, though at first in the same plane as the sun, had somehow received a southward dip out of that plane, so that the angle of the sun's course is greater in winter than in summer.[2] Presently, with the earth-globe, this will appear as the obliquity of the ecliptic, better understood, and meanwhile, even with an earth-disk, some attempt can be made in this way to account for seasonal changes and climates (Anaximander is credited with grasping the obliquity, says Pliny, and so opening the portals of Nature). An antique idea, often to be repeated, was that the heavenly fires are formed and fed by vapours rising from the sea, and a few were so wild as to suggest that the sun is 'quenched' every night and a new one made from such kindled clouds. Some alleged crudities of Xenophanes about many suns at once and a month-long eclipse have been doubted, but without good reason, and Heraclitus could even say that the sun might be as big as a man's foot. The sun is said to turn back at the solstices because of the air condensed by its own heat or for other peculiar reasons.[3]

1 *Met.* II, 1, 354a. See p. 36, n. 1. Diels, *Doxographi Graeci*, 1929, p. 561: Heath, *Greek Astronomy*, 1932, p. 10: Heidel, *Frame*, p. 78: Rey, op. cit. p. 408: Dreyer, *Hist. of Planetary Systems*, 1906, pp. 12, 16. Convex, ibid. p. 14, Rey, p. 405, Gilbert, *Meteor. Theorien des griech. Alt.* 1907, p. 378, but wrongly for concave [see Addenda].

2 Several ap. Diels, op. cit. pp. 338, 377, 563: Heath, op. cit. pp. 29, 37, 39: Dreyer, op. cit. pp. 26–8, 31, 33, with the curious reasons given: Rey, op. cit. p. 442: Gilbert, op. cit. pp. 285, 680: Heidel, *Heroic Age*, pp. 122–3: Berger, *Erdkunde*^{2}, p. 79: Rehm-Vogel, op. cit. pp. 11, 13: C. Bailey, *Greek Atomists and Epicurus*, 1928, p. 152.

3 Early notions of sun ap. Arist. *Met.* II, 1, 353b, 2, 355a: Aet. II, 23: Dreyer, op cit. pp. 24–5, 31, 33–4. Xen., doubted by Berger, op. cit. pp. 190–4 and Robin, *Greek Thought*, 1928, p. 83, but cp. Dreyer, op. cit. p. 19, Gilbert, p. 95. Heraclitus, Gilbert, pp. 448, 461: Rey, op. cit. pp. 336, 411. Anax., Plin. II, 31.

GREEK THEORY TO ARISTOTLE

Even the bold fancy of a drum-like earth did not change the primitive view of its surface as a disk. It was with this fixed horizon that Anaximander 'ventured' to draw the first general map, which, with the 'improvement' by Hecataeus, was later considered the beginning of real geography. The range of the practical knowledge at their disposal has been indicated in the previous chapter. The heart of the map was what was now known as an inner sea with a short strait leading to an outer. As for the framework, Herodotus presently laughs at those who draw the earth perfectly round, 'as if turned on a lathe', and girdled by the Ocean-stream. Aristotle too abuses such maps, evidently still current in his time, for showing 'the inhabited earth'

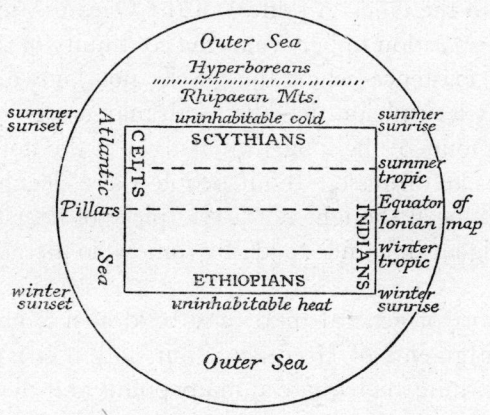

Fig. 10. Frame of the Ionian map.

as round. Their statements are hardly fair: if the round frame, the horizon of the disk, was still called by the name of the mythical Ocean-stream, this was little more than a concession to the old poetic tradition. (If Hecataeus seriously brought the Argo round by the Ocean, was this any longer a stream, as some suppose?)[1] Within the circular rim for quite a distance were unknown parts, either outer seas, mostly unsailed, to which the name Ocean was transferred, or fabulous peoples or deserts of uninhabitable cold or heat. Only inwards came the really known 'inhabited earth', not round at all but a rectangle such as Ephorus gives in his old-fashioned geography after Ionian sources. The horizon provided certain fixed points, like those where the sun rises and sets at solstices, and the map (as on the sketch above) has a kind of tropics of its own: in winter,

---

[1] Some as Jacoby, *F.G.H.* I, 329. Concession, Gilbert, op. cit. p. 398. Hdt. IV, 36: Arist. *Met.* II, 5, 362b. On Anax., Berger, pp. 32–9 (inner sea, ibid. p. 48): Heidel, *Proc. Amer. Acad.* 1921, pp. 239–88. Map, cp. p. 35, n. 1.

says Herodotus, the sun's traverse is far to the south and it stands over inner Africa, while in summer it withdraws towards Scythia. Other ideas underlying the map may be gathered from statements that Asia lies nearer the sun and so is very fruitful and has everything finer and larger, and that India being nearer the sunrise is hottest in the morning.[1] The main axis is a line through the inner sea, already foreshadowing the remarkably accurate Gibraltar–Rhodes parallel of the later geographers. On it are Greece and Ionia, 'midway between the sunrises', with an ideally tempered climate; no doubt the oldest conception had these in the centre of the world, with the famous 'navel of the earth' at Delphi. Some rude attempts are also made to find meridians, like a very wrong one from the Danube mouths through Sinope to the Nile. An effect of the Ocean frame inherited from myth was a predisposition to believe in the continuity of the outer seas and to assume their existence when they were not known. Nowhere does Herodotus betray a suspicion that the earth may not be flat, though there were already rumours of the long winter night of the north and a curious statement, which he dismisses, about people there sleeping six months in the year (this has been thought not a real piece of hearsay but a garbled form of an intelligent inference made by some who already held the globe theory).

Some rough sort of general map may be drawn from Herodotus and even from the fragments of Hecataeus, but only if it is well understood that the data are quite inadequate at many points and that reconstructions may differ widely within certain limits. (Thus nobody really knows how well either drew much of the inner sea itself, and some ascribe to the older writer a Nile flowing from the west, or even a Nile flowing from India round a Red Sea lake.) What both writers have to say of the various countries has already been described. It should be added that Herodotus accepts the outer sea only where it seems to him proved by actual voyages, all along the south from the Indus to Gibraltar (done by Scylax and Necho's men), and not west and north of Europe, though rumours of Tin Islands and a north-flowing river had substance enough. Yet, while so sceptical in this matter, he admits a baseless principle of symmetry. Near the limits of the known are two rivers, marking so to speak the winter and the summer tropics of the Ionian map: they must needs behave as counterparts, the Nile flowing east and north as the Danube flows east and south. Also there can be no Hyperborean people 'beyond the north wind' because there is none 'beyond the

---

[1] Hdt. III, 104: Asia, Hipp. *on Airs*, 19: sun withdraws, Hdt. II, 24, IV, 36. Rectangle, Eph. ap. Str. 34, Ps.-Scymn. 167–82, and Cosmas, 116*b*: Heidel, *Frame*, pp. 12, 17, 27, *Heroic Age*, pp. 125–6, and see p. 37, n. 1.

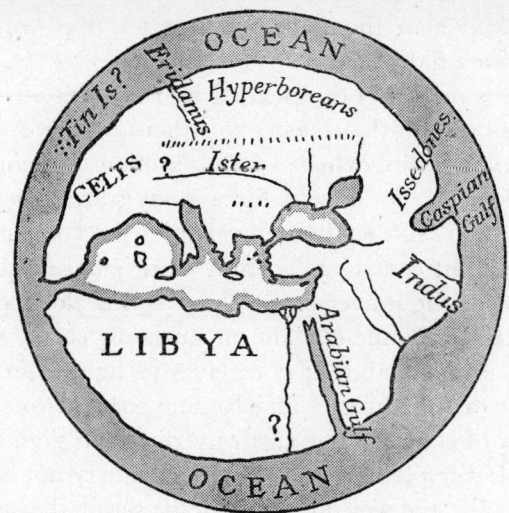

MAP OF HECATAEUS
(*Much of the drawing is very conjectural*)

Fig. 11.

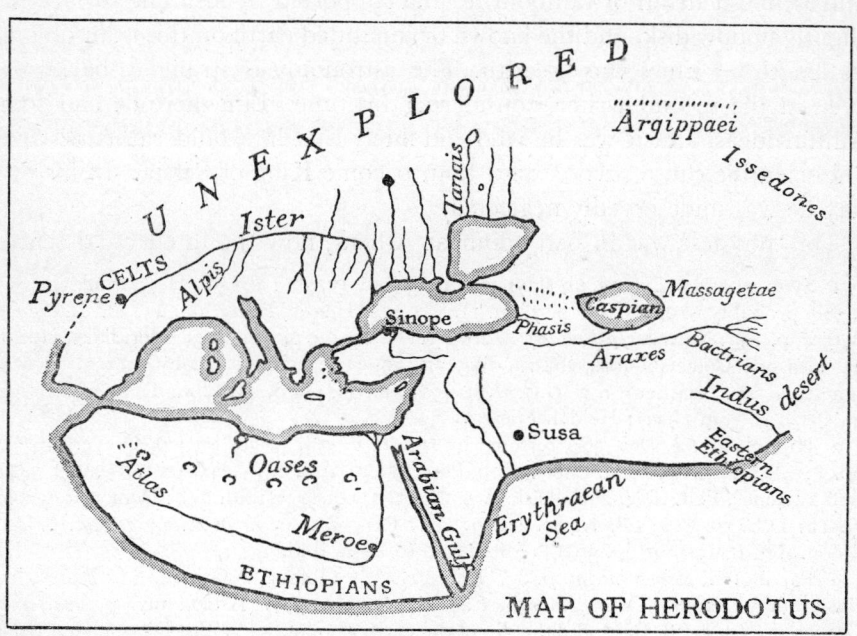

Fig. 12.

south'.¹ (Such strange arguments from symmetry are not unknown much later, as when Magellan thought that America must end in a southern cape because Africa did.)

The historian is only slightly touched by the spirit of Ionian 'physics'. Anaxagoras had brought that science to Athens, where many disliked it so heartily that they had him expelled for his impious opinions. Having seen the fall of a meteorite, he knew it for a stony star, an opinion far better than Aristotle's later. Other heavenly bodies, he concluded, are similar fragments, hurled out centrifugally from an original mass and made red-hot by the whirl of the universe. So the sun is a glowing lump of metal 'bigger than the Peloponnese'. The moon is an earth, with plains and mountains, and even inhabited; it receives its light from the sun, a view credited already to Anaximenes and leading straight to something like a true explanation of eclipses. The earth's surface is a slightly concave disk. So it is too for his disciple Archelaus, though he may not have said exactly that because of this 'the sun does not rise or set at the same time for all peoples, as it ought to if the earth were level' (the effects of concavity would not be those actually produced by the rotundity of the earth but just the opposite).² Ionian science culminates in Leucippus and Democritus, with their many worlds formed by mechanical combinations of atoms. The earth is composed of the heavier atoms coming to rest at the middle, and is like a drum or tambourine and supported by air. The surface is a slightly hollow disk, and the known or inhabited earth on this is an oblong, its length 1½ times the breadth. The astronomy is strangely backward, even in the second writer, considering his time. Elsewhere he had some fruitful ideas, and it was he who said finely that he would rather discover one scientific cause (αἰτιολογία) than become King of Persia. In his own day he was undeservedly neglected.³

For 'physics' was in bad odour at Athens, now the intellectual centre.

---

1 Symmetry, Hdt. II, 33, 49 (Hypernotians, ibid. IV, 36): already Hec., thinks Jacoby, I, 368, probably wrongly (see p. 71, n. 1). Tropics, Heidel, *Frame*, pp. 25, 28. Inference, Berger, p. 195: Nansen, *In Northern Mists*, 1911, I, 20: see p. 113, n. 3. Meridians, Hdt. II, 34, also one Colchis–Persis, ibid. I, 104, VII, 79, Hec. fr. 289, Jacoby, I, 355. Centre, 'ancients' ap. Agathem. I, 2 (*G.G.M.* II, 471): navel, see p. 41, n. 1. Tempered, Hipp. *on Airs*, 12 (from Hec.): Heidel, *Frame*, p. 53.

2 Hippol. I, 9, 4, *Dox.* 564, rejected by Heidel, *Frame*, p. 78 (but cp. Dreyer, op. cit. pp. 33–4). Meteorite, Diog. Laert. II, 10, Plut. *Lys.* 12, Aet. II, 13: cp. Arist. *Met.* I, 7, 344 *b*. Sun a 'stone', Plat. *Apol.* 26 *d*. Disk, Aet. III, 10, 5: concave, ibid. II, 8: Democritus, ibid. III, 10: D.L. IX, 31: Gilbert, op. cit. p. 282: Rey, *Jeunesse de la Science grecque*, p. 442. Moon, Aet. II, 25 (but cp. 30): credited also to Dem. ibid.

3 Farrington, *Science in Ant.* p. 83. Dem. fr. 118. Oblong, Agathem. I, 2: Bailey, loc. cit. misunderstands. Drum, Heath, *G.A.* p. 38, *Dox.* 377. Astronomy, p. 113, n. 3. Dreyer, op. cit. p. 28. Dem. has the dip of the earth as p. 96, n. 2. But D. much less backward than L., Bailey, op. cit. pp. 149–55.

There had been too many conflicting doctrines, and it seemed hopeless to reach truth in this matter. The Sophists, the new professors of culture, discussed most subjects very freely, among others the contrast of Nature and custom (they read Herodotus on such things as Indians eating the dead, and they reflected, like Montaigne, that no opinion was so fantastic that custom had not planted it in some country). But they shunned physics as both unprofitable and indiscreet. There was plenty of superstition left when Nicias could ruin the great expedition to Sicily by his obstinate inaction during an eclipse. It was easy to stir up fits of intolerance against those who 'presumed to explain away the gods as blind forces' (some like Plato's uncle Critias thought them an invention of cunning statesmen to keep the people in order). Socrates was condemned at least partly for an alleged curiosity about things above and below the earth, though he had long since abandoned such studies. Years earlier a comic poet had used him as a stalking-horse for a general attack on them, but the caricature applies more justly to another, Diogenes of Apollonia, who revived air as the primal substance. When young, we hear elsewhere, Socrates had admired this kind of wisdom, and had turned eagerly to Anaxagoras, who said that 'Mind' arranged all things: he hoped to learn whether the earth is flat or round, and why it should be the one or the other, and why it should be at the centre, if it is so. But he had been disappointed: the great man used 'Mind' merely to start the cosmic rotation, and did not make it go on to design everything for the best, but mentioned as causes only air and ether and water and many other absurdities. This reaction of Socrates against materialistic physics and his quest for intelligent design were to have bad effects for science in the many philosophies which sprang from his personality and teachings. His greatest disciple, Plato, had a positive contempt for observation, upon which natural science rests. (Both, it may be said for them, felt that it was not man's chief business to understand Nature but rather to understand and make the best of himself.)[1]

Geography shared in the prejudice against 'physics'. Speculation about unknown parts was disliked, and attempts to measure and map the whole earth were regarded as windy talk and fair game for comedy. Yet we hear of a public 'map having a circuit of the earth': Socrates snubbed the proud Alcibiades by leading him to it and bidding him point out Attica and his own estates (the anecdote is rather dubious). Smaller maps were familiar enough: when the people were fired by thoughts of taking Sicily and even

---

[1] Livingstone, *Greek Ideals and Modern Life*, 1935, pp. 66, 88. Contempt, Farrington, op. cit. pp. 115, 122: Gilbert, op. cit. p. 153. Disappointed, Plato, *Phaedo*, 96a–99c, as is Arist. *Met.* I, 4, 985a. Indiscreet, Plato, *Apol.* 19b: Xen. *Mem.* IV, 7, 6. Diog. mocked in Aristophanes, *Clouds*, 225 (423 B.C.). Forces, Plut. *Nic.* 23: invention, Critias ap. Sext. Emp. *adv. Math.* IX, 54. Custom, Hdt. III, 38.

Carthage, young and old could be seen drawing sketches of those parts. But the current histories avoid discussions of geography except such brief account of the scene of events as appears necessary. So Thucydides limits himself, though remarks on earthquakes and the like show the student of Anaxagoras: to him a Nicias seems grossly superstitious (another free-thinking student was the statesman Pericles, who explained an eclipse to a soldier by holding a cloak before his face). Xenophon has casual phrases betraying a belief in an uninhabitable north and south. Of special geographies by Athenians we hear only of coastal descriptions by Phileas and Euctemon, of which we have nothing or the merest scraps about the strait of Gibraltar and a submarine bank just outside. Yet the second author is known to have observed that the sun's motion was not uniform and the four seasons not quite equal, as did Meton, who was concerned with the calendar.[1]

Elsewhere there was still writing more in the Ionian taste. Damastes copied largely from Hecataeus, and used old properties like the Hyperboreans beyond the fabulous range. Ctesias said that India was very hot and the sun seemed (apparently from certain mountains) ten times larger there than in other lands. Ephorus had typically Ionian notions, as mentioned above, and he set a new fashion for historians by including two books of formal geography. But the framework of his map was already obsolete, and it is surprising only that it had lasted so long, as the theory of the earth-globe had been in the air for some time, just how must be described presently. Until this was applied, of course, nobody could really explain why new stars appeared as one travelled south, or why the polar stars rose higher and the days grew longer as one travelled north: such things were noticed sometimes by practical men like traders, but could not be scientifically valued.[2]

It is only fair to give here some of the acute observations and reasonings on kindred matters: most were made already at this time, to be repeated later with minor elaborations, a few of which may be mentioned in advance to avoid constant recurrence to these topics.

The sea is thought the relic of a vast water-mass which was reduced and made salt by the sun. Animals 'arose in the moist' and emerged on to dry land, said Anaximander, and even men derive from such fish-like creatures;

---

1 Dreyer, p. 93. Scraps ap. Avien. 42, 337, 350: Rehm, *R.E.* VI, 1060: Berger, *Erdkunde*, pp. 239–41. Thuc. II, 28, III, 87, VII, 50. Pericles, Plut. *Per.* 25, Cic. *de Rep.* I, 16, 25. Xen. *Cyr.* VIII, 6, 21, *Anab.* I, 7, 6. Sicily, Plut. *Nic.* 12. Anecdote, Aelian, *V.H.* III, 28. Comedy, Aristophanes, *Clouds*, 201–5. Prejudice, Berger, op. cit. pp. 224–6.

2 Berger, pp. 173, 190–4. Damastes, ibid. pp. 238–9, Jacoby, *F.G.H.* I, 152–6. Copied, Agathem. I, 1. His Red Sea a lake?, p. 82, n. 1: Sieglin, *Schulatlas*, ascribes this also to Hec. Sun, Ctes. ap. Phot. 72, 5: Dreyer, op. cit. p. 172: but cp. p. 210, n. 3.

it is a dazzling guess, but the details do not suggest anything like the theory of evolution, though he might have thought of that, it has been hinted, if he had known of the great apes. Sea-shells and salt deposits found far inland are rightly understood to indicate old sea-bottoms, as in Egypt and the Libyan depression or even the heart of Asia Minor. Fossil 'imprints' of fish and sea-weed at Malta and elsewhere, Xenophanes realizes, must have been made in mud which has become stone. (It is odd that big bones were usually misread as belonging to giants and not prehistoric beasts, though some had an inkling of the truth.) How free all this thinking was! The germ of modern geology was when Steno noted shells and sharks' teeth dug out at Malta; but he was cramped by the absurd Christian time-scale ('the poor world is almost six thousand years old', says Touchstone, and Archbishop Ussher dated Creation 'at the beginning of the night before Monday, the 23rd of October, 4004 B.C.'). Hutton in 1789 demanded unlimited time, and just after him William Smith assigned fossils, often extinct forms, to their own strata, but controversies about the Flood and the like were still not over.[1]

Plato has a vision of the rocky skeleton of Greece once covered with thick soil and many forests. Others have a fair notion of the planing down of the earth's surface by the slow processes of denudation.

Much is said of rivers, though those of the homeland were nearly all mere torrents, drying up in summer. The silting work of rivers was familiar in Ionia itself and elsewhere in the inner sea, where the tides are too feeble to scour the mouths. Later it was still more obvious, when old ports were threatened or had been left miles inland, as in Ionia and at the mouth of the Po. Plainly the Nile had made its own delta, and more: Herodotus guesses that, if diverted, it could fill up the Red Sea in less than 20,000 years (the time is too short, of course, but how intelligent he sounds beside some who were still hindering the progress of geology till well down the nineteenth century!). The big Russian rivers, it was thought, would silt up the shallow Azov quite soon, and in due course, some wildly added, even the Black Sea. The river pushing out the Cilician coast-plain would eventually reach Cyprus opposite. One in Greece which had already overtaken some off-shore islands, would join up the rest (it has not done so because the sea is too

---

[1] Sollas, *Age of the Earth*, 1905, pp. 222–7, 243. Inkling, Suet. *Aug.* 72: cp. p. 375, n. 1. Xenophanes, *Dox.* 566 after Anax. (relic, *Dox.* 351). Animals, Anax. ibid. 430: E. E. Sikes, *Anthropology of the Greeks*, 1914, pp. 48–9. Apes, Myres in *Anthropology and the Classics*, 1908, pp. 128–30, ed. Marett. Shells, etc., Hdt. II, 12: Xanthus praised by Erat. ap. Str. 49, Pearson, *Early Ionian Historians*, p. 123: (Ammon), Erat. ap. Str. 809–10, etc. Berger, pp. 146–51. See p. 156, n. 1 (Strato's theory), p. 43, n. 3. Why sea salt, opinions in Arist. *Met.* II, 1–3, Aet. III, 16, *Dox.* 381: Dreyer, pp. 30, 34.

deep).¹ Other interesting rivers were those which disappeared down swallow-holes in limestone districts like Arcadia, and they suggested some extravagant myths, as of a Greek river passing a long way under the sea to emerge in Sicily. Plato has a fancy picture of underground rivers, and Aristotle, while finding fault, believes in reservoirs of water generated in the earth and helping to maintain rivers.² There was a disposition to conceive the earth as riddled with caverns and channels, and these play a large part in the explanations of volcanoes and earthquakes.

Active volcanoes could be observed in the west, especially Etna, which was sometimes in violent eruption as in 479 and 426. The Lipari islands had others besides Stromboli, with its intermittent puffs, a light-house and weather-glass for sailors. In an island near Naples Epomeo (now long extinct) more than once scared off colonists. Vesuvius played the innocent till A.D. 79, but some could detect it as having once had 'craters of fire', and near-by were Lake Avernus with its vapours and the solfataras of the 'Phlegraean fields'. The older Greek lands had little but hot springs and spurts of gas, and Lemnos oddly has nothing to show why it was the Fire-god's favourite home. But the Aegean had seen a great submarine eruption at Thera about 2000 B.C., and islands were to be ejected here again (in 196 B.C.) and also near Lipari, while a hill was to be upheaved in Greece as late as 282 B.C. There was every readiness to infer similar events by land and sea in pre-historic times. Past activity was easily recognized, as in the 'Burnt Country' of Asia Minor, and later near the Asphalt Lake or Dead Sea, where plenty of signs seemed to confirm the native legend of the disappearance of Sodom and a dozen towns.³ (In fact this last region is not properly volcanic.)

The explanations offered are much the same as for earthquakes, which are closely associated, being noted, for instance, as very frequent in the

---

1 (Achelous), Hdt. II, 10, Thuc. II, 102, Str. 458, Plin. IV, 2, prophecy in Paus. VIII, 22, 11. Cyprus, Str. 53, 536. Azov, Arist. Met. I, 14, 353a; Black, Polybius, IV, 40. Ports, Priene, Str. 579: Spina (Po), Str. 214, Plin. III, 20. Nile, Hdt. II, 10–12. E. C. Semple, *Geogr. of Med. Region*, 1932, p. 106: Newbigin, *Southern Europe*, 1927, p. 175, *Frequented Ways*, 1922, pp. 284–90: E. Ludwig, *Mediterranean*, 1943, pp. 34–5. Torrents, Str. 36, Paus. II, 15. Planing, Theophrastus in Ps.-Philo, *de Aetern. Mundi*, 23, 118–19. Skeleton, Plato, *Crit.* 111 b.

2 Met. II, 2, 356a, I, 13, 349b (reservoirs denied by Perrault, 1674, A. Wolf, *Hist. of Science...in 16th and 17th Centuries*, 1935, pp. 361, 392). Plato, *Phaedo*, 111 d. Alpheus to Sicily, Pindar and Timaeus, rejected by Str. 271: cp. Sen. *N.Q.* III, 26, 5, Plin. II, 225. Even Nile to Delos, Callim. *Del.* 206, Paus. II, 5, 3. Arcadia, Arist. Met. I, 13, 351a, Erat. ap. Str. 389, cp. 215, 275, 371. Glover, *Springs of Hellas*, 1945, p. 5. Semple, op. cit. p. 28. Newbigin, *S.E.* p. 364. Ancients on rivers, Rainaud, s.v. Geogr. in *Dict. des Ant.* 1896, pp. 1523–4.

3 Posidonius ap. Str. 764 (but not volcanic, Jos. *Ant.* I, 9): see p. 172, n. 2. Burnt, Xanthus ap. Str. 628. Upheaved, at Methana, Str. 59, Ovid, Met. XV, 296–306. Islands ejected, Pos. ap. Str. 57, 277: Plin. II, 202–3: Tozer, *Islands of Aegean*, 1890, pp. 99–100. Lemnos, ibid. pp. 270–3, cp. Soph. *Phil.* 911. Vesuvius, Diod. IV, 21, Vitr. II, 6, 2, Str. 247: Epomeo, ibid. 248. Semple, op. cit. pp. 50–4. G. W. Tyrrell, *Volcanoes*, 1931. Much in Humboldt, *Cosmos*, I and V, 1864–5. Lipari, Str. 275–7 and see p. 26, n. 1.

same Burnt Country, and as having become rarer in the Etna region after the opening of volcanic safety-valves. An early suggestion (by Anaxagoras) is that a fiery ether gets into the hollows below the earth and seeks a way out. Aristotle conceives that, besides winds getting in from outside, others are generated by the earth's heat from underground water: they blow through the many passages and shake the earth, and at times they catch fire and burst violently out.[1] The notion of wind, 'vis fera ventorum caecis inclusa cavernis', is echoed through the poets and down to late times.

Minor earthquakes were common in Greek lands, and there were some disasters, as from one which overthrew Sparta in 464, B.C. and others accompanied by tidal waves in Euboea (476 B.C.) and the gulf of Corinth (373 B.C.); the worst was to come in A.D. 17, wrecking twelve cities of Roman Asia. The subject was often discussed from the first, and special books were written by two men both named Demetrius. Early theories were that the earth's crust caved in when too dry or too wet, or that it was shaken when the underground passages were overfilled with rain or other water. But soon the stress was laid on the struggles of imprisoned winds or gases, and from Aristotle this view prevailed. Of the true cause of most earthquakes, the slipping of the crust rocks along lines of previous faulting or fracture, and ultimately the shrivelling of a half-cooled globe, there was never any idea. Attempts were made to observe the range of shocks and to explain why certain regions were peculiarly liable, like indented coasts and off-shore islands—not without good reason, but the large share assigned to the sea may partly reflect the old notion of Poseidon the Earthshaker. Among the after-effects ascribed some were real, such as changes of drainage, but grossly exaggerated. Vast prehistoric earthquakes were too readily assumed. One, it was supposed, had made the Peneus ravine—in fact an ordinary erosion valley—to drain out the lake which had covered the plain of Thessaly. Others with the help of tidal waves had torn off large islands, Euboea and Sicily and even Cyprus, and swallowed up huge areas like Atlantis.[2] The name of Rhegium on the Sicilian strait suggested 'break'

---

1 *Met.* II, 8. Ventigeni crateres, Lucr. VI, 701. Anax., Gilbert, *Meteor. Theorien*, pp. 322–4. Tozer, *Anc. Geogr.* pp. 198–200. Geikie, *Love of Nature among the Romans*, 1912, p. 353. Valves, Str. 258. Burnt, Str. 579, 628. An underground connection Stromboli—Etna, Diod. V, 74: *Aetna*, 445. Vis, Ovid, *Met.* XV, 299: Serv. ad Virg. *Aen.* III, 572, VIII, 423, *Georg.* II, 479: Justin, IV, 1, etc. Capelle, *Neue Jahrb.* 1920, pp. 318–20.

2 Pos. ap. Str. 102: islands, Str. 60, 258 (Sicily perhaps?), Plin. II, 204–5, III, 86, IV, 20. Peneus, Hdt. VII, 129, Str. 430, Sen. *N.Q.* VI, 25, 2. Drainage, Thales ap. Sen. *N.Q.* VI, 6: Str. 578. Theories, *Dox.* 377–81: Arist. *Met.* II, 7–8: Sen. *N.Q.* VI, 5–26: Plin. II, 191–206: Gilbert, op. cit. pp. 293–322: Rainaud, op. cit. p. 1526: Tozer, *Anc. Geogr.* pp. 197–9. Dem. of Scepsis and D. of Callatis, Str. 58, 60. Achaean tidal wave, Arist. *Met.* 340 b, 368 b, Callisthenes ap. Sen. VI, 23, Heraclides ap. Str. 384–5, Plin. II, 206. Capelle in *R.E.* Suppl. 4 (1924), pp. 344–64. Range, Pos. ap. Str. 58. Liable, Str. 447. 'Broken', Aesch. etc. ap. Str. 258: Lucan, II, 435–8, and Peneus, ibid. VI, 343–51.

and was fancifully connected with the supposed fact that the island had been 'broken' off by earthquakes. (And after all the strait does mark a deep fracture of the earth's crust, where there have been bad earthquakes, one of which destroyed Reggio and Messina in 1908.)

A matter long discussed was the influence of climate. There was a theory that a country's situation and conditions largely determine its flora and fauna and even its human inhabitants and their mode of life. It is carried very far in an essay *On Airs, Waters, and Sites*, which is in a collection of writings under the name of the great doctor Hippocrates and is generally accepted as of his school and time (that of Pericles or a few years later, by 410 B.C.?). The author proceeds from an interest in soil and water, climate and exposure, as affecting the health of cities, and he believes that 'both the physique and the character of men follow Nature', meaning the nature of the country. (Some critics, however, detach the geographical half, 12–24, from the preceding, and also suspect many interpolations.) He knows only a narrow strip between what he supposes uninhabitable cold and heat; yet he divides it into three belts with differences of climate, from which he draws sweeping conclusions, though differences of configuration are also brought in and somewhat disturb the argument. The northern belt, Scythia, is cold and wet and a featureless steppe; the cold explains why the wild animals are few and small, the cattle small and hornless, and even why the people are red-haired; because of the steppe they live the monotonous life of nomad herdsmen, and from all the conditions they are big, heavy, and infertile. The southern belt, Libya and Egypt and most of Asia, is hot and dry, and it too is generally level; hence it is very productive, has many and large animals, and peoples black, black-haired, and feeble. The middle belt has marked diversity of seasons and soil and landscape; the peoples are tall and fair, and also strong and spirited and intelligent, for it is change that produces quick wits and hardiness of body and soul. These praises apply, of course, to the Greeks, but not apparently to Asiatics of the same belt, who have been softened by despotic rule. Here another complication is introduced, nurture being strong enough to counteract nature. It is further admitted that even quite far north there may be a sultry hollow like the Phasis valley, where the people are swarthy from the air and fat and sluggish from drinking the tepid marsh water. Altogether a remarkable essay, with a basis of real observation, but not easy to follow and amusingly bold in its theorizing.[1]

---

1 W. H. S. Jones, *Hippocrates* (Loeb), 1923, 1, xxi. Farrington, op. cit. p. 104. Norden, *Germ. Urgesch. in Tac. Germ.* 1923, pp. 53, 105. Berger, *Erdkunde*², pp. 82, 122–4. Pieces in Toynbee, *Greek Hist. Thought*, 1924, pp. 163–8, and see *Study of History*, 1, 251. Wilamowitz, *Lesebuch*, 1901, 1, 199–207. Critics, Edelstein, ΠΕΡΙ ΑΕΡѠΝ *und die Sammlung der Hippokr. Schriften*, 1931. Fully also Diller, *Philologus* Suppl. 1934. Myres, op. cit. pp. 146–7, 162.

There are some remarks of similar tenor in the books *On Regimen*, about the nature of various districts and winds: southern peoples are drier and hotter like their climate, and so on. (Another treatise included in the same medical collection is possibly a good deal older; anyhow it is of no scientific merit, drawing a silly comparison between the seven parts of the earth and those of the body, the Peloponnese with its noble men answering to the head and so on.)[1]

Herodotus has much to say on similar lines, while aware that a nation is not the product of climate alone, or of race alone, but of complex factors including culture and tradition. Greece and Ionia, having the best-tempered climate, he thinks, are the nursery of free men; soft countries make soft peoples; the Libyans are healthy in a heat which is at least equable; the Egyptians are as unique as their climate and their river. So the Scythians are peculiar for the essay *On Airs*, and both may get the doctrine from Hecataeus. Henceforth the influence of climate becomes a commonplace or 'topic'. Plato knows that soil and climate affect a people's temper. Aristotle puts it quite crudely: the men of the cold north are free and brave, those of the hot east are clever, and only the Greeks are all three, and only they are truly civilizable, and so entitled to make slaves and 'living tools' of all barbarians, a view fortunately rejected by his pupil Alexander. Among the Greeks themselves, it is often admitted, some are not so clever as others, as the local fog gets into Boeotian heads, while a bright air gives the Athenians keen wits. All sorts of things are accounted for on these lines. The Ethiopians are black and woolly-haired from their hot desert climate, the Indians black but not woolly-haired as their heat is damper. (Moderns agree after all that black skin and kinky hair are probably specializations evolved in a hot climate, though an Elizabethan captain thinks that, if the Ethiopians are black and woolly-haired as compared with the people of the East and West Indies, it must be because Noah cursed Ham for begetting a son in the Ark.) Posidonius expects to find in the same latitude not only similar plants and animals but peoples similar in body and mind, customs and even language. Strabo sensibly objects that customs may be borrowed and peoples are not always to be explained by their climate, though Nature and Providence have made Europeans the best of mankind. To Pliny his own country seems chosen by its climate as in every other way to rule the world. It is noted that a war-like people may degenerate when it invades a softer country, like the

---

1 Pseudo-Hipp. περὶ ἑβδομάδων, 1–11, between Thales and Anaximander, thinks Roscher, *Philologus*, 1911, pp. 529–38, but cp. Gilbert, op. cit. p. 353: Rey, *Jeunesse de la Science grecque*, pp. 426–8: Rehm-Vogel, op cit. p. 27. Remarks, π. διαίτης, II, 37–8 (Loeb, *Hipp.* vol. 4), but it has 'south pole' ibid.

Celts in Italy or in Asia Minor. One German tribe seems to be less bovine than another owing to local conditions (ipso terrae suae solo et caelo acrius animantur).[1] So the debate goes on, with much that is suggestive. Some moderns have gone very far in the same direction. In temperate lands, says Buckle in 1867, people must work hard for food, and are therefore bold-spirited; Nature is not overwhelming, and there can arise a will to understand it, as happened first in ancient Greece, and even to manage it, as modern Europe has done. 'Le despotisme convient aux pays chauds, la barbarie aux pays froids', says Rousseau, 'et la bonne police aux régions intermédiaires' (remarks not very consistent with his own theory of the 'social contract'). Already in 1586 Bodin had cited Aristotle for climate affecting national characters, to which modes of government should be adapted. Montesquieu had been specially elaborate. Cold Europe, he argued, produces vigorous and hard-working men, needing much food and drink, and with tempers bold and active and free, and Nature adds many mountains, where freedom is easily defended; within Europe the north is particularly valiant, and the English are made by their weather irritable and intolerant of tyranny; southern Asia, too hot and fertile, is the home of soft and slack and timid peoples, and of despotism and slavery and monkish religions. This is important for the development of the modern historical method in political science; but nowadays such large simplifications are out of fashion. Ratzel and others, indeed, stress the influence of environment, including climate as only one of many factors. But this geographical determinism is often overstrained and rouses objections: for instance, islanders have not always been sailors, and the English themselves were shepherds and farmers for long before they really took to the sea; also men have reacted increasingly against their environment, clearing forests and draining marshes and so on, till they are very far from being slaves of Nature. The matter is now rather put thus: a region has possibilities, which are variously chosen and used at various periods. Some peoples have not had the wit or the will to use great natural advantages, while for others adverse conditions have been a challenge (according to Toynbee each of a score of civilizations has been a response to a challenge of some sort).

---

1 Tac. *Germ.* 29. Celts, Livy, XXXVIII, 17, cp. Polybius, IV, 21. Rule, Plin. III, 31. Objects, Str. 103, 823, 826: Rainaud, op. cit. p. 1527. Pos. ap. Str. 33, 41, 96 and in Vitruvius, VI, 1, 1–10, VIII, 3, Manilius, IV, 711–43, Plin. II, 189–90, Ptol. *Tetrabiblos*, II, 2: Reinhardt, *Poseidonios*, 1921, pp. 74–87: Norden, op. cit. pp. 107–15. Wits, Eur. *Med.* 829 as Cic. *de Fato*, 7, *N.D.* II, 6, 17: 'Boeotum in crasso iurares aere natum', Hor. *Ep.* II, 1, 244, cp. Juv. x, 50 (Abdera). All three, Arist. *Pol.* VII, 6, 4: slaves, ibid. I, 6, 1255a. Plato, *Laws*, 747d. Hec., Norden, op. cit. p. 60 as Jacoby, and Anderson's ed. of Tac. *Germ.* 1938, xiv. Hdt. I, 142, III, 106, II, 35, 77, cp. nation, ibid. VIII, 144. Specializations, Fleure, *Races of Mankind*, 1927, pp. 14, 26, 38; *Introd. to Geography*, 1929, p. 75. Ark, Captain Best in Hakluyt, Everyman ed. v, 181.

GREEK THEORY TO ARISTOTLE

The character of a nation is mainly the result of nurture, of many experiences besides climatic, and it can be often made and remade. It is allowed that some climates are overpowering, as in the tropical rain-belt or the Arctic zone. Elsewhere, too, climate has its importance, of course. Has it not made the British adaptable and opportunist and 'humorous grousers'? 'The waterways opened into the Mediterranean and the Baltic have given to Europe', says Fisher, 'a climate so temperate...as to provide the most favourable physiological stimulus to activity and enterprise', except for the cold dark winters of Russia. And again, 'in the western half of Europe man has been assisted both by climate and by geography. Rolling hills or mountain ranges relieve the monotony of the level spaces. Comparatively speaking, the cleansing sea is always a neighbour....Everything facilitates the movement of men, the intermixture of races, and the development of an active habit of thought and enterprise.' (Yet civilization did not begin in Europe, and North America with all its advantages had for ages only a scanty population of Indian hunters, who never managed to tame the bison and develop even a nomadic culture; but then the bison was not tamable, nor anything in America unless the llama.) There seem to be certain best conditions for human energy, a fairly marked seasonal contrast, some rain throughout the year, and variable weather, and within Europe these are found in the north-west rather than the Mediterranean, which was, of course, most praised by the ancients themselves. A great psychologist's view is that in the long prehistoric ages geographical environment was the main factor in producing different races, directly by its influence on each generation and by weeding out the strains least adapted to it, indirectly by determining occupations or modes of life and therefore social organization; with civilization racial change became relatively slight, as the types already formed persisted and men were more able to subdue or adapt their environment.[1]

[1] McDougall, *The Group Mind*, 1920, esp. pp. 200–38. Best conditions, E. Huntington, *Human Habitat*, 1928, pp. 141–6, *Civ. and Climate*³, 1924 (criticized by W. Fitzgerald, *The New Europe*, 1945, p. 237). Kendrew, *Climates of the Continents*³, 1941, pp. 226–7. H. A. L. Fisher, *Hist. of Europe*², 1938, I, 9. Ellen C. Semple, *Influences of Geogr. Environment on the Basis of Ratzel's System of Anthropo-Geography*, 1911, esp. ch. 17: on old exaggerations, ibid. pp. 18–22, R. de C. Ward, *Climate*², 1918, pp. 221–2, Brunhes, *Human Geography*, 1920, pp. 525–8, Hertz, *Race and Civ.* 1928, pp. 300–4, Ernest Barker, *National Character*, 1927, ch. 3, esp. pp. 51, 69–81 (grousers, p. 79): E. E. Sikes, *Anthropology of the Greeks*, 1914, pp. 79–84. Toynbee, *Study of History*, 1934, I, 249–71. G. East, *The Geogr. behind History*, 1938, pp. 12, 37. Febvre, *Geogr. Introd. to Hist.* 1925, esp. pp. 91–8. C. D. Forde, *Habitat, Economy and Society*², 1937, pp. 463–5. Marett, *Anthropology*, 1914, ch. 4. Nurture, Barker, p. 7: Pollard, *Factors in Mod. Hist.*³ 1932, pp. 25–6. On French theories, ibid. p. 153: J. B. Bury, *Idea of Progress*, 1921, pp. 38, 102–3, 146–7: Preserved Smith, *Hist. of Modern Culture*, 1930–4, II, 206–9: E. G. R. Taylor, *Late Tudor and Early Stuart Geography*, 1934, pp. 133–7: A. Wolf, *Hist. of Science...in 16th and 17th Centuries*, 1935, pp. 583–7. Some medieval

One consideration detracts from the value of ancient writings on peoples and their customs. In this literary type as in others they were apt to follow approved models, and they appear unduly ready to transfer old clichés to new peoples. So the accounts of Thracians and Scythians are echoed in those of Gauls and Germans. Here no doubt the early formula held fairly good, and there were fresh reports which seemed to confirm it, though it is odd that the very cattle of Germany should be small and hornless like the Scythian. But some customs are too freely ascribed: too many tribes hold their women in common, or kill off their old men, or have no temples or images of gods. There is also a persistent tendency to idealize the simple life. So, after a pattern older than Herodotus, who knew better, the Scythians are just and honest, need no written laws, and are ignorant of the use of gold and silver. This is glibly repeated about other remote peoples, and the remotest are very near Utopia. Sometimes the colours are palpably borrowed from philosophic Utopias, as when the Scythians are said to have a communism of women 'in Plato's way' (that such group marriage or promiscuity ever existed is quite improbable).[1]

§ 2. THE EARTH AS A GLOBE

Despite some wonderful intuitions the Ionians had remained very backward in astronomy, keeping a flat earth and hardly observing the planets and their movements. Two ancient statements ascribing the earth-globe to Anaximander or even Thales are bad mistakes, and it is shocking that they should be carelessly repeated in some recent books. It was elsewhere, among the western colonists, that the globe was first mooted. Just when and how it appeared, and how it came to be more widely accepted and applied in earnest to geography, all this is still rather obscure. By the accounts it seems to have been reached in a very Greek way, as a by-product of general philosophizing. Before this time, no doubt, Greek sailors going north had seen southern stars set and the Bear rise higher and had noted the lengthening day. These things and the round-edged shadow

---

observations, Kimble, *Geogr. in Middle Ages*, 1938, pp. 176–80. Fleure, *Geogr. Factors*, 1921, p. 5 dislikes the term geogr. 'controls'. See also E. R. A. Seligman, *Econ. Interpretation of History*[2], 1912, pp. 10–15: Viljoen, *Economics of Primitive Peoples*, 1936, pp. 12–22: Teggart, *Theory of History*, 1925, pp. 171–7: C. Dawson, *Progress and Religion*, 1931, pp. 55–9: Goldenweiser, *History, Psychology, and Culture*, 1933, pp. 112–16: P. W. Bryan, *Man's Adaptation of Nature*, 1937, pp. 7–11: Hertz, *Nationality in History and Politics*, 1944, pp. 37–45, 316–19: Carr-Saunders, *Population Problem*, 1922, chs. 15, 17.

[1] Ephorus ap. Str. 300 (Πλατωνικῶς). Kill old, see p. 64, n. 2: women, p. 57, n. 1. Cattle, Tac. *Germ.* 5, cp. Hdt. IV, 29 and Hippocr. (also Str. 307). Schroeder, *de Ethnographiae ant. locis quibusdam communibus*, 1921: Trüdinger, *Stud. zur Gesch. der griech.-röm. Ethnographie*, 1918: and esp. Norden, op. cit. pp. 56 f., criticized by Anderson, op. cit. pp. xxvii–xxxvi, who defends Tac.

at eclipses are presently cited as confirmations of the globe, but not as having suggested it in the first instance.

Pythagoras was an Ionian who migrated to south Italy about 530 B.C. and started what was at first rather perhaps a moral and religious revival than a school of philosophy. He left no writings, and soon became a legendary figure, piously credited with all the discoveries of his sect, so that it was quite uncertain which doctrines were really his. He is nebulous already for Aristotle, who prefers to speak of 'the so-called Pythagoreans' or 'the mathematicians' in general. Unlike the Ionians they did not seek a primal substance but concentrated on the forms of things as more significant. As numbers underlie forms, defining the undefined, so 'they saw in numbers many analogies to things that are and become'. 'They thought that the whole heaven is harmony and number'. (Harmony itself is number, they knew, having discovered that tones are in ratio to lengths of string.) Ten is 'perfect' and embraces the whole 'nature' of numbers; so the bodies moving in the heaven must be ten. As those visible are only nine, namely the heaven of fixed stars, the five planets, and sun and moon and earth, they invented a tenth, the counter-earth. The 'perfect' figures are sphere and circle; so the earth, like the other bodies, must be a sphere and revolve in a circle. Round what? A central fire, for the centre is the 'worthiest' position, and fire is the 'worthiest' to occupy it. (The earth goes round the fire west-east in a day and night, and the sun round the fire in a year.) Why do we never see the central fire? Because our face of the globe is always turned away from it. Or the counter-earth? Because the central fire always lies between. The distances of the bodies are supposed to conform to a musical scale and the movements to produce a literal harmony. It was by such arbitrary and mystical reasoning, not by observation, that 'the Pythagoreans' got their ten moving spheres including the earth. So says Aristotle anyhow, though he allows that they did find a use for the counter-earth, to explain why the moon's eclipses are relatively frequent, and they claimed to account for the observed facts as easily as those who placed the earth in the centre. Elsewhere this peculiar system is attributed specially to Philolaus—of him more presently—who 'held that the earth revolves round the fire in an oblique circle, in the same direction as the sun and the moon'.[1] Alcmaeon, a younger contemporary of

---

[1] (Theophrastus? ap.) Aet. III, 13, 2, II, 7, 7, *Dox.* 377–8: Heath, *Greek Astr.* pp. 32–3: Dreyer, op. cit. pp. 40–9: Duhem, *Système du Monde*, 1913, I, 11–21. Arist. *Metaph.* I, 5, *de Caelo*, II, 13 (and harmony, ibid. II, 9, 291 *a*): Heath, op. cit. pp. 30, 34 and his *Aristarchus*, 1913, pp. 105–15. Eclipses, Reymond, *Hist. des Sciences exactes dans l'Ant.* 1924, pp. 160–2. Mistakes, Aet. III, 10, Diog. Laert. II, 1, rejected by Dreyer, op. cit. pp. 13–14, Berger, *Erdkunde*, pp. 32–4, etc. but repeated in Draper and Lockwood, *Story of Astronomy*, 1940, p. 19, Johnstone, *Study of Oceans*, 1926, p. 32 and even Cambr. *Comp. to Greek Studies*[4], 1931, p. 232.

Pythagoras, is said to have discovered that the planets and the sun and moon have separate orbits west-east opposite to the motion of the heaven of fixed stars. As for Pythagoras himself there is a statement that he was the first to call the heaven a kosmos and the earth round, meaning probably spherical, while Parmenides was the first to do so in writing (according to a better source the latter was the first to do so at all).[1] Each is also credited even with dividing the globe 'after the measure of the heaven-sphere into five circles or zones, arctic, summer, equatorial, winter, and antarctic.'[2] Some have refused the globe itself to either, as Schaefer in a special essay on the development of ancient views about the shape and size of the earth. On the evidence we may perhaps be content with 'the Pythagoreans'. Many moderns, however, refer to Pythagoras himself the 'perfect' globe, though as yet resting in the centre, like Anaximander's drum, of which it may be an improved version. (Burnet goes so far as to suppose that he argued from the round shadow at eclipses.)[3] Yet, if the globe was propounded so early, it is not easy to understand why there is no surely datable trace till Plato, and some now reduce it to his time and deny that so important a discovery was made in such a rough and purely speculative fashion as reported, and that scientific proofs were added only later as afterthoughts.[4]

Parmenides, also of Italy (about 475?), though not of the same school, apparently borrowed its cosmology, or something like it, to describe what he thought an illusive world of appearances. He speaks in high poetic language of many 'crowns' or rings to an outermost of unmixed fire, and the midmost, the earth, is balanced unsupported, recalling Anaximander's drum surrounded by fire-filled wheels. He is usually understood as meaning a globe, and as either repeating it from Pythagoras and being the first to publish it, as mentioned above, or himself reaching it because it is the

---

1 Better, Theophr. ap. D.L. IX, 21 as cp. Favorinus ap. D.L. VIII, 48: Rey, *Jeunesse de la Science grecque*, p. 430. Alcmaeon, Aet. II, 16, Dreyer, op. cit. p. 38: yet his sun flat, ibid. p. 40, *Dox.* 352, 359: Tannery, *Pour l'Hist. de la Science hellène*², 1930, p. 214.

2 Pyth., Aet. III, 14, 1, *Dox.* 378. Parm., Aet. III, 11, 1, *Dox.* 377: Pos. ap. Str. 94, 111: see also p. 113, n. 2, p. 116, n. 3.

3 *Legacy of Greece*, 1922, p. 64, but cp. Heath. Drum, Burnet, *Greek Phil.* 1924, p. 44: Gilbert, *Meteor. Theorien*, p. 282 (P. or a successor?). P. himself, Duhem, p. 5: Heath, *G.A.* XXVIII, *L.G.* p. 113, and *Aristarchus*, pp. 48–9 (and zones, ibid. pp. 64–5): Tannery, loc. cit.: Berger, *Erdkunde*, p. 185: Dreyer, p. 38. P. or one of earliest pupils?, Günther, *Gesch. der Erdkunde*, 1904, p. 22. Pythagoreans, Sarton, *Introd. to Hist. of Science*, 1927, I, 73 (Parm. zones, ibid. p. 85): school started from Anax. and probably early globe, A. E. Taylor in *Eur. Civ.* ed. Eyre, 1935, III, 750–1. Essay, W. Schaefer, 1868, pp. 12–13 here following Forbiger, *Alte Geogr.* I, 45–6.

4 E. Frank, *Plato u. die sogenannten Pythagoreer*, 1923, pp. 67, 71, 184. But cp. Heidel, *Frame*, p. 98: Singer, *Short Hist. of Science*, 1941, p. 21.

GREEK THEORY TO ARISTOTLE

'perfect' figure.[1] Some accept also the ancient statements ascribing zones to him, including a torrid zone which is twice as broad as was later conceived and implies a huge globe. But others reject these as a misunderstanding of something else in an obscure poem, perhaps the rings round the old earth-disk.[2]

Oenopides, about 430 B.C., is said to have 'discovered' the obliquity of the ecliptic or to have claimed this discovery of Pythagoras; rather he may have defined the concept more exactly. Herodotus has an incredulous mention of a northern people who 'sleep' (or have a night of) six months; is he here unconsciously giving as a travel report what was really an inference from the globe theory already in the air? (Elsewhere he has Greece in a temperate belt between too hot and too cold, but with his flat earth is helpless to explain such things, of course.) It is improbable that Xenophanes had said something about a night—not an eclipse—a month long, as Berger supposes. As late as 400 B.C. Democritus still has the earth as a slightly concave disk, quite ignoring the rival theory; from this ignorance some doubt if the globe theory was already current, but his astronomy was strangely backward.[3]

At the same time Socrates explains—or Plato represents him as explaining—how he had once been curious whether the earth is flat or round (meaning no doubt spherical), and had hoped to learn from Anaxagoras. The latter thought only of a concave disk, as we have seen, so that the other suggestion must have come from elsewhere. Socrates proceeds, in the imaginative style of 'myth' in which Plato announces a provisional sort of truth on such uncertain matters, to describe the earth as hanging unsupported in the middle of a spherical universe. The known part from the Pillars to the Phasis, where we dwell like ants or frogs round a pool, is a deep hollow; it is covered with air and mist through which we cannot see the pure heaven, though others, far better and happier than we, can see this from the true surface or the 'pure earth'. This last is a globe, and of quite

---

1 Rey, op. cit. pp. 364, 433–5: Heath, *G.A.* xxx and *Aristarchus*, p. 64 (Parm. first published): Dreyer, p. 20: Gilbert, op. cit. pp. 106, 682. Robin, *Greek Thought*, 1928, p. 90 hesitates, as Bréhier, *Hist. de la Phil.* 1926, I, 62. Only old disk, Heidel, *Frame*, pp. 70, 91. Globe with liquid fire kernel, if Diels right on fr. 12 and Aet. II, 7, 1, Ueberweg-Praechter, *Gesch. der Phil.* 1926, I, 86.

2 So Heidel, op. cit. pp. 76, 80, 91, as Reinhardt, *Kosmos u. Sympathie,* 1926, p. 361 (but R. admits globe). Accept, Berger, pp. 204–13, Rehm-Vogel, p. 12, Heath, *Aristarchus*, p. 66, Rey, p. 439: perhaps Günther, loc. cit.: Wilamowitz, *Lesebuch*, 1902, I, 182: R. de C. Ward, *Climate*², 1918, p. 21.

3 Doubt, Frank, op. cit. p. 185. Ignoring, Rey, op. cit. p. 409. Xen., see p. 97, n. 1. Temperate, Hdt. I, 142, cp. II, 22, IV, 27, Berger, p. 123. Inference, Dreyer. p. 39 after Berger, p. 195 on Hdt. IV, 24. Oen., Eudemus in Theo Smyrn. p. 198, ed. Hiller, Aet. II, 12, 2: Dreyer, p. 38: see also p. 153, n. 1.

extravagant size, as the Mediterranean basin is only a 'small fraction', one of many deep niches. The basin is really the old concave disk, but now put on the surface of a huge globe. Of a scientific division into zones there is no hint, and the globe conception appears still quite novel and tentative.[1] Two young men taking part in the same dialogue are said to have heard the Pythagorean Philolaus, who had come to Greece; but the mention is casual, and there is no word of the globe moving round a central fire, the theory ascribed to him elsewhere. (Burnet cannot accept it as his, and he is almost as shadowy as the founder of his school.) Much earlier, in a comedy attacking Socrates, there are some gibes at attempts to measure the earth, but these hardly seem to concern the globe.[2]

Plato himself met Pythagoreans during his western journeys and learnt that the planets have regular courses in a direction opposite that of the fixed star heaven. His friend Archytas may have attempted to 'measure earth and sea and the numberless sands' (it is unlikely that this reference is a mere mistake for the later Archimedes, who casually mentions an estimate of the globe by somebody). It has been held that only this generation of the school were really 'the mathematicians' and authors of the globe itself and of the 'Philolaic' system, so that Plato may have got the 'perfect' globe from Archytas.[3] If so, he showed no interest in any attempt at precise measurement.

Certainly it was Plato's adoption that gave the globe a wider currency. He is said to have 'removed the odium of physical studies' at Athens, but indeed he was quite averse from them. Nature as revealed by observation seems to him only half-real, a shadowy copy of the unseen but real world of ideal Forms, which can be grasped only by reason: so there is a 'true' astronomy to be sought behind the complexity of the visible movements with which the astronomer deals. (Plato is meagre on them and never knew much.)[4]

---

1 Heidel, *Frame*, p. 78: Frank, op. cit. pp. 184–6. Disk on globe, Rey, op. cit. p. 432. Flat or round, Phaedo, 97*d*–99*a*, niches, 108*d*–111*c*: see esp. Robin's ed. 1926, LXVII. Plato as a literary artist, like Aristophanes, takes liberties with Socrates, who really had no interest in natural science (see Xen. *Mem.* I, 1, 14), thinks A. Platt, *Nine Essays*, 1927, pp. 188–200: much is Plato's own, Cornford, *Before and After Socrates*, 1932, pp. 56, 75 (against Burnet and Taylor).

2 Aristophanes, *Clouds*, p. 204, despite Berger, p. 221, Dreyer, p. 173: see p. 102, n. 1. Burnet, *G.P.* p. 92 and *Early G.P.*[3] p. 297. 'Philolaus' sums up Pythagoreans of 450–400 B.C., Rey, op. cit. p. 307, *Maturité de la Pensée scient. en Grèce*, 1939, pp. 8–9.

3 Frank, op. cit. pp. 71, 77, 186, planets, p. 205: Glotz-Cohen, *Hist. grecque*, III, 467–9 (1936). Measure, Hor. *Odes*, I, 18. Archimedes, see p. 154, n. 1.

4 Dreyer, pp. 60, 67. 'True', already *Rep.* 527–30: Duhem, op. cit. p. 94: Farrington, *Science in Ant.* p. 127, *Science and Politics*, pp. 46, 138: Glotz-Cohen, op. cit. p. 430. Disastrous, Dampier-Whetham, *Hist. of Science*, 1929, pp. 28, 31: Singer, op. cit. pp. 33–4: Platt, op. cit. p. 13: Friend and Feibleman, op. cit. pp. 29, 72: some defence by De Burgh, op. cit. p. 143. See p. 94, n. 1. Odium, Plut. *Nic.* 23.

That way lies no good for natural science, and in fact his influence was to be disastrous for it.

Already in the myth of the *Republic* we hear of the music of the spheres. Latterly his imagination turns more and more to the number-mysticism of the Pythagoreans. In the same vein of 'probable myth' as before, he makes one of them, Timaeus, discourse on the work of the Creator, who is a great Geometer. The heavenly bodies are gods, entrusted with part of the work. Only regular and uniform motions in 'perfect' circles are 'suitable' for such beings, an assumption never to be shaken off till Kepler decided for ellipses. The earth, however, is not one of the revolving bodies but at the centre, with the moon and sun and five outer planets going round it.[1] This seems inconsistent with its rotating about its own axis in twenty-four hours, despite an obscure passage saying that 'the earth, packed round the axis which extends through the universe, was created as guardian and artificer of night and day'.[2] Of special interest for geography is a 'myth' of another kind, that about Atlantis, and in particular his fancy of another continent beyond the Atlantic: here the globe is still conceived as very large. Was he the first also to imagine Opposite-feet or Antipodes? Only one notice gives the credit elsewhere, to 'the Pythagorean Memoirs', meaning the founder himself or some nameless follower, who described the earth as 'ball-shaped and inhabited round about' (περιοικουμένην) and said that 'there are also Antipodes, and our down is their up'.[3]

Eudoxus of Cnidus had studied with Archytas and now drew some inspiration from Plato, though not of his school (about 370 B.C.). Plato set the problem, we hear, how to explain the shocking irregularities of the planets and 'save the appearances', while keeping the assumption of regular circular movements about one centre, the earth at rest. Eudoxus answered with an ingenious system of 26 concentric spheres, moving round differently orientated axes, a beautiful piece of geometry, says Heath, and the first attempt to furnish a mathematical basis for astronomy. Towards the end Plato is said on good authority to have repented of giving the earth the central position of which something else was 'worthier', presumably fire,

---

1 From Archytas, thinks Frank, op. cit. pp. 122, 128. A stage just before 'Philolaus', Rey, *Jeunesse*, p. 413, *Maturité*, p. 8. Motions, *Tim.* 39e, 40a: probable, ibid. 29c, 48d: ratios apparently musical, ibid. 35b, cp. *Rep.* 617b.

2 *Tim.* 40b: Arist. *de Caelo*, II, 13, 293b, 14, 296a: Cic. *Acad. Pr.* II, 123. Not rotation, Heath, *Aristarchus*, p. 174 (cp. *G.A.* XLIV), Dreyer, pp. 71–8, Duhem, pp. 85–9, Rivaud's ed. pp. 59–62: but cp. Cornford, *Plato's Cosmology*, 1937, pp. 120–34. Not round but up and down axis of universe, Burnet, *E.G.P.* pp. 301–3, *G.P.* p. 348, A. E. Taylor, *Plato*, 1926, pp. 448–9.

3 Alex. Polyhistor ap. D.L. VIII, 26. Heidel, *Frame*, p. 84. Plato first, D.L. III, 24 (in *Tim.* 63a, Frank, op. cit. p. 186). Arist. first, thinks Burton, *Disc. of Anc. World*, 1932, p. 47 (habitable S. temp. zone). Huge globe, *Tim.* 24e.

though many deny this and can see no sign of the change in his latest writings.[1]

Eudoxus also wrote a text-book of the stars, which was for long much admired and commented upon. Perhaps his, as many infer, was the earliest known figure for the circumference of the globe, 400,000 stades, which Aristotle accepts rather casually from 'the mathematicians', without explaining how it was got. No doubt the method was to measure the height of a star at two places approximately on the same meridian. Probably the star was Canopus, just above the horizon at Cnidus but rising high in Egypt (Eudoxus is said to have stayed there, observing with the priests). The marked difference in so short a distance indicated that the earth-globe must have a pronounced curvature, and therefore be very small relatively to the universe. The figure is still vastly in excess, however, being over 44,000 miles on the ordinary stade (or 39,000 on the short) instead of the real 25,000 miles.[2]

By now the globe was really being 'divided into zones after the analogy of the heaven-sphere' (on the lines of the diagram), and thus being seriously applied to geography.[3] Even now, if the theory was good enough, there were still no accurate data for placing the tropic on the actual map, much less the arctic circle in a still unexplored north. Eudoxus, says Strabo, not a very good witness on such matters, could determine klimata or latitudes (the word now becomes part of the new globe geography and expresses the fact that a place is warmed by the sun according to the

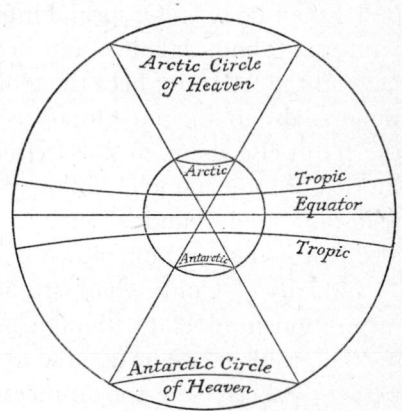

Fig. 13. Zones.

---

1 So Duhem, pp. 90–1, on *Laws*, 821–2, *Epinomis*, 987*b*: Cornford, loc. cit.: Dreyer, pp. 79–84. Theophr. ap. Plut. *Numa*, 11, *Plat. Quaest.* 8. Most accept, Burnet, *G.P.* p. 347, Taylor, *Plato*, p. 450, Berger, *Erdkunde*, p. 182, Frank, p. 205 (perhaps). Set problem, Simplicius on Arist. *de Caelo*, p. 488 (Heiberg). On Eud., Dreyer, op. cit. pp. 87–103: Heath, *C.A.H.* VII, 295: Berger, op. cit. pp. 242–8: Gisinger, *Erdbeschreibung des E.* 1921, and in *R.E.* Geogr. pp. 581–6: Tannery, *Mém. Scient.* 1925, III, pp. 366–8.

2 Arist. *de Caelo*, II, 14, 298*a*. It is E.'s, Berger, p. 265: Tannery, op. cit. VII, 342: Hultsch, *R.E.* VI, 946: Rehm-Vogel, p. 35. Perhaps, Duhem, I, 211, II, 1–4 (very doubtfully): Heidel, *Frame*, p. 97 (or Archytas?, p. 94): Dreyer, pp. 119, 173 (short stade). Burton, op. cit. p. 47 says 50,000 miles, Lambert in *Enc. Brit.* 14th ed. Geodesy about 46,000. Canopus, Str. 119. Cnidus (near Rhodes) is about 400 miles from Egypt.

3 Heidel, *Frame*, pp. 99, 102. Hipparchus *in Arati et Eudoxi Phaen.* I, 11, ed. Manitius: Mette, *Sphairopoiia*, 1936, p. XIII. Eud. first, Frank, p. 186. But Parm. first?, see p. 112, n. 2, p. 113, n. 2.

'inclination' of its horizon to the earth's axis). Aratus, who turned him into verse, stated the ratio of the longest to the shortest day for Greece in general, when it suits only the Dardanelles or thereabouts. If Eudoxus himself did this, he did not understand very well, and should not be credited with the whole method later developed by Hipparchus.[1] Aristotle realized that the tropic was the line on which the sun is at the zenith, casting no shadow, at the summer solstice, but he did not know that this was so at Aswan, as was to be learnt soon after him, and he made uninhabitable heat begin already north of the tropic, before the shadow is thrown to the south. He is blamed later for taking as the line of uninhabitable cold not the fixed arctic circle but the ever visible circle (of Athens), namely the one marking the northward limit of the stars which do not set for that place: this gives a latitude about Leeds or Hamburg and well short of Moscow! It has often been doubted whether he could have been quite so crude; but some are as bad even much later, and Scythia was supposed to become a cold desert only a short way north, and Pytheas had not yet explored northern seas or ascertained that habitable lands reached the arctic circle proper.[2]

Eudoxus stretched the length of the known world to be twice its breadth, and seems among 'the mathematicians' cited as leaving a comparatively narrow Ocean westwards from Spain to India. He is mentioned in a series of notable geographers, and a longish description of the earth, at least eight books with a map, was apparently his, as are most of the fragments under the name, though they are slight (only a few rubbishy scraps are now left for a later Eudoxus of Rhodes).[3] He may be used in various remarks of Aristotle. He drew wrongly the direction of Greece itself, pulling it eastward. Doubtfully authentic is a new theory of the Nile, otherwise ascribed to one Nicagoras or (obviously falsely) to native 'philosophers' or priests: the flood-water is said to come all the way from the south temperate zone of 'dwellers opposite', who live under the winter tropic and have winter when we under the summer tropic have summer (the wording seems loose and the whole has been suspected as an invention of

---

[1] Heidel, p. 98 against Manitius, op. cit., Berger, Gisinger, op. cit. and Heath, *Aristarchus*, p. 192. 'Climates', Str. 390, Gisinger, fr. 71, σχημάτων ἔμπειρος καὶ κλιμάτων cp. τοῖς τε κλίμασι καὶ τοῖς σχήμασι, Ps.-Scymn. 112–14 on Erat. Hipp. op. cit. I, 3, 5.

[2] Doubted, as Bunbury, *Anc. Geogr.* II, 227, Berger, *Fragm. des Erat.* p. 75 and *Erdkunde*, pp. 217, 306–8. Later, Geminus, 4, Manilius, I, 560, Cleomedes, I, 5, Macrobius, *S.S.* II, 6. On zones, Arist. *Met.* II, 5, 362 *b*: Webster in Oxf. transl. ad loc. attempts some defence: Heidel, pp. 86, 96. Arist. blamed by Pos. ap. Str. 94–5.

[3] Jacoby, *F.G.H.* II, 159. Series, Erat. ap. Str. I and Agathem. I, I (*G.G.M.* II, 471): book Plut. *Is. et Osir.* 353*c*. India, Arist. *de Caelo*, II, 14, 298*a*, Str. 64: Heidel, p. 88. Length, Agathem. I, 2, and see p. 215, n. I.

the time of the Ptolemies).¹ In one version the river is supposed to pass under the floor of an equatorial Ocean before 'emerging in our lands'.

Aristotle (384–322 B.C.) did an immense work in organizing knowledge and inspiring his school to collect all previous results and develop the various sciences, now emerging more distinctly from the general background of philosophy. Unlike Plato he values sense-perception and allows that the natural world of change may be the object of science. Sometimes he can study Nature patiently and accurately, as in his wonderful research on animals. But despite this bent he is deeply influenced by his old master's spirit. He approaches 'physics' with the assumptions of his 'first philosophy', seeking for final causes and deducing so much at the cost of observation that the result is a travesty of science.² 'We must collect the facts', he says elsewhere, and sometimes he collects a great many, but not here. The upper world is supposed to be filled with a special fifth element, ether, indestructible and having a 'natural' circular movement: so the outer sphere of the fixed stars, the First Moved and nearest the First Mover or God, has a simple and perfect movement, daily in a circle, while those of the planets are slower and more complex. Below the moon is the world of the four ordinary elements subject to change and decay; they have their natural motions, heavy earth and water down or towards the centre, light air and fire up or away from it, and they seek their 'natural places' and rest there, unless external action causes forced mixtures and movements.

Much of this is both artificial and reactionary, and the insistence on design is specially disturbing in this subject (contrast the moderns who hold that the very existence of the earth is due to an unlikely accident, a disruption caused in the sun by the approach of another star). But at least he accepts the earth as a globe. Some of his reasons are curious: if it was formed by heavy particles moving down from all sides, they must have gathered in this form, and even if it was not, as he thinks, this shape is 'necessary'. He adds, however, two reasons from observation: the earth throws a round shadow on the moon at eclipses—it is not known who first used this argument, though some would ascribe it to Pythagoras himself—and the stars change as one travels north or south. But the earth must have a 'natural place', resting at the centre. So he rejects the current doctrine of its revolving round a central fire, and is forced to go back to the system

---

1 Heidel, op. cit. pp. 100–1, against Capelle, *Neue Jahrb.* 1914, p. 344, who takes N. as 5th century B.C. Aet. IV, 1, 7 ἄντοικοι: Geminus, 16, 26: *Dox.* 386. Priests, Diod. I, 40. Nic., Ps.-Arist. *Inund. Nili*, ed. Rose, p. 248. 'Aliena crescere bruma', Lucan, x, 299. Version, Mela, 1, 54. Greece, Str. 390.

2 Farrington, *Science in Ant.* p. 140 (and *Greek Science*, p. 111): Duhem, op. cit. II, 71: Cornford, *C.A.H.* VI, 333: Dreyer, op. cit. pp. 108–10, 122: Dampier-Whetham, op. cit. pp. 33–6: Hogben, *Science for the Citizen*, 1938, pp. 251, 392.

of Eudoxus, to which Callippus had already added seven spheres; he badly misunderstands this purely geometrical construction as a real machinery and has to increase the spheres to 55, a creaky affair soon discredited by its own complexity and by more knowledge of the planets.[1] But his authority was to keep the earth at the centre almost without question for twenty centuries.

The globe must be of no great size, he knows, and very tiny compared with the universe, as the stars change markedly in quite a short distance. How he accepts a rough estimate, and how he conceives the zones, two of them habitable, has been mentioned above. As for the known inhabited world, its length from Spain to India is to its breadth from Ethiopia to the Azov as over 5:3, to judge from adding up travel items, which he neither thinks very reliable nor troubles to give. The unknown interval left from Spain westwards to India, open sea and impassable, cannot be very great, he says; he adds obscurely that both India and West Africa have elephants, meaning apparently that these countries are not opposite ends of a flat earth but reasonably near each other on a globe, as the similarity in fauna seems to show. (This passage as used by Roger Bacon and borrowed from that writer by Cardinal D'Ailly had a considerable influence on Columbus.) It is evident that Aristotle has no use for Plato's Transatlantic continent. He gibes rather unfairly at the circular inhabited earth of the Ionian maps still current. He seems to avoid pronouncing on a continuous outer sea, though he assumes it south of Africa, where some were already questioning its existence, and north of Europe.[2] Scattered remarks on various regions have been quoted in the previous chapter, and some may be added here. He is interesting on rivers, though it is not quite true that the biggest rise from the highest ranges. Of these he has an exaggerated notion, asserting that the sun shines on the Caucasus peaks for four hours before sunrise and after sunset. He has a theory that the sea basins are progressively deeper from the Azov and Black Seas westwards, and that this and the number of rivers determine a certain flow, a theory soon to be developed by Strato.

1 Dreyer, pp. 112–13, Burnet, *E.G.P.* p. 347, Frank, op. cit. pp. 40, 207, Robin, *Greek Thought*, p. 289: W. D. Ross, *Aristotle*, 1923, pp. 96–9 makes some defence. On earth, esp. *de Caelo*, II, 14, ed. Guthrie (Loeb), 1939: Heath, *G.A.* pp. 90–1: Duhem, I, 211, 220: Heidel, pp. 87–8: Dreyer, pp. 115–18. The math. proofs first in Eudoxus, Kiepert, *Lehrbuch*, p. 4. Not known, Boll, *R.E.* Finsternisse. P. himself, p. 112, n. 3. Accident, Inge, *God and the Astronomers*, 1934, p. 253: J. Johnstone, *Study of the Oceans*, 1926, p. 4. Collect, *Anal. Pr.* I, 30: Whewell, op. cit. pp. 52, 59 (see p. 94, n. 1.).

2 Some, ap. Ps.-Scyl. 112, see p. 90, n. 2. North sea, *Met.* I, 13, 350b: south, II, 5, 363a. Maps, ibid. p. 362b. Spain west, ibid.: elephants, *de Caelo*, II, 14, 298a, Dreyer, p. 118: Berger, *Erat.* p. 89 and *Erdk.* p. 318. Estimate, see p. 116, n. 2: zones, p. 117, n. 2. Columbus, see p. 327, n. 1: Kimble, *Geogr. in Middle Ages*, 1938, pp. 85, 92: A. P. Newton, *Travel and Travellers of the Middle Ages*, 1926, p. 15.

He has no formal treatise on geography and touches on it chiefly in the *Meteorology*, concerned with the world of change below the moon and all the combinations of elements which go on there. The prime cause of the phenomena is the sun according as it approaches or recedes. It warms the earth and its waters and draws exhalations of two kinds. One is a vapour which, when chilled, condenses and returns to earth as rain and in other forms. The other is dry and smoke-like, and causes winds and often ignites and is ejected by the cold air as comets and the like; this is a bad relapse after the Pythagoreans had said that comets were planets appearing at long intervals.[1] (He has also a strange notion that meteorites are raised by hurricanes, against several who had explained them rightly as pieces falling from the heavenly bodies.) Winds play a large part in earthquakes and volcanic eruptions. Altogether there is a good deal of observation, but little is his own, and most is misused for a priori theorizing. 'Certainly remarkable', as a great geologist admitted, are the flashes of insight by which he sees mighty changes in the outlines of sea and land in immense periods, sometimes after a local 'great winter' of excessive rains as in the Greek version of the Flood.[2] On tides he is, it seems, queerly ignorant and wrong. In the inner sea they were hardly noticeable except at a few places like the head of the Adriatic, where the rise is 1–3 ft., and the Syrtis inlet (south of Tunisia), where it is 3–8 ft.; and indeed they were seldom noticed, though Herodotus already mentions a daily tide in a Greek bay (as also at the head of the Red Sea). Currents too were not marked enough to attract attention, except in straits. The apparent flow there is attributed by Aristotle to a 'swinging' of the sea and said to be more visible than where the sea is wide and open. Just outside Gibraltar the sea is described as shoaly and calm and lying in a hollow, though the sentence is suspect (elsewhere he is credited with the statement that winds raised by the sun push forward the Atlantic, and with another that the Iberian cliffs hurl back the sea, whereas most of the coast is really low and sandy). Alexander and his officers had not yet had their adventures with the Indian Ocean tides.[3]

---

1 *Met.* I, 6, 2, cp. 6. Basins, *Met.* II, 1, 13–14, see p. 205, n. 1. Rivers, *Met.* I, 13, 350a. Ranges, see p. 87, n. 2. Meteorology text Fobes, 1919: transl. E. W. Webster, 1923: Comm. of Ideler, 1834–6 and Saint-Hilaire, 1863 still useful. Lones, *Aristotle's Researches on Nat. Science*, 1912. Capelle in *R.E.* Suppl. 1935, pp. 338–44 (Meteorologie).

2 *Met.* I, 14. Lyell, *Principles of Geology*, 1875, I, 20–2: Lones, op. cit. pp. 48–9: C. Dawson, *Age of the Gods*, 1934, p. 4. But cp. p. 43, n. 3. Earthquakes, etc., see p. 105, nn. 1-2. Meteorites, cp. p. 100, n. 2.

3 Suspect, Webster ad *Met.* II, 1, 354a. Swinging, ibid. Duhem, op. cit. II, 267–70: Semple, *Geogr. of Med. Region*, 1932, p. 383: Mieli-Brunet, *Hist. des Sciences, Antiquité*, ch. 35, after Almagià, *Dottrina della Marea*, 1905 (doubt if A. meant tides). Aet. III, 17, Stob. I, 38, *Dox.* 382–3. Push, Berger, p. 351: Tarn, *Hell. Civ.* 1927, p. 249. Cliffs, Arist. criticized by Pos. ap. Str. 153. Hdt. VII, 198 Maliac gulf, II, 11 Red Sea. Adr., Str. 212.

GREEK THEORY TO ARISTOTLE

Not Aristotle's, though containing scraps of matter from him or his school, are various little works passing under his name. The pleasing essay *On the Universe* keeps his fifth element and many of the explanations of natural phenomena, but is full of the more religious spirit of the Stoics and especially of Posidonius. The *Wonderful Stories* is a late collection of titbits from history and natural science, like a statement that the strait of Messina waxes and wanes with the moon; part seems to be good observation from his school, but much is puerile. The *Flood of the Nile* known only in a Latin version from the Arabic, shows signs of being after Eratosthenes, though it has been strongly defended as genuine.[1]

Some things in Aristotle were to be far from healthy for science, like the central earth and the fifth element, which tended to put the upper world beyond research, and the conception that its movements control all changes of the lower. (Plato had begun this with his divine stars, and a pupil of his admired the old wisdom of the Chaldaeans, though Eudoxus rejected its pretensions.) The Stoics were to draw the full implications and give their countenance to astrology. Aristotle led physics astray, but it was not altogether his fault that the worse parts of his science were to be extravagantly respected for some 2000 years.[2]

If at this point we look back over the Greek achievement, it will be seen that geography had really advanced quite far, though in a peculiar way: it had begun as a philosophical speculation, and had still not disengaged itself from that background. But the globe was already an assured fact, and the theory of zones was beginning to be thought out. In the next period there was to be a great effort to develop the science on this basis.

It is worth noting that Copernicus himself was not an observer but argued much like the Pythagoreans and Plato, assuming 'a harmony in the motion and magnitude of the orbs' and basing his system on philosophical grounds of mathematical simplicity.[3]

1 By Partsch, 1909, followed by Rehm, *R.E.* Nilschwelle: see p. 90, n. 1. Moon, *Mir. Ausc.* 55: given in Arist. *Minor Works*, tr. Hett, Loeb, 1936. *De Mundo*, ed. Lorimer, 1933: tr. Forster, 1914. Exhalations, ibid. 4, etc.

2 Singer, op. cit. p. 50: Buckley, *Short Hist. of Physics*, 1927, p. 6. Stoics, Duhem, II, 290, 297. Plato, *Tim.* 38 e, 40 d: astrology already some influence, Boll-Bezold-Gundel, op. cit. pp. 19, 91–3: Jaeger, *Aristotle*, 1934, pp. 132, 151–5. Des Places in *Mélanges Cumont*, 1936, pp. 129–42. Planets now nicknamed Ares, etc., Cumont, *Astrology among Greeks and Romans*, 1912, p. 45, *Religions Orientales*^{2}, p. 240. Cp. p. 158, n. 2, p. 168, n. 1. Eud. ap. Cic. *de Div.* II, 42, 87.

3 Dampier-Whetham in *Background of Modern Science*, Cambridge, 1938, pp. 33–5: H. Dingle, *Science and Human Experience*, 1931, pp. 31–2 (C. cleared the ground for the observer Galileo): Friend and Feibleman, *What Science Really Means*, 1937, p. 49: J. H. Randall, *Making of the Modern Mind*, 1927, p. 229: Armitage, *Copernicus*, 1938, pp. 1, 87–90.

As regards climates, the ancients tend to divide them too sharply by lines of latitude: the amount of solar heat is the chief factor, no doubt, but they often seem not to realize clearly how much it is modified by others, like altitude, mountain-barriers, and the distribution of land and water.[1] Yet, as is discussed above, they do suggest various complications of local conditions as helping to mould the characters of peoples. We shall find Strabo, however, badly misjudging earlier accounts of Britain and deforming the map of Europe, partly because he does not grasp the effect of a maritime climate.

It should be added that some recent writers react against Frank's doubts and defend the old view ascribing the first idea of the globe to Pythagoras himself or at least to the older Pythagoreans. Parmenides is thought to have echoed them, or to have invented the globe as an improvement on Anaximander's drum.[2] As for the zones, the passage crediting them to Pythagoras seems invalidated by another giving them only to 'some Pythagoreans'.[3] Many give them to Parmenides, though it is admitted that with his broad torrid zone he had no clear notion of the tropic and that the relation of the globe to the celestial globe was obscure till Eudoxus, who was the first to draw really definite lines for the zones.[4] Plato in his earlier myth about the known earth as a niche in a huge globe may follow some Pythagorean who combined in this bold way the Ionian disk and the Pythagorean globe; his mention of Antipodes, and the description of the globe as 'inhabited round about', may come from a similar source.[5]

1 R. de C. Ward, *Climate*[2], 1918, pp. 23, 32 (he allows Strabo some fairly distinct ideas on local differences). Cp. Strabo's mistakes about Pytheas, ch. IV: p. 194, n. 2, p. 322, n. 1.

2 Gigon, *Ursprung der griech. Philosophie*, 1945, pp. 86, 285: echoed, Mondolfo in *Archeion*, 1936, p. 8. Older P., Capelle, *Die Vorsokratiker*, 1935, p. 307: also Mieli, *I Prearistotelici*, 1916, I, 289. P. himself, Ninck, *Die Entdeckung von Europa durch die Griechen*, 1945, pp. 47, 54 (by analogy from the heaven globe): Armitage, op. cit. p. 20 (globe at centre): Hyde, *Anc. Greek Mariners*, 1947, p. 8: so Mieli, loc. cit. (perhaps): Günther, *Astronom. Geographie*, 1919, p. 61. On Frank see p. 112, n. 4, p. 114, n. 3: against him E. de Strycker in *L'Ant. classique*, 1940, p. 221, citing Zeller-Mondolfo, *La Filosofia dei Greci*, I, 1938: Cherniss, *Aristotle's Criticism of Presocratic Philosophy*, 1935, pp. 393–6.

3 Galen in *Dox*. 633: Ninck, op. cit. p. 47. See p. 112, n. 2.

4 Ninck, op. cit. p. 46 (on Aristotle's blunder, rightly blamed later, ibid. p. 56). For Parm. also Capelle, loc. cit., Gigon, loc. cit., Hyde, op. cit. p. 9, P. Friedländer, *Jahrb. D. Arch. Inst.* 1914, pp. 101, 108.

5 Gisinger, *R.E.* Oikumene, § 6 and Perioikoi (1937). See p. 115, n. 3. Combined, Friedländer, op. cit. pp. 98–112.

CHAPTER IV

FROM ALEXANDER TO ERATOSTHENES

§ 1. THE EAST

IN a few sensational years Alexander marched to the Indus and back to die at Babylon (334–323 B.C.). He left only a posthumous child, and it may be doubted whether any heir could have held together an empire so huge and shapeless. Yet a great part was kept for a long time under the kingdoms founded by his officers. Though weakened by dynastic wars, they were still prosperous when the shadow of Rome began to fall their way (about 200 B.C.): the Ptolemies were secure and wealthy in Egypt, and the Seleucids, ruling from Syria, were asserting themselves again as far east as Bactria, from which independent Greek kings were soon to re-enter India.

This was the heyday of the 'Hellenistic' period, when Greek civilization was spread far and wide, if often thinly and patchily. There arose a new conception of the civilized world as including many 'barbarians', who had proved educable, though the Successors gave up Alexander's generous policy of fusion and chose rather to keep down their native subjects. It cannot be said that even in this time of close contact the Greeks were what moderns would call good observers of other peoples and cultures. They did not care to read barbarian writings, such as the Old Testament, now partly translated for the use of Greek-speaking Jews. They took little notice when natives like Manetho and Berossus produced from Egyptian and Babylonian records a little real history—mixed, indeed, with uncritical rubbish—and the pieces have been preserved only through the interest of Jews and Christians. The belles-lettres of the new capitals ignored such works as dry and unstylish, with their outlandish names, and preferred worthless writers like Hecataeus of Abdera, who gave the old accounts—with a modernistic flavour—and repeated their bad mistakes (Diodorus, who uses him, still puts dynasty XIX before the pyramid-builders of dynasty IV). It was fashionable enough to praise eastern wisdom, but only when it seemed to coincide with Greek. In return the Jews began to suggest that the Greek was borrowed from theirs, or had caught glimpses of truth from the same Divine Reason which had inspired Moses more fully, an argument later to be echoed without end by Philo and the Christian Fathers.[1]

---

[1] Already Jews of early 2nd cent. B.C. ap. Clem. *Strom.* v, 14, 97, Origen, *c. Celsum*, I, 13. Hec. ap. Diod. 1: mistakes, see p. 66, n. 1. Hec. in Jacoby, *F.G.H.* IIIA, 11–64 and *R.E.* VII, 2750–69: Wendland, *Die hell.-röm. Kultur in ihren Beziehungen zum Judentum und*

Alexander's service to geography is sometimes rather overrated: after all a good deal had been known of the Persian empire before, though surprisingly little by himself at first, it seems, if he thought that the Indus might be the upper Nile. But his triumphant march did, of course, vastly widen the practical horizon, and bring a great increase of direct and detailed knowledge. For the farther parts it long remained the prime source, with a few additions from later contacts with Bactria and India (there was, however, a certain admixture of fable and false information, as about the Caspian 'gulf', which was to be seriously misleading). Several companions left good accounts, which are reasonably fully preserved through later writers who copied them, but we should be glad of some originals like the two 'pacers' who measured the distances and described the countries with their peoples and products. The total gains for geography were well used, first by Dicaearchus, a pupil of Aristotle, and especially by Eratosthenes, who was librarian of Alexandria about 234–196 B.C. He could base his mapping on his own remarkable measurement of the globe. His book has not survived, but the gist, together with the criticisms of Hipparchus, can be fairly well recovered from Strabo.[1]

How the first half of the march compares with Xenophon's may be seen from the map given in that connection (p. 83), and little need be said of these more or less familiar regions. A good deal of inner Asia Minor was left unconquered for the moment, and later, though the Seleucids did much to spread Greek civilization here, it began to pass under half-native kings, while far-wandering Celts settled in Galatia and a kingdom of Pergamum established its right to independence by fighting these invaders. Alexander passed on to Syria, where he first encountered an army under Darius himself, near the port which still bears his name as Alexandretta or Iskanderun. He occupied Phoenicia as the chief base of the enemy's fleet, taking Tyre after a long siege. Jerusalem lay off the line of march now and later, and a supposed visit of Alexander is an invention of the Jews themselves, like some mentions of Jews attributed to writers of this time (yet two of Aristotle's pupils noticed them already and, rather oddly, as a community of 'philosophers'). Egypt submitted readily, and here was built the greatest

Christentum, 1912, p. 116. Already Theophr. and Clearchus on Jews, ibid. p. 195. Few studied barbarian history, Tarn, *Hell. Civ.* 1927, p. 233: E. Bevan in Marvin, *Western Races and the World*, 1922, pp. 60–5. New view of barbarians, Erat. ap. Str. 66: Plut. *de Alex. fort.* I, 6: Haarhoff, *The Stranger at the Gate*, 1938, p. 69.

1 Berger, *Geogr. Fragm. des Erat.* 1880, and *Erdkunde*², 1903, pp. 384–441: Thalamas, *Géogr. d'Érat.* (and *Étude bibliographique*), 1921: Bunbury, *Anc. Geogr.* I, 615–60: Knaack, *R.E.* VI, 358–77 (1909): Gisinger, *R.E.* Geogr. p. 604: St Martin, *Hist. de la Géogr.* 1873, pp. 130–40. Pacers: Diognetus and Baeton, Erat. ap. Str. 574, Plin. VI, 61, Athen. X, 442 b. Sources for Alex., Jacoby, *F.G.H.* IIB, 1929. His march, Tarn, *C.A.H.* VI. Hell. monarchies (301–218 B.C.) in *C.A.H.* VII.

Alexandria, on a site wonderfully well chosen, just west of the delta and away from the river's silt: almost at once it outstripped the older cities and trading centres, Athens and Syracuse and Carthage. A picturesque episode was the excursion along the desert road and inland to consult the oracle at the oasis of Siwa (the story exaggerates the difficulties). Returning to Syria, Alexander passed by Damascus to the Euphrates bend. From there he marched not down the river like Xenophon but eastward to cross

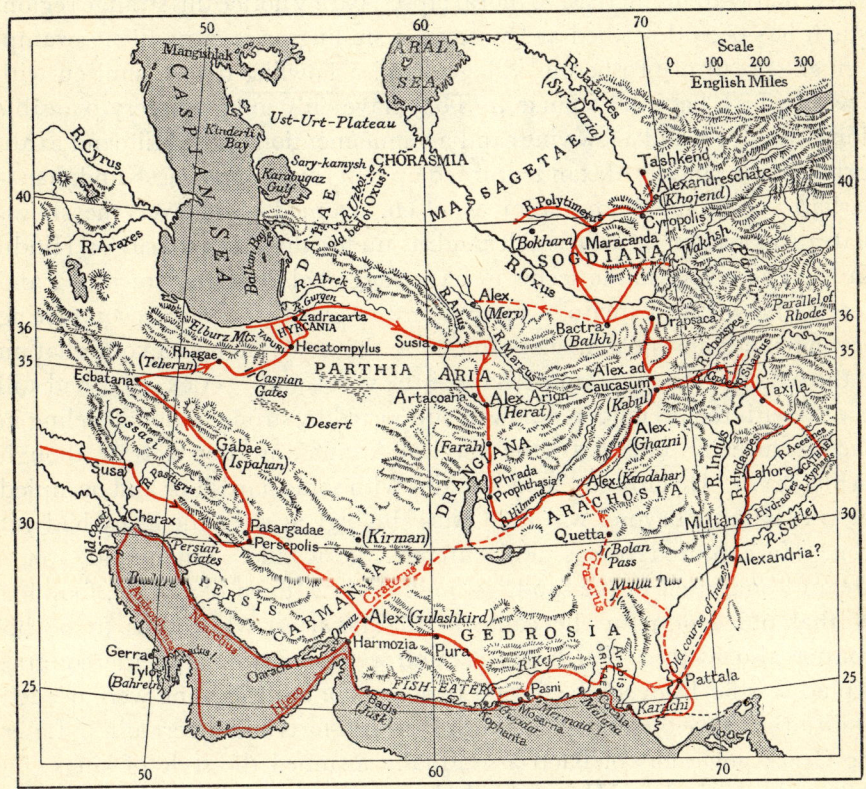

Fig. 14. Alexander's March.

the Tigris above the ruins of Nineveh and win his crowning victory. He let the beaten king escape by the passes to Media, and turned south to take Babylon and the treasures at Susa.

Henceforth the country was far less known (see map above). Pushing through the brigand hill-tribes, he forced the Persian Gates and entered the old national capital in the central plateau of Persis. He then turned sharp north-west by the desert and Ispahan to strike the fugitive king's route at Ecbatana (Hamadan), an old royal residence. He pressed the chase to a pass called the Caspian Gates, which was to be a crucial point for the mapping of these parts. Four days beyond he found the king murdered by a pretender, one Bessus. Having spent some time subduing the Caspian tribes in their wooded hills, he moved eastward to country where the rivers already lost themselves in desert, as at the oasis of Merv; he may himself have founded this place later, and the Seleucids rebuilt it and walled it off against the nomads. He had to make a wide detour south to subject Aria, where he founded Herat, and on to the changing lake-delta of Seistan; the writers, concerned with his increasing moral lapses, barely notice this strange region, which has been described as 'by turns a smiling oasis, a pestilent swamp, a huge spread of prosperous villages, and a howling desert, smitten with a wind which becomes a curse'. (They have only some not very plausible things about tin and a few vines and a vague mention of the Hilmend as absorbed in the sands.) Alexander turned up that river and so past Kandahar—perhaps not named from him as often assumed—and over the snowy plateau to winter in a little Alexandria under the Paropanisus or Hindu Kush. The native name seems to have suggested 'Indian Caucasus', and not, as the writers explain, a mere desire to glorify the hero as conquering beyond the famous Caucasus; some took the new range as a continuation of the old, and the ignorant perhaps as the very same![1] Alexander had still to deal with the pretender, who was supported by strong national feeling in Bactria, already praised as 'the jewel of Ariana', as later of Iran, though partly desert. He crossed the mountains with some hardships and occupied Bactra (Balkh); beyond was the Oxus, the biggest river the army had yet seen. He captured Bessus, and entered Maracanda (Samarcand), on a stream losing itself in the sands as now. Past a 'town of Cyrus', founded by that old conqueror, he came to the Jaxartes, which was to be his frontier also, with a 'Farthest Alexandria' (Khojend). But the country behind was far from subdued, and two years of hard fighting were needed against the brave Sogdian chiefs with their hill-forts and desert allies. Later the Greek governors of Bactria gradually assumed the style of kings (by 228 B.C.): Antiochus III came all the way to assert his suzerainty, but shrank from weakening civilization in the face of nomad enemies and made terms (208–206 B.C.), and presently the Seleucids lost all hold of Iran. The isolated Bactrian kingdom had a short but stirring life, with adventures deep into India; very regrettably only scraps of its story survive (it is remarkable for producing some of the finest of Greek coins). A reaction

---

[1] Bunbury, I, 484: some soldiers, Erat. ap. Arr. v, 3, 2, cp. v, 5, 3. Seistan, Sir T. Holdich, *Gates of India*, 1910, pp. 81, 201–3. Sands, Arr. IV, 6, 6, cp. Curt. VIII, 9, 10. Tin, Str. 724. Merv, Str. 516, Plin. VI, 46–7. Pupils, Clearchus and Theophr.: Bevan in *Legacy of Israel*, 1927, p. 31. Hec. of Abdera on Jews in Diod. XL, 3, Josephus, *Against Apion*, I, 186, II, 43 (not all really Hec.). Vivid Pergamene sculptures of Galatians, including the 'Dying Gladiator', Grenier, *Les Gaulois*, 1945, pp. 27–30.

of the east had begun when a tribe of Dahae nomads beyond the Caspian thrust south astride the main road to found the Parthian Kingdom (248 B.C.); it was to do much against the Seleucids and even the Romans, but as yet it hardly mattered.[1]

Alexander made a short raid on the 'Scythians' beyond his frontier river, and there was one later crossing, by Demodamas, an officer of Seleucus and his son, perhaps to drive back an invasion and cover the rebuilding of Khojend (about 270 B.C.). But no rumour came of the vast regions beyond the roof of Asia. On the contrary, it was believed that the Ocean was quite near, sweeping round from a Caspian 'gulf'. Very strangely this notion of a gulf came into fashion just when knowledge should have improved.[2] For a moment, it seems, Alexander's companions thought otherwise: they took the sea as a lake (perhaps an overflow of the Azov?) and made the Jaxartes pass round north of it to become the Tanais or Don, so that it formed the continental boundary (Strabo says that the motive was to flatter Alexander as having conquered all Asia to the frontier of Europe). But soon they said that it flowed to the Caspian 'gulf'. So did the Oxus too, they declared, thus providing a handy trade-route from India, and all antiquity repeats the statement.[3] Yet it was probably ill-founded. Alexander never touched the lower course, though he received a Chorasmian prince, who offered help to conquer some neighbours, the Colchians and Amazons (later legend brought him to the Caucasus to build gates against the Scythians or Gog and Magog). Just before his death he meant to send an officer, one Heraclides, to find out if the sea was a gulf, but nothing was done.[4] Presently the chief authority was Patrocles, a governor in these eastern parts (about 285–280 B.C.). He asserted that both rivers ran into that sea, and gave the distance between the two mouths (80 parasangs or 2400 stades) among other figures; he thought the sea about the same size as the Black, and misconceived it hopelessly as a squat bottle with a long narrow neck, by which one might sail into the Ocean and so round to India. (Pliny misread him as actually doing this impossible voyage, and even this blunder was to be not without effect on geography, being cited in Elizabethan times as evidence for the

1 Dahae Parni from the Ochus (Tejend), Apollodorus of Artemita ap. Str. 509, 515. Terms, Polybius, x, 49, xi, 34. Jewel, Str. 516. On B. esp. Tarn, *Greeks in Bactria and India*, 1938.

2 Near, Arr. *Anab.* v, 26. Dem. briefly, Plin. vi, 49. Tarn, *J.H.S.* 1940, p. 92.

3 Patrocles ap. Str. 509 (navigable, Aristobulus, ibid.): Str. 73: Varro ap. Plin. vi, 52. Don, see p. 85, n. 1. Flatter, Str. 509–10. Overflow, Plut. *Alex.* 44, some ap. Curt. vi, 4, 18, Arr. vii, 11, 1.

4 Arr. vii, 16. Prince, ibid. iv, 15, 4, and see p. 141, n. 1 (Amazons). Gog, see p. 28, n. 2.

feasibility of a north-east passage to China.)[1] Of the Aral, to which both rivers flow to-day, there is no sure description by any western traveller until the Byzantine envoy Zemarchus (about A.D. 570).

What is to be made of all this? It is certain that two seas already existed, though they had been one in prehistoric times. Also the Jaxartes, from the lie of the ground, can never have run as described. Thus the ancients were all wrong about one river, and they may well have been about the other too. In their defence some hold that a branch did then reach the Caspian by what is thought a dry river-bed traceable across the desert. There is evidence that water has occasionally overflowed in this direction as far as the Sary-kamysh depression, and Arab writers say that, when the Mongols tampered with the Aral dams, it went farther and reached the Caspian, though they had apparently no good tradition that it had ever done so before. (Some, however, accept a branch as existing in Alexander's time and down to the first century A.D., and then again in the thirteenth to sixteenth centuries.) A recent view is that Patrocles mistook the Atrek for the Oxus, and expressed the opinion that goods might be brought down this way from India, and later writers misreported the suggested trade-route as actually in use.[2] If he himself explored this coast, it is not easy to explain his figures and statements. One attempt brings him to the narrow entrance of the Karabugaz gulf to mistake this for the Oxus. Another denies this and brings him only to Balkan bay, the outlet of the Uzboi, which may or may not be an old river-bed. Another supposes that he passed the Oxus, which was really here, and that at Kinderli bay, though the distance is exaggerated, he somehow assumed the mouth of a river (the Jaxartes); perhaps too he went on to Mangishlak and mistook the eastward turn of the sea for the Ocean, as the presence of seals may have appeared to confirm.[3] But it seems likely that he never left the southern part of the sea, and that for the rest he misread native talk about the two great rivers, which in fact both flowed, as to-day, to the Aral (some of the things said then and later may have been rumours of this second sea but misapplied to the Caspian or the Azov or a supposed Ocean thereabouts). Whatever bad work or hearsay lay behind this egregious report of Patrocles, his

---

1 Plin. II, 167, VI, 58, cp. Erat. ap. Str. 69, 74. Figures, Str. 507–8, 518: Plin. VI, 36. Passage, E. G. R. Taylor in Newton, *Great Age of Discovery*, 1932, p. 214.

2 So Tarn, *Greeks in Bactria*, pp. 112–13, 488–93, after Kiessling, *R.E.* IX, 466, against Herrmann, ibid. Kasp. Meer. Accept, as Kaeppel, *Off the Beaten Track in the Classics*, 1936, p. 79: and similar Le Strange, *Lands of Eastern Caliphate*, 1905, p. 455: Barthold, *Nachr. über den Aral-See*, 1910 (from Russian): Huntington, *Pulse of Asia*[2], 1919, pp. 337–49, see p. 80, n. 1. Hennig, *T.I.* p. 185 denies the Caspian branch and gives up the figures.

3 Herrmann, *R.E.* X, 2283: seals, Str. 513. Karabugaz, K. J. Neumann, *Hermes*, 1884, pp. 165–95 as cp. H. Wagner, *Gött. Gel. Nachr.* 1885, pp. 209–27.

official position gave it respectability, and the Caspian 'gulf' was accepted as proved, with baneful results for the whole map of Asia for a long time to come.[1]

Returning across the mountains, Alexander started for India; there were no Persians left in the old Indus province, but he meant to take all they had held, and more. The main body went by the Khyber Pass, while he himself raided the fierce hill-tribes on its northern flank (a few names are easily recognizable in the modern, like Swat). Beyond the Indus Taxila was the first of many populous cities of an ancient civilization which astounded the invaders. On the Jhelum he overcame the brave rajah 'Porus', and founded two cities. There was more hard fighting to the Beas, where the weary men refused to go on, however near they might be to the Ocean. Sometimes the Indian plain is described as four months' march; he is also said to have heard of a strong kingdom only twelve days away on a bigger river than any yet, surely the Ganges and not merely the Sutlej as Tarn has argued. Various writers seize the chance for more or less wild speeches: one makes the men complain of being dragged into another world and beyond sun and stars and to an Ocean full of monsters and brooded over by perpetual darkness, 'immobiles undas in quibus emoriens Natura defecerit'. After a fit of sulks Alexander was forced to turn back and downstream. In storming a city of the Malli (not Multan) he was badly wounded, and the further progress was very slow. The geographers, not allowing for this, made the lower Indus too long; there are, too, some pardonable mistakes on the five rivers and their mutual relations, and various names are hard to place; also the main stream then had a different course, and the coast was well north of its present line. The delta suggested comparison with the Nile's. Alexander sailed down both arms, where the tidal bore caused some alarm.[2] He decided that Nearchus should explore the southern Ocean, while he would march west keeping in touch. He had already sent off Craterus with a large force by the Bolan pass.

Several companions left descriptions of the country which on the whole do not deserve the incredulous sneers of later writers. The new province

---

[1] Misread, Tarn, *Hell. Civ.* 1927, p. 194, and in *J.H.S.* 1901, pp. 10–29 (but details?): Aral, ibid. p. 21; cp. obscurities in Str. 509–10, 512–13.

[2] Arr. *Anab.* vi, 19: on tides, Ones. ap. Str. 693, Arr. *Ind.* 21, Curt. ix, 9, etc. Old course, Tarn, *C.A.H.* vi, 413 and map. Mistakes, e.g. Arr. *Anab.* vi, 21. Ocean near, ibid. v, 25–6, but cp. Nearchus ap. Arr. *Ind.* 3, Str. 689. Complain, Curt. ix, 3, 8; 4, 18. Sutlej, Tarn, *J.H.S.* 1922, p. 93, *C.A.H.* vi, 402 (on Diod. xvii, 93, xviii, 16). Hill-tribes, Arr. *Ind.* 1, Str. 697–8: Mookerji, *Hindu Civilization*, 1936, pp. 282–4. On site of Aornos, Sir M. A. Stein, *Geogr. J.* Nov. 1927, and *On Alexander's Track to the Indus*, 1929, pp. 115–16, 151–4. On Alex. and India, *Hist. grecque* (ed. Glotz), iv, 137–60 (1938).

was evacuated almost at once, and passed under a native king who had seen Alexander and been inspired to seize power at Patna. Seleucus advanced threateningly to the Indus and beyond, but made a treaty ceding the valley and even part along the Kabul. His envoy Megasthenes (about 300 B.C.) wrote an account which was long to be the standard authority. The next envoy, Deimachus, over-estimated the size of this land, talked of monstrous peoples, and seemed to Strabo a worse liar than most; one Dionysius sent from Egypt is merely a name.[1] Strangely there is no western mention of Asoka, the greatest of his dynasty, who ruled down to Mysore and scattered Buddhist sermons in stone over his empire; he even sent missions as far as Syria and Egypt (258 B.C.), as is known only from his side and not from the recipients. Antiochus III met a 'king of the Indians' in the Kabul region and made an alliance, borrowing some elephants, but presently Bactrian kings were again to invade India.

The writers are good on plants and animals, with some mistakes and exaggerations. Megasthenes describes well the capital and the efficient government, less well the caste system. Various customs are observed like widow-burning (strangely ascribed to one tribe only) and the ascetic practices of the Gymnosophists, the 'naked philosophers' or fakirs. But there is still a good deal of the old Utopian stuff about a happy and long-lived people. Many repeat, if they do not always believe, native rumours (often chiming with Greek fancies) of queer tribes in remote parts, pygmies and men who have one eye, or no nose or mouth, or feet turned backwards, or long ears in which they wrap themselves to sleep. Among things surprising to Greeks were the summer rains of the upper Indus, but they seemed to confirm those generally thought to cause the swelling of the Nile.[2] (The statements about the rains differ, excusably enough: really the Punjab grows wheat with winter rains, and its rivers are fed by the snows of the Himalayas, while the summer monsoon rains fall heavily farther east along that range and on the Ganges basin and are much slighter over the Indus, so that Lahore has only 18 inches yearly to Calcutta's 59.)

---

[1] Plin. vi, 58: Deim., Str. 70, 76. Meg. envoy, Arr. *Anab.* v, 6, 2: much in Str. 702–13, Arr. *Ind.*, Diod. II, 35–42, etc. McCrindle, *Anc. India as described by Meg. and Arrian*, 1877, and his similar later works: Bevan, *C.H.I.* I, 400–23. Many of sources in *F.G.H.* IIB: Meg. in old *F.H.G.* II, 397–439. On Meg. a huge article by O. Stein, *R.E.* Meg. (1931): a Dutch book by Timmer, 1930, rev. by Cary, *C.R.* 1931, p. 226. De la Vallée Poussin, *L'Inde anc. et l'Empire des Maurya*, 1930. Moreland and Chatterjee, *Short Hist. of India*, 1936, pp. 49–52.

[2] Nearchus ap. Str. 690, Aristobulus, ibid. p. 692: Arr. *Ind.* 1 and 6, 4, *Anab.* VII, 7, 9: two rainy seasons, Diod. II, 36, 4–5. Queer tribes, even Meg. ap. Str. 70, 711, Plin. VI, 70 (Pygmies), VII, 22–6: Baeton, ibid. VII, 11, etc. Bevan, op. cit. p. 423. Castes, ap. Arr. *Ind.* 11–12, Diod. II, 40–1, Bevan, op. cit. pp. 409–11. Kaeppel, op. cit. pp. 108–11. Aborigines called 'noseless' already in Rigveda, Mookerji, *Hindu Civ.* 1936, p. 70.

Something was learnt of the geography beyond the Indus valley. A 'royal road' gave 10,000 stades to Palibothra (Patna); the items are obscurely reported in two accounts which cannot be reconciled. Past the capital the Ganges continued 6000 stades eastward, it was said, the final southward bend being not realized. The great Snowy Range was known as Emodus and Imaus (Himalaya, the abode of snow), but it was supposed to run due east instead of south-east. Megasthenes could name 58 big rivers, including about a score of Ganges tributaries, and 118 peoples with their chief cities, the number of their fighting men and elephants, and other details; but for their placing Pliny's crowded and telegraphic summary is not of much use.[1] (He does attempt a certain order, hill tribes between Indus and Jumna—six named, including one with many tigers—and so on.) Some of the details are picturesque, like a city-moat guarded by crocodiles. The pygmies are said to be in the mountains of the famous Prasii, the people round the capital itself (Patna).

Peninsular India is cut off from North by a belt of wooded ranges like the Vindhya. It was only slowly that there came some hearsay of southern kingdoms. There is surprisingly early word of Taprobane or Ceylon, ill-placed and vaguely large, with gold and pearls and elephants. (According to its own tradition Buddhism was introduced by a son and daughter of Asoka.) A puzzle is a cape Tamaros—also Tamus, with a curious sort of doublet Tabis—where the huge wall of snowy mountains is said to end in the eastern Ocean, with some possible islands beyond: a cape of Burma is later mentioned as Temalas, and some think it the same, but this seems very dubious. (When the gallant Elizabethan seamen were trading round to the White Sea and pushing on eastwards, it was gravely discussed how far north 'the huge promontorie Tabin', apparently taken as Cape Chelyuskin, might reach before the coast turned south-east to give a passage to Cathay.) The Indians had their own happy people 'beyond the north wind', the Uttara Kurus, and someone picked up their fable and even the name, as Attacori.[2] It is often supposed that India already imported silks from China, but, if the editing is duly discounted, what Nearchus noticed

---

1 Plin. VI, 64–78, mainly from Meg. Figures in Arr. *Ind.* 5, 2 (rivers), 7, 1. Road, Erat. ap. Str. 689 and Plin. VI, 62: Berger, *Erat.* pp. 158, 227: though Berthelot, *L'Asie... d'après Ptolémée*, p. 311 tries to reconcile.

2 Amometus ap. Plin. VI, 55: Rohde, *Griech. Roman*², p. 233: see p. 36, n. 1. Same, Herrmann, *Land der Seide*, 1938, p. 41, and *R.E.* Tamaros: cape in Erat. ap. Str. 519 (doublets, Mela, III, 60, 68, 70, Plin. VI, 53): Bunbury, I, 666. Cathay, E. G. R. Taylor, *Tudor Geography*, 1930, pp. 97–8, 130: Hakluyt, Everyman ed. II, 213, 224, V, 107–8, 121, 126: see also p. 128, n. 1, p. 199, n. 2. Ceylon, Ones. ap. Str. 691, Erat. ibid. 690, Plin. VI, 81–3: on the figures, Berger, *Erat.* pp. 233, 237: Tennent, *Hist. of Ceylon*, 1860, pp. 6–9. Pepper already Theophr. H.P. IX, 19–20, only as drug, Tarn, op. cit. p. 371.

was really a local wild silk, and he did not use the word 'serica', nor did another companion speak of Seres or Silk-men. A native mention of such imports has been put about 300 B.C., but is doubtful in date and otherwise.[1]

Leaving India, Alexander meant to keep near the fleet and help it with stores, but was pushed inland by the coast hills at Ras Malan, and for a time the forced marches were a nightmare of thirst and hunger in the sand-dunes. No line was reasonable in summer for a large force with many non-combatants, and his was not the best. (The accounts are none too clear in topography: Strabo talks of keeping within 500 stades of the coast, and another is careless.) In Carmania Craterus rejoined him, having had apparently no difficulty, even in taking elephants across the last desert stretch (it has been argued that the climate must have worsened since and that otherwise Alexander could not have brought an army through a region where to-day a small caravan can scarcely find water and forage).[2]

For the fleet we have a full summary of the detailed report of Nearchus himself. There was a long wait at Karachi for the change from the summer to the winter monsoon (October); then he started with many doubts and fears, which seem strange enough if he knew of the old voyage of Scylax and if the natives used these winds (he was able to pick up a pilot on the way). Nothing terrible happened, though food ran short and a few ships were piled on the surf-beaten coast: there were no mermaids, and no monsters except some spouting whales, which were easily scared off. The tedious stretch of miserable 'Fish-eaters' was counted as more than 10,000 stades, a bad overestimate from days taken. It was a relief to see a little cultivation again in Carmania. Presently the Arabian cape was sighted, and Onesicritus, second in command, was for cutting across, but fortunately was overruled. Entering the gulf, they rested at a pleasant spot Harmozia, short of the barren island destined to be so famous as the Portuguese station of Ormuz. Nearchus made a trip inland to find his master, who received him with tears of joy and bade him carry on to the head of the gulf. They passed several islands, one with a pearl-fishery, and along Persis, where the hills rose steeply to the inner plateau (the three zones are well described). After Bushire the coast was low and shoaly, and they crept round tricky sandbanks into the Euphrates and back a little up the Karun (end of

---

1 Grousset, *Hist. de l'extrême Orient*, 1929, I, 36: Pelliot, *T'oung Pao*, 1912, p. 727: though Herrmann, op. cit. p. 25 and *R.E.* Seres, Sinae accepts. Nearchus ap. Str. 693, as G. F. Hudson, *Europe and China*, 1931, p. 60, Tarn, *Greeks in Bactria*, p. 120 (cp. Herrmann). Seres ap. Str. 701 is 'some say', not Onesicritus.

2 Huntington, *Pulse of Asia*, 1919, pp. 316–20. Str. 721–3: Arr. VI, 23–6: careless, Plut. *Alex.* 66. Tarn, *C.A.H.* VI, 415 seems too kind to Alex. Sir P. Sykes, *Hist. of Afghanistan*, 1940, I, 68 (route as Tarn). Craterus, Str. 721, 725.

FROM ALEXANDER TO ERATOSTHENES

January 324 B.C.). The whole voyage had taken two months of actual sailing apart from long halts.[1]

Alexander founded a port, and improved the water communications of Babylonia (the writers have some confusions about the rivers, the harder to sort out as there have been changes in the courses since, largely, it seems, owing to the silting of the Karun). He also sent officers to explore the west side of the gulf and beyond. One reached Gerrha, a place of transit for incense, and islands opposite (Bahrein) with pearl-divings and mangrove-forests growing below high tide: some coincidences of names suggested a queer notion that this was the original home of the Phoenicians. Another officer managed to round the great southern cape, but came back to report an endless desert coast beyond. Nearchus would have continued the work but for the king's death. Others had reached 'Happy Arabia' from Egypt; its fragrant wares are well described, though not without traces of the old fables, and soon a surprising amount is known about the chief tribes and their towns. An incense-road led 70 days or 12,000 stades up the side towards Palestine, which country the Ptolemies long tried to hold against their Syrian rivals partly because of the profits of this trade. It is strange to see the owl of Athens finding its way (see Plate I D) into the Sabaean and other Arabian coinages.[2]

Arabian waters had room for another Utopia. Euhemerus (about 300 B.C.) professed to sail south to three Panchaean islands and to find an inscription there confirming his view that gods are merely old rulers or benefactors magnified by popular tradition. The Utopian form is inspired by a tale of Hecataeus of Abdera, to be discussed presently, but the placing is very different. The account of islands and people is fairly sober in order to win credit for the theory. This last, neither new nor profound, had a certain success, but few took the geography seriously,

---

[1] Hennig, *T.I.* 1, 165. Zones, Arr. *Ind.* 40, Str. 727. Figures, Str. 720, Arr. *Ind.* 25 29, 38: overstated, Berger, *Erat.* pp. 249–51. Voyage in Arrian, *Indica*, 21–42, ed. Chantraine, 1927: *G.G.M.* 1, pp. 306–69, Tabulae xv: text, Roos, 1928 (with map). Plin. VI, 96–100, 109 is a jumble (from Ones. through Juba). Bunbury, 1, 525–51: Tozer, 141–3: Glotz, *Hist. grecque*, IV, 165–8 (1938). Pilot, Arr. *Ind.* 27: Tarn, op. cit. p. 367. Tomb of King 'Red' (Erythras) on island, Str. 766, Arr. *Ind.* 37, Curt. VIII, 9, 14, X, 1, 14: see p. 81, n. 2, p. 7, n. 1.

[2] G. F. Hill, *Coins of Arabia, Mesop. and Persia*, 1922, pp. 45, 77: *C.A.H.* X, 247: Rostovtzeff, *Soc. and Econ. Hist. of Hellenistic World*, 1941, plate LXXIX, 3: J. G. Milne, *Greek and Roman Coins*, 1939, p. 62 and plate XI (not direct trade but slow spread of a reputed coin-type). Road and tribes, Erat. ap. Str. 767–9, Plin. XII, 63–4, Berger, pp. 439–41, but E. wrong on cinnamon, Tarn, *Hell. Civ.* p. 196: see p. 298, n.1. Wares already Theophr. *H.P.* IX, 4; *C.P.* II, 5, 5. Officers, Arr. *Anab.* VII, 207–10, *Ind.* 43. Kiernan, *Unveiling of Arabia*, 1937, pp. 22–3. Phoen., Str. 766. Ant. III (not IV as Plin. VI, 147, 152) thought of annexing Gerrha, Tarn, op. cit. p. 213. Bab. rivers, Bunbury, II, 314: Str. 728–9 is obscure, citing Polycletus, Nearchus and Onesicritus: see p. 286, n. 3.

though 'Panchaean odours' were to become a commonplace of poetry. The story, after its kind, borrowed local colour where it pleased, among other places from Ceylon (not unknown since for spicy breezes). Some other mentions of 'Happy Islands' off Arabia may be more real and contain a rumour of Socotra.[1]

If Alexander had lived, the southern Ocean might have been better used. As it was, the Successors were too concerned with watching each other and keeping the balance of power in the inner sea. So they left the Indian trade to Arabian middlemen, though the Ptolemies did much voyaging within the Red Sea and for a short way outside.

Such in general was the new information about the east. When the task of mapping was approached, there were great difficulties. No observations for longitude were feasible, and the few available for latitude were very vague or wrong: at the summer solstice the sun cast no shadow in the upper Punjab, it was said, or cast a shadow southward either at the Fish-eater coast (so Nearchus, probably misreported) or in south India, where the Bear was not seen (so Megasthenes correctly, though another denied the fact).[2] The most reliable figures were along Alexander's line of march, but he had made wide detours, and the items were often grossly exaggerated. The most striking feature of Asia seemed a broad mountain-spine running due east, the Taurus–Elburz–Hindu Kush–Himalaya; this is much too schematic, of course, and the last section very wrong, as it should bend away south-east. The central parallel, already foreshadowed in the Ionian map, was the axis of the inner sea from Gibraltar to Rhodes, and thence south of the Taurus; it was now continued through the Caspian Gates and along the base of the Indian mountains (previously pushed far north on a level with the Caucasus). On the whole this is remarkably correct, and the credit belongs to Dicaearchus.[3] Eratosthenes followed him, and tried to get another parallel as follows (see Fig. 15). Because Ethiopia and south India had similar climates, plants and animals, and black peoples, he put them on a line; the method was rough, and the result not good, as the parallel of Meroe should pass near Bombay. Between this line and the northern mountain-wall he fitted in the reported Indian distances, only

---

1 Theophr. *H.P.* IX, 4, 4: Agatharchides, 103 (*G.G.M.* I, 191). Euh. ap. Diod. V, 41–6, VI, 2: Eus. *P.E.* II, 2, 59–60: Jacoby, *F.G.H.* I, 300–13 and *R.E.* VI, 952–72, esp. 958–61. Colour, Rohde, *Griech. Roman*[2], pp. 237–41. H. J. Rose, *Greek Lit.* 1934, pp. 368–9, *Greek Mythology*, p. 6. Geffcken in Hastings, *Enc. of Rel. and Ethics*, 1911, V, 572–3.

2 Deimachus ap. Str. 76–7: N. ibid. and ap. Arr. *Ind.* 25: Ones. ap. Plin. II, 183 (Punjab): Meg. ap. Diod. II, 35, 4: Heidel, *Frame of Anc. Greek Maps*, 48, 104, 126: Berger, *Erat.* 180–3: Bunbury, I, 534, II, 382. Middlemen, Tarn, *Hell. Civ.* p. 196.

3 Dic. fr. 55 Müller: Agathem. I, 5 (*G.G.M.* II, 472): Bunbury, I, 628: Berger, *Erat.* pp. 166, 173–5: Heidel, op. cit. pp. 48, 111 (Caucasus). On D.'s line Boll. *R.E.* V, 341.

at the cost of twisting the peninsula round to point south-east. The Indus, giving one side, was supposed to flow south, and was badly overestimated from the slowness of Alexander's passage downstream. So its mouths were pulled far below the tropic, and with them the Fish-eater coast, and it seemed fitting that this wilderness should be on a line with the Arabian-Saharan desert belt.[1] But this made a mess of the Persian gulf, dragging most of it south of the tropic too, a position irreconcilable with other data such as the course and length of the Euphrates.

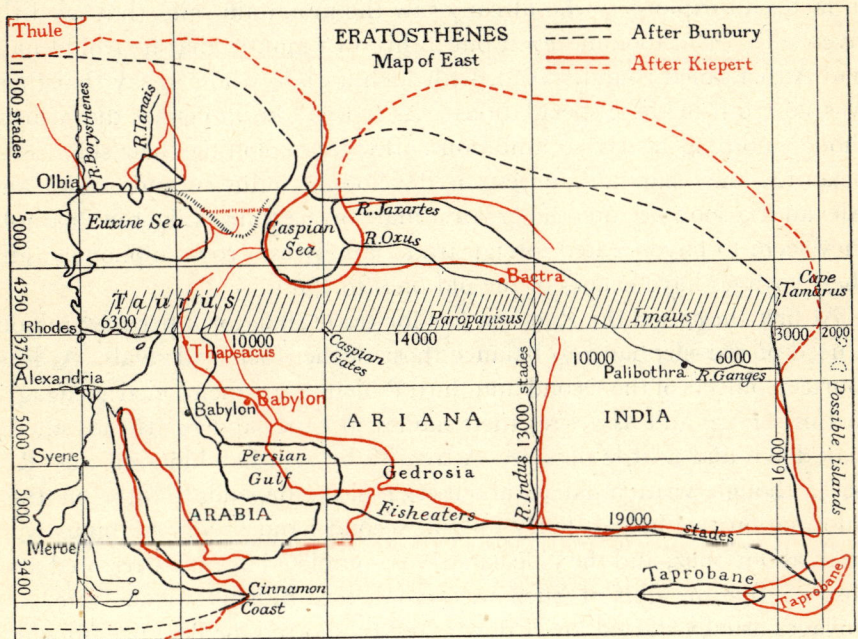

Fig. 15. Eratosthenes: map of the East.

Thus the mapping of Eratosthenes worked westwards from India. The second 'section' was the great slab called Ariana or Iran. Its coast having been overstretched owing to the slow voyage of Nearchus, the northern side was made to agree by not allowing enough for Alexander's wide detour in this region. (The detailed figures given for his march hereabouts differ incurably.) Bactria, as lying beyond the broad mountain belt, was pushed much too far north. The third working section had the mess just indicated: how the mapper dealt with it cannot be surely made out from Strabo's long and obscure discussion, reporting the severe criticisms of Hipparchus, but it appears that Babylon was very wrongly pulled well

---

[1] Erat. ap. Str. 133. Meroe line guesswork, says Hipparchus ap. Str. 133 and 77. Mapping of India, Berger, *Erat.* pp. 224–37: astr. data, ibid. pp. 177–82 (see p. 134, n. 2).

south of the latitude of Alexandria.¹ It is strange that after the several voyages already reported the shape of the Persian gulf should have been so ill-conceived.

§ 2. AFRICA

There was plenty of guessing about what might have been if Alexander had lived. He would have attacked Carthage, among others, and done much for African geography. He would have ascertained the sources of the Nile (unreliable seem two late statements that, inspired by his old tutor, he did in fact send explorers, who already saw the mountain rains that swell the river). It is said too, and even put in his own mouth, that he would have had Africa sailed round.² And, with such a man, who can say that there was no truth in these speculations? As it was, the Ptolemies did a little, though nothing nearly so ambitious. Besides exploiting their submissive peasants, they had an interest in developing industry and trade, and Alexandria soon became the greatest mart of the time. Like the Pharaohs they seem to have treated foreign trade largely as a royal monopoly, and their voyages have echoes of the old ones to Punt.

At first they used the Red Sea less for trade than for a peculiar reason, a need of war-elephants to balance those of their Seleucid rivals. At least fourteen officers of the second and third Ptolemies are mentioned as engaged in this service and as giving their names to capes and roadsteads all the way down and a little outside. A treatise by Agatharchides on the 'Red Sea', though written later (about 132 B.C.), depends mostly on their information: we have it fairly fully at second hand.³ New harbours were built about Suez, and the Nile canal was completed or rather restored after disuse. But the gulf of Suez was avoided as difficult to navigate, and voyages usually started lower down, at Myoshormos or Berenice, to which ran desert roads equipped with cisterns and military posts (traffic along these very old routes was now easier as camels had probably been introduced). The ports for the hunting-grounds began with Ptolemais, about Port Sudan, and another was Adulis, near Massawa, the best harbour,

1 Str. 89, but obscure and contradictory, 77–91, 134, 727, 746: Berger, *Erat.* pp. 259–64: on P.G. ibid. pp. 273–82. Incurably, ap. Str. 514, Plin. VI, 45, Berger, op. cit. p. 243, though Berthelot, *Asie*, p. 95 tries to cure.

2 Arr. *Anab.* V, 26, some ap. VII, 1, 2: Plut. *Alex.* 68. Bury, *Hellenistic Age*, 1925, p. 8. Nile, Ps.-Arist. *Inund. Nili*, Lucan, X, 30, 272–5: Bolchert, *Arist. Erdkunde*, p. 58. Rains, Photius, *Bibl. Cod.* 249: Joh. Lydus, *de Mensibus*, IV, 104, cp. Pos. ap. Str. 790, who does not say that Callisthenes witnessed the rains.

3 Excerpt from two books and epitome in Photius, and paraphrase of a piece in Diod. III, 12–48: *G.G.M.* I, liv–lxxiii and 111–95 and Tabulae VI–VIII. Officers, Erat. and Agath. via Artem. ap. Str. 768–76, 789. On Agath. Bunbury, II, 51–61: Berthelot, *Afrique sahar. et soudanaise*, pp. 215–18: Schwartz, *R.E.* I, 739–41: Leopoldi, *De Ag. Cnidio*, 1892: Hyde, *Anc. Greek Mariners*, 1947, pp. 196–200, 202.

where an important inscription has been found. The natives, accustomed to kill elephants for their meat and ivory, had to be taught to take them alive; sometimes, we hear, they sawed trees, so that the beasts leant on them and fell, to be easily caught as they could not rise with their jointless legs! (Aristotle had attacked notions, perhaps going back to Ctesias, that elephants have no knee-joints and sleep standing). The African elephants are not really smaller than the Indian, as stated, or afraid of them. They have a bad name now as untrainable; yet they were evidently used both by Egypt for a time and by Carthage (some shown on coins have the large ears and sloping back of this breed). By this hunting, then, the whole unalluring coast became quite minutely known all the way to the strait, which is well described with its island stepping-stones. The general run is somewhat misconceived as due south for 9000 stades to Ptolemais, and thence too markedly south-east for 4500 stades. Unaccountably divergent and bad are some figures from one Timosthenes, an admiral of Ptolemy II, if they are properly reported.[1]

The outer coast is drawn more easterly for 5000 stades to the Cape of Aromata or Perfumes (Guardafui). It is arranged in a rather artificial succession of Myrrh and Frankincense and Cinnamon Coasts, though the last name is often applied to the whole. The 'cinnamon' is said to be brought from inland. The Cape had been barely rounded, and the mapper could only presume that the coast soon turned abruptly west. So he drew an imaginary line to the point reached by Hanno down the other side of the continent. We hear nothing yet of direct voyages to India. Apparently there was no thought except of coasting, and that was too long to be worth while; how the monsoons came to be used we shall see later.

Upstream the Ptolemies did not attempt conquest beyond lower Nubia, but their influence extended farther, for instance to the Ethiopian king who would not die at the order of his priests, after the ancient practice, and massacred them instead, an act which is also told of some modern negro kings. There were still gold workings in the Nubian desert, with convict labour under appalling conditions. Several travellers are named as leaving

---

1 In Plin. VI, 163 (strait garbled ibid. and 170). Erat.'s figures in Str. 768. Jointless, Agath. 53, Diod. III, 27, Str. 772 (not Plin. VIII, 8), Ambrose, *Hex.* VI, 5, 31: 'an old and grey-headed error even in the days of Aristotle, and as for the manner of their venation... we shall find it to be otherwise than by sawing of trees', Sir T. Browne, *Pseudodoxia*, 1646, III, ch. 1. Arist. *de Incessu Anim.* 709 a, H.A. 498 a: Pease, *Class. Phil.* 1939, p. 372. African smaller, Polybius, V, 84, Plin. VIII, 27, Livy, XXXVII, 40. Roads, Str. 815, Plin. VI, 102–3: J. Ball, *Egypt in Class. Geographers*, 1942, pp. 68, 83 and appendix by G. W. Murray, ibid. pp. 183–5: see p. 273, n. 3. Hunting, Diod. III, 18, 40: Jennison, *Animals for Show and Pleasure in Anc. Rome*, 1937, pp. 37–40: camels, ibid. p. 33. Tarn, *H.C.* pp. 197–9. Canal, Str. 804–5, Diod. I, 33: completion wrongly denied by Plin. VI, 165. Inscr. *O.G.I.S.* I, 199: perhaps a Berenice here, Tarn, loc. cit. Coasting, cp. p. 176, n. 1.

accounts of southern parts. The triangle between Nile and Atbara is the 'island' of Meroe, and details are given of 'another island' between the main Nile and the Blue, with the Sembritae, the old 'Deserters'. Various tribes west of this stretch are named only from their customs as eating roots or seeds, locusts or elephants or ostriches, using big dogs to hunt buffalo, or the like. Against an old Utopian notion it is pointedly observed that such primitive savages are short-lived. Strange animals are noted such as the giraffe and rhinoceros, which might be seen in royal processions and zoos as well as at home.[1] Hunters or traders from the coast had now actually witnessed the rains long since assumed as causing the Nile flood, and had seen or heard of the lake amid mountains which was the source of the Blue Nile (Tana). A hint that the main stream comes 'from some lakes in the south' is remarkable, but seems only a guess, or at best a rumour of the sudd swamps, not of the great lakes.[2] The theory of a western Nile was for the time being discredited. But one notion, briefly ascribed to Dicaearchus, sounds archaic, that the flood-waters come somehow from the Ocean: it is hardly right to find here a knowledge of the fact that the rains come with winds from the southern sea.

The Nile was supremely important for the mapping of Eratosthenes. Its course, generally north except for one big loop, provided his chief meridian. Aswan gave the tropic, having a well which was lit down to the bottom at noon at the summer solstice. He drew two southmost parallels, through Meroe and through the Sembritae-Cinnamon Coast, the latter being continued, not unhappily, east to Ceylon. The distance from Aswan to Alexandria was his basis for measuring the globe. At least one traveller, Philo, already under Ptolemy I, had made a useful observation, that at Meroe (as at Ptolemais) the absence of shadow occurred not at the summer solstice but 45 days before and after, and the mapper fixed the place 11,800 stades from the equator, one of the very best of ancient determinations.[3]

1 Athen. v, 201, Diod. III, 36: Hubbell, 'Ptolemy's Zoo', *Class. Journ.* 1935, pp. 66–77: Jennison, op. cit. pp. 28–35. At home, Agath. 39, Plin. VII, 28. Tribes, Agath. 50–61, Diod. III, 15–47, Str. 770–2, Plin. VI, 191–3: Fischer, *R.E.* Sebritae: Berthelot, loc. cit. and p. 241: Hennig, *Terrae Incognitae*, I, 187–94: Pliny badly conflates three writers, Rossini, *Aegyptus*, 1925, pp. 5–21. Diod. III, 2–11 is mostly Agath. as gold ibid. 12–14: Ball, op. cit. p. 52. King and priests, Diod. III, 6, Str. 822: Wainwright, *Sky-Religion in Egypt*, 1938, pp. 52, 62: Frazer, *Golden Bough*, abridged ed. 1925, pp. 265–74: Seligman, *Eg. and Negro Africa*, 1934, p. 21: Budge, *Hist. of Ethiopia*, 1928, I, 52.

2 Bunbury, II, 613, 663: some confusion of names of rivers between Erat. and Str. 786: Berger, *Erat.* pp. 302–7. Rains, Erat. ap. Str. 786, 789, 98. Lake Psebo, Artem. ap. Str. 822, and mountains, Agath. 84, Diod. III, 41. Island Phebol a misuse of this?, see p. 274, n. 2.

3 Str. 77, Plin. VI, 171, II, 183: Berger, *Erat.* pp. 147–8, *R.E.* Erat. VI, 365–6. Archaic, Dic. in Joh. Lydus, *de Mens.* IV, 107: hardly, Rehm, *R.E.* Nilschwelle, p. 589, against Berger, *Erdk.* p. 376.

Cyrene was attached to Egypt and gave her some famous men like the librarian-geographer himself. It has been mentioned above how the desert oracle of Ammon was made still more famous by a visit of Alexander, round which fables soon gathered. Carthage now played her biggest part and carried war by sea and land even to Italy. Her small home territory, the original tiny 'Africa', was early raided by a Sicilian tyrant in 310 B.C., and again by a Roman consul in 258, and it was there that she was finally beaten by Scipio in 202 B.C. Westwards were the Numidians or Nomads; one of the two kings prevailed as Rome's ally and got a vast domain from the Moorish border to the Cyrenaic, with the task of watching Carthage. The geographical accounts are still strangely defective. A big book *On Ports* by Timosthenes, already cited as an admiral of Ptolemy II (about 260 B.C.), showed marked ignorance of these western coasts, and few of the fragments of Eratosthenes concern them. The northward projection towards Carthage is very poorly realized. The figure for the coast beyond to the strait (8800 stades) is fairly good—in fact better than Strabo's 13,500—but the direction is misconceived as slightly north-west. Little seems known of the Atlas hinterland, and still less of Hanno's outer coast, which is hopelessly misdrawn as running south-east. A periplus written for one Ophellas, tyrant of Cyrene, apparently talked of hundreds of vanished Phoenician colonies a little beyond the strait, and was used by Eratosthenes, too trustfully according to a later judgment.[1] The origin of the name 'Africa' is still obscure; it was to be extended to the whole continent, as 'Libya' had been.

§3. EUROPE

Alexander is said to have received envoys from as far west as Spain, and later historians liked to guess what might have happened if he had lived to attack not only Carthage but Rome. As things turned out, his successors had quite enough trouble keeping the balance of power among themselves in the eastern Mediterranean. Macedonia, indeed, had a frontage in another direction: she had the hard task of defending herself and Greek civilization against the northern tribes, including new swarms of Celts on the middle Danube, who had already sent envoys to Alexander. A minor king related to him, Pyrrhus of Epirus, came to champion the western Greeks, and won ground for a moment from Carthage in Sicily, but was engaged in south Italy and driven out by Rome, which thus attracted the

---

[1] Strabo's, 826: Gsell, *Hist. anc. de l'Afrique du Nord*, v, 14. S.E., as later Str. 119–20, 130, 825, Mela, I, 20, Dion. Per. 174, 270. Projection, Berger, *Erdk.* p. 423. Figure, Erat. ap. Plin. v, 40: see p. 182, nn. 1–2. Ignorance, Str. 93: Dubois, *Examen de la Géogr. de Strabon*, 1891, pp. 251–2. Ammon, Callisthenes ap. Str. 814, Plut. *Alex.* 27, Curt. IV, 7. Name Africa, Gsell, op. cit. VII, 3–5 (1928).

serious attention of the Greek world for the first time. Timaeus, a Sicilian who lived long as an exile at Athens, wrote a history which was to remain a standard authority on the west, though he was not a traveller and later writers could sneer at his arm-chair knowledge of the more distant parts.

The barbarian powers now took the front of the stage. Rome and Carthage, having become neighbours across the strait of Messina, were drawn into a long war (264–241 B.C.). It was fought out mainly in Sicily and on the sea, where the Romans had everything to learn, building fleets on the model of their enemy's quinqueremes. (Ships had become much bigger, though a few extravagantly big ones mentioned were more for parade than practical use.)[1] At last Rome won, and was left with Sicily as her first overseas 'province'; soon afterwards she seized a chance to grab Sardinia and Corsica. In a second war (219–202 B.C.) the whole western Mediterranean was involved. The able generals of Carthage had turned for compensation to Spain, with its great resources in minerals and fighting men, hitherto hardly more than tapped from Gades. They occupied the south and south-east with a base at New Carthage (Cartagena), and Hannibal pushed into the unknown interior as far as Salamanca. The Romans had tried to bargain for a limit at the Ebro, but he was bent on revenge. Soon he was on the Rhône, and he crossed the Alps, though with heavy loss. (There has been a vast debate on the question by which pass he came down, apparently on the district of Turin, and where, if anywhere, he pointed to the promised land below: many argue for the Col du Clapier, a minor pass south of the Mont Cenis, or for the Cenis itself, but Livy's mention of the Durance on the route, if correct, seems to point to the Genèvre.)[2] He was joined by thousands of the Po Gauls, whom Rome was only in process of subduing. He won resounding victories and ravaged far and wide, but he could not break the solid Roman federation. His brother, who had destroyed an army in Spain and crossed the Alps quite easily, was overthrown before reaching him. At last he was forced to

---

1 Heichelheim, *Wirtschaftsgesch.* p. 569. Arm-chair, Polybius, XII, 25. Guess, Livy, IX, 17–19. Spain, Arr. *Anab.* VII, 15, 4–6: Diod. XVII, 13: from Rome, Clitarchus ap. Plin. III, 57. On Timaeus' geogr. of west a work by J. Geffcken, 1892. Celts to Alex., Str. 301–2, *C.A.H.* VI, 355.

2 So Partsch, *R.E.* Alpes, 1894, Preller, *Scottish Geogr. Mag.* 1926, pp. 350–9, with surveys of literature. Polybius, III, 39, 48–56: Livy, XXI, 35–7. Clapier, Colonel Perrin, 1887: Colin, 1904; Spenser Wilkinson, 1911; Berthelot in *Rev. Ét. Anc.* 1935, pp. 185–204, 1936, pp. 35–8. Cenis, Jullian, *Hist. de la Gaule*, I³, 485–6 (1914), Bourgery, *Rev. Phil.* 1938, p. 120. Both, Knoflach, *Klio*, 1932, p. 404. Some go as far south as the Col de l'Argentière, Freshfield, 1883, H. B. George, *Relations of Geogr. and History*, 1910, pp. 212–14, or as far north as the Little St Bernard, Mommsen, Kiepert, W. W. Hyde, *Roman Alpine Routes*, 1935, pp. 197–210. On the passes generally, Str. 208: Jullian, op. cit. pp. 41–50 (Genèvre most used): G. East, *Hist. Geogr. of Europe*, 1935, pp. 130–2.

FROM ALEXANDER TO ERATOSTHENES

return home to be defeated by Scipio, who had cleared Spain and carried the war into Africa. Two new provinces were made in Spain, Hither and Further.

In the Adriatic Rome had done some police work against the Illyrian pirates, and Macedonia, resenting this interference so close by, had made an alliance with Hannibal. This was to draw the Roman arms upon herself and presently upon others: it was the beginning of the end of the greatness of the Hellenistic kingdoms.

A description of the Black Sea as like a Scythian bow and having a circuit of 23,000 stades goes back to this time, if it is not older. One Macedonian general raided over the lower Danube, perhaps as far as Olbia, to be killed by the Scythians, and presently a king invaded the Getae and was captured. There began already a legend about Alexander and some very vaguely placed Amazons, that he received their envoys and sent them back to their queen to announce his coming, or that she herself came to visit him, but the earliest and soundest historians said nothing of them, as Arrian remarks, and he thinks those women-warriors must have died out before Xenophon, who would otherwise have met them. Of northern parts Greek ideas were still very hazy. But a current version of the return of the Argonauts may be partly discounted as consciously archaistic: it is by the learned poet Apollonius of Rhodes, who was librarian of Alexandria just before the geographer. The heroes pass up the Danube and out by the supposed branch into the Adriatic, then up the Eridanus–Po to stormy Celtic lakes under Hercynian mountains; here they nearly enter a northern branch, a sort of shadowy Rhine, but instead turn west down another (the Rhône) —the old amber-river has become this strange composite. Elsewhere the Danube is said to rise vaguely 'from desert places', apparently about the wooded Hercynian mountains, or in the fabulous Rhipaean range. Some made the heroes sail up the Don and haul their ship to another river, flowing to the northern Ocean, which was presumed to be quite near, sweeping westwards from the Caspian 'gulf'.[1]

The mappers took as the axis of the inner sea a parallel Gibraltar–Rhodes, which is remarkably accurate, except that it should pass through

---

[1] Tim. ap. Diod. IV, 563–4. Desert, Erat. in Schol. Ap. Rhod. IV, 284: Hercynian, Erat. ap. Caesar, B.G. VI, 24. Po-Rhône already Eur. ap. Plin. XXXVII, 32? Adr. branch, see p. 48, n. 2, p. 88, n. 1: so perhaps Erat. ap. Str. 47, 317, Hipp. ap. Str. 57: denied by Tim. ap. Diod. IV, 56, 7. Lakes, Ap. Rhod. IV, 627: for his geography a monograph by Delage, 1930: Pearson, Amer. J. Phil. 1938, p. 443: Mooney's ed. 1912, p. 15. Bow, Erat. (not Hec.) ap. Amm. Marc. XXII, 8, 10, Plin. IV, 76, 86, Val. Flaccus, IV, 728. Amazons, Arr. Anab. VII, 13 (and see p. 127, n. 4): visit, Curtius, VI, 5, 24, Justin, II, 4, 33. Mac. raids, Zopyrion and Lysimachus, C.A.H. VI, 394, VII, 82. Early Illyrian wars, Ormerod, Piracy in Anc. World, 1924, pp. 169–80. For Ap. Rhod. see also p. 168, n. 3.

the northward projection of Africa, and not through Messina but 2° south of it. The total length of the sea is badly exaggerated (by some 550 miles, on the ordinary value of the stade). The distribution of the items is hopelessly wrong, as on the sketch, the western basin being much too short relatively to the eastern, 8000 as compared with 13,500 stades, though a trifle improved from Dicaearchus, who had said 7000. (This disproportion

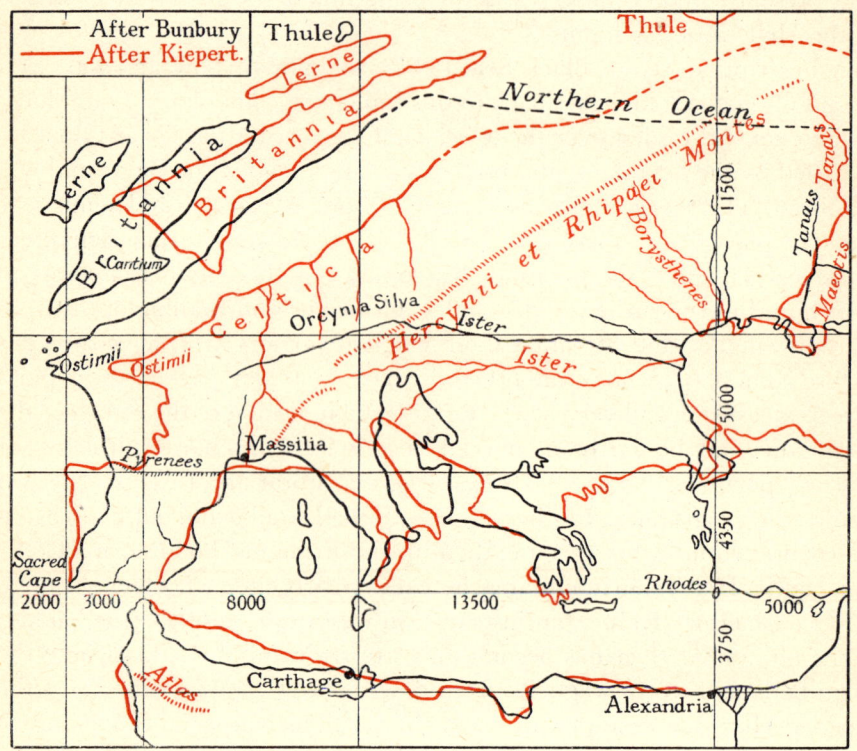

Fig. 16. Eratosthenes: map of the West.

was soon to be duly censured and fairly well corrected to 13,200 and 13,600 stades.) Both writers exaggerated the breadth of the western basin. An early figure for the Adriatic is 10,000 stades, but how the sea was drawn is obscure. An attempt at a meridian Rome–Messina–Carthage is very unsuccessful. Such errors badly distorted the outlines of Europe, but the drawing is ill preserved because the writers were later despised as still ignorant of the west and not worth considering by those who had the advantage of Roman knowledge.[1]

[1] Str. 93: meridian attacked, ibid. 92. Censured, Polybius ap. Str. 105 (and breadth): corrected, Artem. ap. Plin. II, 242 and ap. Agathem. I, 15. Adr., Dic. in Polybius, loc. cit., Berger, *Erdk.* p. 379.

FROM ALEXANDER TO ERATOSTHENES

For the outer sea there was the report of Pytheas of Marseilles. We have only scraps, chiefly from two writers who lose their tempers whenever they quote such an arrant liar. Of his date nothing is really sure except that he is not mentioned by Aristotle, who has some occasion to deal with such geographical matters, but was mentioned by that writer's pupil Dicaearchus, which suggests something vaguely around 320 B.C.[1] This first reference was already distrustful, it seems. Yet he was respected by Timaeus and by Eratosthenes in his mapping, which is unfortunately ill recorded by the two prejudiced witnesses. What did the man really claim to have done and seen and heard? Nearly every fragment about him is beset with doubts, but moderns, after being misled by his ancient detractors, now agree at least that he was not a liar.[2]

He certainly had interests in science, as he noted against Eudoxus that there was no star precisely at the pole; also he made a very accurate shadow-reckoning at home, and on his voyage he observed the lengthening of the day and took heights of the sun, from which the astronomer Hipparchus could calculate the latitudes. For once it seems that an ancient journey may be ascribed, as many admit, purely or mainly to scientific curiosity. Nothing is really known, however, of the circumstances. His ancient enemies sneer at him as a poor private man without the means for his alleged voyage; in reply it is often guessed that he had the backing of his city, anxious for better touch with the source of tin, though supplies were already coming in handily enough over Gaul. How he managed to run the presumed Carthaginian gauntlet at the straits is quite obscure (some try to date him from a temporary weakening of Carthage, but the argument is thin).

[1] Dic. in Str. 104. Scraps, esp. Polybius ap. Str. 63, 104, 190 and Strabo himself: Artemidorus also hostile, ap. Str. 63. De Navarro, *C.A.H.* VII, 53, thinks *c.* 325–3: 330–25, Müllenhoff, Beckers, etc.: *c.* 345, Much, *R.E. Germani* (1918), p. 552, Schütte, *Our Forefathers*, 1929, I, 29, after Sieglin: *c.* 310–06, Cary-Warmington, *Anc. Explorers*, p. 33.
[2] Misled, as Sir G. C. Lewis, *Astr. of Ancients*, 1862, pp. 467–83. But cp. Müllenhoff, *Deutsche Alt.* I (1870), ch. 2: Bunbury, I, 590–603: Tozer, pp. 153–64: Berger, *Erat.* pp. 73, 372–9, etc. and *Erdkunde*[2], pp. 332–67: Rice Holmes, *Anc. Britain and the Invasions of Julius Caesar*, 1907, pp. 218–30: Nansen, *In Northern Mists*, 1911, I, 43–73: Jullian, *Hist. de la Gaule*, I[3] (1914), pp. 416–29: Cary-Warmington, op. cit. pp. 33–40: Hennig, *T.I.* I, 120–36: Malye, *Bull. Ass. Budé*, Oct. 1933, pp. 34–47: Angus in *Greece and Rome*, 1934, pp. 165–72: Kaeppel, *Off the Beaten Track in the Classics*, 1936, pp. 121–9: V. Stefansson, *Ultima Thule*, 1942, pp. 9–79 (much after a book by Broche, 1935). Sir Clements Markham, *Lands of Silence*, 1921, pp. 26–9, thinks of a six years' voyage. Monographs by Hergt, 1893, G. Mair, 1893–1906, Matthias, 1901–2, Kähler, 1903: I do not directly know Bessell, 1858, Callegari in *Riv. Stud. Ant.* 1903–5, Sphyris, 1912, Blasquez in *Bol. Soc. Geogr.* Madrid, 1913. Also Hübner, *R.E. Britanni* (1899), p. 863: Gisinger, *R.E. Geogr.* 594–6 (1924): H. E. Burton, *Discovery of Anc. World*, 1932, pp. 53–5: H. Philipp, *Tac. Germania*, 1926, pp. 42–54 (following Sieglin): S. Casson, *Greece and Britain*, 1943, pp. 26–35. Elton, *Origins of English History*[2], 1890, pp. 12–73.

He can vaguely be followed round to the north side of Spain, and so (across or coasting?) to a cape Kabaion with a people called Ostimii or something similar; hereabouts were several islands, the furthest being Uxisame, three days off (from where?). All this recalls the Oestrymnian cape and islands of the early periplus (p. 54), whether the name is connected or not. The island specially named is often taken (rather riskily) as Ushant. The cape is the projection of Brittany, no doubt, without our needing to believe that a river Oust and a bay of Cabestan reflect the ancient names, as Berger supposes. The mapper duly accepted the projection, whereas the sceptics were to make a sad mess of the coast by flattening it out.[1]

From here he may have crossed direct to the Cornish mines, like the old seamen of this coast and the later Veneti whose oaken ships with leather sails Caesar was to admire. Pytheas was the first to mention the name of the Brettanic or rather Prettanic isles. It seems to be Priten or the 'tattooed' or 'painted people'; but another meaning has been suggested ('channel people' from the same root as fretum) and it may not even be Celtic at all, but from some local native name, just as the Romans picked up 'Graii' and extended it to the Greeks. He may have also mentioned the older name of 'Albion', which is of obscure origin and no longer confidently explained as akin to the Latin albus and referring to the white cliffs of Dover. (The Celts had come in perhaps only a century or little more before, in the Iron Age, some hold, though others add earlier waves of Bronze Age invaders to account for the Goidelic dialects of Ireland and Scotland and Man, which have qu where the Brythonic has p.) It is generally understood from the scrimpy texts that he coasted all the sides, but in what order and with how many landings to explore cannot safely be made out. Anyhow he realized the island as a triangle, named the corners, capes Belerion (Land's End), Kantion, and Orcas (opposite the Orkneys), and estimated the sides; they are in a fairly good proportion 3:6:8, but in the total nearly double the truth, perhaps, some suggest, because his figures in days of slow coasting were later clumsily translated into stades at an average rate which was here much too high. The mapper had some trouble with this huge island, but seems to have fitted it in as 'stretched obliquely along' the continent, so that its northern corner pointed north-east. The voyager must have sighted and heard of Ireland, and it appears on the map as a big island Ierne, longer than it is broad, 'lying along north of Britain'.[2] The people are said

[1] Str. 64, 148, 195. Berger, *Erat.* pp. 213, 268–72. Scientific, Holmes, p. 220, Berger, *Erdk.* pp. 353–8, Müllenhoff, I, 307–13, etc. Shadow, Str. 115: other data, ibid. 75, Berger, op. cit. p. 148. Star, Hipparchus, *in Arati et Eudoxi Phaen.* I, 4, 1: Heath, *Greek Astr.* p. 119: Nansen, op. cit. p. 47.

[2] Str. 201: Diod. v, 32 has 'Irin' (Erin): some Irish really cannibals, Ridgeway, *E.A.G.* II, 51 (1931): Grenier, *Les Gaulois*, 1945, p. 221. Britain, Pol. ap. Str. 63, 104:

FROM ALEXANDER TO ERATOSTHENES

to be much wilder than their neighbours, and promiscuous in sexual intercourse—a stock charge against lowly tribes—and even to be cannibals.

The following is the gist of various things which Pytheas may have said about Britain, though the statements may contain some later elements: (*a*) In these northern parts—towards (and including?) Thule, of which more presently—they thresh their corn indoors in large barns, as the climate is dull and wet; they make bread, and those who have both corn and honey brew a drink from them; northwards nearer the frozen zone animals become scarce or fail, and so do cereals except millet (oats?), though there are wild fruits, vegetables and roots. (Strabo, despite his prejudice, cannot help feeling that these things sound sober enough and queerly unlike the old fables about happy Hyperboreans.) (*b*) The people are numerous and under many chiefs, who use chariots in their occasional wars. They have mean dwellings of logs or thatch, and are simple in diet and ways. They store the corn-ears in cellars and grind some as required. The country is extremely cold as it lies under the Bear—a mis-statement which can hardly be original. (He is not cited as saying anything about physique: it is only a later writer who remarks on a swarthy people in Wales who may have come from the direction of Spain, a speculation now generally accepted for the origin of the earlier population.) (*c*) The people of Belerion are more civilized from their dealings with traders. They dig out tin ore with much work and skill, hammer it into pieces like dice, and cart it at low tide to an island Ictis, from which traders (presumably Gallic) take it across to Gaul and then on horseback thirty days to Marseilles and Narbonne.[1] (*d*) There is tin in an island Ictis (or Mictis), six days inwards from Britain—whatever that may mean—and the natives sail to it in hide boats. Pliny cites Timaeus, and can hardly mean the Isle of Wight, which he knows as Vectis; yet some have thought of this, even as once joined to the coast opposite. Others argue for an old 'isle' of Thanet, six days from Cornwall. But far the most are for St Michael's Mount, off Cornwall itself. The name is good Celtic and connected with the Muir n' Icht or

---

placing and figures, Diod. v, 21: Berger, *Erat.* pp. 208, 372–82 (sides translated, Müllenhoff, p. 381, Hergt, pp. 26, 44, but B. doubts). Celts only in Iron Age, Schütte, op. cit. I, 117: only 5th cent.?, Wheeler in *Eur. Civ.* 1935, II, 278: cp. Hubert, *Celtes*, 1938, p. 159 early and Brythons 6th cent.: how early (Goidels)?, Childe, *Prehistory of Scotland*, 1935, p. 167: Goidels in late Bronze, *Enc. Brit.* ed. 14, Britain. Priten, Collingwood and Myres, *Roman Britain and the English Settlements*, 1936, p. 31: but fretum, Constans, *Encicl. Ital.* s.v. Britannia, 1930: local, J. Fraser (see p. 357, n. 1). Albion, Hübner, *R.E.* Britanni, 1899, against Holder: see p. 54, n. 1.

1 (P. ap. Tim. ap.) Diod. v, 22, 38, which is not merely from Posidonius as Ridgeway, op. cit., O. Davies, *Roman Mining*, 1935, p. 142, etc., suppose, comparing Pos. ap. Str. 147: it is partly Pos. and the overland trade began *c.* 300, thinks Cary, *J.H.S.* 1924, p. 175. (*b*) is (Tim. ap.) Diod. v, 21. (*a*) is Str. 201. Swarthy, Tac. *Agr.* 11, see p. 235, n. 2.

English Channel, as is Caesar's Portus Itius. (*e*) Tin is found in Britain, but Pytheas is an unblushing liar, for Scipio (the younger?) could learn nothing worth mentioning about the island from the traders of Marseilles and Narbonne, to which the tin came, or those of a port Corbilo on the Loire. (But the traders may have wanted to keep their secrets?)[1] (*f*) He says that above Britain the sea rises 80 cubits (perhaps wrongly reported). This has been variously referred to tides which rise about half that amount in the Bristol Channel or to high tides (or rather storm-waves?) in the Pentland Firth. (*g*) He says that the flood-tide occurs when the moon waxes and the ebb when it wanes. He cannot have said anything so absurd, and the law of the half-daily Ocean tides is known to Eratosthenes; it seems that Pytheas was the first to connect the tides with the moon, however faultily in detail.[2] (*h*) It seems likely that he should be credited with some at least of the islands mentioned before the Roman invasion of Scotland, 30 or 40 Orcades or Orkneys, 7 Haemodae, 30 Haebudes, and 'Dumna, Bergi, and greatest of all Berrice, from which there is sailing to Thule' (the sailing is from the Shetlands, some understand, while others take Berrice, or Nerigon according to a very dubious variant, as Norway).[3]

He also went along the continent to some point beyond where Celt-land was supposed to merge into 'Scythia', for the name Germans had not yet been heard of (they had remained so obscure, it has been argued, because they were under Celtic domination). According to his enemies he claimed to have gone 'as far as the Tanais', whether this is an unfair sneer or he used the name for some German river: it is hard to believe, as some explain, that he really mistook the Elbe for a northern outflow of the Don, such as was used by the Argonauts in one fanciful version of their story. We hear vaguely of an aestuarium or stretch of tidal coast named Metuonis, apparently reaching 6000 stades from the Ocean (from Ushant, some understand). He mentioned two German tribes without knowing them

[1] Polybius, III, 57 and ap. Str. 190. Younger?, no, the Scipio of 218 B.C., thinks Grenier, *Les Gaulois*, 1945, p. 151. Secrets, Hencken, *Archaeology of Cornwall*, 1936, p. 173. Route new then?, Cary-Warmington, op. cit. p. 125, Collingwood in Frank's *Econ. Survey of Anc. Rome*, 1937, III, 46. (*d*) Plin. IV, 104. St. M., Holmes, op. cit. pp. 499–514, Hencken, pp. 171–6, Davies, p. 145, Rickard, *Man and Metals*, 1932, I, 316–26: so Bunbury, Tozer. Thanet, Angus, op. cit. p. 170, after Elton and Rhys. Wight (joined, C. Read), Ridgeway, Hergt, p. 29, Hübner, loc. cit. Icht, Davies, loc. cit. Müllenhoff dismisses the six days as a confusion with Thule.

[2] Duhem, *Système du Monde*, II, 271. Singer, *Short Hist. of Science*, 1941, p. 52. Erat. ap. Str. 55. (*g*) is Pseudo-Plut. *Plac.* III, 17 (but not known to Timaeus, ibid., Berger, pp. 351–2). (*f*) Plin. II, 217: Bristol, Holmes, p. 224 as cp. Angus and (waves), Tozer, p. 159, Cary-Warmington, Casson, op. cit. p. 33.

[3] As Broche. Shetlands, Hergt, p. 48 (who makes Thule Norway). Plin. IV, 104: see p. 247, n. 1. Nansen, op. cit. pp. 56, 106: all Pytheas apparently and Haem. = Shetlands, ibid. p. 90. Orcades (Celtic) already P., Childe, op. cit. p. 266.

as such. One was the Gutones, or Guiones, as some read, comparing the Inguaeones later mentioned for this North Sea coast. The other was the Teutons, who brought the amber washed up by the sea on an island Abalus a day offshore. (Some reject the first name as a corruption of Teutons, and so leave only one tribe.) All this brings him to the Elbe, many agree, and the island may be Heligoland.[1] Elsewhere he, or Timaeus using him, is said to have named an island (the same one?) Basilia, and one Xenophon of Lampsacus of some uncertain date before Pliny talked of a vast island Balcia three days off: this is generally suspect as a mere exaggeration of the same, but has been defended as referring to Jutland or south Sweden. There were later Gutones on the other amber-coast beyond the Vistula, but a fancy that Pytheas went so far deserves little consideration. Whether certain Horse-feet and Ear-sleepers and other fabulous peoples go back to him is very dubious.[2]

A sun-height in Celtic country was interpreted by Hipparchus as giving the latitude of 54° (which is that of the Yorkshire coast or the Elbe mouth), and two other statements as giving 58° and 61°, where the longest days were 18 and 19 hours (these answer respectively to the top of Scotland and to north Shetland–Bergen). What did Pytheas really say about Thule? According to the two bitterest critics he heard that it is the northmost of the British isles, six days north of Britain, and near or only one day from the 'frozen' sea, if it was not conceived rather as the 'curdled' sea; in these parts there is something—he had seen it himself from a distance—neither land nor sea nor air but a blend of them, like a sea-lung, in which land and sea and everything floats, and which is in some sort the bond holding all things together, something impassable for men or ships (the wording is very mysterious); there is habitable land up to 'the utmost parts about Thule', where 'the summer tropic is the same as the arctic circle'.[3] He

---

[1] So Detlefsen, *Entdeckung des germ. Nordens*, 1904, p. 12: Hennig, *T.I.* p. 132: Beckers, *Rhein. Mus.* 1929, p. 59 (from Ushant, ibid. p. 55): Elbe, Bunbury, I, 598, etc. Only Teutons, Müllenhoff, Much in *R.E.* Germani. Guiones, Detlefsen, p. 7, cp. Inguaeones, Plin. IV, 96, Ingaevones, Tac. *Germ.* 2. 'Tanais', Pol. ap. Str. 63, 104: Don, Wilamowitz, *Lesebuch*, 1902, I, 226, Gisinger, loc. cit., Burton, loc. cit. Island, Tim. ap. Diod. V, 23 (Basilia), Plin. IV, 94, XXXVII, 35. Probably from P. is Mela on sinus Codanus = German-Jutland coast, thinks Beckers, *Geogr. Zt.* 1936, p. 293: cp. p. 241, n. 2. Domination, D'Arbois de Jubainville etc., denied by Elston, *Early Relations between Celts and Germans*, 1934, pp. 55–7.

[2] Mela, III, 56, Plin. IV, 95 his?, Müllenhoff, p. 483, Rohde, *Griech. Roman*, p. 188. Vistula, Mair, op. cit. (Gutones, etc), and still Broche and Rickard, op. cit. p. 295. Balcia, P.? ap. Xen. ap. Plin. IV, 95: Abalcia, Solinus, 19, 6. Sweden, Detlefsen, op. cit. p. 23, Nansen, p. 101: Jutland, Hergt, p. 34, Jullian, op. cit. p. 422. Same, Beckers, pp. 53–9.

[3] Str. 63, 104, 114, 195, often citing Polybius: one day, Plin. IV, 104. Latitudes, Hipparchus ap. Str. 73: hours, Cleomedes, I, 7, 37, II, 1, 18: Geminus, 6, 8. Thule only hearsay, Burton, loc. cit.

came to these parts, it is thought, says Geminus just after mentioning the parallel of 18 hours: anyhow he states in his book on the Ocean that the barbarians pointed out where the sun went to sleep for a short [summer] night of three or two hours. Another version understands them as referring rather to the long winter night. Did they show where the sun set behind a sacred mountain or island? And was it the place where the sun set at their shortest night? Or did they mean the place where the sun sleeps all 24 hours at least once in the year, namely, the arctic circle?[1] And was he himself in the latitude of 21 or 22 hours, which is above $63\frac{1}{2}°$ or $64\frac{1}{2}°$? Cleomedes says that he is thought to have been in Thule, which is on the arctic circle and which has, it is very wrongly added, a month-long day (Pliny once carelessly says that it has a day of six months, though elsewhere rightly one of 24 hours). Lastly there is what seems to some an unmistakable description of the midnight sun, possibly from the experience of Pytheas.[2]

And the result for the map? Before him uninhabitable cold was supposed to begin not far north of the Black Sea. Now an interval of 11,500 stades was allowed from there to the parallel of Thule, which was put at or near the arctic circle and possibly on the same meridian as that sea, though others draw it in much farther west (see the map). His enemies ruin this map by utterly rejecting any habitable land in such high latitudes and perversely clinging to old notions. Sometimes Thule was understood to be the Shetlands, as when a Roman fleet reached the Orkneys and 'saw Thule from a distance'. A late historian applied the name to Scandinavia, perhaps rightly, according to a view now prevalent. An Irish monk of the ninth century put it in Iceland, where some of his brethren had stayed, a day south of the frozen sea.[3]

Pytheas can hardly have seen the frozen sea himself: indeed, some think that he need not have gone beyond the Shetlands and interpret the rest as hearsay. Before him queer things had been said of 'sluggish' Ocean waters, and more were said after, as of a sea 'stiff for rowers' north of Scotland; there is one beyond south Sweden 'almost immobile, by which the known world is girdled'; natives of Jutland spoke of a 'dead sea' northward, and the Argonauts, coming west from the Caspian 'gulf', had to tow their ship through a dead or Cronian sea. The notion continues in the medieval Lebermeer. It may have started from the fears of seamen caught in calms

---

1 Jullian, loc. cit.: Holmes, p. 226. Geminus, 6, 9 as cp. Cosmas, p. 149 B: Berger, *Erat.* pp. 150–1. Shortest, Nansen, p. 50.

2 Mela, III, 57, Nansen, p. 62, Sir G. Macdonald in *R.E.* Thule: but Hennig denies and cp. Bunbury, II, 353. Cleom. I, 7, 37. Plin. II, 186 as cp. IV, 104.

3 Dicuil, *de Mensura Orbis*, ch. 7. Scand., Procopius, *Bell. Goth.* II, 14–15. Fleet, Tac. *Agr.* 10. Meridian of Black, Nansen, p. 76 as Müller, Kiepert and most, but cp. Bunbury, St Martin, Forbiger: uncertain, Berger, *Erat.* pp. 207–8.

FROM ALEXANDER TO ERATOSTHENES 149

or adverse currents in a foggy sea.¹ The 'sea-lung' has given desperate trouble. Elsewhere a shell-fish is so named (not a jelly-fish as often said), but the point of comparison is obscure, and some deny that it is referred to here at all. What he saw and compared to a 'sea-lung' has been very variously explained; some say a glare of light or phosphorescence on the sea, or the play of colour of the northern lights, many think of the freezing sea or ice-bergs or muddy drift-ice perhaps seeming to confirm hearsay of such a sea, others suggest a low fog over the sea (looking like a jelly-fish, Masson says) or over Frisian sandbanks (looking like a spongy human lung).² If he saw drift-ice in winter in Norway, the description is strangely obscure, and Nansen thinks it rather a rumour of the polar sea, coloured by older fancies of what there might be at the limit of the world, 'a region of darkness and mists, where sea and land and sky were merged into a congealed mass'.

And what was this Thule? Merely the Shetlands, some conclude, heard of as the 'northmost of the British islands', and misplaced too far north, but this is very unlikely. Most discount the phrase and look elsewhere. Many think of Iceland, usually as known only by hearsay; the very latest discussion (Stefansson's, after Broche) argues that he actually reached Iceland, saw the midnight sun as described from its north coast, and went on one day to find himself in a thick fog among mush ice, which rose and fell in a way suggesting the breathing of a jelly-fish. Certainly Iceland is near the frozen sea, though it is far more than six days from Britain and it has no bees for the honey-drink.³ Norway has bees, and also reaches north to the arctic circle (it has oats well up the coast, and barley can

---

1 J. G. C. Anderson's ed. of Tac. *Germ.* on ch. 45, cp. Sen. *Suas.* 1, 1. Partly from ice melting on the sea, Much, *Germania des Tac.* 1937, p. 400. Scotland, Tac. *Agr.* 10: Jutland (Cimbri), Philemon ap. Plin. IV, 95, Detlefsen, op. cit. p. 24. Cronian, *Orphic Argonautica*, Rohde, *Griech. Roman*, p. 223: cp. also Plut. *de Facie in Orbe Lunae*, p. 26. Before, as by Himilco q.v. and cp. *immobiles undas*, Curtius, IX, 4, 18 (cited p. 129, n. 2). Hearsay, Günther, *Gesch. der Erdkunde*, 1904, p. 52: Wilamowitz, op. cit. p. 225.

2 Kähler, op. cit., Hennig, p. 135. Masson, *Ministère de l'Instr. publ. Section de Géogr.* 1923, pp. 55–66, rev. in *Isis*, 1925, p. 177. Fog (off Norway), Hergt, p. 74, Cary-Warmington, Angus: some northern sea-fog, Casson, op. cit. p. 20. Freezing, Ridgeway, 1, 370: icebergs, Bessell, ice-sludge (and fog?), Matthias, p. 17, Markham, p. 29, cp. Nansen, 1, 67. Lights, Gerland, 1894, ap. Berger, p. 348, Gisinger, *R.E.* Geogr. p. 596. Glare, Tozer. Shell-fish, Arist. *H.A.* V, 15, 21, *de Part. Anim.* IV, 5, 43, Plin. IX, 154: not relevant, says Jullian.

3 For I. are Bessell: St Martin, *Hist. de la Géogr.* 1873, p. 104: Berger, p. 364, heard of from Britain, as Kähler (from Shetlands): reached, Mair: yes possibly, Gisinger, loc. cit. ('hearsay' of Str. 104 refers only to frozen sea): reached in 6 days, Broche, Stefansson: passed probably round I., Berthelot, *Rev. Arch.* 1932, p. 8: Philipp, op. cit. p. 51 (hearsay). For Shetlands, Müllenhoff, 1, 385, Kiepert, Bunbury, Tozer, Matthias, op. cit., Haverfield, *Enc. Brit.* 1911, Thule. Columbus on Iceland, Fiske, *Discovery of America*, 1920, 1, 382–3, and see below, p. 340, n. 1.

ripen in the long summer days right up to and within the circle). He could hear of Norway in north Scotland, where the natives may have pointed in that direction, but many now agree that he went himself—from Britain direct or from the Elbe?—and that he sailed up to the line of a 3–2 hours' night, about Trondheim, and was there told of a place farther north where you could *see* the sun go to bed and rise again (?), or even that he went on himself to see the midnight sun.[1] But much of the case for Norway rests on the assumption that the text cited as (*a*) about bees and oats in vague northern parts really applies to Thule. If this is duly discounted, a hearsay of Iceland seems to suggest itself as the more plausible solution. When next we learn anything definite of Iceland, about A.D. 825, it is called Thule and has had Irish hermits, soon to be followed by a Norse colony, which led to another in Greenland and several voyages to the American coast (about A.D. 1000). Columbus seems to have meant Iceland by Thule, and even to have claimed, very dubiously, to have been there himself.

These chilly seas could be used for a rather silly Utopia. Hecataeus of Abdera found a new home for the Hyperboreans in Helixoia, a large and fertile island over against the Celtic coast; there they are visited by Apollo, who is attended by flocks of singing swans from the Rhipaean mountains; besides spurious rivers and the like there is an outer sea called Amalcian, which Pliny understands to be frozen, though this seems to go ill with so favoured a people. By its position the island sounds like a vague Britain with a flattering climate, though we need not believe that the round temple echoes hearsay about Stonehenge. A recent writer suggests that (even in name!) it is Heligoland, the amber island, endowed with the size of Britain or Scandinavia; the whooper swan, which migrates that way, was early connected with Apollo, and one remembers the old hearsay of a German river brought by the amber-trade, the Eridanus, which was later wrongly identified as the Po or Rhône. It is not certain that Hecataeus knew of Pytheas or set out to parody him.[2] A writer who did this, some think, was

[1] Nansen, p. 62, Macdonald, loc. cit. Trondheim, Jullian, op. cit. p. 422, Malye, loc. cit. Hennig, p. 120: Shetelik and Falk, *Scand. Archaeology*, 1937, p. 190: Singer, loc. cit. Norway, also Holmes, p. 226 (hearsay), Hergt, p. 68 (bees, etc.), Cary-Warmington, Kaeppel, op. cit.: *C.A.H.* VII, 53 (De Navarro) and XI, 50 (Ekholm): Gjerset, *Hist. of Norwegian People*, 1927, p. 24. Markham, loc. cit. Possibly to arctic circle, Sarton, *Introd. to Hist. of Science*, 1927, I, 126, 144. Bed, so Angus, op. cit. p. 172.

[2] Tomaschek, *R.E.* I, 1716. Berger, *Erdk.* p. 349. Hec. ap. Diod. II, 47–8, Str. 299, Plin. IV, 95, Aelian, *N.A.* XI, 1: name H. in Steph. Byz.: *F.G.H.* IIIA, 15–18. Rohde, *Griech. Roman*[2], pp. 226–9. Hubert, *Celtes*, 1932, p. 30. Stonehenge, Allcroft, *Nineteenth Century*, Apr. 1920, as Stukeley long before: Philipp, op. cit. pp. 54–6 after Sieglin, who connects the name with the Lexovii of the Seine: Casson, op. cit. p. 20: Grenier, *Gaulois*, 1945, pp. 338–9. Heligoland, Krappe, *Class. Phil.* 1942, pp. 353–70 (but where does he get Helioxoia?). On Hec. see p. 123, n. 1. Britain, also Hennig, *Hist. Zt.* 1928, pp. 1–33, cited by Oldfather on Diod. ad loc. (Loeb): Déchelette, *Arch.* II, 411.

one Antiphanes of Berge, of whom little is known except that he became proverbial as a sort of Munchausen and that Pytheas was wronged by being mentioned in the same breath.¹ Theopompus, a historian fond of pretentious digressions, had a forcible-feeble Utopian tale of which some details are obscure: he used Plato's Transatlantic land, a fourth continent 'outside this world', for placing certain happy and long-lived Meropes, who invaded the Hyperboreans but found them comparatively so wretched that they withdrew in disgust.²

There is no hint that any Greek of this time attempted to follow the track of Pytheas to Cornwall, but the coins of his city now spread deeper into Gaul, and it has been argued that the overland tin-trade there increased, and flourished from about 300 to 50 B.C., being largely in native hands.³ With Roman expansion northward his report should have been better understood, but it had bad luck. His enemies had some excuse for doubting habitable lands far north; for, while not quite unaware that a maritime climate is milder than a continental, they had no idea of the Gulf Stream and how much north-western Europe benefits by the warm wet winds from the Atlantic.⁴ It was hard to swallow not only Thule but a Britain lying well beyond the latitude of south Russia, which seemed next door to a frozen waste. We ourselves do not always remember that Bergen is much less cold in winter than Belgrade, and that our island is on a level with Labrador and Kamchatka.

1 As by Str. 102: Bergaean=lying, ibid. 47, 100, 104. Ps.-Scymn. 652. Parodied, Knaack, *Rh. Mus.* 1906, pp. 135–8 (*c.* 300: at latest 3rd cent. B.C., Rohde, op. cit. p. 251).

2 Ap. Str. 43, 299, Aelian, *V.H.* III, 18, and parodied in comedy *Meropis*. Obscure, Rohde, op. cit. pp. 221–3. Bury, *Anc. Greek Historians*, 1909, p. 166.

3 Cary, *J.H.S.* 1924, pp. 176–8, followed by Tarn, *Hell. Civ.* p. 204. But cp. De Navarro, *Antiquity*, 1928, p. 431.

4 See pp. 194, 255 and p. 358, n. 1. Britain less cold, Caesar, v, 12. Open sea islands milder, Ps.-Hippocr. *On Regimen*, II, 37: cp. p. 153, n. 1 (Theophr.). Dubois, *Géogr. de Strabon*, 1891, pp. 257–63.

CHAPTER V

THEORY IN THE SAME PERIOD

A NEW development of theory about the globe was the supposition that it rotates on its own axis. The priority is given to one Hicetas of Syracuse, who thought, we hear, that the earth rotates, while the sky of fixed stars is stationary, as are the sun and moon(!)—a bad garbling of the original, which referred only to daily movement and meant that the earth by rotating produces the same succession of day and night as if it rested and the sky moved. (The statement was to be known to Copernicus and encourage him to broach his daring theory, while he oddly missed the important texts about the only two ancients who really did anticipate himself.) Apparently Hicetas said that the earth rotates at the centre of the universe, and he cannot have kept a counter-earth as one mutilated text alleges.[1] Ecphantus, perhaps a disciple (not before 400?), seems to have followed suit. Heraclides of Pontus, a pupil of Plato who had heard some Pythagoreans, made the earth rotate on its axis in (not exactly) twenty-four hours. He also realized that two planets, Venus and Mercury, as they appear markedly brighter at some times than at others, cannot revolve in a 'perfect' circle round the earth, and he made them revolve round the sun, and the sun itself round the earth, as Tycho Brahe was to do. He thus boldly rejected the assumption that the heavenly movements are all concentric. Some credit him with the further suggestion that the earth may move round the sun, but the text is corrupt and perhaps really refers to Aristarchus, and, even if it does not, can hardly be accepted against that writer's claims.[2] Tannery and others have questioned whether Hicetas and Ecphantus are anything more than characters appearing in a dialogue of Heraclides.[3] Aristotle does not mention any of the three, and has the earth stationary, as already described.

1 Aet. III, 9 (and some ap. Diog. Laert. VIII, 85). Frank, *Plato u. die sogenannten Pythagoreer*, 1923, p. 215 ascribes the 'Philolaic' system to Hic., but Rehm-Vogel, op. cit. p. 47 deny. Rotates, Theophr. garbled by Cic. *Acad. Pr.* II, 123, Aet. III, 13, 3, *Dox.* 378. I follow T. H. Martin, *Mém. Acad. Inscr.* XXX, 2 (1881): similar Dreyer, *Hist. of Planetary Systems*, 1906, pp. 50–1, 123–7. On Cop. Humboldt, *Cosmos*, II, 691.

2 Refers to A., Heath, *Aristarchus of Samos*, 1913, p. 282 (this doubted by Duhem, *Système du Monde*, pp. 410–18), or someone before A., Berger, *Erdk.* p. 98, even someone in circle of Archytas, Frank, op. cit. p. 138. Credit, Schiaparelli: Heiberg, *Math. and Phys. Science in Ant.* 1922, p. 46: denied by Dreyer, op. cit. pp. 131–5. Heard Pyth., Diog. Laert. V, 36.

3 Tannery, *Mémoires Scient.* 1925, VII, 249–57: Frank, loc. cit.: possibly, Rey, *Jeunesse de la Science grecque*, p. 390. But real, *Dox.* 492, 506, *Vorsokr.* I, 441: Robin, *Greek Thought*, p. 64. Both known to Heraclides, Sarton, *Introd. to Hist. of Science*, 1927, I, 94, 119, 141.

The school of Aristotle did much to develop the sciences, now more clearly marked off from each other. His successor Theophrastus founded botany on a very respectable accumulation of observed material, including good reports by Alexander's companions on things like the banana, the spreading banyan, and the mangroves of tidal beaches; his study of the distribution of plants has its bearings on geography. He wrote also on minerals, winds, and weather-signs, and had occasion to note the contrast between maritime and continental climates. He had very good ideas on slow geological changes, including even the process of denudation. Of great value was his survey of earlier 'physical' doctrines, which was freely used by later compilers: through them it is the source of much of our information, and as such it has been brilliantly restored by Diels in his *Doxographi Graeci*. A fellow-student, Eudemus, did a like service for the history of geometry and astronomy. He is the first to mention the figure of 1/15 of a circle (or 24°) for the obliquity of the ecliptic, and ascribes it to 'other astronomers' since Oenopides. There seems to have been some time-lag before it was really applied to geography. Pytheas, indeed, was intelligent enough to know that he was doing much for geography by testing the zone theory and pushing the limit of the habitable so far north. He could read the proportion of pointer and shadow at Marseilles at noon of the summer solstice as $120:41\frac{4}{5}$, which gives an angle of 19° 12′, and, if the obliquity is added, a latitude of just over 43°, very near the truth. But it is not clear that he could already express latitude in this way, as was presently to be done, or fully understood the relation of his observations to latitude.[1] How he may have connected them with the still very rough effort to measure the globe there is nothing to indicate.

The will of Theophrastus contained a provision for the safe keeping of the maps in his school. A nephew of Aristotle, Callisthenes, historian and victim of Alexander, found room for various digressions on matters like earthquakes, the causes of the Nile flood, and the Libyan depression. A pupil of Aristotle who gave some special attention to geography was Dicaearchus. It has been indicated how well he drew the 'diaphragm' or great central parallel through Rhodes, along which the inhabited world

1 Heidel, *Frame of the Anc. Greek Maps*, pp. 99, 106, criticizing Berger, *Erdk.* p. 339, Gisinger, etc. (see p. 117, n. 1). Oen., p. 113, n. 3. Figure by 'others', Theon after citing Eudemus, Heath, *Greek Astr.* xxxvii: Heidel, op. cit. pp. 72, 102. P. latitude direct by pole height, Müllenhoff, *Deutsche Alt.* i, 310, Nansen, *In Northern Mists*, 1911, p. 47. Shadow, Str. 134. Climates, Theophr. fr. v, *de Ventis*, 7. *Hist. Plant.* iv, 1–8 (banyan, iv, 4, 4, etc.): Tozer, *Anc. Geogr.* p. 200: Bretzl, *Botan. Forsch. des Alexanderzugs*, 1903: ed. Hort, Loeb, 1916. On his 'meteorology' Strohm, *Philologus*, 1937, pp. 249–68, 403–28. Also a history of astronomy, Diog. Laert. v, 50. Th. on winds, J. G. Wood, *Greeks on Winds*, 1894: Sir D'Arcy Thompson, *C.R.* 1918, pp. 49–56. Changes, Ps.-Philo, *de Aet. Mundi*, 118–22, 138–41: see p. 104, n. 1.

was henceforth measured. He himself counted the length as $1\frac{1}{2}$ times the breadth, but few of the details are preserved. Soon after him it is mentioned (by Archimedes) that 'some have attempted' a new estimate of the globe, and Berger and most suggest him as the likely author. A few, however, do not care to trace the source, while one guesses Eudoxus as 'at least probable'; another thinks rather of Aristarchus, here concerned only to give a rough maximum to show that the earth is very small relatively to the universe, or of someone else not long before the great effort of Eratosthenes.[1] The method, a very crude one, is explained as follows. Aswan and Lysimachia, on the Dardanelles, were assumed as on a meridian—really they are about 6° apart—and the difference between the zeniths of the constellations overhead was calculated as 1/15 of the meridian. The required circumference was therefore 15 times the distance between the two places. This was taken as 20,000 stades, which is far too much (Eratosthenes presently made it only 13,100). But, even if the ground distance had been accurate, the constellation method could hardly have been satisfactory. The result, 300,000 stades, though a great improvement on the only previous estimate of 400,000, is still very excessive (over 33,000 miles instead of the real 25,000). It has been argued that, with the obliquity known as 1/15, the figures agree with a distribution of zones and distances as shown on the above diagram. This gives the breadth of the known world as 40,000 stades, and the length would then work out as 60,000 stades.[2] Dicaearchus cannot have altogether distrusted Pytheas, if he thus accepted habitable land to near the arctic circle. Among other work, he measured some of the chief mountains of Greece with a primitive theodolite; the results are ill reported, but they were evidently not very good, though at least reasonable as compared with earlier and later exaggerations of such heights. One purpose may have been to show that the highest were just

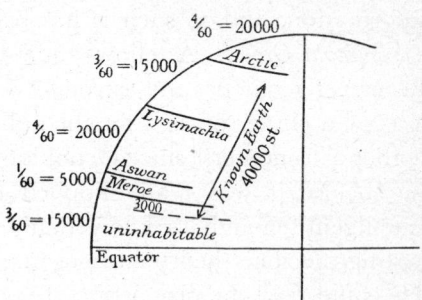

Fig. 17. Dicaearchus: zones.

---

1 Heidel, op. cit. pp. 120, 129, 134. Archim. *Aren.* 1, 8. Likely Dic., Berger, *Erdk.* p. 370: Rehm-Vogel, p. 35: Gisinger, *R.E.* Geogr. p. 599: Martini, *R.E.* v, 559 (doubted by Kubitschek, ibid. Suppl. VI, 33): Tarn, *Hell. Civ.* 1927, p. 246: Sarton, op. cit. p. 145. Cannot trace, Tannery, *Rech. sur l'Hist. de l'Astr. anc.* 1893, p. 110 and Duhem, op. cit. II, 4. Eud., Thalamas, *Érat.* p. 134. Length (as Democritus), Agathem. 1, 2. Call., see p. 136, n. 2, p. 139, n. 1. Will, Diog. Laert. v, 51.

2 Berger, op. cit. p. 374. Method (Posidonius ap.) Cleom. 1, 8: very rough, Dreyer, op. cit. p. 173.

a roughening of the surface of the globe, 'mere dust on a ball', and as negligible as the greatest sea-depths. He connected tides with winds raised by the sun, not yet apparently with the moon. His writings included a minutely detailed account of Greece with 'tabulae', more likely maps than lists, which was still consulted by Cicero as the best authority. Some topographical pieces extant under his name are not his, though one may go back to his type.[1]

Strato, head of the same school from 287 B.C., showed a marked interest in 'physics' and an independent mind with a bent for experiment: so he broke with Aristotle's 'natural' movements of two elements up and two elements down. What concerns geography is a notable theory based on the long familiar fact of the Dardanelles current. Aristotle had conceived the Black Sea as fed by many big rivers and overflowing into the deeper Aegean, with a series of still deeper basins westwards to Gibraltar. In amplification of this it was now argued that the Black Sea had been a lake until, its bed being gradually raised by silt, it flooded over into the Mediterranean. The latter too had been a lake, swollen by many rivers, until it burst out through the narrow land-bar; then its level fell, uncovering the southern coast to its present outline and leaving shells and salt deposits far inland, while at the strait itself there is a submarine reef. Eratosthenes accepted the outbreak and even thought it quite recent, after Homer's time, when sea covered the isthmus of Suez, as he supposed, a confusion of the argument rightly attacked by Hipparchus. Others had reasonable objections, pointing out, for instance, that the exit of neither the Black Sea nor the main sea had really such a steady outward current as the theory postulated. Strabo, our chief informant, seems to accept with the modification (borrowed from Hipparchus) that the sea-bottoms were raised not by silt, which is never carried far from river-mouths, but by slow periodic movements of elevation. As late as 1803 one Bory de St Vincent believed that the sea broke out suddenly through the strait, and argued that it flooded an Atlantis hitherto connecting the islands from Madeira to the Azores and Cape Verde. Moderns admit a land-bridge at Gibraltar, and that the sea once extended farther inland. But it was a shrinking lake, like the Caspian to-day, or rather there were two such lakes with another land-bridge over Sicily. More water was lost through evaporation than was added by both rainfall and rivers together, and so it is still, the level of the sea being

---

[1] *G.G.M.* I, 97–110, 238–43: *R.E.* v, 562, VIII, 424: see p. 204, n. 3. Cic. *Ep. ad Att.* vi, 2. Roughening, Pos. ap. Cleom. I, 10, 56, Gem. 14. Heights, Str. 388, Plin. II, 162, Apul. *de deo Socr.* 8, Theo Smyrn. 124–5, ed. Hiller, Plut. *Aem. Paullus*, 15, 5–7, Bunbury, I, 617, Berger, op. cit. p. 380: Capelle in *Stoicheia*, v (1916) and *R.E.* Meteorologie, p. 352. Exaggerations, Arist. see p. 87, n. 2, Pol. ap. Str. 208–9 (Alps), Artem. ap. Str. 203, Plin. v, 80.

maintained only by an upper current of less saline water from the Atlantic: if the strait were closed again, the sea would not fill to overflowing but would gradually dry up. With the Black Sea Strato was nearer the truth: there the supply of fresh water exceeds the evaporation and the upper current is outwards, though there is a salter undercurrent. As for sea-depths, the ancients knew very little, of course, and the supposed arrangement of ever-deepening basins does not occur in fact. And it was a case not of a lake breaking out but the Ocean breaking in, after all more like the popular fancy that the Pillars of Hercules had been torn apart to let in the Atlantic.[1] It seems that the Mediterranean was once a land-area with two big lakes, while an ice-cap extended as far south as Central Europe. Then the ice melted and the Atlantic rose and burst through the limestone dike at the strait. The subsidence which brought the Ocean far in was after the raising of the young fold mountains which nearly surround the basin, including the Atlas. The eastern strait which partly drained out a once vast Black-Aral sea was opened not suddenly but by slow erosion.[2]

Strato was the tutor of the second Ptolemy, the real founder of the great library and research institute or 'Museum' at Alexandria. Here science now made its chief home, flourishing under liberal patronage and becoming increasingly specialized. In several fields like medicine great progress was made. Mathematics had a golden age with Euclid and Archimedes and others. Astronomy profited from this study and from improved instruments and the use of Babylonian observations. There was a notable effort to make a science of geography. Not all the sciences advanced: for instance zoology strangely declined from the high level of Aristotle into mere compilation of paradoxa or curious facts, which were often fables. Some keen minds were applied to mechanics and such things, hitherto left to despised craftsmen, and for a moment it was perhaps just possible that some useful machines might come long before their time, but the cleverness was largely wasted. Scholarship was busy on old writers, Homer being specially favoured. The new literature was mostly bookish and uninspired, and hardly tried to reflect the bigger world opened by Alexander. There were some attempts to make poetry of science, from snakes and bees to stars. Aratus, about 275 B.C., versified the star-chart of Eudoxus, soberly if not

1 Plin. III, 3–4, VI, 1: Val. Flaccus, I, 587–90, cp. II, 617. Strato in Strabo, 49–51, 64–6: objections, ibid. 51–2, 56–7: Erat. ibid. 38. Berger, *Erat.* pp. 57–68, *Erdk.* pp. 382–3, 390–2. Capelle, *R.E.* Straton, 1931, esp. pp. 299–300. Black overflows, Arist. *Met.* II, 1, 254*a*. Polybius, IV, 39–40 refers to such theories. (On sea-depths odd statements Fabianus ap. Plin. II, 102, Oppian, *Hal.* I, 82–5.) Atlantis, Moreux, *L'Atlantide*, 1924, p. 52.

2 On geol. history E. Ludwig, *Mediterranean*, 1943, pp. 20–5: P. Lake, *Phys. Geogr.* 1936, p. 152: Newbigin, *Med. Lands*, 1924, pp. 26–30. Erosion, Frazer, *Folk-lore in the Old Testament*, 1919, I, 167–71, 360, citing Huxley. See p. 43, n. 3 for a mythical anticipation of Strato's theory.

always with full understanding, adding some more popular matter on weather-signs. He ignored astrology, but, if he was widely read from the first, it was largely because of the growing interest in that pseudo-science. He begins by describing the axis round which the heavens turn, with the earth poised in the middle, and the two poles, one invisible, the other standing high above the Ocean (meaning the horizon). He then gives the northern constellations, beginning with the Bears and including the zodiacal signs themselves (26–320): the southern follow (320–453). He will not discuss the planets, but explains the circles of the celestial sphere, such as the tropic of Cancer, with the turning-point of the sun in summer, the corresponding tropic of Capricorn, and the equator (all this 480–524), and the zodiacal belt with the ecliptic, in which are the apparent paths of the sun and moon and chief planets (its obliquity causes variation in the length of day and night at different seasons and latitudes).

The great Archimedes concerns us chiefly by mentioning the new estimate of the globe discussed above: he gives it casually in a popular essay, the *Sand-reckoner*, designed to show that very large numbers can be expressed. (Greek science suffered badly from the lack of a good system of notation like ours, which comes from the Arabs or through them perhaps mainly from India.) A pupil of Strato was Aristarchus of Samos, who was observing already in 281 B.C. and lived probably till about 230 B.C. In an early work, alone extant, he tried to reckon the relative distances of the sun and moon from the earth: here he assumed these as constant, though evidence to the contrary was already available, and did not yet question the central earth.[1] Later he published, says Archimedes, 'the hypotheses that the fixed stars and the sun remain motionless and that the earth revolves about the sun in the circumference of a circle, the sun lying in the middle of the orbit'. 'He attempted to save the appearances', says another, 'by supposing the heaven to remain at rest and the earth to revolve in an oblique circle, while it rotates at the same time about its own axis and is put in shadow according to its inclinations.' No one is named as accepting this startling theory at the time, and only one afterwards, Seleucus, who lived among the Babylonians but was really a Greek (about 150 B.C.): he is said to have 'expressed it as a definite opinion and not merely a hypothesis' (perhaps he argued that the sun, being the greatest mass, should be the centre of gravitation). The popular philosophies were hostile, when they noticed Aristarchus at all: Cleanthes, head of the Stoic school (about

---

[1] Evidence, Farrington, *Science in Ant.* pp. 181–5: Duhem, op. cit. I, 398. On A. see Heath, *Aristarchus of Samos*, 1913: Duhem, I, 418–23, II, 17–26: Dreyer, pp. 136–48. Aratus, tr. G. R. Mair, Loeb, 1921: Boll-Bezold, *Sternglaube u. Sterndeutung*³, revised by Gundel, 1926, p. 21: Kroll, *R.E.* Lehrgedicht, VII, 1842–57.

263–233 B.C.), protested that the man who had dared to move the hearth of the universe should be tried for sacrilege. (It was uncomfortable, as it was to be again after Copernicus, that men should no longer feel themselves the centre of all things but be reduced to what Lord Balfour called 'a brief and discreditable episode in the life of one of the meaner planets').[1] Scientists too were adverse, even Archimedes and presently Hipparchus, and they seemed to have good reasons. The new doctrine did not in fact 'save the appearances'—it could have done so only by making the earth revolve not in a circle but an ellipse. On the other hand the current astronomy did save them by a system of eccentric circles and epicycles: inherent already in Heraclides, it was now outlined by the 'great geometer' Apollonius of Perga, and was to be adopted by Hipparchus and Ptolemy. Against rotation seemed the absence of parallax: if the earth rotated, a place on its surface was in very different positions at different times, but a fixed star as viewed from it always gave the same angular distance, at least with the instruments available (parallax was not in fact measured till 1832–8, so minute an angle being difficult to observe). Aristarchus anticipated this objection, and rightly answered that the star's enormous distance cancelled the effect of the change of the observer's position; but others preferred to believe that the observer was always at the same point of space on an immobile earth. So his brilliant achievement dropped into limbo till Copernicus, whose own was to meet plenty of resistance and to prevail only because of a new instrument, the telescope, as used by Galileo, and because there was a Kepler to correct his still 'perfect' circles into ellipses. On geography Aristarchus had no influence, unless perhaps by inventing an improved form of sun-dial, otherwise ascribed to Berossus. This man, a Babylonian priest, helped science by publishing a list of his countrymen's observations, and injured it by transplanting their astrology at a moment when both popular superstition and the trend of philosophy favoured its acceptance.[2] In its home, strangely enough, it was being largely superseded, under Greek influence, by a scientific astronomy.

Eratosthenes of Cyrene was called to Alexandria as a royal tutor and then for long was head of its famous Library (about 234–196 B.C.). Scholar and poet, he was a man of many interests, too many for him to be first rate

---

[1] Cited by Gilbert Murray, *Essays and Addresses*, 1921, p. 185. Cleanthes in Plut. *de Facie in Orbe Lunae*, 6, D.L. VII, 174. Sel. in Plut. *Plat. Quaest.* 8, 1, Heath, *G.A.* p. 109: Duhem, I, 423, II, 71: Dreyer, p. 140 thinks S. affirmed only rotation, not the rest. Mass, Frank, op. cit. p. 44, from Aet. II, 24, 8, III, 17, 8. The texts on A. are Archim. *Aren.* I, 4 and Plut. *de Facie*, loc. cit., Heath, *G.A.* pp. 106, 108. Tarn, *Hell. Civ.* p. 241.

[2] Duhem, II, 274: Riess, *R.E.* II, 1810. B.'s school at Cos (before 268 B.C.), Vitr. IX, 2, 6, questioned by Schnabel, *Berossos*, 1923, p. 10 but cp. Boll-Bezold, op. cit. p. 23. See p. 168, n. 1, p. 121, n. 2, p. 218, n. 1. On Apoll. Tannery, *Mém. Scient.* III, 323–5: Tarn, op. cit. p. 242.

THEORY IN THE SAME PERIOD

in anything, it was thought (he had a nickname 'Beta'). But his best work was in geography, and was unquestionably of the highest value. He found geography in a very unsatisfactory condition, and undertook to make it a science by really measuring the globe and fitting the 'inhabited earth' on its surface. His treatise, the *Geographica* in three books, is lost, but the contents, with the criticisms of Hipparchus, are fairly fully known through Strabo. He opened with a sketch of the history of the subject, beginning from the early Ionian maps, rather than from Homer, whom he dismissed as knowing very little and romancing a great deal. In the second book he came to the globe, giving the usual proofs and perhaps adding another from the fact that the same eclipse occurs at different times for different regions; all this he treated at undue length for Strabo, who has hardly any taste for that side of the matter. He then referred to his famous measurement of the globe, but only briefly here, as he had explained it already in a special essay. This too is lost, and Strabo does not seem to have understood it, but the method is recorded elsewhere (only once, as it happens, and in a writer rather out of the way, or it would be far more widely known). It deserves an honourable place in any history of geography or of all science.

At Syene or Aswan (S on the diagram) at the summer solstice the noonday sun was vertical, lighting a deep well all the way down; the ray R falling on the pointer G cast no shadow on the bowl of the dial. Alexandria (A) was taken as being on the same meridian, because the Nile flowed nearly due north; there at the same moment rg, assumed parallel with RG, made a shadow Aa, which was read as 1/50 of the circle of the bowl. The pointers if continued downwards would meet at the centre of the globe C, and the angle ACS = the angle Aga. Therefore the arc subtending it, AS,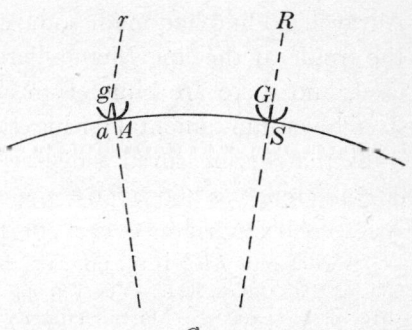

Fig. 18. Eratosthenes: measurement of the earth.

must be 1/50 of the great circle of the earth (the fraction, equivalent to 7° 12′, is very near the truth). He was well aware of the chances of error, except indeed the fact that the earth is not a perfect globe but slightly flattened at the poles (a fact which, of course, has been known only since Newton). Alexandria, being at the western arm of the delta, might lie somewhat off the line—really it is some 3° westward—and the absence of shadow occurred not only at Aswan itself but for a stretch of 300 stades (really it is 37 miles north of the tropic). But he checked by further observations, this time at the winter solstice, when there were shadows at both places, and the difference of the shadows gave the same fraction as before. It remained to get the ground-distance. How he worked here we are not told, but a figure more than usually exact might be expected in an old home of land-surveying. The items apparently came to something so near 5000 stades that he adopted this round number. (The distance by river is given elsewhere as 5300 stades, which he may have reduced to get the direct: it is notable that Ball, himself a surveyor in Egypt, regards his figure as a rough itinerary measure, not an exact one from official surveys as Berthelot thinks.) The required circumference was therefore 50 times this ground distance, or 250,000 stades. So Cleomedes explains, no doubt rightly enough in principle. All others like Strabo give the result as 252,000, and, if the above account is reliable, it is inferred that the geographer himself added the 2000 in order to get a figure divisible into 360 degrees or rather into 60 parts (as degrees begin only later, with Hipparchus). But most accept the larger figure as original, in which case the account cannot be strictly accurate in detail. It is suggested that the fraction may be simplified for a popular audience, 1/50 instead of 10/504, or the ground distance may be (from 5040 stades), or both: one writer has contended that he said 48 × 5250 stades, though this seems arbitrary.[1] It should be added that a few have conceived the procedure a good deal differently. A traveller Philo had made some excellent observations of shadows beyond the tropic at the line Meroe–Berenice, which the geographer must have used, and there are hints of an ancient notion that a calculation in this stretch was fundamental for his estimate; some, relying too much on these, think that he measured a degree hereabouts as 700 stades, and thus the circumference as 360 × 700 = 252,000 stades, and incidentally the distance Aswan–Alexandria as over 7° or 4982 stades.[2]

[1] Viedebantt, *Klio*, 1915, pp. 211–16. Simplified, Forbiger, I, 180, Rehm, *R.E.* XI, 688 (or 5040 stades, Rehm-Vogel, p. 44). Original, most as K. Miller, *Erdmessung im Alt.* 1919, p. 5, against St Martin, *Hist. de la Géogr.* 1873, p. 139, Kiepert, *Lehrbuch*, p. 5, Berger, *Erdk.* p. 410, Heath, *Aristarchus*, p. 339, Dreyer, p. 175, Thalamas, *Géogr. d'État.* p. 162, Berthelot, *Rev. Arch.* 1932, II, 2–7, J. Ball, *Egypt in Classical Geographers*, 1942, pp. 35–42. Schaefer thinks Hipparchus added 2000 (essay cited, p. 112, n. 3). Ivor Thomas, *Selections illustrating the History of Greek Mathematics*, 1941, II, 266–73 (follows Heath). Cleom. *Cycl. Theor. Meteor.* I, 10, 52–5 (using Posidonius), Heath, *G.A.* pp. 109–12. Well, Str. 817, Plin. II, 183. Essay, Hero, *Dioptr.* ch. 35, Schöne: Galen, *Inst. logica*, 12 (contents). Works on Erat. see p. 124, n. 1. On method, Bunbury, I, 621–5: Berger, *Erat.* pp. 99–142, *Erdk.* pp. 406–12: Nissen, *Rhein. Mus.* 1903, pp. 231–45: Thalamas, op. cit. pp. 133–64. Briefly in Singer, *Short. Hist. of Science*, 1941, pp. 70–1: W. Shepherd, *Science Marches On*, 1939, p. 102, etc.

[2] Müllenhoff refuted by Berger, *Erat.* pp. 137–40 and Thalamas, op. cit. p. 92, as similar older views by Bunbury, I, 684. Hints, Plin. VI, 171, Martianus Capella, VI, 598, Simpl. ad Arist. *de Caelo*, II, 14, 16. On Philo see p. 138. Plin. II, 183 repeats the ground-distance as 5000 stades. Mart. Cap. speaks of 'mensores regios Ptolemaei' (falsely for Aswan-Meroe, *R.E.* VI, 365). 5300, Str. 786.

Whatever the details, the method was brilliant. How good was the result? Unfortunately we are not sure what his stade meant, or anybody's for that matter, and this troublesome doubt pervades the whole subject of ancient geography and makes it hard to handle. (Measurements have always been a terrible nuisance, as anyone may learn if he inquires into the complicated history of the English mile.) The stade was originally a furrow-length or furlong and always counted as 600 ft. On short distances like race-courses it was measured out, though even here it differed according to the foot-unit used. The stade was regularly translated into Roman figures as 125 paces or 625 ft. or 8 to the Roman mile: this answers to an ordinary stade of 185 metres or about 607 English feet. There was, however, another reckoning as $8\frac{1}{3}$ to the Roman mile, which gives the Attic stade of 177·6 metres.[1] In practice long distances were not measured out, of course, but calculated by the time taken to cover them at the normal rates of a light traveller, an army, or a ship. Sometimes there might be a well-worn 'royal road', with halts fixed by what men or horses could regularly do; yet even for such the figures given are notably discordant. For Alexander's march we hear of specially trained 'pacers', whose stade may have been rounded to 200 paces and so a good deal shorter than the ordinary. It is astonishing that ancient writers, even geographers, betray hardly any uneasiness about the value of travel reports in stades which might be a very variable quantity; or rather, perhaps, they were so conscious of the looseness of such figures that it did not seem worth while to argue in what stade they were expressed.[2] Eratosthenes in his mapping had to make the best of many distances given by others in such terms. Did he mean ordinary stades, even in his most scientific effort, the measurement of the globe? Strabo shows no suspicion to the contrary, and translates his figures into Roman at the usual rate. So does Pliny: once he adds that the schoenus is 40 of his stades, or 5 Roman miles, while some have given 32 stades to the schoenus (an eastern unit of not very certain value). Underlying this remark has been seen a special stade counted as 1/32 of an Egyptian or 1/40 of a Hellenistic-Roman schoenus, and equal to 300 of the local cubits or 157·5 metres (really over 9 and not 8 to a Roman mile). Such a unit is thought likely for 'the royal measurers of Ptolemy' or the old surveys used to obtain the ground distance, which on this basis becomes reasonably

---

[1] Pol. ap. Str. 322 and VII, fr. 57 and so Posidonius, Kubitschek, *R.E.* Karten, x, 2080. Cp. 8 stades 'as most', Str. 322, Plin. II, 85, Pol. III, 39, 8, Varro ap. Cens. 13: a little less, Plut. *C. Gracchus*, 7. Mile, J. W. Gregory, *Story of the Road*, 1931, p. 190: Jervis, *World in Maps*, 1938, p. 15.

[2] Hultsch, *Griech. u. röm. Metrologie*², 1882, p. 44: Berger, *Erat.* p. 136. Itin. stade say 160–8 m., Thalamas, op. cit. p. 158. Discordant, Tannery, *Mém. scient.* III, 56, comparing Hdt. v, 52 and Xen. *Anab.* II, 2, 4.

accurate, while on the ordinary stade it is badly overestimated. Anyhow many since D'Anville, and the great bulk of recent authorities, have taken the short stade as meant.[1] On this the circumference of 250,000 stades works out at 39,375 kilometres, and that of 252,000 stades at 39,690 km. or 24,662 miles, less than 200 miles short of the actual! Or the diameter is only 50 miles less than the real polar! Even with some discount for a happy cancelling out of various errors, it is very wonderful, if true, and should be cried from the house-tops as the best thing in ancient science, a thing never really improved on till Picard in Newton's time. But it seems too good to be true. On the ordinary stade, at 177·6 metres, the result is 44,400 or 44,755 km., which is 11–12% too much, and at the higher reckoning of the stade the excess is still greater.[2] Even so this was the only really sound attempt to measure the globe in ancient times. To Pliny already it seemed an *improbum ausum*, an unconscionable impudence of Greek speculation, and its fame rang down the darkening Roman centuries, and was never quite forgotten in the Middle Ages. (As for Newton there is a curious story, derived from friends of his and often repeated since, that at first he used the current seamen's figure of 60 miles to a degree of latitude: so he found his calculations for gravitation not coming right and laid them aside till some years later, when he had heard of Picard's new and very exact estimate, 69·1 statute miles. But Newton himself nowhere states what figure he originally assumed, and it does not seem obvious why he was unaware of several figures already available, one only a fraction of a mile too much and two of about 67 miles, like Snell's in a treatise of 1617 aptly called *Eratosthenes Batavus*.)

On the globe thus measured the zones were arranged as follows. The tropic and the arctic circle (with Thule) were fixed on the usual estimate

1 So St Martin, op. cit. p. 138, Tannery, op. cit. III, 62–3, Hultsch, op. cit. pp. 60–3, Dreyer, loc. cit.: Heath, *Aristarchus*, p. 340, and in *Legacy of Greece*, 1922, p. 126: Berthelot, op. cit. pp. 1–2 and *Afrique*, 1927, p. 223: Rehm-Vogel, p. 44: probably, Tarn *Hell. Civ.* 1927, p. 247: Cary, *Hist. of Greek World* (323–146 B.C.), 1932, p. 344 (method, ibid. pp. 407–8): K. Miller, op. cit. p. 7: S. Günther, *Gesch. der Erdkunde*, 1904, p. 23. Schoenus, so Viedebantt, loc. cit.: Oxé, *Rhein. Mus.* 1938, p. 60: Plin. XII, 53. 252,000 st.=31,500 m.p. (Roman miles), ibid. II, 247.

2 Heidel, *Frame*, p. 124, says $13\frac{3}{4}$% (similar Raisz, *General Cartography*, 1938, p. 17): less than one-seventh, Bunbury, I, 625, Tozer, p. 172: Ball, loc. cit.: Nissen, op. cit. p. 241 chooses 177·6 metres. Barber in *C.A.H.* VII, 263, gives about 28,000 miles as cp. real 24,860: so Bury, *Hell. Age*, 1925, p. 21. About 30,000, L. D. Stamp, *The World*[8], 1935: 25,700, Stembridge, *The World*, 1940, p. 3. About 29,000, Burton, *Discovery of Anc. World*, 1932, p. 56. About 24,000, Dampier-Whetham, *Hist. of Science*, 1929, p. 52. Almost exact or 20% too large acc. to stade, Schlesinger in *Development of the Sciences*, ed. Woodruff, Yale, 1923, p. 136. Newton story e.g. in Sir D. Brewster's *Life*, 1855, I, 26, 290–2: cp. doubts of Dampier-Whetham, op. cit. p. 429, A. Wolf, *Hist. of Science...in 16th and 17th Centuries*, 1935, p. 151. Snell, etc., E. G. R. Taylor, *Late Tudor and Early Stuart Geography*, 1934, p. 81. Preserved Smith, *Hist. of Mod. Culture*, 1930–4, I, 117–18, II, 32.

THEORY IN THE SAME PERIOD

of the obliquity of the ecliptic as 1/15 of the great circle (or 24°): two texts seem to ascribe a more accurate one, 11/166 or 23° 51′, but should not be so interpreted. The known 'inhabited world' filled the whole temperate zone between, and overlapped the tropic half way to the equator, its total breadth being 37,800 stades. Elsewhere he says 38,000, which seems only a round number, though some explain the discrepancy by using the texts just mentioned, which would add 200 stades to the temperate zone.[1] In some early verses he had taken the 'torrid' zone literally, but he now describes it as inhabited for the overlap to the Cinnamon Coast at least. A statement that he spoke of the equator itself as habitable, like some later, is probably a mistake of Strabo's for Posidonius.[2] The same verses had assumed both 'dwellers opposite' and Antipodes in the south temperate zone, and he still believed in these as a matter of theory, but they were beyond the reach of practical geography, and his present business was to map the known lands.

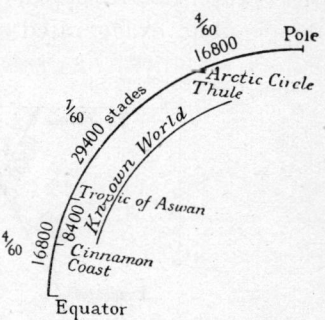

Fig. 19. Eratosthenes: zones.

He regarded the known earth as an island. The outer sea might be taken as continuous, he thought, because similar tides were observed on several of its coasts, as in the Atlantic and Indian Oceans. Besides, it had been sailed in most parts(!). Where it had not been sailed, it might be assumed to exist, as eastwards and westwards from the Caspian 'gulf', supposed to have been proved a gulf by Patrocles, and along the south of Africa (clearly he had no use for the story of Necho's seamen). A view that he suggested a doubt of the continuous Ocean, as some did before and after, seems wrong.[3] He compared his own outline of the known earth to a chlamys or sleeveless cloak.

To fit the known earth on the globe he calculated its breadth and length along two great lines intersecting at Rhodes. The breadth line is a prolongation of the supposed meridian stretch used in his measurement of the globe. How far it is from being a real meridian may be seen from the red

---

[1] Bunbury, 1, 664 from Ptol. *Almag.* 1, 1 and Theon Alex., who are explicit. St Martin, p. 136, Thalamas, op. cit. p. 122: so Dreyer, p. 176, Singer, op. cit. p. 76, Schlesinger, op. cit. p. 137, but cp. Berger, *Erat.* p. 131.

[2] Strabo, 97. Berger, *Erat.* p. 85: see p. 177, n. 1, p. 210, n. 1, p. 214, n. 1. Verses, Hermes fr. 19: Berger, op. cit. p. 87: see p. 219, n. 3. Tarn, op. cit. p. 248 and *C.Q.* 1939, p. 193 wrongly accepts the mild equator as E.'s: so St Martin, op. cit. p. 133 (high, as Nile rises there).

[3] Berger's, *Erat.* p. 89: see p. 208, n. 2. Continuous, ap. Str. 56. Uniform tides, ap. Str. 5, questioned by Seleucus and Hipparchus, ibid. p. 6. Cloak, Str. 113, 118.

line of Fig. 20 as compared with the real meridian of Alexandria. Along it are given his distance items, and a cross marks places for which good astronomical observations were available. A notable correction, from an observation of his own, was the stretch Alexandria–Rhodes, which skippers had exaggerated as 4–5000 stades. The next is grossly excessive,

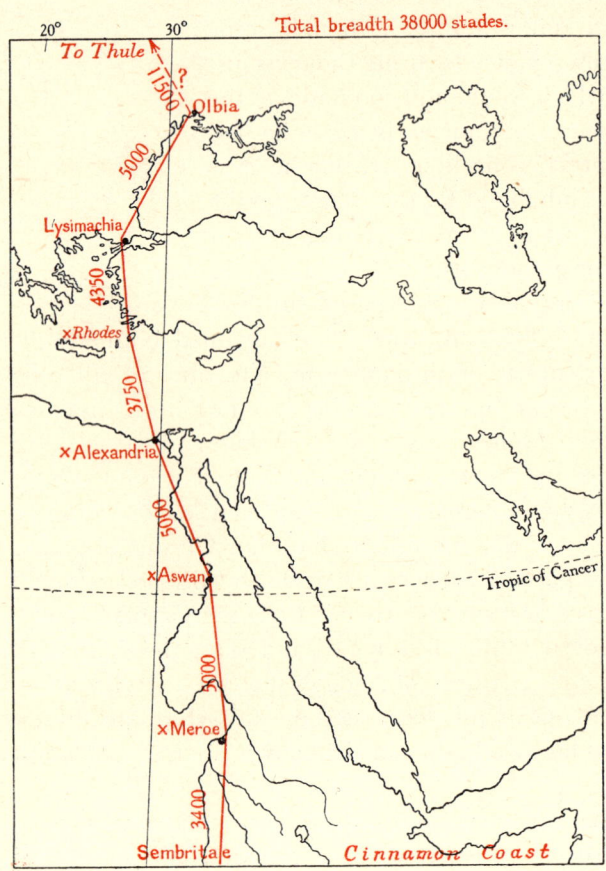

Fig. 20. Eratosthenes: latitudes.

though the placing of Lysimachia (=about 43°) is much better than the datum (=48°) used in the crude estimate of the globe made before his time.[1] By a cancelling of errors Olbia comes off quite well, only $1\frac{1}{2}$° too far north. How he dealt with Thule has already been discussed (perhaps the red line should be drawn due north from Olbia).

The length was worked out along the great central axis adopted from

---

[1] See p. 154, n. 2. Berger, *Erat.* pp. 143–55, *Erdk.* pp. 414–16, Bunbury, 1, 639. Rhodes, Str. 125.

Dicaearchus. How far it diverges from a real parallel may be shown roughly as follows. There are glaring errors about Messina and the Indian mountains, but on the whole it is remarkably good. At best, however, it is a band rather than a line, for he can speak of it as the parallel of Rhodes or of Athens, though he knows these places to be 400 stades apart in latitude

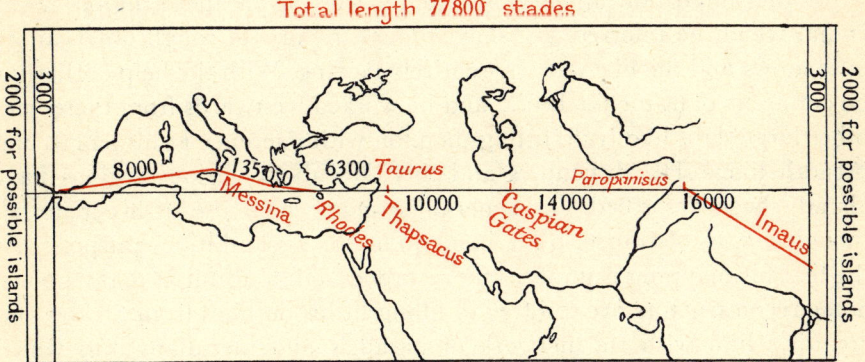

Fig. 21. Eratosthenes: length-line.

(really they are much more).[1] As for the items, there is still a bad disproportion between the two basins of the Mediterranean, which is rather odd (though Strabo later has a disproportion here of another kind and even far worse). The ancients never had any practical means of fixing

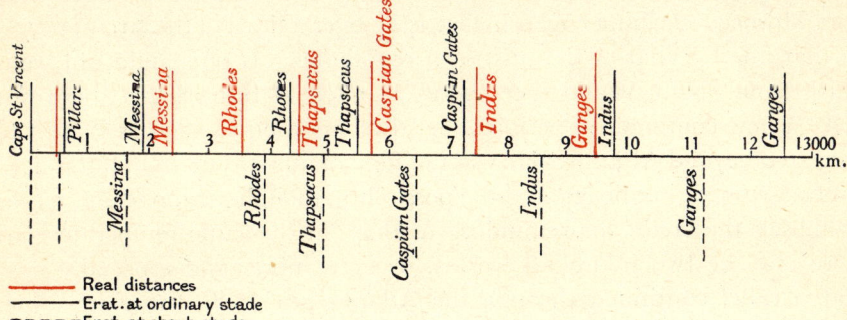

Fig. 22. The same.

longitudes: they could only work with travel data like Alexander's march and manipulate them to guess distances along a parallel. It is not surprising that the eastern items are badly exaggerated. The whole length from Cape St Vincent to the Ganges mouth is made 70,800 stades: on the ordinary stade (of 177·6 metres) this is an excess of some 1900 miles, and a considerable excess even on the short stade, as indicated on the diagram. A further

[1] Str. 35, 39, 79. On the length line, Str. 64, 92–3: Bunbury, I, 627–30, 642–3: Berger, *Erat.* pp. 152–4, *Erdk.* pp. 416–19: about one-third in excess, Tozer, p. 173.

3000 stades are allowed for the projection of India, and 2000 more at each end of the map for possible islands. The grand total is roundly 78,000 stades so that the length is rather more than twice the breadth: perhaps a certain prejudice for such a proportion was partly responsible for the outer additions.

Another important line for his mapping was the parallel Ethiopia–south India, which he inferred so riskily, though reports of rough observations of shadows and the like were not entirely lacking. With the help of this line he got a sort of frame for India, and he worked westwards from there with other large slabs like Iran, fitting them on with reference to his length and breadth lines. His difficulties and mistakes about various regions have already been described. In general he made good use of his material, though it was, of course, quite inadequate for his ambitious purpose. At the best his mapping is imperfectly recorded and doubtful at many points. Some reconstructors are too free in filling in his outlines from Strabo and crediting him with the network of parallels and meridians into which Hipparchus transformed his cruder working sections.[1] After all he had only a few such lines. As for the projection, he drew his lines straight and intersecting at right angles, without attempting anything better.

He realized that the known earth occupied lengthwise little more than a third of the way round the globe, which was under 200,000 stades on the parallel of Rhodes. (The fraction is surprisingly accurate, as the Old World from Morocco to China covers in fact 130°, over a third of the circuit nearly on that line.) What of the unknown remainder? If one could sail westwards from Spain, would there be a clear sea to India? Or would one strike a new continent of perioikoi or 'dwellers round', such as Plato had suggested beyond Atlantis? He was not fond of idle speculation, but it need not be assumed that he ignored the possibility, though Strabo seems to take to himself the credit for reminding us that 'in the same temperate zone there may be two inhabited worlds, or even more, and especially near that parallel continued through the Atlantic sea'.[2] So the older writer is generally thought to have preferred the other view, that one could sail all the way west to India 'if the width of the Atlantic sea did not prevent it'.

---

1 As Thalamas, op. cit. pp. 4, 209 complains: E.'s σφραγῖδες or πλινθία not rectangles, Rehm-Vogel, p. 43. Riskily, see p. 134, n. 2, p. 135, n. 1 (shadows, ibid.): Berger, *Erdk.* p. 420. Straight, ibid. p. 428. Parallels and meridians, Berger, *Erat.* pp. 189–209. Med., cp. Strabo's map sketched on p. 194, Dubois, op. cit. p. 355.

2 Str. 64-5, cp. 118 εἰ περιοικεῖται: Berger, *Erat.* p. 87, *Erdk.* p. 398: Thalamas, pp. 222, 232. Probably Erat., Tarn, *Hell. Civ.* 1927, p. 249: cp. p. 213, n. 2. Bury, *Hell. Age*, 1925, p. 21 agrees with Berger's doubts. Clear sea, Fiske, *Discovery of America*, 1892, reprint 1920, I, 369.

Brilliant as was this effort in geography, it was far from being common knowledge, and even long afterwards there were many otherwise cultivated men who ignored the very fact of the globe. The prevailing philosophies, absorbed in ethics, were not of a scientific temper. The Epicureans, indeed, adopted the mechanistic physics of Democritus in order to rule out interfering gods, and they rejected the fifth element and the superstition of astrology. But this did their astronomy no good, and they were queerly indifferent to scientific truth: so long as lightning was not a tantrum of Zeus, it might be almost anything you please. It is vain and mad, they said, to assert that the sun must move from one cause; perhaps it passes under the earth, perhaps it is quenched daily and a new sun formed, very probably it is about the same size as it appears—a childish outburst of petulance against the divine stars. (This absurdity is not from Democritus, who said that the sun was large.) Their earth seems to be the old flat disk or shallow tambourine 'riding on air'; they deny the globe and laugh at Antipodes who have night when we have day and walk feet uppermost without tumbling downwards into the sky. All this is sadly un-Greek, it has been said, and part of a general 'failure of nerve'.[1] Anyhow a rationalism so blandly careless could do little for science, for which some of these opinions were a downright slap in the face.

The Stoics believed in a fiery aether pervading the universe as a sort of life-force and sustaining its orderly motion and the balance and 'sympathy' of all its parts. This matter is somehow active and conscious, a Spirit or Reason working where the rival school sees only chance combinations of atoms. It moves the divine stars in their stately measure round the earth; it causes the sun to mark day from night and to bring the seasons by going northward or southward; it even allows floods and earthquakes and eruptions for the economy of the whole. Such is the great Order to which man, whose own soul is a spark of the divine fire, should willingly conform himself, as he will have to obey anyhow ('ducunt volentem fata, nolentem trahunt'). It is a manageable universe with everything moving round the earth and with man as the moral centre. In general the Stoics borrow their cosmology from Aristotle, with the globe and Antipodes. So much the better for geography, but they, too, show little scientific insight, and they make dangerous concessions to divination and astrology. Sometimes they revert to old Ionian fancies, as when they think of an ocean along the

[1] Gilbert Murray, *Five Stages of Greek Religion*², 1925, p. 142: astrology, ibid. p. 178, Farrington, *Science and Politics in Anc. Greece*, 1939, p. 140. Earth, Epicurus ap. Diog. Laert. x, 74: Lucr. v, 434, 449, 495. Antipodes, Lucr. I, 1052–82. Sun, ibid. v, 650–79, size, 564–91. Various phenomena, ibid. vi. C. Bailey, *Epicurus*, 1926 (sun, Letter II, 91–2, etc.), *Greek Atomists and Epicurus*, 1928, pp. 359–63 as cp. Dem. ibid. p. 149, sun large, Cic. *de Fin.* 1, 6, 20.

equator because it seems wanted to feed the sun with its evaporation.[1] Of other schools, the Cynics have no use for any knowledge not immediately translatable into conduct, and the Sceptics would suppress the desire to know as vain and unhappy, like the Indian fakirs whom their founder Pyrrho had seen.

All these schools were to continue on the same lines for several centuries. How strangely insecure were the best gains of ancient science, including the earth-globe, when a respected philosopher like Epicurus could treat them so cavalierly! And his many followers went on repeating him, long after the globe had been not only proved but strikingly well measured, and after one or two had even made it go round the sun!

Astrology was to put the various countries under the influence of special signs of the zodiac, and traces have been detected of an early scheme of this kind, going back to an Egyptian of about 200 B.C., and even much further, to a time when western lands like Britain were not in the view.[2]

The learned Alexandrine poets have little of interest for our matter except the above-mentioned verses on zones by Eratosthenes himself, here apparently competing with Aratus. He laughed at the traditional localizings of the adventures of Odysseus, but others liked geography of this antiquarian cast, and wrote such things as 'a list of rivers' and just-so stories on the legendary origins of place-names and customs. An epic on the Argonauts has stretches of versified periplus like a catalogue of peoples along the south coast of the Black Sea, the same old series.[3] These writings have small value for the new knowledge of their own day, and still less for its brilliant science.

[1] Cleanthes ap. Gem. 16, 21, Cic. *N.D.* II, 40 and 118, III, 37,: Macr. *Sat.* I, 23, 3, *Somn. Scip.* II, 10, 10: Cleom. I, 6, Plin. II, 46, 'sidera humore pasci', Lucan, x, 255, 'Oceano pasci Phoebumque polumque': Berger, *Erat.* p. 23: Dreyer, p. 159. Eruptions, Ps.-Arist. *de Mundo*, 5–6, 396*b*–400*a*: stars, ibid. 2, 391*a*, 392*a*. Insight, Farrington, op. cit. pp. 114–16. Manageable, G. Murray, *Essays and Addresses*, 1921, pp. 98, 184. Bevan, *Stoics and Sceptics*, 1913, pp. 109–18. A bad step back about planets, Dreyer, loc. cit.

[2] Cumont, *Klio*, 1909, pp. 263–73, oldest astrol. chorography: similar Boll-Bezold, op. cit. p. 64 (Egypt under Aquarius, etc.).

[3] Apoll. Rhod. II, 345–409: for his geography see p. 141, n. 1: Wilamowitz-Moellendorff, *Hell. Dichtung*, 1924, II, 185–91. Rivers, Callimachus ap. Str. 397: in prose, as *Marvels according to Localities*, etc., Callimachus, ed. Mair, Loeb, 1921, p. 12. E.'s verses, p. 163, n. 2: E. Schwartz, *Charakterköpfe aus der ant. Lit.* 1919, II, 84–6.

CHAPTER VI

THE ROMAN REPUBLIC

HAVING prevailed against Carthage, the Roman Republic was now drawn into a career of aggression resulting in the mastery of an orbis terrarum round the inner sea. The first advances seemed rather the logic of events than deliberate policy, but appetite grew with easy triumphs, and the ruling class became more and more predatory. Senators had little respect for trade, and it is not proved that commercial motives counted much, but there was plenty of spoil from wars and the misgovernment of rich provinces. In the end Rome took credit to herself for 'sparing the conquered', and some could defend her dominion as well earned, 'patrocinium orbis terrae verius quam imperium'; but the conquest was ruthless enough, and the eastern lands suffered badly, especially when involved in the agonies of Roman civil wars. We need not follow the whole ugly process in detail except where it brought gains for geography, as in the northern hinterland, hitherto poorly described by the Greeks. In the east it was merely a case of taking over some relics of Alexander's heritage: the scenes were novel to the Romans themselves, but their campaigns added little to general knowledge, unless about corners like Armenia and the Caucasus. Their writers sometimes talk naïvely as if their dominions included 'all lands not inaccessible'. But for exploration, beyond the range of their arms, they did nothing as yet, and it was no credit of theirs if a few new reports came, like the first ill-understood rumours of the Chinese 'Silk-men'.

Their wars were told in general and special histories with such account of the scenes as was thought to the purpose. Romans themselves produced no formal treatise on geography till Varro right at the end of the period, and his is known only indirectly as used in later works. Much of our matter concerning the subject comes from Strabo, who wrote in the early Empire but drew freely on writers of this time.

§1. THE EAST

The intervention of Rome was soon disastrous for the Hellenistic kingdoms. Macedonia was humbled and ordered to keep her hands off Greece (197 B.C.). Antiochus III, encroaching in the same direction, was driven out and pursued into Asia Minor. He was still a Great King, who had carried his arms as far east as Bactria, and his host included Indian elephants and Arabian camels and picturesque contingents from the Dahae and other peoples 'barely heard of by name' ('nominibus gentium vix fando auditis'); yet he was easily overthrown, and had to give up everything north of the Taurus. A consul made a lucrative march round the evacuated country and inland to beyond Ankara, where he robbed the Galatian robbers of their hoards. The Senate was slow to annex, but enjoyed dictating to kings. An envoy was able to stop short Antiochus IV invading Egypt (168 B.C.). In the same year a restive Macedonian king was vanquished and deposed. Among the hostages taken for the good behaviour of Greece was Polybius, who became the friend of leading Romans and the chief historian of his times; he asked himself how these exceptional barbarians had subjected 'almost all the inhabited world' in half a century, and answered that they deserved their success by their sound character and government, though he found cause to complain of their brutal power-politics. Soon Macedonia was definitely annexed, with Greece to be under its governor's eye (146 B.C.). The kingdom of Pergamum, long a favoured ally, was taken over as a province of 'Asia' (133 B.C.), and bled by greedy proconsuls and greedier tax-farmers. Rhodes had her sea-trade ruined to favour Delos, which became a huge slave-market, though a statement that it dealt with ten thousand slaves a day is no doubt over-coloured. The pirates who supplied it went unchecked, except that a strip near their chief base in Cilicia was occupied in 103 B.C. (it was to come more into the limelight when they were at last swept from the sea and rounded up in this corner in 67 B.C.).

Strained and corrupted by this unscrupulous imperialism, the Republic fell into civil disorders. The chance to rescue the east was seized by Mithridates, king of Pontus, with the help of his son-in-law, who had enlarged Armenia at the cost of the last feeble Seleucids. But presently Lucullus pushed him back to Pontus and out of it, took his ally's new city of Tigranocerta (somewhere near the upper Tigris), and pressed on till within sight of the capital and Mount Ararat. There his hard-driven troops mutinied, and he had to retreat, on a line somewhat east of Xenophon's. The ground was lost for the moment, but his successor Pompey had an easy task: the Armenian submitted and was left with a reduced kingdom, while Mithridates fled round to the Crimea (65 B.C.). Pompey followed as far as the Caucasus (it was to be reached again later by Antony's general Canidius).[1] Rome was still reluctant to annex countries too far inland and

---

[1] In 36 B.C., Str. 500: *C.A.H.* XI, 71. L.'s campaigns, Eckhardt, *Klio*, 1909, pp. 400–12, 1910, pp. 192–231: Ormerod in *C.A.H.* IX, 365–71: Debevoise, *Pol. Hist. of Parthia*, 1938, pp. 70–5: T. R. Holmes, *Roman Republic and the Founder of the R. Empire*, 1923, esp. I, 192–9 (site of Tigranocerta, ibid. pp. 409–25). R. conquest in A.M., see Broughton in Frank's

difficult to hold, and only one province was added, 'Bithynia and Pontus', the rest being left to 'client' kings.

The whole great block was not yet called 'Asia Minor', a happy name not apparently invented before late antiquity (Orosius). The old mistake about the narrow neck had been corrected long since, but some could still repeat it and talk of 1500 stades when others said 3000. The Taurus is conceived to run due east and to be not so much a range as a mountain-belt often 3000 stades broad and including whole nations like Armenia. The main road is described as from Ephesus east past Apamea, a great trade-centre, and Mazaca (Caesarea) to the Euphrates crossing. Some inland parts are still rather vague in Strabo, though he had travelled a good deal there from his native Pontus. The outline is somewhat misconceived, the northward bulge being exaggerated and the Aegean coast continued north too far.[1] Armenia with its 'mountain-plains' is well described from eye-witnesses. He forgets even to mention the southern and longer arm of the Euphrates, and presently it is treated as a tributary as it is to-day. There is some confusion about the lakes—Urmia seems given twice under different names. The Tigris is brought from an 'icy Niphates', which took the fancy of Roman poets (as a mountain or a river), and it is strangely supposed to flow in a visible current through Lake Van and then for some way underground.[2]

The Caucasus isthmus is sometimes underestimated by more than half as 1500 stades. The old glamour of the Argo clings to Colchis, in which Strabo has also some family interest. Dioscurias is still wrongly thought the easternmost place on the Black Sea. New details are given of native kingdoms, especially the Iberian, with its strongholds about Tiflis guarding the main pass. Eastwards were Albanians, partly nomad, who sacrificed human victims to the moon, and above this people some contrived to have Amazons. The Kur, though said to have its own mouth into the Caspian,

---

Econ. Survey, IV, 1938, pp. 505–34. March of Manlius, 'per Axylon quam vocant terram', Livy, 38, 18. Slaves at Delos, Str. 669: Rostovtzeff, *Soc. and Econ. Hist. of Hellenistic World*, 1941, II, 794. Cilicia, Ormerod, *Piracy in Anc. World*, 1924, ch. 6. Naïvely, see p. 223, n. 1. Sparing, Virg. *Aen.* VI, 853: Cic. *de Off.* II, 27. Trade, ibid. I, 42, 151. Pol. I, 1, VI, 56: Glover, *Springs of Hellas*, 1945, ch. 6. (For the cherry from Cerasus see p. 228, n. 1: Plin. xv, 102, Tert. *Apol.* 11, Amm. Marc. XXII, 8, 16.) Ant.'s forces, Livy, xxxv, 48, xxxvII, 40.

1 Str. 632, bulge, 645: mistake also on Lycia, ibid. 677. Road, Artem. ap. Str. 663 (without distances) and Plin. II, 244. Neck, Artem. ap. Plin. VI, 7: better, Erat. ap. Str. 68. For Strabo, XII–XIV on A.M., esp. Bunbury, II, 292–305. Name first Orosius, I, 2, 14.

2 Armenia, Str. 527–33, Bunbury, II, 287–91. Witnesses like Theophanes, who accompanied Pompey. Lake U. in Str. 523, 529. S. arm as Arsanias in Plin. V, 84. Niphates, Hor. *Odes*, II, 9, 20: river in Lucan, III, 245, Juv. VI, 409. Tigris, Lucan, III, 261–3. On Strabo's sources in Bk. XI K. J. Neumann, 1881.

may have already joined the Aras, as Pliny presently says and as it does to-day; we hear of a trade-route upstream and so across the watershed to the Phasis. In this connection Pompey's companions repeat the old and probably wrong notion of Indian wares coming down the Oxus to the sea. Caspian water was brought to him, it is said, when three days' journey away, and seemed comparatively sweet, a fact which was explained by the inflow of big rivers. The sea was generally assumed to be a gulf, but one writer somehow reverted to the first idea of Alexander's companions about the Tanais passing round north of a lake.[1]

Pompey turned south to annex Syria, where the Seleucids could be treated as defunct. Antioch was to be the hub of the Roman East, though not comparable in trade with Alexandria, being fifteen miles upstream and reachable only by boats from an indifferent port (to-day long silted up). Large parts of the country were still left to native rule, including the Jews with their high priest and a Nabataean Arab kingdom controlling the inner caravan-route leading north to Damascus. The name Syria was often conveniently used for the whole stretch, and 'Hollow Syria' was sometimes loosely extended, though properly the valley between the two Lebanons, called the Bekaa or 'depression' to-day and sadly run to swamp. (The country eastwards from Euphrates to Tigris was often called Syria too, but Syria 'between the rivers', ἡ μέση τῶν ποταμῶν, or Mesopotamia.) Much of the good description of Syria comes from Pompey's friend and historian, the philosopher Posidonius, who was born here. There are striking accounts of famous places like Tyre, with its high houses and smelly dye-works, and Jerusalem, in a land no better than a quarry and neglected till the 'Egyptian priest' Moses chose it for his temple, a temple with no images. Among natural curiosities are underground rivers, signs of old volcanic action to confirm the legend of Sodom, and the dismal Asphalt Lake, not yet mentioned as the Dead Sea (heard of long since as so salt that a man floats and no fish can live). There is some confusion with the Sirbonian bog near the border of Egypt, and a bad blunder of Strabo's about the Jordan reaching the Mediterranean (a muddle with the Litani?).[2] A writer

[1] Polybius, III, 37–8: Berger, *Erdk.* p. 523. Oxus, see p. 127, n. 3, p. 128, n. 2: Varro on C. in Mela, III, 38, Plin. VI, 38. Iber. and Alb., Str. 499–500, Bunbury, II, 279–82: W. E. D. Allen, *History of the Georgian People*, 1932, pp. 60–4. Isthmus, Artem. and Pos. as cp. 3000 in Str. 491. Kur own mouth, Theophanes ap. Str. 501, cp. Plin. VI, 26. Diosc., Str. 497. Strabo's grandfather governor of Colchis under Mithridates, ibid. 499. Amazons, Theoph. ibid. 503–4.

[2] Str. 755: bog, confusion, 763, cp. 760 (Plin. v, 68 rightly). Lake, Arist. *Met.* II, 3, 359: 'fama nihil mergi', Plin. v, 72. Syria, Str. 749–60, Judaea, 760–4: Bunbury, II, 317–19. Sodom, Pos. ap. Str. 764, see p. 104, n. 3. Name Syria, Str. 749, cp. 754, 756, Plin. v, 66: differently Hölscher, *Palästina in der pers. u. hell. Zeit*, 1903, p. 12. Honigmann, *R.E.* Syria (1932). Μέση, Diod. XVIII, 3, 31, Arr. v, 25, 4. Mesop., Plin. loc. cit.

interested in the Jews and other eastern peoples was one Alexander Polyhistor, evidently from his fragments a busy but uncritical compiler, and another authority was Nicolaus of Damascus, Herod's secretary.

The stage was now set for the endless feud with the Parthians, who had risen high from small beginnings as a Transcaspian desert tribe. Antiochus IV might have stopped them, but he died on the way at Ispahan, and they had occupied Media by 160 and even Babylonia by 141 B.C. with a new capital at Seleucia there. The first diplomatic contact with a Roman general was in 92 B.C.; presently Lucullus had made a threatening gesture, and Pompey would not recognize an Euphrates frontier. Crassus sought military fame here and proposed to dictate terms in Seleucia, though a statement that he dreamt of Bactria and India and the outer sea is wild; anyhow he had hardly begun the attack through the Mesopotamian desert when he was overthrown near Harran (53 B.C.) and Syria itself was very nearly lost. (We hear of some prisoners from his army drifting as far east as Merv.) Caesar meant to wipe out the disgrace; Antony resumed his design and penetrated through the Armenian mountains to a place southeast of Tabriz, but was forced to retreat. His adventure brought some details of a corner hitherto little noticed, Media Atropatene, whose name remains as Azerbaijan. The Parthian question was left to give repeated trouble to the Emperors, and no satisfactory frontier was ever found. Naturally there were books on a people which appeared 'in some sort a rival of Rome', but they are lost. One was by Apollodorus of Artemita, a place east of the Tigris and now under their rule (about 100 B.C.): it was used by Strabo in a special treatise, itself lost, and more slightly in his *Geography*. Another by an unknown eastern Greek, about 85 B.C., was used through Trogus by a late writer, Justin, who thus becomes an important source for eastern history.[1]

From these come a few precious scraps about the Bactrian kings, otherwise known chiefly from their interesting coins. They renewed the invasion of India, reaching parts well beyond Alexander's limits, and their picturesque story would be far more prominent if any adequate account had survived (it has been brilliantly pieced together by Tarn). Demetrius, starting in 183 B.C., took the whole Indus valley; his coins show him with an elephant's scalp or a solar topee and have 'the invincible Maharajah' in the native language and script (Plate II, A, B). Then a general and kinsman, Apollodotus, advanced along the coast past Barygaza (towards Bombay) and

---

[1] Tarn, *Greeks in Bactria and India*, 1938, pp. 44–50. Atropatene, Str. 523–4, from Antony's officer Dellius: Plut. *Ant.* 37–51: Dio, XLIX, 24–31: T. R. Holmes, *Architect of the R. Empire*, 1928, pp. 124–8: Tarn in *C.A.H.* x, 71–5: Debevoise, op. cit. pp. 125–8. Crassus, ibid. 79–95. Merv, Plin. VI, 47. Wild, Plut. *Crassus*, 16.

also inland to Ujjain; another general, Menander, pushed from Alexander's final river to Muttra and even Patna. The two were meant to join hands, but Demetrius had to turn back home, to be killed by Eucratides, who had been sent by his Seleucid cousin to recover Bactria (167 B.C.). This man too began conquests towards India, but returned and was killed, probably by a son of his victim with Parthian help; yet his own son Heliocles foiled this rival and kept the kingdom. Menander, left independent in India till his death (towards 145 B.C.), held parts as far as Barygaza; he found his way into the native literature, and had legends of the Buddha and of Asoka transferred to him.[1] His son lost part of the Punjab to Heliocles, and the southern provinces no doubt fell away. Then Bactria itself, 'drained of men' by these adventures, was overwhelmed by nomad invaders. They are detailed as Sacarauli, Asii, Pasiani, and Tochari, or as Saraucae and Asiani (or reges Thocarorum Asiani).[2] How the Chinese annals help to explain some of them will be mentioned presently. Others were the old Sacae or Scythians, who now invaded Parthia and killed two of its kings (128, 123 B.C.) and settled in 'Sacastene' or Seistan. When the Parthians attacked them, most drifted away to found an 'Indoscythian' kingdom on the lower Indus, from which they pushed upstream (about 80 B.C.), though various Greek princes continued in parts close-by till at least 30 B.C. (One prince ruling at Taxila had an envoy as far as Gwalior, who left a record there professing himself a devotee of a native god.) There is a vague statement that strong Bactrian kings—especially, it seems, Euthydemus (about 200 B.C.)—had extended their power up to the Phryni (or rather Phauni?) and Seres, perhaps over the grim watershed to Kashgar, and also, Tarn suggests, north to Ili to gain contact with the middlemen for Siberian gold. The Phauni have often been equated with the Huns, even in name.[3] No word yet of silk, and the Chinese date the opening of direct trade later, after the travels of an envoy of theirs in 128 B.C.; yet the name Seres is generally understood as derived from the Chinese word for silk. After a longish interval silk begins to be mentioned as used for Parthian flags,

---

[1] Plut. *Mor.* 521 d, Tarn, op. cit. 263. Men. to Isamus=Jumna or Son?, Apoll. ap. Str. 516, to Patna, Str. 698. Ap. and Men., Justin, prol. XLI. Seltman, *Greek Coins*, 1933, pp. 235–6, cp. Tarn, op. cit. p. 139 (some by Dem. II in his father's name).

[2] Apoll. ap. Str. 511: Justin, XLI, 2, XLII, 1 (and prologues). Tarn, op. cit. ch. 7. Junge, Saka-Studien, *Klio* Beiheft, 1939. Debevoise, op. cit. pp. 54, 59. *C.A.H.* IX, 582.

[3] As Tomaschek, perhaps rightly, says Minns, *Scythians and Greeks*, 1913, p. 122: Huns, A. Herrmann, *Land der Seide*, 1938, p. 27 (and Seres in Tarim). Siberian, Tarn, op. cit. pp. 84, 111, 121 (these Seres=Wu-sun at Issyk). Apoll. ap. Str. 516. Plin. VI, 55 has Phuni et Focari (Tochari). Huns, Sir P. Sykes, *Quest for Cathay*, 1936, p. 25 (and B. kings perhaps reached Khotan). Envoy, Rapson, *Anc. India*, 1914, pp. 134, 156.

PLATE II

A, B. Coins of Graeco-Bactrian invaders of India (see p. 173).

D. Athena on a seal-impression found in Chinese Turkestan (see p. 311).

C. Coin of Augustus with Capricorn and globe (see p. 203).

E. Britannia welcomes Carausius (see p. 356).

LIBRARY
STATE TEACHERS COLLEGE
WAYNE, NEBRASKA

awnings at Caesar's shows, and Cleopatra's dresses.¹ The Seres seem, at least at first, to be conveyors of silk in the Tarim basin rather than the Chinese themselves.

Indian wares are named as coming, like nard and cinnamon and ivory, but the traffic was nearly all indirect, it seems, and brought no detailed knowledge of the Indian coast. The Seleucids founded new colonies at the head of the Persian Gulf, but left the sea-trade mainly to middlemen at Gerrha and Ormuz. For the Ptolemies we have evidence of 'cargoes of incense and other wares' moving along the desert road (in 130 B.C.), of an official with an eye on 'the Indian and Red Sea' (in 62 and 51 B.C.), and of a loan to importers of goods from Somaliland, all showing a certain interest in shipping to the strait and a little way beyond. Trade was still active so far, though elephants were no longer required as by the early kings, whose efforts were now recalled in the book of Agatharchides. But the outer sea was left to middlemen in Yemen. The wealth of these Sabaeans is exaggerated, and it is told how, lest they should be too happy, they get head-ache and nose-ache from an excess of fragrance, and their trees are infested by purple snakes.² For through voyages to India there is one circumstantial story of a bold adventurer, Eudoxus of Cyzicus, about 120 B.C. He seized the chance of an Indian pilot, the sole survivor of a ship driven into the Red Sea (so Indians, we gather, competed in the Ocean trade). He sailed with presents suitable for native kings and duly returned with spices and precious stones, to be robbed of his profits by the royal monopoly (though he must surely have known of its regulations before he started). He was sent again, 'better equipped', and this time came back only after being blown far down east Africa, and thereby hangs another tale, of which more later. All this, if vague about places, is credible enough, and he may only have coasted, though some suggest that his Indian pilot probably knew and used the monsoon. If the voyages were not followed up, that was due, Strabo implies, to the weakness and anarchy of the later Ptolemies: hardly twenty ships a year ventured then even a little beyond the straits, he says, and it appears that they were content to pick up Indian wares at places like Aden. Perhaps some went farther: anyhow Cleopatra in her despair thought of sailing away to India, after dragging her fleet across the isthmus (the canal was unusable, it seems, because of the low

---

1 Florus, I, 46 (III, 11), Dio, XLIII, 24, and (dresses), Lucan, X, 141: Tarn, p. 120. Ideas of Seres and silk, Yule-Cordier, *Cathay and the Way Thither*, 1915, I, 16, 20. Name, Soothill, *China and the West*, 1925, p. 8.

2 Agatharchides ap. Diod. III, 47. Trade still, ibid. III, 18: Tarn, *Hell. Civ.* 1927, pp. 198–9. Road, *O.G.I.S.* I, 132, official, ibid. 186, 190: Rostovtzeff, op. cit. II, 924, 928: loan, ibid. p. 922. Wares, Pol. XXX, 25–6, Athen. V, 201 b, Tarn, *Greeks in Bactria*, pp. 361, 366: colonies, ibid. pp. 17, 66: Gerrha, ibid. 367, also Indian ships to O., p. 260.

176 HISTORY OF ANCIENT GEOGRAPHY

Nile).¹ Just after the Roman annexation there was a boom in sea-trade, as seen by Strabo himself visiting Egypt in 25 B.C. One Hippalus gave his name to the south-west monsoon, as the first western skipper to cross the open with these regular winds or perhaps to make some improvement on the original short cut. He is often dated after Strabo, who does not mention him, but the monsoon sailings may have begun well before, to give time for so marked a development of shipping as that writer observed. Pliny describes three stages: at first sailing was only with the wind straight behind to the Indus mouth, but with experience bolder short cuts were found, to a port north of Bombay and at last diagonally across to Malabar and the pepper ports. This final route was recent in his day (A.D. 77), but the second had been used 'long' (perhaps since 60 B.C.?) and the first for 'a generation' before that. Tarn favours this dating without caring how Hippalus comes in (elsewhere he counts him about 100 B.C. and as discovering the monsoons, probably known long before to the Indians). He was just after Eudoxus, thinks Rostovtzeff, if he did not actually sail with that pioneer. Several now agree to date him quite early, before 70 B.C. Others make him do the first stage soon after Strabo's visit, under Augustus or Tiberius, while many have put him as late as A.D. 50.²

Mere romancing is the tale of one Iambulus preserved by Diodorus. He was taken by Ethiopians and set adrift with a companion to reach, if lucky, a happy isle lying due south. In four months they reached a large round isle, in a group of seven of the same size. It has ripe fruits all the year, a reed producing fine wool, and another with a vetch-like fruit which puffs in boiling and makes a delicious bread. There are some 'incredible' animals. The people are tall and handsome and long-lived, with flexible bones and split tongues; they have wives and children in common, and write downwards, and are learned in star-lore. The guests stayed seven years, but were then expelled. After four months' sailing they were cast up, one dead, on India; the other was taken many days to the king at Patna, who liked Greeks and gave him the means to go home by way of Persia. All this would hardly be worth repeating in detail if Lassen had not seriously

1 Plut. *Ant.* 69. Aden, Peripl. 26 (on Periplus see p. 228). Str. 118, 798. Eudoxus, Pos. ap. Str. 98–100. Monsoon, Hornell, *Antiquity*, 1941, p. 248: so Rostovtzeff, op. cit. pp. 926–9, and apparently Dessau, *Röm. Kaiserzeit*, 1924, I, 381. E. story has absurd details and is not proven, Tarn, *Hell. Civ.* pp. 199–200.

2 As Schoff, *Periplus*, 1912, H. G. Rawlinson, *Intercourse between Western World and India*, 1916, p. 109, Friedländer, *Life and Manners*, 1909, I, 306, and many. H. after Strabo, A. C. Johnson in Frank's *Econ. Survey*, 1936, II, 344: Warmington, *Commerce between R. Empire and India*, 1928, pp. 44–8 (Tib.): Charlesworth, *Class. Quart.* 1928, pp. 92–100 (about 10 B.C. and stage 2 also Augustus), cp. his *Trade Routes*, 1926, p. 60 (about A.D. 50). Early, Otto, *R.E.* VIII, 1661: Hennig, *T.I.* I, 226–8: Rostovtzeff, loc. cit.: Tarn, *Greeks in Bactria*, pp. 368–9 and *Hell. Civ.* p. 198. Plin. VI, 100–6.

THE ROMAN REPUBLIC 177

found the place in Bali, in the East Indies, with sago as the bread-reed. It is only another Utopia, a rather silly and pointless one, with some local colour perhaps from early rumours of Ceylon. Notable is the very feature about which Diodorus hesitates, the mild climate so near the equator, reflecting an improved notion of what had been taken too literally as the 'torrid' zone.[1]

A piece of an Alexandrian farce, perhaps of this time but more likely later, has a Greek girl being rescued from a barbarian king, here an Indian, a burlesque of an old tragic motif; the king's words have been supposed to be Kanarese, a language of the west coast, but seem merely gibberish, as one would expect.[2] Some liked to praise Indian among other eastern sages, and fancied Pythagoras to have been a pupil of the Brachmanes as well as of an Assyrian Zaratos.

APPENDIX: THE CHINESE HORIZON

The last feeble Chou was now set aside and the Ts'in (or Ch'in) duke of the northern marches took the title of 'First Emperor'. It was he who decreed the burning of the books in order to make history begin with himself, and also the joining up of older walls into a Great Wall 'ten thousand li long' (the present imposing remains in some parts are much later repairs and elaborations). It is commonly accepted that the name of China is due to this remarkable tyrant. Almost immediately after him began the glorious Han dynasty, which was to reign for over four centuries, from 206 B.C. to A.D. 220, except for a short break of usurpation at the beginning of our era. It is excellently recorded by the historian Szu-ma Ch'ien, who wrote about 90 B.C., and in its copious official Annals, the Early and Later Han. All devote special 'chapters' to relations with the Hiung-nu nomads and the 'western countries', and these are available in several translations, a very recent being De Groot's with a critical commentary.[3] Evidently the translation is a difficult business, indeed, and the layman does not always

---

[1] Improved, Pos. ap. Cleon. 1, 6, 31 (not Erat., see p. 163, n. 2): H. J. Rose in *Class. Quart.* 1939, p. 9 misunderstands, and Tarn, ibid. p. 193 dates too early. Story in Diod. II, 55–60: for theory, see p. 215, n. 3. Bali, Lassen, *Ind. Alt.* III, 255. Sumatra, Gerini, *Ptolemy's Researches on Eastern Asia*, 1909, p. 593. Rohde, *Griech. Roman*², 1900, pp. 241–58: W. Richter, *Iambulus*, 1888. I. writes many paradoxa, Lucian, *V.H.* 1, 3.

[2] Barnett, *J. Eg. Arch.* 1926, p. 13, against Hultzsch, *Hermes*, 1904, p. 207. Later, Warmington, op. cit. pp. 132, 332. Oxyrh. Pap. III, 413: Powell and Barber, *New Chapters in Greek Lit.* 1921, I, 121: H. J. Rose, *Handbook of Greek Lit.* p. 347. Sages, Alex. Polyhistor ap. Clem. *Strom.* I, 15, 69, III, 8, 60.

[3] *Chin. Urkunden zur Gesch. Asiens*, I (Hunnen), 1921, II (Westlande), 1926, esp. II, 9–45. Later Han by Chavannes in *T'oung Pao*, 1906–7. Se-ma Ts'ien, *Mémoires hist.* ed. Chavannes, 1895–1905: his ch. 123 transl. by Hirth, *J. Amer. Or. Soc.* 1917, pp. 89–152. Earlier translations by Wylie, *J. Anthr. Inst.* 1881–2, Kingsmill, *J.R.A.S.* 1882. On the sources, Cordier, *Hist. gén. de la Chine*, 1920, I, ch. 2. Wall, De Groot, I, 41, 44, cp Cordier, I, 206. Name China, see p. 313, n. 3.

know what to make of these reports, but in general their contribution to history is clear enough.

The Wall was stoutly defended, but at its western end a people called the Yue-chi were badly mauled by the nomads (176–165 B.C.). Many of them fled away behind the Tien-shan to the Wu-sun in Ili and farther still, pushing some Sai or Sacas over the Jaxartes. Even here they were dislodged by their enemies with Hiung-nu help, and presently they came into the ken of western writers as destroying the kingdom of Bactria in the way already mentioned: probably among the invaders named they are the Tochari and Asii. It is now known that in the Tarim basin, the present Chinese Turkestan, there were then and long survived Indo-European languages, an East Iranian and two dialects of another which was surprisingly of a centum or western type: it appears that the speakers of this 'Tocharic' called themselves Arsi.[1] Thus the Yue-chi seem, before their flight, to have been the easternmost wanderers of Indo-European speech. The Emperor Wu-ti was anxious to know what had become of these old allies, and sent Chang K'ien to ascertain. This brave man was captured by the enemy, but escaped after ten years and went on to Ta-wan (Fergana) to find the lost people encamped north of the Oxus and in process of conquering Ta-hia or Bactria (128 B.C.). If they had no further interest as allies, they might still be useful for trade, and now and on a second mission to the Wu-sun he sent out officers to gather information about the considerable kingdoms beyond. His master was already driving back the nomad power and clearing the western roads. A regular traffic began not only with the Tarim oases but with the countries beyond the great watershed. Quite soon (114–108 B.C.) some ten large caravans a year were reaching Ta-wan, and when one was mishandled a punitive expedition went all the way: so long had China's arm suddenly grown. To cover the main road the Wall was continued by an earth-work with brick watch-towers to a point near the old terminal lake of the Tarim; the region became utter desert later, and the extension was quite forgotten till it was seen in 1900 by Bonin and explored in 1907 by Sir Aurel Stein.[2] From its famous 'Gates' the road

1 Grousset, *Hist. de l'extrême Orient*, 1929, I, 303: Herrmann, op. cit. p. 28. Invaders, see p. 174, n. 2 and esp. Tarn, op. cit. ch. 7, 284–6: races and languages, pp. 287–90: T. A. Sinclair, *C.Q.* 1924, pp. 119–26: G. F. Hudson, *Europe and China*, 1931, pp. 60–4: Grousset, op. cit. I, 59–60, 208–14: Yule-Cordier, op. cit. I, 35: Minns, op. cit. pp. 121–2: Cordier, op. cit. I, 224: Junge, op. cit. esp. pp. 96–105 (see p. 174, n. 2). Attack on Yue-chi, De Groot, I, 76–9: their name, ibid. p. 47. Vernadsky in *Byzantion*, 1944, pp. 81–6 (Asiani = Wusun, Asii = Alans), *Anc. Russia*, 1943, p. 83.

2 Sir M. A. Stein, *Ruins of Desert Cathay*, 1912, II, chs. 53, 58, etc.: *Serindia*, 1921, chs. 14–20: *On Anc. Central-Asian Tracks*, 1933, pp. 167 f. Cordier, op. cit. I, 235. Punitive, ibid. De Groot, I, 152, 155. Chang K'ien, ibid. II, 9–19: Yule-Cordier, pp. 37–9: Cordier, pp. 226–34: C. P. Fitzgerald, *China*, 1935, pp. 176–85: E. H. Parker, *Thousand Years of the Tartars*, 1895, pp. 34–6. Lou-lan site found by Hedin, 1901.

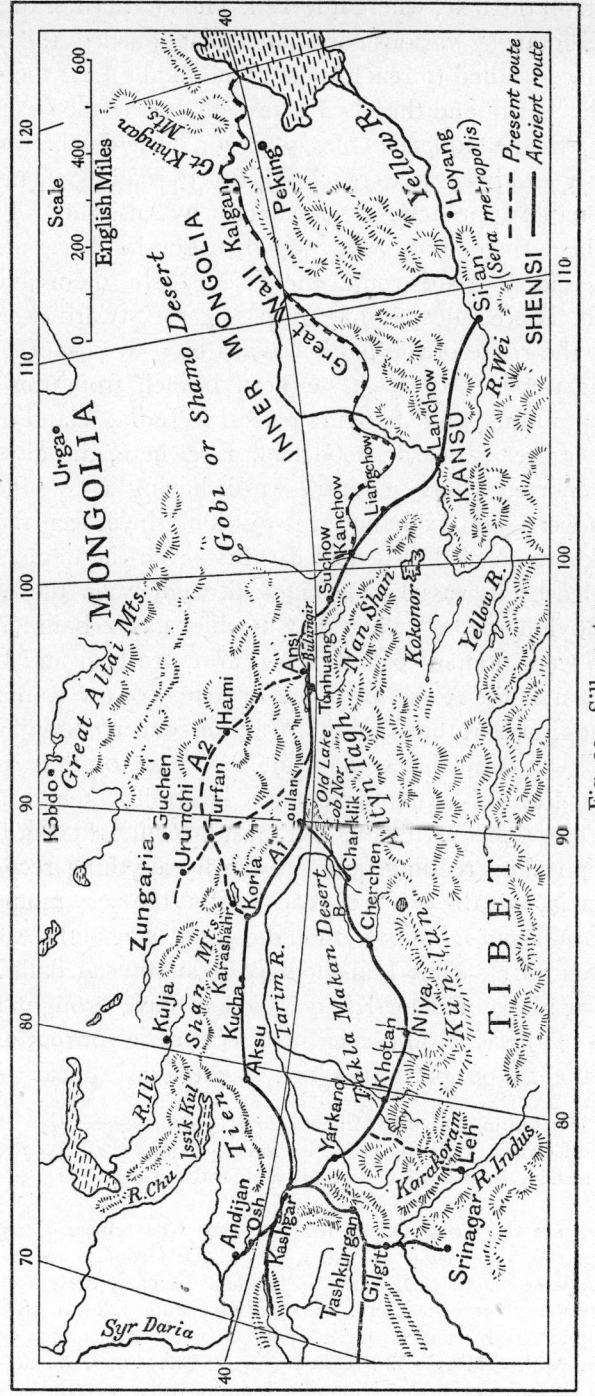

Fig. 23. Silk routes.

ran to Lou-lan on the lake, where it forked. The southern branch (B on the map) led to Khotan by various oases later abandoned to the desert when the Kun-lun rivers failed to reach them. The middle (A1, long preferred) passed near the Tarim and then by the present northern oases to Kashgar, and on it were the headquarters of a governor (near Kucha from 60 B.C.). There was early another way to reach this 'north road', by Turfan; to-day the only reasonable approach is a wide detour by Ansi-Hami-Turfan (A2), and so it has been since about A.D. 250, when Lou-lan became impossible. Such were the old silk-roads round the Tarim basin, themselves long and dreary enough. There followed difficult passages westward over the roof of Asia. Besides the route of the first caravans there was another by Tashkurgan to the upper Oxus.[1] A southern branch from this went over 'head-ache mountains' and 'hanging passes' to India, a land of which the Chinese pioneer already heard a good deal. Elsewhere, nine days west of the Yue-chi, he reported a large country An-si, having a town Pan-tu, with which envoys were soon exchanged: it has long since been recognized as Parthia, the kingdom of the Arsacid dynasty (even the names are said to answer). Ruled by its vassals was Tiao-chi, vaguely on the western sea, apparently Babylonia. On 'a great marsh, which has no banks(?) and is the northern sea' were nomads called Yen-ts'ai or An-ts'ai and later A-lan, commonly taken as the Aorsi and Alans of writers of the Roman empire.[2] The sea in question is in that case the Aral, misconceived somewhat as the Caspian 'gulf' was from the Roman side. We hear too that An-si envoys offered jugglers from Li-kan, and the name has been taken to mean Syria, though this is questioned. In general it must be confessed that the Chinese accounts are puzzling reading, and say hardly anything recognizable of Greeks in Bactria, but the explorer reached it at the very moment of their ruin. A name O-ik-san-li has been thought a rendering of the Alexandria at Herat (or in Seistan?), while Lan-she may be another at Balkh, though it is a doubtful reading. Chang K'ien is said to have brought home from Ta-wan seeds of the vine, and even its Greek name (βότρυς as p'u-t'ao), and so too the grape pattern which begins to appear on Chinese

[1] Roads, A. Herrmann, *Die alten Seidenstrassen*, 1910: *Lou-lan*, 1931. De Groot, II, 47–8, 114: Yule-Cordier, pp. 58, 98: Chavannes, *T'oung Pao*, 1907, pp. 167–70: Cordier, p. 255: Stein, *Desert Cathay*, chs. 34–5, 46 and in *Geogr. J.* 1925, pp. 377–403, 473–501.

[2] Hirth, *China and the Roman Orient*, 1885, p. 139: Chavannes, *T'oung Pao*, 1905, p. 558, 1907, pp. 168, 195 (A-lan): Cordier, p. 254: De Groot, I, 229, II, 15–16, 105: Minns, loc. cit.: Rostovtzeff, *C.A.H.* XI, 94: though Teggart, *Rome and China*, 1939, p. 201 denies Aorsi = Y. or ever there. Parthia, Kingsmill, *J.R.A.S.* 1882, p. 81 (first to equate An-si and Arsak): Parker, loc. cit.: De Groot, I, 231, II, 17, 33, 93: Hirth, op. cit. p. 36 (and Mulu = Merv): Yule-Cordier, p. 23: Chavannes, op. cit. 1907, p. 177. (Parthia already De Guignes, before Gibbon.) India, Cordier, p. 230.

mirrors.¹ The name Ta-hia has been equated with Tochari or Dahae or explained quite differently. Many of these and other details seem very dubious, but anyhow the fact remains that the horizons of China and the west had now overlapped. The connection thus formed between the two worlds was at best slight, both now and later, and neither ever had more than a vague notion of the other. But the silk-trade was real, and it was to have important consequences for the map: the 'inhabited world' was to be extended far east, in fact much too far, and the exaggeration of Asia was to encourage Columbus to think his enterprise feasible.

§2. AFRICA

Carthage, having recovered a modest prosperity, too much for her suspicious enemy, was now brutally destroyed (146 B.C.), and her small domain annexed as a province of 'Africa'. Close-by was Numidia; here a strong king had taught many of his people to settle down, with some civilization borrowed from Carthage. A few places had Roman traders, but the steppes and mountains were not inviting. Only a troublesome pretender forced intervention. The war with Jugurtha was fought mostly near the province (112–105 B.C.); at last he was betrayed by his Moorish ally, who was rewarded with a western slice of the kingdom. Otherwise it was left alone until Juba chose the wrong side in the civil war, when Caesar gave away another slice and annexed the rest as New Africa (46 B.C., presently to be restored for a short time to Juba's son). He also revived Carthage, as a Roman city, and the province began to be an important source of corn and olive-oil.

Early attached to 'Africa' was the strip eastwards past the 'three cities' or Tripolis, including the one to-day called Tripoli. Beyond was a long gap of utterly desert coast, hardly mentioned in history except when one Roman army plodded along it to fight another (Caesar's) in Tunisia. A later poet takes this cue for a fearsome catalogue of African snakes, including the dreaded basilisk, and invokes against them a tribe of snake-charmers, the Psylli, said elsewhere to have perished long since fighting the south wind and its sand-storms.² Cyrene, long a dependency of the Ptolemies,

1 Hirth, *Fremde Einflüsse in der chin. Kunst*, 1876, pp. 8, 12: H. A. Giles, *Civ. of China*, 1911, p. 35: De Groot, II, 11, 35. Name already, Kingsmill, op. cit. p. 93: Wilhelm, *Short Hist. of China*, 1929, pp. 121–2: questioned by Pelliot. Herat, De Groot, I, 231, II, 92: Seistan, Tarn, op. cit. p. 347. Lan-she, ibid. p. 298, Specht, *J. As.* 1883, p. 322, Herrmann, *Seidenstrassen*, p. 48, but De Groot, II, 95 reads Kamsi (Wylie Keen-she). Syria, Hirth, *C.R.O.* pp. 36, 141 (and already Wylie), but Hyrcania, De Groot, II, 18, 93.

2 Hdt. IV, 173. Snakes, Lucan, IX, 700–838. Psylli, ibid. pp. 891–938 (cp. Hdt. IV, 173), Plin. VII, 14, XXVIII, 30. Cato's march, Str. 836, Plin. V, 22, Plut. *Cato Minor*, 56. Mirages, Diod. III, 50–1. Trade of Africa, Haywood in *Econ. Survey of Anc. Rome*, ed. Frank, IV, 3–118 (1938). Basilisk, Plin. VIII, 78, etc.

had three ports renamed after them or their wives (one is Tolmetta to this day, while Benghazi is a corruption of Berenice). It was bequeathed to Rome in 96 B.C., but not taken over till 74 B.C. Egypt itself was far too rich a prize for any Roman politician to trust any other with its taking, and so it escaped somehow until Cleopatra perished with her lover in the last civil war (30 B.C.).

The new reports of Africa are not very satisfactory. For the parts above Egypt there is Agatharchides, using mainly the information of the period just before, as given in the previous chapter. He discussed the various theories of the Nile flood, as did Posidonius, who accepted the summer rains of the Ethiopian mountains, now reliably attested. A poet refers to the sources of the Nile as a mystery. The Romans had their own way of exhibiting strange animals, and an occasional giraffe and hippopotamus already appeared in the shows of Caesar's time. For the Atlas region it was easy to improve on all former accounts, but campaigning did not go deep inland, and we hear little of exploration. Polybius, who was with his friend Scipio at the siege of Carthage, was given some ships to reconnoitre westward to the straits: he talked of 8800 stades (repeating an earlier figure) with four 'Nomad' tribes including the Maurusii. Strabo has a hurried and poor chapter in his last book. He relies too much on obsolete descriptions, mainly one on the old coastal scheme by Artemidorus (about 100 B.C.); he adds a little from Posidonius, who had no personal knowledge, except that he once landed by accident, on a voyage from Spain to Italy, and watched some monkeys.[1] The ports close to Carthage and the province are, of course, minutely detailed; yet the northward bulge is still not properly realized (even Hipparchus places the city at 32° 40' or 4° too far south). The coast to the straits is still misconceived in direction. Its length is even worsened, probably after Artemidorus, to 13,500 stades: the western or Riff section, as 5000 stades to the Molochath (Mulwia), is badly exaggerated in proportion to the rest, 6000 to Cape Tretum and 2500 to Carthage.[2] There is talk of fertile land and many rivers and towns, but there are few names like Iol, the capital of Juba II, and a port at Oran. Behind are deserts and big lakes and marshes and mountains: there are a range all along from the outer sea to the Syrtis and others running parallel, with some forests in Maurusia (the source of the citrus-wood so

---

1 Str. 144. Chapter, Str. xvii, 3 (825–40). Strenger, *Strabos Erdkunde von Libyen*, 1913: Gsell, *Hist. anc. de l'Afrique du Nord*, v, 18–20: Berthelot, *L'Afrique sahar. et soudanaise*, 1927, pp. 235–50. Pol. iii, 33, cp. Liv. xxiv, 29, Maurusios Numidas: figure as Erat. ap. Plin. v, 40, see p. 139, n. 1. Agath., see p. 136, n. 3: on Nile ap. Diod. i, 36–41: Pos. partly in Seneca, see p. 273, n. 1. Mystery, Tib. i, 7, 23. Giraffe, etc., Plin. viii, 69, 96.

2 Str. 827, 829, 832: Artem. guilty, Strenger, op. cit. pp. 74, 78: he or Pos., Gsell, op. cit. v, 2. No clear account of the restored Carthage, complains Mahaffy, *Greek World under Roman Sway*, 1890, p. 219.

THE ROMAN REPUBLIC   183

fashionable for round tables). This does give some impression of the configuration, the coast or Tell Atlas with fertile valleys, the poor plateau-steppe of the shotts or salt lakes, where the nomads grazed their flocks, and the bolder Saharan Atlas, still partly wooded to-day: such is the general picture, though in detail each range is broken and complex and both converge into a jumble of hills at the eastern end (the really high mountains are the Great Atlas at the western). Strabo speaks of plenty of wild beasts, including elephants, and gives this as a reason why the people took to nomadic habits in a cultivable country, a queer echo of the old notion of a wild-beast zone (it is true that panthers and the like were supplied to the Roman arena, and elephants did exist here until they were killed off). The people, he says, are great horsemen, polygamous, and otherwise like nomad Arabs. Inland all along are Gaetulians, the greatest of Libyan nations, reaching east to the Garamantes, who are fifteen days from the oasis of Ammon. Ten days from these are some western Ethiopians, and near them somewhere Nigritae and Pharusians; the last have summer rains and on occasion raid to the Moorish coast, a month away, with water-skins slung under their horses (some think they were in south Morocco towards the Draa).[1]

There is a pamphlet by Sallust, who had a certain local interest as the first governor of Caesar's new province: he writes on the old war with Jugurtha, and is chiefly concerned with its reactions on home politics. The topography is slight enough to leave doubts on battlefields, and a short digression on the lands and peoples is very sketchy, with borrowings from Posidonius: there are some good touches like the 'savage and harbourless sea' and the scarcity of rain and other water (it does not appear that the climate was noticeably better then than now). He mentions the river Mulucha (or Mulwia) as the frontier between Numidians and Moors, but a military operation so far west seems unlikely. The hinterland is vague, wastes and mountains with wild beasts and Gaetulian nomads, and then some 'Ethiopians' to the torrid desert. Altogether he knows little.[2]

Polybius, who seems to have given a detailed account of Hanno, is understood to have continued his own reconnaissance some way down the outer coast. It is disputed how much of a jumbled passage of Pliny's is

1 Gsell, op. cit. I, 295 with Nigritae west from Nigris=Jedi. Str. 826, 828. Garam., ibid. 835: Gaet., ibid. 829 (first Artem.). Beasts, (Pos. ap.) Str. 833. Ranges, Str. 826: lakes, ibid. 828, 835. Configuration finely in Belloc, *Esto Perpetua* (*Alg. Studies*), 1906, pp. 12, 56–8: S. H. Roberts, *Hist. of French Col. Policy*, 1929, I, 176. Elephants, Plin. VIII, 2, 32: Juv. x, 150, XI, 125: Bovill, *Antiquity*, 1929, p. 417.

2 Gsell, op. cit. V, 17, VII, 124–6. Climate, Belloc, op. cit. pp. 109–11. At most perhaps very slightly more rain, Gsell, I, 99: Bovill, op. cit. pp. 414–23: Jane Soames, *Coast of Barbary*, 1938, pp. 24–7, citing Gautier, etc. Sall. *Jug.* 17–19. Pos. (cp. Str. 171), Strenger, op. cit. pp. 61, 92. River, *Jug.* 92. Site of Muthul?, ibid. 48–54. Question of Mulucha, Gsell, v, 2–4: Last, *C.A.H.* IX, 127 accepts the operation.

from him and how much from Agrippa. It has some distances and many new names as far as rivers with crocodiles and hippopotami, which sound like Hanno's and are now called Darat and Bambotus. The latter has been thought the Senegal or the Gambia (so Aly, though he denies that Polybius was there). If he put Cerne opposite the Atlas at the end of Mauretania, he was very wrong; Gsell takes the above passage as mostly not his, and cannot say where this Atlas and Cerne are supposed to be, while the Darat is only the Draa. Some wildly credit him with a voyage rivalling Hanno's to the Senegal or beyond (one carries him even to the Niger delta). Others bring him at least past Cape Ghir or about to the Draa.[1] Strabo, though well disposed to him, says nothing of any voyage of his at all. His own account of the coast, still misconceived to run south-east, is very feeble. Near the strait are a headland Cotes (Cape Spartel), actually supposed the westernmost point, and the Atlas, which the natives call Dyrin—a genuine form of their name for 'mountains'. He has Tangier and two places a little past, but practically nothing more: he regards Cerne as a fable, and has none of the new names mentioned above. These may be largely hearsay from Cadiz seamen who fished and traded down to 'Ethiopia'. No doubt they reached some of the islands too. A rebel general in Spain heard from them of Fortunate Isles, to which he thought of retiring as a last refuge. (Thus the old bright sunset Isles of the Blest were being lent a local habitation, though for most still an airy nothing, a place where all go who have lived pure lives.) The islands are described as two, close together, very fertile and with a perfect climate, and are variously placed 'not far from the Pillars' or 10,000 stades from Africa. The figure, tolerable only for the Azores, may well be discounted, and the rest is mostly taken as indicating Madeira and Porto Santo, not the Canaries to which the old mythical name was presently to be applied. Madeira may have been found once before.[2] It was destined to several rediscoveries, one by an Englishman eloping with a lady about A.D. 1370, it is said, though this tale is now rejected.

[1] Strenger, op. cit. pp. 27–32, punctuating Plin. v, 9–10 otherwise than Detlefsen, *Geogr. Afrikas bei Mela u. Plin.* p. 17: Ghir, Ruge, *R.E.* II, 2119. Bunbury, II, 329, 432 is rightly reserved. To Senegal, Cary-Warmington, p. 52: Kaeppel, op. cit. p. 54: Hennig, *T.I.* I, 196–9 (or Verde): Niger, Berthelot, op. cit. pp. 263–7. Cerne, Pol. ap. Plin. VI, 199: Gsell, op. cit. III, 389–93 (Draa also, VIII, 260). Darat=Rio de Oro and B.= Senegal, *G.G.M.* I, xxxi. Aly, *Hermes*, 1927, pp. 331 f. Cichorius, *Rh. Mus.* 1908, pp. 220–3 seeks to prove that Panaetius was with Pol.

[2] P. 78, n. 1. (Pos. via Sall.?) ap. Plut. *Sertorius*, 8: Pos. ap. Str. 150. Traded, Coelius Antipater (after 123 B.C.) ap. Plin. II, 169. Fished, Pos. ap. Str. 99. Coast in Str. 825–7, 829. Dyrin also Pos. ap. Plin. v, 13 (ad Dirim), Vitr. VIII, 2, 6: 'mountains', Gsell, *Hérodote*, p. 110: Steinhauser, *Glotta*, 1936, pp. 229–38 (derives even Atlas and Atarantes from same word). Pure, Plaut. *Trin.* p. 549: Rohde, *Psyche*, Engl. ed. 1925, p. 537. Madeira, Fischer, *R.E.* VII, 42, citing a diss. on ancient reports of Canaries by

THE ROMAN REPUBLIC 185

A remarkable story is told of the Eudoxus already mentioned as sailing twice to India (p. 175). On the way home from the second venture (about 116–115 B.C.) he was blown far down east Africa, where he jotted down some native words. He also found a wreck and brought back its figure-head, which suggested thoughts of the Cadiz ships fishing down Morocco and of one in fact just reported missing. He resolved to go as it had presumably gone, and so to complete the round of Africa. He raised the means to fit out three ships, and started from Cadiz, with such confidence that he took some of its famous dancing-girls as presents for Indian kings. Forced by his crew to keep too near a dangerous coast, he ran his best ship aground, but made a fifty-oar of the relics and went on. He reached an Ethiopian people speaking the language noted before, in fact the same people, it seems implied, though only 'next Maurusia', which leaves a long gap unexplained (Berthelot supposes that he reached a Congo tribe akin to the Bantus of the eastern side). He now returned, having ear-marked an island as future winter-quarters, where he might sow seed. Equipping a large merchant-ship and a fifty-oar, he started again. What happened to him this time they may know at Cadiz, says Posidonius—which is puzzling, as he had stayed there about twenty years later, but perhaps he heard the story only after his visit and could no longer inquire personally? Strabo thinks that he was deceived by a fabrication. There is no word of any names or distances reported by the voyager, and no other evidence (a version that he went from the Red Sea to Cadiz is mere garbling by a careless writer). For Posidonius the essential point is the figure-head, which he accepts as coming from Cadiz and so proving a continuous sea round Africa. Yet that a Spanish fishing-boat should have wandered round to east Africa, or even drifted to it as a wreck, is utterly unlikely, though Pliny produces a still wilder tale of Spanish wrecks being found in the Red Sea by a fleet of Augustus. Apparently the second venture ended in disaster, and just because of this lame conclusion most do not care to reject the story wholesale.[1] There is some likeness to the obscure expedition of the

---

Curt Müller, 1902, pp. 7, 21. Canaries, thinks Bannerman, *Canary Islands*, 1923, p. 4. Rediscoveries, Beazley, *Prince Henry the Navigator*, 1895, pp. 109–10 (and of Canaries, ibid. pp. 107–8): Prestage in A. P. Newton, *Travel and Travellers of the Middle Ages*, 1926, p. 204: *Portuguese Pioneers*, 1933, p. 5.

1 Vivien de St Martin, p. 151: Bunbury, II, 74–9: Berger, *Erdk.* pp. 569–74 (though sceptical): Strenger, op. cit. pp. 32–6: Hennig, *T.I.* 1, 218–25: Jacoby, *R.E.* VI, 929–30. Berthelot, op. cit. pp. 237–8: Cary-Warmington, pp. 98–103: probably considerable foundation, Mahaffy, *Greek World under Roman Sway*, 1890, pp. 48–52. Denied by Grote, ch. 18 (*re* Necho): Chassang, *Hist. du Roman dans l'Ant.* 1862, p. 137: Sir G. C. Lewis, *Astronomy of Ancients*, 1862, p. 507: 'nugator', Klotz, *Quaest. Plin. Geogr.* 1906, p. 84: Tarn distrusts Pos., see p. 176, n. 1. Pos. ap. Str. 98–100: Strabo is hostile, 100, 103. Garbling, Nepos in Mela, III, 90, Plin. II, 169–70. Wrecks, ibid. 168.

Vivaldi brothers in A.D. 1291. They started with two galleys to go 'by the Ocean sea towards the parts of India', but disappeared after Cape Nun in Morocco (a name long read as 'no', because if one went beyond there was no return); a son made a vain search right round to the Somali coast, it is said (very dubiously). In 1455 another Genoese, in the service of Prince Henry of Portugal, professed to hear from (descendants of) survivors that one ship had stranded in the sea of Guinea, while the other had gone on to a town of Ethiopia inhabited by Christian subjects of Prester John. Such are some of the queer things said of voyages down this side of Africa. Anyhow Eudoxus had no effect on mapping, and there was no idea of the enormous southward extension of the continent. Posidonius himself drew the coast as running south-east and then east to the last point discovered from the Red Sea. Strabo is no better, and he can assert that Africa is smaller than Europe and far less populous, because the greater part is desert and most of the rest sparsely inhabited by nomads. Some odd things in Diodorus about Amazons fighting the people of Cerne are hardly worth mentioning except as a wild vagary.

The Portuguese, by the way, took quite a long time to grope down to the Guinea coast, and it is not proved that they planned from the first to round Africa to the Indian Ocean, or indeed until some twenty years after Henry's death, when the pace suddenly quickened.[1]

§3. EUROPE

In Spain the Greeks had had only a few minor coastal colonies, and they had known little of the inner mass, a high and bare table-land, fringed and crossed by ranges and held by warlike brigand tribes. After driving the Carthaginians out, the Romans had plenty of work to conquer the country from their bases of Hither and Further Spain in east and south. It was a long business with ugly aggressions and reverses. The Celtiberians were not subdued till Scipio razed their chief stronghold, Numantia, among the bleak hills at the source of the Douro (133 B.C.); Polybius attended him here too and wrote a detailed account. From the southern province there were early pushes to the middle Tagus, but it was often raided by the Lusitanians, who produced a national hero in the shepherd-king Viriathus (147–138 B.C.). On his death a general Brutus overran them and reached the

---

1 J. A. Williamson, *Ocean in English History*, 1941, p. 10, but cp. Prestage in Newton, op. cit. p. 214: Vivaldi, Kimble, *Geogr. in Middle Ages*, 1938, p. 108 (sceptical, after Beazley): how far south?, Prestage, p. 203, and see his *Portuguese Pioneers*, 1933, p. 121. Diod. III, 52–5. Smaller, Str. 824. Shape, Pos. ap. Str. 830–1, slightly different from Erat. ap. Str. 825.

north-west corner, while his ships co-operated from Gades, the first Roman fleet to appear in the Atlantic. Caesar, when governor here, made a similar land and sea expedition (61 B.C.). Spain was heavily involved in the cause of the rebel general Sertorius in 81–72 B.C., and again in Caesar's civil wars in 49 and 45 B.C. The fierce Biscay hillmen were still independent when the Republic ended.

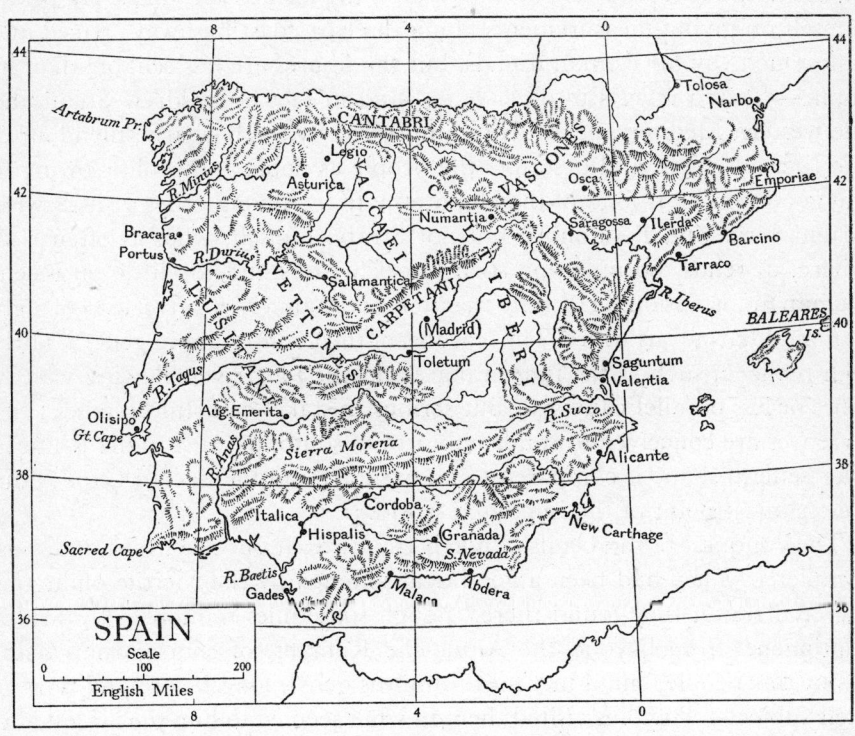

Fig. 24.

By that time Romanizing, begun early with settlements of veteran soldiers, had gone very far, especially in the south. Gades was a busy port, and its ships were the largest to be seen in the Italian harbours and nearly the most numerous. The country seemed one of the richest in the world. Among exports were oil and wine and corn, salt-fish, fine wool and textiles. Above all Spain was still the great land of mining. The writers are loud in praise of its many minerals, and describe their working with interesting detail: the silver mines near New Carthage are said to have employed 40,000 slaves. In what is told of the people some traits of the later Spaniards seem already recognizable, including a tendency to regional isolation and disunion produced by the configuration, though Strabo foolishly ascribes it to a morose pride.¹ He also thinks, more sensibly, of barren mountains as a natural home of brigandage. Livy remarks that this, the earliest province on the mainland of Europe, was the last to be completely subjected, as no country was more suited 'locorum hominumque ingeniis' for outbreaks of guerrilla fighting.

The discovery of this and other western lands was not so new as Polybius makes out, but it was easy to improve on the former accounts. He prides himself on giving measurements along the east coast highway 'paced and milestoned' by his Roman friends, but the figures are less reliable than he thinks—Strabo reverts to older ones—and in fact he misdrew Spain and the western Mediterranean. He is impressed by the barbaric splendour of the Iberian chiefs, and describes the people as noble and prolific owing to the good air (he is fond of the climate motif). Among other visitors were Artemidorus and Posidonius, but not Strabo himself, who, as often elsewhere, depends too much on such Greek writers and too little on recent Roman information. He refuses, after his manner, to give lists of ugly names of barbarous tribes. The features of the country are in general fairly well realized, such as the inner ranges and the long rivers flowing west in more or less parallel canyons. But serious mistakes can still be made: the Pyrenees are conceived to run from north to south, parallel to the Rhine!² The general shape is compared to an ox-hide, and the Sacred Cape is the westernmost point of the inhabited world.

The conquest of the Gauls of north Italy was at once resumed and soon completed. They had been a good deal softened by their fertile plain and the civilization they found there, though sometimes reinforced by wilder contingents from beyond the Alps. The Romans, of course, knew a lot about this people, 'nata in vanos tumultus gens', long before and now as their subjects. Polybius visited them in what seemed to him the largest and richest plain in Europe, and was impressed by the great crops and herds and the brave and handsome people, living in villages under chiefs who

---

1 Str. 158: Pollard, *Factors in Modern History*³, 1932, p. 60: Madariaga, *Spain*, 1930, 24: J. B. Trend, *Civ. of Spain*, 1944, pp. 12–16: Fouillée, *Esquisse psychologique des Peuples Européens*⁶, 1921, pp. 141–2. Configuration, ibid. pp. 15–20, Altamira, *Hist. of Spanish Civ.* 1930, pp. 4–6: W. Atkinson in *Spain*, ed. Peers, 1929, pp. 1–4. Minerals, Pol. III, 37, x, 10, 11, Pol. and Pos. ap. Str. 146–8, Diod. v, 36. Gades, Str. 160, ships, ibid. 144. D. Brutus, Str. 152–3. On wars, Schulten, *C.A.H.* VIII, ch. 10. C. H. V. Sutherland, *Romans in Spain*, 1939. Van Nostrand in *Econ. Survey of Anc. Rome*, ed. Frank, 1937, III, 121–224. O. Davies, *Roman Mines in Europe*, 1935, pp. 94–114.

2 Str. 127, 137, 177. Bunbury, II, 239–45. Pol. III, 39 and ap. Str. 105–7. People and chiefs, Pol. XXXIV, 8, 19. Misdraws, F. Braun, *Entwicklung der span. Provinzialgrenzen*, 1909, pp. 50–4 and see p. 142, n. 1. On sources of Strabo III, Zimmermann, 1886. Tribes, Str. 155. Ebro flows south, ibid. 175. Guerrilla, Livy, XXVIII, 12, so XXIV, 42. Ugly, Str. 155, cp. 177.

THE ROMAN REPUBLIC

liked to have as many dependents as possible. In Gaul itself the Romans intervened to help their old friends of Marseilles against local tribes in 154 and again in 125–124 B.C. This led to fighting with much bigger peoples behind, especially the Arverni in Auvergne, against whom the jealous Aedui were willing to help (123–121 B.C.). So was acquired a southern province from Geneva to Toulouse, with the much-needed road to Spain, guarded by two colonies at Aix and Narbonne. It was soon swarming with business men, and began to be quickly Romanized. Its wares took the old routes of Massalia, though some stern tribes like the Belgic Nervii and the Germans would not admit its insidious wine; the coins of the Republic became familiar on the Rhine, where they were long preferred to later currencies.[1]

The new province was only just in time to save Italy itself from an unforeseen danger, a big German migration, the first to be recorded because of its impact on the civilized world. The tribes concerned were the Cimbri of Jutland and their neighbours the Teutons, whom Pytheas had reached by sea long before. The movement was at least partly due, it was said, to a special 'great tide' or inroad of the Ocean, a story which some doubted or ignored, though there had been earlier rumours of 'Celts' fighting the sea.[2] Passing up the Elbe, the migrants jostled the Celtic Boii in Bohemia and beat a Roman general pushing from the Italian frontier. They turned west to the Celtic Helvetii, who were then in Baden as well as Switzerland but restless under German pressure and ready to provide help to invade Gaul. Thus reinforced, they overthrew several armies in the province, one with great loss at Orange (105 B.C.). The Cimbri now drifted into Spain and, on being resisted there, back again. They planned a grand attack on Italy, but it had had time to prepare, and the Teutons were destroyed on the Riviera road, and the Cimbri after penetrating by the Brenner Pass (102–101 B.C.). Thus already the south saw these warriors, tall and fair and with blue or grey eyes, and their fierce women, who killed themselves by the ring of waggons rather than be taken (among them were grim priestesses who used to cut the throats of prisoners). But the name German was not at first heard of, and they seemed only specially big and blond and wild Celts or 'Celtoscyths', as someone called them, probably Artemidorus, while Posidonius guessed that some had wandered long since to the Black

---

1 Tac. *Germ.* 5. Wine, Caes. *B.G.* II, 15, IV, 2 (and I, 1, 3). Swarming, already Cic. *pro Fonteio*, 5, 11: many at Orléans, Caes. VII, 3. Gallic wars in Italy, Pol. II, 14–35, people, ibid. 14–17, Grenier, *Les Gaulois*, 1945, pp. 116–17. Romans said 'Massilia'.

2 P. 89, n. 1. Pos. ap. Str. 292–3, 102 (text?): Diod. v, 32 and Plut. *Mar.* 11 ignore tide. Cp. Artem. via Livy in Florus, I, 37 (III, 3) 'cum terras eorum inundasset Oceanus': Norden, *Germ. Urgesch.* 1923, p. 463: Jullian, *Hist. de la Gaule*, III, 56 (1929): Last, *C.A.H.* IX, 141 (one cause).

Sea to appear as Homer's Cimmerians. Many were to go on talking of Germans as Celts long after they should have known better.[1] Some still argue that the Cimbri were Celtic-speakers and even Cymry, though the theory has been often demolished.

An early visitor, before the province began, was Polybius; he gives some figures and claims to have followed all Hannibal's route, including the pass on which there is such debate. Yet he draws the Alps too straight and the course of the Rhône not very well. He had heard about the Alpine lakes and a port on the Loire. Posidonius came and saw something of the Gauls and described them picturesquely (about 90 B.C.). They are quarrelsome and addicted to tribal wars; the gentry have many vassals and fight from chariots like Homeric heroes; the table manners are dreadful, and some customs as grisly as the Scythian, for they hang the heads of enemies on their horses' necks or nail them on their doors. But there is some barbaric art and culture, with Druid priests and seers and bards: writing is known, and these people, though vain and truculent, seem clever and teachable.[2]

Much fuller knowledge came with the conquest in 58–51 B.C., of which the great account is Caesar's own. When he took over, the province was seriously threatened. An encroaching German king, Ariovistus, had taken much land from the Sequani, who had called him in against their Aeduan neighbours. The Helvetii were again moving. Caesar beat them on and beyond the Saône and sent them back home to serve as a buffer. He then marched up the Doubs to rout the German near the Gap of Belfort and hurl him over the Rhine, which he announced as the new Roman frontier. But the Belgic tribes had no use for a foreign champion, and drew him north to the Sambre, where the toughest of them fought hard. The west gave a deal of trouble, notably the Veneti, with their strongholds on capes; they had a big fleet of stout oaken ships with leather sails, and the oared galleys built against them on the Loire won only by the luck of a dead calm off Quiberon. The Channel tribes were saved meanwhile by their marshes and woods: we learn of a great forest from the sea to Lorraine of which the present

---

1 Str. 290, 295, Diod. loc. cit., Ps.-Scymn. 109 (Cimm. ibid. 166, 175). Artem. ap. Str. 293 and Plut. loc. cit. Pos. ap. Str. loc. cit. Celts, Cic. *de Prov. Cons.* 32. Germans, *C.A.H.* IX, 140: not pure G.?, Piganiol, *Hist. rom.* 1939, p. 149: Celticized?, Hubert, *Celtes*, p. 192. Demolished, J. Fraser, *Proc. Brit. Acad.* 1927, against H. Peake, *Bronze Age and Celtic World*, 1922. Elston, *Earliest Relations between Celts and Germans*, 1934, pp. 117–21, against Feist. C. and G. hardly distinct yet, Grenier, op. cit. p. 93 and names of chiefs Celtic.

2 Pos. ap. Str. 197–8, Diod. v, 28–9, and Athen. IV, 151*e*, 154*a*, VI, 246*c* (Pos. fr. 15–17, Jacoby, *F.G.H.* IIA). Reinhardt, *Poseidonios*, pp. 26–30. Grenier, op. cit. pp. 203–12 and in Frank's *Econ. Survey*, III, pp. 403–5 (1937). Pass, p. 140, n. 2. Pol. III, 39, 48. Rhône, ibid. 47, II, 14, 16. Hyde, *Roman Alpine Routes*, 1935, p. 11. Burton, *Discovery of Anc. World*, 1932, p. 57. Loire, see p. 194, n. 1, p. 146, n. 1. Lakes, ap. Str. 209.

Ardennes are only a relic—if the passage is genuine. An officer, Crassus, dealt with the Aquitanians, partly akin to their neighbours of Spain. Already the despatches were dazzling the home public with 'unheard-of names of warlike nations'.[1] But the north rose, and one force was destroyed

Fig. 25.

there, and another barely rescued. Then a national leader appeared, Vercingetorix, of the Arverni, who fought very well till besieged and taken at Alesia (in the Côte d'Or). The country did not stir when the army was withdrawn for the civil war. Caesar had done a mighty work, far more lasting than Alexander's: Gaul was to be a Latin civilization, which would absorb many barbarian invaders. How much of this he himself foresaw is another matter.

[1] Cic. de Prov. Cons. 33 (in 56 B.C.). Arduenna silva, v, 3, cp. vi, 29, Rhine-Nervii (interpolated?). T. R. Holmes, *Caesar's Conquest of Gaul*[2], 1911, and *Roman Rep. and Founder of R. Empire*, II, 1923: Hignett in *C.A.H.* IX, 537–73: Jullian, op. cit. III: Hubert, *Les Celtes depuis l'Époque de La Tène*, 1932: Grenier in Frank, op. cit. pp. 411–58 and *Gaulois*, 1945, pp. 383–408: F. B. Marsh, *Hist. of R. World* (146 to 30 B.C.), 1935, ch. 12.

Only tribal jealousies and unstable feudal conditions had made the conquest possible, as he knew. On the people he echoes and modifies Posidonius. Chariots are now disused in most parts in favour of cavalry; the Druids are still strong, but are rarely allowed human sacrifices. The Gauls are greedy for news and rash to act on rumour; they go lightly to war but soon lose patience if things go wrong. They are clever, have excellent ships and mines, and can imitate anything. Mommsen's account of them as lazy, tipplers and brawlers, incapable of organization and politically useless, and so on, is a masterpiece of national prejudice, and almost everything he says can be easily turned against the Germans; yet most recognize that there is a good deal of the future French in the ancient sketch.[1] Napoleon saw in them frivolity, credulity, and other faults, and thought he could trace these to the Gauls.

Caesar's geography is very sparing, usually just what is needed to explain events; some passages going a little beyond this minimum are suspected by the editors as interpolations (partly also for linguistic reasons), like one which makes the Meuse rise in the Vosges and has an unintelligible muddle of two views about the Waal and Rhine.[2] Yet enough is said to cover the country with names, many easily recognizable in their modern forms, Remi—Rheims, Ambiani—Amiens, Matrona—Marne, and so on, while not enough to show how he conceived the mapping: for instance he does not mention the Breton projection as such, and speaks of Britain as 'opposite' the stretch from the Loire to the Channel.

Strabo is minute on the old southern province, but for the rest has little that is not from early sources or from Caesar, whom he does not use carefully at first hand. He thinks the Garonne as long as the Loire. In his blind prejudice against Pytheas, and perhaps encouraged by the apparent silence of Caesar just mentioned, he denies the Breton projection and flattens the outer coast to run north-east from the Pyrenees to the Rhine.[3]

1 J. M. Robertson, *The Germans*, 1916, pp. 58–62 (on Mommsen): McDougall, *The Group Mind*, 1920, pp. 229–30: Fouillée, *Psychologie du Peuple français*[6], 1921, pp. 148–9: Oman, *On the Writing of History*, 1939, p. 186: Grenier, *Gaulois*, p. 23. Set characterization, Caes. *B.G.* VI, 13–20, and remarks, III, 18, IV, 5. Ships, III, 8: mines, III, 21, VII, 22. Minerals disappointing, Str. 190–1, Davies, op. cit. p. 76. Barzun, *Race*, 1938, p. 31 cites *Maximes et Pensées de Bonaparte*, p. 193.

2 IV, 10: the right view is a gloss, Constans' ed. (1926). Most bracket, I, 1, 5–7 (though similar errors in Str. 199, Mela, III, 12). Editors, Meusel, Holmes, 1914, Klotz, 1927 (and *Cäsarstudien*, 1912, pp. 27–56, and in *Rhein. Mus.* 1934, pp. 66–96). Beckmann, *Geogr. u. Ethnogr. bei Cäsars B.G.* 1930, defends (too obstinately).

3 Str. 129, 195, 199: Berger, *Erat.* p. 217: so already Artem. 'Opposite', Caes. *B.G.* III, 9. Strabo used C. as used in an excursus in the history of Timagenes (cited by Amm. Marc. XV, 9, 2), thinks Klotz, *Cäsarstudien*, pp. 57–135. For Str. on rivers see p. 233, n. 1.

THE ROMAN REPUBLIC

On Britain Gallic traders could not or would not tell Caesar much, even about the nearest part, where the people were very recent Belgic immigrants and obviously in close touch with their kinsmen. He had to deter them from sending help, and probably he meant to do more. In the reconnaissance of 55 B.C. he barely held his landing-ground while repairing many ships battered 'at the full moon, which makes the Ocean tides highest, as our men did not know' (it is hard to believe that none of them knew the connection between the two). Next year he brought a much stronger force and crossed the Thames, but was given no pitched battle, and retired after taking an oppidum 'protected by woods and marshes' (near St Albans). The sea had again done its part by destroying forty ships at anchor, and he left with hostages and a promise of tribute. At home his adventure to the remote island, 'almost another world', 'penitus toto divisos orbe Britannos', caused a great sensation, though extravagant hopes of plunder in gold, silver, and pearls were disappointed. Cicero's brother meant to write about it, a fine subject, thought Cicero: 'quos tu situs, quas naturas rerum et locorum, quas gentes, quas pugnas... habes!'[1]

There is a set description in Caesar, apparently unknown to later writers like Tacitus and now often suspected, though defended by Collingwood as substantially genuine. The Britons have a blue war-paint, and still cling to chariot-fighting. For money they have bars of iron from the coast parts or use imported copper. Tin is oddly said to be found 'inland', meaning inwards from the straits of Dover? (The tin of Cornwall was still worked, and no doubt called for by the Breton ships, but its secret was well kept, so it seems; Scipio about 135 B.C. had known of a tin trade passing over Gaul, but could learn nothing worth mentioning about Britain from the traders concerned.) Cantium, being nearest Gaul, is far the most civilized part, and remarkably populous, with well-stocked farms (yet probably life was mainly pastoral even here). The inner or northern tribes sow no corn but live on their cattle; a dozen men or more have a wife in common—this sounds like a bad rumour, and who are these people, the earlier Celtic invaders or some natives there before them? The island is less cold than Gaul, and has shorter nights, as measured by the water-clock. It is a triangle, the nearest side being about 500 Roman miles and the others reported as 700 and 800. (This is a marked improvement on Pytheas, but the directions are not good.) The third side has no land opposite

---

[1] Cic. *ad Q.fr.* II, 15, 4: plunder, Cic. *Ep. ad Fam.* VII, 7. World, Vell. Pat. II, 46, orbe, Virg. *Ecl.* I, 66. Campaigns in Caes. *B.G.* IV, 20–38, V, 2–23. Tides, IV, 29. T. R. Holmes, op. cit. II, ch. 10 (1923), and *Anc. Britain and the Invasions of Julius Caesar*, 1907: Hignett, *C.A.H.* IX, 560: Jullian, op. cit. III, 336–64: Collingwood and Myres, *R. Britain and the English Settlements*[2], 1937, pp. 34–53. Belgic, c. 75 B.C., ibid. p. 26: c. 100, Wheeler in *Eur. Civ.* 1935, II, 260.

northward, while its (Kentish) corner looks towards Germany; the second faces the west and Ireland and Spain! Ireland (Hibernia) is half the size, 'it is thought', and lies beyond a sea as wide as the Channel, with Mona half-way (here Man, it seems, though later Anglesey). Presently Agrippa overestimated Ireland as 600 miles by 300, and Livy somehow got a different notion of Britain as a long rhomboid. One writer talks vaguely of two large islands, Albion and Ierne, with many small ones round.[1]

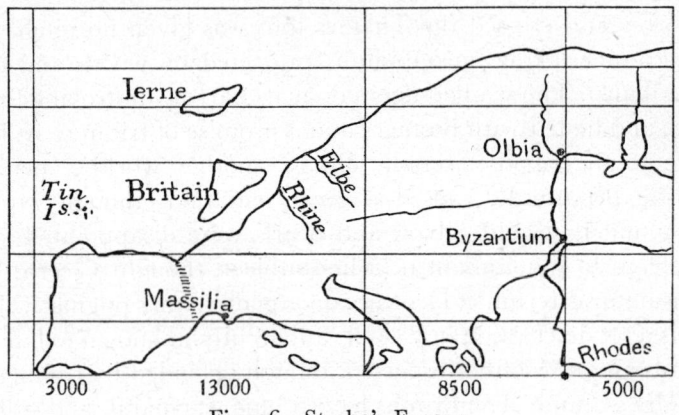

Fig. 26. Strabo's Europe.

By Strabo's time tolls were being paid in Gaul on British corn and cattle, hides, slaves, hunting hounds, gold and silver and iron (there is strangely no word of tin as a current export). Of geography he makes a startling mess, because after Polybius he rejects every word of Pytheas and his high latitudes. He places a vague Ireland north of Britain and near the line of uninhabitable cold, which he pulls far down. He flattens Britain to suit, making the southern side actually the longest and drawing it parallel to the misconceived straight coast of Gaul.[2] The climate is said to be not so much snowy as rainy and foggy, the sun being seen for only three or four hours about noon. With Thule, of course, he will have nothing to do, and Caesar has only a faint echo of anything like it. A poet talks of 'ultima Thule', probably with no clear idea of what he means; his ancient

1 Ps.-Arist. *de Mundo*, 393 *b*: several smaller islands, Caes. *B.G.* v, 13. Livy ap. Tac. *Agr.* 10. Agrippa ap. Plin. iv, 102 (and Britain 800 × 300 m.p.). Placing similar in Tac. op. cit. 10, 20, 24, Dio Cass. xxxix, 50, etc. Caes. v, 12–14: genuine, Collingwood, op. cit. p. 476: Barwick, *Philologus* Suppl. 1938 (C. added 12–13 in margin for a second ed.): but cp. Klotz, *Cäsarstudien*, pp. 43–9. Tin, Collingwood, op. cit. p. 70. Scipio, see p. 146, n. 1. Pastoral, Birnie, *Econ. Hist. of British Isles*, 1935, p. 14.

2 Str. 72, 115: Bunbury, *Anc. Geogr.* ii, 250: Berthelot, *Rev. Arch.* 1933, pp. 9–12 (and on Agrippa's map, which restored the Breton projection). Exports and climate, Str. 199–200. Klotz, op. cit. pp. 128–35. On Pytheas, see p. 151, n. 4. Thule, see p. 218. n. 2. Virg. *Georg.* i, 30, and Probus and Servius ad loc.

THE ROMAN REPUBLIC

commentators explain it as either the farthest of the Orkneys or beyond that group.

Posidonius had mentioned tin not only in Britain but also in the north-west corner of Spain and in the Tin Islands, whatever these were meant to be. (It must be conceded that all the later writers conceive them as somewhere apart from Britain, but they may have been wrong in so interpreting the early reports, and the tin may have come mainly from Britain, though probably some also from Spain.) Strabo describes them as a group of ten lying well north of the corner mentioned and in the latitude of Britain; the people wear long black coats and stride about with sticks like tragic Furies, and they have tin and lead and hides to barter. Formerly only the Phoenicians of Gades did the trade, taking such care to conceal the route that one skipper, when followed by Romans, ran his own ship and theirs aground, and was publicly compensated for his loss (this incident, if not legendary, as Gsell hints, was presumably after 205 B.C., when the Romans acquired Gades). But in time, Strabo continues, the secret was discovered: Publius Crassus crossed a sea wider than the British Channel and found the people working shallow mines. Later Pliny puts the islands sixty miles west of the corner, and Ptolemy, too, maps them thereabouts. Pliny mentions tin also in north-west Spain, and archaeologists hold that so much was got there that it supplanted the Cornish workings for the next two or three centuries.[1] But it seems that the association of the islands with Spain is a confusion, part of the old legend of the Tin Islands. Crassus sounds like Caesar's officer in west and south-west Gaul, and some believe like Holmes that he crossed to Scilly or Cornwall, where he was told that tin was found 'inland' (Strabo, being in a haze about Tin Islands, may misunderstand the whole business). Others think of an earlier Crassus who served in north-west Spain in 95 B.C., and he is supposed to cross either to the off-shore islands (so Hennig) or most often to Scilly or Cornwall.[2]

---

1 Haverfield and Taylor, *Vict. County Hist. of Cornwall*, v, 19–21: Cary, *J.H.S.* 1924, p. 168: Hencken, *Arch. of Cornwall*, 1936, p. 172: Collingwood, op. cit. pp. 70, 230, *C.A.H.* XII, 289 and *Econ. Survey*, ed. Frank, 1937, III, 46–7: Albertini, *C.A.H.* XI, 493. Plin. IV, 34, XXXIV, 47, 156. Pos. ap. Str. 147: latitude, Str. 156. Skipper and Crassus, Str. 175–6: after 146 B.C.? Lewis, *Astronomy of Ancients*, 1862, p. 452: story probably from Pos., Casson, *Greece and Britain*, 1943, p. 11. Tin in Britain, Pos. loc. cit., Diod. v, 22, 38: see p. 146, n. 1. Rickard, *Man and Metals*, 1932, I, 304 cites Borlase, *Tin Mining in Spain*, 1897, p. 24. Tin Islands, see p. 55, n. 3, p. 232, n. 1.

2 Cary-Warmington, p. 42: O. Davies, *Roman Mines in Europe*, 1935, p. 142: Hencken, op. cit. p. 168. Offshore, Hennig, *T.I.* pp. 229–34, Philipp, *Tac. Germania*, 1926, p. 38. This Crassus also Jacoby, *F.G.H.* (Str. 175–6 is Pos. fr. 115), Norden, *Germ. Urgesch.* 415, Haverfield, *R.E.* Kassiterides. Caesar's Crassus, Mommsen, Bunbury, II, 244, Berger, p. 355 (Strabo misunderstands, being mistaken on Tin Islands): Holmes, p. 493 (Scilly): Nansen, *In Northern Mists*, 1911, I, 27: Ridgeway, *E.A.G.* I, 609 oddly takes him to islands off Spain. Gsell, op. cit. IV, 116. Tin Islands, Breton as Mela, Siret, see p. 55, n. 3.

It is all very puzzling, but rumour had had altogether too long a start with the Tin Islands, and the geographers never knew what they were talking about on this matter.

Of Germany something was learnt from Caesar's brief raids in 55 and 53 B.C. After hunting out two tribes which had drifted over the lower Rhine, he crossed below Coblenz and ravaged the 'villages and crops' of the Sugambri, who retired into their 'solitude and forests'. The Suebi, who blackmailed the more civilized Ubii on the river (about Cologne), had abandoned their 'towns' and withdrawn out of reach. On the second occasion they went far, to a vast forest Bacenis dividing them (meaning here the Chatti of later writers in Hesse?) from the Cherusci. They are mentioned in the host of Ariovistus apart from the Marcomanni—themselves really Suebi—and they are the fiercest and largest nation, it is said. All Germans live for war, and each tribe judges its own importance by the width of the 'solitude' it can make round itself: the Suebi have one of 600 miles, meaning Bohemia, it seems, from which they had driven the Celtic Boii and to which they were to withdraw about 9 B.C. when threatened by the Roman advance.[1] (The suggestion of Lebensraum is grim, though it was easy then to find large stretches of uninhabited bog or forest for such a Mark or frontier zone.) It may be noted that, while proclaiming the Rhine as the frontier, Caesar himself allowed some tribes of the defeated king to remain along the west bank. Among the others it is surprising to find one if not two from Jutland, though he gives no hint of knowing that they came from such distant parts.

There is a curious question about the name Germani, never used by the Germans themselves and of uncertain derivation. A group of tribes which had crossed the Rhine into Belgium were so called by their Celtic neighbours; probably they were Germans who became Celticized there, though Caesar seems to imply that they were Celts and a few like Müllenhoff still take them as Celts invading from the original Celtic home. Anyhow it was from this group that the name was extended to Germany, perhaps already by Posidonius, who may thus have revised his earlier opinion about the Cimbri and Teutones.[2] Caesar insists that the Germans are quite unlike

---

[1] Str. 290, Tac. *Germ.* 42 (Marcomanni). Solitude, *B.G.* IV, 3, VI, 23. C.'s raids, IV, 16–19, V, 9–10, 28. Jutland, Harudes, *B.G.* I, 38, 51, and perhaps Sedusii, 51, read Eudusii, Eudoses of Tac. *Germ.* 40, Jutes. Zone, R. E. Dickinson, *The German Lebensraum*, 1943, p. 46.

[2] Norden, *Germ. Urgesch. in Tac. Germ.* 1923, pp. 70–8: J. G. C. Anderson's ed. 1938, pp. xxi, xxxix. Name, some ap. Tac. *Germ.* 2: group, Caes. *B.G.* VI, 32 (Celts), V, 27. Müllenhoff, *Deutsche Alt.* II, 153–62, 189–206: so Holmes ed. of *B.G.* 1914, p. xxxi. Schütte, *Our Forefathers*, 1929, I, 17–28. Frahm, *Klio*, 1930, pp. 186–92. Much, *R.E.* Suppl. 3, Germani (1918), p. 546. Good discussions in Elston, op. cit. (see p. 190, n. 1). Grenier, op. cit. p. 164.

the Celts in language, religion, and customs. When not fighting, he says, they hunt a great deal. They raise cattle, and have only a little agriculture, re-allotting the land every year, lest private property should weaken the will for war and cause jealousy and faction (rather, it may be understood, the tribe each year marked out part of its land for crops and kept the rest as common pasture).[1] Traders are little needed except to buy spoil, and only the Ubii, softened by Gallic trade, import wine. These barbarians are big and hardy, chaste when young, and scrupulous in hospitality.

Caesar's geography is meagre, but he confirms the Hercynian Forest, 'known by hearsay to some Greeks', though it is less gloomy than they suppose and has open patches: it is nine days wide and extends eastward sixty and vaguely more to the Dacians and beyond (this indicates the whole series of wooded ranges from the Black Forest to the Carpathians). The passage is one of those most often questioned, and almost certainly not his is the note on the many strange beasts, reindeer and huge wild bulls and elks; the last have jointless legs, and are taken by sawing through the trees they lean against, a story told elsewhere of elephants. One editor argues that Caesar used a clerk to compile this matter from Greek geographers.[2]

A Danube frontier was beyond the vision of the Republic, and the river was still far from being perfectly known in all its course. From the head of the Adriatic there were early friendly relations and trade with a Celtic kingdom of Noricum (in Austria), which had gold and iron (here at Hallstatt had been the first known iron-working in Europe). Caesar is rather vague on the Danuvius in these parts, and several have questioned whether he understood it to be the same river known lower down as the Ister, our Danube. It is odd that some could still repeat the old blunder of a Danube branch to the Adriatic. Along the coast was a rather vague sub-province of Illyricum, attached to north Italy, but after many petty wars control of Dalmatia was little more than nominal.[3] Macedonia was not always well protected against the northern barbarians, the Dardanians and the fierce Celtic Scordisci (Belgrade way), despite many victories credited to governors in 'illa uberrima supplicationibus triumphisque provincia'. However some

---

1 IV, 1, VI, 22, generally like Tac. *Germ.* 15, 26, Anderson, ad loc.: Ekholm, *C.A.H.* XI, 50: more settled in Tac., Birnie, op. cit. p. 21: see p. 242, n. 1. Character, *B.G.* VI, 21–4 and (Suebi) IV, 1–3. Str. 291 denies agriculture and compares nomads.

2 Constans, op. cit. XIV: jointless, Plin. VIII, 39, and see p. 137, n. 1. Caes. *B.G.* VI, 25–8. Forest, also Str. 207, 290, 292: 'invia atque horrenda', Livy, IX, 36. Bulls, uri, also Tac. *A.* IV, 72.

3 Ill. wars, *C.A.H.* IX, 107: Ormerod, *Piracy in Anc. World*, 1924, pp. 181–5. Noricum, Pol. ap. Str. 208–9: iron, ibid. 214: Davies, *R. Mines*, pp. 165, 175: Chilver, *Cisalpine Gaul*, 1941, p. 35. Branch, even Hipp. ap. Str. 57: Nepos in Mela, II, 57, 63 and Plin. III, 127: denied by Str. 57, Diod. IV, 56, 7: see p. 48, n. 2, p. 88, n. 1, p. 141, n. 1. On Caesar Brandis, *R.E.* Danuvius, Cavaignac, *Hist. gén. de l'Ant.* 1946, p. 485.

counter-raids were carried along the Morava and finally to the Danube, in 112–110, 100 and 75 B.C. The Thracian kingdom was made client in 73 B.C., and a general penetrated through the mountains to the lower Danube, where he checked the Bastarnae, though they crossed again and beat a proconsul in 61 B.C. First mentioned well before, as hired by the last Macedonian kings, they were long wrongly described as Celts: they seem to be the 'Galatae' who appear in an inscription, along with Sciri, as attacking the old Greek colony of Olbia about 212 B.C. Only later were they recognized as Germans from the Vistula, the first of their race to reach the Black Sea and to figure in history (apart from those visited by Pytheas). Still more formidable were the Dacians, especially when a strong king conquered far along the river.[1] Caesar meant to deal with him, but it was left for his heir to realize a Danube frontier. Some still contrived to find the noble savage hereabouts and used him as a foil for a corrupt civilization: so a poet praises the Scythians roaming in carts on the steppes and also the stern Getae, who change their common land every year and till it by rotation (much as Caesar says of the Germans, and the tone anticipates that of Tacitus on the same people).

The former Scythia was now rather Sarmatia, with Roxolani described as having corselets of raw ox-hide and wicker shields. The Crimea came into some limelight when its Greek cities sought help from generals of Mithridates, and later when the old king fled thither through various tribes from the Caucasus.[2] A son, who helped to destroy him, was allowed to keep it as a sort of client, until he took advantage of the civil war to recover much more and was defeated in Pontus by Caesar himself. The geography is vague and poor. Strabo is brief, being little interested in such remote and barbarous parts. The Azov was now better conceived as small compared with the Black Sea, but everything north of the Roxolani near-by was unknown, and it was doubted whether any people could live in such a cold wilderness. Roman poets talked as if the 'Scythians' lived like Eskimos, and they

---

[1] Str. 303–4, Suet. *Jul.* 44, etc.: Pârvan, *Dacia*, 1928, pp. 156–7. Bastarnae, Dem. of Callatis ap. Pseudo-Scymn. 797, Str. 306, Plin. IV, 81, Tac. *Germ.* 46: *C.A.H.* XI, 59. Celts, Pol. as Livy, XL, 57, XLIV, 26. Inscr., *C.I.G.* 2058 (*Sylloge*³, 495): Rostovtzeff, *C.A.H.* VIII, 561: Minns, *Scythians and Greeks*, 1913, p. 124: L. Schmidt, *Gesch. der deutschen Stämme*, 1910, pp. 459–61: Schütte, op. cit. I, 92, 241: Grenier, op. cit. 122 (Celts). Sciri of Vistula, Plin. IV, 97. Geogr. accounts, see p. 250, nn. 1–2. Mac., Cic. *in Pis.* 38, 44, 97.

[2] Str. 496: Appian, *Mithr.* 102. Generals, Str. 306, 309, 312, Rostovtzeff in *C.A.H.* IX, 228. For Strabo's geogr. of Crimea, E. v. Stern, *Hermes*, 1917, pp. 1–28. Bastarnae in M.'s armies, Appian, op. cit. pp. 15, 69, 71. Rox., Str. 306. Sarmatians, Vernadsky, *Anc. Russia*, 1943, ch. 3: his attempt to derive 'Russia' from Rox-olani seems very dubious, 76, 87, 278. Getae, Horace, *Odes*, III, 24, 9–16, cp. Caes. *B.G.* IV, 1 (p. 197, n. 1): Glover, *Springs of Hellas*, 1945, p. 53. Scythians just, Trogus ap. Justin, II, 2, 5–10.

clung to old properties like the Rhipaean mountains, which Strabo dismissed as a fable. (Rather in their vein is Pope's

> Lo! where Maeotis sleeps, and hardly flows
> The freezing Tanais through a waste of snows,

which he himself liked best of all his lines.) While some questioned the northern Ocean as a mere assumption, most accepted it and put it quite near, even within 200 miles.[1] A careless and credulous writer, Nepos, had a story about some Indians being driven by a storm past the Caspian 'gulf' to Germany, and of this no one has made any reasonable sense. Some have seen a confusion with Venedi (or Slavs). Several have cited cases of Eskimos being blown as far as Europe, and have hinted that some such castaways may have been mistaken as Indians and supposed to come from the east. (Strabo does not mention the business, though he refers vaguely to certain voyagers spoken of as going round from India to the Caspian, and adds that, if historians do not agree on the fact, the voyage seems possible at least, from what Patrocles said.) Even this wild tale of Nepos is not without importance for the history of geography: some Elizabethans used it, understanding 'Germany' to mean Norway, as evidence of a northern passage round Asia, and gallant efforts were made to find

> the imagined way
> Beyond Petsora eastward to the rich
> Cathaian coast,

a hopeless voyage which was to be carried out first by a steam-whaler in 1878–9. Others like Gilbert even contrived to read the story as supporting a north-west passage round Canada, and Frobisher brought home an Eskimo whose Tartar features seemed to prove that Asia had actually been reached.[2]

The northward advance of the Romans had been a defensive reaction against barbarian inroads. After some groping they had pushed suddenly

---

[1] Pos. ap. Str. 491 (but cp. Agrippa ap. Plin. IV, 81). Questioned, Pol. III, 38. Wilderness, Str. 306, 493: Artem. ap. Plin. II, 246 (but cp. Isid. ap. Plin. IV, 102, 1250 m.p. to Thule). Rhipaean (in Latin texts often Riphaean), Str. 295: Virg. *Georg.* III, 349–83, IV, 517: Dion. Hal. XIV, 3. Azov, Str. 310, 493: rightly reduced in Pol. IV, 39. Poor stuff in Diod. II, 43–6.

[2] Sir W. Foster, *England's Quest of Eastern Trade*, 1933, p. 53. Gilbert in Hakluyt, Everyman ed. V, 104–9: E. G. R. Taylor, *Tudor Geography*, 1930, p. 33. Asia, ibid. pp. 33, 131. Also Taylor in Newton, *Great Age of Discovery*, 1932, p. 221. Eskimos, Forbiger, *Alte Geogr.* 1844, II, 4: Hennig, *Terrae Incognitae*, I, 235–8: some, ap. Winsor, *Christopher Columbus*, 1894, p. 127: Plischke in *Pet. Mitt.* 1916, pp. 93–5, who cites Gomara 1553 and Wytfliet 1597. Nepos in Mela, III, 45, Plin. II, 167 (N. is credulous, ibid. V, 14). Venedi, Schafarik, *Slav. Alt.* 1842. Str. 518, 74, see p. 128, nn. 1–2.

and decisively to the Rhine; elsewhere they were only fumbling towards the Danube. They had already passed well beyond the Mediterranean climate and the sphere of a Mediterranean power, and had reached some country with which the Greeks had never been really familiar. Thus, now and later, several of their campaigns were almost advances of knowledge, and at least a few traders went well beyond the legions. Of other explorers we hear very little: the Romans had not the necessary curiosity even for geography, where they might have done something.[1] They built their famous roads right over the conquered lands: such was 'via illa nostra per Macedoniam et usque ad Hellespontum militaris', 711 of their miles to Byzantium. But they cared little for travel beyond the limits of civilization: in this sense they hardly deserved the description 'avidam ulteriorum semper gentem', and they compare ill with what an Elizabethan called 'the searching and unsatisfied spirits of the English', noted already by Caxton as born under the domination of the moon, 'which is never steadfast but ever wandering'. Even frontier officers did not spend their furloughs in the wilds, it seems, or write books about their adventures: otherwise we should probably have some traces (there are a few in the next period, as of two men who strayed far into the Sahara).

One odd matter, just how had 'a big white bear' come to the royal zoo in Egypt? A polar bear, whose journey 'must have been exciting', it is suggested, but this is not likely despite one such bear which seems to have reached a medieval Sultan of that country, and an expert on animals ancient and modern is content with a mere albino from Syria or Thrace.[2]

Here may be mentioned a few verses sometimes taken too seriously as proving a horror of the sea among the landlubber Romans or the ancients in general. There is a curious tirade against the impious man who first dared to cross the estranging sea, defying its storms and monsters. This is hardly more than a mannerism in an old Utopian vein, and the same writer talks elsewhere of greedy merchants venturing to the frozen north and the tropics and India.[3]

1 S. N. Miller in *Eur. Civ.* ed. Eyre, 1935, II, 507, 510. Defensive, ibid. pp. 370, 376: E. C. Semple, *Infl. of Geogr. Environment*, pp. 66, 362. Danube a makeshift, see p. 249, n. 2.

2 Jennison, op. cit. p. 34 (see p. 138, n. 1). White bears from Thrace in Paus. VIII, 17. Polar, Tarn, *Hell. Civ.* 1927, p. 251. Athenaeus, V, 201 c. Avidam, Livy, IX, 38, 5. Via, Cic. *de Prov. Cons.* II, 4: length, Plin. IV, 46: also Str. 322-3. Romans not adventurous, Warde Fowler, *Rome*, 1912, p. 11: Sir C. P. Lucas, *Greater Rome and Greater Britain*, 1912, pp. 69, 74.

3 Horace, *Odes*, III, 24, 36-41: *Ep.* I, 1, 45. Tirade, *Odes*, I, 3, 9-24, cp. *Epod.* 16, 57-60, Ov. *Met.* I, 94, Hesiod, *Op.* 236. Seriously, as by H. B. George, *Relations of Geogr. and History*, 1910, p. 78.

After Caesar's withdrawal from Britain a minor general is invited by a very minor poet to conquer that island and a second part of the world beyond the sun—

> Te manet invictus Romano Marte Britannus
> teque interiecto mundi pars altera sole.

This extravagance does not refer to Thule or any western land but to the southern hemisphere ('solus utroque idem diceris magnus in orbe').[1]

Presently in the exercises of schoolboys Caesar was made to debate the chances of conquering Britain, and to wonder what the Ocean was like, whether Britain was an island and how big it was, 'nam tum ignorabatur': these things hardly deserve attention except as suggesting that many people knew little or nothing of Pytheas (Caesar himself has only a distant echo of that ancient mariner).[2]

As for the 'Indian' castaways mentioned above, whom several have explained as blown from America, an old editor scorns such guesses and opines that Britons dyed dark blue were mistaken for Indians![3]

By now the writers of Rome talked as if her fame or even her conquests covered the entire 'orbis terrarum' (sometimes 'orbis terrae'). The phrase was so closely identified with 'the inhabited earth', 'a sort of great island which we call the orbis terrae', that it could not without awkwardness be applied to the globe, 'illum globum...quae terra dicitur'. One writer speaks of a ball, 'pila terrae', in denying the primitive notion of the navel of the earth at Delphi; but neither 'pila' nor 'globus' became popular, and no new term for the earth as a globe was invented. The word 'orbis' began to be freely used also in a restricted sense, meaning only 'region'.[4]

---

1 Pseudo-Tibullus, IV, 1, 149–50, cp. 176. A writer in *Quart. Rev.* 1893, II, p. 12 seems to misunderstand this of the west.

2 See pp. 194, 218. Exercises, Quintilian, VII, 4, 2.

3 'Indians', p. 199, n. 2. Editor, Isaac Voss, *Mela*, 1700, ad loc. America, Gaffarel, *Rev. de Géogr.* 1881–2, as A. von Humboldt and others long before: Cavaignac, *Hist. gén. de l'Antiquité*, 1946, p. 455: possible, Hyde, *Anc. Greek Mariners*, 1947, p. 162.

4 Common from Ovid on, S. Reinach, *Cultes, Mythes et Religions*, 1908, I, 184–94. Ball, Varro, *L.L.* VII, 17: J. Vogt, *Orbis Romanus*, 1929, p. 7. 'Globum', Cic. *de Rep.* VI, 15: island, Cic. *N.D.* II, 165. On the concept 'orbis terrarum' see also p. 217, n. 3, p. 220, n. 2, p. 223, n. 1, and essays by R. Richter and R. Friedrich, both 1887, and mine in *Univ. Birm. Hist. J.* I, 1947.

CHAPTER VII

THEORY IN THE SAME PERIOD

THE endless commenting on Homer had some curious developments for geographical theory. It was very perversely argued that he already knew all about the globe; he was also supposed to have, like the Stoics, an Ocean which covered the whole torrid zone and so could feed the sun uniformly in its different positions. Prominent in this strange aberration was Crates, who was the royal librarian at Pergamum and came once as its envoy to Rome in 165 B.C. He explained Menelaus as wandering round to the south side of Africa and finding Ethiopians 'in two parts', there and on the opposite bank of the equatorial Ocean, while the Erembi were cremni or 'dark people', really Indians (somebody else changed the text to 'Arabs').[1] Crosswise there is another Ocean or interpolar gulf, he conceives, so that water occupies more than half the surface of the globe. In this gulf he puts many of the peoples visited by Odysseus: the nightless giants were at the latitude of some very short night such as Pytheas reported, while the dayless 'Cerberians'—rather than Cimmerians—were at the pole, with a six months' night and a cloudy sort of six months' day. Against the usual Stoic view of tides as a sort of breathing in and out, he explains them as a collision of waters due to a back-flow of the currents from the ice of the poles, and he credits the old poet as meaning nothing less by his 'back-flowing' Ocean.[2] In this very odd way Crates came by his earth with two inhabited worlds in each hemisphere. Strabo says that to represent the earth one should make a globe 'like that of Crates', and to depict the known earth clearly upon the surface a big globe is needed, not under ten feet in diameter; but this statement does not quite prove that Crates made a show-piece of such a size. How he drew the known inhabited world in detail there is hardly any information (the sketch is quite conjectural). In fact his symmetrical scheme of the globe, 'orbis quadrifariam duplici discretus Oceano', bore little relation to any known geographical facts, and was hardly better than an idle fancy of misguided

---

[1] Str. 31, 42: see p. 24, n. 1. Sun, p. 168, n. 1. C.'s fragments now best in Mette, *Sphairopoiia*, 1936. Berger, *Erdk.* pp. 441–58. Kroll, *R.E.* XI, 1634–41 (1922).

[2] Macrobius, *Somn. Scip.* II, 9, 8: Duhem, *Système du Monde*, II, 273. Breathing, Athenodorus ap. Str. 173. Cimm. etc., Geminus, 6, 10–21: Mette, op. cit. pp. 75, 82, 265–6, 283: Gellius, XIV, 6, 3: Sen. *Ep.* 88, 7. Most of surface, Plut. *de Facie*, 935 d. For some curious echoes of this theory of tides, Kimble, *Geogr. in Middle Ages*, 1938, pp. 155, 164–5, 234.

scholars: they merely showed a 'more accurate ignorance' than others who talked vaguely of several such islands or continents.[1] But the notion had its fascination, especially in the uncritical days of declining science, and through Macrobius it passed down to the Middle Ages. According to some it is still traceable in the decoration of the royal orb. A globe, occasionally with certain crossing bands, figures as a symbol of power on Roman coins, a few of 76 B.C. and the end of the Republic, more commonly in the Empire. Augustus has it with his birth-star, the sign of Capricorn,

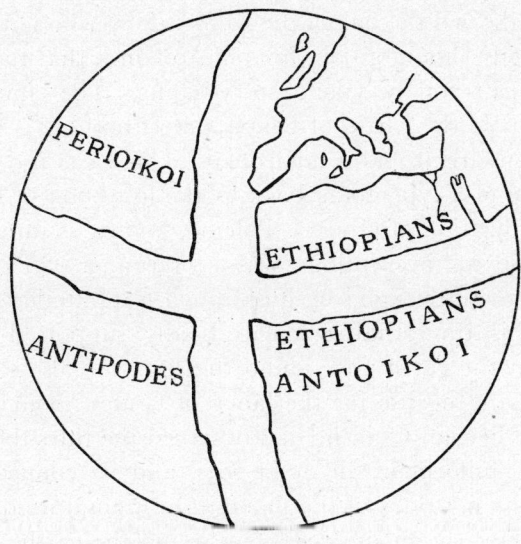

Fig. 27. Orb of Crates.

and on his and later types it appears, often with a rudder and horn of plenty, in token of the providential rule of the gods and a god-like Emperor (Plate IIC). The ruler holds a globe or receives it from Jupiter or sits on it, or Victory sits or stands on a globe; yet the globe may have stars, and seems, rather surprisingly, to be nearly always the heaven rather than the earth, while a statue of like design is described as carrying 'sphaeram aeream formatam in speciem poli'. That the globe may be the earth is admitted only doubtfully and in a few cases; a writer who thinks otherwise is puzzled to explain why the Romans should like the earth-globe so much on coins and so little elsewhere, being inclined to relapse to a flat 'orbis

---

[1] Housman on Manilius, I, 246: cp. Ps.-Arist. *de Mundo* 3 (several), Berger, *Erat.* p. 89. Big globe, Str. 116 (in Str. 12 a celestial globe is meant). Orbis, Eumenius, *Const. Caes.* 4. Macr. op. cit. II, 5, 6, II, 9, 4: Gem. 16, 1–3: Cleom. I, 2: Mart. Cap. VI, 603. E. L. Stevenson, *Terrestrial and Celestial Globes*, New Haven, 1921, I, 7–8, with drawing, resembling Kretschmer's.

terrarum'.[1] As for the sort of earth-globes which we use, practically nothing is heard of them in ancient times.

A more harmless pedantry than that of Crates was the elaborate commenting on Homer's catalogues of places. A Demetrius, about 150 B.C., wrote with a strong local interest on the Trojan allies, to the tune of thirty books on sixty lines! He had his own notion of Troy itself as not the site later and now generally accepted but another a few miles away. Apollodorus dealt with the Achaean list in twelve books, often cited by Strabo. On the wanderings of Odysseus he shared the sensible view about finding the cobbler who sewed the bag of the winds: those who put the adventures round about Sicily should go on, he said, to admit that the poet removed them to the Ocean 'for the sake of story-telling'. The same writer's was a verse description of the earth, of which almost nothing is known, as some apparent citations are probably not from it.[2] There was also some intelligent local description of a type going back to the lost book of Dicaearchus on the 'life' or civilization of Greece. Polemo, known as interested in works of art and as copying inscriptions, was a forerunner of Pausanias, if he is not proved to have been used by him, much less plundered wholesale.[3]

It was at this time that Seleucus boldly supported the theory of Aristarchus that the earth goes round the sun. He also said good things about tides, having no use for the fancy of Crates about them. Born in a colony on the Persian Gulf, he had observed the tides there. He denied that they were uniform in all outer seas, and he connected them, like Pytheas, with the positions of the moon. On the nature of the attraction he was less happy: the moon, revolving round the earth and contrary to the earth's own revolution, he said, affects the air between, which presses on the Ocean and transfers to it its wave-like motion.[4] Posidonius was

1 K. Miller, *Mappaemundi*, 1895, III, 129–31. Heaven, Grueber, *Coins of R. Rep. in Brit. Mus.* 1910, I, 529, 576, II, 358: Mrs Strong in *J.R.S.* 1916, pp. 32–5: Schlachter (and Gisinger), *Der Globus*, 1927, pp. 69–79. Earth sometimes?, ibid. p. 67: Mattingly, *Coins of R. Empire in B.M.* 1923, I, cxxxix: S. F. Hill, *Guide to Exhib. of R. Coins in B.M.* 1927, p. 42, child of Domitian on earth-globe (but is this right?). *C.A.H.* Plates IV, 198 a, 200 f, does not say which. Sphaeram, Amm. Marc. xxv, 10, 2. Orb, Berger, p. 458. Globe on later coins, Mattingly, op. cit. II, xix, III, xxii–xxiii.

2 Jacoby, *F.G.H.* IIB, 1118: on catalogue, ibid. 1087–1104. Ocean, ap. Str. 298. Sensible, see p. 25, n. 1. Dem. of Scepsis ap. Str. 599, 602, and often on Troad: *Fragments*, ed. Gaede, 1880. W. Leaf, *Strabo on the Troad*, 1913: Bunbury, II, 48–9: Schwartz in *R.E.* IV, 2807–13. On Apoll. ibid. I, 2863–71: Atenstädt, *Rhein. Mus.* 1933, pp. 115–44. Site, Vellay, *Controverses autour de Troie*, 1936, still questions like D.

3 Sir J. G. Frazer, *Pausanias's Descr. of Greece*, I, lxxxiii–xc (1913). Local, ibid. pp. xliii–xlviii: Heiberg, *Maths. and Phys. Science in Class. Ant.* 1922, p. 78: see p. 155, n. 1.

4 Aet. III, 17, Stob. I, 38 (*Dox.* 382–3): Str. 6, 174: Duhem, op. cit. I, 424, II, 272–3: Dreyer, *Hist. of Planetary Systems*, 1906, p. 140: Reinhardt, *Poseidonios*, 1921, p. 123: Heath, *Aristarchus*, p. 302: Tarn, *Greeks in Bactria and India*, p. 43 and *Hell. Civ.* 1927, p. 249: Berger, pp. 561–2: and see p. 211, n. 2. For S., p. 158, n. 1.

THEORY IN THE SAME PERIOD

presently to take up the matter after watching the tides at Cadiz. It is not easy: even now tides are very hard to explain in detail, and some seas have one a day, not two, while account must be taken of the kind of coast.

If geography was to progress, the urgent need was to test and correct the mapping of Eratosthenes. To begin this task was one of the minor activities of Hipparchus. He observed about 161–126 B.C., partly at Rhodes, and was the greatest of ancient astronomers. It was probably he who discovered the precession of the equinoxes, by comparing older observations made in Alexandria about 300 B.C., though some claim priority for a Babylonian, Kidinnu, and the Greek certainly used data from that quarter. In general, he raised the science to a far higher level than before, but it was fateful that for the reasons already mentioned he set aside the suggestion of Aristarchus and kept the earth in the centre, developing the system of epicycles and eccentric circles. He is responsible for the bulk of the matter in Ptolemy, who expounded him and often filled in gaps and brought his star-catalogue up to date. Nothing survives directly except a youthful commentary on the mistakes of the popular poem of Aratus and its authority Eudoxus. His work on geography is known mainly through Strabo, who does not always understand him or enable us to do so: it consisted of three books, closely following and examining the three of Eratosthenes. Even the famous measurement of the globe did not escape his criticism, how serious is not clear.[1] He approved the arc method, of course; he was conscious that the meridian was not quite right and that it was hard to get the ground-distance accurate, but he seems to have accepted the grand total, at least provisionally. A statement that he added 26,000 stades may rest on a misunderstanding, though some think that he did perhaps make this allowance for possible errors in the method. One writer argues that he improved the details to 50·4 × 5000 stades (which some ascribe to the original calculation).[2] Anyhow Hipparchus can find little fault with the result. But he goes on to attack the whole mapping procedure with a sharpness which Strabo often resents as nagging and unfair. He has no trouble in showing how easy it is to go wrong when one tries to deduce

---

1 Only hints in Str. 63, 113, 132: Cic. *ad Att.* II, 6, a Serapione et ab H. reprehenditur: Vitr. I, 6, 11: Berger, *Erat.* pp. 105–6. H.'s fragments, ed. H. Berger, 1869. Bunbury, *Anc. Geogr.* II, 2–15: Berger, *Erdk.* pp. 458–87: Rehm in *R.E.* VIII, 1677–80: Dubois, *Examen de la Géogr. de Strabon*, 1891, pp. 302–12. Kidinnu, Schnabel, *Berossos*, 1923, p. 237: B. Meissner, *Bab. u. Ass.* 1925, II, 418: Fotheringham: denied by Kugler, L. W. King, *Hist. of Babylon*, 1915, Heath in *Legacy of Greece*, p. 132.

2 Viedebantt, *Klio*, 1915, p. 202 (and see p. 160, n. 1). Allowance, Tannery, *Recherches*, p. 116 and Heath, op. cit. p. 344, defending Plin. II, 247: no, Berger, *Erat.* p. 130, *Erdk.* p. 466: Dreyer, p. 175: Thalamas, *Géogr. d'Érat.* p. 163.

straight distances (along a parallel) from round-about journeys like Alexander's march. He studies the various working-sections of the map in detail, and proves that their construction involves impossible triangles; for instance, one side drawn from the Caspian Gates to near the mouth of the Persian Gulf cannot be a meridian, as supposed, but must run south-east (this correction is sound). He hates the guess-work of putting Ethiopia

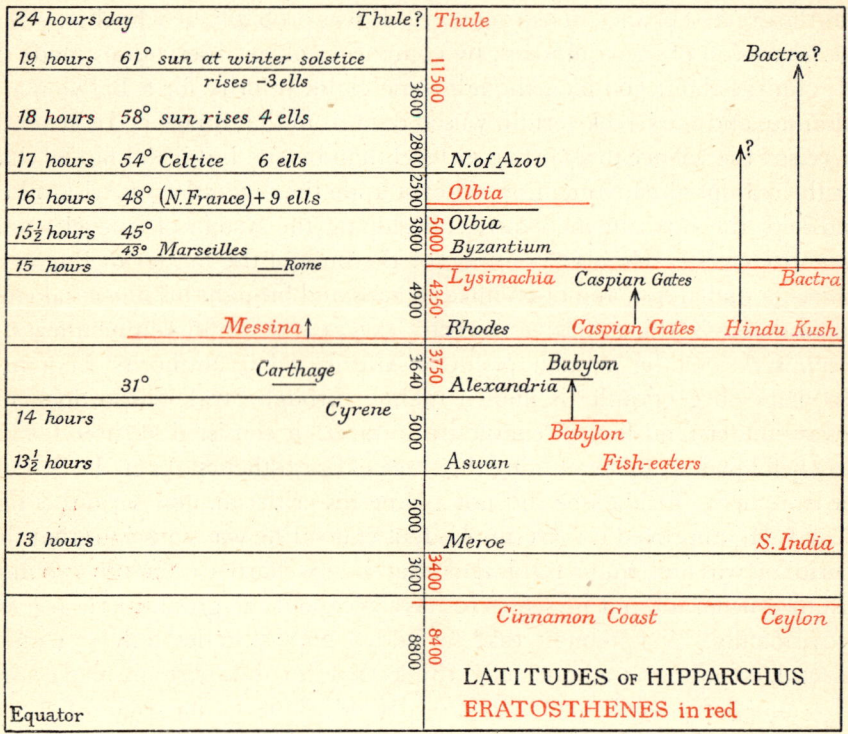

Fig. 28.

and south India on a parallel merely because they have similar products and peoples, without any check from accurate observations (yet after all he seems to accept the result, or at least Strabo assumes him to do so).[1] He insists that the essential ground-work of a map must be observations, as many and as good as possible, far more of them than the very few hitherto available. In principle he is quite justified, of course. He himself could contribute some: he had the skill to make what could be made of the data of Pytheas for high latitudes, and he did his best to elaborate the

[1] Str. 77, 133: Berger, *Erat.* p. 189. Triangles, ibid. p. 185: Str. 86: resents, Str. 79, 87. Berger, *Erdk.* pp. 464–5.

scheme of parallels, especially for Europe, though not without making bad mistakes. How he dealt with the breadth-line of the inhabited earth as drawn by Eratosthenes may be shown as on the diagram (Fig. 28). There is little change in the lower part up to the main parallel of Rhodes (Messina is now rightly removed northward off this line, though not enough). He places Byzantium badly, 2° too far north, being misled by a faulty shadow-reading which seemed to agree with the excellent one of Pytheas for Marseilles. Olbia is rightly pulled some way south. How exactly he located the high latitudes is very ill reported: the distance figures after Olbia are wrong, as they lead to 52 and 56, not 54 and 58° as they are supposed to do. The line beyond, that of the 19 hours' day, is said to pass through south Britain, not north Britain as one would expect and as many would like to read; the text should stand, but it is only part of Strabo's garbling of everything connected with Pytheas. In Asia an observation enabled a good correction for Babylon. But much of the criticism is unhappy and even downright perverse: sometimes, rather than accept the over-hasty new constructions, he will be content with older and worse maps. He attacks the remarkably good main parallel drawn eastwards from Rhodes along the base of the Taurus–Elburz–Hindu Kush: he wrongly pushes the Caspian Gates well north on an old view that the mountains may bend away north-east from about the longitude of Babylon. He makes the Indus flow south-east, and seems to believe a wild figure for India, and so to carry Bactria outrageously far north, though it is a land of vines, as Strabo remarks (the modern map shows it on a line with south Italy): but it is not quite clear if this step back is fairly ascribed to him.[1] In general, with his table of latitudes he made a good beginning of the necessary work for the sort of map he had in view. The work was never in fact to be adequately done even by Ptolemy's time. Moderns were not to find it too easy: they could get the height of the pole-star, the only method which Columbus mentions; where it failed, as in the tropics, the Portuguese used the sun, but with rough results until Zacuto prepared tables of the sun's declination.

As for longitudes, a very few fixed points would have saved Eratosthenes from enormous mistakes, but not even Hipparchus could supply such determinations, nor anyone else in ancient times. He knew indeed of a theoretical means. A famous eclipse during Alexander's crowning victory near Arbela (beyond the Tigris) had been observed also at Carthage, at

---

[1] Berger, *Erat.* p. 148: Str. 72–5. Indus, Str. 87. Bend away, ibid. 81–2: old maps, ibid. 69, 71. Correction, ibid. 88. Table of latitudes, ibid. 131–5: Ptol. 1, 7, 9: Berger, *Erdk.* pp. 473–6. Keep 'South' Britain in Str. 75: Jacob, *Rev. de Phil.* 1912, p. 149. Declination, J. A. Williamson, *The Ocean in English History*, 1941, p. 8.

a time said to differ by three hours or 45°; but he prudently thought this datum too inaccurate to use (in fact the distance is some 33°). Only a few others of the kind are ever mentioned, four hours between Persia and Spain, three between Armenia and Italy.[1] The practical difficulties, when there were no good and portable time-pieces, were too great to allow of any tolerably useful results. The very modern way is to compare local time, as determined by sun or stars, with Greenwich time carried in a watch or nowadays easily got by wireless; before this there were only laborious methods, including the use of eclipses, as is told of Amerigo Vespucci in Venezuela.

As regards plane projection, there is some hint that Hipparchus anticipated Ptolemy, at least in principle, and thought of an improvement, with the meridians as straight lines converging towards a central one and crossing straight (if not curved) parallels. But probably he did not publish any maps of his own. The whole purpose of his work was critical, to show that mapping was premature without a much larger and better basis of astronomical observations, such a basis, indeed, as was not to be provided till modern times.

He did not think that a continuous outer sea was necessarily implied by uniform tides, even if these could be proved against the recent denial of Seleucus. Insisting that Ceylon had not been actually sailed round, he raised the doubt, we hear, whether it might be not an island but rather 'the first part of another world'. Some had already suggested that the sea might not continue round Africa, and he was prepared at least to consider the possibility of land at unexplored parts.[2] Ptolemy was to go further and positively to map the Indian Ocean as a closed basin, though not, by the way, with Ceylon as part of the supposed 'terra australis'.

What Hipparchus wanted to begin was a long effort of patient work on his own lines. But the best conditions for science were past, even in Alexandria, and the wind blowing from Rome was unhealthy. Geography was not to develop on the scientific side nearly so well as it had promised. Yet already it had become too technical for the taste of general writers and readers, and there was a reaction to older kinds of treatment. Polybius

---

[1] Plin. II, 180, Cleom. 1, 8, 41. Arbela, Plut. *Alex.* 31, Plin. loc. cit., Ptol. I, 4, 2, who accepts 45°, IV, 3, 7, cp. VI, 1, 5: Str. 7 is vague. Berger, *Hipp.* pp. 29–32. Timepieces, Mieli-Brunet, *Hist. des Sciences: Antiquité*, p. 544: Hogben, *Science for the Citizen*, 1938, pp. 228, 81 (Amerigo).

[2] Berger, *Hipp.* 79, *Erdk.* p. 461. Suggested, some ap. Ps.-Scyl. 112. Ceylon, Mela, III, 70, Plin. VI, 81: Fiske, *Discovery of America*, 1920, I, 308: wrongly ascribed to H., thinks Malavialle in *Annales de Géogr.* 1900, pp. 251–7. Tides, Str. 6. Projection, Str. 117 vaguely: Kiepert, p. 6: Berger, *Erdk.* pp. 476–8, 632, *Erat.* p. 200: Tozer, *Anc. Geogr.* p. 343: Schöne, *Die Gradnetze des Ptol.* 1909. Critical, Str. 93.

values the subject in his way as useful for understanding the practical world and events: it is necessary for all educated men, especially those of the governing class like his noble Roman friends. He gives it indeed a fair amount of space, not only many digressions but a whole formal book of his history (xxxiv, mostly lost). Historians should know their ground as well as generals, he insists, and he prides himself on his own travels: he has been at pains to see much of the west, which was little known till opened up by the Romans, as the east had been by Alexander. He tries to account for the greatness of Rome by the abundant resources of Italy as well as by sound character (Strabo follows him in this as in many other views). He has an eye for geographical situation, and gives good sketches of districts, like the plains of the Po and Campania, and of various towns, Sinope and Sparta and Acragas: he explains how winds and currents have made Byzantium always important, though exposed on the land side to barbarian attacks. In this connection he refers to theories of the Black Sea outflow, and he thinks that the whole sea will in the end silt up as its Azov appendage is already doing. He stresses the influence of climate on national character —an old topic, but his phrasing on 'assimilation to environment' sounds remarkably modern. He shares the common crotchet of overrating Homer's knowledge, and is very perverse about it.[1] He rejects Pytheas wholesale, and so limits the breadth of the known world by beginning uninhabitable cold not far north of the sea of Azov. A Don–Nile meridian is not an improvement on the previous Dnieper–Nile. (He keeps the Don and Nile as the continental boundaries.) He doubts the Ocean assumed in the north, and somehow rightly denies a Caspian 'gulf'. Whether there is sea east of Asia or all round Africa no one knows for certain, he says, reasonably enough on the kind of evidence then available. He does not care to discuss astronomy, though a general should know more than the Athenian Nicias who ruined the great expedition to Sicily by his old-fashioned superstition about an eclipse. He does not understand that there must be a fixed arctic circle, but has a better notion of the 'torrid' zone, which many still took literally as too hot to live in, at least beyond the Cinnamon Coast. Actually it is hottest and driest at the tropics, he thinks, and becomes more habitable farther south, where there are not only mountains catching the Nile rains but apparently a plateau (which Strabo denies) shelving up towards the equator. All this was probably in the special geographical book of his history, though Geminus credits him with a separate treatise on the habitable

---

1 See p. 26, n. 1. Climate, Pol. IV, 21: see p. 108, n. 1. Byzantium, Pol. IV, 38, 43–5: sea, 39–40 (cp. p. 104, n. 1). Plains, Pol. II, 15, III, 91: towns, IV, 56, V, 21, IX, 27. Rome, VI, 50, Str. 286–8. Reaction, Berger, p. 490: on Pol. ibid. pp. 499–525, Bunbury, II, pp. 16–42: K. Miller, *Mappaemundi*, 1898, VI, 124–7 with P.'s map of Mediterranean: Dubois, op. cit. pp. 295–7.

equator.¹ (It is quite true that—owing to clouds—the heat can be less at the equator itself than near the tropics: the equatorial belt is wet and on each side is a fringe with summer rains, for the rains here 'follow the sun'.)

Among those with a crude view of uninhabitable heat was Agatharchides, who should have known better, as he said so much of the Red Sea coast and the tribes inward to the upper Nile and also discussed the various explanations of the Nile flood: he cares little for theory, though he mentions how the Great Bear is seen in Arabia and how it guides the nomads on their journeys. (Most of his writings are lost, however, including an *Asia* in 10 books and *Europe* in 49!) Of a big work by Scymnus, about 185 B.C., only a few tiny scraps remain. An extant verse account of part of the inner sea was once ascribed to him with no good reason and is now labelled as Pseudo-Scymnus, written about 110 B.C.; among many sources it mentions Eratosthenes with respect, but is not concerned with theory.² Most quoted later is the geography of Artemidorus, in eleven books on the coastal plan of description (about 102 B.C.). It was handy for many careful statements of distance, it appears, and said a lot about customs and famous men and events, a kind of matter liked by Strabo, who used him very freely, notably on the old Greek lands of Asia Minor. He plumes himself on travelling as far as Spain. For the east he accepted Eratosthenes as still standard, while venturing to check his figures along the great length-line: he reduced the total slightly, to 68,544 stades, but the items deserve little consideration except for a much better proportion between the two basins of the inner sea. He had no use for Pytheas, and so cut the breadth-line drastically to 30,000 stades. Even Strabo can censure his innocence of science and his assertions that in Spain the night comes down suddenly and the setting sun looks very big: Posidonius, however, also notes this illusion, and thinks it due to the sun being seen through dense and misty air. (The sun does seem larger on the horizon than when high up, and this is so, as an Arab writer explains, because we compare it when low with near terrestrial objects.)³

1 Gem. 16, 32. Pol. ap. Str. 97: habitable, also Pos. ibid. (see p. 214, n. 1) and Panaetius and one Eudorus, *Comm. in Aratum Reliquiae*, ed. Maass, 63, 97, Berger, *Erat.* 83: see p. 163, n. 2, p. 177, n. 1. Ocean, Pol. III, 38: on north sea, p. 199, n. 1. Caspian, p. 172, n. 1. Eclipse, Pol. IX, 19. Meridian, Pol. IV, 39, Str. 107–8, 492, Plin. IV, 77, Berger, *Erdk.* p. 521, Burton, p. 57. Boundaries, Pol. III, 37, 59.

2 *G.G.M.* I, 196–237: Gisinger, *R.E.* V, 672 (the real S. ibid. p. 661): Berger, *Erdk.* pp. 493, 530: Bunbury, II, pp. 69–74: Hoefer, *Rhein. Mus.* 1933, p. 67. Mahaffy, *Greek World under Roman Sway*, 1890, pp. 56–60. Addressed to Nicomedes (probably II) of Bithynia. Torrid, Agath. 79, and ap. Diod. III, 38: stars, ibid. 48, II, 54: Nile flood, ap. Diod. I, 36–41. On Agath. see p. 136, n. 3.

3 Al Hazen, Hogben, op. cit. p. 135: Pos. ap. Cleom. II, 1, 66–7 and Str. 138. Censure, Str. 172. Length and breadth, Plin. II, 242, 246, IV, 102. Bunbury, II, 61–9: Berger, *Erdk.* pp. 525–8 and in *R.E.* II, 1329: K. Miller, op. cit. VI, 127–30, with map showing A.'s distances. Daebritz, *De Art. Strabonis auctore*, 1905. Stiehle, *Philologus*, 1856. Dubois, op. cit. pp. 313–17.

A man of many interests, including geography, was this same Posidonius (about 135–51 B.C.). He settled at Rhodes, where he had studied under Panaetius, and like him he won the favour of high Roman circles for a modified kind of Stoicism. He described his friend Pompey's eastern wars and continued Polybius in a large-scale history, which was later often quoted. He travelled westwards to Gaul and Spain in order to inform himself on peoples and customs, while he paid some attention to other matters, staying a month at Cadiz watching sunsets and tides. Among his writings were works on physics and 'meteorology', the universe, the Ocean, the size and distance of the sun, and a commentary on Plato's *Timaeus*, which brought that strange book again into prominence; none is directly preserved, but they underlie a great deal of what his own and the next few generations have to say on natural science. He was not an original thinker or scientist, though he had 'a bent for explaining causes and much of Aristotle's manner', a feature which Strabo dislikes.[1] It is from Aristotle that he develops his 'meteorology', after the pattern of his school. He heightens to a mystical tone their belief in the universe as an organism pervaded by a vital force and showing 'sympathy' in all its parts. So the tides are 'in sympathy with the moon': he himself observed the daily and monthly periods and heard of specially strong yearly tides near the equinoxes, and he tried to explain the dependence on the moon's phases, using Seleucus but also going back to Aristotle's sun-raised wind (his discussion was often repeated with more or less understanding and hardly improved on till the sixteenth century).[2] The moon is supposed to affect many other things like trees and shell-fish and the blood of men, an old and persistent superstition, as when Falstaff dies 'e'en at the turning o' the tide'. The sun is praised as vastly important, causing by its light and heat most of the phenomena of earth and air; it produces day and night and the seasons, while from the various inclinations (*klimata*) of the earth's surface to its course come the differences of all lands and of their waters, human races, animals and plants, and even minerals. Its tropical heat is said to ripen the gems of Arabia (there are curious echoes of this long afterwards, when it is

1 Str. 104. Fragments in Jacoby, *F.G.H.* IIA, 222–317 (much concerns history rather). Schmekel, *Philosophie der mittleren Stoa*, 1892, pp. 238–90: Hicks, *Stoic and Epicurean*, 1910, pp. 130–46: Bevan, *Stoics and Sceptics*, 1913, pp. 85–118. Not original, Dobson, *Class. Quart.* 1918, pp. 178–95. Berger, *Erdk.* pp. 550–82: Bunbury, II, 93–100. Capelle, *Neue Jahrb.* 1920, pp. 305–24.

2 Duhem, *Système du Monde*, II, 280, 286, 361: Mieli-Brunet, op. cit. p. 657, after Almagià: Schmekel, op. cit. p. 286: Reinhardt, *Poseidonios*, pp. 121–4: Tarn, *Hell. Civ.* 1927, p. 249: Berger, op. cit. pp. 560–6: Sarton, *Introd. to Hist. of Science*, 1927, I, 183–4, 204. Pos. ap. Str. 55, 173–4: Sen. *N.Q.* III, 8 (closely): Plin. II, 212, who understands little, as does Ps.-Arist. *de Mundo*, 396a: Ptol. *Tetrabiblos*, I, 1: Cleom. II, 1, 54, II, 2: Aet. III, 17, 9. Seleucus, see p. 204, n. 4.

believed that 'the influence of the sun doth nourish and bring forth gold, spices, stones and pearls'). So too he accounts for large animals 'of double nature' like the camel-bird and the camelopard, namely the ostrich and the giraffe.[1] The stressing of the secret harmony between nature and life was unhealthy for science: like most of his creed, except his own master, he defended divination, and he opened the way for astrology, which was already invading in force from its eastern home. It is often suggested that he was tainted by the air of his Syrian birthplace, but he left it early, and his mysticism is explainable from ordinary Stoic doctrine.

On the size and distance of the sun he gets far nearer the truth than any ancient before or after, but by lucky guesses. The weakness of his science is glaringly exposed in a new estimate of the globe, though it seems not very seriously meant: he wants only to illustrate the point that the size of the earth can be read directly from the heavens and that compared with them it is tiny. A bright star, Canopus, is visible from Rhodes just above the horizon—really it is more than just above—and it is high up at Alexandria; for the difference of height he accepts an old and bad figure, $1/48$ of the zodiac circle or $7\frac{1}{2}°$ (the real is $1/60$ or $5\frac{1}{4}°$). The required circumference should therefore be 48 times the distance between the two places, if they are on a meridian, as is still assumed. On the popular seamen's figure for this item, 5000 stades, the total is 240,000. But, he adds, if one accepts the correction of Eratosthenes, 3750 stades—he ignores the further reduction of Hipparchus—the total will be 180,000, which he seems to prefer. He naïvely fails to see that the correction was got only from an astronomical observation, and from one quite different and far more accurate, $1/62\frac{1}{2}$ or $5\frac{1}{3}°$, expressed by the geographer only on the basis of his own globe measurement as $252,000/62\frac{1}{2} = 3750$ stades. If this is rightly reported, any attempt at defence is quite useless, as Reinhardt admits (Schmekel mildly notes 'various errors' and Tarn more severely 'some strange assumptions'). It is not a case of one estimate expressed in terms of two different kinds of stade, though some still allege that he meant 180,000 stades of 210 metres = 240,000 of 157·5 metres. One writer argues that he is badly misreported, that he never gave the smaller total at all, and the other only in a rough attempt to popularize the method of Eratosthenes,

---

[1] Diod. II, 48–54 (Pos. fr. 114, Jacoby), cp. Plin. xxxvII, 8: Reinhardt, op. cit. p. 205. Sun, Cic. *N.D.* II, 49. Vis vitalis, ibid. pp. 24, 32: Reinhardt, op. cit. pp. 175, 202 and *Kosmos und Sympathie*, 1926. Echoes, Barlow, 1541, cited by E. G. R. Taylor in A. P. Newton, *Great Age of Discovery*, 1932, p. 200. Tides and life, Cic. op. cit. 50, *de Div.* II, 33: Plin. II, 220–1. 'Luna alit ostrea', Lucilius ap. Gell. xx, 8, 4, Manilius, II, 93, Plin. xI, 196. Stemplinger, *Ant. Aberglaube*, 1922, pp. 15–17. Frazer, *Golden Bough*, abridged ed. 1925, pp. 34–5. A grain of truth, Eisler, *Royal Art of Astrology*, 1946, pp. 138–43.

THEORY IN THE SAME PERIOD 213

which he really accepted along with its result.[1] Yet Strabo talks of his lower figure as the smallest possible measurement, as compared with the older geographer's (he makes no attempt to explain the method). The figure, taken in ordinary stades, is, of course, very much (at best about a sixth) too small.

On the basis of the same figure the parallel of Rhodes worked out at 140,000 stades (or a trifle over), and the length of the inhabited world from Spain east to India had been given as 70,000 or just half. What of the unknown half? Sailing west from Spain, would one strike India, or something else on the way? India, at the opposite end of the long inhabited earth, seemed to him in a sense antipodal to Spain. Yet treatises which otherwise owe him a good deal say that probably there are several other continents, some larger, some smaller than ours, or that there are 'dwellers round', unreachable by us over an unsailable Ocean full of monsters, and having winter and summer when we have ours, though the day begins later for them.[2] He regards the Ocean all round our inhabited earth as proved by the uniform tides and by actual voyages, including the Spanish wreck recently found by Eudoxus in east Africa. North of the Black Sea he puts the Ocean quite near, so that the breadth-line of the known world is reduced to under 30,000 stades, in agreement with the view then current.

He understands that there must be a fixed arctic circle, and that one should not use the arctic circle of Rhodes.[3] At the tropic, where the sun lingers in the zenith about half a month, there is a desert belt from the Sahara across Arabia towards India. The equator is actually less 'torrid', being cooled by the long nights, here equal to the days, and it is comparatively well watered and fertile (his master Panaetius is cited with one Eudorus, an Academic, as talking of cooling by etesian winds and by the vapour from the equatorial Ocean). The idea of a mild equator was thus not quite new, but it should not be ascribed to Eratosthenes, as it sometimes

---

1 Viedebantt, *Klio*, 1915, pp. 207–31, 1920, p. 94. Allege, as Oxé, *Rhein. Mus.* 1938, p. 59: different stades also Dreyer, op. cit. p. 177, Miller, *Erdmessung im Alt.* 1919, p. 12, but cp. Kubitschek, *R.E.* Suppl. vi, 43–5 (Erdmessung). Schmekel, op. cit. p. 285. Tarn, op. cit. p. 248. Reinhardt, *Poseidonios*, p. 196: Thalamas, *Géogr. d'Érat.* p. 130: Heath, *Aristarchus*, pp. 345–7. 'Faulty', *Legacy of Greece*, p. 131: astonishing levity, Nissen, *Rhein. Mus.* 1903, p. 231. Not serious, Schaefer, op. cit. p. 23. Cleom. 1, 10, p. 90, Ziegler (Jacoby, Pos. fr. 97): Str. 95. A bad step back, Berger, *Erdk.* pp. 577–82, Rehm, *R.E.* xi, 688. Berthelot, *Rev. Arch.* 1932, ii, 17–19 is much too kind. About one-seventh too small, Fiske, *Discovery of America*, 1, 374.

2 Treatises, Ps.-Arist. *de Mundo*, 392 *b* (unlike Arist. cp. p. 120, n. 1) and Cleom. i, 2, 12, 15 ('dwellers round' also Gem. 16, 7). Half, Str. 102. Would strike India, Tarn, op. cit. p. 249: see p. 166, n. 2. India, Hamilton, *C.Q.* 1934, p. 52 (from Plin. vi, 57, opposite Gaul).

3 Str. 95, Cleom. 1, 7, 34 (but 1, 2, 12 contradictory).

is after a slip of Strabo's. New and strange is a fancy that there is a difference of climate also by longitude; from the east, which the rising sun passes quickly over, there is an increasing dryness westwards to the Atlas region, which has notably few and small rivers. As for unknown parts, the south temperate zone is doubtless not only habitable but inhabited, as 'Nature loves life' and abhors a vacuum (this is Aristotle's principle that Nature does nothing in vain, and, as a medieval writer says of the same zone, 'if it is habitable, then it would be vain unless it were inhabited'). So there are both 'dwellers opposite', who may be called Ethiopians, and Antipodes, who can walk on the earth below us, since all heavy bodies are attracted towards the centre of the globe.[1]

He is strong on the old theory of climatic influence on the physical and moral characters of peoples, and carries it to a point where it easily merges with astrology (much later writing on both subjects attaches to his). He is interested in matters of physical geography like earthquakes and volcanic action, and has a grandiose conception, after Aristotle, of many elevations and subsidences before the present distribution of land and sea: parts now inhabited were once seas, while seas now cover what were peopled continents (he seems to think of Atlantis).[2] Here again he was not always critical enough, and at best hardly more than a conveyer of some good science.

We hear of an epitome of his meteorology by one Geminus. Under this name (an odd one for a Greek) we have an *Introduction to the Phenomena*, and a datum in the text seems to point to about 70 B.C., and thus perhaps, the editor thinks, to a pupil of Posidonius, from whom the similar matter in Cleomedes is expressly derived. But our book often differs markedly from the supposed teacher, so that Reinhardt denies his influence, and some treat the author as earlier, about 140 B.C., or at least as repeating the science of that time.[3] He has the older globe-measurement, and very peculiar figures for the length (100,000 stades) and the breadth of the inhabited earth. He has the arctic circle of Rhodes, and cites some as taking the torrid zone literally, though he does not do so himself. A chapter explains how the length of the day changes according to latitude, and it

[1] Gem. 16, 2, 16, 19–20 and 26–7, Cleom. 1, 2, 22. Rivers, ap. Str. 830. Mild, as Polybius (p. 210, n. 1). Slip, Str. 97: Berger, *Erat.* p. 85: see p. 163, n. 2, p. 177, n. 1: Reinhardt, Pos. 63, 189. Pan. and E. in *Comm. in Aratum Reliquiae*, ed. Maass, p. 97: some say habitable, Achilles, ibid. p. 63. Albertus Magnus, *c.* 1280, cited by Kimble, *Geogr. in Middle Ages*, 1938, p. 84.

[2] Str. 810: see p. 104, n. 3, p. 105, n. 2: climate, p. 109, n. 1. Attaches, e.g. Manilius, Ptolemy's *Tetrabiblos*.

[3] Of just before Hipparchus, Dreyer, op. cit. pp. 130, 151: of H. chiefly, Sarton, op. cit. pp. 202, 212: early, Berger, *Erat.* p. 109. Denies, Reinhardt, op. cit. pp. 178–83. Ed. Manitius, 1898. Tittel, *R.E.* vii, 1026. Pupil, so Heath, *L.G.* p. 131.

has an interesting mention of Pytheas. To his credit he rejects astrology.[1] Much of the same matter is handled far less expertly in the *Cyclic Theory of the Heavenly Bodies* by one Cleomedes of unknown date, perhaps the second century A.D., who professes to take most from Posidonius, and can be treated as a summarizer of his, if not a disciple. Occasionally he prefers the commoner Stoic tradition, as when he rejects the habitable equator, saying that the tropic has a longer pause to cool and is reached by etesian winds. He is a not very intelligent compiler, with a clumsy arrangement and some naïve arguments and blunders. He makes easy play (after his original) with the silly statements of the Epicureans that perhaps the sun is only as big as it looks and is quenched in a sizzling Ocean. Among the proofs of the globe is the one from ships, how they are seen when approaching land or receding from it. He alone is detailed on the famous measurement of the globe and also on the new one (p. 212) which was so bad a travesty.[2]

Theodosius wrote an excellent text-book of spherical geometry and also 'on days and nights' and their changes in length, and on 'habitations' or the positions of stars at various times and latitudes (his date is vague, after Hipparchus but not necessarily after Posidonius?). One Alexander Lychnus versified geography and the movements of the heavenly bodies, and was looked into by Cicero and imitated by a Roman versifier. The historian Diodorus, who wrote about 60–30 B.C., is himself dull and uncritical, but preserves useful material on various things like Chaldaean astrology and the Nile problem. He cites statements on shadows and stars in India and elsewhere, and the Utopia of Iambulus, 'most temperate, we are told, considering that it lies at the equator'; day and night are always of the same length, and at noon there is no shadow. Elsewhere he remarks that it is only fourteen days' sail from the ice of the Azov to Alexandria and ten more up the Nile to the fringe of uninhabitable heat.[3]

The Romans themselves were still parvenus in science, as indeed they were always to remain. A people of farmers, a disciplined patriotism had

---

[1] On Pytheas, ch. 6 (similarly Cleom. I, 5 and 7, II, 1). Torrid, some ap. Gem. 16, 25, but cp. 16, 21. Rhodes, 16, 7. Length, 15, 4, based on globe-measurement of Eudoxus, Gisinger, *R.E.* Geogr. 583, not of Dicaearchus as Berger, p. 370.

[2] Cleom. I, 10. Proofs, I, 8, pp. 72–87 (ship also Str. 12, already Erat.?). Sun, II, 1, 91. Torrid, I, 2, 12, I, 6, 3 (cp. Pos. p. 210, n. 1). Ed. Ziegler, 1891. Reinhardt, op. cit. pp. 183–6: Duhem, *Système*, I, 470–2: Rehm, *R.E.* XI, 679–94 (on measurement, p. 688): Tannery, *Mém. scient.* III, pp. 351–3 (disciple?, so Sarton, op. cit. p. 211). M. Arnold, *Quaest. Pos.* 1903 and Boericke, *Quaest. Cleom.* 1905, put 2nd cent. A.D.

[3] III, 34, 38: shadows etc. II, 35, 4 (see p. 134, n. 2), III, 48: Utopia, II, 56 (see p. 177, n. 1): Nile, p. 210, n. 2: astrology, II, 29–31. His travels slight, despite I, 4. Queer stuff about Amazons attacking Atlantians near Cerne, III, 52–7, see p. 186, n. 1. Alex., Cic. *Ep. ad Att.* II, 22, 7, Str. 642, and see p. 218, n. 2. Theod. date, Str. 566, Vitr. IX, 8, 1: anywhere in 150–70 B.C., Ziegler, *R.E.* Theod. 1934, against Fecht who edits π. οἰκ. *Abh. Gött. Ges. Wiss.* 1927. By 20 B.C., Heath, *L.G.* p. 132. T.'s matter mostly old, Sarton, loc. cit.

raised them high, and now too suddenly there had come empire and wealth. They had had no education or literature worth mentioning until they began to be civilized by conquered Greece. Their religion, which Polybius admired as useful for keeping the common people in order, had streaks of gross credulity about portents and the like: even later during an eclipse soldiers could make a din of horns and trumpets to free the moon from witchcraft. It is the more surprising to hear that as early as 168 B.C. one Gallus was an intelligent student of astronomy. Before a battle he warned the army that an eclipse of the moon would happen next night from the second to the fourth hour, a natural occurrence due to the moon being hidden by the earth's shadow; after the event his wisdom seemed superhuman (another version is that he merely explained the cause when the eclipse had begun). He was presently consul and retained to old age a passion for measuring heaven and earth, it is said, giving the distances to the sun and moon and stars 'after Pythagoras'. If so, he was very unlike old Cato, who shied at everything Greek and himself taught his son all that a good Roman should know, war and farming, oratory and law, and some homely medicine including magic spells. (It is curious to find him warning his tenants against astrologers, and a praetor of 139 B.C. banishing these 'Chaldaeans' from the capital.) The national poet admitted that it was not vouchsafed to Romans

to trace the motions of the skies
with learned rod, and tell the stars that rise,

but claimed that their task was to conquer and rule the world and impose the habit of peace. Far from showing any originality in pure science, they were slow to learn it from others or even to acquire any sense of its value: their instinct, quite complacently defended, was to think of mathematics as measuring and counting and to boast of being 'practical'.[1] At the best they were to remain dilettanti, and the only question for us is to gauge is how much they could assimilate from their Greek teachers.

What they sought from Greek philosophy was a basis of judgment in morals, and philosophy had long been tending that way anyhow, giving 'physics' only a secondary place. The Epicurean creed found a fervent champion in the poet Lucretius, with all its bold rationalism and its bland indifference to scientific truth in detail. So he attacks the 'perverse' theory that there are Antipodes who walk head downwards and cannot tumble

---

1 Cic. *Tusc. Disp.* I, 5. Virg. *Aen.* VI, 849. Praetor, Val. Max. I, 3, 3. Gallus, Plin. II, 83, Cic. *de Sen.* 49: eclipse, Livy, XLIV, 37, Plin. II, 53, other version, Cic. *de Rep.* I, 15, 23, Val. Max. 8, 11. Fotheringham, *Historical Eclipses* (Halley Lecture), 1921, pp. 29–32 rejects Livy's 'sensational story'. Witchcraft, Tac. *Ann.* I, 28, cp. Livy, XXVI, 5, 9, Mart. XII, 57, 15, Juv. VI, 442. Religion, Pol. VI, 56: so Scaevola (through Varro) ap. Augustine, *C.D.* IV, 27. Cato, *Agric.* 5, 4.

THEORY IN THE SAME PERIOD

into the lower sky, and that 'when they see the sun we behold the stars of night, and they share with us time about the seasons of heaven and pass nights equal in length to our days'. Less against the Roman grain was Stoicism with its divinely created universe, where harmony already reigned, so that the chief virtue was a calm resignation. Cicero inclines to it as best for most people, and he can even for political purposes uphold its defence of divination, which he attacks elsewhere—a bad atmosphere for science![1] He professes himself of the New Academy, which had quite departed from Plato and now 'followed the probable'; from this standpoint he can freely discuss the rival doctrines for the education of his countrymen (his great service to the western world was to provide it with a philosophical vocabulary). In physics he is only a dabbler, girding at the contradictions of the Greeks and their boldness in handling such mysteries, a note often to be heard in later Roman writers. But at least he keeps the globe; it is tiny in relation to the universe, and at rest in the centre, 'terra...locata in media mundi sede, solida et globosa, et undique ipsa in sese nutibus suis conglobata'. Once he does note (in a muddled way) that some have made it rotate on its axis.[2] There are five zones, only two habitable—no word here of the recent view of a mild equator. The inhabited earth from Spain to the Ganges is an oblong island filling part of the north temperate zone, which also contains doubtless another continent of 'dwellers round'; in the 'south zone, unknown to us, which the Greeks call the opposite earth', are both dwellers opposite and Antipodes. The show passage in this kind is the dream in which Scipio hears the music of the spheres; he sees the globe with its four island-worlds separated by Oceans, and all three besides ours having people, 'partim obliquos, partim aversos, partim etiam adversos...nobis'. These echoes of Crates were to be repeated through the commentary of Macrobius to the Middle Ages. Cicero thought of writing on geography, but found it a 'rather obscure science', too technical to stylize, and he drew back after a look into Tyrannio and Serapio, a critic of Eratosthenes ('between ourselves I hardly understand a thousandth part').[3] He did a translation of Aratus on the stars and began one of Plato's *Timaeus*. He argues sensibly against astrology, though what he says of 'sympathy' is not entirely against it. An adept was his friend Nigidius, who sought (with some Greeks of the time like Alexander

---

[1] Farrington, *Science and Politics in the Anc. World*, 1939, pp. 206 (Cic. *Laws* as cp. *de Div.*), 116. Antipodes, Lucr. I, 1052–67: see p. 167, n. 1.

[2] See p. 152, n. 2: *Acad. Pr.* II, 123. Girds, ibid. 122, *Timaeus*, I, I. Centre, *N.D.* II, 98, *Orat.* III, 78.

[3] *Ep. ad Att.* II, 4 and 6–8: *de Orat.* I, 61. Crates, see p. 203, n. 1. Zones, *Tusc. Disp.* I, 68, *N.D.* II, 66. Antipodes also *Acad. Pr.* II, 123. Oblong, *N.D.* II, 164. Dream, *de Republica*, VI. Macr., see p. 383, n. 2.

Polyhistor) to revive Pythagorean number-mysticism: he was 'a keen and diligent investigator of things which Nature seems to have wrapped in darkness'. Astrology had been strongly attacked by Carneades, whom Cicero follows, but by now its victory was almost complete.[1]

The historians give some description of countries and peoples and customs, but hardly touch geographical theory. Caesar (if the chapter is his) found the nights in Britain shorter by the water-clock, and could learn nothing about islands opposite credited by some with a winter night a month long, a strange echo of the talk about Thule. Once he mentions Eratosthenes, but only on the great German forest. It would be interesting to know what were the Druid teachings 'de mundi ac terrarum magnitudine' and what exactly Caesar had learnt of tides. Nothing is known of a poem called 'Iter', about a journey to Spain (on another occasion, while crossing the Alps, he wrote on grammar!). A diligent versifier, of whom only a few odd lines survive, was Varro of Atax, who wrote on the Argonauts and translated Aratus and probably imitated Alexander Lychnus.[2] Little remains of M. Terentius Varro (116–27 B.C.), the 'most learned of the Romans' and the first with their naïve faith that they were capable of one-man encyclopaedias. He had a whimsical humour, as the pieces of his satires show, but he read and wrote far too much, like Pliny, who used him often and on various subjects. Geometry and astronomy (with a large streak of astrology) each had its book among his nine *Disciplinae*. Geography had three books in the *Antiquities*; one was probably much used by Virgil for his lovingly minute catalogue of places in the oldest Italy. An *Ora Maritima* sounds like a coastal description, but the few scraps suggest something more technical on navigation (elsewhere he seems to have written on tides and weather-signs). To him goes back, no doubt, much that is common to Mela and Pliny both in arrangement and matter. Nepos is cited for some credulous things like the Indians blown past the Caspian 'gulf'; they may come from his miscellaneous writing rather than any special book on geography.[3]

[1] On N., Cic. *Tim.* 1, 1, Serv. ad Virg. *Georg.* 1, 19, 43, 218, Schol. Lucan, 1, 639, indices of Plin. VI–XI, XVI. On astrology, Cic. *de Div.* II, 87–99, *de Fato*, 8: Lynn Thorndike, *Hist. of Magic and Experimental Science*, 1929, 1, 269–74. C. quotes his own Aratus, *N.D.* II, 104–14.

[2] *Chorographia* (?) ap. Priscian: indices of Plin. III–VI: lines in Serv. ad Virg. *Georg.* I, 375, 397. Erat. in Caes. *B.G.* VI, 24. Druids, (Pos. ap.) Caes. VI, 14, Mela, III, 19. Tides, p. 190, n. 1: Klotz, *Cäsarstudien*, p. 22. Iter, Suet. *Jul.* 56. Britain, Caes. V, 13 (cp. the garbling in Plin. II, 186–7): Berger, *Erat.* p. 150: Bunbury, II, 128, 381: Nansen, *In Northern Mists*, 1911, 1, 80. Tac. *Agr.* 12, *Germ.* 45 is less intelligent.

[3] See p. 199, n. 2. Tides, etc., Varro, *L.L.* IX, 26, Vegetius, V, 11: Varro's science elementary and useful, Boissier, *Étude sur...Varron*, 1861, pp. 322–31. His astrology and number-mysticism in Censorinus, 8, 13, etc., Gell. III, 10. Italy, Rehm, *Das geogr. Bild des alten Italiens in Vergils Aeneis*, 1932, pp. 104–6. On geogr., Reitzenstein, *Hermes*, XX, 514f.: H. Dahlmann in *R.E.* Suppl. VI, 1231–2 (1935).

Romans must have seen the maps of Greek geographies, and used travel and campaigning maps, as later, though clear mentions happen to be lacking for this time. Maps of a sort seem implied in a general's complaint of arm-chair critics who know exactly which pass to use, how to bring up supplies and so on. Once Varro finds his friends looking at Italy painted on a temple wall, but this may be rather a picture, and so an earlier temple 'tabula' or 'forma' of Sardinia. Representations of conquered towns, rivers, and mountains carried in triumphs did not apparently include maps.[1] Sallust notes that a few writers divide the 'orbis terrae' into two parts (semi-circles) and call the western half Europe, including Africa, and the eastern Asia; to whom he refers is obscure, but the remark was cited several times later and led to a queer form of medieval map. Varro mentions the division into north and south by the length-line of Eratosthenes. He speaks not quite intelligently of the arctic circle, 'inter circulum septentrionalem et inter cardinem caeli', where there is a six months' day or night and the sea is really unsailable because it is frozen.[2]

The attitude to Greek theory can be curiously naïve. The poets are familiar enough with the globe and its five zones, determined by those of heaven and two of them habitable. Virgil echoes some verses of Eratosthenes, who accepted Antipodes, and yet in the same breath he can say that the southern hemisphere may be never lit up, or that when we have morning it may be evening there—a bad confusion with the western hemisphere, of course. (The lines were once quoted with fine effect by Pitt, speaking against the slave trade, as the dawn crept through the windows of the House,

> Nos ubi primus equis Oriens adflavit anhelis
> illic sera rubens accendit lumina Vesper.)

Virgil thought of explaining earthquakes and eclipses, the courses of the heavenly bodies, and 'why winter suns make such haste to dip in Ocean', but wisely did not pursue these topics. Propertius, in a rather cheap imitation of this passage, reserves such subjects for the time when he will be too old for love, and Horace has something in a similar tone.[3]

---

1 Kubitschek, *R.E.* Karten, § 11. Tac. *Ann.* II, 41. Sard., Livy, XLI, 28, 8 (referring to 174 B.C.). Varro, *Res Rustica*, I, 2, 1. Tabulae of Dicaearchus, see p. 174, n. 1. Critics, Paulus in 168 B.C. on Macedonia, Livy, XLIV, 22.

2 Varro, op. cit. I, 2, 3–4: north (Europe) and south (Asia), *L.L.* V, 31. Cp. Sall. *Jug.* 17, 3: same notion, Lucan, IX, 413, where Housman cites *G.G.M.* II, 495, *G.L.M.* 71, Oros. I, 2, 1: see too Aug. *C.D.* XVI, 17. For 'Sallust maps', Beazley, *Dawn of Mod. Geogr.* I, 631–2, K. Miller, *Mappaemundi*, III, 110–15, J. K. Wright, *Geogr. Lore of Crusades*, p. 65.

3 Hor. *Ep.* I, 12, 14–20. Prop. III, 5 (IV, 4), 23–39. Virgil, *Georg.* II, 475–82, cp. *Aen.* I, 742–6. Zones, *Georg.* I, 233–51: confusion also Manilius, I, 242–5, Housman, ad loc. Zones, Pseudo-Tibullus, IV, 1, 152–9, Hor. *Odes*, I, 22, 17–22, Ovid, *Met.* I, 44–51. Never lit, like Lucr. V, 650–5.

Another feature of Roman writing is a marked taste, not only in poets, for obsolete notions like the mountains of the north wind and even the Nile flowing from India. Also no poetry has had a more intemperate passion for the music of place-names. Apart from reckless things like calling an Indian river 'Medus Hydaspes', there are long catalogues with more sound than sense, as when Arimaspians and other fabulous or vaguely remote barbarians are supposed to take an interest in a Roman civil war.[1] Both now and later there is also an extravagant way of talking about Roman conquests and 'hoc orbis terrae imperium', as if it embraced 'all peoples and tribes by land and sea'. Such claims arouse ironical thoughts. Yet the same writers sometimes expressly mention the globe, and must have been aware that a large part of its surface was quite unknown. Even a Greek, while talking glibly of the five zones, could describe Rome as mistress of all lands not inaccessible or uninhabitable and of all seas, not only that within the Pillars but also the Ocean, so far as it is sailable![2]

Many wild guesses resting on a mere jingle of names could still be repeated. Thus the Medes were traced to a son of Medea by Jason, and another Argonaut was invented to found Armenia. It is even said that some Medes were in the army of Hercules, when he went to the Pillars, and later degenerated into 'Moors'. There are various popular fables of other kinds. A king of Macedonia climbed the Balkan mountains, hoping, it is said, to confirm a 'wide-spread opinion' that the Black and Adriatic seas, the Danube and the Alps could all be seen from there; but he saw nothing except thick fog. This notion of two seas being visible is repeated for other inland mountains, as in north Greece and the heart of Asia Minor. But then some believed in a man who stood at the west end of Sicily and counted the enemy ships leaving the port of Carthage 135 Roman miles away! This is absurd, of course, though the African mountains can be seen from the island on a clear day.

For a practical people the Romans had little talent for industry and commerce, and in various ways were strangely uninventive: it has been shown that they failed even to devise a harness which did not half-choke a horse.[3] It was practical to do much more in the way of exploration than

1 Lucan, III, 245–95: Antony has Bactrian allies, Virg. *Aen.* VIII, 688, etc. Nile, Virg. *G.* IV, 292, Lucan, X, 292 (from Seres!). Mountains, Virg. *G.* III, 352, IV, 518 (see p. 199, n. 1): Varro in Mela, I, 115, III, 36, Plin. IV, 78: Trogus ap. Justin, II, 2, 1. Medus H., Virg. *G.* IV, 220. Rant in Ps.-Tib. IV, 1, 140–6. Prop. V, 3, 7–10. Even Milton ends in vacant sonority, R. W. Chapman, *Portrait of a Scholar*, 1920 (Proper Names in Poetry).

2 Dion. Hal. I, 3, 3 (zones, II, 5, 3): Diod. I, 4, 3. Extravagant, Cic. *de Imp. Cn. Pompeii*, 53, 56. Ovid, *Fasti*, I, 85 (with Frazer's note), II, 135, 684, *Trist.* I, 5, 69, III, 8, 51: Prop. IV, 11, 57: Mart. XII, 8, 1. See p. 223, n. 1.

3 Lefebvre des Noettes, *L'Attelage: le Cheval de Selle à travers les Âges*, 1921: Fisher, *Hist. of Europe*, I, 93. Talent, Warde Fowler, *Rome*, pp. 14, 124. Balkan, Pol. ap. Livy,

they did. If any science could have interested them, geography should have, but their own writers were to contribute nothing important. Some had little use for the elementary fact that the earth is a globe, and thought of a map as a string of names along a road. And at least the Romans made good roads: already we hear how straight and solid they were, and measured out with milestones, which took away much of the weariness of a journey, as was presently remarked—'facientibus iter multum detrahunt fatigationis notata inscriptis lapidibus spatia'.[1]

Astrology could easily adapt itself to current science, with the globe in the centre of the universe, and it did not exclude some intelligent ideas of geography. It made much, for instance, of the 'seven climates' or parallels from Meroe to the Dnieper mouth, with a longest day rising at half-hour intervals from 13 to 16 hours, though its treatment of such things is loose enough.[2]

A later historian professes to envy those who wrote of the Republic and its great wars with plenty of scope for geography ('situs gentium') and other kinds of picturesqueness. In fact Livy, spacious as he is, does not follow Polybius in giving a whole book to geography, and he cares little for such digressions. Once he pauses to speculate what would have happened if Alexander had turned west, and elsewhere he has some of the usual rhetoric about that king stopping only when nothing was left to conquer, in India, 'qua terrarum ultimos fines Rubrum mare amplectitur'. He has local descriptions, of course, as of New Carthage, the Peneus ravine, and the site of Rome with its bracing hills, 'ad incrementum urbis natum unice locum' (this last more patriotic than true, but Cicero says much the same). When he came to a new country like Britain he had to give some account of it, and a lost book contained 'situm Germaniae moresque'. He has some remarks on a southern climate softening northerners and on people being generally like their places, as cultivators differ from ruder hillmen ('cultorum molliore atque ut evenit fere locis simili genere'). He knows at least that an eclipse of the sun is due to the moon, but one looks in vain for any statement clearly implying that the earth is a globe.[3]

XL, 21–2 (on Philip, 181 B.C.), see p. 49, n. 2: also Boion and Argaeus, some ap. Str. VII, fr. 6, 538, see p. 288, n. 4. Moors, Sall. *Jug.* 18. Medus, Str. 526, some ap. Diod. IV, 56. Armenus, Str. 503, 530, Justin, XLII, 2, 10, 3, 8. Heniochi (Charioteers) near Dioscurias, Plin. VI, 26, etc. Ships, some ap. Plin. VII, 85, who cites Varro and Cicero: 'it is said', Str. 267.

1 Quint. IV, 5, 22. Roads, Plut. *C. Gracchus*, 7.
2 As ap. Plin. VI, 212–20, citing Nigidius at 217: much from Serapion, thinks Honigmann, *Die sieben Klimata und die* πόλεις ἐπίσημοι, 1929, rev. by Gisinger, *Gnomon*, 1933, pp. 96–101.
3 Eclipse, XXXVII, 4, 4 and see p. 216, n. 1. Places, IX, 13, 7: climate, XXXVIII, 17 (Galatians). Shape of Britain, ap. Tac. *Agr.* 10. Rome, V, 54, 3, like Cic. *de Rep.* II, 3–6. Local, XXVI, 42, XLIV, 6. Alex., IX, 16–19: India, XLV, 9, XLI, 52 (world 'ab Gadibus ad mare Rubrum', XXXVI, 17). Envy, Tac. *Ann.* IV, 32–3.

CHAPTER VIII

THE GREAT DAYS OF THE ROMAN EMPIRE

§1. TIMES AND WRITERS

AFTER the civil wars order was restored by Caesar's heir, who ruled as Augustus (27 B.C.–A.D. 14). What he established was not an hereditary monarchy, but in practice men of his house succeeded till it died out with Nero. Then for a bad year several armies raised up their generals in turn, one of whom founded a new quasi-dynasty, the Flavian (A.D. 69–96). Another break was tided over quietly, and there followed a remarkable series of able rulers down to Marcus Aurelius. Only with his degenerate son does the Decline begin. For two centuries the 'ring of lands' had enjoyed such a continuous peace as it had never known before.

There were wars, but nearly all at the outer edges and designed to secure good frontiers against the barbarians, especially in the north. Augustus pushed to the Danube all along, and had ambitious thoughts of the Elbe, but a sharp reverse made him fall back on the Rhine. He left his successors the advice to call a halt and consolidate within the already acquired 'bounds of Ocean and distant rivers'. On the whole they obeyed, but there were some expansions. It was thought worth while to take in Britain, perhaps less for its own sake than to ensure the Romanizing of Gaul. There was a slight advance to an outpost line in south Germany, and beyond the Danube Trajan added the large bastion of Dacia. Impatient of the usual compromise with Parthia, he annexed the Armenian buffer-kingdom and even carried his arms for a moment to the Persian Gulf. Hadrian at once abandoned these eastern gains as untenable, keeping only 'Arabia'. In the south, though Mauretania was early taken over, the desert gave little trouble, and there was hardly any boundary line at any time. It is with Hadrian that there begins a general defensive policy, expressed in some parts by walls, 'loca in quibus barbari non fluminibus sed limitibus dividuntur'.

The Empire was really more than a 'ring of lands' round the inner sea. Northwards it extended well beyond the zone of Mediterranean climate and culture. Here were needed the strongest armies of defence, too far from the centre and exposed to gradual barbarization as local recruitment became usual. Here the first signs of strain appeared and the ultimate breach was to come; but as yet there were only faint misgivings of possible danger. The writers are deeply conscious of the greatness of the

THE GREAT DAYS OF THE ROMAN EMPIRE

Empire, and often talk as if everything outside were a mere barbarian fringe, left free only because not worth the taking: when Jupiter surveys the world from his Capitol, he sees nothing that is not Roman, and the sun would never set on the Empire if Rome had not turned to civil wars instead of annexing the few countries outstanding, Parthia and India, Germany and the Sarmatian nomads! For Gibbon it was 'the most numerous society that has ever been united under the same system of government', and he imagined a population of 120 millions, certainly far too much. Beloch's special study of the statistics, which are inadequate and hard to interpret, gives only 54 millions, no doubt erring considerably in the other direction. Recent writers say not over a quarter of the present numbers in the same area, or at the most a third, 70 or 80 millions.[1]

Behind the wall of the legions was what Pliny calls 'the immense majesty of the Roman peace'. Having made a prey of so many lands, the conquerors had decided to renounce aggression and check the swift decline caused by their plunder and misrule. The government was now far better organized, and went on working even under bad Caesars. The eastern provinces, which had suffered much, began to recover, and in the west there was a rapid development of town-life and civilization. Travel was freer and safer than it had ever been or was to be again till the nineteenth century. There was a great mingling and assimilation of races. Trade was considerable with peace reigning in so large an area, the levelling of customs barriers, and the making of new roads: it is all one continuous land and people, says a Greek admirer. Yet in many ways this mighty state was not a healthy one. The mischief of the past had been too serious, and even the great days of the Empire were at best an Indian summer rather than the golden age proclaimed by some of its writers, though others from the first have gloomy undertones and a consciousness of decadence, like Livy ('ut iam magnitudine laboret sua').[2] Social and

1 S. N. Miller in *Eur. Civ.* ed. Eyre, 1935, II, 456: quarter, H. S. B. Moss, *Birth of the Middle Ages*, 1935, p. 4: perhaps 70 in Constantine's time, Fisher, *Hist. of Europe*², 1938, I, 97, after Bury, *Invasion of Europe by the Barbarians*, 1928, pp. 37–8. Grenier, *Gaulois*, 1945, p. 227 and C. Jullian give Gaul alone over 20 m. Beloch, *Bevölkerung der röm. Welt*, 1886. Delbrück in 1907 gave 60 or 65: a discussion in Lot, *Fin du Monde antique*, 1927, pp. 75–80. Nomads, Lucan, VII, 421–36, I, 14–20. Capitol, Ovid, *Fasti*, I, 85: fringe, Aristides, XIV, 28, Appian, praef. 7, Paus. I, 9, 5, cp. Petronius, 119, 1, Sen. *de Benef.* III, 33, 3, Claudian, *Stil.* III, 138–40, and see p. 220, n. 2. Limitibus, *Vita Hadr.* 12.

2 Livy, praef. 9: Hor. *Epod.* 16, 2, *Odes*, III, 6, 46–8: Sen. ap. Lact. VII, 15: Florus, I, 1, 4, 8: W. Rehm, *Die Untergang Roms im abendländischen Denken*, 1930: Eva M. Sanford, *Amer. J. Phil.* 1937, pp. 437–56. Summer, Toynbee, *Study of History*, 1939, IV, 509 (the Augustan rally, ibid. p. 62). Admirer, Aristides, loc. cit., so Epict. III, 13, 9, Tert. *de Anima*, 30. On communications and commerce, G. H. Stevenson in *Legacy of Rome*, 1923, pp. 141–69: Friedländer, *Roman Life and Manners* (Engl. 1909), I, ch. 6. Immense, Plin. XXVII, 3: 'commercio rerum ac societate festae pacis', XIV, 2: similar Vell. Pat. II, 126.

economic life was infected by a legacy of slavery on an appalling scale. Rome itself was a parasitic growth with a pauper rabble expecting free bread and shows. All were not so idle elsewhere, and there was even a limited mass-production of wares in small factories. But there was little industrial progress, and the government showed hardly any intelligent care for such matters; in fact, the economic organization was low, and commercial motives were quite secondary in imperial policy. Land-transport remained very slow and too dear for trade in cheap and heavy goods to be much more than local; for urgent travel and news there were, of course, many relays of horses, but these took long enough. Ships were not very notably faster or safer than before, or better able normally to face winter weather, even the corn-ships on which the food of the capital depended. These were of about 250 tons, with good rigging, and an added sprit-sail enabled sailing with a beam wind. From the ports near Rome it was seven days at the best to Cadiz, and to Alexandria nine, and usually perhaps double that, while the return might take double that again and often longer still. Lucian's big ship (too big to be true) takes 70 days from Egypt to the Piraeus against the wind. The most vividly described voyage is St Paul's, in one Alexandrian ship, overcrowded with 276 on board, from Lycia past Crete to be storm-driven on Malta, and later to Puteoli by another, 'which had wintered in the isle'.[1] Despite such conditions, however, there were luxuries which repaid distant trade, and some were sought outside the Empire and brought gains for geography. We hear of a few traders who went far beyond the legions, like the man who got through to the Baltic amber-coast and those who learnt something of the long silk-road to China; by sea there was the important development of the monsoon trade to India.

Apart from many historians who tell of frontier wars, the gains for knowledge are recorded in a series of writings of very various quality. The first and far the most comprehensive and interesting is Strabo's *Geography* in 17 books. How it was published and how it escaped the notice of Romans like Pliny is still somewhat obscure, but the bulk may have been written about 7 B.C., as Pais argued, and revised long after in extreme old

---

[1] Acts xxvii. 5–xxviii. 13: J. H. Rose, *Man and the Sea*, 1935, pp. 54–7. Clowes, *Sailing Ships*, 1930, I, 35–8 and Plate V. Lucian, *Navis*, 7. Ship with 600 (?), Jos. *Vita*, 5. Winter sailing rare, Philo, *Leg.* 29, Jos. *A.J.* XVI, 15, Tac. *Ann.* III, 1, IV, 6, 6, Suet. *Claud.* 18. Speed, Alex., Plin. XIX, 3, Cadiz, Ps.-Scyl. 3: Charlesworth, *Trade Routes and Commerce of R.E.*[2] 1926, pp. 23, 153: Stevenson, op. cit. p. 163. Transport, Heichelheim, *Wirtschaftsgesch. des Alt.* 1938, pp. 570, 573, 730: mass-wares, ibid. pp. 693, 695. Secondary, Miller, op. cit. II, 442: low, ibid. pp. 445–53, industry, pp. 435–9: Lot, op. cit. p. 86: Fisher, op. cit. pp. 84, 94. Rostovtzeff, *Soc. and Econ. Hist. of R.E.* 1926. Oakeshott, *Commerce and Society*, 1936, pp. 28–31. E. T. Salmon, *Hist. of Roman World* (30 B.C.–A.D. 138), 1944, pp. 253–7.

age (there are insertions concerning A.D. 18, though a mention of Juba's death in A.D. 23 may be interpolated). His travels, from his own Pontus as far as Aswan and Rome, were certainly not remarkable either in range or thoroughness. (He was never farther west than Etruria, and seems not even to have visited Athens!) His work is largely a compilation from Greek writers like Artemidorus; while giving the Romans the credit of opening up the west and north, he does not use their recent information so fully as he should there or elsewhere (for instance, he knows nothing of a Saharan campaign of 19 B.C.). He had written a long history to supplement Polybius, and he has a similar conception of the value of geography (if we had his history he would probably seem to us more of an historian than a geographer). He means to give neither a technical treatise like Eratosthenes nor a mere coastal guide for traders quite ignorant of science: he writes for readers of liberal education, and especially generals and rulers, who are interested mainly in 'the inhabited earth' as the scene of history, and little in unknown regions outside, though they should have a modicum of science about the globe and its zones. He is justifiably proud of his big design, and seems the first to have attempted the picture on so large a canvas. Judged as descriptive his work has great merits, though not always well planned or executed, being tedious in parts and unequal in its distribution of matter. Only one book is allowed to all Africa, as against eight for Europe and six for Asia; of these Greece and his native Asia Minor have three each, of which far too much is occupied with rambling discussions of the accuracy of Homer's catalogues. When he handles the scientific side his faults are still more conspicuous. Yet we owe him a vast debt for having survived and thus preserved much of what is known on the whole subject: a story of its development would hardly be possible without him. A recent valuation rightly gives most space to an analysis of his sources but seems rather too severe.[1]

The first Latin geographer extant is Pomponius Mela, who hails from south Spain and indicates his time of writing as A.D. 43. After a glance at the world in general, he says, he will describe the various lands more fully (this has been often misread as a promise to write a fuller account later). What he gives is an outline in three very short and sketchy books. It is

---

[1] Honigmann, *R.E.* Strabo (1931). H. L. Jones, 8 vols. 1917–33 (Loeb). Transl. Hamilton and Falconer, 1854–7 (reprint 1912), Tardieu², 1886–94. Esp. Bunbury, *Anc. Geogr.* II, 209–39 and detail, 239–338. Berger, *Erdk.* pp. 533–50. M. Dubois, *Examen de la Géogr. de Strabon*, 1891 (too kind as cp. Müllenhoff). Much in Rainaud, *Geogr.* in Daremberg-Saglio, *Dict. des Antiquités*, 1896. A general essay in Glover, *Greek Byways*, 1932, pp. 223–59. Not Athens, Mahaffy, *Greek World under Roman Sway*, 1890, pp. 190–2. On date, etc., G. C. Richards in *Greece and Rome*, 1940, pp. 79–90, and see p. 288, n. 2. Various dissertations on sources of separate books.

bad work, concerned only to show how cleverly he can write up an unreadable subject, with ingenious points and rhetoric to the current taste. On the old coastal method he starts from Gibraltar and goes first anticlockwise round the inner sea, giving the islands separately, and then clockwise along the outer Ocean, with the islands in two lots. This scheme is often awkward, and inland parts come off badly, some like Dacia being not even mentioned. He 'adds things worth knowing about the countries and peoples', with a leaning to strange customs and animals. He uses obsolete sources, and quite uncritically, stating as facts all sorts of discarded fancies like Griffins and Amazons and headless people and the Danube branch to the Adriatic. As reflecting the new knowledge of his own time he is of little use except for the first obscure mention of Baltic waters. As recent confirmation of the northern Ocean he cites the wild story about the Indians blown past the Caspian 'gulf' to Germany. Altogether poor stuff and poor writing, aping the manner of Sallust, and with much borrowing apparently from Varro. The whole is only some 86 pages.[1]

Next comes the relevant section of 'that immense register where Pliny deposited the discoveries, the arts, and the errors of mankind'. He had served on upper and lower Rhine and as a procurator in Spain and elsewhere, and was an advocate and a trusted counsellor of Emperors; in the end he was commanding a fleet off Naples when, partly from a genuine curiosity, he went too near the eruption of Vesuvius (A.D. 79). He had found leisure to write on many things, including large-scale histories of the German wars and his own times (both lost). His nephew tells of his incredible industry, how he was always reading or being read to, how he made extracts and left a mass of closely-written note-books. He conceived a grandiose plan which no one man had ever attempted, even a Greek, as he boasts: he would write an encyclopaedia of Nature and all its products and their applications in the life and arts of men. It is done in 37 books as follows: I, contents and list of sources; II, cosmology and meteorology; III–VI, geography; VII, man and his characteristics and powers, physical and mental (including some oddities of remote peoples); VIII–XI and XXVIII–XXXII, animals and the medicines derived from them; XII–XXVII, plants, with a stress on those important in agriculture, and plant medicines; XXXIII–XXXVII, minerals and their uses in medicine and the fine arts. (There are all sorts of cross-references, and some things are added in

---

[1] In Parthey's ed. 1867. Ed. Frick, 1880. Bunbury, op. cit. II, 352–68: H. E. Burton, *Discovery of Anc. World*, 1932, pp. 76–81. Summers, *Silver Age of Latin Lit.* 1920, pp. 289–92. 'Dicam alias exactius', I, 2, cp. 'nunc exactius dicturo', 24. A reconstruction of M.'s map in K. Miller, *Mappaemundi*, 1898, VI, 102–7 and Taf. 7: also Jervis, *World in Maps*, 1938. I have not seen a diss. by Fink, 1881, or a transl. and comm. by H. Philipp, I, 1912.

THE GREAT DAYS OF THE ROMAN EMPIRE 227

unexpected contexts, like a long and dry attempt to explain the uses of astronomy for agriculture and the calendar in xviii.) Truly, as his nephew calls it, 'opus diffusum, eruditum, nec minus varium quam ipsa Natura'. The execution, of course, falls far short of the design: he was no master of all the sciences, but only a tireless reader and note-taker. He states that he used about 2000 volumes and 100 select authorities; actually the indices cite 473 writers, over two-thirds of them Greek. But many were consulted only occasionally or at second hand; in various blocks of matter he relied on a few main sources, with a predilection for Romans, especially omnivorous bookmen of his own breed like Varro, while other parts read like what they are, mosaics of cuttings. The style is sometimes as dry as the facts, but often he tries to adorn his 'barren matter' with epigram and rhetoric, and there are spurts of whimsical moralizing, as in frequent tirades against luxury.

The four books on Geography are even queerer than the rest.[1] He follows the coasts like Mela, but on a somewhat different scheme, hardly less awkward. Starting from Gibraltar he goes clockwise round the inner sea to the Don, cuts overland across the supposed Rhipaean mountains (at iv, 94), and returns by the northern and western Ocean; starting again, he goes anti-clockwise round the inner sea to the same river, crosses the range again (at vi, 33), and returns by the eastern and southern Ocean (the islands are inserted in various groups). The books consist mainly of rigmaroles of names, some with short descriptive labels, on a formula something like this: towns of the Sabaean Arabs on the Red coast, four (named), inland four (named) including one 'to which they convey incense'. Most of these details would now be simply entered on maps, leaving room in the text for some description better worth while; as it is, heaps of obscure names are given, while leading features are omitted. He knows that geography should be more than 'bare place-names', but can find space for little else, and often the placing is jumbled or uncertain. For each region he professes to use the best sources; in fact he is mainly compiling from compilers like Varro, and with little critical sense. In the general preface he claims to add on all subjects much that is not in his authorities, because 'life' or civilization has discovered it since their time.

---

[1] Critical ed. by Detlefsen, 1904, and see his *Geogr. Afrikas bei Mela u. Plin.* 1908: *Anordnung der geogr. Bücher des P. u. ihre Quellen*, 1909. Transl. Bostock and Riley, 1855–7, 1898, Rackham (Loeb), vol. II, 1942. Bunbury, op. cit. II, 371–87 and detail, pp. 387–442. Klotz, *Quaest. Plin. Geogr.* 1906. Summers, op. cit. pp. 300–10. L. Thorndike, *Hist. of Magic and Experim. Science*, 1929, I, 42–99. Wethered, *Mind of the Anc. World; a Consideration of Pliny's Nat. Hist.* 1937, esp. chs. 17–18. Dannemann, *P. u. seine Naturgeschichte*, 1921 (mostly excerpts). J. Wight Duff, *Lit. Hist. of Rome in Silver Age*, 1927, pp. 347–85.

This means new geographical details from extensions of the Empire, new wares brought to serve its increasing luxury, new materials and medicines and such like. The range of his work is so vast that from it, more than any other we get an impression of the manifold business and complexity of this ancient world. Much was done to naturalize plants, for instance, and we hear that the cherry brought from Pontus by Lucullus has now reached Britain. There is curious information on all sorts of things, mining in various parts, how rabbits overran the Balearic islands, how troops are used against locusts in Syria, how two huge obelisks were shipped to the capital, the export of table-ware from 'insignibus rotae officinis', the eider-down of the geese the Germans call 'gantae', how paper is made, a special manure in Gaul and Britain, useful medicines learnt of on remote frontiers, a pigeon post, lighthouses and aqueducts, and what not. There are valuable census statistics for the towns of some provinces; otherwise the best matter for geography comes from recent campaigns, as in the Atlas, and developments of trade, especially the monsoon sailings to India.

A nameless Graeco-Egyptian skipper engaged in these voyages seems to be the author of a periplus of the 'Red Sea', meaning both our sea so called and the Indian Ocean. He knows the nearest coast of India all down, and has some hearsay of the farther side and even of China. It is a valuable document, detailed about wares given and taken, times and ways of sailing, local conditions, and other practical matters. It used to be put a few years after Pliny's sketch of the same trade, but the references are now held to favour an earlier date, probably about A.D. 50.[1]

There is a school geography in excruciating pseudo-epic verse by one Dionysius, dubbed for this work Periegetes, meaning tourist or guide. He wrote, as now proved from an acrostic it contains, in Alexandria and under Hadrian, who reigned A.D. 117–38. He describes the known earth as a sling-shaped island, and proceeds to deal with the Ocean and its gulfs, including the Caspian, and then the continents; he is brief on Africa and rather less so on Europe (ll. 174–269 and 270–446) and, after clumsily inserting the islands of the inner sea and the Ocean, he gives Asia far more fully (ll. 620–1166, in the main from Eratosthenes). He seems to drag in as many mythological allusions as possible, and treats as realities all kinds

---

1 J. G. C. Anderson in *C.A.H.* x, 253, 881: Tarn, *Greeks in Bactria and India*, 1938, p. 148: Charlesworth, *Class. Quart.* 1928, p. 93 (date A.D. 40–70 and perhaps A.D. 50–65), see also his *Five Men*, 1936, pp. 146–55. Ed. Müller, *G.G.M.* I, xcv–cvi, 257–305, Fabricius, 1883, Frisk, 1927: tr. and comm. McCrindle, 1879, Schoff, Philadelphia, 1912. Cherry, Plin. xv, 102: rabbits, ibid. VIII, 217, cp. 104 (also Polybius, XII, 3, Str. 163, 168): locusts, XI, 106: obelisks, XXXVI, 70: Samian ware, XXXV, 160–1: gantae, X, 53: paper, XIII, 68–80: manure, XVII, 42: medicines, XXV, 21, 77, XXVII, 2–3: lighthouses, etc. XXXVI, 83, 101: post, X, 110. Cherry, see p. 170, n. 1.

of old fancies like the mountains of the north wind, the amber-river, the sunset isle, Amazons and Arimaspians.[1] Only a few things have any value for times near his own, a hint of a recent campaign in Libya, the warlike Alan horsemen, the southern Scyths of the Indus delta, and the Seres who produce silk (in a very queer way).[2] This curious piece of doggerel was to be popular in the Decline and twice translated and often commented upon. It is hardly significant except as the sort of rehash of older matter served up in school teaching.

Yet just then ancient geography was reaching its widest horizons, and there were still men who sought recent reports and tried to improve on former mapping. Marinus of Tyre is known only indirectly through Ptolemy, who used him as the latest and most careful geographer 'of the time' (the expression leaves his precise date rather uncertain, perhaps about A.D. 110?). He gathered new data from the land and sea trade to the Far East and from certain remarkable journeys into the Sahara and past Zanzibar, and he applied them boldly to extend the known earth, so that it made a much more imposing show on the surface of the globe. Ptolemy corrects him by re-interpreting the same material, though he hints vaguely at a few still newer reports.[3] He freely admits his large debt, and the older writer must also be credited with many of the blunders committed, especially in misreading Roman sources, as in the bad mess made of Germany.

Claudius Ptolemaeus (Ptolemy), who worked at or near Alexandria, had already written the *System of Astronomy*, which was to be so renowned among the Arabs and in the Middle Ages as 'the greatest' or *Almagest*: some observations recorded seem to cover A.D. 127–41, and the publication was probably just after. It was from this angle that he approached geography and made the most ambitious of ancient efforts to map the known world, about A.D. 150. His book is almost wholly unreadable and hardly meant to be read: it consists mainly of long lists of places, each with its figures of latitude and longitude, from which anyone with enough patience can construct the maps for himself. Unfortunately, such matter was peculiarly liable to corruption, and a painful labour of editing is still needed before

[1] Respectively ll. 315, 289–92, 558, 773, 31, and cp. Erembi, 963, Trinacie, 467. Ed. *G.G.M.* II, xv–xl, 103–76. Bunbury, op. cit. II, 480–90 (wrongly dates about A.D. 90). Knaack, *R.E.* V, 915–24 (1903). Date proved by Leue, *Philologus*, 1884, p. 175. A diss. by U. Bernays, 1905. Much probably from Alex. Lychnus, see p. 215, n. 3.

[2] Respectively, 208–10 (Nasamones destroyed by Domitian): 306–8: 1088: 749–57 (Seres).

[3] *Geogr.* I, 17, 4. Latest, ibid. I, 6, 1. On M., Bunbury, II, 519–45: Berger, pp. 593–616: Honigmann, *R.E.* XIV, 1767–96, with map (1931). Cp. Herrmann's reconstruction, *Pet. Mitt.* 1930 Suppl. pp. 45–54. Kubitschek, *R.E.* Karten, §§ 28–9 (1919). Tozer, *Anc. Geogr.* p. 338.

we can be sure of having the best possible text and maps closely akin to his—for he certainly drew maps for his own use, and it was off these that he transcribed his figures. Whether he published maps is disputed. It is another question whether the various maps in medieval manuscripts have any authority as going back to his published ones (if any) or at least to early drawings from his text. J. Fischer has given a sumptuous facsimile of a famous parchment, Codex Urbinas Gr. 82, and its 27 maps, besides many from other manuscripts. Stevenson's translation has 27 maps from the Ebner MS. of about 1460, the basis of those in the early printed editions of the time of Columbus, which swarm with errors. The mere look of Ptolemy is formidable to the ordinary student, and a great difficulty in using him is the lack of any complete critical edition and commentary.[1] The sketch-maps in the following pages omit masses of details and names and are meant only to give an idea of outlines and important features (often even these cannot be safely drawn from the data, like the middle courses of rivers). It is still another question how much real knowledge the maps represent: what, for instance, is to be thought of all these names so confidently placed in the heart of India or Scythia? It will be seen how startling were the errors which Ptolemy and others could still make about familiar countries; but we must consider with special interest what they say of regions hitherto vague or quite unknown.

§2. EUROPE

The best civilizing work of the Romans was done in France and Spain, where it was to survive wholesale barbarian invasion, while in Britain it was thinner and weaker. But the outstanding fact about them is that they failed to conquer the Germans, who were to wreck their Empire. 'Hinc movet Euphrates, illinc Germania bellum'—it is the constant refrain of their history, and the northern frontier was more important than the eastern.

In Spain it was left for Augustus to subject the Biscay hillmen and relieve the country of war and even of its chronic brigandage. He re-

---

[1] C. Müller, 1883, continued to Bk. v by C. T. Fischer, 1901, with volume of 19 maps (8 of Asia missing). Partial editions, Cuntz, *Galliae Germ. Raetia Noricum Pannoniae Italia*, 1923: Renou, *Géogr. de Ptol. L'Inde*, 1925. J. Fischer, 4 folios, Leyden, 1932. E. L. Stevenson, New York, 1932, without Greek or commentary and with many errors, as J. Ball, *Egypt in Classical Geogr.* 1942, p. 86, says. A handy but bad text, Nobbe, 1843–5. Forbiger, I, 402–32 with maps of world and continents: Bunbury, op. cit. II, 546–636: Berger, pp. 616–48. *R.E.* Geogr. §§ 42–5, Karten, §§ 30–58. Schnabel, *Text u. Karten des Ptol.* 1938. Detailed works on P.'s India, McCrindle, 1885 (reprint 1927), E. Asia, Gerini, 1909, C. and S.E. Asia, Berthelot, 1930, Africa in his *Afr. sahar. et soudanaise*, 1927, pp. 299–413. Book I transl. with notes by H. von Mžik, 1938.

THE GREAT DAYS OF THE ROMAN EMPIRE 231

organized the provinces. The Hither, renamed after its capital at Tarraco, was greatly extended to include the newly conquered north and the three legions there (soon only one was needed, at a place which still bears its name as Leon). The Further province, rich and highly civilized, became 'Baetica', being essentially the valley of the Baetis or Guadalquivir. A western province was detached as Lusitania; the chief place was a colony of veterans at Merida (Augusta Emerita), but there was a town of Lisbon, and a 'Port' was to be the origin of Oporto, and indeed of 'Portugal'. Nearly everywhere in the peninsula Romanizing was thorough, helped on by many colonies, whose names often survive like Saragossa (Caesaraugusta). The Iberian language early died away in the south, though elsewhere it lasted longer. The many small clans tended to develop towns on Roman patterns: Pliny talks of 500 or more 'civitates' and 'populi', and Ptolemy names some 66 tribes and 380 'cities' (he uses the word very freely). Trade prospered more than ever, and Gades was one of the greatest harbours in the Empire, sending its ships not only to Italy but to the Rhine.[1] Plenty is said of the minerals for which the south had always been famous, and new workings were opened in the north-west: it became for a time the chief Roman gold-field, and had iron, lead, and silver, and also tin, so much apparently that the Cornish supply could for long be almost neglected. One town was noted for water which favoured the making of steel, and Toledo blades were already reputed.[2] There was no early capital answering to Madrid, a place chosen later for its central position but with nothing else to recommend it. Comparatively little is heard of the north and north-west, which are outside the Mediterranean climate and to-day among the most important parts of Spain.

The writers are naturally full on so old a province, but can still make bad mistakes in geography, though the notion of the Pyrenees as running north–south is soon corrected. Mela, himself hailing from near Gibraltar, has some new details on the north-west, and is the first to mention the Lisbon projection as such, but Pliny is confused here. Ptolemy almost

---

[1] Dessau, *Gesch. der röm. Kaiserzeit*, 1930, II, 2, 460. Gades, Str. 160. Language, ibid. 151, cp. 'sermone patrio', Tac. *Ann.* IV, 45. Cantabrian war, Str. 165, *C.A.H.* X, 116: brigandage, Vell. Pat. II, 90, 4. On provincial boundaries Braun (see p. 188, n. 2), Str. 152, 166. Plin. III, 6–30, IV, 110–20. Books on Spain, p. 188, n. 1: Bouchier, *Spain under R. Empire*, 1914: Syme, *C.A.H.* X, 342–5, Albertini, ibid. XI, 491–501. Altamira, *Hist. of Span. Civ.* 1930, pp. 26–35. Sutherland, *Romans in Spain*, 1939, chs. 7–11. Thouvenot, *Essai sur la Prov. rom. de Bétique*, 1940. Trend, *Civ. of Spain*, 1944, pp. 16–19.

[2] Grattius, *Cyneg.* p. 341. Water of Bilbilis, Mart. IV, 55, XII, 18, 9: Plin. XXXIV, 145. Cornish, see p. 195, n. 1. Minerals, p. 188, n. 1: Plin. IV, 112, XXXIII, 78, 95, XXXIV, 4 (Marian copper), 156 (tin), etc.: gold, O. Davies, *R. Mines in Europe*, 1935, pp. 68–78, 97–9: tin, ibid. p. 147: Charlesworth, *Trade Routes*, pp. 157–62. Tin, Cary, *J.H.S.* 1924, pp. 168, after Haverfield.

ignores it, and his map is distorted by the very old misconception of Cape St Vincent as the westernmost point (some explain that his cape is a conflation of that and Cape Roca from two different nautical guides). He makes the Pyrenees end westward in an imaginary headland. How he may have come by his group of Tin Islands has already been discussed. Dionysius has 'Western Islands' with tin somewhere hereabouts; otherwise he dismisses Spain absurdly with a couple of obsolete names.[1]

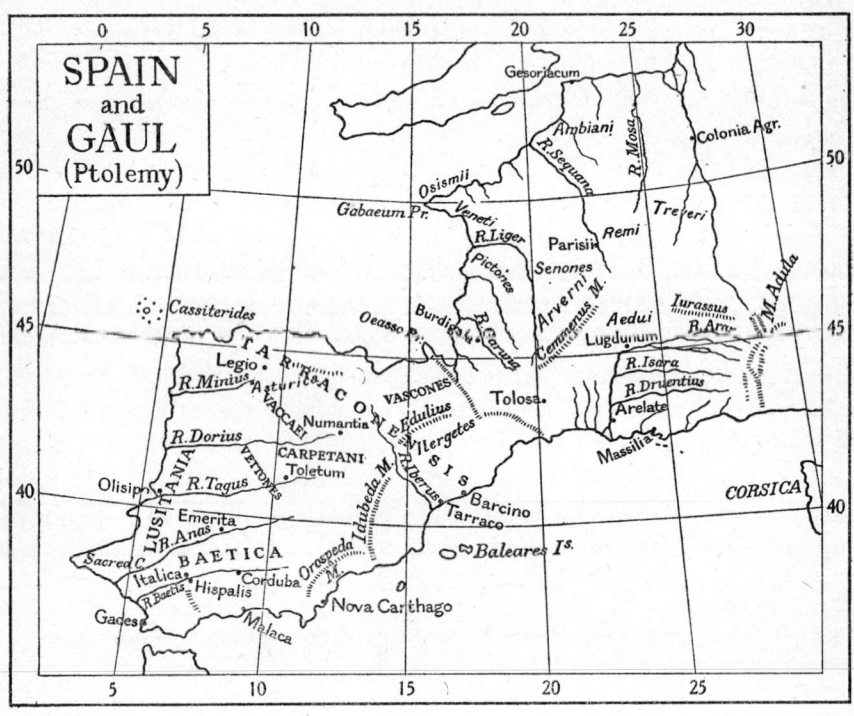

Fig. 29.

Augustus had still to clear some troublesome tribes from the Alpine passes, which are now better described. (Yet the writers have still some curious mistakes about the Alps, calling Monte Viso the highest peak and not even mentioning Mont Blanc.) In Gaul little work remained but to mop up in outlying parts, the Channel coast and near the Pyrenees, and to check some German raiding. The old southern province was already becoming 'Italia verius quam provincia'. The rest Augustus organized in three parts meant to be fairly equal in size and not coinciding with

[1] Dion. Per. 328. Islands, ibid. 563: Ptol. II, 6, 76: Plin. IV, 119: see p. 55, n. 2. Projection, Mela, III, 7: Plin. IV, 113 (and confusion still Solinus, 23, 5). Pyrenees, see p. 188, n. 2: corrected by Mela, II, 85 (no, Braun, op. cit. p. 38), Plin. IV, 110. Bunbury, op. cit. II, 359, 390 (Ptol. ibid. 586). Ptol. II, chs. 4–6.

Caesar's three racial divisions. He extended Aquitania north to the Loire to include some Celtic tribes, and Belgica a long way south-east to Geneva. The central and purely Celtic area was named after Lugdunum (Lyons), founded in 40 B.C., the only Roman town deliberately imposed on Gaul: it was the capital of the whole country and the seat of an assembly representing the 60 (or 64) cantons. These had their own centres, Lutetia of the Parisii, Avaricum of the Bituriges, and so on, which gradually approximated to Roman towns (it is the tribal names which have survived as Paris and Bourges, Arras and Amiens, Rheims and Rennes, and many others). The protecting legions were camped at the outer edge on the Rhine. Freed from German invasions and their own feuds, the people settled down willingly to their fate, except for two very partial and half-hearted revolts (in A.D. 21 and 70). The Celtic language was doomed to die out, though some was still spoken at Trèves, it seems, as late as the fourth century (Breton is not a survival but the result of a backwash of refugees from Britain in Anglo-Saxon times). At the price of this swift denationalization the country prospered under the Roman peace. Besides plenty of land-produce it had manufactures such as textiles and pottery. Trade was helped by Agrippa's system of roads radiating from Lyons to the Rhine, by Paris to the Channel, and south-west to Bordeaux, already a flourishing place on a 'sea-lake' of the Ocean. There were also wonderfully handy river-ways, with only short portages between, over the low central watershed, and we hear of a governor who thought of improving the system by a canal between Saône and Moselle. (The central plateau has never seriously hindered the communications of the three great basins round it or impaired the unity of France.)[1]

The geographers have some surprising blunders about a country so important and familiar. Strabo wrongly makes the tributaries of the Rhône, the Saône and Doubs, come from the Alps like the main river, and he should have used Caesar better and Agrippa's roads branching from Lyons. It has been explained how badly he drew the outer coast, suppressing the Breton projection. Mela soon restores this, but Pliny is rather obscure here and Ptolemy has a poor idea of its size, and no idea of the Norman peninsula. He also breaks up the coast southward into deep bays.

---

1 Fleure, *Human Geogr. of W. Europe*, 1918, pp. 56–7: Marriott, *Short Hist. of France*, 1942, p. 6. Canal, Tac. *Ann.* XIII, 53. Rivers, Str. 189. Roads in 38–37 B.C., Str. 208. Burdigala, ibid. 190. Cantons, ibid. 182, Tac. *Ann.* III, 44, Ptol. II, 7–10. Passes, Str. 208: tribes, Plin. III, 133–8: Syme in *C.A.H.* X, 347–51: W. Hyde, *R. Alpine Routes*, 1935. Mistakes on Alps, Mela, II, 4, 4, Plin. III, 117: Chilver, *Cisalpine Gaul*, 1941, p. 35. Italia, Plin. III, 31. Jullian, *Hist. de la Gaule*, IV–VI, 1914–20: routes, ibid. V, ch. 3, Charlesworth, *Trade Routes*, p. 183. Albertini in *C.A.H.* XI, 501–10: Grenier in Frank's *Econ. Survey*, 1937, III, 509–62.

Inland his matter is very defective: for instance, he still has the false drawing of the rivers mentioned, and quite ignores other big ones like the Aisne and Marne already known to Caesar; he misconceives the Loire, puts the Parisians on the latitude of its mouth, and so on. The general shape and proportion of length to breadth are not good. Much in his map is almost inexplicably bad, and two special studies differ widely about the stade used and in their accounts of his procedure and mistakes of distance and of orientation. The last kind are commonest, it seems, but there are also confusions of the Gallic league with the Roman mile: so Berthelot, who thinks that the distances are mostly calculated from one town to the next and not referred to certain starting-points like Boulogne as Cuntz argues.[1]

Augustus was expected to invade Britain, but it was not thought worth while till Claudius in A.D. 43. The advance was rapid to the Welsh hills and the Humber, where it paused. In A.D. 61 the governor was away attacking Mona (Anglesey) when the eastern tribes rose and stormed the chief settlements at Colchester, London, and St Albans before he could master the revolt. We have a life by Tacitus of his father-in-law Agricola, governor in A.D. 78–85. He completed the conquest of Wales, and pushed north to establish a line on the Forth-Clyde neck. He went on to beat a Caledonian host at a Mons Graupius, somewhere beyond a last camp east of Dunkeld and perhaps near Forfar or Brechin, while he may have marched to near Aberdeen (the name Grampians seems a mere misreading of the old but does not help to locate the battlefield). He even sent a fleet from the Tay to the Orkneys, if not farther (before this three brig-loads of German deserters had slipped off home, apparently from the west coast and round the north). But he was recalled, though a complaint that 'Britain was thoroughly conquered and at once let drift' seems hardly fair, as excavation shows that the Scottish ground was held against attacks for some twenty years (hence, too, Ptolemy's surprising knowledge even of these parts).[2] After a northern rising, in which the York legion was probably destroyed by the Brigantes, Hadrian came himself and built his wall over the high moors between Tyne and Solway (A.D. 122). Twenty years later Pius 'removed the barbarians and made another wall' between Forth and Clyde. (One likes to think of the centurion at Auchindavy who set up

1 Ptol. II, 7–10. Cuntz, *Galliae*, etc., 1923 (stade 185 m.). Berthelot, *Rev. Ét. anc.* 1933, pp. 293–303, 425–35, 1934, pp. 51–69 (stade 157·5 m.). Projection, Mela, III, 23 (and island of Sein, ibid. 16), Plin. IV, 107, Bunbury, II, 392. Tributaries, Str. 192, 204. A curious catalogue of names with the Vosges as a river, Lucan, I, 392–465.

2 Tac. *Hist.* I, 2: Sir G. Macdonald, *Roman Wall in Scotland*[2], 1934, 2 and in *J.R.S.* 1937, pp. 93–8. Tac. *Agricola*, ed. J. G. C. Anderson, 1922. Rising of Boudicca, Tac. *Ann.* XIV, pp. 31–9. Brechin, Collingwood and Myres, *R. Britain and the English Settlements*[2], 1937, p. 115. Aberdeen, Syme, *C.A.H.* XI, pp. 151–8. Orkneys, Tac. *Agr.* 10: deserters, ibid. 28.

THE GREAT DAYS OF THE ROMAN EMPIRE 235

an altar 'Genio Terrae Britannicae'.) The same Emperor had to punish the Brigantes for invading a certain district by depriving them of much of their land.¹ Vague troubles continued, and under Commodus everything was lost beyond the older wall or its Cheviot outposts (A.D. 180 or soon after).

It has been explained how Strabo from notions of his own made a mess of Britain. Mela, writing in A.D. 43, goes back to Caesar, but has rather surprisingly heard of the Orkneys and seven Aemodae 'opposite Germany', apparently the Shetlands. Obscure are the date and credentials of one Philemon, who repeated too readily some hearsay from traders about Ireland. Pliny adds thirty Haebudes, and already has a rumour of a great forest where wild Caledonians live on grass and berries and game. He is careless enough to put the Isle of Wight, like Man, between Britain and Ireland. He does not really know what to make of Thule. Tacitus is sketchy in geography, having only eleven names, of which four cannot be safely placed, like a river Tanaus. London appears already as a busy place of trade (it had arisen where two small hills rising above the marshes commanded the lowest crossing of the Thames, and there is no proof of a pre-Roman town there). Britain is described as rainy and foggy but not very cold, and as fertile except for vine and olive; it has a few very poor pearls, and gold and silver and other minerals (no word of tin). He misplaces it on old lines, and talks of Ireland as half-way between it and Spain. He believes, no doubt rightly, in an old migration of dark people from Spain to Britain. He has a notion of the north part as wedge-shaped, and of long sea-lochs running into the mountains. The big limbs and red hair of the Caledonians suggest a wrong guess of German origin (the name of their chief is Celtic). The fleet 'discovered' the Orkneys, which cannot be right, and 'first confirmed' Britain as an island; it also 'saw at a distance' something understood to be Thule, here no doubt the Shetlands, and reported a 'sluggish' sea thereabouts: perhaps this was a belt of calm and fog, but taken as the beginning of the strange dead sea rumoured to exist beyond the known world, 'immotum mare et quasi deficientis in suo fine Naturae pigra moles'.² Some poets talk loosely of Britain itself as Thule. Dionysius has only four lines, queerly old-fashioned, with a vague and large Britain and an Ireland 'above' it almost lost in the haze. Finally we

---

1 Paus. VIII, 43, 4: *Vita Ant. Pii*, 5, 4: Macdonald, op. cit. pp. 7–10. Collingwood and Myres, op. cit. pp. 140–9. Centurion, A. R. Burn, *Romans in Britain*, 1932, p. 131.
2 Sen. *Suas.* I, 1: Tac. *Agr.* 10, cp. *Germ.* 45: see p. 149, n. 1. Wedge, *Agr.* loc. cit.: Ireland, ibid. 24: pearls, ibid. 12. Tanaus, ibid. 22: *C.A.H.* XI, 151, 156. Islands, Mela, III, 54, Plin. IV, 103. Caledonians, *Agr.* 11. Dark, ibid. Philemon criticized by Marinus, cp. Ptol. I, 11, 7. Site of London, L. D. Stamp, *The World*⁸, 1935, pp. 241, 306. K. Miller, *Mappaemundi*, 1898, VI, 111 tries to draw the map of Tacitus, as does Singer, *Short Hist. of Science*, 1941, p. 105.

have Ptolemy's map, vastly more detailed than any previous account and with a quite remarkable number of names. He knows many even far north like the Loxa (or Lossie?) and the Varar (the Farrar or Beauly). The Ituna is the Eden, near the Selgovae of Solway and opposite the Vedra or Wear; but Morecambe is not a genuine survival of his Moricambe (in fact the place used to be called Poulton and was renamed after the identification was suggested in Whitaker's *History of Manchester* in 1771). The mysterious northmost Camp oddly named as Winged has been thought meant for Agricola's near Dunkeld. Many of the names in Scotland are

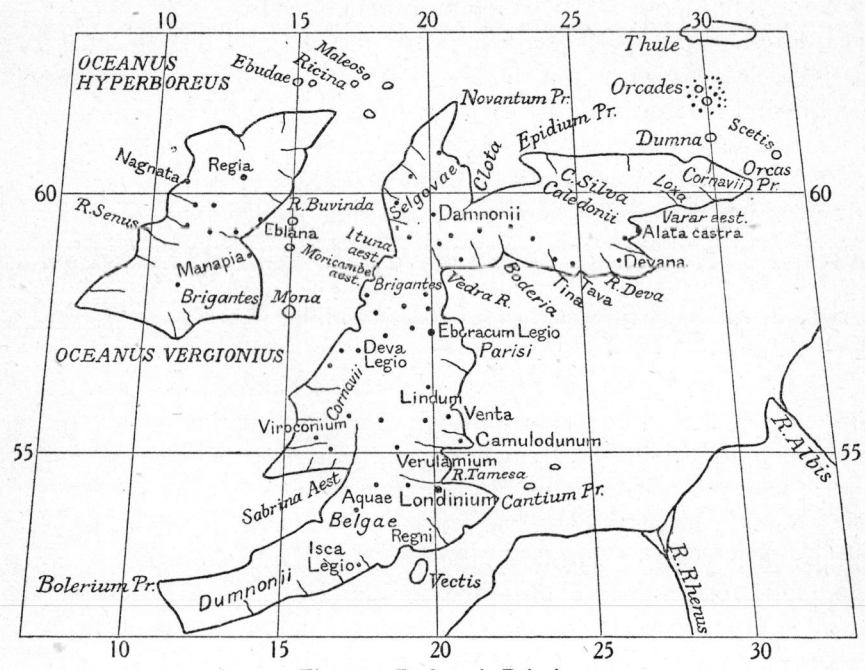

Fig. 30. Ptolemy's Britain.

decidedly Celtic: notable are Cornavii in Caithness as well as round Wroxeter and Damnonii on the Clyde besides Dumnonii in Devon. A legion is mislaid Exeter way instead of at Caerleon on Usk. As for the general shape of Britain, it is good except that he twists Scotland round to point east (Cape Novantum is certainly the Mull of Galloway, though so badly misplaced). The twist arises probably not from a misfitting of sectional maps, as one writer supposes, but from an effort to get Scotland in comfortably south of Thule. This is drawn as a large island at about 63° or the latitude of the 20 hours' day: it seems pulled thus far south to suit the fleet's Thule or the Shetlands, though they are in fact only 60° at the lower end. There are no Haemodae, and the Ebudae, properly belonging to

THE GREAT DAYS OF THE ROMAN EMPIRE

Scotland, have got badly shifted towards Ireland, far from Dumna (apparently Lewis) and Scetis (Skye?), which are themselves misplaced. Britain had already figured in the *Almagest*, with several place-names including one recognizable as Catterick, and with 'Little Britain' at 58–61°, the Ebudae at $19\frac{1}{2}$ hours or 62°, and Thule beyond.[1]

Agricola thought of sending a legion to take Ireland and 'remove liberty from the sight of Britain', whose traders used to cross to the nearer part. (It has been inferred from some verses that an attempt was actually made, but this is very dubious.) Strabo places the island absurdly far north. For Mela it is an oblong nearly as large as Britain and vaguely 'above' it, and so very emerald that the cattle have to be prevented from over-eating and bursting. Pliny makes it much shorter than Britain, though about as wide, and only thirty miles from Wales. Ptolemy has it fairly good in shape and size but still too far north, so as to lie wholly above Wales. Among his surprising number of names several rivers like the Buvinda or Boyne are easily recognizable; of the ten 'cities', including seven inland, only Eblana or Dublin seems reasonably certain. It is notable that Celtic tribes like the Brigantes are confined to the south-east. Probably there were no Roman ships or regular trade going to Ireland, though some coins reached it, perhaps for slaves and hides.[2] A strange question is raised by a pot of grey ware with some Latin scribbling, as a trawler dredged it up from fishing grounds 150 miles west of Ireland!

Utopian fancy could still play with these chilly waters, and wildly enough. A tale represented as heard from a mysterious stranger in Carthage has an island Ogygia five days west from Britain, with three others spaced out northwards, one of them the prison of the deposed elder god Cronos and a mild and pleasant place, though it has a day of 23 hours for a month on end. Only 5000 (?) stades beyond is a new world, a continent so great that its rivers silt the Atlantic and make it hard to cross (it does not suit

---

[1] II, 6. *Geogr.* II, 3 (and Ireland, 2). Bunbury, II, 582–5 (P.'s Thule is Shetland). Pulled, Nansen, *In Northern Mists*, 1911, I, 117. Misfitting and names, H. Bradley, *Archaeologia*, 1885, pp. 379–96: Celtic, Quiggin in *Enc. Brit.* ed. 11, Celtic Lit.: on names also J. Fraser, *Inaug. Lecture*, Oxford, 1923, p. 12: Childe, *Prehistory of Scotland*, 1935, p. 262: A. B. Scott, *Pictish Nation*, 1918, pp. 9–11 (Skye, etc.): W. C. Mackenzie, *Scottish Place-Names*, 1931, questions Lossie, Farrar, Solway, Novios-Nith, but accepts Malaios-Mull and perhaps Scetis-Skye (Nobbe reads Maleos). Dunkeld, I. A. Richmond, *Proc. Ant. of Scotland*, 1922, pp. 288–300 (but cp. the placing?). Dion. Per. 566–9. Poets, Silius, III, 597, XVII, 417, Statius, *Silvae*, IV, 4, 62, V, 1, 90.

[2] Collingwood in *Econ. Survey*, ed. Frank, 1937, III, 118. Haverfield, R. Objects in Ireland, *E.H.R.* 1913, pp. 1–12. Tribes, R. A. S. Macalister, *Arch. of Ireland*, 1928, 17, *Anc. Ireland*, 1935, p. 125: Hubert, *Celtes*, 1932, p. 239. Bunbury, II, 580–1. For Strabo, see p. 194, n. 2. Mela, III, 53 (bursting, said also of Babylonia, Curtius, V, 1, 12). Plin. IV, 104, reducing Agrippa, ibid. 102. Tac. *Agr.* 24. Inferred from Juv. II, 159 by McElderry, *C.Q.* 1922, pp. 151–62.

the author to sink a huge Atlantis to explain the presumed shoals). The people there know of our old world or 'inhabited earth' as an island, and every generation they send envoys who pay their respects to Cronos and sometimes come on to visit us, like the stranger who appeared in Carthage. This curious fiction of Plutarch is obviously in a 'mythical' vein like Plato's with hints from Hecataeus of Abdera and others; possibly too there is a flavour of Celtic legend, about a god or hero resting from his labours in an otherworld island like Arthur's Avallon or the one visited by Saint Brandan. The idea of Cronos ruling in the Isles of the Blest goes back to an interpolated line in Hesiod. An extravagant romance by one Antonius Diogenes brought its characters to see the 'wonders beyond Thule', places of six months' and even perpetual night. He seems to be early in this kind and among the writers burlesqued in Lucian's *True Story*. The latter's nameless hero sails from Gibraltar, curious about the limits of the Ocean and peoples who might dwell beyond. After being storm-driven for some eighty days, he reaches a wooded island with a river of wine, and so on. We leave him finally in 'the continent facing our own', but between he has been in many queer places, including a whale's belly and the moon; so far as it touches geography the skit is superficial and rather pointless, and a sea which suddenly freezes and thaws is hardly more plausible than one of milk with an island of cheese.[1]

Of Germany there was ample chance to learn a good deal. Augustus made a long effort to conquer it, thinking of nothing less than an Elbe frontier and putting his own step-sons Drusus and Tiberius in charge of operations. Their first task was to force a more direct communication with the Rhine: one moved north down the Inn, while the other converged from the west on Lake Constance, and the mountain region so enclosed became a province of 'Raetia and Vindelicia' (15 B.C.). Incidentally an old question was settled, the source of the Danube being found in the Black Forest. Soon after, it appears, Noricum was quietly annexed as part of the same plan and also as useful for its iron and gold.[2]

---

[1] Lucian, *V.H.* II, 2. Platt, *Nine Essays*, 1927, pp. 107–12. Ant. Diog. excerpt in Photius, *Bibl. Cod.* 166: Rohde, *Griech. Roman*[2], 1900, esp. pp. 269–92: 1st cent. A.D., so Schmid, *R.E.* I, 2615, though some 3rd cent. Plut. *de Facie in Orbe Lunae*, 26–9: *de Defectu Oraculorum*, 420a, (isle of Cronos). Rohde, 230: W. Hamilton, *C.Q.* 1934, pp. 24–30. Celtic, Grenier, *Gaulois*, 1945, p. 369: E. K. Chambers, *Arthur of Britain*, 1927, pp. 218, 230: J. Rhys, *Celtic Folklore*, 1901, II, 493–5, *Studies in Arthurian Legend*, 1891, pp. 367–9. Hes. *Op.* 169: Rohde, *Psyche*, Engl. ed. 1925, p. 76. Pot at Cardiff, *J.R.S.* 1934, p. 220, noted by J. A. Williamson, *Ocean in English History*, 1941, p. 14.

[2] *C.A.H.* X, 350: Miltner, *Klio*, 1927, p. 209. Gold, Str. 214: iron, Hor. *Odes*, I, 16, 9, *C.I.L.* III, 4788. Danube, Str. 207, 292. Plin. IV, 101, Tac. *Germ.* 6, 33: Mela, II, 79 is careless. Raeti, etc., Plin. III, 133. On R. Switzerland book by Stähelin[2], 1931. Route of Drusus, Chilver, *Cisalpine Gaul*, 1941, p. 36 (though Brenner also used).

THE GREAT DAYS OF THE ROMAN EMPIRE 239

In 12 B.C. Drusus sailed out from the Rhine by a canal and two 'vast lakes', later to be merged in the Zuyder Zee (after a great inroad of the Ocean in the thirteenth century, it is often said, but in general outline the sea was there apparently some time before). He reached the Weser, but on the return was stranded on the sand-banks by the unfamiliar tides. By land he penetrated through Chatti and Cherusci to the same river, and even through the 'Hercynian Forest' to the Elbe, but on the way back was accidentally killed (9 B.C.). To escape encirclement the Suebic Marcomanni withdrew from the Main to the old 'home of the Boii' (Bohemia), and their able king Marbod won strong allies along the Elbe, like the Semnones and Langobardi (Lombards), and beyond to the Gutones or Goths of the Vistula. Tiberius marched about without getting a pitched battle (8-7 B.C.); in the next few years, it seems, one general pushed from the upper Danube to the Elbe (or the Saale mistaken for it?), and another to tribes on the east side of Marbod, the Cotini and Anartii, to form relations against him.[1] In A.D. 4-6 Tiberius from the Rhine marched to the Langobardi, while his fleet entered the Elbe after exploring along to the cape of Jutland, from which came envoys of the once famous Cimbri (his men are said to have 'looked out upon or heard of an immense sea to Scythia and frozen parts').[2] Transferring to the Danube command, he launched a grand converging attack on Marbod, but was pulled back by the revolt of the provinces behind, Pannonia and Dalmatia, only recently subjected. There was another shock when three legions of Varus, marching back from the Weser, were destroyed by the wily Cheruscan Arminius in the Teutoburg forest (A.D. 9, the exact site of the battle has been vastly debated). Augustus now abandoned all thought of conquest, too readily, it seems, but his decision is a turning-point of history. (In judging his policy it should be remembered that he had a sketchy knowledge of the country and thought of it as almost all swamp or forest.) Tiberius as Emperor allowed his nephew Germanicus some campaigns to the Weser (A.D. 14-16), but he took no adequate revenge, and had more mishaps from the sea: two legions were nearly drowned by a flood tide, and his ships were blown on to the islands and some even to Britain, survivors telling of whirlpools and strange birds and monsters, 'whether they saw these things or imagined them in their fright'—so Tacitus, who may echo some remarkable verses by an eye-witness, though these may concern

---

1 Dessau, *Inscr. Sel.* 8965: Syme, *C.A.H.* x, 367, xi, 84: Miltner, op. cit. p. 213. General, Domitius, Dio, lv, 10*a* (Saale, some infer from Vell. Pat. ii, 106, Tac. *G.* 41): *C.A.H.* x, 365. Lakes, Tac. *G.* 34, *Ann.* i, 60, ii, 8, xiii, 54: Plin. iv, 101, xvi, 5. M.'s allies, Str. 290, with some obscure names. M. praised, Vell. Pat. ii, 108-9. On the geogr. development of the Rhine delta a thesis by Norlind, 1912.

2 Plin. ii, 167. Mon. Anc. 26: Vell. Pat. ii, 106: Str. 293.

rather the previous adventure of Drusus. (Pliny cites some reports of mermen and mermaids in these waters. The Ocean gave a good chance to declaimers, but they did not take it well, a critic thinks: 'nam aut tumide scripserunt aut curiose'.) We hear of a string of 23 islands including Borkum and one with glaesum or amber which recalled the old report of Pytheas: certain 'Pillars' mentioned are perhaps his Heligoland. Some found in one name an absurd reason for bringing Odysseus to the Rhine.[1]

The conquest had miscarried, and it was a poor salve to Roman pride that the name of Germany (Upper and Lower) was applied to the military commands along the left bank, with no better excuse than that a few German tribes had been transplanted there, 'ut arcerent, non ut custo-direntur', as the Ubii already by Agrippa in 38 and others by Tiberius in 8 B.C. Eight legions were more than enough to hold the bridge-heads of Cologne and Mainz. The Germans, left to their own quarrels, soon murdered Arminius and expelled Marbod, whose kingdom fell into a sort of clientship. They might be formidable, it was thought, if they could achieve unity and discipline, but happily there seemed less chance of this than of sapping them by the insidious influences of civilization. Some control was still kept beyond the lower Rhine, and the Batavians were freely levied and even allowed to serve under their own chiefs till a mutiny which shook the frontier at a critical moment of civil war (A.D. 70). From the upper river there was a gradual advance to an outer line of forts covering a shorter communication with the Danube and nipping off the barbarian salient pointed at the heart of Gaul. The first pieces of continuous barrier were by Domitian; his work was reorganized by Hadrian, and Pius added a new line in front, as he did in Britain. Soon after him Marcus Aurelius began to have serious trouble in defending this German and Raetian 'limes'.[2]

Of the writers Strabo is still vague on placing, vaguer than he should be, as about Jutland: once he says loosely that the coast is unknown beyond the Elbe. He exaggerates the difficulty of the country, 3000 stades or more to that river through marshes and jungles, but he can name other 'forests' branching from the Hercynian—itself not too thick to enclose some good country—and also tribes of Marbod's alliance as far as the

---

[1] Some ap. Tac. *G.* 3. Pillars, ibid. 34. Anderson ad loc., Detlefsen, *Entdeckung des germ. Nordens*, 1904, p. 43. Plin. IV, 97, XXXVII, 42 (Glaesaria or Austeravia): glaesum, Tac. *G.* 45: Burchanis, Str. 291. Monsters, Tac. *Ann.* II, 23: verses of Pedo ap. Sen. *Suas.* I, 15 (Edward ad loc. thinks Drusus). Mermaids, Plin. IX, 9–10: Juv. XIV, 283: Paus. X, 4, 4. Sketchy, as John Buchan, *Augustus*, 1937, p. 313 insists.

[2] On the Limes Fabricius, *R.E.* XIII, 572–604 (1926): B. W. Henderson, *Five R. Emperors*, 1927, chs. 5–6: Syme, *C.A.H.* XI, 158–68, 181–4: R. Germany and Raetia, Stade, ibid. pp. 526–39. Sapping, Tac. *G.* 15, 42, cp. 33, 37, *Ann.* II, 26, 62: Sen. *de Ira*, I, 11, 4. Client, Tac. *Ann.* II, 63, XII, 29, Plin. IV, 81. Arcerent, Tac. *G.* 28: Ubii, Str. 94, others, Dio, LV, 6. L. Schmidt, *Gesch. der deutschen Stämme*, 1910 (²1934). G. Schütte, *Our Forefathers*, 1929–33.

Gutones (he does not name the Vistula, but Agrippa already does).¹ Mela is the first extant to speak of a vast Codan gulf full of islands large and small, the largest and most fertile being Codanovia: the gulf seems in name the Katte(n)gat, but many take the description as applying only to the tidal North Sea coast or at least as partly confused with that. Pliny calls the island Scadinavia—clearly Skåne or south Sweden—and says that the known part alone holds an enormous nation, the Hilleviones (if the text is right), so that they may well call it 'alterum orbem', while a second island is hardly smaller! An immense range Saevo, 'not inferior to the Rhipaean', is said to 'form' the gulf: it seems an idea of mountains in south Norway, presumably sighted by the fleet from Jutland way. He also gives several names not safely identified, Latris (Zealand?) and so on. Thus, rather obscurely, the Baltic coasts come into record, while the sea is misconceived as part of the Ocean and Scandinavia as an island.² Both writers seem to use another, perhaps one Philemon, who wrote probably after the voyage to Jutland. Pliny cites him for amber being dug up in 'Scythia' and for a sea called 'dead' by the Cimbri to a certain cape, perhaps in Norway just opposite rather than their own Skaw (some have put it elsewhere, beyond the North Sea): it is questioned whether they meant the tideless and frozen Baltic or only shared the old notion of a 'sluggish' sea. (A modern historian imagines that one could then have met men in Gaul who had coasted 'east into the Baltic and north past the Norway Capes and could speak of an ocean curdled like milk and great bearded sea-monsters with ivory fangs'.) We hear also of a knight who started from about Vienna and travelled up the Marus or March and altogether 600 Roman miles almost due north to the amber coast near the Vistula mouth to fetch amber for Nero's shows; from him must have come much of the knowledge concerning the eastern Germans, and finds of coins and wares prove the continued use of this amber trade-route, though some explain them rather as booty.³ Elsewhere Pliny has scattered

1 Agr. in Mela, III, 33, Plin. IV, 81, 100. Str. 290. Vague, ibid. 128, 207: distance, 292: Jutland, 293–4. Bunbury, II, 259. Huge old oaks, Plin. XVI, 6.

2 Plin. IV, 96–7. Mela, III, 31, 54: N. Sea, Schmidt, op. cit. I, 51, Ekholm, *C.A.H.* XI, 51, Beckers, *Rhein. Mus.* 1939, p. 64 (in M.'s source): confused, Müllenhoff, *D.A.* I, 489. Detlefsen, op. cit. p. 30, Nansen, op. cit. I, 91, 95. Katte(n)gat, etc. Detlefsen, p. 31. Range, Müllenhoff, IV, 45, Nansen, p. 102. Latris = Zealand, Tastris = N. Jutland, Beckers, *G. Zt.* 1936, pp. 292–304. Singer, *Short Hist. of Science*, 1941, p. 103 tries Mela's map.

3 Schmidt, op. cit. p. 45, but trade, Anderson on Tac. *G.* 45, Cary-Warmington, *Anc. Explorers*, pp. 118–19, Schütte, op. cit. I, 19, II, 17: *C.A.H.* XI, 70, 72, Plates V, 19 (wares rare on E. Baltic). Plin. IV, 81 (Marus), XXXVII, 45. *C.A.H.* X, 415, 418. Norway, Detlefsen, op. cit. pp. 3, 24, Beckers, op. cit. p. 63 (and sluggish), cp. frozen (to Skaw), Hergt, *Pytheas*, p. 40. Philemon ap. Plin. IV, 97 (and amber, ibid. XXXVII, 33): date, Kroll, *R.E.* Philemon, 1938, against Detlefsen who puts *c.* 100 B.C. Chauci fishermen, Plin. XVI, 2–4: Herc., ibid. 6, animals, VIII, 38, birds, X, 132. Walrus, John Buchan, op. cit. p. 309.

notes on Germany, some showing personal knowledge, as on the wretched fishermen of the barren North Sea coast; he talks of the Hercynian forest with its huge old oaks, its big animals, elks and wild oxen and horses, and its strange birds.

Tacitus tells of some wars with the Germans at their due places in his history, using a big book by Pliny (now lost). He had written in A.D. 98 a special essay 'De Origine et Situ Germanorum', the best of the kind that survives from ancient times. He describes first the Germans as a whole and their public and private life (1–27), then the individual tribes and their specific differences (28–46). He does not claim personal knowledge, and writes apparently from books and oral reports. He wishes to inform his countrymen on a people who had checked their arms and were potentially more dangerous than the more obvious rival, Parthia. His style and temper incline him to point the moral of their freedom and virtue against Roman decadence, but this is hardly his main purpose. He does not conceal their failings: they are disunited (and long may they be!); they gamble wildly and drink deep, a vice to be encouraged by selling them wines; they have private blood-feuds; they incline to form war-bands under successful leaders, and, when not out to slay and plunder, they mostly gorge and sleep, for 'with a strange inconsistency they love indolence and hate peace'. Some things are idealized, like their religion, and they had more taste for Roman money and wares than is said, and had more and worse-treated serfs and slaves. He follows an old literary type and is not quite free from its clichés.[1] (A good deal of the character described has often been recognized as persisting in modern descendants, including even the English, who have been much modified by later blending, among other factors of a highly varied historical experience.) The geography is subordinate and impressionistic, with hardly any names but tribal. The country is 'in general wild with forests or hideous with swamps', but has fertile parts. The Hercynian Forest crops up at various points and finally unnamed as a 'continuous ridge' (the Sudeten) dividing Suebia. He knows of the Angles and other northern tribes, one probably the same as the later Saxons, who all meet in an island of the 'Ocean' (meaning the

---

[1] Despite the defence of Anderson, Tac. *Germ.* 1938 against Norden, op. cit.: see p. 110, n. 1. Money, Tac. *G.* 5, wine, ibid. 23: more trade than he knows, Brogan, *J.R.S.* 1936, p. 195. Econ. conditions, *C.A.H.* XI, 71–2. Much, *R.E.* Suppl. 3, Germani, 1918, and ed. of Tac. *Germ.* 1937. More agriculture than often thought, G. East, *Hist. Geogr. of Europe*, 1935, pp. 51–8: see p. 197, n. 1. Character, E. Ludwig, *Germans*, 1942, p. 16: Fouillée, *Esquisse psych. des Peuples européens*[6], 1921, pp. 248–50: Boutmy, *English People*, 1904, pp. 59–63 (sport, betting and drinking!): McDougall, *The Group Mind*, 1920, p. 230. Tac.'s bad influence on modern race-superstition, Barzun, *Race*, 1938, pp. 11, 27–8: H. Fyfe, *Illusion of National Character*, 1940, p. 193.

Baltic or North Sea?) to worship a certain goddess, but he places them only vaguely as 'protected by rivers or woods'. The German race is indigenous, he thinks, and has remained unmixed, as the uniform physical type shows. He cites native lays, known already to Pliny, about Mannus (the first Man) and his three sons, from whom derive three great stocks, Ingaevones 'nearest the Ocean', Istaevones apparently near the Rhine,

Fig. 31.

and Herminones inland; more sons were added as ancestors of the Suebi, 'Vandilii' and others, evidently later eastward expansions of the race (Pliny counts Suebi and 'Vandili', including Gotones, in the third stock).[1] In the detailed account Tacitus ignores this scheme for a quite different division between non-Suebic tribes in west and north-west (chs. 29–36) and Suebic in east and north (38–45). Here the name is stretched beyond reason to cover even the Angle group (presumably Ingaevones) and many tribes as far as the Gotones, with no better excuse than the fact that some had been allies of the Marcomanni; these last were the real

[1] Plin. IV, 99–100: Tac. G. 2–4. Herm., already Mela, III, 31. Herc., Tac. G. 5, 28, 30 and ridge, 43. Reudigni, ibid. 40 = Saxons of Ptol. II, 11, 7: Eudoses Jutes, see p. 196, n. 1.

Suebi, with some neighbours, said to meet for human sacrifice in the forest of the Semnones, who claimed to be their oldest and chief tribe. The details of eastern peoples are remarkable. The great Lugian nation—really the same as the Vandals—meet in a certain grove, among them the grim Harii, who have black shields and dye themselves black, but strangely not the Burgundians, mentioned already by Pliny. Eastwards are Gotones, another ominous name: it was not known till long after, from their own tradition, that they had come from Götaland in Sweden, as the Burgundians from Bornholm and the Silingae Vandals from Zealand.[1] Beyond these Goths are Aestii, who sell amber, a fossil tree-resin dug up on their coast or washed up by the sea, and have sold it 'since Roman luxury gave it repute' (really they were not Germans at all but Balts, and their name was to pass to the Finnish Estonians). South and east of them are Veneti, or rather Venedi, in a wide area of woods and hills, brigands like the Sarmatians but not living like them on horses or in waggons: they are the Slavs or Wends, as the Germans call them, in their oldest known home, probably about the middle Vistula. Farther along are Fenni, very poor and primitive, using bone-tipped arrows and sleeping under shelters—perhaps Finland way, though a late writer says similar things of the Lapps as Scrithifinni or 'ski-ing Finns' and they are still 'Finns' to the Norwegians. The series ends in fabulous peoples with human heads on bestial bodies. The 'Suebic sea' is part of the open Ocean, and furs come from its unknown waters. It has vast islands, no 'Scadinavia', oddly enough, but strong tribes of Suiones (Swedes) under an over-king, with fleets of peculiarly shaped oared galleys; no doubt they crossed to their Gothic kinsmen, from whom the amber traders heard of them, and some Roman coins and wares reached their home (a large proportion of the coins have been found in the island of Gotland). Vaguely next are Sitones under a queen, destined to become in medieval legend a 'land of women', apparently Finnish (or later to be Finnicized) Kvaens in north Sweden misread as 'women' (compare 'queens'). Beyond the Suiones is a sea sluggish and almost immobile, and the last gleam of sunset continues to the dawn. There are already hints of the Vikings to come, and also of German pirates, as we hear of Chauci raiding Gaul.[2]

[1] Tradition in Jordanes, 9, 25 (6th cent. A.D.): Paulus Diaconus on Lombards. Ekholm, *C.A.H.* XI, 60–1. Schmidt, op. cit. pp. 29–30, 326, etc.: Svanström and Palmstierna, *Short Hist. of Sweden*, 1934, pp. 6–7. On connotations of 'Suebi', Frahm, *Klio*, 1930, pp. 192–210.

[2] Tac. *Ann.* XI, 18. Amber, Tac. *G.* 45. Suiones, ibid. 44: ships, Schmidt, op. cit. p. 40, Gjerset, *Hist. of Norwegian People*, 1927, p. 22. Wares, ibid. p. 18, Cary-Warmington, pp. 127–8, Shetelik and Falk, *Scand. Archaeology*, 1937: *C.A.H.* XI, 61, Plates V, 11 (Gotland). Ski-ing, Procopius, *B.G.* II, 15: Fenni in Scand., Müllenhoff, II, 39–75: not Lapps, Ekholm, *C.A.H.* XI, 66, Nansen, op. cit. I, 112: see p. 356, n. 1. Finns, Vernadsky, *Anc. Russia*, 1943, p. 101. Ptolemy writes Guthones, Venedae, Finni.

THE GREAT DAYS OF THE ROMAN EMPIRE 245

Ptolemy's map is puzzling in many ways. It is hard even to draw, as the text places long rivers only by their sources and mouths and strings tribes loosely 'above' or 'below' each other. There are 69 of them and 95 'poleis'! No doubt the host of new names represents a considerable accretion of knowledge, especially from trade, but we have not his working

Fig. 32.

material and cannot judge how far they may be subdivisions of old tribes, or may reflect movements since their day, or may be mistaken. Probably the traders' routes used often cross in confusion: a recent account tries to reconstruct eight such itineraries. There are sometimes bad doublets or two inconsistent placings of the same tribe as of the Langobardi and the Burgundians. Schütte talks of a chaos of names mutilated or doubled or invented. Müllenhoff thought that Ptolemy, or rather Marinus, made an appalling jumble by conflating two accounts, one of Augustus' time, giving the chief peoples from west to east, and another more special one of Trajan's. Schmidt agrees that the map is contaminated from two and that the 'towns' are a mess. The 'Cimbric peninsula' (Denmark) is exaggerated and wrongly pointed north-east, and it has as many as eight tribes: the Fundusii are a misreading from a Latin source of the Eudusii (Eudoses in Tacitus), who are the Jutes, and on the neck are Saxons but not Angles, who are wrongly moved up to the middle Elbe. For the Lugians and others a comparison with Tacitus is perplexing; among new names are the Silingae (Vandals), who were to give their name to Silesia. The ranges are queerly conceived, the Abnoba or Black Forest being shifted north and the 'Hercynian Forest' now limited to a short eastern stretch and so on. The Rhine itself is ill drawn, with no Lake Constance and no sharp bend to the north. On the Baltic coast, wrongly made due eastward and too long, no river is safely identified, though the Viadus is usually assumed to be the Oder; the Vistula is curiously short and bad, rising from a misplaced range. And the 'poleis'? Some are Roman ones in the salient or falsely transferred from the Roman bank; even hereabouts there can be wild blunders, one place being a Latin phrase misunderstood as a town (Siatutanda from 'ad sua tutanda'). What of all the rest where previous writers speak at most of villages or a few oppida, like Mattium, the chief place of the Chatti, and a settlement of traders under Marbod's castle?[1] Yet some names are interesting such as two ending in 'ford' and several in the Celtic -dunum or 'town', like Lopodunum (Ladenburg in Baden) and others much farther east, a legacy from the old Celtic cradle in these parts. As for the general shape, the country is exaggerated by a third. The North Sea islands described do not exist, while the string known before is omitted. Scadinavia and Suiones do not appear, but instead three small Scandian islands (three of the Danish) and a larger, Scandia proper, of only moderate size, yet with six tribes, including the Gutae (of Götaland or south Sweden) and another recognizable as Hedemarken in east Norway; it is badly misplaced opposite the Vistula, because the traders had heard of it from the amber coast there. (Pliny already had 'Scandiae'— besides Scadinavia—but falsely applied to British islands, including one

---

[1] Tac. *Ann.* I, 52, II, 62: 'vici', *Germ.* 16. Siat. from *Ann.* IV, 72. 'Towns', G. East, op. cit. pp. 126–7. On map of Ptol. II, 11, Bunbury, II, 588–90: Müllenhoff, IV, 50–4: Detlefsen, op. cit. pp. 58–62: Schütte, op. cit. I, fig. 8, *Scottish Geogr. Mag.* 1914–15, *Ptolemy's Maps of N. Europe*, 1917: Schmidt, op. cit. pp. 10, 45. Eight, Steche on P.'s Germany, 1937 (inaccessible to me), rev. by Hyde, *Class. Weekly*, 1938, pp. 176–8. Doublets, Ptol. II, 11, 9 and 17: II, 11, 18 and III, 5, 20. Suebus=Oder, Richmond, *Scottish Geogr. Mag.* 1923, 99–102 (Saxonum Ins.=N. Frisian and Alociae=land north of Lümfjord).

THE GREAT DAYS OF THE ROMAN EMPIRE 247

Dumna, which Ptolemy puts near the Orkneys.)[1] The amber people is not mentioned, though two tribal names may be subdivisions of it, and beyond the Vistula begin Sarmatians; the coast turns north only gradually and ends in unknown land, at a point answering to the Gulf of Finland but put too far north on a line with Thule.

The Danube frontier was essentially the work of Augustus. In his early days he had himself pushed from the head of the Adriatic to the Save

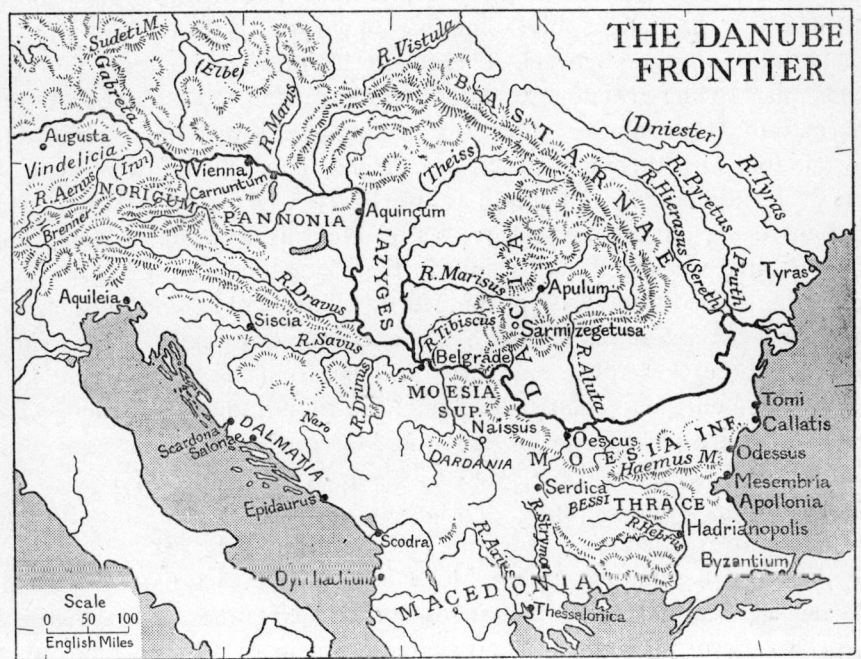

Fig. 33.

(35–33 B.C.). From this base Tiberius dealt with the Dalmatian hillmen and the fierce Pannonians (12–9 B.C.), but they rose behind him when he was moving on against Marbod, and it took three years of hard fighting to subdue them (A.D. 6–9). From Macedonia M. Crassus early reached the lower Danube (by way of Sofia) and drove out the encroaching Bastarnae (29–28 B.C.); yet a province or military zone of Moesia was not established till a good deal later, some time before A.D. 6. Raids alarmed the poet Ovid in his wretched exile (A.D. 8–18) at Tomi, an old

---

[1] Plin. IV, 104, Detlefsen, op. cit. p. 63: see p. 146, n. 3. Haedini, Nansen, op. cit. p. 119, Gjerset, op. cit. p. 26: K. Malone, *Amer. J. Phil.* 1934, pp. 362–70. Some see a corruption of Suiones in Favonae (Schütte) or Levoni; Malone finds migrant Suiones in the Sulones near the Vistula, III, 5, 20. Finni wrongly pushed to Vistula, Much, op. cit. p. 415. Celtic, Grenier, *Gaulois*, p. 82.

Greek colony 'inter inhumanae nomina barbariae', where he had to learn to speak 'Getic and Sarmatian' (he complains bitterly of the arctic cold and of various savages swarming across the frozen river, and describes them as bearded, wearing trousers and hides, and using poisoned arrows).[1] A Thracian client kingdom was allowed to remain, with the duty of watching the lowest reach, but it failed to keep order without frequent intervention and was annexed in A.D. 46. Moesia was extended downstream and later divided into two commands. A far-wandering tribe of Sarmatians, the Iazyges, had sometime in A.D. 20–50 thrust itself into the plain (of Hungary) between Theiss and Danube, where they found a congenial roving-ground like later invaders from the steppes. Other Sarmatians were among those threatening the lower river, and were formidable with their mailed cavalry. Here many enemies were kept off partly by diplomacy and subsidies: we hear early too of masses of barbarians being admitted as settlers, as by Plautius, a legate of Nero. The Dacians had weakened after a split in their kingdom, and a counter-raid could be pushed some way up the Maros.[2] But troublesome raids culminated in a serious attack on the camps, and Domitian replied by invasion; after a general was killed, another won a victory near the Iron Gate Pass in A.D. 88, but peace had to be bought with subsidies, and there were reverses upstream from the Iazyges and Marcomanni. Trajan resolved to finish with Dacia, and came twice in person (A.D. 101–7); the reports are rather vague on topography, but picturesque details are given in the reliefs of his own column at Rome. He penetrated the difficult country by the same pass and also up the Aluta to the Red Tower, took the capital Sarmizegetusa, and forced the king to suicide. He annexed the kingdom, expelling most of the people and replacing them by veterans and other settlers, including Dalmatian miners. The rich gold mines and hoards were probably a strong motive for the conquest, but mainly he wished to add a huge natural bastion to the river defences, and most approve this work. It was not an offensive base, and the part occupied was limited. The northern frontier was never defined, though a legion was moved forward to Apulum (Alba Julia or Karlsburg); presently we hear of a

---

1 Ovid, *Tristia*, III, 10, v, 7, *ex Ponto*, IV, 9–10, etc. Zone, Dio, LV, 29: *C.A.H.* X, 367, 804: Syme in *J.R.S.* 1945, p. 109. Tib., Vell. Pat. II, 110–16 (who served there), Dio, LV, 28–34. Crassus, ibid. LI, 23–7, Liv. *Ep.* 134–5, Florus, II, 26: *C.A.H.* X, 117–18. Iapydes to Save, Suet. *Aug.* 20, Str. 207, 314–15, Liv. *Ep.* 131–2, etc.: *C.A.H.* X, 84–8.

2 Str. 303–4, Mon. Anc. 30, Suet. *Aug.* 21: *C.A.H.* XI, 84, cp. X, 367: Miltner, *Klio*, 1937, 226. Settlers, Str. loc. cit.: Plautius, Dessau, *Inscr. Sel.* 986, *C.A.H.* X, 775, 802, XI, 85: cp. later case, Dio, LXXII, 3. Subsidies, *Vita Hadr.* 6. Iazyges, Tac. *Ann.* XII, 29, Plin. IV, 80, *C.A.H.* X, 804: they kill the old, Val. Flaccus, VI, 122–8. Mailed, Tac. *Hist.* I, 79. A Thracian war in A.D. 25, Tac. *Ann.* IV, 46–51. Outliers of steppes, East, op. cit. 42: Mackinder, *Democratic Ideals and Reality*, 1919, p. 122.

THE GREAT DAYS OF THE ROMAN EMPIRE 249

division into three districts, Apulensis, Malvensis, and Porolissensis.[1] There was still some trouble here, but the first serious strain came rather from the Germans. The Goths behind had begun to move southward, jostling the Vandals, who pressed others towards the upper river. There is an ominous ring about these attacks, 'Victualis et Marcomannis cuncta turbantibus, aliis etiam gentibus, quae pulsae a superioribus barbaris fugerant, nisi reciperentur bella inferentibus.... Gentes omnes ab Illyrici limite usque in Galliam conspiraverant'—there follows a portentous list of tribes all along and even to the Don. In hard wars, A.D. 167-80 with a brief interval, Marcus Aurelius drove them back and invaded their lands, and he would have made a province of Marcomannia, it is said, and another of Sarmatia (adjoining it in Hungary), and so would have pushed the frontier to the great ring of the Bohemian and Carpathian mountains; but he died in harness at the camp of Vienna, and the gains were abandoned by his worthless son. Henceforth the long Danube line, like the Rhine, was in danger. Except for wide swamps towards the mouths it is not a 'natural frontier' and never was, and a recent writer does well to protest against the assumption of any vast wisdom in its choice.[2]

The geographers are never so full or accurate as one would expect from these events. Strabo gives a good account of the Adriatic coast fringed with islands and backed by ranges, altogether 6600 stades to the strait. He knows something of campaigns inwards to Pannonia and of roads opened over the Save to the Danube. He has a good deal about the wild Dardanians in their dirty caves—elsewhere they are said to wash only on three occasions in their lives—and about the brigand tribes of the Haemus, a range which is still made too high and long. On Moesia he is very poor except for a mention of the Iron Gate rapids: most of his space is wasted on a rambling defence of Homer as already knowing these parts. The Dacians, recently 'quite humbled' by their own factions and by the Romans, are the people once described as Getae, he says; the country has a river Marisus and mountains, and stretches from the Hercynian Forest

---

1 *C.I.L.* III, 1457. Wars, Dio, 68, 6–14. Approve, as Longden, *C.A.H.* XI, ch. 5: B. W. Henderson, *Five R. Emperors*, 1927, chs. 10–11. Reliefs, *C.A.H.* Plates V, 3, 37–41, 85. See also G. A. T. Davies, *J.R.S.* 1917, pp. 74–97, 1920, pp. 1–28: Homo, *Haut-Empire*, 1933, pp. 453–64: Paribeni, *L'Italia Imperiale*, 1936, pp. 310–26. Alföldi, *C.A.H.* XI, 77–89: Pârvan, *Dacia*, 1928: East, op. cit. pp. 44–7. Gold, O. Davies, *R. Mines in Europe*, 1935, pp. 198, 205. Domitian's war, *C.A.H.* XI, 168–71, 175–8, 185–7. Central Dan. provinces, ibid. pp. 540–54. A diss. by Borszak on anc. knowledge of Carpathian basin, 1936: on geogr. of Pannonia A. Graf, 1936.

2 Toynbee, *Study of History*, 1939, V, 591–5: see p. 200, n. 1. Marcus, Homo, op. cit. pp. 564–73: Weber, *C.A.H.* XI, 349–65: Albertini, *L'Emp. rom.* 1929, pp. 210–12. *Vita Marci*, 14, 22, 24. Vague trouble, *Vita Pii*, 5, 4: a startling raid of Costoboci (of Galicia) to Greece?, Paus. V, 34, 2. Goths move, Schmidt, op. cit. pp. 40, 53, 356–8.

to the Dniester, though he cannot tell the exact boundaries.¹ Mela with his coastal scheme never even mentions Dacia, and he can repeat old fables like the Danube branch to the Adriatic and the mountain from which that sea and the Black are both visible. Pliny describes the whole block of lands with a lot of names and figures, but the arrangement is not good and he is rather brief on parts along the Danube. It is said to have sixty tributaries, about half of them navigable. For the Dacians and others beyond the river he has very little. Ptolemy is surprisingly bad. He narrows the upper provinces absurdly by drawing the Adriatic coast too easterly and bringing the Danube too near. There are many errors in detail, and

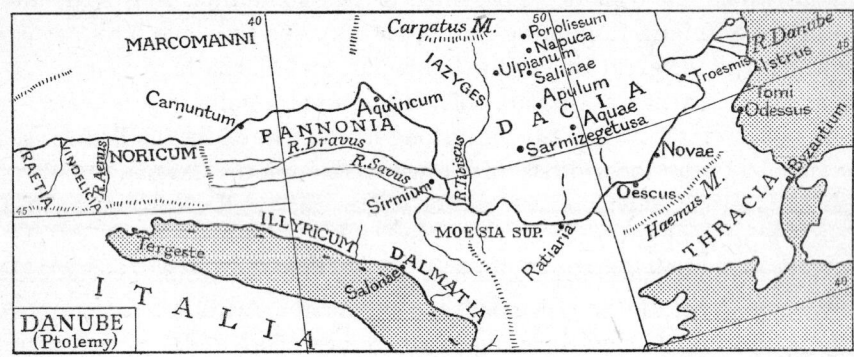

Fig. 34.

some misplacings, as of Vienna, are really too bad to be true and may be ascribed to a faulty text.² Dacia is given as many as fifteen peoples and forty-four 'notable towns', including several Roman settlements, but he ignores the river Marisus and the mountains of the plateau, the Transylvanian Alps. Yet far northward he can name the Carpathians, where he puts the sources of the Theiss and Dniester.

The governors of Moesia could extend their protection over the old Greek colonies along to the Crimea, which was useful as a granary for their army and for other eastern legions. Augustus had imposed a king there; 'so our friendship was sought by the Bastarnae and Scythians and kings of the Sarmatians on either side of the Don'. We hear of troops sent in A.D. 47 to support the client king, who had the Aorsi as allies against a rival backed by the Siraci, another tribe between Don and Caucasus.

1 Str. 303–5. Moesia, ibid. 295–303, of which 296–302 on Homer: Bunbury, II, 263–4. Homer's 'Mysians' still in Dion. Per. 322. Campaigns, Str. 314–15. Adr., ibid. 314–17: Liburnia and Dalmatia, Plin. III, 139–45, 150–2. Dard., Str. 316: Nic. Dam. fr. 107d. Haemus, Str. 313, tribes, 318.

2 Kubitschek, R.E. Karten, x, 2071. Mela, II, 2, III, 63: Bunbury, II, 357. Plin. III, 146–9: Danube and beyond, IV, 79–81: Mac., ibid. 33–9, Thrace, ibid. 40–50: Bunbury, II, 397.

THE GREAT DAYS OF THE ROMAN EMPIRE 251

Plautius, Nero's governor, boasts of compelling the 'Scythians' to raise the siege of a Crimean town, and just then the kingdom, it seems, was taken over directly for a few years (A.D. 63–8). Later Arrian makes the king's death an excuse for detailing the north coast of the Black Sea as well as the south where his own province was (this section of his periplus is now

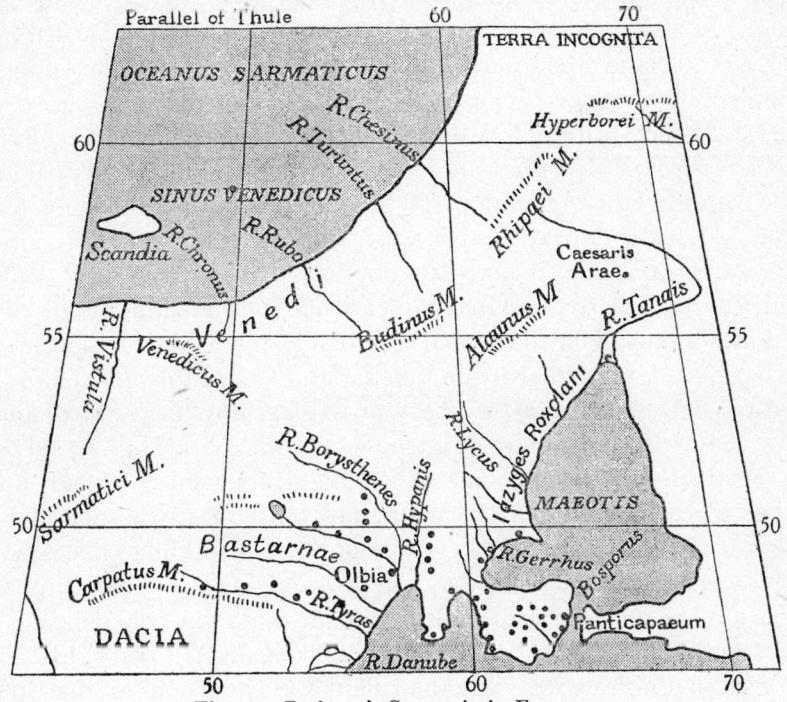

Fig. 35. Ptolemy's Sarmatia in Europe.

defended as genuine after many attacks). Presently Pius sent a force to protect Olbia, which was still a Greek town, it appears (at least an exiled orator says he found the people enthusiasts for Homer). The Aorsi were early replaced by the Alans, who had probably drifted from the Aral region, where they were just within the Chinese horizon; their westward movement was perhaps a chief cause of the pressure of their Sarmatian kinsmen against the Danube.[1] Little is said of the northern hinterland:

[1] As Roxolani, Tac. *Hist.* I, 79, III, 24: list in *Vita Marci*, 22: Schmidt, op. cit. p. 54. Alans, see p. 290, n. 4, p. 318, n. 3: Chinese, p. 180, n. 2: *C.A.H.* x, 777. Aorsi already Str. 492, 506. On Sarmatians Rostovtzeff, *C.A.H.* XI, 91–104. Arr. *Periplus Ponti Eux.* 17–25, ed. Roos. Olbia, *Vita Pii*, 9, 9: Dio Chrys. *Or.* 36: on this, Mahaffy, *Greek World under Roman Sway*, 1890, pp. 273–6: D. R. Dudley, *Hist. of Cynicism*, 1937, pp. 152–3 (and D.'s lost Getica). Directly, B. W. Henderson, *Nero*, 1903, p. 224: *C.A.H.* x, 775, 802, XI, 85: Minns, *Scythians and Greeks*, 1913, p. 599. Plautius, see p. 248, n. 2: Minns, op. cit. pp. 447, 469, 599. Troops, Tac. *Ann.* XII, 15–21. Siraci, also Str. 506: *C.A.H.* x, 753 (Bosporan kingdom, ibid. pp. 265–70). Aug. quotation, Mon. Anc. 31.

no traveller is named as going even a short way there, and the writers are content to repeat and garble old matter. Strabo doubts if any can live in the cold desert behind the Roxolani of the Azov (so the exiled poet puts the 'ultima terra' there, and 'ulterius nihil est nisi non habitabile frigus'). That sea may be quite near the northern Ocean, if not an inlet of it, thinks Pliny: some allow a big stretch of land up to the latitude of Thule, but this is a mere guess, he says. He makes a mess of the old tribes and rivers, and he and Mela state baldly as facts things which Herodotus disbelieved. Both restore the fabulous Rhipaean range as the source of the Don, and Dionysius brings two rivers from it, though the Don oddly from the Caucasus.[1] It flourishes still in Ptolemy, with a Hyperborean doublet, while various other mountains of his seem to have little more reality. (Even in Hakluyt's day people were still guessing about his northern range, and were now inclined to put it as far as they knew along the Arctic coast.) The rivers to the Baltic are not safely identified: possibly the northmost is meant for the Dvina. The best feature of the map, which here overlaps into Asia, is the Rha or Volga, rightly made to approach the Don bend and flow to the Caspian. The Azov is still grossly exaggerated, and the Black Sea itself is too far north anyhow, and the shape not so good as the old 'Scythian bow' would suggest. Of the tribes vaguely placed 'above' or 'below' each other many are old names, often queerly misplaced, many are otherwise unknown. If they were not mixed with things like Amazons and 'Alexander's Columns', they might be credited as coming from new travel reports, but a recent defence on this line is not convincing, and others agree that Ptolemy (and Marinus) filled blanks with very little scruple and even that his lists are worse than Pliny's.[2] The Chuni on the Dnieper have been thought some Huns who pushed west early with the Alans, but others deny that these came to the notice of western writers. The Unni of Dionysius on the north-west Caspian are probably only a misreading of a name in a much earlier source.[3] The same writer is full of the old geographical weeds, Amazons and Arimaspians, Colchians from Egypt, and the like, and he still has the Caspian 'gulf', opening into the strange

1 Dion. Per. 314, 663. Mela, I, 12, 115, 117, II, 1, III, 36. Plin. IV, 78, 88, 94, VI, 33. Rivers, ibid. IV, 93, tribes, ibid. 25–6, Azov, II, 167. Bunbury, II, 356, 400. Strabo, see p. 199, n. 1. Spalei on Don in Pliny=Spali of Jord. 28 (Slavs), Vernadsky, *Anc. Russia*, 1943, p. 104. Inlet, some ap. Lucan, III, 277–9. Ultima, Ovid, *Trist.* III, 4, 51.

2 Müllenhoff, *D.A.* 1892, III, 91–100: Honigmann, *R.E.* Marinus, XIV, 1793. Defence, Teggart, *Rome and China*, 1939, pp. 183–91. ·On Alex. and Amazons, cp. p. 127, n. 4, p. 141, n. 1. Asaei, Ptol. v, 9, 16=Alans, Vernadsky (see p. 178, n. 1). He gives Ptolemy's map. op. cit. 88. Hakluyt, Everyman ed. I, 112, II, 332.

3 Dion. Per. 730, cp. Uitii in Erat. ap. Str. 514, as Kiessling, *R.E.* Hunni, VIII, 2593: Bunbury, II, 486 was already very dubious. K. defends Chuni of Ptol. III, 5, 25: Huns too, Minns, 123, Berthelot, *L'Asie...d'après Ptol.* p. 216, Schmidt, op. cit. p. 104: Sir B. Pares, *Hist. of Russia*³, 1937, p. 10, but cp. De Groot, *Chin. Urkunden*, I, 238. See p. 318, n. 3.

curdled or dead northern sea, where the sun is dark and clouded.[1] Pausanias has some curious digressions, on the Sarmatian nomads, supposed ignorant of iron and wearing corselets made of hoofs, on the way of hunting the 'Celtic' elk—sober compared with one in an often suspected passage of Caesar—and on the great north sea which has tides and monsters and ends in something vaguely 'unsailable'.[2]

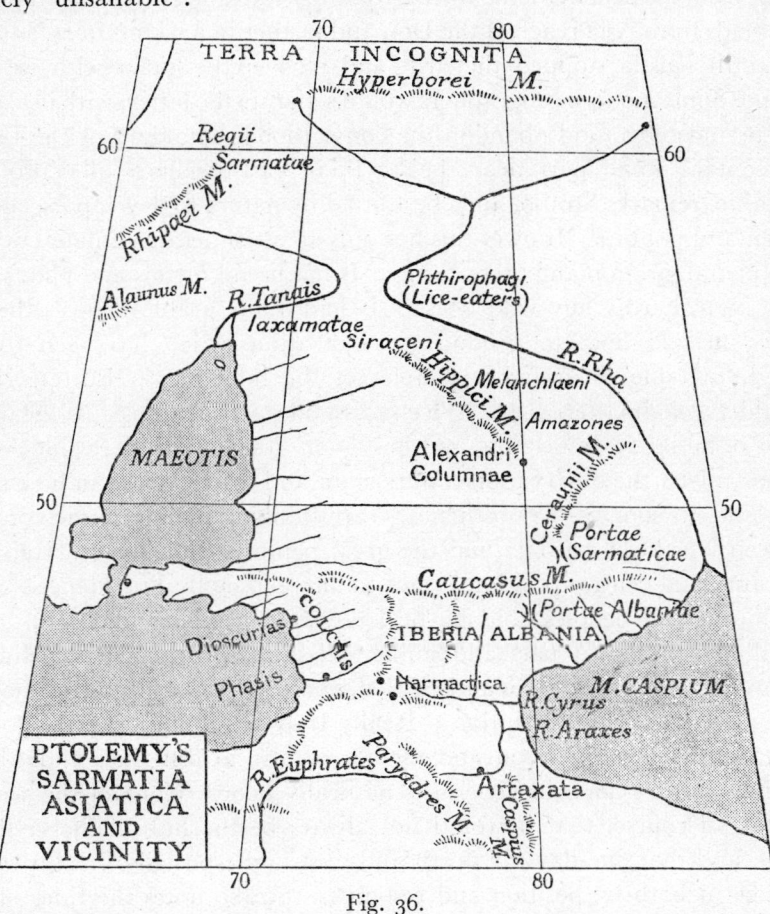

Fig. 36.

To-day Europe has two boundary lines, along the Caucasus and the Urals. The latter fade away towards the Caspian and have never been a serious obstacle to repeated invasions, while the very steppe and climate of Asia overlap far westwards; so it was for centuries the fate of Russia to be bullied by Tartar Khans and hardly to remember that she belonged to Europe at all (she had taken some steps towards civilization under Scandinavian leaders). The ancient writers had no clear knowledge of the

1 Dion. Per. 49: weeds, ibid. 659, 773 (Amazons), 31, 689.
2 Paus. I, 4, 1 (frozen, Frazer ad loc.): elk, IX, 21, 3, V, 12, 1 (cp. Caes. B.G. VI, 27, Plin. VIII, 39): bison, X, 13, 1–3. Sarm., ibid. I, 21, 5.

Urals anyhow, and it is excusable if they fumbled with the continental frontiers. After the old idea of the river Phasis, some still thought of the Caucasus isthmus, but nearly all chose the Don like Ptolemy.[1] They were not so very wrong: physically Europe is a mere peninsula projecting from the huge land-mass of Asia, to which nearly all Russia belongs by climate, being remote from the benefits of the warm Atlantic winds and currents, and plenty of nomads from Asia reached the Don and farther in ancient times, as often later until Russia stopped the drift and recovered contact with western Europe. Some modern geographers would separate the latter, with its varied climate and relief, and abandon the conventional boundary of the Urals.

Except a 'small part near the Scythian cart-dwellers' all Europe is habitable, remarks Strabo, and 'best fitted by nature to develop excellence in men and polities'. It owes this not only to a temperate climate but to a varied configuration and other things. It has useful metals and plants and cattle, with hardly any wild beasts. It had many arable plains—though Greece needed few—to produce a civilization which has been strong enough to tame the rougher peoples of the hilly parts. Europe is for Manilius 'maxima terra viris et fecundissima doctis artibus'. It is far the fairest of all lands, says Pliny, and has a very long coast-line, while Africa has few inlets (the observation is important and truer even than he knows, as he and his source—Eratosthenes?—are thinking mainly of the contrast between North Africa only and the great peninsulas opposite). Italy, by its beauty and central position, seems to him chosen by Providence to rule and mother all peoples, and he praises its fertile plains and sunny hills and shady forests. A poet adds minerals: so does Strabo, whose similar panegyric has been extravagantly called, in a very recent jargon, a 'masterpiece of geopolitical description'. Really Italy has to import a third of its grain, and is poor in wood and metals, as also in fisheries. Indeed the Mediterranean region in general is naturally poor.[2] None of the writers dreamt, of course, that it would not always be the hub of the civilized world, and that one day the north and west and especially Britain would far excel it both by position and resources. Strabo notes the tides of the nearest part of the Ocean, between Gibraltar and the Tagus, and how they scour the river-mouths and carry ships conveniently in. In fact, they were

[1] Mela, I, 8, II, 1, Plin. III, 3, Arr. *Peripl.* 19, Ovid, *ex Ponto*, IV, 10, 55, Manilius, IV, 677, Lucan, III, 273–6, IX, 411–19: see p. 59, n. 2. Isthmus, Ps.-Arist. *de Mundo*, 393 *b*, some ap. Dion. Per. 19–22. On Russia and Europe, C. Dawson, *Judgement of the Nations*, 1943, p. 143. Newbigin, *Frequented Ways*, 1922, pp. 13–15.

[2] P. 45, n. 1: G. East, *Med. Problems*, 1940, pp. 16–18. Italy, Plin. III, 39–41, XXXVII, 201–2: minerals, Virg. *Georg.* II, 165, Str. 286. Weigert, *Generals and Geographers: the Twilight of Geopolitics*, 1942, p. 81. On climate, cp. p. 109, n. 1. Coast-line, Plin. III, 5, cp. Africa, ibid. v, 1, Str. 130. Europe best, Str. 126, Manilius, IV, 686, and see p. 322, n. 4. Humboldt, *Cosmos*, 1864, I, 295–6, 482. Kendrew, *Climates of the Continents*[3], 1941, pp. 226–7.

THE GREAT DAYS OF THE ROMAN EMPIRE 255

to matter vastly more farther north, and most of all where they flowed up the gently graded British channels. But as yet these outer coasts lay in shadow, with an impassable waste of sea beyond. They were hardly included in the praises of Europe, though their climate, tempered by Ocean winds, was better for the energy of men, and they had other advantages. They are not so cold as they ought in theory to be, and the reason—quite unknown then, of course—is the Gulf Stream, which brings Mexican waters to warm Britain and even to keep open Norwegian harbours past the arctic circle; or rather perhaps we should thank the winds, which cause the northward drifts of water and carry rain and mild air in winter deep inland, as happens nowhere else in such high latitudes.

It will have been seen in some of the above maps that even familiar parts could still be surprisingly ill drawn, like the Italian boot, pulled badly eastwards. The western Mediterranean is much too wide in Strabo (and still in Ptolemy) with no idea of the African projection, and he narrows the eastern basin and puts Crete on a level with the south end of Greece.

Of merely local interest and uncertain date (not necessarily before the sack of Byzantium in the civil war of A.D. 196?) is a minute description of the old and famous sea-passage of the Bosporus: it is by one Dionysius of that city. A poet talks of the strait as made by Neptune's trident 'and', he prudently adds, 'the long work of time' (this in still another version of the old Argo story).[1]

A question of climate arises from certain ancient descriptions. Already before Gibbon some thought them, after due discount, enough to show that Europe was once distinctly colder and wetter, and they ascribed this (quite wrongly) to the amount of forest then uncleared. Recently some have argued that within ancient times there were fluctuations of rainfall so considerable as to be a major cause of events like early migrations and even the decline of the Roman Empire. This last suggestion has been firmly denied, and the whole matter seems still very dubious.[2]

[1] Val. Flaccus, II, 617: see p. 156, n. 1. A list of Black Sea rivers, Ovid, *ex Ponto*, IV, 10, 45–64 (so sea less salt). Dionysius in *G.G.M.* II, i–xv, 1–101. Ed. Güngerich, 1927. Berger, *R.E.* v, p. 971. Greece itself distorted, Str. 92. Tides, Str. 140, 142–3, 151. Mackinder, *Britain and British Seas*[2], 1915, pp. 35–41, 168–70: Fairgrieve, *Geography and World Power*[7], 1932, p. 162: H. J. Randall, *History in the Open Air*, 1936, p. 26: L. D. Stamp, *The World*[8], 1935, pp. 204, 211: A. A. Miller, *Climatology*[3], 1944, p. 46.

[2] Denied, by N. H. Baynes in *J.R.S.* 1943, p. 30, against E. Huntington: in general H.'s *Civ. and Climate*, 1915, pp. 225–32, *Pulse of Asia*[2], 1919, pp. 369–70, *Human Habitat*, 1928, pp. 149–55, etc., partly supported by C. E. P. Brooks, *Climate through the Ages*, 1926, and in *Enc. Brit.*[14], s.v. Climatic History. David Hume's essay *Of the Populousness of Ancient Nations* (1741). Syria may have declined from neglect rather than decrease of rain, H. C. Butler in *G.R.* Feb. 1920: East, *Hist. Geogr. of Europe*, 1935, pp. 193–4. R. de C. Ward, *Climate*[2], 1918, ch. 11 (no appreciable change in E. Med., says Eginitis, ibid. p. 349). Miller, op. cit. pp. 288–9. Carr-Saunders, *Population Problem*, 1922, pp. 301–3 (doubts Huntington). J. W. Gregory, *G.J.* 1916, I, 321–45 (Cyrenaica much as now).

CHAPTER IX

THE SAME: AFRICA

THE little 'Africa' (roughly Tunisia) was one of the most thickly populated provinces, with plenty of towns old and new, the restored Carthage being soon the biggest of them all and the second in the western half of the Empire. There were many Libyan clans allowed their own headmen under the eye of special prefects: Pliny counts twenty-six such 'nationes' and Ptolemy names thirty-nine. In general 'Africa' prospered. Its cultivation was helped by reservoirs and aqueducts, wherever water was scarce, and, with the nearer and richer part of Numidia, it supplied a third or more of the bread which left the rabble of Rome 'free for races and shows'. Olive-oil, figs, and dates were produced, and vineyards spread until checked by a protectionist decree in favour of home wines.[1] Among the exports were salted tunny and fish-sauce, sponges, a purple dye, a fine marble, hides from the nomads, and citrus-wood, favoured for expensive tables, from the mountains of the hinterland, and wild beasts for the arena. The defence was not very hard, being mainly designed to keep out the untamed nomads in and beyond the Aurès: the military command was early detached from the proconsul and finally became a separate province of 'Numidia'. A single legion was enough, except once when an able chief disciplined his tribe and attracted help from both Mauri and Garamantes (A.D. 20–23, the campaigns are described with little detail of topography). Under Trajan the headquarters were moved west to Timgad, a show-place to-day with its forest of broken columns, and presently to Lambaesis, commanding the northern slopes of the range and the mouth of the long flanking defile by which the railway now winds steeply down to Biskra and the desert. Gradually roads and posts were pushed down this way to the sheer southern face of the mountain-wall and the last oases near the Jedi and the salt lagoons.[2] Only here in all

---

[1] Suet. *Dom.* 17. Corn, Josephus, *B.J.* II, 16, 4: Juv. VIII, 118: Tac. *Ann.* XII, 43. Nationes, etc., Plin. V, 29–30. Trade, see p. 181, n. 2. Albertini, *C.A.H.* XI, 481–90. Syme, ibid. X, 346–7, XI, 145–50. Citrus, Plin. XIII, 91–3: marble, XXXVI, 49.

[2] *C.A.H.* XII, 86. On frontiers, Gsell, *Hist. d'Algérie*, 1929, pp. 22–5: Windberg, *R.E.* Numidia, 1937. Campaigns with Musulamii, Tac. *Ann.* II, 52, III, 20, 73, IV, 23–5: *C.A.H.* X, 643: Cagnat, *L'Armée rom. d'Afrique*², 1912, I, 9–24. Road to open up Saltus Aurasius, *C.I.L.* VIII, 10230, 2728: Bryant, *Reign of Ant. Pius*, 1895, p. 70. Sherwin-White, 'Geogr. Factors in Roman Algeria', *J.R.S.* 1944, pp. 1–10. A. M. Scott, *Barbary*, 1921, pp. 85–97.

THE SAME: AFRICA

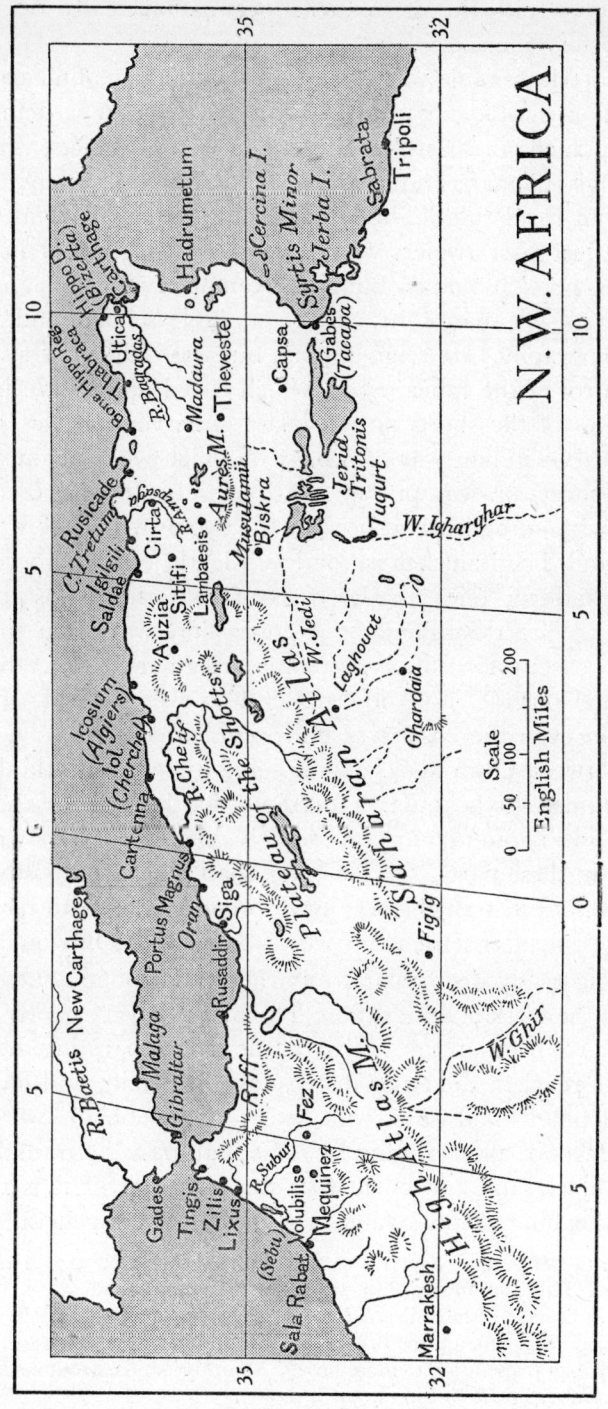

Fig. 37.

the Atlas region did the permanent occupation really open up the mountains to the Sahara.

The whole of Mauretania was given to Juba II in lieu of the eastern part of his Numidian heritage (25 B.C.). Scattered Roman settlements were early planted, chiefly in coast-places east and west of Algiers, with outliers as far as Tingis (Tangier) and a few miles beyond, where they were 'exempted from royal rule'. The king had his rather artificial capital at Iol-Caesarea, just past Algiers which was later to grow at its expense, and a 'spacious port' at Saldae (Bougie). Roman in education and married to a daughter of Cleopatra, he was an amiable scholar and writer on history and geography. He reigned long, but was disliked as a vassal and had little control of the inner tribes, which roved for pasture in the forbidding plateau of the shotts or salt-lakes. Intervention was sometimes needed, as in a Gaetulian war of A.D. 5, of which we hear only vaguely. His son and successor was put to death in A.D. 40 and the kingdom annexed, not without fighting: it became the two provinces of Mauretania, Caesariensis and Tingitana (more or less Algeria and Morocco).[1] New colonies were added, one at Algiers itself, but there was little town development or direct Romanizing even a short way from the Tell or coast region: except for supplying some irregular troops, the steppes really remained outside, and no frontier was ever defined. In the far western section even the coast was not occupied continuously, the communication between Oran and Tangier being by sea. Thus the Riff tribes were left untamed to be often a nuisance locally and to the Spanish province opposite: some of several vaguely mentioned wars with Mauri seem to refer to these parts. On the outer coast the last outpost was about Rabat, and behind it, though there were broad valleys with rivers fed by the Atlas snows, the last settlements were about Fez.[2] Only one general is named as going really deep inland anywhere hereabouts, Suetonius, the same who did the work of annexation. The march is very poorly reported, but seems to have been up the Mulwiya, the river separating the two new provinces. He reached the Atlas in ten days, it is said, and found dense forests with elephants and other wild beasts (the elephants were soon to disappear). Beyond, after crossing by some high pass, he tramped over a hot desert of black sand and burnt rock to a river Ger. This is a form of a native name meaning simply 'water-course', but is here generally taken as

[1] Plin. v, 11: *C.A.H.* x, 660. Gaetulicus, Dio, LV, 28. *C.A.H.* x, 347. Tingis already, Str. 827, Iol, etc., ibid. 831: towns, Plin. v, 19–21. Mommsen, v, 645.

[2] Plin. v, 5. Nuisance, Calpurnius, *Ecl.* IV, 40: *C.I.L.* II, 1120, 2015. Wars, *Vita Hadr.* 5, 12: *Vita Pii*, 5, 4, Paus. VIII, 43 (see Bryant, op. cit. p. 73): *Vita Marci*, 21–2. Also *C.I.L.* III, 5212: Eph. v, 1043 (expedition to mountains). Mauri brigands, Fronto, *ad Ant. P.* 3, 8. For the frontier, Fabricius, *R.E. Limes*, 1926, p. 667.

meaning the Wadi Ghir, which runs south-east into the Sahara.¹ The raid was presumably to punish some desert tribe for helping the rebels; anyhow it sounds impressive, and the original memoir is a regrettable loss. (Near-by is the gorge of the Zis, where the Foreign Legion was opening a way only in 1931, and we hear of 'valleys of black glittering shale with hills that might have been made of coal'.)

The ancients never had any single name for the whole great block of land between sea and desert, which we call Barbary and the Arabs call the Maghreb or Island of the West. Really it belongs to Europe, though twice torn from it for long periods, by the Phoenicians and Arabs. Under the Romans it faced towards the inner sea, and their desert outposts were the southern frontier of Europe.

The general descriptions are surprisingly poor, considering the opportunities. Strabo's chapter is hurried and not good for the time of writing, even if a reference to the death of Juba II (about A.D. 23) may be an interpolation. He draws mainly on matter which belongs to the previous period, and it has been considered already in that connection. He is alone in extending the name Atlas all along in the modern way, all others confining it to the highest parts near the western coast and having various special names elsewhere, more or less 'unpronounceable except for native tongues'. Mela is very poor, and even omits the recent occupation of the two Moorish provinces; he has some obsolete stuff, as on the Triton river and lake, and strangely misplaces the river Mulucha (to east of Oran). Pliny gives in his curt way some valuable details of towns and colonies, but, except for the notice of the Ger campaign cited above, he is bad on the whole hinterland, like Mela. There is vague hearsay of mountains and deserts, and worse still are the echoes of old rumours of swarming beasts and monstrous peoples. Such is *tota Gaetulia ad flumen Nigrim*—of this river more presently—and it is doubtful if he has any clear notion of what he is talking about, though that people, *natio frequens multiplexque Gaetuli*, seems in him and others fairly well distinguished from negro peoples to the south, with whom it sometimes mixed to form 'Black Gaetulians'. A poet has a curious catalogue of African tribes; so has another, wrongly adding to Juba I the kingdom of Juba II, and he gives an impressionistic sketch of the country. Dionysius is brief and negligible. Ptolemy has plenty of names, but leaves us wondering, as often, what his data were and how much he mishandled them. His mountain ranges bear little relation to

---

1 Plin. v, 14–15, Dio, LX, 9. So Vivien de St Martin, *Nord de l'Afrique dans l'Ant.* 1863, pp. 106–8: Tissot, *Géogr. comparée de l'Afrique rom.* 1884–8: Mommsen: Cagnat, op. cit. p. 30: Gsell, *Hérodote*, 1916, p. 213. Pass 4–5° long. west, St Martin, or 8–9°, Ball, cited by Ruge, *R.E.* Atlas, II, 2118: to Zis, O'Connor, *Nat. Geogr. Mag.* 1932, p. 281. Zis, S. Sitwell, *Mauretania*, 1940, pp. 128, 169. Elephants, Plin. VIII, 2, Aelian, IV, 10, etc.

the facts. He shockingly misconceives the run of the whole north coast. The proportion of the two Mauretanias is much better than before, but the length covers 5° and 15° (instead of 3° and 8°). Strange to say, the old

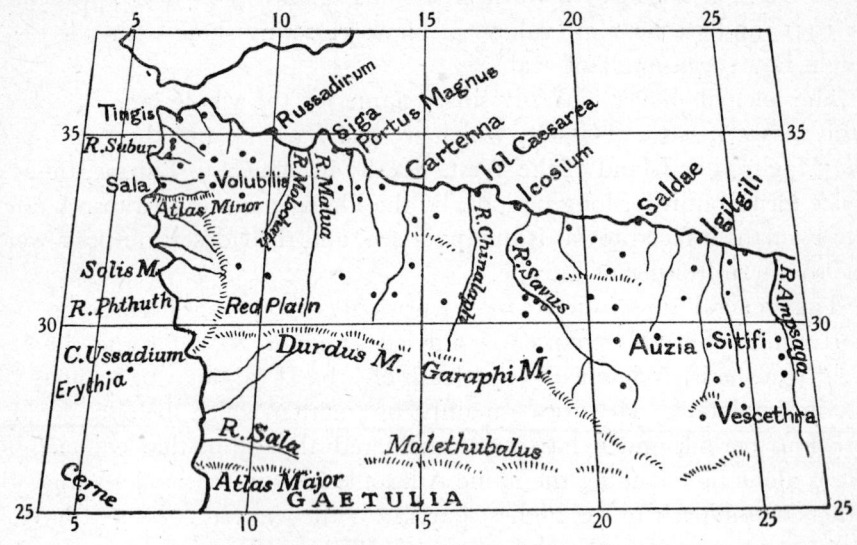

Fig. 38. Ptolemy: N. W. Africa (*a*).

'Africa' is worst of all. The projection, long obstinately underestimated, is flattened almost to nothing, so that Carthage is only 1° north of the latitude of Alexandria and the Syrtis becomes a small inlet. Inland he

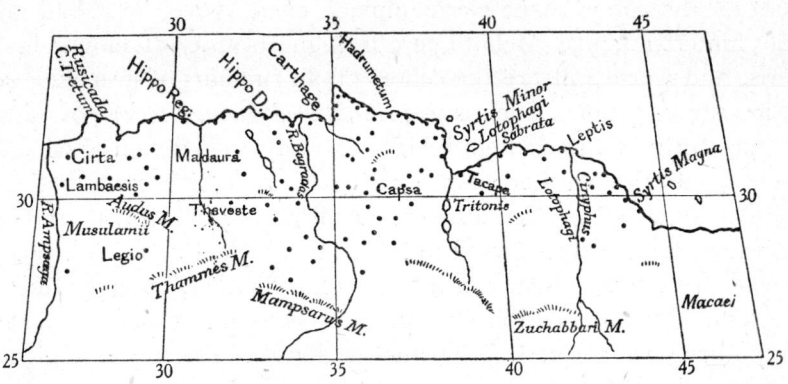

Fig. 39. Ptolemy: N. W. Africa (*b*).

makes a dreadful mess. The river Bagradas is lengthened out of all reason and wrong in direction, while the lakes which should lie well south of its source are put westwards and strung out along the old and half-fabulous river Triton. He misplaces the camp-towns and the Aurès frontier, and his queer drawing opens an artificial gap (between Capsa and Theveste), which he fills with dubious names.[1] The whole coast from the straits to the Little Syrtis is stretched over 33° instead of 16°, and any allowance for his faulty degrees still leaves a wild exaggeration. It is odd that the ancient attempt to map the Atlas region was throughout so very unhappy.

On the outer coast hardly anything is said that is recognizably both new and accurate. There is no explicit mention of Roman trading or exploring beyond the few Moroccan stations. If these places had good information or hearsay, it does not seem to reach the writers or is hopelessly muddled with old reports and fables (anyone who wants a bad headache should compare the lists of names). Pliny cites some rivers and distances to bold mountains overhanging the sea, presumably the High Atlas, and he adds some rubbish about 'the most legendary mountains of Africa', the peak rising from the desert in Herodotus, and the Pans or Satyrs whose flutes and cymbals Hanno is supposed to have heard hereabouts. Mela too has little but such echoes. Strange things are made of Cerne, and the hairy women become 'Gorgons', breeding without males. There are thrown in gardens or islands of the Hesperides and the isle of the 'red' sunset Erytheia, which figures still in Ptolemy.[2] He draws the coast south, or slightly south-east, and so quite misconceives the shape and size of Morocco. He has a Lesser and a Greater Atlas well apart, with a range Durdus (Durnus?) between, which suggests the native name previously reproduced as Dyrin: the Greater, though placed so far south, may be the High rather than the Anti-Atlas, while his Lesser, put close beyond Rabat, does not really exist. On the distant parts he seems guilty of every sort of mess, both from his faulty gradation and because he does not really know what to make of Hanno or of anything told since, mostly dubious hearsay (Fig. 44). His Daradus is only the Draa, some believe, and the sharp cape beyond is only Juby, misplaced vastly too far south, as are the Canary Islands opposite. Others think of the Senegal and Cape Verde, though in that case the Islands should not be opposite. He puts Western Horn and the Chariot of the Gods in the region of 10–5° north, which agrees

---

1 Berthelot, *L'Afr. sahar. et soudanaise: ce qu'en ont connu les Anciens*, 1927, p. 340 (on Ptolemy, pp. 299–413, Mela, ibid. 251–5, Pliny, ibid. 261–95). Dion. Per. 185–203. Poet, Silius, III, 231–324: on his sources J. Nicol, 1936 (much from Varro): another, Lucan, IV, 668–96 and sketch, 420–30. Mela, I, 20–37, from Varro or Nepos, Gsell, *Hist. de l'Afrique du Nord*, 1927, V, 22–3: on Mulucha, ibid. 2–4 (see p. 183, n. 2). For Strabo, see pp. 182–3. Atlas, Str. 826.

2 Plin. V, 5–10, VI, 199–205 (much from Agrippa, not Polybius, see p. 184, n. 1). Mela, I, 22–8, III, 93–9. Columbus thought of Gorgon Islands off C. Verde, and Hesperides in W. Indies!, Elton, *Career of Columbus*, 1892, p. 78.

surprisingly well with modern placings. He ends with a 'western gulf' (with Fish-eaters and western Ethiopians) and then 'unknown land', after his manner elsewhere. Most, however, assumed that the Ocean continued round Africa, and some supported this with garbled versions of actual voyages, those of Eudoxus and of Hanno, who is once very carelessly said (by Pliny) to have sailed on 'to the borders of Arabia'.[1] Hanno's voyage had been too early for the globe geography, and later it was seldom thought out in that connection: none seems to have suggested that he could not enter the torrid zone, often described as uninhabitable. Not ancient is the Arab notion of seas here kept boiling by the sun; the Portuguese had it too, and thought that any Christian would turn black beyond Cape Nun (or Non), so called because there was no return.

About the Happy Isles fairly good reports, though with obscure figures, are cited from King Juba and one Statius Sebosus, who may be between him and Pliny (hardly of the end of the Republic as Bunbury supposed). There are five, including Canaria and another, 'misty and called after its perpetual snow', undoubtedly Teneriffe; the details are curious, big dogs and lizards, many birds and fruits, date-palms and tall trees, papyrus, honey, a mountain pool—the crater of Palma, some suppose—and traces of buildings. Ptolemy maps six, half with new names, and puts them too far out, drawing his prime meridian through four of them as the westernmost known land. He seems to use the same reports with various misunderstandings and corruptions of names, and not to include the westernmost outliers, Palma and Ferro. (The last, however, is usually taken as on his prime meridian.) Some locate in the same group certain islands which Juba is said to have 'discovered' and found useful for purple-dyeing (perhaps from a lichen growing there), but the reference is obscure, and others put them just off Morocco, while a few have thought of Madeira. Altogether the Romans did very little for the map hereabouts; it has been guessed that, if they had not controlled the Red Sea trade-route, they would have tried to get round Africa, but the enterprise sounds very unlike them.[2]

[1] Plin. II, 169–70. Mela, III, 90–6 from Nepos (on Hanno and Eudoxus). Draa, Burton, p. 105, Kiepert, Bunbury, II, 621 after St Martin, op. cit. pp. 425–61, *Hist. de la Géogr.* p. 208: Senegal, Berthelot, op. cit. p. 319, Migeod, *J. Afr. Soc.* 1915, pp. 414–22. Arab and Port. notions, Beazley, *Prince Henry the Navigator*, 1895, pp. 118, 172, 262. Kiepert finds the Senegal in the Stachir, Forbiger in the Nias.

[2] Guessed, H. A. L. Fisher, *Hist. of Europe*, I, 413. Off Morocco, Gsell, op. cit. VIII, 256 after Vidal de la Blache: Aly, *Hermes*, 1927, p. 344. Canaries, Bunbury, II, 175, 203, after D'Anville. Madeira, Kiepert, Mommsen. Crater, thinks Bannerman, *Canary Islands*, 1922, p. 5. Plin. VI, 202–5. Sebosus, Klotz, *Quaest. Plin. Geogr.* 1906, pp. 85, 144 and *R.E.* Sebosus (cp. Bunbury, II, 172). Mela, III, 102 is vague. C. T. Fischer, *R.E.* Fort. Insulae VII, 42–3 (1912) after Curt Müller, 1902.

Such was the scanty gain of geography from the Atlas provinces. From Cyrenaica, with utter desert close behind, little could be expected. A general of Augustus had to chastise the Marmaridae (about Tobruk), and in A.D. 86 one Flaccus crushed the Nasamones for revolting against tribute; this people had an ill fame as plundering the wrecks stranded in the Syrtis.[1] The writers have plenty of old matter to borrow, if little fresh to add. Strabo at least saw the 'table-like plain' of Cyrene from the sea. We hear of three campaigns against locusts every year. A poet places the oracle of Ammon too far west and south, and describes an old march along the

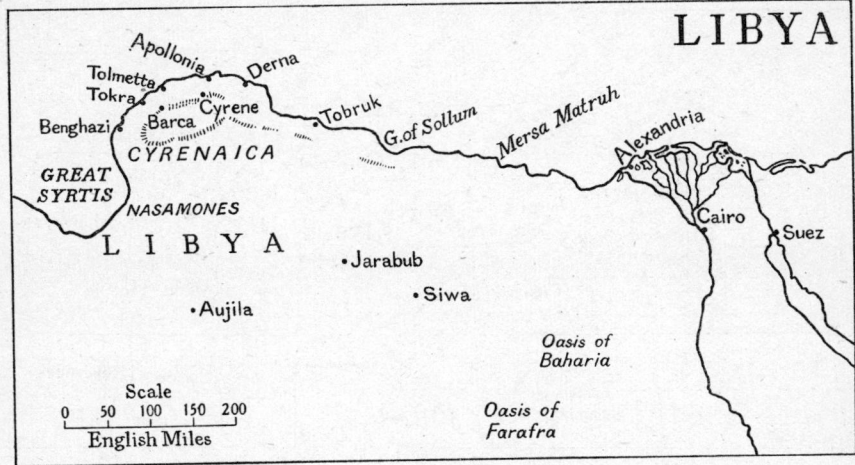

Fig. 40.

dismal coast with its shoals and fierce sandstorms and a host of snakes, real and fabulous. Against these last he summons the local Psylli with their strange powers, and such snake-charmers were called in to suck the poison from Cleopatra's wound. Pliny has confusions on the two Syrtes and the fabulous Lake Tritonis, which others also place in this western region. Odd things are said of the silphium: the nomads had spitefully destroyed the roots, and the Romans had used it as fuel to reduce the supply and raise the price, so that it was extremely rare already in Nero's time. The silphium district is said to be a long narrow strip, and Ptolemy still maps one but mislays it far inland beside a 'wild-beast country', a relic of the one in Herodotus. His coast outline is not too well

---

1 Curtius, IV, 7, 20, Lucan, IX, 441–4, Silius, III, 320 (who have Tritonis lake hereabouts, cp. Dion. Per. 266: see p. 68, n. 2), Flaccus, Dion. Per. 208–10, Zonaras, XI, 19, vaguely Statius, *Silvae*, IV, 8, 12: *C.A.H.* XI, 25: Cagnat, op. cit. p. 41: Gsell, *L'Emp. Domitien*, 1894, p. 234. M. fought by Quirinius, Florus, II, 31 (IV, 41), *C.A.H.* X, 347. Mela, I, 27–42. On Cyr. Romanelli in *C.A.H.* XI, 667–74.

drawn, and the tribes are often queerly placed, while some desert lakes and rivers are imaginary fillings of blanks. (He uses 'Libya' in a very narrow sense for the coast just west of Egypt, but his 'inland Libya' stretches almost across the continent.) In general the accounts of the hinterland are a copy of the old series of oases from Ammon westwards with various garblings and misplacings like Pliny's of Augila.[1]

It was from an unpromising part of the coast that some real pioneering was done. This was the strip of Tripolis attached to 'Africa', three towns,

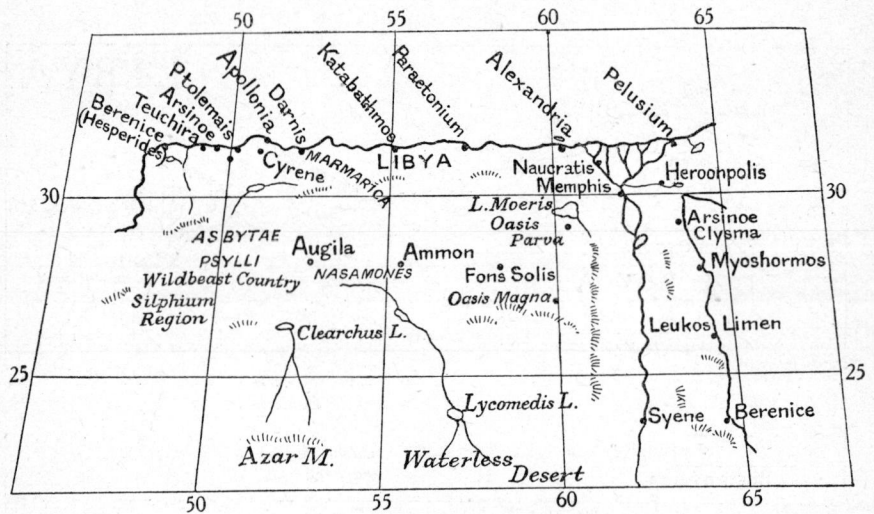

Fig. 41. Ptolemy's Cyrenaica-Egypt.

as the name means, and an arid plain back to a better plateau with some ravines and water. Far behind were the Garamantes in the oases of Fezzan, whose name appears already as Phazania. A proconsul Balbus in 19 B.C. made remarkably deep inroads. One was to Cidamus (Ghadames), where a small garrison was long maintained. Another was over long burnt-looking Black Mountains and then desert to Garama itself, which is Jerma near the present chief place Murzuk; the distance was 25 days in all on this detour, apparently by Sokna. He showed at his triumph images of some thirty towns, tribes, rivers, and ranges hitherto unknown (a few names seem identified as far as Rapsa, which is Ghat). Strabo is badly out

---

[1] Str. 791 (Ammon), 799, 813–14, 822: Plin. v, 45: Mela, 1, 23, 43–7 is bad. Silphium, Str. 837, 839, Plin. v, 33, XIX, 38–9, XXII, 10, cp. Arr. III, 28, 7. In general, Str. 835–9, Plin. v, 28–9, 31–4. Poet, Lucan, IX, 303–18, 431–62 (and Ammon, ibid. 511–30): see also p. 181, n. 2, p. 90, n. 1. Cleopatra, Suet. *Aug.* 17: Dio, LI, 14. Locusts, Plin. XI, 105. 'Libya', Ptol. IV, 5, 26, 31. Steier, *R.E.* Silphion, 1927 (not yet definitely identified): Melin in *Libia*, I, 8–13, 1937 (does it still exist?).

of date by not knowing of this expedition, and like others he uses 'Garamantes' in a vaguely large way.¹ There are no details of another campaign under Augustus against the same people. These punishments did not prevent them helping a bold nomad chief on the Aurès frontier or raiding down to the three ports. Once when they had been chased back from

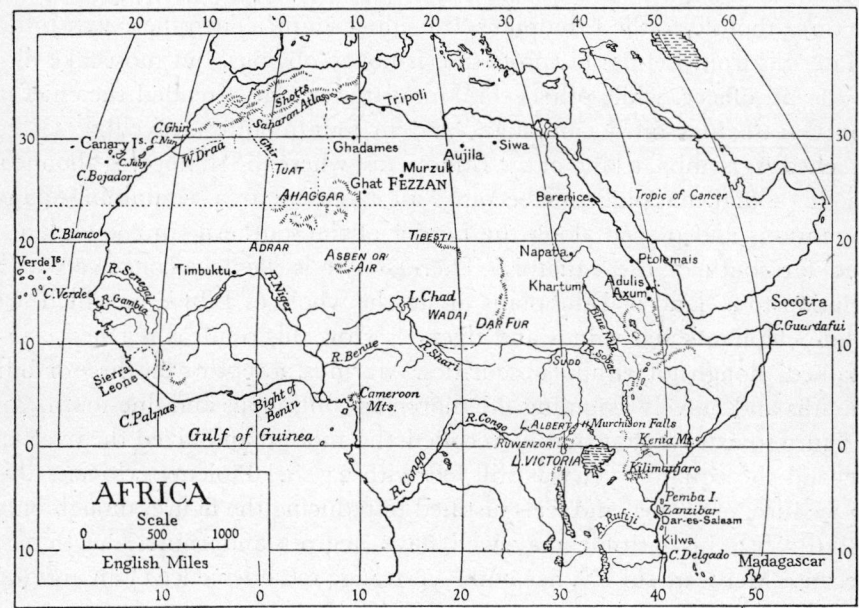

Fig. 42.

Leptis, blocking the water-holes behind them, a new route was opened: this was shorter by four days, and presumably the direct one over the 'red plateau'. Ptolemy, after Marinus, has striking things to say. He knows of routes of 30 and 20 days, perhaps the same as those indicated, though he somehow places Garama 8° too far south.² He adds a tantalizingly brief notice of two men who had explored a long way beyond. Their relations with the native kingdom are not clear, and there is no word of their

1 Str. 835, Livy, XXIX, 33, Virg. *Aen.* VI, 794 (and *Ecl.* VIII, 45 extremi G.). Balbus, Plin. v, 35–7 (copied by Solinus, 29): *C.A.H.* x, 346 curtly (as 'spectacular'). Names, Dessau, *R.E.* VII, 751–2, citing Barth, Duveyrier and Tissot: F. R. Rodd, *People of the Veil*, 1926, p. 323: Bovill, *Caravans of the Old Sahara*, 1935, p. 18: garrison, ibid. Piccioli, *Magic Gate of the Sahara*, 1935, p. 287. On Tripolitania, Cagnat, *En Pays romain*, 1927, pp. 255–82. Garamantes often in poets, Lucan, IV, 334, Silius III, 103, etc. On modern roads, Casserley, *Tripolitania*, 1943, who refers to Balbus, p. 90, but not to Ptolemy's travellers.

2 Ptol. I, 10, 2: on routes, Gsell, *Hérodote*, p. 149. Opened in war of A.D. 70, Tac. *Hist.* IV, 50, cp. Plin. v, 38. Nomads, Tac. *Ann.* III, 73, IV, 23, 26. Campaign of Quirinius, Florus, loc. cit., Romanelli, *La Cirenaica Romana*, 1943, pp. 76–9.

difficulties except a hint of forced marches between wells: it is not said that camels were used, but they were now available hereabouts, as many had been among the spoils of Juba I when beaten by Caesar. Septimius Flaccus, who 'took the field' from the province, was evidently an officer, and perhaps, many infer, the same legate who cut up the Nasamones, though this may well be doubted, as it is by Gsell. Anyhow, he 'went from the Garamantes in three months to the Ethiopians, travelling south'. Then there was Julius Maternus from Leptis: his profession is not so obvious, but most take him too as an officer, while others think of a trader. He attended the chief of the Garamantes on a campaign, and in four months, travelling south, reached Agisymba, a land of the Ethiopians, where the rhinoceros abounds. In the actual mapping this becomes an extensive area, containing many mountains and placed along the border of the southern 'unknown land' and far south of the equator.[1] There too it is vaguely conceived with relation to a 'land of Ethiopians along the whole of Libya, in which are white elephants and rhinos and tigers'! How this result is reached is explained, though not without obscurities. Marinus, accepting the three or four months and naïvely assuming the march as continuous and due south, got a figure so extravagant that he recoiled and more than halved the overlap beyond the equator, yet was still left with 24° S.! Ptolemy criticizes this procedure, of course, and feels justified in reducing the figure, though only to $16\frac{1}{4}$° S.: this latitude may well have negroes and rhinos, he thinks, because Meroe at $16\frac{1}{4}$° N. has both—a strange recrudescence of an antique kind of argument from symmetry.[2] It is clear that such manipulations deserve no respect, and that the point reached must have been well short of the equator. The route has been variously identified. St Martin, after the explorer Duveyrier, traced it south-west to the oasis of Asben or Air in the heart of the great desert, and this is now confidently supported by Windberg; yet it seems an unlikely place for the animals concerned. Most go south to the region of Lake Chad or somewhere between it and the Niger, at about 14° N., while Berthelot carries on a little farther to the Benue. Some who think of the Chad plain include Wadai east of it to provide the required mountains. Two recent writers on the Sahara make the route south-east to Tibesti, to which Arabs and Turks were to penetrate; the time taken is not too great in certain conditions, and a Barditus range

---

1 IV, 9, 5 (white elephants, ibid. 4): notice of the two Romans in I, 8, 5–6, wells, I, 10, 2. Legate, Cagnat, *L'Armée rom. d'Afrique*, p. 42, Berger, p. 588, Kubitschek, *R.E.* x, 2059, but cp. Gsell, *L'Emp. Domitien*, p. 237. Trader, Norden, *Urgesch. in Tac. Germ.* 1923, p. 440: *C.A.H.* XI, 145: but officer, Cagnat, loc. cit., Albertini, *L'Empire rom.* 1929, p. 114 (probably to Sudan). Camels, *Bell. Afr.* 68: Bovill, op. cit. p. 21. At least Maternus to Sudan, Dessau, loc. cit. Fezzan probably occupied by then, Rodd, loc. cit.

2 I, 9, 8–10. Halved, I, 8, 3, I, 14, 6: Bunbury, II, 524: Berger, p. 600.

THE SAME: AFRICA 267

is found in a modern Bardai.[1] Probably there, too, were the people raided by the Garamantes of Herodotus. Perhaps ancient Sultans of Fezzan, like modern, pushed their slaving expeditions not only that way but south towards Chad. (Columbus, by the way, thought of the Cape of Good Hope as 'in Agesimba'!) It remains obscure what interest the two Romans had in straying so very far afield. If one at least was an officer of rank, the suggestion that he brought troops on such a wild-goose chase seems absurd. Nor are these alluring routes for a trader. Perhaps both were envoys or attachés, men of the adventurous frontier-officer type, accompanying the chief to satisfy an exploring curiosity unusual in their countrymen. If either really crossed the great desert, it is astonishing that Ptolemy should dismiss the feat in a few lines and have the queer notions about to be mentioned on Saharan rivers. Yet it is hard to deny that through friendly relations with the desert people there did come some hearsay, if not direct knowledge, of the fertile Sudan beyond.

An old theory was revived in a new form by Juba: it may be sketched as in Fig. 43, very roughly and with all sorts of reserves on directions and distances. A lake in his own kingdom of Mauretania has crocodiles and fish like the Nile's: so the Nile must rise there, not far from the Ocean. Then it passes underground 'some days' to emerge in a second lake, and again under the desert for 20 days (directions are not given). It wells up in a third lake as the Nigris—*fonte illo quem nigrum* (read *Nigrim*) *vocavere*— and now flows east, with creatures and plants and a flood like the Nile's and with fertile land and forests and wild beasts on the south side; at last it turns sharply north to become the Nile itself. So Pliny; Mela has another name, Nuchul, and there are others still more obscure in the queer version of Vitruvius. Strabo already has something similar, without naming Juba as the author, and he cites a vague notion of underground stretches from Posidonius, to whom some would therefore trace the theory.[2] What suggested the strange upper course between a series of lakes? The Jedi,

[1] Rodd, op. cit. pp. 322–7 ('punitive expeditions'): Bovill, op. cit. p. 19. Berthelot, op. cit. p. 408. Chad or near, Kiepert, *Lehrbuch*, 1878, pp. 11, 223 (at most 12° N.), Bunbury, Norden: *C.A.H.* loc. cit.: not S. of Chad-Wadai, Tomaschek, *R.E.* Agisymba, 1894 (after A. Roscher and Kiepert): Kanem or Bornu, Sir H. H. Johnston, *Colonization of Africa*², 1913, p. 48. Asben, St Martin, op. cit. p. 219: Windberg, *R.E.* Niger, 1936 (who denies camels used). Cary-Warmington, p. 182 deny that Flaccus got through to the Sudan.

[2] Strenger, *Strabos Erdkunde von Libyen*, 1913, p. 70 and Honigmann, *R.E.* Libye, p. 162, from Pos. ap. Str. 275: Str. 826, 829. Juba ap. Plin. v, 51–3, 44, VIII, 77. Mela, I, 50, III, 96 (cp. Orosius, see p. 270, n. 2). Vitr. VIII, 2, 6–7 (Granger's notes absurdly make the lakes Albert and Victoria Nyanza). Also Paus. I, 33, 6 vaguely, Dio, LXXV, 13. Dion. Per. 215 has Nigretes but only a westward loop of the Nile, 222–3: but cp. Bunbury, II, 488. Nigritae, see p. 183, n. 1: Plin. v, 43: Mela, III, 103–5. Juba revives (with a patriotic twist) the theory of Promathos, Rehm, *R.E.* Nilschwelle: see p. 77, n. 2.

think some, which rises in the Saharan Atlas (though hardly near the outer sea) and ends in lagoons like the Shott Jerid. Was it supposed to be continued by the Igharghar, one of the wadis, mostly dry or with underground water, which ran far south into the Sahara? Windberg, after Duveyrier, insists that a Moorish king must have known of this great water-course all the way to its source on the north slope of the Ahaggar (or Hoggar), in a lake which has crocodiles to-day, while another desert river (the Tafasasset), flowing from the opposite slope, is the supposed continuation from this lake Nigris (he does not believe that our present Niger has anything to do with the matter). Others think of the Ger, which Suetonius reached from

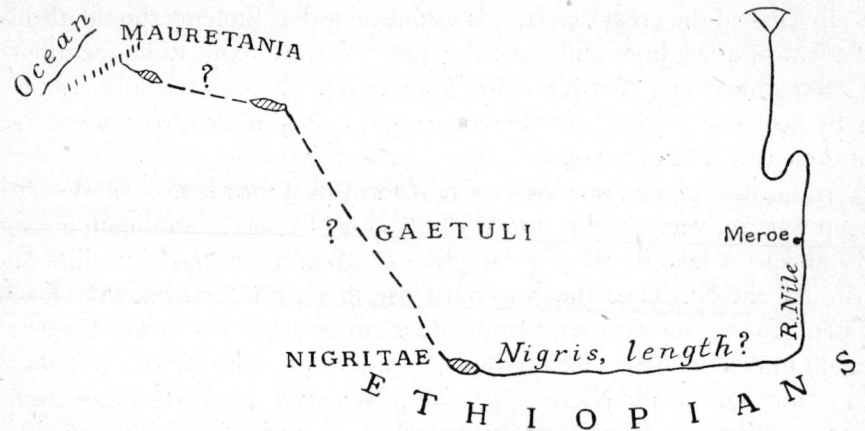

Fig. 43. Juba's Nile theory.

the High Atlas (p. 258), though it does not occur to Pliny to connect it with the theory now in question. (So Berthelot confidently finds the second lake in the Tuat, which is hardly in Mauretania.)[1] It seems that 'Nigris' like 'Ger' is a transcription of a native (n)gir meaning simply 'water' and liable to be applied to many rivers or wadis. Plainly the ancient writers have very little idea of the vast width of the desert, and some like Gautier argue that their 'Ethiopians' here were only people of negro affinities living within the Sahara itself. And yet there seems a hint of the fertile Sudan beyond it, not only above Egypt but also in the west. Thus possibly there was a vague rumour—brought by slaving caravans from Timbuctoo?—of the great southern river which moderns have chosen to call the Niger as an echo of this very theory.[2] The Arabs called it the Nile of the negroes, and the

[1] Berthelot, op. cit. pp. 254, 282. Same, Hennig, *Terrae Incognitae*, p. 104. Jedi, Gsell, *Hérodote*, pp. 214–24 and *Afrique du Nord*, VIII, 254 after St Martin. Jedi and Igharghar, Cary-Warmington, p. 183: Windberg, loc. cit.

[2] Berthelot, loc. cit. (too confidently) finds the third lake in the Niger at its Saharan elbow. Not improbably Niger, Cana, *Enc. Brit.* ed. 14, Niger: confused with an Atlas river, Kiepert, p. 11. Gautier cited in *Enc. Brit.* Sahara, which is vague on ancient knowledge.

fancy of a connection with the Nile was not finally abandoned till the journeys of Clapperton and his companions in 1822–30.

Quite different and still harder to explain is the notion of Ptolemy. He covers the desert with two sprawling inland river-systems, connected with each other only through a watershed range and not connected in any way with the Nile. (So in general, though in detail they are rather variously mapped from his peculiar wording.) Their names seem derived from the same native word for water already noticed. The western is the Nigeir; it rises in a lake near the Ocean but well south of the 'Greater Atlas', so

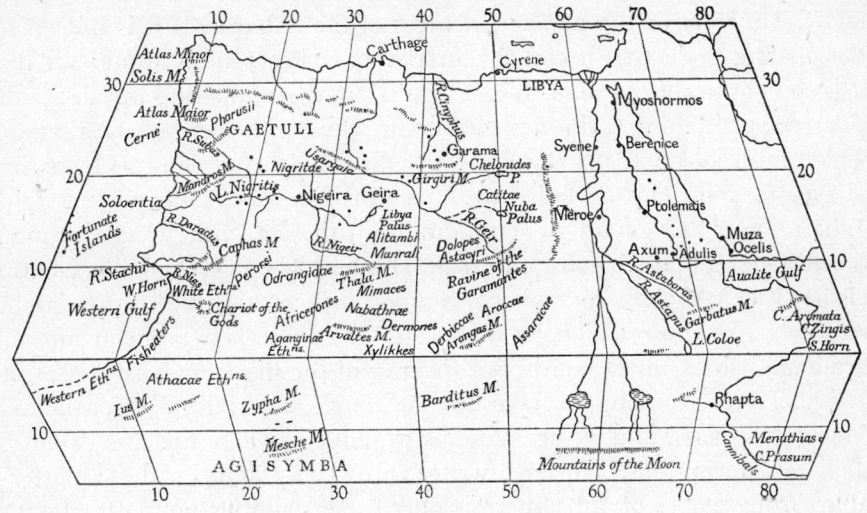

Fig. 44. Africa (Ptolemy).

that it has only a faint resemblance to either the Nigris or the Ger of previous writers. The eastern river is called the Geir; it has obviously nothing to do with the Ger, being placed far eastward and associated with the Garamantes. The watershed is conceived as far enough north to send a river (the exaggerated Bagradas) to the coast near Carthage, and the source-lake of the Nigeir is after all north of the Daradus. Many after St Martin take this to be only the Draa, and they conclude that the whole mapping rests on nothing better than reports of northern desert wadis.[1] Windberg explains the Geir as being the same as Juba's river from a lake Nigris in the Ahaggar, while the Nigeir is the Ger of Suetonius continued far south-east to the same range. But many since the Arabs have credited Ptolemy with some hearsay of our Niger. Berthelot finds Nigeira east of

[1] Bunbury, II, 618–25. Ptol. IV, 6, 8–14 (rivers, 13–14). Borchardt, *Pet. Mitt.* 1928, p. 28 makes Nigeir = Ger and Geir = Igharghar. Geir is both these on Kiepert's map, but Nigeir is our Niger.

Timbuctoo and the Libyan lake on the lower Niger, and he explains the Geir as a combination of rivers west and east of the Chad basin, which as yet contained no lake, he thinks. (There is a notion that Chad is a comparatively recent lake, because it is only slightly saline, but this fact can be explained differently.) Another finds Chad in Lake Nuba at the east end of the Geir system, north of the 'ravine of the Garamantes' and strangely near the Nile.[1] Another actually connects Nuba with the Nile as the sudd swamps of Lake No, where the Bahr el Ghazal comes in from the west. Such attempts at exact location carry very little conviction. But it seems hard to deny that at least something in all this business refers to the Sudan and not merely to the northern fringes of the Sahara. If it is indeed so, the placing in degrees becomes remarkably correct; many would say that it is too correct to be plausible. There is another desperate puzzle: if the rivers have anything to do with the Sudan, why does Ptolemy put Agisymba, which most locate about Chad, so very far from them? (But we have seen above, p. 266, why he failed to reduce the figures of Marinus enough.) Where too did he get all these mountains in the far south, none ever mentioned before, that we know of, except Hanno's Theon Ochema or Chariot of the Gods? Anyhow he makes a wonderful mess, and there are no rivers remotely like those which he draws, though there is a basin of internal drainage, Chad, in the south, far apart from the shotts or salt-lakes of the north. Here, as often, we have not the rough material on which he and Marinus worked, and we are at a loss to judge its value and the extent of their misconceptions. No later writer throws any light on these matters: apart from echoes of Juba there is only some sonorous nonsense about a river Gir thought to be the upper Nile and to flow past Garamantes and cave-dwelling hunters who have ivory and ebony.[2] In the end the Peutinger map draws south of the hills of Cyrene a queer lake Nusap and a 'marsh like the Maeotis (Azov) through which the Nile passes', also farther west flowing past Nasamones and Garamantes a river which 'quidam Grin [sic] vocant, alii Nilum appellant: dicitur enim sub terra Etyopum in Nilum ire lacum'.

There were other and far more promising lines of discovery, namely from Egypt, both by sea and land. Only now did Egypt reap the full advantage

---

[1] Hennig, op. cit. p. 348. Berthelot, op. cit. p. 336. J. Ball, *G.J.* LXX, 210 puts the 'Tortoise Marshes' (north of Nuba) at Kufra, with no river Geir, but he mistranslates, ibid. p. 512. Cana, *Enc. Brit.* ed. 14, Niger, thinks Geir possibly the Shari, and Nigeir unidentifiable: *Enc. Brit.* Africa, Ptol. had heard of our Niger. Lake No, Honigmann, *R.E.* Libye, pp. 158, 163 (and Nusap of Tab. Peut.): Nero's men not beyond this (p. 273, n. 1). Saline, Huntington, *Civ. and Climate*³, 1924, p. 327, but cp. Suggate, *Africa*², 1933, p. 105.

[2] Claudian, *Laud. Stil.* 1, 252 and *Idyll*, 4, 21 (*in Nilum*). Echoes, Oros. 1, 2, 29–31: Tab. Peut. drawn in Spruner-Menke, *Atlas Ant.* XXXI: see p. 362, n. 1.

of its position for transit trade: Alexandria, after declining under the last worthless Ptolemies, at once took its place as easily the greatest market of the Roman world. Egypt was important also as the chief granary of the hungry capital, and the Caesars therefore kept it tightly in their own hands. It was still a favourite goal of tourists, and we have a long and interesting chapter by Strabo, who travelled upstream with the prefect Aelius Gallus (27–25 B.C.). He gives a brilliant sketch of Alexandria with its broad streets and fine buildings, its renowned lighthouse, and the great harbour, with another on a lake behind receiving endless wares by canals from the Nile. He details the towns, all worshipping some animal without knowing why. He saw all the usual sights, as presently did the prince Germanicus, and he describes them well. (He happens to be the first to mention the famous statue which made a musical sound at dawn.) But little was understood of the history: so an obelisk was read as saying that a king had ruled as far as Bactria and India, which is all wrong. At Aswan Strabo saw the supposed bottomless fountains of the Nile—he unjustly accuses Herodotus of believing in them—and the celebrated well which was lit up by the tropical sun at the summer solstice.[1] An essay by Seneca *de situ et sacris Aegyptiorum* is lost, though we have his discussion of theories of the Nile flood. Pliny is too busy with lists of names to give much else. (What an *otiosa ac stulta ostentatio* are the Pyramids, and after all we are not sure of the very names of their builders!) His distances are often inaccurate. Ptolemy has curious errors in detail even about his native country, and his false gradation makes it much too short. It may be noted, as an echo of an old puzzle, that some still counted Egypt to Asia rather than to 'Libya' or Africa.[2] He himself pointedly rejects the Nile as a boundary, though even after him some continued to prefer it to the isthmus.

Upstream there was a good chance of exploring, and it was not quite neglected. The fighting needed was not very serious. An early prefect, Petronius (24–22 B.C.), did enough to warn off frontier raiding: he took some places, cut across the desert to avoid the river loop, and destroyed Napata, but did not push on to Meroe. Nothing was annexed now or later

1 Str. 785–819, 824: animals, 812–13, well, 817, 'abysses', 819: Alexandria, 791–4, market, 798, Ptolemies, 796–8. Germ. in A.D. 19, Tac. *Ann.* II, 59–61: obelisk, ibid. 60, Str. 816. On R. rule here, A. H. M. Jones in *Legacy of Egypt*, 1942, ch. XI. Statue, Str. 816, etc.: Mayor's note on Juv. xv, 5. Strabo on Egypt, J. Ball, *Egypt in the Classical Geographers*, 1942, pp. 53–70.

2 Mela, I, 20 and 49, Plin. V, 48, VI, 191 as cp. Str. 685, Ps.-Arist. *de Mundo*, 393 b, Dion. Per. 10–25: see p. 66, n. 1. Plin. V, 47–64 (on Nile, 51–8). Essay, Servius ad Virg. *Aen.* VI, 154. Pyramids, Plin. XXXVI, 75. Boundary, Ptol. II, 1, 6, IV, 5, 13: Nile or isthmus, Agathemerus, I, 3. Pliny on E., Ball, op. cit. pp. 72–84, who respects Ptolemy's work, ibid. pp. 101–30. For Plutarch on Eg. myths, Mahaffy, *Greek World under Roman Sway*, 1890, pp. 312–13.

except the stretch to short of Wadi Halfa. The Ethiopians actually encountered are described sometimes soberly as the lowly nomads they were, though old fables still cling to the name.[1] Nero was vaguely credited with plans of conquest here: it has been suggested that he thought rather of the Axum kingdom (in Abyssinia), which controlled the ivory trade, but this is very dubious.[2] A scouting party of his soldiers had gone up the river and found Meroe quite a small place and the country poor by nature and not entirely because the Romans made a desert and called it peace. Beyond they saw some herbage and forests and tracks of elephant and rhinoceros. They went much farther to immense swamps, choked with vegetation and impassable even for boats, and they saw apparently a big waterfall between two rocks. What this was is obscure: the Ripon Falls, somebody guesses, but these are broad and are mere rapids and much too far south, while the nearer Murchison Falls are narrow and impressive (some think of the Fola rapids below these). The rest plainly refers to the sudd or block of floating vegetation above the Sobat junction, about 9° N., never to be described again till reached by Egyptian troops in 1839 and penetrated by Samuel Baker in 1862 (the barrier of this great sponge was not really mastered till after 1900). Seneca alone mentions the final adventure, as heard personally from two of the scouts, and he has no hint of any motive other than discovery: he was Nero's minister and former tutor, and the men may have been sent at least partly because he had stirred in Nero an ambition to solve the old Nile problem. The swamps rather strangely confirm him in a wrong explanation of the flood already rejected by Aristotle, as welling up from underground lakes, supplied not from rain, he thinks, but by seepage from the sea. Otherwise the discussion, of which parts are missing, is largely after Posidonius. It was closely followed by his nephew Lucan, who dismisses the underground lakes, however. It is notable, too, that Lucan quite ignores any form of the alleged western Nile. He considers the view ascribed to Eudoxus that the river may come all the way from a south temperate zone and carry the winter rains of that zone (*aliena crescere bruma*). A new argument against snow is that it would melt in spring, not in summer, and could not cause so long a flood. Mela and Pliny give, beside the above report of Juba's, a bad summary of other theories, as if several were equally valid, even the damming of the current by winds. Yet eye-witnesses had long since proved that the flush came down the Blue Nile from heavy summer rains in the Ethiopian mountains: so Strabo knew, and for any other views

[1] As Mela, III, 85–8, Plin. v, 46, VI, 182, VII, 21: soberly, Str. 787, 819–23. Petronius, ibid. 820–1, Mon. Anc. 26 (ed. E. G. Hardy, pp. 123–5), Plin. VI, 181: *C.A.H.* x, 241–3: Budge, *Hist. of Ethiopia*, 1928, I, 59–60. Headless Blemmyes, Mela, I, 48, cp. 23.

[2] As J. G. C. Anderson says, *C.A.H.* x, 779, 880, against Schur, *Klio* Beiheft, 1923. Plans, Plin. VI, 181, Tac. *Ann.* xv, 36, Suet. *Nero*, 19, 35, Dio, LXIII, 8.

he refers us rather casually to two writers of his time (both now lost).[1] The knowledge of the rains still left plenty of doubts about the main stream, and at first there was little idea of its length, as the southern Ocean was 'generally thought' only some 600 miles beyond Meroe. Strabo takes his account from Eratosthenes. Pliny understands the 'island' of Meroe too literally (as does Ptolemy). He gives a jumble of many southern tribes from older writings, including the Deserters or Sembritae and an unknown 'caput eorum in insula Sembobitin' (various other places have some reality). The sun's heat, he thinks, may well nourish strange animals and peoples, including the Pygmies long since reported in the source-marshes; for Mela these are extinct, killed out by the warring cranes, and for Strabo a fable, while Ptolemy ignores them.[2] The latter's mapping is very remarkable, and how he came by it must be explained presently. The place-names may be compared with Pliny's, but he queerly misplaces the 'Sebridae' to the left bank, and the Soboridae seem a false doublet of them.

When Egypt was drawn into the Roman peace, its sea-trade increased greatly both in quantity and range: the most important was with India, but some went down the African coast, which became known well beyond previous limits. As before, the gulf of Suez was not apparently much used, or the Nile canal, despite a renovation by Trajan. Far more is heard of ports lower down, Myoshormos and Berenice, and the old desert roads from the Nile, which were now restored with cisterns and guard-stations.[3] The Red Sea had long been minutely known, but a new feature was a kingdom founded by Arab immigrants in Abyssinia: the capital was at Axum, a week inland from its port of Adulis, the chief market for ivory, tortoise-shell, and slaves. Some strange beasts also came from these parts, and the rhinoceros of the African species is correctly described as the 'Ethiopian bull' with two horns on his nose. The general run of the coast is still wrongly drawn as south to Adulis and then sharp east to the strait. The 'Cinnamon coast' beyond to the Cape of Perfumes (Guardafui) had

[1] Str. 790: rains, 786. Mela, I, 53–4: Plin. v, 55. Lucan, x, 188–331: Sen. *N.Q.* IV a, 2. Scouts, ibid. VI, 7, 2 and 8, 3–5: Plin. VI, 184–5, XII, 19. Ripon, Hennig, *T.I.* pp. 306–9. Fola, Budge, op. cit. p. 100: falls above 5°, Langenmaier, *Pet. Mitt.* 1916, pp. 10–12. Dessau, *Röm. Kaiserzeit*, 1930, II, 646 oddly treats the data of the scouts as hearsay. Sponge, E. Ludwig, *The Nile*, 1940, pp. 82–5. On Mela see p. 323, n. 1. Bruma, Lucan, x, 299: see p. 118, n. 1. Snow, (Pos. ap.) Sen. IV, 2, 21, Lucan, x, 219.

[2] Str. 821: Mela, III, 81, cp. Plin. VI, 187, x, 58–60. Island, Plin. v, 53, cp. Str. loc. cit. Tribes, Plin. VI, 178–97, VII, 31. 'Generally', ibid. 196. See p. 138, nn. 1–2. Ptol. IV, 7, 29, 33 (Nobbe): Fischer, *R.E.* Sebritae (1923). Pygmies also Ovid, *F.* VI, 176, Gell. IX, 4, 10, Athen. 390 b, and see p. 281, n. 3.

[3] Str. 815, Plin. VI, 102–3, 168: *C.I.L.* III, 6627 (Dessau, *Inscr. Lat. Sel.* 2483): *C.A.H.* x, 245: G. W. Murray, *J. Eg. Arch.* 1925, pp. 138–50. Ports, Str. 770. Canal, ibid. 805: Plin. VI, 165 is wrong (see p. 137, n. 1): 'Trajan's river', Ptol. IV, 5, 54. A voyage from Suez, Lucian, *Alex.* 44.

never been quite so thoroughly worked as now, and the Skipper of the Periplus can give many details of its little ports and their wares. Ptolemy has again a good idea of the distance, but misconceives the outline badly, with an exaggerated projection on the way (at Mosylon, as probably Pliny already).[1] The cassia and cinnamon of this place are mentioned elsewhere, in a materia medica.

Formerly the Cape of Perfumes had been barely passed, and it was assumed that the coast turned westwards just beyond. But the Skipper knows much farther: from Opone (Ras Hafun) for 12 days south and southwest are first a Rocky Coast and then a low one of 'Beaches', terms which the Arabs still use to-day; there follow 7 days of Azania with some rivers and roadsteads (the Benadir or port region), then two more south-southwest to a point off which—only 300 stades off—is a low wooded island Menuthias, with crocodiles and turtles. Two days on is the last mart of Azania, called Rhapta after its 'sewn' boats (such boats of planks bound with cords are a recurring motif in later accounts of Zanzibar and the Indian Ocean in general). Rhapta is said to be a great centre for ivory and tortoise-shell, and subject to a certain 'tyrant' of south Arabia, from whom it is rented by some of his merchants. Ptolemy is inconsistent about the island: he mentions it as 'lying near', while his figures mislay it far out and southward. Some have therefore thought wildly of Madagascar, but clearly enough the place is either Pemba or Zanzibar or perhaps a confusion of both ('low and wooded' seems rather to suit the first). Zanzibar has often been subject to Sultans of Muscat, and the first half of the name is the same as appears in Azania and in Ptolemy's cape Zingis, while the second half means 'sea'. Pliny talks of the 'Azanian sea', though he begins it too far north, including not only the island of Socotra but waters within the Red Sea.[2] Rhapta should be about opposite Menuthias or a little beyond. Thereafter the Skipper's information fails, and he supposes the coast to turn west, on the usual assumption of an Ocean surrounding the continent.

1 Plin. VI, 174. Adulis, ibid. 172, Periplus, 3. Roman luxury in tortoise-shell, Plin. IX, 12, 39. Rhino, Martial, *Spect.* 22: Paus. V, 12, 1, IX, 11, 2, as cp. Plin. VIII, 71, 74, Oppian, *Cyneg.* II, 553: giraffe, Paus. IX, 21, Plin. VIII, 69. Jennison, *Animals for Show and Pleasure in Anc. Rome*, 1937. M. medica of Dioscorides, I, 13–14. Huntingford, *Anthropos*, 1940–1, pp. 209–20 wildly puts Ptolemais and Adulis outside the strait.

2 Plin. VI, 172. Periplus, 15–18. Pemba, Ingrams, *Zanzibar*, 1931, *Arabia and the Isles*, 1942, p. 4: either or both, Bunbury, II, 553: either or Mafia, Coupland, *East Africa and its Invaders*, 1938, p. 17: P. or Mafia, Herrmann, *R.E.* Menuthias, 1931. Madagascar, Glaser, Vidal de la Blache, *Ann. Géogr.* 1894, p. 243, C. Peters, *Eldorado of the Ancients*, 1902, p. 312: Johnston, op. cit. p. 44 (in Ptolemy, but Z. in Periplus). Phebol in Ps.-Arist. *de Mundo*, 393 *b* is hardly Madagascar as Capelle, *Neue Jahrb.* 1905, p. 539: it is Socotra, Bolchert. *Arist. Erdkunde*, p. 93, or unknown, Grohmann, *R.E.* Phebol, 1938: see p. 138, n. 2. Sewn boats, Hakluyt, Everyman ed. III, 203, IV, 246, VII, 157: Prestage, *Portuguese Pioneers*, 1933, p. 257.

But he had done well: quite suddenly he had added a long stretch hitherto unknown, though most of this was only hearsay, it seems, from Arab merchants. The next writer, Marinus, as used by Ptolemy, can name four Greek skippers who had themselves sailed down so far or even beyond. One, Diogenes, had been blown south to near Cape Rhaptum in 25 days, another nearly the same distance in 20 days, which he translated extravagantly as 20,000 stades. A third, Dioscorus, went past Rhapta 'many days', or 5000 stades as he judged, along a land of cannibals to a cape Prasum (at best probably Delgado, 11° S.). From these data Marinus inferred a figure so enormous that he hastily halved the overlap past the equator and still reached 24° S., to square with his placing of Agisymba, the farthest point reached on the inland line (just how he worked is rather obscure).[1] Ptolemy makes his usual criticisms and arbitrary reductions, and gets a latitude nearly equal to his own placing of Agisymba at $16\frac{1}{4}$° S. Rhapta itself he puts at 7° S., which is remarkably near the truth. Such was the notion of this coast. Arab trade went so far here because it was blown up and down by handy monsoons, and already there is a hint of the odious slaving which was to run like a scarlet thread through the history of these parts.

The skipper Diogenes is strangely said to have been driven south 'to the lakes from which the Nile flows'. Presumably this means to some port where he heard of lakes from the Arabs trading up country for slaves and ivory: that he himself explored far inland is not probable.[2] Ptolemy maps two lakes accordingly, at the level of Rhapta. He also supposes them to be fed by head-streams from the snows of certain Mountains of the Moon. No doubt the coast hearsay included a rumour of some snowy mountains, but it was no more than a rumour, and the range which he draws is nothing actual but rather what seemed necessary to supply water enough for so mighty a stream.[3] It was from the same coast that modern discovery proceeded. Two German missionaries at Mombasa heard from Arab traders of snowy mountains 10–30 days inland, and in 1848–9 they saw Kilimanjaro and Kenya. They also picked up talk of lakes, from which they wrongly inferred one huge 'sea of Unyamwezi', a name which, curiously enough, means Land of the Moon. The mountains referred to are only isolated peaks and far short of the lakes, and so did not satisfy everybody as really answering to the ancient description. Burton was now commissioned to go to 'the reported lake of Nyassa' and north to a range marked

---

1 Ptol. I, 7: some confusion here, Bunbury, II, 526, Berthelot, op. cit. p. 229. Detailed maps in *G.G.M.* Tabulae 8, 12 (compared with Periplus).

2 Despite Hennig, op. cit. p. 346, Johnston, loc. cit. and J. N. L. Baker, *Hist. of Geogr. Discovery*, 1931, p. 29. Ptol. I, 9, 1, 4, and I, 17, 6. 15°, ibid. IV, 8, 1 as cp. $16\frac{1}{4}$° (p. 266). Slaving, etc., Coupland, op. cit. pp. 15–18.

3 So Bunbury, II, 616 sensibly. Ptol. IV, 8, 3.

as the probable source of the Nile. In 1857 he went with Speke by the beaten track of the Zanzibar Arabs to discover Tanganyika. Speke, leaving him ill, pushed north to 'the unknown lake of Nyanza', which he found and named Victoria. In 1860 he came again with Grant and heard of a western lake (Albert) and, though a negro king would not let him near, he guessed its shape and size very well: it was really he who broke the back

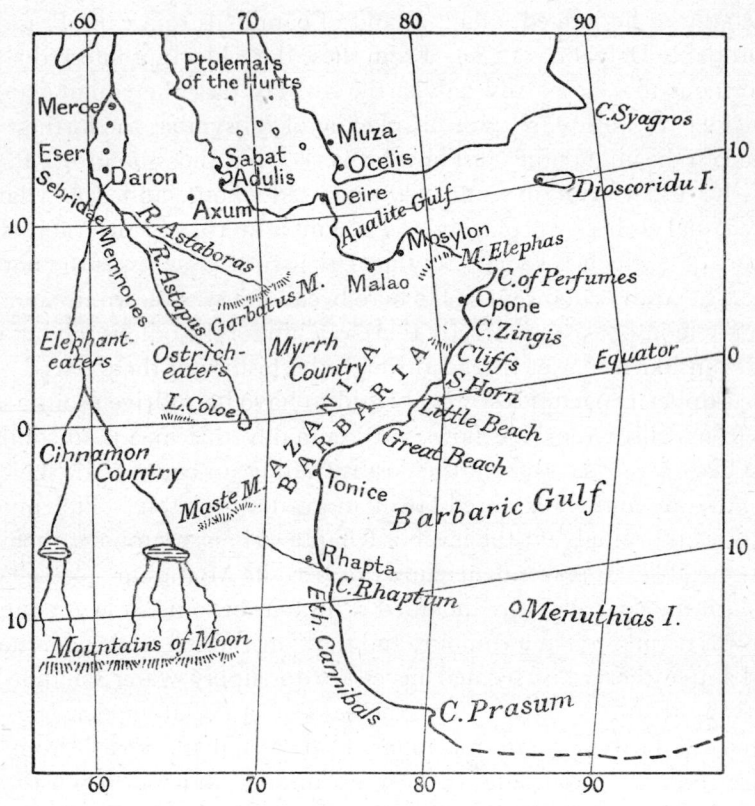

Fig. 45. E. Africa (Ptolemy).

of the Nile problem. Presently Baker reached this lake from the north, and overrated its size (1864). Close by is Ruwenzori, the 'rainy mountain', with 30 miles of glaciers and snowy peaks, generally veiled in heavy cloud and mist; when visible, it 'floats in the sky like an exaggerated lunar landscape'. For many years it proved singularly elusive, being never glimpsed by Baker or apparently by Gordon's officers or at first by Stanley; later, in 1888, a boy pointed to a mountain covered with 'salt', and he saw what seemed a silvery cloud, till he slowly realized what it was—'it now dawned upon me that this must be Ruwenzori'. Already in Speke's time the Arabs had talked of a wonderful snowy mountain, rarely seen, evidently this remote and inaccessible range.¹ So too it may have had its part in the ancient rumours, but it is idle to see in Ptolemy's map more than a happy guess from the vaguest hearsay. One writer concludes that the mountains are almost entirely his invention, only the east end answering to something real, the Livingstone mountains north-east of Nyassa. A few have suspected, with no good reason, that the mountains are a mere interpolation in his text. As for the mysterious and entrancing name, did the natives have one sounding like Selene, the Moon, or did they explain the snow, as they are said to do to-day, by saying that the mountains draw the moonlight down?² Or what else is behind it? Anyhow his range held its place on maps till these very modern explorations. Of the Pygmies, to-day on the slopes which send the headwaters to Lake Albert, he said nothing, despite old legend, and they were to remain fabulous until Schweinfurth confirmed them in 1870.

Such were the ancient limits of detailed report of Africa, and reflection on them does not encourage belief in the two brief and vague stories of circumnavigations by Necho's seamen and Eudoxus. Anyhow they were now so completely ignored that Ptolemy could prolong the coast from about Delgado eastwards as the southern coast of an Indian Ocean supposed to be a closed basin. Probably most did not follow him in this drawing, and kept the traditional shape of Africa as a peninsula. They were right, as it happened, but they knew very little, and many talked carelessly of impassable heat—so precarious was the gain of knowledge southward. The prejudice for a literally 'torrid' zone was strangely obstinate, it may seem, but so it was to be again a century and more after Marco Polo had travelled thousands of miles in tropical seas on his way home from China.

The great south land which Ptolemy invented with such trifling excuse was to cause a deal of trouble. The Arabs failed to disprove it, because they did not venture beyond Mozambique, from the fear, as Marco Polo says, of never returning against the current. Vasco da Gama passed round the Cape to their Zanzibar colonies, and thus exploded the fiction of any great south land so far as its connection with Africa was concerned. In the far

---

1 Sir H. H. Johnston, *Nile Quest*, 1904, p. 139: Stanley, ibid. pp. 227, 260: others, ibid. pp. 186, 233, 250. J. Buchan, *The Last Secrets*, 1923, pp. 105–25. P. M. Synge, *Mountains of the Moon*², 1938.

2 Ludwig, *Nile*, p. 41. P.'s mainly Ruwenzori, Johnston, op. cit. p. 28: Perrot, *Pet. Mitt.* 1918, p. 25: Hennig, op. cit. pp. 357–63: perhaps, Cary-Warmington, op. cit. p. 177: R. as Stanley and most since, Filippo de Filippi, *Ruwenzori* (Exped. of Duke of Abruzzi), 1908, pp. 4–8 and L. Hugues, ibid. pp. 289–301 (lakes are Victoria and Albert or Albert Edward or a fusion of both): Ball, op. cit. (rev. *J.H.S.* 1943, p. 126). Interpolation, Simar, *Géogr. de l'Afrique centrale dans l'Ant. et au moyen Âge*, 1912. Invention, Langenmaier, op. cit. (and name from Unyamwezi: Kilimanjaro is P.'s Maste farther N.). Huntingford, loc. cit. queerly understands Mountain of the Moon (Kilimanjaro).

south-east Marco Polo had spoken of a number of big islands rather than a continuous land, but the notion was to die very hard: even early modern mappers disposed to challenge Ptolemy, like Mercator, kept a southern continent, partly because it seemed needed for the earth's balance, a strange reappearance of the old fad for symmetry. The map opposite shows how strong was the prejudice for this supposed land about 1600, even long after Magellan had passed through his straits and Drake had followed him. Explorer after explorer was misled, and mappers were still fumbling with a 'terra australis nondum cognita' till Cook crossed the Antarctic Circle in 1772; the big island of Australia was the somewhat poor answer to the age-long question, and its very name is an echo of Ptolemy's mistake.[1]

Some ancients made a good observation that Africa has few inlets, as compared with Europe, and they suggested this, more truly than they knew, as a reason for its retarded development.[2] In fact, though thrice the size of Europe, it has a coast shorter by some 4000 miles. With its smooth outline and a high-plateau rim close behind, so that access up the rivers is soon checked by rapids, Africa seems to hold off the sea. It was long regarded chiefly as an obstacle on the way to India. Until very modern times the difficulties of vast deserts and unhealthy forests were too formidable, and penetration of the hinterland was very slight, so that the ancient accounts kept their prestige far longer here than for other parts of the world. The Arabs had a notion of a western Nile or Nile of the Negroes flowing from the same Mountains of the Moon as the other Nile. Henry of Portugal and his officers in 1445 were convinced that the Senegal was this western Nile, 'for the water comes with such force into the sea as to sweeten it'. which sounds like a queer echo of a very antique statement.[3] In 1490 Pedro de Covilham reached Abyssinia, thinking he had found the fabulous Christian kingdom of Prester John; the Portuguese sent a force which saved the country from Mohammedan invaders (1543), and were allowed to remain about a century, during which two Jesuits visited the source-lake

---

1 Heawood, *Geogr. Discovery in the 17th and 18th Centuries*, 1912, pp. 10–13, 71–6, 235–44: E. G. R. Taylor, *Tudor Geography*, 1930, pp. 118–19, *Late Tudor and Early Stuart Geography*, 1934, pp. 4, 33, 69: E. Prestage, *Portuguese Pioneers*, 1933, pp. 310–13: A. Wolf, *Hist. of Science...in the 16th and 17th Centuries*, 1935, pp. 375, 378: J. H. Rose, *Man and the Sea*, 1935, ch. 7: Beaglehole, *Exploration of the Pacific*, 1935, pp. 4–11: H. van Loon, *Home of Mankind*, 1933, p. 378, *Story of the Pacific*, 1940, chs. 7–10: G. A. Wood, *Discovery of Australia*, 1922, ch. 1: J. A. Williamson, *Ocean in English History*, 1941, pp. 145–76 (Polo, ibid. pp. 6–7): Buchan, op. cit. p. 129: Rainaud, *Le Continent austral*, 1893. See p. 318, n. 2.

2 Inlets, Str. 130, 121–2, Plin. v, 1: see p. 254, n. 2, p. 109, n. 1, p. 322, n. 4. Semple, *Infl. of Geogr. Environment*, pp. 117, 254. Van Loon, *Home of Mankind*, pp. 395, 400.

3 P. 77, n. 2 (Euthymenes). Beazley, *Prince Henry the Navigator*, 1895, pp. 109, 220, 253, 274: Payne in *Cambr. Mod. Hist.* 1907, I, 11: Prestage, op. cit. pp. 74, 106. Perham and Simmons, *African Discovery*, 1942, pp. 25, 80 (on Park).

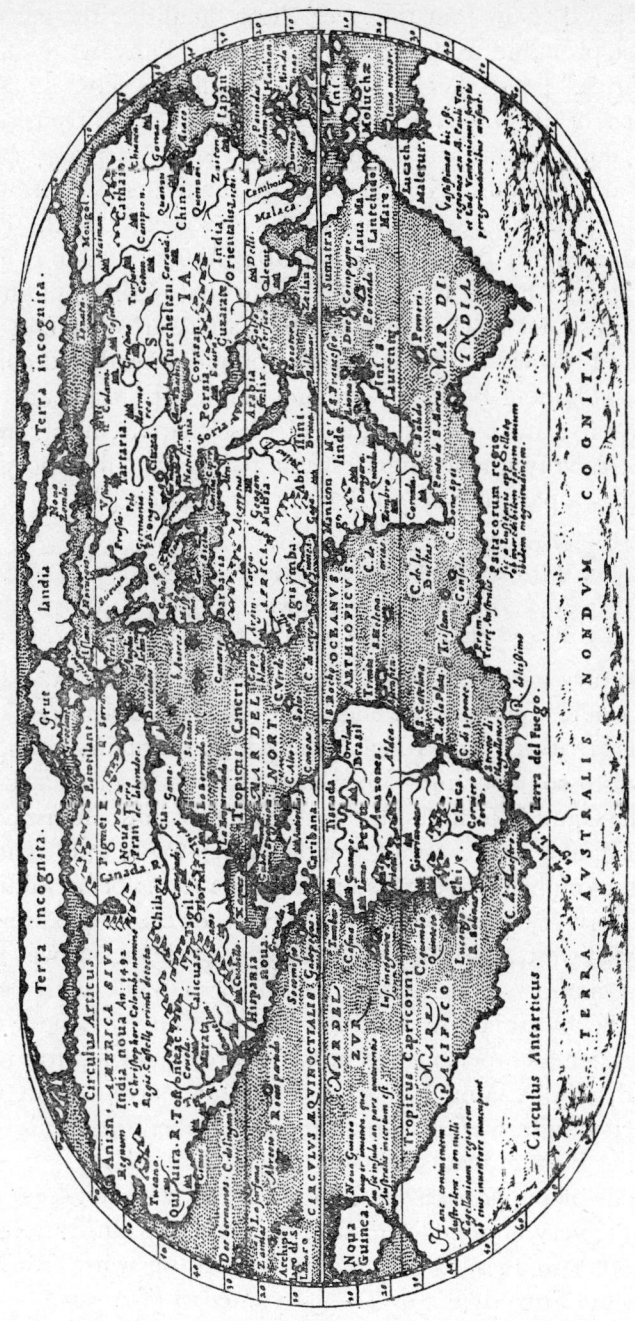

Fig. 46. Porro's map (from Ortelius) for Magini's Ptolemy, 1596–8.

[From Heawood, Geogr. Discovery in 17th and 18th Centuries

of the Blue Nile. Yet Ludolf could write in a history of Ethiopia, translated in 1684, as follows: 'Now that the river Niger should be the left channel of Nile is most probable from hence, for that as Pliny writes, and experience confirms, it partakes of the same conditions with it, agrees in colour and taste of the water, it produces the same sort of reed, the same sort of papyr, and the same sort of animals, and lastly encreases and overflows at the same seasons. Neither does the name itself contradict the conjecture in regard that, as we have said, Nilus itself is by the Hebrews and Greeks call'd Niger. But as to what the Egyptian related to Herodotus, that the left channel flow'd toward the south, that perhaps might be for such a certain distance of land, not but that afterwards it might vary its course, and wind toward the west. Which opinion, after I had communicated to the most famous Bochart, so highly skill'd both in the ancient and modern geography, and the best judge of these matters, he wrote me in answer, il est tres vray que le Niger est une partie du Nile; most certain it is that Niger is a part of Nile.' Presently Swift noted that

> Geographers in Afric maps
> With savage pictures filled their gaps,
> And o'er unhabitable downs
> Placed elephants for want of towns.

Most of his century had very little interest to spare for Africa, except the Guinea slave-trade. Towards the end James Bruce rediscovered the lake of the Blue Nile (1770–2), but wrongly believed this the main stream, though D'Anville tried to convince him otherwise. In 1795 Mungo Park pushed inland from the Gambia to find the Niger 'glittering in the morning sun as broad as the Thames at Westminster and flowing slowly to the eastward'. It was a thrilling moment in the history of exploration: before him no one knew where the river began or ended or even its direction (he himself had thought it flowed west). In 1805 he followed it far down but was killed at Bussa, so that mappers were still bemused for a while with echoes of Ptolemy, and the lowest course was finally proved only by Lander in 1830. His former master Clapperton had made a great journey from Tripoli to Lake Chad, while Laing had from the same starting-point reached Timbuctoo. How light was thrown on the great lakes and the Mountains of the Moon has been indicated above.

The multitude of papyrus-scraps found in Egypt does not seem to have yielded anything very notable for distant travel; a few illustrate the trade known from other sources, as does a tariff of tolls on wares from Arabia and the opposite 'Trogodyte' (or Troglodyte) coast of Africa.[1]

[1] Oxyrh. Pap. 1, 36. Cp. the loan mentioned on p. 175, n. 2. On trade, Mitteis-Wilcken, *Grundzüge u. Chrestomathie der Papyruskunde*, 1, 1, 262–9 (1912).

As indicated above, the ancients probably had no inkling of Madagascar, and what happened there never got into record. To judge from its language colonists were perhaps already coming all the way from Java and thereabouts; a seaworthy outrigger-boat helps to explain such remarkable voyages, like those of the Polynesians in other directions.[1]

Hardly worth mentioning, except to show how gullible some ancients were, is a hoax played on Pausanias when inquiring about Satyrs. A certain Carian solemnly told how he was driven by storms into the Atlantic and came to islands where there were such wild men, with red hair and tails little shorter than those of horses. An odd modern or two have taken this yarn seriously as meaning a visit to the old African 'Gorillas' or even to savages in the West Indies![2]

In spite of their rejection by most of the geographers the Pygmies and the migrant cranes with which they fought continued to flourish as a commonplace of poetry.[3]

A recent translator of Ptolemy observes that the route from Fezzan to Lake Chad is really almost due south like his route to Agisymba, which is probably the region south-east of the lake with the Shari swamps and the Guera and Bongo massif, or perhaps a larger region including Tibesti with its ranges.[4] With regard to the map of E. Africa (p. 276) the same writer insists that in the data of the voyages two passages of Book I conflict with each other and both with the mapping of Book IV: in fact Ptolemy draws the coast badly, being 6° wrong about the Cape of Perfumes and leaving too little room from there to Cape Rhaptum, of which Cape Prasum may be a mere doublet.[5]

---

1 Hornell, *J.R. Anthr. Inst.* 1934, pp. 309–11: Lord Raglan, *How Came Civilization?* 1939, pp. 119, 147: Marett, *Anthropology*, 1914, p. 114: Goldenweiser, *Anthropology*, 1937, p. 488. The writer in *Enc. Brit.* ed. 14 Madagascar talks of 'many theories' and gives no date.

2 Lafitau, 1724, and L. de Rosny, *Antilles*, 1886: Gorillas, Schubart, 1875: all cited by Frazer on Paus. I, 23, 5–6. Glover, *Springs of Hellas*, 1945, pp. 73–4 has a strange notion that perhaps Ireland is meant! 'Wild men' also in Paus. II, 21, 5.

3 Lucan, III, 199–202, V, 711–16, VII, 832–4: Juv. XIII, 167–70. A mosaic found in Rome shows pygmies attacking hippopotami in a Nile landscape, H. S. Jones, *Companion to R. History*, 1912, pl. LXXII.

4 H. v. Mžik's transl. of Ptolemy, Book I, 1938, p. 28. See p. 267, n. 1.

5 Mžik, op. cit. pp. 33–4, 57–9, on the passages in p. 275, n. 2: Rhaptum probably somewhere Mombasa–Rufiji.

CHAPTER X

THE SAME: ASIA

IN Asia the Romans held only a remnant of Alexander's empire, and their wars were confined to the very old stage of the Near East, while the farther lands appear in their historians usually as a vague background from which emerge Parthian kings and reinforcements. What is told of these parts is largely a repetition of previous matter. Yet we hear of traders who passed right through Iran to establish direct contact with the Silkmen. By sea many went to Malabar and one or two to Malaya and beyond. On both lines came some knowledge which was real, if never very sure or well digested, and there even began a notion, dim but recognizable, of China. These gains meant a lengthening of Asia, all the more important because it was greatly overestimated by Marinus and Ptolemy, a mistake fateful for geography above all by its influence on Columbus. As for the nearer and familiar countries, the descriptions of this time could have little that was new, except about changed political conditions, but they are often fuller than any before which survive, and are of interest especially for the mapping, which is still far from perfect.

The Roman area was little more than a coastal frontage, even when it was deepened for the better organization of defence. This was done by gradually annexing the vassal kingdoms, Galatia in 25 B.C., Cappadocia in A.D. 17, Commagene in 17–38 and definitively in 72, and East Pontus in 63. Thus the hinterland was effectively occupied to the general line of the upper Euphrates, a line in itself formidable enough to need little work of fortification. The eastern legions, at first concentrated behind the bridge-head of the Syrian bend, were now better distributed. Key-points were Samosata, Melitene, where the highway from Ephesus and Caesarea crossed the river, and Satala, on the immediate flank of Armenia and with a road from a useful sea-base at Trapezus. The enemy in view all along was Parthia. This empire, loosely feudal and semi-barbarous, was often weakened by civil wars and had little offensive power. It was not really a serious rival, as some observers liked to think, not without malice (others shrewdly said that the Germans were more dangerous). But it could give endless trouble on an unsatisfactory frontier, though after all this frontier was remarkably stable, varying only within a narrow range. The chief cause of quarrel was Armenia, which Parthia regarded as an appanage, while Rome wanted to have the 'bestowal of the kingdom' without attempting to occupy a country so poor and difficult. There was too a matter of prestige. Augustus was fully expected to avenge Crassus, and the poets talked wildly of imminent conquests to the Caspian and India and even the Silkmen, but he was content with a diplomatic victory and twice sending princes to invest his Armenian nominees.[1] Tiberius sent one also and

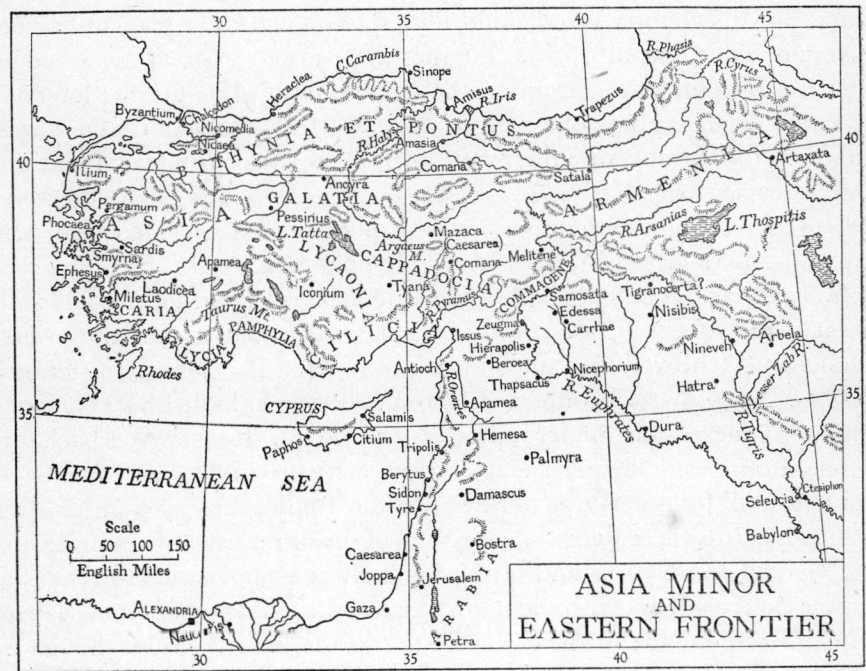

Fig. 47.

checked a Parthian intervention. After a change of kings Nero's general Corbulo marched in, burnt Artaxata, and moved round by some little-known country near Lake Van to occupy Tigranocerta. But another general, invading from Cappadocia, was badly beaten, and now the Parthian candidate was recognized at the cost of his coming to Rome to pay homage.[2] This arrangement of nominal suzerainty worked for 50 years, till a breach of it offended the warlike Trajan, who forthwith invaded and

[1] Poets, Virgil, *Aen.* VI, 794, VIII, 729: Horace, *Odes*, I, 12: Ovid, *A.A.* I, 197: Prop. IV, 4, 1–9, V, 6, 79–84. Rival, Greeks in Livy, IX, 18, 6, Str. 515, Trogus in Justin, XLI, 1, Dio, XL, 14: cp. Tac. *Germ.* 47. Aug. and Parthia, Anderson, *C.A.H.* X, 254–65, 273–83. Formidable, Hogarth, *Wandering Scholar in the Levant*, 1896, pp. 134–7. Stable, Toynbee, *Study of History*, 1934, I, 75.

[2] Tac. *Ann.* XIV, 23–6, XV, 1–17, 24–31: Anderson in *C.A.H.* X, 758–73: Schur, *Klio*, 1925, pp. 75–96 and Beiheft, 1923: B. W. Henderson, *Nero*, 1903: V. Chapot, *Frontière de l'Euphrate*, 1907: Debevoise, *Pol. Hist. of Parthia*, 1938, ch. 8.

annexed Armenia. He also attacked direct through Mesopotamia and crossed the Tigris to make another province of 'Assyria'; he even took the enemy capital, Seleucia, and sighed for Alexander's youth as he gazed on the Persian Gulf and a ship leaving for India. (If he had a fleet on the 'Red Sea', it was more likely meant against pirates than to ravage 'Indiae fines' as stated.)[1] He could put on his coins the proud legend *rex Parthis datus*. But the country rose behind him, and he had to retreat, intending to resume later, but died of his fatigues (A.D. 117). So great a war, soon after the Dacian, was a strain on the empire, even at its height; anyhow Hadrian at once abandoned the conquests as untenable. Conflict was staved off till Marcus Aurelius, whose armies recovered Armenia and again took Seleucia, bringing back a terrible plague (A.D. 161–4). At the very end of the century Septimius Severus more or less repeated Trajan's exploits, and he kept control of north Mesopotamia.

In Syria various patches had been left to local rule, and Pliny could still count many *tetrarchias in regna discriptas barbaris nominibus*, but they were gradually taken over, and all by about A.D. 100. The Jews gave serious trouble. Augustus had confirmed Herod and even enlarged his kingdom, but later annexed part under a procurator (A.D. 6). It was given back for a time, but there followed a long story of tactless handling and fanatical resistance, till Jerusalem was stormed and the Temple destroyed in A.D. 70; even afterwards there were violent risings of the dispersed Jewries in Egypt and Cyrene and Cyprus and of the remnant at home (A.D. 116, 132–5). On the desert side was the client kingdom of the Nabataean Arabs. Their caravans came down to the Red Sea to tap the incense trade, though a customs officer at the port of Leuce Come was not theirs, it seems, but Roman and intended to discourage this evasion of the Egyptian route.[2] Finally Trajan annexed most of the kingdom as a province of 'Arabia', meaning only this north-western edge of the vast peninsula (A.D. 106). A legion was placed at Bostra with forward posts to cover the outer slopes of the Hauran. This high plateau caught some sea rains, and they were well used with aqueducts and reservoirs to produce plenty of corn: here the work of Rome has been highly praised. Other posts were pushed south to defend the 'new road' past Petra to the Red Sea, *a finibus Syriae usque ad*

---

[1] Eutropius, 8, 3: Henderson, *Five R. Emperors*, 1927, p. 330, but cp. *C.A.H.* XII, 233. Ship, Dio, LXVIII, 28. Work of Flavians, Henderson, op. cit. ch. 4: *C.A.H.* XI, 137–45. Trajan, Debevoise, op. cit. ch. 10: *C.A.H.* XI, 236–50. Marcus, ibid. pp. 345–9. Severus, ibid. XII, 9–18.

[2] Periplus Maris Erythraei, 19. Roman, Charlesworth, *Trade Routes of R.E.* 1926, p. 43, Schur, *Klio* Beiheft, 1923, p. 46: but cp. Schoff ad loc., Warmington, *Commerce between R.E. and India*, 1928, p. 16. Caravans, Str. 781. Tetrarchies, Plin. v, 74, 82: Str. 753, 755–6.

mare rubrum.[1] Petra, finely set in a gorge of the desert hills, has many rock-tombs showing a peculiar veneer of Hellenistic or Graeco-Roman civilization; 'the eye recoils', says Doughty, 'from that mountainous close of iron cliffs in which the ghastly waste monuments of a sumptuous barbaric art are from the first an eyesore', but he was a lover of the open desert, and others have a kinder opinion of the place, if it is hardly the 'rose-red city half as old as time' of the prize-poem. A similar amalgam was Palmyra, far out on the desert road from Damascus. After an unsuccessful raid by Antony it was not really independent 'between two empires', as Pliny describes it, and probably from Hadrian it had a strong Roman garrison, but it enjoyed certain privileges for its caravan-trade, which went as far as the head of the Persian Gulf. Where the route crossed the Euphrates there was another 'caravan city', Dura-Europos, now well-known as a sort of Pompeii of the Syrian desert.[2] In general, except for the tragic clash with the Jews, Syria was prosperous. Much land was cultivated which later reverted to desert, so that some insist that there must once have been a considerably larger and better distributed rainfall. Antioch early became 'not far short of Alexandria in power and size', though not well placed to rival it in trade, despite an effort to improve its port at Seleucia (this has long since silted up and disappeared). Industry flourished especially in the old Phoenician towns, as famous as ever for purple and glass, and their shipmen were again conspicuous and had offices in Italian ports and probably farther away. The Jews were not yet prominent as money-makers. Pliny must have written on them at length in his lost history; as it is, he has a few phrases on Jerusalem that 'was' and another place 'now a second tomb', the pleasant Jordan losing itself in the pestilential Asphalt Lake, and so on. Tacitus can still talk of rites borrowed from Egypt and the worship of an ass's head.[3] (Christianity, when it began to attract some notice, seemed only another form of Jewish superstition.)

1 Dessau, *Inscr. Lat. Sel.* 5834, 5845: Chapot, op. cit. pp. 247, 259. Praised, by Mommsen, v, 476, Sir G. A. Smith, *Hist. Geogr. of Holy Land*, ed. 1926, pp. 611–38. Annexed, Dio, LXVIII, 14: *C.A.H.* XI, 237–8. Brünnow and Domaszewski, *Die Provincia Arabia*, 1904–9: Musil, *Arabia Petraea*, 4 vols, 1907–8.

2 Rostovtzeff, *Dura-Europos and its Art*, 1938: *Caravan Cities*, 1932: on inscriptions in *Mélanges Glotz*, 1932, II, 713. *Orientis Gr. Inscr. Sel.* II, 629, 632. C. P. Grant, *Syrian Desert*, 1937, pp. 59–63. Raid, Appian, *B.C.* v, 9: Plin. v, 88. Petra, Str. 779, Plin. VI, 144 (distances muddled). Books on Petra by Dalman, 1912, Sir A. Kennedy, 1925, M. A. Murray, 1939. Musil, op. cit. II, 41–150: Kammerer, *Petra et la Nabatène*, 1929: Hölscher, *R.E.* Petra, 1937.

3 Tac. *Hist.* v, 2–5. Plin. v, 70, 73: Jordan, ibid. 71. Offices, *C.I.L.* v, 1601, *O.G.I.S.* 594–5. Antioch, Str. 750: port, Paus. VIII, 29, 3. Mommsen, v, ch. 10 (and Jews, ch. 11). Bouchier, *Syria as a R. Province*, 1916. Cumont in *C.A.H.* XI, 613–48. Heichelheim in *Econ. Survey*, ed. Frank, 1938, IV, 123–257. Rainfall, Huntington, *Mainsprings of Civilization*, 1945, pp. 536–42, citing H. C. Butler, *Geogr. Rev.* Feb. 1920: see also p. 255.

Strabo still has some bad slips on the geography, and makes the coast turn from southward abruptly westward at Joppa. Ptolemy treats the whole region in two sections, a very long Hollow Syria, with as many as 108 'towns' —16 in the district of Palmyra alone—and a 'Syria Palaestina also called Judaea' with 43 towns and reaching to the sea. The run of coast, rivers, and ranges is often surprisingly far from accurate. He adds a third chapter for Arabia 'Petraea', the new province; it has some 30 towns and villages, a few like Rabbath-Ammon (Philadelphia) being careless doublets of places already mentioned in Syria. It is of interest to find the name Saracens appearing.[1]

The country eastwards was dealt with in various accounts of the Parthian wars, now lost, like Arrian's with its ten books on Trajan. Some seemed to a critic models of how history should not be written, and he mocks their fancy geography and descriptions 'more frigid than Caspian snows'. The same wars heightened the usual interest in Alexander, of whom we have a history by Curtius, brief and picturesque, and another by Arrian, the fullest and best which has survived, but following the old sources and not remarkable for any new geographical matter. The best thing extant for topography is a series of stages and distances from Zeugma, 'the Ferry', down the Euphrates to the beginning of Babylonia at Hit (25th stage), and presently across to the Tigris at Seleucia. (This route, however, involved paying tolls to many petty sheikhs, and some traders preferred to take a line through the desert well off the river, as modern travellers have often done for similar reasons.) The 'Stages' is by Isidorus—Pliny once by a slip calls him Dionysius—a man sent ahead to gather information for the young prince Caius Caesar, soon to be killed in Armenia (A.D. 4). He came himself from Charax, a port and colony of Alexander's on the Persian Gulf but already left miles inland by the rapid silting there.[2] Mela and Pliny describe the Euphrates as largely used up for irrigation or lost in marshes and as reaching the sea only through the Tigris, while one rather obscure discussion implying separate mouths seems an echo of older writers.[3] The upper Tigris is still misconceived as passing through Lake Van and then a tunnel under the mountains, and Pliny blunderingly doubles the lake and

---

1 Ptol. v, 17: rest in 15–16. Str. 749–65: slips, see p. 172, n. 2. On Plin. v, 66–90, Klotz, *Quaest. Plin. Geogr.* 1906, pp. 159–63, Detlefsen, *Geogr. Bücher des Plin.* 1909, pp. 81–7.

2 Plin. VI, 139–40: slip, ibid. 141. Ed. *G.G.M.* I, 244–56 and Tabulae, 9–10: Schoff, 1914. Bunbury, *Anc. Geogr.* II, 163–5: Weissbach, *R.E.* Isidorus, 1916: Tarn, *Greeks in Bactria and India*, 1938, pp. 53–5. Tolls, Str. 748: modern, C. P. Grant, op. cit. pp. 26–7, 169: *Desert Route to India, Journals of...1745–51*, ed. Carruthers (Hakluyt Soc.), 1930. Gertrude Bell, *Amurath to Amurath*[2], 1924, pp. 108–10, checks the stages part of the way (Nicephorium–Hit). Frigid, Lucian, *How to write History*, p. 24.

3 Str. 529 after Erat. 729, citing three writers of Alexander's time: see p. 133, n. 2. Cp. Mela, III, 77, Plin. V, 90, VI, 124, 130. Bunbury, II, 290, 366, 409, but cp. Tarn, op. cit. p. 61.

the whole process.[1] Much of what is said of Babylonia and its neighbourhood is, of course, very well-worn matter. Ptolemy has many oddities, especially in the drawing of the rivers. He gives for Mesopotamia 69 'towns and villages', for Assyria 34, and for Babylonia 30, not including a good many on the right bank of the Euphrates counted to Arabia Deserta.[2]

Let us turn back to Asia Minor, of which the bulk was held and kept clear of war, especially when the client kingdoms were taken over in the way

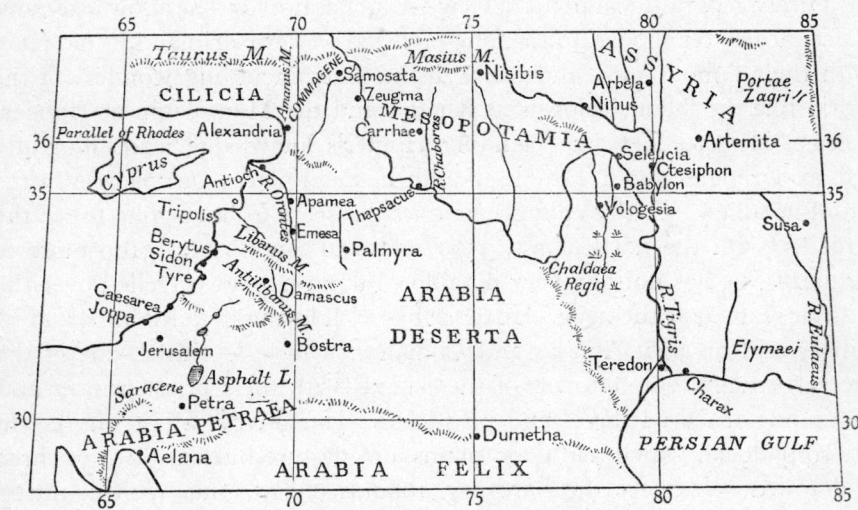

Fig. 48. Ptolemy: Near East.

described. The old province of 'Asia', after suffering so much in the Republic, now enjoyed decent government and unbroken peace and prosperity. Ephesus was the greatest mart of 'Asia short of Taurus', though its harbour was threatened with silting: the second place in trade was Apamea, on the high road running east to the Euphrates crossing, and many other towns were rising in importance. On the south coast the Lycians were permitted independence as a league of cities until A.D. 43; the piratical days of Rough Cilicia were long over. In the mountains close behind the troublesome Pisidian tribes were early tamed.[3]

No one had yet thought of the name 'Asia Minor', a good one for all this

1 Plin. VI, 127–8, cp. Str. 529: Dion. Per. 988: Lucan, III, 261–3, VIII, 439. Ptol. v, 13, 7: two other lakes, ibid. 8. Huntington, *Pulse of Asia*, 1919, p. 354 goes astray about them.

2 Ptol. v, 19: rest in 18, 20, VI, 1. Str. 736–48. Plin. VI, 41–2, 117–41 (and 'Arabia', v, 86–90): Klotz, op. cit. pp. 193–7.

3 Str. 569, Plin. v, 94, Tac. *Ann.* III, 48, Dio, LIII, 26: Anderson in *C.A.H.* x, 270–3. Lycia, Str. 664: outbreaks, Suet. *Claud.* 25. Cilicia, Tac. *Ann.* VI, 41, XII, 55. Towns, Str. 577, 579. Ephesus, ibid. 641, high road, 663 (from Artemidorus). On Roman A.M. see Keil and Cumont in *C.A.H.* XI, 580–613: Broughton in *Econ. Survey*, ed. Frank, 1938, IV, 593–916 (Empire): roads, ibid. pp. 860–8.

mass of land except the deeply indented western coast, which looks towards and rather belongs to Europe. Strabo conceives a 'great peninsula', and he gives it three whole books, an excellent piece of historical geography and his best; himself of Pontus, he had visited a good deal, and his local descriptions have been praised as 'marvellously lucid and accurate'.[1] (It is unlikely that, as Pais supposed, he revised his work at home, because he does not mention the new provincial status of Cappadocia, A.D. 18.) From the purely geographical point of view—which is not his—he allows excessive space, nearly two books, to the long-civilized western strip and its old cities with their famous men and other distinctions, including wonders of the world like the fallen Colossus at Rhodes and the Mausoleum at Halicarnassus. His crotchet for defending Homer's knowledge leads him into tedious wrangles about Troy itself and the dead places and peoples in the list of its allies. (Oddly enough, he does not seem to have gone to see the Troad.)[2] On the north coast, 3500 stades to Sinope and 3100 more to Trapezus, he has nothing very notable. Inland he had travelled over the eastern plateau at the neck. He describes with loving detail Pontus and its valleys and his own Amasia and Comana, 'a little Corinth', one of the several strange temple-towns of these lands with their priest-princes and thousands of sacred slaves and prostitutes. He conveys a fair impression of Cappadocia, which had good plains and pasture but only two or three real towns. Next are the bare dry uplands of Lycaonia with countless rough-woolled sheep and the big salt-lake Tatta.[3] He had not visited the western plateau and is sketchy on some parts like the core of the old Phrygian kingdom. He is intelligently interested in matters like the silting work of rivers, and rightly connects the frequent earthquakes with the signs of former volcanic action to be seen especially in the 'Burnt Country': one place near had daily shocks and twelve cities of 'Asia' had just been laid waste. There are still bad mistakes on outlines and distances: the western coast is made much too long and continued north to opposite Byzantium, and he exaggerates the bulge into the Black Sea. But he does not narrow the neck absurdly, as some still do, except that he repeats a local fable that the seas on both sides are visible from the inland peak of Argaeus.[4] Pliny

1 Sir W. M. Ramsay, *Hist. Geogr. of A.M.* 1890, pp. 73, 96. Str. xii–xiv (on west xiii and most of xiv). Peninsula, Str. 533.

2 Leaf, *Strabo on the Troad*, 1923, p. xxviii. Troy, Str. 593–5, Leleges, ibid. 611–13, Halizones, 549–54, etc.: 'dead places', Plin. v, 121–3, 127. Against Pais, J. G. C. Anderson in *Anatolian Studies (to Ramsay)*, 1923, pp. 1–13: and see p. 225, n. 1.

3 Str. 568. Capp., ibid. 533–40, Amasia, ibid. 546. Travels, 535–6. Figures in 543–8. On treeless plateau cp. Cic. *pro Flacco*, 41, Vitr. ii, 1, 5: Axylos, Livy, 38, 18.

4 Str. 538. Cp. Artem. ap. Str. 678, Plin. vi, 7 (200 R. miles), and still Dion. Per. 861–5: see p. 79, n. 2, p. 87, n. 1. Bulge, Str. 545: W. coast, ibid. 584, 655. Silting, etc., see p. 104, nn. 1 and 3, p. 105, n. 1.

has his usual staccato summary, overcrowded with minor names, and is of little use unless for the areas of the Roman 'conventus' or 'iurisdictiones' He makes some bad blunders and duplications. He plumes himself on fresh figures for the two halves of the north coast—3720 and 3240 stades, as compared with Strabo's above—and on details of Cappadocia due to recent campaigns from that base.[1] Arrian, himself a Bithynian and legate of Cappadocia, gives a detailed periplus of the same coast, using an older, by one Menippus; the genuineness of the whole need not be doubted, though he is chiefly interested in the eastern corner attached to his own command. A new version by Valerius Flaccus of the hackneyed Argo epic had repeated the traditional series of peoples hereabouts, including the Chalybes still working hard at their steel. Ptolemy has a host of names filling his map: there are 77 'towns' for Little Armenia alone! But the outlines are far from good, and the details are severely criticized by Ramsay, who has constantly to discard him in favour of Strabo. Often he has tried to combine several sources of different dates and so fallen into all kinds of contradictions and duplications. He deals with the map in eight sections, Bithynia and Pontus, 'Asia proper', Lycia, Pamphylia, Cilicia, a big Galatia and a big Cappadocia both reaching right across from the last named to the Black Sea, and Little Armenia ('Great Armenia' is handled separately, in connection with the Caucasus lands). A writer who attempts to detect his methods in constructing this map finds that he makes the whole area half again too large, and that few of his placings rest on astronomical observation, while some are very wrong indeed.[2]

At Trapezus there was a small fleet to deal with pirates, and a protectorate extended round the corner to the Phasis and even Dioscurias, 'the end of our dominion'. An old mistake that this place was the easternmost point of the sea was now duly corrected, but Pliny does not know that it is the same as Sebastopolis. Various kings of the Lazi and others in these parts were appointed or confirmed by Trajan and his successors. Hadrian, a great tourist, came to Trapezus and climbed what was taken to be the hill from which Xenophon's men had hailed the sea. Arrian, as his legate, reports on his inspection of the forts all the way round, including Phasis, where he was not convinced by the Argo's anchor. The coast is minutely detailed with slightly reduced figures and some new names of tribes. Ptolemy has a rough map of 'Pontic Cappadocia' and then Colchis, which he gives ten towns and villages, among them an Aea lingering from the

---

1 Plin. VI, 23. Figures, ibid. 4–12. His account, V, 91–151, VI, 1–11: Klotz, op. cit. pp. 163–78, Detlefsen, op. cit. pp. 113–18.

2 Cronin, G.J. 1905, pp. 429–41. Ramsay, op. cit. pp. 68–73, 95–6. Ptol. V, 1–8. Arrian, *Periplus*, 12–16, ed. Roos. G.G.M. I, 370–423 (cp. Epitome Peripli Menippi, ibid. 563–73). Val. Flaccus, V, 140–53, cp. Mela, I, 105–7.

Argo fable.¹ The Phasianus or pheasant from these parts had by now been naturalized in Italy.

For Armenia there is more detail from recent campaigns and 'the sending of kings as suppliants and princes as hostages'. Yet the Tigris-Van mistake continues as mentioned above. Ptolemy extends the country to the Caspian and gives it three lakes and as many as 84 'towns'. He makes the Aras both join the Kur and have a separate mouth, a compromise between earlier statements.²

The Caucasus kingdoms were still often involved with Armenia and like it 'protected by our greatness against foreign powers'. Their passes were not always secure against the Sarmatians raiding southward. Among these the Aorsi were now replaced by the Alans, apparently a new wave arriving from the east. In A.D. 36 some Sarmatians (already Alans?) were 'let in by the Caspian road'.³ Nero is said to have intended an expedition to the 'Caspian Gates'. It was against the Albanians, according to one version, which some accept as referring to the pass of Derbend close to the Caspian sea. But Pliny thinks he meant the Caucasian Gates, the pass of Dariel, and so most take the enemy as the Alans. A few years later a Parthian king even suggested co-operation in defence, but Vespasian refused, though he sent a force to help the Iberians at that pass.⁴ Later the Alans raided into Media and Armenia, and Arrian, legate of Cappadocia, tells how he mobilized his two legions in fear of their attack. He thinks the Caucasus about as high as the Alps, an understatement. Ptolemy has two passes called Gates, both badly placed, and gives Albania many rivers and 28 towns and villages, as compared with only ten for Iberia. For him Asia reaches beyond the Caucasus to the Don, and his mapping here has been sketched above in connection with the eastern edge of Europe. The new Argo epic has the Gates, and its catalogues of tribes include the Alans and partly reflect a

---

1 Ptol. v, 6, 6–7 and v, 10: Manrali = Mingrelia? Arr. *Periplus*, 1–11 (figures cp. Plin. vi, 12–14): detailed maps in *G.G.M.* Tabulae, 16–18. Kings, Dio, LXVIII, 9, Eutr. 8, 3, Arr. op. cit. 11, *Vita Hadr.* 21, *Vita Pii*, 9, 6. Corrected Arr. 11 as cp. Str. 497. Pirates, Tac. *Hist.* III, 47–8, Jos. *B.J.* II, 367. Ormerod, *Piracy in Anc. World*, 1924, p. 26.

2 Ptol. v, 13 (see map, p. 253): cp. p. 172, n. 1. Armenia, Str. 527–33, Plin. vi, 23–8. Tigris-Van, see p. 287, n. 1. Pheasant, Plin. x, 132.

3 Tac. *Ann.* vi, 33. Alans then, Jos. *Ant.* XVIII, 4, 4, Taübler, *Klio*, 1909, pp. 14–17, but reading dubious, Teggart, *Rome and China*, 1939, p. 222. Protected, Tac. *Ann.* IV, 5: involved, ibid. VI, 32, XI, 9–11.

4 *C.I.L.* III, 6052, Chapot, op. cit. p. 219, Debevoise, op. cit. p. 201, cp. p. 224, Trajan a guard near Caspian G., Arr. *Parth.* VIII, fr. 6. Refused, Suet. *Dom.* 2, Dio, LXVI, 15. Nero, Plin. VI, 40, Suet. *Nero*, 19, Dio, LXIII, 8: Tac. *Hist.* I, 6, Albanos, defended by Schur, op. cit. p. 65, but Alans meant, Mommsen, Rostovtzeff, *Iranians and Greeks*, p. 117, Taübler, op. cit. p. 22, Anderson, *C.A.H.* X, 777. Alans, Sen. *Thy.* 630, Lucan, VIII, 223 (antedated). Jos. *B.J.* VII, 244–51 has confusions. Dar-i-Alan = gate of Alans, Vernadsky, *Anc. Russia*, 1943, p. 194.

current interest in these parts. Pliny reports a queer variety of opinion on the width of the isthmus. At the main pass he has a rock fort 'to prevent the entry of innumerable peoples', and oddly talks of actual iron gates. These, or a brazen wall, got into the legend of Alexander: by sundry confusions he was supposed to have come here and made gates to bar out the Scythians or the Gog and Magog of Jewish tradition.[1]

Of contemporary Iran the writers usually seem to know very little: it is hardly more than a dim vista behind the figures of Parthian kings. A counsellor of Augustus is supposed to worry what is happening in Bactria or even among the Silkmen, but this is not to be taken seriously. Once there is word of direct contact, when rebels in Hyrcania sent their own envoys to Nero; it has been suggested that he sought to improve the occasion to establish an independent silk-route across the Caspian, but this is not very plausible. There is a more dubious notice of a Bactrian embassy to Hadrian. Isidorus continues his 'Stages' eastwards into Iran, though with less detail than before: it is not quite certain that he travelled himself. The route is by the Zagros pass to Hamadan and thence on something like Alexander's tracks. There is a similar detour south by Herat and round to an Alexandria in 'White India'. This is probably Ghazni (rather than Kandahar). He describes it as the end of the Parthian empire, wrongly for his own time, when it was under a Saca ruling from India, while nearer home, in Seistan itself, the sub-kings had ceased to be even nominally vassal to Parthia (he seems to be using an earlier document, in fact a Parthian official survey of about 100 B.C.).[2] It is curious that he says (and knows?) nothing of silk, and there is no reason for an assumption that Chinese merchants were met at Kandahar. Pliny's account is clumsily arranged, first the northern provinces, then some next India, then the south coast with a bad summary of Nearchus: there are ragged ends, repetitions, and obscurities, and the whole is a poor compilation from earlier compilers. The new historians of Alexander give little impression of having any fresh knowledge of the ground, as when Curtius remarks that the old colonies about Merv have now forgotten their origin (they had done so long since). Yet an overland silk-trade was going on: Ptolemy, after Marinus, knows of a Syrian merchant, one Maes Titianus, as sending his agents right through

1 A. R. Anderson, *Alexander's Gate, Gog and Magog...*, 1932, pp. 15, 20. Plin. VI, 29–31, 39. Val. Flaccus, V, 603, tribes, VI, 33–162 (Alans, 42). Ptol. V, 11–12. Arrian, *Periplus* and *Mobilizing* and *Tactica*, 4: Dio, LXIX, 15: Pelham, *Essays in R. History*, 1911, pp. 212–33. Gog, see p. 364, n. 2.

2 Tarn, op. cit. pp. 53–5, 204, 344. *G.G.M.* Tabulae, 10. Bunbury, II, 165. Bactrian, *Vita Hadr.* 21, 14, accepted by Debevoise, op. cit. p. 241. Hyrcania, Tac. *Ann.* XIV, 25: suggested by Schur, op. cit. pp. 35, 66. Vista, Tac. VI, 36, 44, XI, 8–10 (river Sindes is Tejend?). Silkmen, Hor. *Odes*, III, 29, 27. Chinese met, Charlesworth, *Trade Routes*, p. 103, cp. Tarn, *Hell. Civ.* p. 206 (silk meanwhile by India).

to Bactria, by what arrangement with the Parthians is not explained. The geographer's map of Iran has plenty of names, including some 20 districts or tribes and 80 towns and villages in Media alone. But here as elsewhere he tries to combine accounts of various times and quality, at the cost of many misplacings and blunders and duplications. As a whole Iran is drawn 9° too wide and $5\frac{1}{2}$° too long, and the eastern parts especially are very wrong. He has an Arian lake of sorts, but on the wrong river and much

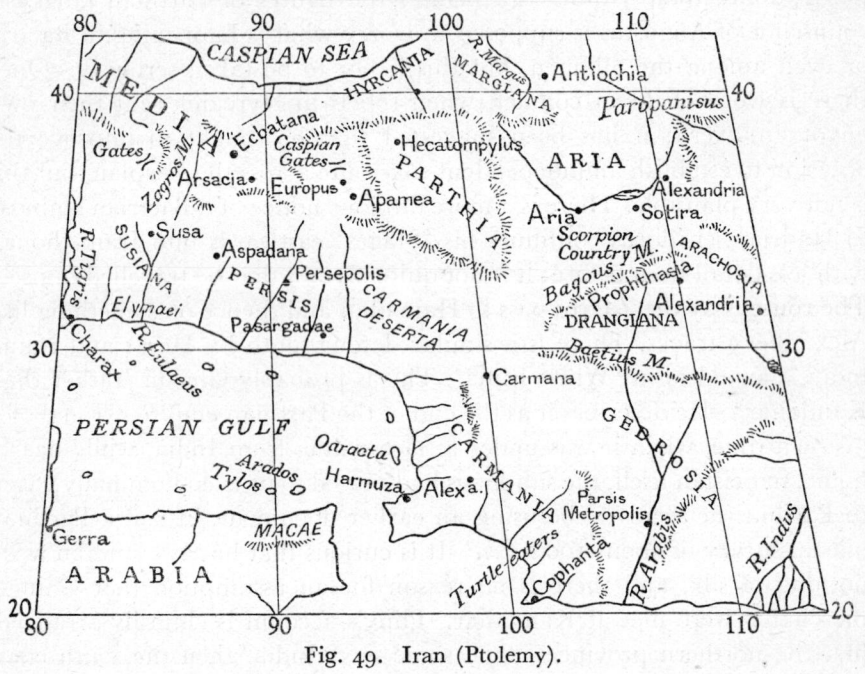

Fig. 49. Iran (Ptolemy).

too far north, while he makes the Arachotus a tributary of the Indus. The run of the Persian Gulf is badly misconceived on old lines, though the head is now put on the right latitude. Little is heard of this sea from others, as the shipping for India passed it by: the Periplus is very brief here, mentioning a port at the head now used instead of Charax, one engaged in pearling, and other divings at the mouth (various writers are interested in pearls and their origin).[1]

The Yue-chi invaders of Bactria consolidated themselves under strong kings, the Kushans, and they too, like the Greek kings before them, proceeded to advance on India (Chinese sources still know something of

[1] Plin. IX, 114, Athen. 93a, citing Isid. etc. Peripl. 35–6. Map, Ptol. VI, 2–6, 8–12, 17–21. Maps of coast in *G.G.M.* Tabulae 14, 15. Duplications as Arsacia-Europus, etc., Tarn, op. cit. p. 231. Berthelot, *L'Asie centrale et sud-or. d'après Ptol.* 1930, p. 159. Maes, Ptol. I, 11, 7. Plin. VI, 41–9, 92–100. Forgotten, Curtius, VII, 10, 15.

them and their progress by way of Kaofu or Kabul). Probably about
A.D. 50 they ended an East Parthian kingdom which had extended itself
from Seistan to the upper Indus. On their coins, some apparently inspired
by gold ones of the Roman Empire, they have the title Shah of Shahs or
Rajah of Rajahs in Greek script, and an amazing medley of gods, Iranian
and Indian and Greek. They adopted Buddhism in a certain form, and
began to spread it along with the native art of Gandhara (the Peshawar
district), which had learnt to represent the Buddha as a sort of 'Apollon

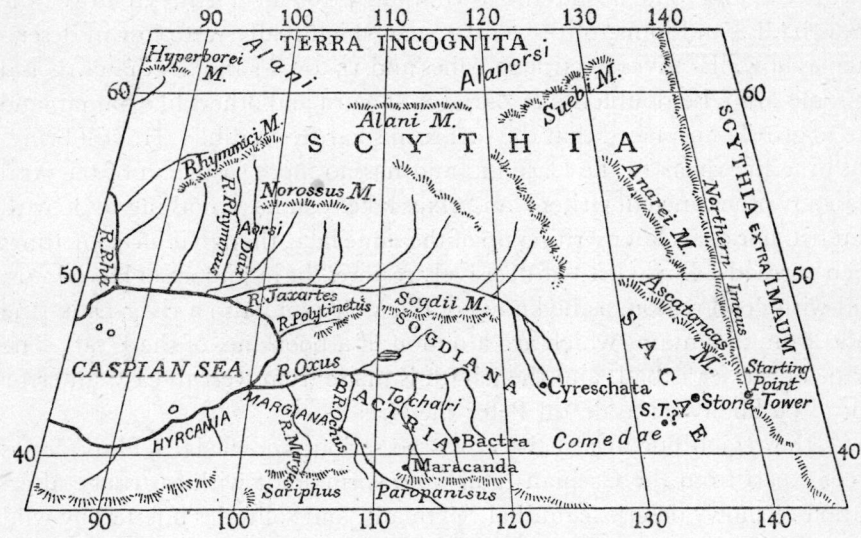

Fig. 50. East of Caspian (Ptolemy).

asexué', in types and drapery derived from Greek sculpture. But the
western writers of the time know almost nothing of this strange history.
They have only vague Tochari, as before, except for a hint of warlike
Bactrians through whom some Chinese silk drifted down to ports in and
beyond the Indus delta; this last is called Scythia or Indoscythia and has
for a moment 'Parthian' princes.[1]

There is much helpless repetition of the old Alexander matter, as on the
'Tanais' (Jaxartes), over which he was thought to cross into Europe, and
on the Caspian: 'some have believed it not to be a closed sea', says Curtius,
who himself seems to double a Caspian lake with a Hyrcanian. Most have
no doubt of the view, which Patrocles had appeared to establish, that the

---

[1] Peripl. 38, 47: Ptol. vii, 1. Tarn, op. cit. p. 232. Silk, Peripl. 49. Chinese, *T'oung Pao*, 1907, p. 191, De Groot, op. cit. ii, 100. Gold, Warmington, op. cit. pp. 297–8. On problem of Kushan chronology, Tarn, op. cit. p. 338, Grousset, *Hist. de l'extrême Orient*, 1929, i, 61, Teggart, op. cit. p. 115. Art, Grousset, ii, 81–2 (after Foucher), Codrington in *Legacy of India*, 1937, p. 80 (from Roman rather than Greek).

sea is a gulf with a long narrow neck to the northern Ocean. So Pliny makes both the great rivers flow to the Caspian, and talks of Indian trade coming to it down the Oxus. But at last there was some new information to consider, from the commercial travellers of Maes. Bactra (Balkh) had long since been placed, with surprising correctness, on the great Rhodes–Caspian Gates parallel. Marinus saw no reason to alter this, and calculated the journey from Syria as straight along the parallel for 24,780 stades. But Ptolemy wrongly conceives that the latter part of the road diverged sharply north-east, and so he pushes the town some 5° too far north. He draws the Oxus badly, and joins to it several rivers which really were lost in deserts then as now. He gives Bactria 13 tribes and 15 towns, and Sogdiana 12 and 9; some are false doublets like Zariaspa–Bactra and others like Samarcand are so grossly misplaced that the text seems hardly credible. He still brings both the big rivers to the Caspian, and has no more suspicion of the Aral than any other ancient writer: an 'Oxus lake' can have nothing to do with that sea, nor can a later writing up of the same lake, though it has sometimes been misread.[1] But at least he decisively restores the inland sea of Herodotus, and with good reason, as he knows of the Volga and also a river Daix (the Jaik) from mountains which are a notion, if a poor one, of the Urals. The shape of the sea is bad, and the length is made from west to east, an error not to be finally set aside till Peter the Great.

Of the region northward there was no serious knowledge. Pliny draws a coast east from the Caspian 'gulf' and sprinkles it with a strange alternation of snowy deserts, cannibal Scythians, and solitudes infested by wild beasts, while on a more inward line he has a jumble of 22 tribes, including the old Issedones and Arimaspians. (The poets, of course, make great play with such names, and one writer somehow knows that the Griffins have spots like leopards.) Ptolemy's Scythia fades northward into unknown land, and few of his ranges and tribes seem to have much reality. If he is right about a closed Caspian, some ascribe this to a renewal of trade passing north of the sea, but the rest of his map has little proof of any notable gain from such a route (a recent attempt to find more value in his matter seems unconvincing).[2] As for the huge rivers struggling through the frozen wastes to the Arctic Ocean, no ancient ever heard of them. Later ages were to ignore Ptolemy's unknown land in favour of Pliny's northern sea sweeping

---

[1] Amm. Marc. XXIII, 6, 59, misread by Barthold, *Nachrichten über den Aral-See*, 1910, p. 8. Rivers, Plin. VI, 52: see p. 127, n. 3, p. 128, n. 2, p. 172, n. 1. Curtius, VI, 4, 1–8, cp. VII, 3, 21. Gulf, Mela, III, 38, Plin. VI, 38, Dion. Per. 706. Zariaspa, Tarn, op. cit. p. 231.

[2] Teggart, op. cit. pp. 191–6, 206–10: see p. 252, n. 2. Ascribe, as Berger. Plin. VI, 50–1, 53 (cp. Mela, III, 59): from Agrippa, thinks Herrmann, *Land der Seide*, 1938, p. 46. Poets, Lucan, III, 280–3, Val. Flaccus, VI, 131: spots, Paus. VIII, 2, 7, cp. I, 25, 6.

past a cape Tabis, and there was a gallant but hopeless effort to find a north-east passage through these icy waters to Cathay; so Mercator's map about 1585 draws the river Ob—and for lack of anything better Ptolemy's Oechardes too—flowing into *Oceanus Scythicus qui et mare Tabin*.

Remarkable things are said of a silk-road going far eastward from Bactra. But before trying to gauge the worth of this report it is desirable to consider all that had been heard by another route, that of the Indian Ocean.

Quite a lot was learnt of Arabia. Half the people there lived by trade, said Pliny, and half by robbery or bakshish for the safe-conduct of caravans (he can give the cost of bringing a camel-load all along the Incense Road). The Sabaeans of the south-west had grown rich by selling transit wares and their own perfumes, and it was complained that they bought nothing in return. Here Augustus committed an aggression surprising in him: presumably his object was both to loot their hoards and to clear the way for the direct sea-trade to India now rapidly developing (25 B.C.). The campaign was entrusted to Aelius Gallus, prefect of Egypt, who bungled it, partly from ignorance of the geography. He lost many transports on reefs and shoals, and landed absurdly far north. Thus he set himself painful marches, made longer, it was suspected, by the misguidance of his Nabataean allies. We hear of marches of many days to a land of their kinsmen with scanty grain and dates, through it for 30, and then for 50 days through desert nomads. Reaching better country he took Negrana (Nejran) and at a wadi 6 days on easily routed an ill-armed enemy; he took some more towns but for lack of water had to raise the siege of Mar(s)iaba, the stronghold of a tribe subject to 'Ilasaros' and only two days from the Incense Country. Pliny talks of 'Mariba' being destroyed, and has this in one tribe, Maribba in another, and Marelibata in a third, while Ptolemy has only a Mara; it has been questioned whether the town of Gallus is the same as Marib with the famous dam east of Sana. The outward journey had filled 6 months; the retreat was in 9 days to Negrana, 11 more to Seven Wells, then through peaceful country to certain villages, lastly by a desert with few water-holes to the port of Egra, altogether 60 days (the accounts are not good and leave the route very doubtful).[1] After heavy loss from hardship

1 Str. VI, 780–2: Plin. VI, 159–62 (and cp. 157, 155): Mon. Anc. 26, ed. E. G. Hardy, 1923, pp. 121–3: Dio, LIII, 29. Hoards, Hor. *Odes*, I, 29, 35: Virg. *Aen.* VIII, 705. Route, Glaser, *Gesch. u. Geogr. Arabiens*, 1890, II, 43–66, followed by Gardthausen, *Augustus*, 1894–1901, I, 789–96, II, 453–5. Same as Marib, Hogarth, *Penetration of Arabia*, 1905, p. 14, Dessau, *Röm. Kaiserzeit*, 1924, I, 380–1, but no, Glaser, p. 57, *C.A.H.* X, 247–53, Kiernan, *Unveiling of Arabia*, 1937, pp. 25–8. Route, Medina–E. of Mecca–Karna, G. W. Bury, *Arabia Infelix*, 1915, p. 7, and finally checked outside Radman 14° 33′, 45° 14′. I have not seen H. Krüger's diss., 1862. A trade war, Hitti, *Hist. of Arabs*, 1940, p. 46. Various Lives of Aug. avoid detailed discussion. Cost, Plin. XII, 63–5.

Tabin, Oakeshott, *Founded upon the Seas*, 1942, pp. 23, 29, and see p. 131, n. 2.

and disease there seemed little gain to show; yet an impression had been made. How and when it was followed up is not clear. The young prince Caius Caesar, for whom Juba wrote a special description, had thoughts of conquest here, and we learn casually of a fleet of his in the Red Sea, but it is expressly said that he 'had only a glimpse of Arabia'. Yet 'not long before' the time of the Periplus some 'Caesar had subjected (or destroyed?)' Aden—the text is sound enough, and the old editors had no right to emend to 'Elisar' or some other local king. This port, once a meeting-place of ships

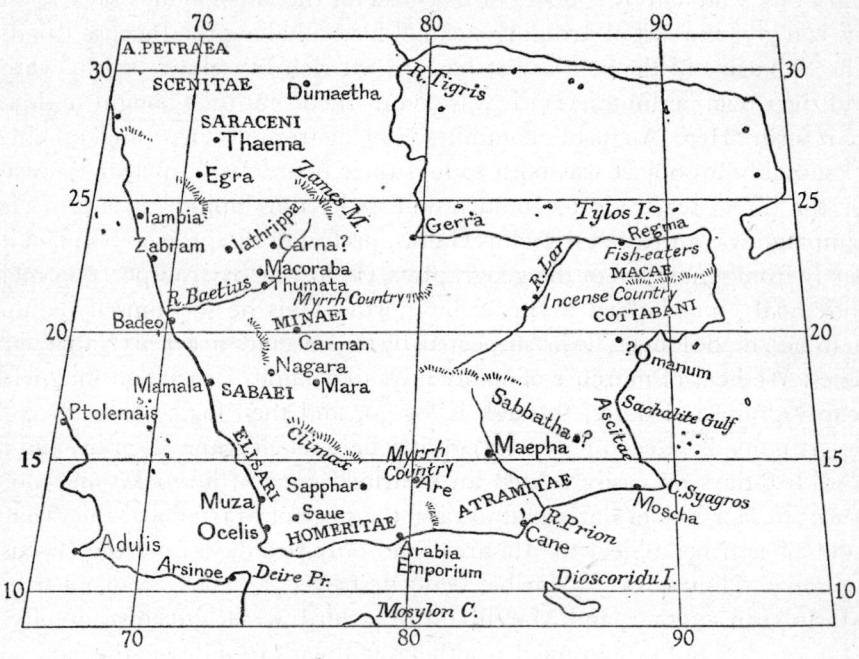

Fig. 51. Arabia (Ptolemy).

from west and east, had thereafter sunk to a village, and the king of the Homerites and Sabaeans to a 'friend' or client.[1] (If it was 'destroyed', it is active again on Ptolemy's map as 'Arabia emporium'.) Mommsen inferred that the humbling was done by the fleet mentioned or soon after, and many follow him, while some think rather of Claudius or Nero. Anyhow the ports thereabouts were freely used by the ships from Egypt (they left with the handy north-west winds at midsummer). The chief for local wares was Muza, 12 days from the inland capital Sapphar, but ships for India preferred Ocelis nearer the strait. The next kingdom, the Frankincense Country of the Atramitae or Hadhramaut, was ruled from Sabbatha

[1] Peripl. 23: 'Caesar', ibid. 26 (Eudaimon Arabia or Happy A. is Aden). Fleet, Plin. II, 168. Glimpse, ibid. VI, 160: Juba, ibid. 141.

or Sabota, a place said to have 60 temples; ships put in at Cane and the cape beyond (Syagros or Ras Fartak), whence they cut across the Ocean with the monsoon. The same kingdom controlled the island of Socotra, where it allowed a settlement of traders.[1]

Thus there was a good practical knowledge of Arabia, though some could still exaggerate its wealth and repeat old fables about winged snakes and

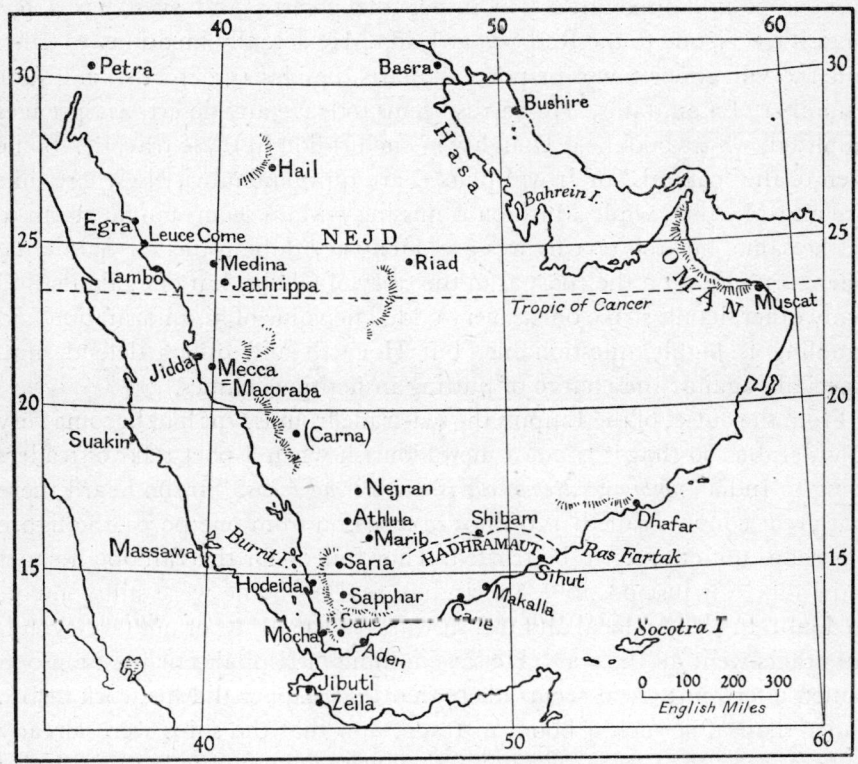

Fig. 52. Arabia (modern).

cinnamon-birds (Pliny thinks that they were invented to raise prices, and that really the cinnamon grows in Africa across the strait, with cassia in the hills beside the 'cinnamon plains', and he does not believe that Alexander's seamen smelt the spicy breezes when still out of sight of land). The name Happy Arabia is oddly extended to nearly the whole mass of the peninsula, Petraea and Deserta being confined to the northern fringe. The circuit is estimated at 4000 miles or more. As far as Syagros the Periplus is full and

[1] Peripl. 30–1: Schur, op. cit. p. 47. Plin. VI, 153 places it well. Ports and sailings, Peripl. 21–30, Plin. VI, 101–4 (some discrepancies as cp. 154–60). Mommsen, V, 611, Firth, *Aug. Caesar*, 1903, p. 281, Charlesworth, *Class. Quart.* 1928, p. 99: perhaps, Warmington, op. cit. p. 15. Claudius, Rostovtzeff, *Soc. and Econ. Hist. of R.E.* 1926, p. 513. Nero, Schur, op. cit. p. 46.

Ptolemy's drawing fairly good, though he seems to misplace Moscha (Dhafar?) short of the cape. Beyond this the coast was seldom visited, and the mapping is worse, while the eastern side is badly misconceived like the rest of the Persian Gulf. Off the coast the accounts bear little relation to each other or to the facts. Pliny gives a portentous rigmarole of names, mostly from Juba, but is confused and obscure. Ptolemy sprinkles any number of inhabited places in impossible deserts, and even has a few longish rivers, one to the Red Sea at Jidda. He actually mentions 57 tribes and 150 villages or towns or ports or marts, besides 13 capitals, and quite a number of mountains. He hardly seems to leave any desert, as Sprenger admitted, whose book was Doughty's 'enchiridion in these travels'. Some even of the 'capitals' or 'royal places' are quite unknown elsewhere, like Are and Maepha, while Mariaba is missing—Mara seems too far north to be the same, but the text figures are often very dubious, as for Sabbatha. There is no Egra on the coast as in the story of Gallus, but one inland, and many other details strike one as very odd. The value of his information and handling is highly questionable, but Hogarth and others defend him, especially against the charge of putting in fictitious names.[1]

From the outset of the Empire the sea-trade from Egypt had become very considerable, so that it is not a mere flourish when a poet talks of traders going to India—*impiger extremos curris mercator ad Indos*. Strabo heard there that great convoys sailed, 120 ships in a season from one port—the figure is perhaps not entirely to be trusted. They sailed 'for the Ethiopian capes and India' (or just possibly 'the Indian sea'?). Some were still content, no doubt, to pick up local and transit wares at the straits or not far beyond, but others went all the way. He says nothing of Hippalus or the monsoon named after him; yet it seems likely that that skipper did his work before rather than after such a boom in trade, and that the ships were already cutting across the Ocean. Probably they were going not only to the Indus mouths but with the wind less straight behind to Barygaza (Broach, where there was an early British factory in 1616, soon outshone by Surat and Bombay). Thus 'India was brought nearer for gain', as Pliny says. Not long before him (or perhaps about A.D. 50) came the final improvement in the use of these regular winds, a diagonal cut from the straits to the Pepper Coast of south-west India; it took 40 days, we hear, though this

---

[1] Hogarth, op. cit. pp. 15–23 and Kiernan, op. cit. p. 33, after Sprenger, *Alte Geogr. Arabiens*, 1875. Charge, Bunbury, II, 610. Ptol. VI, 7 (as cp. Petraea and Deserta, V, 17, 19). For his map, *G.G.M.* Tabulae, VIII, XIII: Müller's *Ptolemy*, 1901: Hitti, op. cit. p. 47: Montgomery, *Arabia and the Bible*, 1934, pp. 73–5: I have not seen Berthelot in *Mélanges ...Desrousseaux*, 1937, pp. 1–10. Carman(?) in VI, 7, 34 besides a Carna, 31. Sabbatha, 38. Plin. VI, 141–62: circuit, 156: 150–1 out of order, *G.G.M.* I, LXXI, Detlefsen, op. cit. p. 139. Glaser, op. cit. II, 73–113. Invented, Plin. XII, 85–8, 95: see p. 82, n. 1, p. 133, n. 2.

seems slow. The return was with another monsoon in December or January and helping winds inside the Red Sea at that time. Not easy to fit into this account of steadily increasing experience and skill is a brief notice of a freedman engaged in collecting the Red Sea duties. He was blown 'past Carmania' in 14 days(?) to Ceylon (some would emend to 40, and infer that he cannot have known about the monsoon).[1] He is said to have shown some coins to the king, who admired them so much that he was moved to send envoys to Claudius. We hear later of the same duties, the *vectigal maris Rubri*, in a rescript of Marcus and Commodus with a list of wares concerned, and an orator praises the great Empire which draws the produce of Happy Arabia and India.

Already Augustus had received envoys, at least twice, it seems, and perhaps from both north India and the Pandya kingdom in the far south (the texts are rather obscure on the matter). They brought a letter in Greek and various presents, an armless boy, a turtle and a big 'partridge', a python and tigers, and with them came a 'sophist' or wise man of Bargosa (Barygaza?), who later burnt himself on a pyre at Athens. A few mentions of embassies to Trajan and his successors are very brief and vague.[2]

If any Roman was ever sent in return, he is not known to have written of what he saw like Megasthenes. Various travels to India were later ascribed to this period, but all are very dubious. So the sage Apollonius of Tyana is made to visit the wise Brahmans and to see or hear strange things; these are told with some touches of scepticism, and the local colour is seldom very plausible.[3] Thomas is in early tradition apostle of Mesopotamia and buried there, but in *Acts* current from the third century he is supposed to convert a king in north-west India and to be martyred there or farther south. The story is usually admitted to be fabulous, belonging to a kind of Christian romance which has its pagan counterparts, like the travels of Apollonius just mentioned. But again there is some interest in the local colour used, here very slight, a real king's name, a possibly real town, and

---

1 Warmington, op. cit. p. 43: Plin. VI, 84. Stages in use, ibid. pp. 100–6, cp. Peripl. 39, 57. Hippalus, see p. 176, n. 2. Final, Tarn, op. cit. p. 369: A.D. 50–5, Charlesworth, op. cit. p. 97. Direct sailing general only after this cut, Schur, op. cit. pp. 50–2. Shipping, Str. 118, 798: figure doubted by Rostovtzeff, *Hell. World*, II, 929. Ad Indos, Hor. *Ep.* I, 1, 45.

2 Dio, LXVIII, 15, *Vita Hadr.* 21, *Vita Pii*, 15, 4. For Aug. see Nic. Dam. ap. Str. 719, cp. 686, Dio, LIV, 9: 'often', Mon. Anc. 31: Suet. *Aug.* 21, Oros. VI, 21, 19, Florus, II, 34: *C.H.I.* I, 597: Tarn, op. cit. p. 321. H. G. Rawlinson, *Intercourse between India and the Western World*, 1916, pp. 107–9. Warmington, op. cit. pp. 35–7, 95, 99, 102. Rescript, Digest, 39, 4, 16, 7. Orator, Aristides, XIV, 94–5 K.

3 Some about Taxila, Tarn, op. cit. pp. 164, 360: Sir J. Marshall, *Guide to Taxila*, 1921. Life by Philostratus tr. Conybeare (Loeb), 1912, Phillimore, 1912. Reitzenstein, *Hellenistische Wundererzählungen*, 1906, pp. 41–5. Whittaker, *A. of Tyana and other Essays*, 1906, pp. 11–19. Thorndike, op. cit. ch. 8. Bidez, *C.A.H.* XII, 614.

little else. A general statement implying that Christianity had reached India by about A.D. 200 is doubtful. So is the alleged visit of Pantaenus, despite the fact that his pupil Clement of Alexandria knows the name of the Buddha and something about Buddhism: perhaps he went only to Axum or south Arabia, which were already sometimes loosely referred to as a sort of nearer 'India'.[1] Yet, however all this may be, the sea-trade was real, and the information from it new and good.

Plenty is said of the wares, many light and costly enough to repay such long voyages. There were above all spices like pepper—we hear all about its kinds and prices—also nard and other perfumes, and a little Chinese silk, which had drifted down from the overland route. There were pearls from the Ceylon strait, and various gems, sapphires, beryls (with an Indian name), and diamonds from two inland districts which Ptolemy can place. More humdrum things were not despised, like cottons and 'the reed honey called sacchari' or sugar. The ships carried some goods to exchange, such as wine and glass and metals, but a great deal was paid for in cash. Already Tiberius complained sourly of the drain of specie for 'stones', and Pliny growls about the money given away to Arabs and Indians and Silkmen— 'so much our luxury and our women cost us'—a million a year of good coinage lost for things to be sold at Rome at a hundred times that amount.[2] Coin-finds in India are sufficient to illustrate the reality of the drain, and give an impression of it as chiefly to the Pepper Coast and as highest in the early reigns; but this is rather misleading, because the natives preferred the first mintages with which they became familiar and asked for them long after, as the Germans continued to like the coins of the Republic. In the

1 So Harnack, *Mission und Ausbreitung des Christ.* 1902, p. 444, Duchesne, *Early Hist. of Chr. Church*[2], 1914, pp. 92, 243, Rawlinson, op. cit. p. 141, Kiernan, op. cit. p. 36, Latourette, *Hist. of Expansion of Chr.* 1938, I, 107: doubtful, Zeiller, *L'Empire rom. et L'Église*, 1928, p. 109, Burkitt in *C.A.H.* XII, 479. J. Stewart, *Nestorian Missionary Enterprise*, 1928, pp. 105–6 defends against Mingana. Pantaenus, Eus. *H.E.* V, 10, 2. Clem. *Strom.* I, 15, 71, III, 7 (stupa). General, Tert. *adv. Jud.* 7. Thomas, cp. earlier versions in Eus. op. cit. III, 1, Clem. op. cit. IV, 9. Dahlmann, *Die Thomas-Legende*, 1912, and others defend, see Latourette, p. 108, Stewart, op. cit. pp. 102–4. Apostolic romance, Duchesne, pp. 328, 373. J. K. Wright, *Geogr. Lore of Crusades*, 1925, pp. 74, 379. Rapson, *C.H.I.* I, 578–9 doubts T.'s visit: mythical, V. Smith, *Early Hist. of India*[2], 1908, pp. 218–22, Garbe, *Indien und das Christentum*, 1914 (Chr. began in 4th century). Farquhar, *Bull. Rylands Library*, 1926, pp. 80–111 and 1927, pp. 20–50 inclines to believe. Wild legend, Kellett, *Story of Myths*, 1928, pp. 219–23.

2 Plin. VI, 101, XII, 84. Tib. in Tac. *Ann.* III, 52. Wares, Periplus, passim: silk, ibid. 39, 49: pepper, ibid. 56, Plin. XII, 26–7 (sugar, ibid. 32, nard, 42, etc.): Dioscorides, I, 7, 68, V, 92: Warmington, op. cit. passim. Drain, *C.A.H.* X, 247: G. F. Hudson, *Europe and China*, 1931, pp. 98–100: Mattingly, *R. Coins*, 1928, p. 182: H. J. Loane, *Industry and Commerce of City of Rome*, 1938, p. 50 and in *Class. Phil.* 1944, pp. 10–21 (on Vespasian's *horrea piperataria*): G. H. Stevenson in *Legacy of Rome*, 1923, p. 169. Beryls, Prop. IV, 7, 9, Ptol. VII, 1, 86: diamonds, ibid. 65, 80.

north the Kushans received and imitated some Roman gold.[1] The drain should not be overrated, though it was palpable, as the supply of precious metals was limited. In the days of the East India Company there was again to be much talk of the drain of bullion for luxuries, even after Europe's reserve of silver had been greatly increased from Mexico and Peru: it was grumbled that Europe 'bleedeth to enrich Asia' and 'all nations bring coin...and this coin is buried in India, and goeth not out', but some defended the trade as bringing a balance of treasure when the wares were re-exported to other countries. Bernier about 1670 had a theory that all gold and silver coinage, after circulating elsewhere, comes at last to be absorbed in India.

For geography the trade brought clear gains, though the writers were slow to use them and long continued to repeat the standard accounts. Strabo knows of the traders but does not try to learn what such illiterate persons may have to say. Mela does not even notice them, and garbles the old matter, with a taste for fancies like gold-ants. Seneca's lost essay was plainly copied from Megasthenes.[2] But at least one gives what he himself knows, the Skipper of the Periplus. He is practical and detailed on the whole western coast. He describes it as running south all the way, a great improvement on the earlier drawing. He tells of the ports and their wares, their approaches and local conditions: he knows, for instance, of the tidal bore and the pilot service at the Narbada mouth below Barygaza. Muziris is in one kingdom (the Chera), and Bacare and Nelcynda, which get pepper from Cottonarice, are in another, Pandion's (the Pandya at the south end). He has heard of some inland places in touch with the coast. One is Ozene (Ujjain), said to be no longer a capital, though presently Ptolemy can name a king there, apparently a Saka satrap. There are, too, Paithan, from which onyx comes down, and a district whose name survives as 'Deccan' and means 'south country', as he rightly explains. (It belonged to the Andhra kingdom extending thither from the south-east: this is not probably

---

1 Warmington, op. cit. pp. 297–8: see p. 293, n. 1. On coins, Sewell, *J.R.A.S.* 1904, p. 591, esp. pp. 620–36, criticized by Schur, op. cit. pp. 52–6, Warmington, pp. 278–96, Rostovtzeff, *Soc. and Econ. Hist. of R.E.* p. 513. Modern complaints of drain, J. A. Williamson, *The Ocean in English History*, 1941, pp. 97, 102–5, 183: W. H. Moreland, *From Akbar to Aurangzeb*, 1923, pp. 52, 60–1: Oakeshott, *Commerce and Society*, 1936, p. 147: Horrocks, *Short Hist. of Mercantilism*, 1925, pp. 59–65: Sir W. Foster, *England's Quest of Eastern Trade*, 1933, p. 289: E. G. R. Taylor, *Late Tudor and Early Stuart Geography*, 1934, pp. 103–4: A. Wolf, *Hist. of Science...in 16th and 17th Centuries*, 1935, pp. 614–18: G. N. Clark, *Seventeenth Century*, 1929, pp. 25–9: Haney, *Hist. of Econ. Thought*[3], 1936, pp. 119–21: W. Cunningham, *Growth of English Industry and Commerce*, 1938 ed. Pt. I, pp. 258–61: M. Beer, *Early British Economics*, 1938, pp. 140–54.

2 Sen. ap. Plin. VI, 60, with figures from Meg. (cp. Arr. *Ind.* 7). Mela, III, 62–9. Traders, Str. 686.

the people mentioned elsewhere as Andarae, but Ptolemy even gives the special title of the dynasty.) We learn that the coins of Graeco-Bactrian kings were still current at Barygaza, but of history the Skipper is ignorant enough to suppose that Alexander himself had reached the Ganges. Pliny has some kindred information on the monsoon routes and the same pepper-markets; Muziris is said to be undesirable owing to a bad roadstead and the neighbouring pirates, while Becare of the Neacyndi receives pepper from Cottonara. Ptolemy's text has Bacarei, with Melcynda. It has been recognized as Vaikkarai, the port of Kottayam, and Muziris seems therefore to be Cranganore rather than farther north, as once placed, at Mangalore.[1] (There is some confirmation from the Indian side, as Tamil poetry preserves a tradition of the foreign visitors at Muchiri and other places.) Pliny knows too that Pandion's capital is inland at Modura (now Madura). Otherwise he gives old outlines and figures, with some complaint of discrepancies in the accounts, and makes a jumble of tribes and places from Megasthenes. He hardly even attempts to compare this matter with the new, so that it is obscure, for instance, where he puts *Perimula celeberrimum Indiae emporium*—apparently on the south-east coast, but in that case his figure is all wrong, and Lassen finds it in the Ceylon strait, McCrindle near Bombay.[2] Dionysius is almost worthless. He has the old shape with much wretched stuff about reed jungles, gold from deserts and rivers, gems, and the wanderings of Bacchus, who set up two pillars by the Ganges and the eastern Ocean; there is nothing recent except a mention of 'Scythians' at the Indus delta.[3]

Of Ceylon the Skipper has only slight hearsay: it is vaguely enormous and has pearls and gems, tortoise-shell and muslins. Pliny names the first three wares. After giving old rumours, he adds some notions said to have been gathered from the envoys sent to Claudius. The island has a flank to India of 10,000 stades and lies four days off with an island of the Sun halfway; Palaesimundum, the chief of 500 towns is on a river flowing south, while another flows north from the same lake (an irrigation tank?). The rest is Utopian: slavery and law-suits are unknown and centenarians

---

1 As once Lassen, Müller, *G.G.M.* Tab. 14, etc., and still Wecker, *R.E.* Limyrice, Berthelot. Corrected after Yule by McCrindle, *Anc. India as described by Ptolemy*, 1885 (reprint 1927, p. 52): V. Smith, *Oxford Hist. of India*², 1923, p. 143: L. D. Barnett, *Antiquities of India*, 1913, p. 13. Bacare, Peripl. 55, Plin. VI, 105, Ptol. VII, 1, 8. W. India, Peripl. 38–58: coins, ibid. 47. Andarae, Meg. ap. Plin. VI, 67. Andhra, Ptol. VII, 1, 82: Ujjain, ibid. 63, Grousset, op. cit. I, 66.

2 O. Stein, *R.E.* Perimula: cp. Aelian, *N.A.* xv, 8. Plin. VI, 56–80: Klotz, op. cit. pp. 188–90: Detlefsen, op. cit. pp. 125–31. Tamil, Schoff, op. cit. p. 205, Warmington, p. 58, Mookerji, *Hist. of Ind. Shipping*, 1912, Rawlinson in *Legacy of India*, 1937, p. 16.

3 Dion. Per. 1088: shape, 1131, cp. 621, 887 (from Erat. somewhat altered): pillars, 1164, etc. Bunbury, II, 488.

ordinary. Some had a more reasonable idea of the size, comparing with Britain. Ptolemy has a new name, Salice, akin to the modern. He stretches the island to 2° S. instead of 6° N.! Oddly such wild exaggerations were to persist in the Arabs and Marco Polo; it has been suggested that they began with a misunderstood unit of measure. But at least he gets the shape fairly

Fig. 53. India.

well, and also the position, close off Cape Cory. The men are said to wear their hair long; there are tigers—so Pliny too, but wrongly—and elephants, and the wares are beryl and jacinth, gold and silver and other minerals, and rice, honey, and ginger, but strangely not cinnamon even yet. The number of names is astonishing, and shows detailed information, though only a few are quite safely identifiable, like the 'Ganges' (Mahavelli ganga), one inland capital (the ruins at Anuradhapura) and Malaea (meaning 'mountain', Adam's Peak) above the 'elephant grounds'. He sprinkles the seas around with exactly 1378 islands, names a score, and maps them with amusing confidence. Dionysius has old stuff as usual: the island is vaguely broad and under torrid Cancer, and it has elephants, while the monsters of its seas can swallow whole ships.[1]

The east side of India was poorly known. There are dubious statements that a few ships reached the Ganges already in Strabo's time, and vaguely 'many' later. The Skipper is fairly detailed only to a pearl fishery opposite

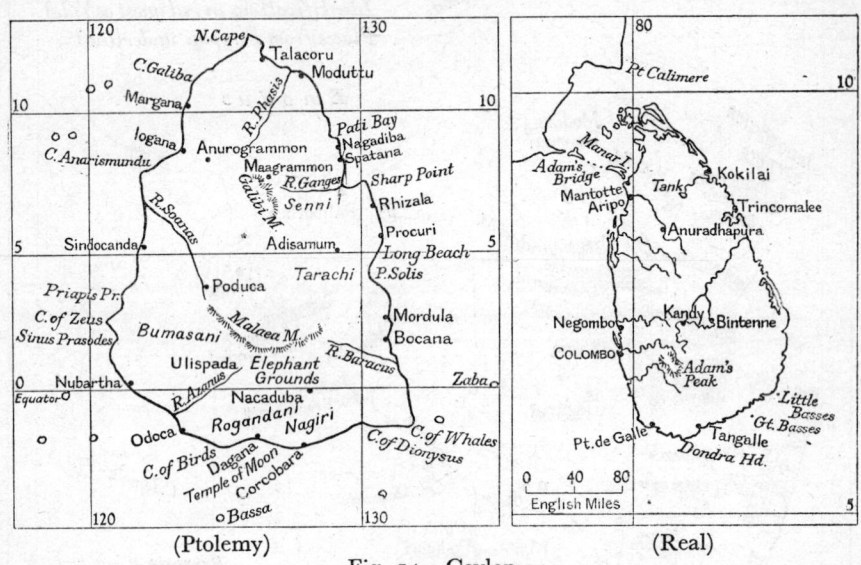

Fig. 54. Ceylon.

Ceylon and another bay there with a town inland. He is usually thought to blunder here and continue the southward trend of the coast too far, well past Comorin, but this may be due to a textual error. Beyond he has hearsay of three ports, a coast running east (instead of north-east as it should), a district Masalia with fine cottons (about Masulipatam), another with ivory and near some cannibals, and a Ganges port with fine muslins and spikenard.[2] Ptolemy by his time has much more, including the Chaberus or Cauvery river and various details for the Chola (or Chora) kingdom, which was to give its name to the Coromandel coast: he has the name three

1 Dion. Per. 592–605: whales also Aelian, *N.A.* XVI, 17. Britain, Str. 130, Ps.-Arist. *de Mundo*, 393b. Peripl. 61. Plin. VI, 81–91: pearls also, IX, 106. On Ptol. esp. Tennent, *Ceylon*, 1860, I, 559–61. McCrindle, op. cit. p. 287. Berthelot, op. cit. pp. 357–71 is too confident. Unit, Kiepert, *Lehrbuch*, 1878, p. 13. Herrmann, *R.E.* Taprobane, 1932 (disliked by Berthelot). Few coins found, Warmington, op. cit. p. 63. On the ruins Lord Holden, *Ceylon*, 1939, p. 26.

2 Peripl. 60, 62–3. Error in 59, deleted by Frisk as cp. *G.G.M.* Tab. XI, Tozer, *Anc. Geogr.* p. 275, etc. Ganges, Str. 686, 'many', Dion. Per. 709–12. No coins of this time, Warmington, p. 111. Visitors from Ganges at Alexandria, Aristides, *Or.* 32, 40.

times over, as the Soringae, the Soretae of Orthura (old Trichinopoly), and the Sorae, oddly said to be nomads under king Arkatos, really of Arcot.[1] Unfortunately he somehow got an utterly wrong notion of the whole coastline. The west side, so well conceived by the Skipper, is now travestied as forming an exaggerated cape just beyond Bombay and then running eastward to Comorin! It even continues in that general direction to a supposed southmost projection at Palura and a port near-by, from which one can cut across the open sea (that is, over the Bay of Bengal to Burma). These places are really about Ganjam, about four-fifths of the way

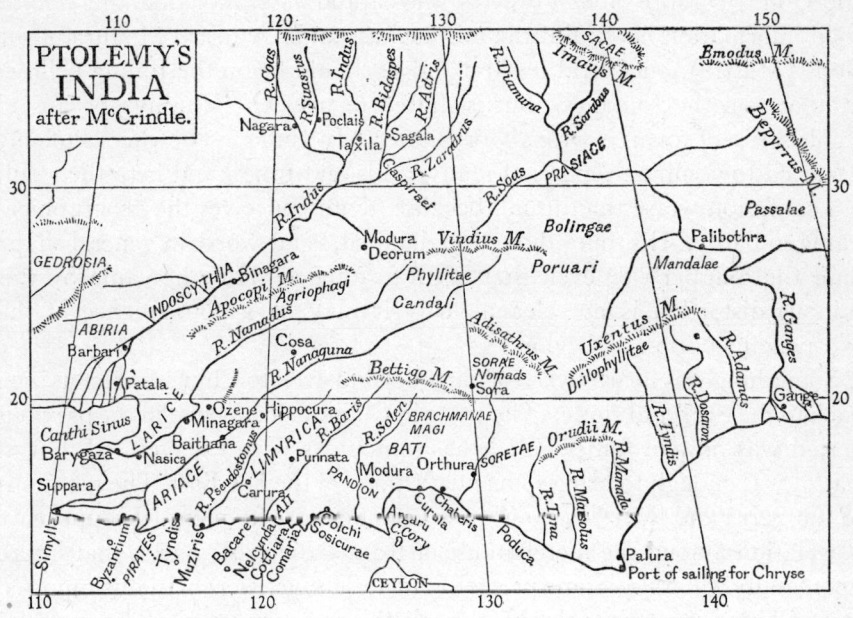

Fig. 55.

up what we know to be the eastern side (or more than half-way, according to Berthelot, who places them just beyond the Godavari mouth). Thus he all but annihilates the great peninsula. His many names evidently include an accretion of new information, but the distortion of the outline makes such a mess that few can be safely located. Of the ranges the Vindius is clearly the Vindhya, rightly near the source of the Narbada but otherwise misplaced. The Bettigo and others represent the Western Ghats, all wrong in direction and pushed absurdly far inland. So they send long rivers to the nearer side, whereas all the long rivers should run to the farther. Those beyond the Cauvery are drawn queerly short, and their identity is much disputed, though the Manada seems at least in name the Mahanadi. The

1 McCrindle, op. cit. pp. 65, 162, 185.

Ganges has a good delta for the first time, but the course is bad and much else is careless: only three tributaries are named out of a score previously known, and the Jumna is absurdly reduced. The Indus is now better drawn as running south-west, though too markedly so; its lower course is far too long at the expense of the upper basin with the five rivers. There is an amazing number of inland tribes and towns. Some have brief labels like Punnata with beryls, Mysore way, and Cosa 'where are most diamonds', perhaps near Baitul north of the Tapti's sources (two tribes thereabouts, the Phyllitae and Candali, have often been guessed as the aboriginal Bhils and Gonds). More often a town is 'the capital of' this or that king—some good information here. But the misplacing can be wild: so Modura of the Gods (Muttra), once held by Menander, should be on the Jumna (Pliny's Methora on the Jomanes), but is shifted to near the Vindhya because a whole series of towns is wrongly orientated. In India as elsewhere Ptolemy has tried to combine reports of many kinds and times, and here the result is a confusion worse than usual, because he misconceives the geographical frame so badly. His map, though so detailed, is far worse in general shape than the Skipper's or even that of Eratosthenes. How he came by this ruinous distortion is not clear: partly it may be a consequence of the extravagant notion of Ceylon.[1]

Something was heard by sea of parts beyond even to China, but let us turn back to the overland route. The trade in Chinese silk opened in the previous period was now in full swing; it has sometimes been exaggerated, but at least it was enough to bring some new reports of the Far East. The mentions of the Seres and their 'sericum' now become more frequent. It appears in Revelation among the merchandise of Rome 'the great harlot that sitteth upon many waters'. (Some pieces found at Palmyra were actually imported from China, one writer thinks, though this is questioned.) The material was admired as lighter and finer than the Coan. Moralists thought it improper for modest women, and Tiberius banned it to men as effeminate, and Marcus Aurelius to his wife as extravagant, being then worth its weight in gold. But it continued to be worn, though always costly.[2] In origin it was

---

[1] Kiepert, loc. cit.: Bhils, ibid. p. 40. Orientated, Tarn, op. cit. p. 245: Hellenistic matter, ibid. pp. 230–51. Methora, Plin. VI, 69, cp. Arr. *Ind.* 8, 5. Lassen, *Ind. Alt.* 1858, III, 94–284: St Martin, *Étude*..., 1860: Cunningham, *Anc. Geogr. of India*, 1871: Yule in Smith's *Atlas of Anc. Geogr.* 1885, largely followed by McCrindle, op. cit.: Berthelot, op. cit. pp. 257–356. Renou, *Géogr. de Ptol. L'Inde*, 1925 (text only, and map after Venetus R.). E. A. Johnston, *J.R.A.S.* 1941, pp. 208–22 (P. partly uses an Indian source: M. possibly is Mahanadi: Maisolus is Kistna).

[2] Tib. in Tac. *Ann.* II, 23, Dio, LVII, 15. *Vita Marci*, 17. Improper, Sen. *de Benef.* VII, 9, 5, *Ep.* 90, 15: Plin. VI, 54. Coan, see p. 86, n. 2, p. 132, n. 1. Exaggerated, as Schmitter, *Rev. Arch.* 1939, pp. 73–102 says. Rev. xviii. 12. Imported, R. Pfister, *Textiles de Palmyre*, I–III, 1934–40: questioned by Flanagan, *Burlington Mag.* 1935, pp. 92–3, Schmitter, loc. cit.

supposed a 'fleece' or down combed from leaves, 'a natural error less marvellous than the truth', says Gibbon, 'and slowly corrected by the knowledge of a valuable insect, the first artificer of the luxury of nations'. (A wild worm does spin its threads on trees, from which they are gathered to make a coarse silk, but the western writers for long say nothing of any Chinese worm, though, oddly enough, a wild silk-worm was known at home, the Coan.) The people were at first very hazily placed, somewhere beyond Bactria and towards the eastern Ocean, between Scythians and Indians, the last of men 'wherever they are', as Seneca says. In general probably they were not Chinese but middlemen in the Tarim basin, to-day Chinese Turkestan.[1] Yet these were after all Chinese subjects for much of the time. What is told of them is strange enough. Only a bad historian makes them send envoys to Augustus, who is extravagantly credited with thoughts of conquering them. Elsewhere they are said to be mild and very shy, awaiting rather than seeking commerce, and doing a dumb barter in a desert or at a certain river. (Dumb barter is familiar enough, when one of the peoples concerned is of a very lowly type, and sometimes when both are, but ancient writers seem to overdo this motif and may well be wrong in ascribing such trade to the Silkmen.) There is a queer report of them as tall, red-haired and blue-eyed, and living 'beyond the Hemodus', (Himalaya)—all this apparently got from envoys of Ceylon. Yule gave it up, and why Ceylon should have anything to do with a people so remote remains obscure (a notion of confusion of Seres with the neighbouring Cheras of south India is not plausible). But the Tarim people, it is now known, were once of Aryan language and kinship; to-day they speak Turki, but European types are still found among them. Of western writers it is the Skipper, curiously, who has the first clear mention of a trade-route from the Seres to Bactria, from which a branch line took some silk down to the Indian ports.[2] Details come with the Syrian merchant Maes, on whose information Marinus and Ptolemy worked. His travellers seem to have gone on from Balkh to a place called Stone Tower, a little short of

[1] Debevoise, *Pol. Hist. of Parthia*, p. 205. Fleece, Virgil, *Georg.* II, 121, Sen. *Thy.* 378 and *Phaedra*, 397, Petronius, 119, Silius, XIV, 664: Plin. loc. cit. *depectentes frondium canitiem*: Dion. Per. 754 (oddly from flowers).

[2] Peripl. 64, to ports, ibid. 39, 49. Ceylon, Plin. VI, 88. Yule-Cordier, *Cathay and the Way Thither*, I, 200. Cheras, Warmington, op. cit. pp. 37, 257, H. G. Rawlinson, *India*, 1937, p. 37, after Kennedy, *J.R.A.S.* 1904. Shy, Mela, III, 60 (desert also Dion. Per. 752), Plin. VI, 54 (both after Varro?), Sen. *de Benef.* VII, 9, 5. Envoys, Florus, II, 34 (IV, 12): conquering, Horace, *Odes*, I, 12, 56, cp. III, 29, 27. Ovid, *Am.* I, 14, 5, oddly has *colorati*... *Seres*. Dumb, Viljoen, *Economics of Primitive Peoples*, 1936, pp. 219–20: in W. Africa, Hdt. IV, 196. See p. 74, n. 1, p. 367, n. 2. P. J. H. Grierson, *The Silent Trade*, 1903: Seligman, *Veddas*, 1911, p. 6. Hoyt, *Primitive Trade*, 1926, pp. 133–4: Boas, *General Anthropology*, 1938, p. 398: J. W. Page, *Primitive Races of To-day*, 1938, pp. 15 (pygmies and negroes), 28 (Semang and Malays).

another named only as 'the starting-point of the traders for Sera'. The route is described, somewhat obscurely, as a zig-zag including a climb up through the gorge of the Comedae. This name was located by Yule from Chinese and Arab sources as belonging to the valley of the Surkhab, a tributary of the Oxus. 'Stone Tower' should be near, probably about Darautkurgan, where the Alai trough opens a way to the river of Kashgar.

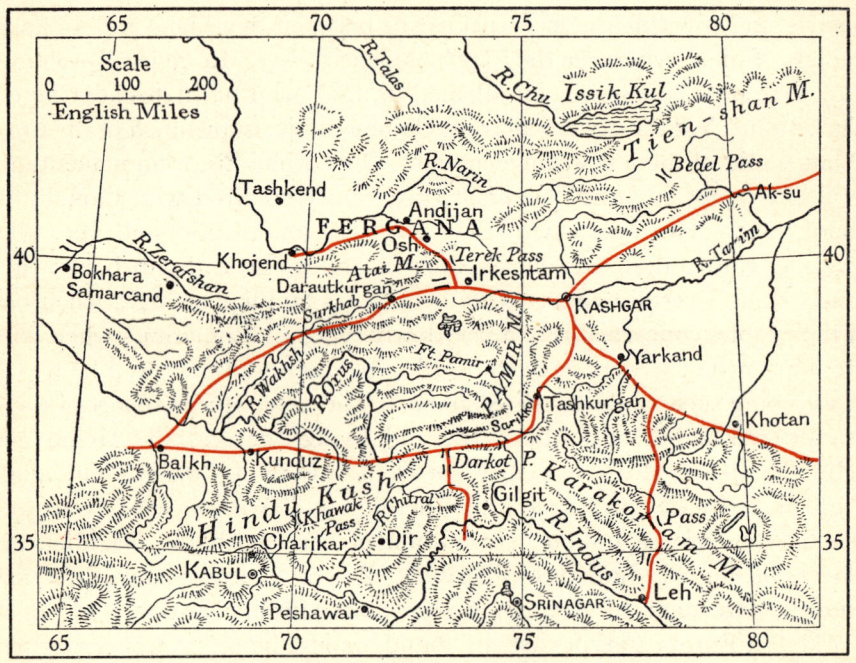

Fig. 56. Silk-roads over the Roof of Asia.

The 'starting-point' may be Irkeshtam, on the present Russian-Chinese frontier, where another road comes in by the Terek pass from Fergana. (Some, however, find it at Kashgar itself, and Berthelot goes far on to near Kucha.)[1] Ptolemy puts it on a range branching north from the main Imaus (or Himalaya) and dividing his two Scythias; this may be taken as a notion of the Pamirs and Tien-shan, which lie between the two Turkestans, Russian and Chinese. His map (p. 293) has Stone Tower just short of it at

[1] Berthelot, op. cit. p. 201. Kashgar, Herrmann, *Land der Seide*, 1938, p. 111, as Friedlaender. Yule-Cordier, op. cit. pp. 190–2. Irk., Richthofen, *China*, 1877, 1, 496, Sir M. A. Stein, *Anc. Khotan*, 1907, I, 55 (hesitates on S.T.). D. already Lullies, 1887, Tomaschek, 1888: Minns, *Scythians and Greeks*, 1913, p. 114: Hermann, *Seidenstrassen*, 1910, and op. cit. pp. 102–6: Stein, *On Anc. Central-Asian Tracks*, 1933, p. 295, accepted by Sir P. Sykes, *Quest for Cathay*, 1936, p. 49, *Hist. of Afghanistan*, 1940, p. 121. Barger, *G.J.* 1938, p. 387 (not necessarily main route, and where exactly S.T.?). D. is the S.T. of Ptol. VI, Berthelot, loc. cit.

135°, on his gradation, but in the preliminary discussion in Book I he makes it 132°: he does not explain the discrepancy, nor can anyone else. Chinese sources and modern travellers have much to say of another route leading from the upper Oxus itself to Yarkand through the mountain-trough of Sarikkol, where there is a fort called Tashkurgan, meaning 'Stone Tower'. Some have guessed this to be his place, but it can hardly be, as it is not reached from the gorge of the Comedae.[1] The ancient map, we must confess, gives a poor idea of all this tremendous roof of Asia and what a modern poet describes (not very accurately) as

> the aerial mountains which pour down
> Indus and Oxus from their icy caves.

That the agents of Maes went on from Stone Tower is often assumed, but it seems more likely that the rest of their report was hearsay gathered from 'the traders to Sera the capital'. Anyhow they told of that city as seven months from Stone Tower. Marinus believed them and oddly took the journey as continuous and straight east: so he made the distance 36,200 stades and fixed the terminus at 228°. Ptolemy discounts by half for the usual exaggerations of traders, for divergences from the parallel, and for many rests, besides halts due to the bad weather presumably frequent in such northern parts. Thus he contrives to reduce the figure to $177\frac{1}{4}°$. Even so the stretch remains far too great. (The agents really meant seven months there and back, it has been suggested, and Marinus misunderstood.)[2] Ptolemy proceeds to complain that the report gave no details worth mentioning; yet where else did he get the many things entered on his maps of 'Scythia outside Imaus' and Serica? From the fact of the silk-trade it is hard to doubt that they reflect some genuine information of the routes through Kashgar and Khotan to some northern city of China, probably Si-an. But the perversions of the mapping are such that scarcely a name can be placed with any confidence. It is not even clear how he means the rivers to be drawn. And what are they? The Oechardes looks remotely like the Tarim, as it seems in a basin between northern and southern ranges (Tien-shan and Kun-lun?). Already D'Anville in 1768 put most of the

---

[1] Guessed, Rawlinson, *J.R.G.S.* 1872, Lassen, II[2], 540: Stein at first (*Sand-buried Ruins of Khotan*, 1903): still Charlesworth, *Trade Routes*, pp. 103, 107, Warmington, op. cit. p. 133, Berthelot, loc. cit. (that of Ptol. I, 11 only): Grousset, *Hist. de l'extrême Orient*, 1929, I, 65, 242: Coédès, *Textes d'Auteurs grecs et latins relatifs à l'extrême Orient*, 1910, p. xxi. Cordier, *Hist. gén. de la Chine*, 1920, I, 273 denies. Gerini, *Ptolemy's Geogr. of E. Asia*, 1909, p. 66 thinks of Khotan.

[2] Herrmann, op. cit. p. 108. Ptol. I, 12, 17: maps, ibid. VI, 15-16. Agents went, Herrmann, Stein, *C.-Asian Tracks*, p. 26, etc.: no, Hudson, *Europe and China*, p. 85, Warmington, loc. cit. For the silk-roads see above, Fig. 23 (p. 179).

names in the Tarim and north-west China. Serica is mainly the Tarim, thinks Yule, or north China, thinks McCrindle, who is sceptical on all details. Herrmann suspects 'Scythia outside Imaus' as an artificial filling of a bad gap opened by Ptolemy's own handling (it should be remembered that he is dealing very freely with his source Marinus). The Thaguri are often taken as a relic of the old Tochari, and a still older people are the

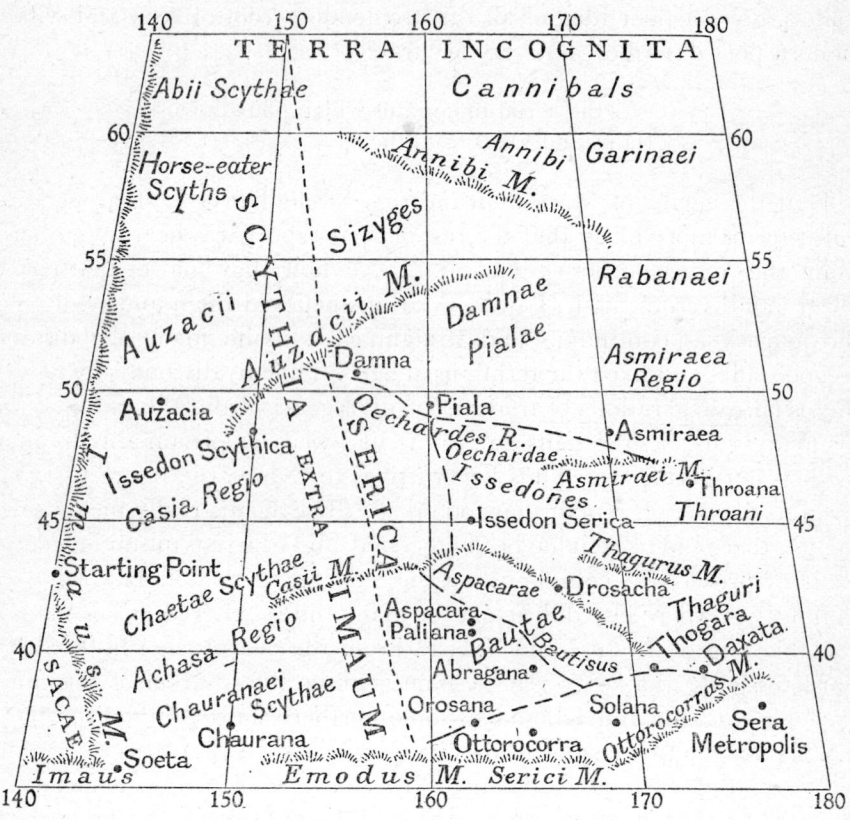

Fig. 57. Ptolemy's Serica and vicinity.

Issedones, but those who know his constructions elsewhere will not have too much faith in this fixing of a wandering name. The two towns he calls Issedon have been very variously placed at Kashgar or somewhere eastwards, 'the Scythian' at Aksu (Minns) or Kucha (Herrmann), 'the Seric' about Lop-nor (both these writers) or within the Wall of China (Tomaschek, Berthelot). Certain resemblances of names like Casia–Kashgar, Auzacia–Aksu, and Chaetae–Khotan have sometimes been used, but very unsafely. Yet the Bautae southward are plainly the Tibetans, who still call themselves Bod; what their river is meant for is obscure. The Ottorocorrae are the happy northern people of Indian fable heard of earlier as the Attacori.[1]

Recent explorers, and especially Sir Aurel Stein, have revealed ample evidence of the strange meetings and minglings of influences on these tracks of Central Asia. Among the traders were Sogdians, who have left documents at the western extension of the Wall. Indians were strong along the road from Khotan, bringing their Buddhism and its sculpture, which long retained obvious traces of its half-Greek beginnings. Their tablets have impressions of seals which were exact copies, if not actual specimens, of Graeco-Roman art, including a quite classical Athena (Plate II D). There have even survived pieces of the silk itself dropped in transit. Yet all this hardly proves that Roman subjects knew these distant roads directly, and the bad mapping rather proves the contrary. Somewhat flimsy is an attempt to show that the report of Maes was derived partly from a translation of a Chinese road-book for the Tarim and that the Chinese unit of measurement was misread at thrice its real value. There is little evidence from coins—apparently only one authentic find in China, of sixteen coins dating from Tiberius to Aurelian, which turned up near Si-an. If some of the drain of cash was for silk, most of the money probably stuck in the hands of middlemen, Parthian and Indian. Odd mentions of other Seric wares, hides (or furs?) and choice iron or steel, are rather puzzling but hardly matter.[2]

The Chinese annals again tell something of the west. A usurper (A.D. 9–23, between the two Han dynasties) lost the Tarim province, where the oases fought each other and fell into dependence on the Hiung-nu. But a brilliant general, Pan Ch'ao, recovered each in turn and helped a colleague to beat back the nomad power (A.D. 73–91). He stopped a Kushan army which had crossed the Pamir, and he won expressions of homage from as far west as Fergana, though it is a misreading to suppose, as some have done, that he himself advanced to the Caspian.[3] The silk-roads became more active than ever and 'foreign traders knocked daily at

---

[1] See p. 131, n. 2. Iss., see p. 62, n. 1. Minns, op. cit. p. 110, etc. accept. Gap, Herrmann, op. cit. p. 149. Yule-Cordier, pp. 15, 194. McCrindle, op. cit. pp. 294–300. Berthelot, op. cit. pp. 229–54, and Hudson, op. cit. pp. 83–5, are too confident. B. gets Iss. Scythica at Guchen, N.E. of Urumchi: Kiepert's map has it at Karashahr, and I. Serica at Ansi (cp. at Khotan Richthofen).

[2] Plin. xxxiv, 145. Coins, Bushell in *Academy*, 1886, p. 316. Road-book, Herrmann, *Lou-lan*, 1931, and *R.E. Seres*, 1923. Athena, Stein, *C.-Asian Tracks*, fig. 46, *Anc. Khotan*, title-page, *Ruins of Desert Cathay*, I, ch. 23: *C.A.H.* XI, 9, XII, 97 and Plates V, 132 *d*: Tarn, op. cit. p. 365 (from Seleucia rather than R. Empire?). Sogdians, Stein, *C.-Asian Tracks*, p. 188, *Ruins of Desert Cathay*, II, 113. Silk pieces, ibid. I, 381, II, 126, *C.-Asian Tracks*, pp. 100, 119: Schmitter, op. cit. (p. 306, n. 2). See also Seligman, 'R. Orient and Far East', in *Antiquity*, 1937, pp. 5–30. Chinese mention Buddhism first in 2 B.C. (rather than A.D. 65), Cordier, I, 263.

[3] Some, Richthofen, *China*, 1877, I, 469, V. Smith, *Oxf. Hist. of India*², 1923, p. 129, and still C. P. Fitzgerald, *China*, 1935, p. 191. Denied by Yule-Cordier, p. 40, Chavannes,

the Barriers'. This new greatness hardly outlived the next governor, his son. But once again contact had been made with lands beyond the roof of Asia. Pan Ch'ao received envoys from the Parthians, and himself sent one in A.D. 97. This man, Kan Ying, came to Tiao-chi on the great sea (Babylonia). He heard of Ta-ts'in, lying 'in the west of the sea' and trading by sea with both the Parthians and India. He had thoughts of going on but gave them up on hearing that the voyage, first south and then north, might take from three months to two years! It appears that this means the long detour round Arabia, and that he was kept in the dark about the only sensible route, overland to Syria. The name seems a vague compliment to a 'Great China' of the west, and most hold after Hirth that it refers to the eastern Roman provinces, and especially Syria.[1] Queer things are said now and later of Ta-ts'in: it is large and populous, having over 400 cities and a big capital An-tu with five palaces (Antioch); the king is chosen for merit and deposed if unsuccessful; the people are tall and handsome and honest; there is a postal route, and lions are dangerous except to caravans. The 'curiosities' or wares are pearls and coral and amber; a later list gives drugs and perfumes, textiles, gems and glass (mistaken as a precious mineral). Sometimes there is a nebulous phrase about 'the western sea which is the same as Ta-ts'in' (the rivers west of Khotan are supposed to flow into the western sea, apparently part of the great Ocean on the west side of the earth). But once at least we hear of direct touch, and by sea. In A.D. 166, after Ta-ts'in had long been hindered from intercourse by the An-si (or Parthians) between, its king An-tun sent envoys; they came to the Tongking frontier, though with disappointing presents, not jewels or glass or other 'curiosities' expected but ivory and tortoise-shell and rhinoceros horn, apparently picked up on the way. The king has long been accepted as Antoninus (Marcus Aurelius), but the men were probably only merchants from Egypt or Syria, who posed or were mistaken as envoys.[2] But, if even one or two merchants reached so far, we turn with interest to what the western writers have to say on the sea-route beyond India.

Herrmann, *Seidenstrassen*, p. 8, Teggart, *Rome and China*, 1939, p. 144. Later Han Annals in Chavannes, *T'oung Pao*, 1906, pp. 210–69, 1907, pp. 149–234. Grousset, op. cit. pp. 217–18, Teggart, pp. 137–46. Cordier, *Hist. gén. de la Chine*, I, ch. 11.

[1] Bury's ed. of Gibbon (ch. 40), IV, App. 12: Hirth, *China and the R. Orient*, 1885: Pelliot, *J.As.* 1921, p. 139, etc., but Herrmann, *Land der Seide*, pp. 6, 91–2 thinks T. is Arabia. On K.Y. see Chavannes, op. cit. 1907, p. 178 (knocked, ibid. p. 216): De Groot, *Chin. Urkunden*, II, 94: Hirth, p. 39, detour, p. 169: Hudson, op. cit. p. 84: Yule-Cordier, p. 41. Ta-ts'in, ibid. pp. 42–6. On a later name Fu-lin, see p. 367, n. 1. Some spell Ta Ch'in.

[2] Hirth, op. cit. pp. 42, 174–8. Chavannes, op. cit. 1906, p. 178, 1907, p. 185. Yule-Cordier, pp. 51–2: Grousset, I, 243: Hudson, p. 89: Warmington, p. 130, etc. But really envoys (as Yule in 1866, Richthofen, I, 512), Oertel in *C.A.H.* XII, 235. Gowen and Hall, *Outline History of China*, 1926, p. 98 talk of 'commissions from Rome'. Ta-ts'in, Hirth, p. 40: list, ibid. p. 73: capital, see p. 367, n. 1.

The old map had drawn the coast from the Ganges' mouth north past the end-cape of the great central range of Asia and then westwards to the Caspian 'gulf'. Room had been left for some possible outlying islands. Such in popular fancy were Chryse the Golden, near the rising sun and paved with gold, some said, and an Argyra or Silver to balance it. Old writers had them off the Ganges and Cape Tamus, says Mela. Pliny has one rich in gold and another rich in silver, both queerly placed off the Indus. But he also has a Cape Chryse and some names which seem to come from genuine hearsay and to anticipate Ptolemy's, though Berthelot despises his confused notes.[1] The hazy Golden Island was already being transferred to a real, if still dim, Farther India. So Josephus found Ophir hereabouts (this placing was to be accepted by Columbus, and as late as 1567 a Spanish expedition from Peru discovered the 'Solomon Islands'). The Skipper knows that ships of the east side of India sail over to a land Chryse with fine tortoise-shell: its gold mines and an island off it, 'Chryse' too, may be relics of fable. Yet the Indians themselves had a name meaning 'golden land' for Burma, and this notion may, some think, embody a rumour of Sumatra. What follows is remarkable. Beyond Chryse and well to the north the sea ends in a country with a very great city not far inland called Thina, from which silk is carried overland, some finding its way down from Bactria (and also from Tibet, it seems) to Indian ports. The city may not be quite the same as Sera, but he clearly knows the people to be the same as the Seres of the overland trade. Here then we have the first European mention of China as approached by sea.[2] The name is a form of that by which China has always been known when so approached. Its age and origin are debated. Some think it a local Malay name for the southern part, Cin 'in the language of the islands', as Marco Polo says. But most trace it to the Emperor who burnt the books and built the Wall, or even to the Ts'in dukes already famous before him.[3] The Skipper's hearsay came without doubt from Indian seamen: they had been trading eastwards with the monsoons perhaps since the third century B.C. and by now were founding colonies everywhere as far as Java and Indo-China. Java-dvipa is a Hindu name,

---

[1] Berthelot, op. cit. p. 373. Plin. VI, 55. Herrmann, *Land der Seide*, p. 32 (Psitharas=Ptolemy's Aspithras, etc.). Tomaschek, *R.E.* Cambari and χρυσῆ Χερρόνησος. Indus, Plin. VI, 80. Mela, III, 70: see p. 131, n. 2. Sunrise, Dion. Per. 587.

[2] Peripl. 64, Chryse, ibid. 63, ships, 60. Yule-Cordier, pp. 183–5. Sumatra, Herrmann, op. cit. pp. 37, 63, 74: Warmington, p. 71 (and perhaps Java). G. E. Harvey, *Hist. of Burma*, 1925, pp. 9, 310. Jos. *Ant.* VIII, 164: see p. 30, n. 1.

[3] Soothill, *China and the West*, 1925, p. 15. Discussion, Yule-Cordier, pp. 2–7: Pelliot versus Laufer in *T'oung Pao*, 1912–13: Herrmann, op. cit. pp. 38–9: Cordier, op. cit. I, 213: Grousset, p. 206: Couling, *Enc. Sinica*, 1917, etc. Malay, Richthofen, op. cit. I, 504–10 (and Yule later).

known to Ptolemy and also to the Chinese, who in A.D. 132 received envoys from 'Yetiao'.[1]

Ptolemy, after Marinus, gives a place on the east side of India as a regular 'port of sailing for Chryse', and he knows of at least one seaman, Alexander, who had gone far in the tracks of the native traders, and this well before the 'envoys' of An-tun. His detailed map reflects an accretion

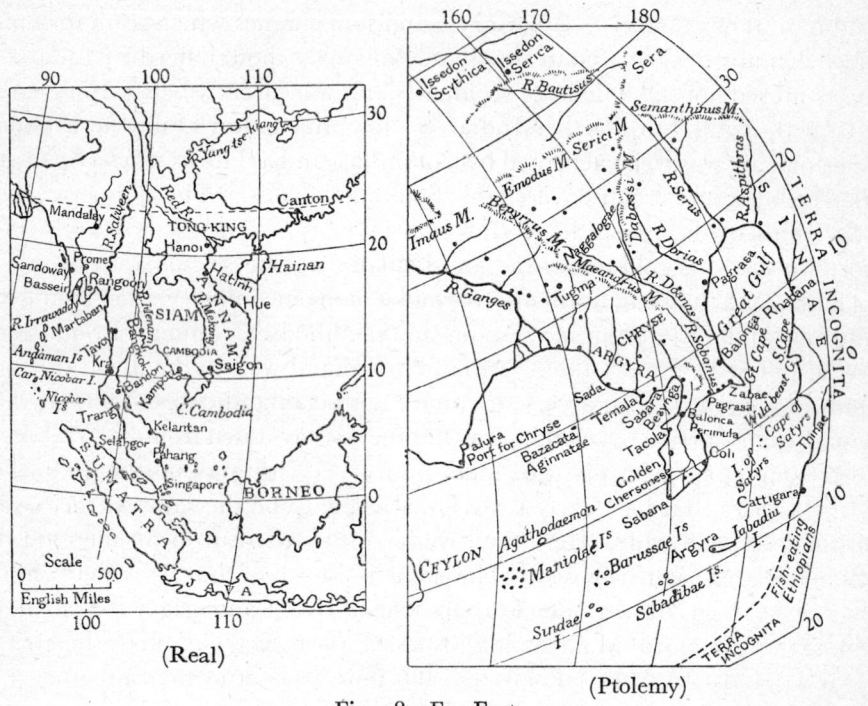

Fig. 58. Far East.

of reports, but we have only glimpses of this working material, and it is hard to say how good it was and to explain his constructions and perversions.

He maps Chryse inland behind an Argyra. Both seem to represent Burma, a Burma unduly lengthened but with a recognizable shape and with the rivers fairly right in direction. Here he goes out of his way to give some curious descriptive notes. Some people are said to be small and fair with thick hair and blunt noses, near a district 'where they say the best malabathrum is produced'—the Skipper has a similar account of a shy people

[1] Grousset, p. 154. Trade and colonies, Hornell in *Antiquity*, 1941, p. 250: Hudson, op. cit. pp. 76, 89: Gerini, op. cit. pp. 7, 734: Furnivall, *Netherlands India*, 1939, p. 6: Quaritch Wales, *Towards Angkor*, 1937, pp. 23, 26: Mookerji, op. cit. pp. 148, 155. Ptolemy's Perimula a colony of Pliny's Indian one?, Lassen, III, 249, McCrindle, p. 201. Hennig, *Terrae Incognitae*, I, 355–6 and *Klio*, 1930, p. 268.

THE SAME: ASIA

doing a dumb barter in the same leaf near the frontier of Thin, somewhere upper Assam way. There, too, are the Naggalogae, correctly explained as meaning 'naked people' (Naga log). At one inland capital 'there are said to be bearded cocks and white crows and parrots'. Another, Tugma, is thought to be Tagaung in upper Burma.[1] The mountains are not well conceived. A Golden Island no longer appears, but instead there is a Golden Chersonese or Peninsula, pointing south and ending at a port Sabana. It seems the Malay Peninsula, with the port at or near Singapore. But, if so, it must be confessed, it is queerly shortened and provided with a fantastic river-system. McCrindle is sceptical, after Yule, and sees only a misconception of the Irrawaddy delta between Besynga (Bassein) and Sabana (about Martaban).[2] Marinus estimated the distance from Cape Cory (opposite Ceylon) to the Golden Chersonese as 61°, carelessly adding up the sailing items as if all on one parallel. So says Ptolemy, who allows for divergences and exaggerations and thus reduces to about 35° (see Fig. 59).

The rest of the map (Fig. 58) has caused endless trouble. It is quite unlike the description of the Periplus. The Sinae have a capital Thinae, a little behind a port Cattigara, but they are put south of the Seres, as if they were a quite different people. Their coast does not go round far north, but is pulled far south to join an imaginary land enclosing the Indian Ocean. If this is discounted as due to a preconceived theory—of which more later—and if the final stretch is pivoted round northwards on the head of the 'Great Gulf', the outline begins to look at least remotely like the modern. Some, however, regard this appearance as deceptive.

For these farthest parts it is not clear either what the seaman Alexander said or how the two geographers used him. The coast is 20 days to Zabae near the Great Cape; it has Pirates with skins like hippopotamus-hide, and in the hills behind are tigers and elephants. But the direction? It is dubiously understood as 'facing south', that is running east, from (the neck of?) the Golden Peninsula, and many accept the cape as what it looks, the south point of Indo-China, with Zabae at or near Kampot. Berthelot, however, takes the coast as 'running north' to a town and cape near Bangkok, and Berger as 'running south' (he even finds Cattigara no farther than Singapore, like St Martin).[3] The last stretch from Zabae to Cattigara

---

1 Harvey, op. cit. p. 10 after Yule. Cocks, Ptol. VII, 2, 25. Nagas, ibid. 18, McCrindle, p. 223, Berthelot, p. 399. Argyra, VII, 2, 3, 17, 22. Chryse, ibid. 17, 23. People, ibid. 15, same as Peripl. 65, Herrmann, op. cit. pp. 37, 62: McCrindle, p. 218.

2 McCrindle, pp. 198–9, 208. But cp. Lassen, III, 232, Berthelot, p. 376, Herrmann, *R.E.* Sinae. Schnabel, *Text u. Karten des Ptol.* p. 49 suspects Sabana as a doublet of Sabara.

3 Berger, *Erdkunde*, pp. 607, 622: St Martin, *Hist. de la Géogr.* p. 205. Berthelot, p. 391, cp. Yule-Cordier, p. 193, McCrindle, p. 203, etc. Gerini, op. cit. pp. 7, 169 reaches Z. at Saigon.

is 'some' or vaguely many days, which Ptolemy rather casually takes as some twenty, 'sailing over southward and more to the left' (south-south-east?). The actual map inserts here a Great Gulf going far north. For the longitudinal distance he reduces Marinus very drastically as usual, in fact to less than half, and he adds a cryptic remark suggesting some fresh information since.[1] The capital Thinae is on the last meridian, and the map ends in swamps overgrown with large reeds and in *terra incognita*. It is all very puzzling. If the Great Cape is what it seems, the Great Gulf should be the China Sea, the southward pull of the coast should be discounted, and Cattigara should be well north on the outskirts of China or even within it. Many think it is—even in name perhaps—the Kiao-chi reached by An-tun's 'envoys', Hanoi in Tongking, most say, or according to Hirth Hatinh in north Annam. Several go on to Canton or beyond as far as the Yangtse mouths.[2] On the other hand many take the Great Gulf as that of Siam, including the Perimulic as a mere bay. Herrmann argues that it is a false doublet of the Gulf of Siam and inserted by Marinus, who made a mess by conflating two sources, Alexander's log and an Indian itinerary expressed in a native measure which he misread at twice or thrice its real value; the final port, he concludes, was about Saigon, and visited rather than owned by the Sinae.[3] (It is notable, indeed, that the text gives two places called Pagrasa, short of and beyond the Great Cape, and a Balonga besides a Balonca, as is shown on the map.) The capital 'has neither bronze walls, they say, nor anything else worth mentioning', a remark not yet plausibly explained. The place is often accepted as Lo-yang (Ho-nan), the capital of the time, or the earlier one, Si-an, but it may be rather some great southern city like Nanking. Clearly the mapper fails, unlike the Periplus, to realize that the Sinae are the same people as the Seres of the overland trade.

It is hard to understand why so very little was heard of the big islands. Iabadiu is said to mean 'barley island', quite rightly, and to be rich in gold

---

1 Ptol. I, 17, 5: Bunbury, II, 604. Ptol. I, 14, 1–4: map of Sinae, ibid. VII, 3. Marinus had stretched his data to get the east end in the longitude already got for Sera, Bunbury, II, 537.

2 Canton, Lassen, III, 98, Forbiger, II, 479, McCrindle, p. 246 (hesitatingly), H. Clifford, *Further India*, 1904, p. 8 (possibly). Beyond, Gerini, p. 302, Berthelot, p. 414. Yangtse, Kiepert, p. 44, Hennig, op. cit. p. 344. Hanoi, Richthofen, I, 508, Yule-Cordier, p. 193, Grousset, p. 243, Hudson, p. 88: Herrmann, *R.E.* Kattigara (but later for Saigon, *Land der Seide*, pp. 76, 83). Hatinh, Hirth, op. cit. p. 47, *Chin. Stud.* 1890, I, 19: Hennig previously, *Von rätselhaften Ländern*, 1935, p. 154.

3 Saigon, as above. Bunbury, II, 606 stopped in Cochin-China. Capital, Si-an, Herrmann, op. cit. pp. 39, 64 (as in Periplus, but Sera is Liang-chou). Lo-yang, Minns, Hennig, *Klio*, 1930, p. 262. Nanking, Fortiger, Berthelot, Warmington, pp. 64, 129. Ptol. doubles Gulf of Siam, Laistner in Newton, *Travel and Travellers of Middle Ages*, 1926, p. 21 (Catt. probably Hanoi).

and have a Silver-town or Argyra at the west end. Size and position are not good for anything, but the name indicates Java. Many, however, think it wholly or partly a notion of Sumatra. Three groups of Cannibal islands seem those off west Sumatra. A desperate suggestion is that the seamen went down this side and round without realizing Sumatra as an island. Another thinks that Alexander missed the strait by landing and crossing at the isthmus of Kra and going on in a native ship.[1] Islands of Satyrs, who 'are said to have tails such as they draw those of satyrs', have been very variously placed, sometimes in Borneo with its orang-utans (one writer has found Cattigara itself there). Of the nearer islands one said to have much shell and a naked people, the Aginnatae, may be the largest Andaman. The isle of Agathodaemon has been sought from Little Andaman (Yule) to Sumatra. A haze of fable hangs over the Maniolae, which have a magnetic stone and should not be approached by ships with iron nails, a persistent legend of these seas (Pliny already has a mountain which attracts iron but near the Indus). They lie roughly like the Nicobars but seem largely mythical. Hennig, who shifts them to the Philippines (Manila!), sees in the notion a proof that Chinese seamen were already using the compass, but this is very flimsy.[2] We hear from Marco Polo and others of the nailless ships of the Indian Ocean, built of such hard woods that cords and wooden pins had to be used instead of iron nails.

The Chinese had held Tongking since at least 111 B.C., and had recently suppressed a revolt there, in A.D. 42. The annals mention envoys from India in A.D. 159 and 161, and one rather dubious report has been taken to mean that they had sent their own by sea already to eastern India (one writer reads the place as Abyssinia, but this is fantastic).[3]

Just after Ptolemy, Pausanias has somehow heard that the Seres keep an insect in specially built houses and feed it for four years(!) on millet and reed, till it bursts and they find threads inside it. Is this glimmer of the truth connected with An-tun's 'envoys'? Anyhow it did not prevail against the usual fancy of silk as combed or gathered from trees. His idea of the

---

1 Hudson, op. cit. p. 89: suggestion, Hennig's, *T.I.* p. 341 and *Klio*, 1930, p. 264, denied by Herrmann, op. cit. p. 65. I.=Sumatra, Bunbury, II, 608, 644: Yule, *Marco Polo*, II, 266: Gerini, p. 458 (on poor grounds, thinks Wecker, *R.E.* India, p. 1290): Ferrand and Krom ap. Herrmann, loc. cit., who agrees. Mixed, Cary-Warmington, p. 169. Islands, Ptol. VII, 2, 26–31. Groups, Gerini, p. 379.

2 *Klio*, 1930, p. 274. Mythical, McCrindle, p. 242. Ptol. VII, 2, 31. Plin. II, 211. Borneo, Volz, *G.Z.* 1911, pp. 31–44. Satyrs there, Kiepert's map, Hennig, Moss, *Birth of Middle Ages*, p. 90: Bali and others, Lassen: Anamba, Gerini, p. 707, as Forbiger. Nails, Sir T. Browne, *Pseudodoxia*, 1646, II, ch. 3. Payne in *Cambr. Mod. Hist.* 1907, I, 29.

3 Herrmann, *Zt. Ges. Erdk. Berl.* 1913, p. 553, believed by Teggart, op. cit. p. 109. Huang-chi, A.D. 2. India, Pelliot, *T'oung Pao*, 1912, p. 457, Ferrand, *J.As.* 1919, II, 45, Hennig, *T.I.* p. 270. Not beyond Malaya, Laufer, 1914. Envoys, Yule-Cordier p. 51.

placing is wild, but a river Ser with a delta may be Ptolemy's Serus, in Indo-China, though some have thought it a rumour of the Yangtse or even the Yellow River.[1] About the same time an astrologer mentions a certain Schine (very briefly, as under the influence of the Crab); the name, otherwise unknown, is supposed to mean China. Oddly enough two inscriptions about a well-to-do Italian silk-merchant (*negotiator sericarius*) are of A.D. 168.

What led Ptolemy to pull the last stretch of coast southwards till it fades into 'Ethiopian' Fish-eaters—oddly far afield—and *terra incognita*? A report of some real southward turn, as at the peninsula opposite Hainan? Or of land to the east like the island of Borneo? Or a rumour of big islands, wrongly strung together as one continuous land?[2] Rather, perhaps, no good excuse at all, but a prejudice for land boundaries and for inhabited lands in the south temperate zone. Anyhow the result was a great imaginary southern land enclosing an Indian Ocean basin. It was to cause much trouble, and the long effort to prove or disprove this *terra australis* was to end in the discovery of Australia.

It has been mentioned in an earlier chapter that Hun pressure was perhaps already indirectly felt in Europe. One Hun chief, who would not be a vassal of the Chinese, had withdrawn far west and ruled on the Jaxartes, till overtaken by their vengeance (53–36 B.C.—there has recently been a picturesque suggestion that they met some Roman soldiers, escaped prisoners of the Parthians, fighting on his side). Some of the Yen-ts'ai or Aorsi seem to have fled from him over the Volga. A second movement of the same people, now called Alans (about A.D. 50), is also traced to a Hun retirement before the Chinese.[3] A few wares may have travelled very far in the reverse direction, to the heart of Mongolia: pieces of textiles found there, of about the first century B.C., are thought markedly Greek in design and actually the work of Greek craftsmen, perhaps of the Crimea.[4]

---

1 As St Martin, op. cit. p. 213: Yangtse, Nissen, *Jahrb*....*Altertumsfreunde im Rheinland*, 1894, p. 14. Paus. VI, 26: see Frazer's note. Yule-Cordier, pp. 21, 202. Bunbury, II, 658. River is Menam, Herrmann, op. cit. p. 26. Another glimmer, Pollux, VII, 17. Envoys, Kiepert, p. 44. Combed, Solinus, 50, Amm. Marc. XXIII, 6, 67, Mart. Cap. VI, 693, etc.

2 G. A. Wood, *Discovery of Australia*, 1922, p. 6 (see also p. 274, n. 2.). Hainan, Berthelot, p. 403. Borneo, Hudson in Sir P. Sykes, *Story of Exploration*, p. 339. Schine, Vettius Valens, p. 9 Kroll: Cat. Cod. astrol. II, 95. Merchant at Gabii, *C.I.L.* XIV, 2793, 2812 (Dessau, 5449, 7601).

3 Teggart, op. cit. p. 220, Kiessling, *R.E.* Hunni, 1913, 2600, Aorsi, ibid. 2587–92, after Hirth (but Teggart, p. 153 denies). See p. 290, n. 4, p. 180, n. 2, p. 251, n. 1. Chief beheaded, otherwise West might have heard of Huns earlier, De Groot, op. cit. I, 209, 225. Romans, Dubs, *Am. J. Phil.* 1941, pp. 322–30, and *T'oung Pao*, 1940, pp. 64–80.

4 Kozlov expedition of 1924–5, north of Urga, as reported by Yetts, *Burlington Mag.* 1926, pp. 168–85: Teggart, op. cit. pp. 212–13: Grousset, op. cit. I, 239.

THE SAME: ASIA

Where the modern satirist chooses to 'survey mankind from China to Peru', his pattern had *a Gadibus usque Auroram et Gangen*, from Spain eastwards to India, but Juvenal might have gone farther, to China itself. Some ancients had, as is shown above, a fair idea of the full extent of the Old World, indeed an exaggerated idea, a fact highly important for the discovery of the New. Yet some still talked as if nothing had been learnt since Alexander. That king, especially at the moment in India when he wept for more worlds to conquer, was a popular subject for schoolboys and overgrown schoolboys practising their eloquence. We have specimens of the things said, and they are not remarkable for geographical detail or for good sense. He has reached the end of the world; will he attempt the Ocean, vast and mysterious, *immotum mare*, full of great beasts and brooded over by perpetual darkness, with no stars or only unknown ones? (Such things are easily invented, remarks a commentator drily, as the Ocean cannot be sailed anyhow.[1]) Will Alexander try to find another world (*alium orbem*) in or beyond the Ocean? Some deny that there is any land habitable or worth while, even if reachable. The phrase 'another world' was often very loosely used, as for Britain explored by Julius Caesar, and the declaimers could hardly have explained what they had in mind, apparently nothing so scientific as 'dwellers opposite' in a south temperate zone.

[1] Elder Seneca, *Suas.* 1, ed. W. A. Edward, 1928: Curt. IX, 6, 20, Quint. III, 8, 17, Sen. *Ep.* 119, 8, Juv. x, 168 with Mayor's note. See p. 129, n. 1. Britain, Vell. Pat. II, 46, Florus, III, 10. Ganges, Juv. x, 2, cp. Tyriis cum Gadibus Indos, Lucan, x, 456: ab Gadibus ad mare Rubrum, Livy, 36, 17.

CHAPTER XI

THEORY IN THE SAME PERIOD

THE last three chapters have described what this period has to say about the world in various directions. It includes some notable gains of knowledge, chiefly from excursions of trade, to the Baltic and Zanzibar and along the silk-road and the monsoon sea-route. Of exploring curiosity, adventurous or scientific, there is still little sign: possibly it had a share in one or two journeys, like those into the Sahara and up the Nile. Even as a practical people the Romans might well have done more for geography, but they were too incurious here also. Perhaps the frontiers were long and uncomfortable enough without looking for more trouble outside. Anyhow there seem to have been few counterparts of the modern types, officers and others, who wander into the back of beyond and write books on their experiences of savage men and beasts. There was no Geographical Society to approve such doings, and no one thought of climbing something never climbed before. The ancients had their love of Nature, and especially of their own countryside, but no taste for seeking out wild and distant scenery. Forests like the German seemed gloomy and formidable, and there is barely a word to spare for the beauty of rugged mountains: it could be said that no charm of spring or summer ever comes to the Alps, and even for Virgil they are hardly more than 'lofty'.[1] There is nothing perhaps quite in the tone of the seventeenth-century tourist who speaks of them as 'high and horrid and disfigured by snow', or of Johnson on the Highlands, 'a wide extent of hopeless sterility', but mountains were just barriers and attracted little interest for their own sake. Very seldom are they described as beautiful, and then only because they contain fertile valleys.

On geographical theory the Romans can only copy, often without real understanding, and even Greeks were now failing to advance the subject. Hipparchus had set the urgent task, to gather plenty of observations, at least of latitude, as the necessary substructure of an improved map. But Strabo can only complain that nothing has been done. Ptolemy, indeed,

---

1 Geikie, *Love of Nature among the Romans*, 1912, pp. 283 f., though criticized by Fairclough, *Love of Nature among the Greeks and Romans*, 1930, pp. 201, 218, 262. Sir D'Arcy Thompson, *Science and the Classics*, 1940, pp. 38–9. Humboldt, *Cosmos*, 1864, II, 372–96. W. P. James, *Lure of the Map*, 1920, pp. 66–70. Alps, Silius, III, 479–99. Ramsauer, *Die Alpen in der griech. u. röm. Lit.* 1901, pp. 47–50. 'Beautiful', Plato, *Crit.* 118b, *Hymn Aphr.* 78: E. E. Sikes, *Roman Poetry*, 1923, ch. 4. For early English indifference to mountain scenery, B. Penrose, *Urbane Travellers*, 1942, pp. 8, 64, 239. Incurious, Miller in *Eur. Civ.* ed. Eyre, II, 507–8.

after Marinus, makes a brave attempt to extend and correct the map, using all the recent gains of travel and approaching the work as an astronomer; but the material of genuine observations is totally inadequate for his purpose.

Strabo writes for general readers of a liberal turn of mind, who want neither a guide-book nor a treatise on mapping but an intelligent account of the various known lands, with a stress on those which have mattered most for civilization. The bulk of his seventeen books is such a description, and one of great interest, if unequal, sometimes clogged with too much history, and not always up to date, especially in taking advantage of Roman information. Yet he does try to handle the scientific side also, and rather more than he professes, mainly in a rambling introduction of two books. There is a sketch of the progress of exploration, ill-proportioned and often wrong-headed; he wastes space defending Homer's supposed knowledge, ignores Herodotus as a mere fable-monger, believes in a Caspian 'gulf' as proved, while he has no use for Hanno's Cerne or for anything said by Pytheas, and so on.[1] The concurrent development of theory is poorly explained, and he has plainly little stomach for the task. Educated readers know without needing proofs, he assumes, that the earth is a globe and rests in the centre of the universe. (He mentions the familiar ship proof.) He ascribes to Parmenides the five zones determined by those of heaven, and gives an account of later discussion, himself wrongly dismissing the view that even the unknown equatorial part of the 'torrid' zone is habitable. He accepts the famous measurement of the globe while passing over its method as too technical for his readers (rather than because of his own incompetence to explain it, Dubois thinks). He says nothing of the bad attempt of Posidonius. He tells how Eratosthenes drew the known earth as a 'cloak-shaped' island in an Ocean with several gulfs including the Caspian, and how he placed it on the globe and built his map round two main lines of length and breadth, also how his effort was criticized, sometimes too sharply, by Hipparchus.[2] For all this important matter he is a prime authority, of course, though his explanation is not very connected or clear. His own objections are often niggling, and his innovations far from improvements. Unlike both the geographers mentioned he rejects Pytheas wholesale, and thereby ruins the map of Europe. Worsening a bad blunder of Hipparchus, he drags Marseilles

---

[1] Cerne, Str. 47: Herodotus, ibid. 508. On Homer, ibid. 15–47 and often elsewhere: see p. 25, n. 1, p. 26, n. 2, p. 27, n. 2. Analysis of Bks I–II in Bunbury, *Anc. Geogr.* II, 219–35. Books on Strabo, see p. 225, n. 1.

[2] E. defended in Str. 69–70, etc.: H. 'carping', ibid. 93. Ocean, ibid. 4–5, 112, island, 113, gulf, 121. E's lines, 112, 120. Zones, 94–5, 97, 110–11, much from Pos., see p. 214, n. 1. Ship, Str. 12: M. Dubois, *Examen de la Géogr. de Strabon*, 1891, pp. 281–2: S. visibly bored with the scientific side, ibid. p. 347.

down to 2° S. of the latitude of Byzantium, and he draws the line of uninhabitable cold only 4000 stades beyond the Black Sea and just above Ireland, thus greatly reducing the breadth of the inhabited world (to 30,000 stades).[1] He would like to reduce the length to suit, but can only omit the Breton peninsula and the presumed outlying islands, leaving the rest practically unchanged as 70,000 stades from Spain to the Ganges. He realizes that this fills little more than a third of the circumference on that parallel, and that the unknown remainder may well contain another inhabited world or even more than one; but he does not care for the four symmetrical worlds of Crates, though liking the fancy of an equatorial Ocean.[2]

He is aware that the only true mapping is to place the earth on an actual globe; this should, he thinks, be not less than ten feet in diameter, if it is to show the known part in sufficient detail. On the question of plane projection (τὸ εἰς ἐπίπεδον γράφειν) he is very rough: for ordinary purposes 'it will make little difference' if we draw the meridians as straight lines like the parallels, and it is not worth while to make them converge on the pole. As for the observations on which a map should be based, he complains of their absence even for well-known countries of Europe, and he can add nothing.[3] This side of the subject is not his métier. He takes an interest, however, in such matters as earthquakes and volcanoes, the silting action of rivers, and the theory of an over-filled lake which burst open the strait of Gibraltar. He is casual on the Nile problem, and he understands little on tides, though citing Posidonius. He modifies the latter sensibly on the influence of climate and environment: some national habits may be acquired otherwise, picked up from neighbours, for instance, or imposed by government, as when a Numidian king taught many of his nomads to settle. Besides a temperate climate, Europe and especially Greece owe their superiority in civilization to other factors, like their having a long coast-line, while Africa has few inlets: the observation (not likely his own) is striking, and moderns say something very similar.[4]

1 Str. 114–15, Ireland, ibid. 72. Bunbury, II, 229. Cinnamon Coast, 8800 stades from Equator as cp. Erat. 8300, Str. 95, 118 (why?), Bunbury, p. 232. Ruins, see p. 151, n. 4.
2 Str. 821. Third, ibid. 113: may well, 65, 118: Bunbury, II, 224. See p. 166, n. 2.
3 Str. 71. Projection, ibid. 109, 116–17. Bunbury, II, 232–3.
4 Str. 121–2, 126 (Greece, ibid. 334): see p. 254, n. 2, p. 278, n. 2: Semple, *Infl. of Geogr. Environment*, 1911, pp. 117, 254, 394. Otherwise, Str. 525, 833: see p. 108, n. 1: a diss. by Rid, 1903. Volcanoes, p. 104, n. 3, p. 105, n. 1: a diss. by Serbin, 1893: Lyell, *Principles of Geology*, 1875, pp. 23–5. Tides, see p. 202, n. 2, p. 211, n. 2. Silting, p. 104, n. 1. Lake, Str. 51, see p. 156, n. 1. Nile, p. 273, n. 1. *Geogr.* mentioned by Athenaeus, 121 A, 637 F. Praised by Rainaud, *Geographia* in Daremberg-Saglio, 1896. 'Statuesque', Str. 13–14.

In general his science is secondary and of little value except for the earlier work he uses. Yet he deserves every credit for the largeness of his design and for what he himself calls his philosophic conception. His synthesis has been highly praised as alone coming near to the modern idea. It is he who has saved much of the material which makes the history of the subject possible. In this period, strangely enough, his *Geography* seems to have quite escaped notice; a Ptolemy, concerned only with mapping, may well have passed it by, but why Roman writers missed using it—to their own great loss—is hard to understand.

Mela dismisses science in a few paragraphs. The earth is a globe, resting in the centre of the universe, and with five zones: he does not even mention any attempt at measuring its size. Our known earth is an island considerably longer than it is broad (he will not spoil his style by giving figures). It lies almost wholly within the north temperate zone. The south temperate is habitable and no doubt inhabited: he cites Hipparchus for a suggestion that Ceylon may not be a huge island but the northern fringe of a world of 'dwellers opposite' there. The Nile may rise among these Antichthones (or Antoikoi) and be swollen by the rains of their winter, then pass under an equatorial sea to emerge among us in our summer; but he gives a liberal choice of other theories and apparently inclines to a western Nile like Juba's.[1] Thule has short bright nights in summer and none at the solstice, and short dark ones in winter (some bad misunderstanding here); there are Hyperboreans with a six months' night and a day as long. Tides may be caused by the moon, if they are not a breathing of the universe or something else.[2] The remark about the opposite earth is not without importance, as Mela was much read later, and a reminiscence of it may have contributed (besides Ptolemy's map) to the persistent notion of a great *terra australis*.

Pliny is a bookworm, too busy reading and compiling to understand anything properly. On every subject he gives beside serious science worthless fables, which he feels equally bound to record (*prodenda quia sunt prodita*). He can say that the hippopotamus slims by bleeding itself on a reed, and he has countless things even worse. Often, indeed, he adds a doubt or denial, as about the phoenix and horse-headed birds in Ethiopia, griffins and the swan-song, but often he believes, or has no idea whether he should believe or not. He can be free-thinking about the gods, and he dislikes some features of astrology, though he does not really reject it—here and elsewhere he

[1] Mela, III, 96–7 (from deserts, ibid. 1, 50): from S. temp. ibid. 1, 54, see p. 118, n. 1. Hipp. see p. 160, n. 2. Antichthones, also Mela, I, 4. Science, ibid. 1, 2–24.

[2] Mela, III, 2, cp. reasons in Lucan, I, 409–17: see p. 202, n. 2, p. 211, n. 2. Hyp., Mela, III, 36, Thule, ibid. 57. Midnight sun?, see p. 148, n. 2. T. australis, Fiske, *Discovery of America*, 1892 (reprint 1920, II, 126).

leaves us with conflicting impressions.¹ *Fragilis et laboriosa mortalitas*—the only certainty is that nothing is certain, *nec quicquam miserius homine aut superbius*. Pliny is already akin to the men of the Middle Ages who found his tomes such a rich pasture of confused feeding.

He gives the usual cosmology, largely no doubt from Posidonius, though with notable differences (his universe is not liable to periodic destruction but eternal, as the Neo-Pythagoreans think). There are strange undertones, a naïve awe of the clever Greeks and almost a sneaking sympathy for the common Roman who needs persuading that the earth is not flat. The globe hangs at rest in the centre—for some queer reasons—and the Ocean does not fall off, which is all very wonderful. A star visible just above the horizon at Rhodes is quite high at Alexandria, and an eclipse is seen in one country hours earlier than in another; so the curvature must be very marked, and the globe tiny in relation to the universe. Inventions of the most exquisite Greek subtlety are the zones and the parallels of latitude with the longest day lengthening gradually northwards till it becomes 24 hours at Thule and 6 months near the Pole (once he says carelessly 6 months at Thule). The middle zone is literally 'torrid' and uninhabitable for the short way beyond the Ethiopians to the equatorial Ocean.² The south temperate is presumably inhabited. The vulgar doubt the Antipodes and ask why they don't fall off, but the Antipodes might as well ask why we don't. (Here he thinks fit to mention a fancy 'acceptable even to the unlearned' that the earth is an irregular globe, something like a pine-cone!) He knows of the old 'science of sun-dials' and the well at Aswan lit by the tropic sun, but he does not explain how shadows were used by Eratosthenes to measure the globe. That was an *improbum ausum*, an unconscionable impudence, 'but so subtly argued that one has not the heart to doubt', and he 'sees that it is generally approved', except that Hipparchus makes a small increase (this last assertion is probably a misunderstanding).³ He accepts the known earth as an island, and supports a continuous Ocean with downright misstatements, that Hanno sailed round to the borders of Arabia, Eudoxus from the Red Sea to Spain, and Patrocles from the Caspian gulf to India, also the wild story of Indians driven past that 'gulf' to Germany. For the

---

1 L. Thorndike, *Hist. of Magic and Experimental Science*, 1929, I, 95–6, despite Plin. II, 23, 28. Gods, ibid. 14–27, XXVIII, 10. Prodenda, II, 85. Slims, VIII, 96. Phoenix, etc., ibid. X, 3–5: 136: 61. Books on P. see p. 227, n. 1: full bibliography by H. Le Bonniec, *Rev. Ét. Lat.* 1945, pp. 204–52.

2 Plin. II, 172, Ocean as Stoics, ibid. 166, 170. Days, ibid. 186–8. Star Canopus, ibid. 178. Zones again, VI, 211 (out of connection). Thule, ibid. IV, 104. Eternal, II, 1: a comm. on II by D. J. Campbell, 1936. On his cosmology, Bickel, *Philologus*, 1924, pp. 355–69: Kroll, 1930.

3 II, 247 (out of connection): see p. 205, n. 2. Dials since Anaximenes, Plin. II, 182–6. Antipodes, ibid. 161.

THEORY IN THE SAME PERIOD 325

length and breadth of the known earth he cites from secondary writers various figures, which deserved little respect, without attempting to judge between them.[1] Even within this 'inhabited world' much has to be subtracted, he complains, for useless desert and marshes and mountains and encroaching gulfs: how small really is the earth, the scene of man's glory, and in the end he gets six feet of it! (The Emperor Marcus Aurelius is also struck by the thought of this narrow stage of human fame, only a part of the inhabited world, itself a very little part of the whole earth, which is itself a mere point in the universe.)

Pliny enlarges on the wonders of Nature and her 'crimes', like earthquakes and eruptions; he repeats much good theory, but often imperfectly or with bad blunders and strange credulities. The great Hipparchus, *paene consiliorum Naturae particeps* and *nunquam satis laudatus*, ended the fear of eclipses by publishing a list of their regular occurrences for six centuries; yet the sun was pale for a year after Caesar's murder. Earthquakes can be omens of disaster, like meteors, and were common in a bad year when Hannibal was laying Italy waste. He can suppose that a meteorite was once predicted.[2] On tides he hardly knows what his own explanations mean. For the Nile flood various obsolete fancies seem as 'plausible' as the summer rains. Like Mela he repeats rumours of monstrous peoples, with dogs' heads or no heads or huge ears or the like, and other peoples very long-lived or with unusual powers: Nature in sportive mood can produce almost anything, he allows, though man's faculties are admirable enough without our believing all these marvels.

He admits that under the Roman peace, when all seas and lands are open, science is not being maintained, much less advanced. He ascribes the fact in a vague way to a vulgar materialism so general that travel, for instance, is now undertaken only for gain.[3] These complaints seem rather beside the point: few ancients had ever been explorers, and the Romans had no interest in science, or were at the best dabblers, like Pliny himself, incapable of original work and often of grasping what others had already done.

Seneca values science highly, indeed, though almost only because it enlarges the mind, as Macaulay notes, and because it improves our morals by revealing the wonderful plan of Creation. The lessons he draws are often

---

1 See p. 210, n. 3. Length, Plin. II, 242: breadth, ibid. 245, IV, 102, where Isidorus respects Erat., Berger, *Erat.* 16. Patrocles, etc., Plin. II, 167–70 (Indians see p. 199, n. 2, p. 201, n. 3). On Pliny's measurements, K. Miller, *Mappaemundi*, 1898, VI, 135–40.

2 Plin. II, 149: pale, ibid. 98: Hipp. ibid. 53, 95. Volcanoes, ibid. 236–8. Earthquakes, 192–211. Disastrous comets, 91. On climatic influence, II, 189–90: see p. 109, n. 1. Marcus Aurelius, IV, 3, cp. VI, 33.

3 Plin. II, 118. Marvels, ibid. VII, 32: many fables in VII from one Isigonus, etc. Nile, Plin. V, 55. Tides, II, 212–42: E. de Saint-Denis, *Rev. de Phil.* 1941, pp. 134–62.

forced enough, but he has an open mind and real curiosity. A youthful interest in earthquakes was revived by new shocks, those which damaged Pompeii in A.D. 63 (he died in A.D. 65 and did not know that they heralded its destruction by Vesuvius). The *Natural Questions* is a rambling discourse, but less so than appears from the present disorder of the books. He considers various phenomena, mostly of the atmosphere, such as wind and rain and snow, and a few of heaven and earth, meteors and comets, springs and rivers, and earthquakes, the last explained by the common doctrine of imprisoned air. In general the science is taken from Aristotle and Posidonius, often indirectly. There is much about exhalations from the earth, some of them feeding the sun. It is not denied that the stars are divine and that 'the fortunes of peoples depend on the slightest motions' of five planets; meteors, too, announce the future. He has no use for horoscopes, indeed—*quid refert providere quod effugere non possis?* On comets he chooses the right view against Aristotle.[1] Little anywhere is his own except the moralizing, but his statement and judgment of theories are more competent than Pliny's. While accepting the globe as at rest in the centre of the universe, he at least mentions that some have believed in its rotation. He loosely describes the torrid zone as uninhabitable, and does not seem sure whether Antipodes actually exist (here he has an echo of Virgil). The known 'inhabited earth' is an island broken into by Ocean gulfs and made useless in parts by burnt or frozen deserts; he does not give figures.[2] He is interested in the recent explorers of the Nile and the problem of its flood. Quite unusual in a Roman—and little justified by the rate of progress in his own day or by his Stoic creed—is his faith in the progress of discovery and science: other planets will swim into our ken, and 'posterity will wonder at our not knowing things so obvious', and in later ages the Ocean will 'unveil new worlds' and Thule will not be the farthest land, this in some verses which were well known to Columbus.[3] The globe is tiny compared with the heavens, and from Spain west to India is only a few days with a

---

[1] Sen. *N.Q.* VII: stars, ibid. II, 10, meteors, I, 1. Sun, II, 5, 2, V, 8, 1, VI, 16, 2. Earthquakes, VI, 5–21 (youthful, VI, 4, 2). Ed. Oltramare, 1929: transl. J. Clarke with notes by Sir A. Geikie, 1910. Gummere, *Seneca the Philosopher*, 1928, pp. 49–62. Mieli-Brunet, *Hist. des Sciences: Antiquité*, 1935, pp. 721–33: Dill, *Roman Society from Nero to Marcus Aurelius*, 1904, pp. 300–5. Horoscopes, Sen. *Ep.* 88, 14: fortunes, *Dial.* VI, 18, 3. For Aristotle on comets, see p. 120, n. 1.

[2] Sen. *Dial.* VI, 18, *N.Q.* I, prol. 7. Antipodes, Sen. *Ep.* 122 (cp. Virg. *Georg.* I, 233–41): but *Phaedra*, 940, *orbemque nostris pedibus obversum colas*. Rotating, *N.Q.* VII, 2, 3, *an mundo stante terra vertatur*.

[3] Sen. *Medea*, 376–80. Gummere, op. cit. pp. 84, 116, citing E. G. Bourne, *Seneca and the Discovery of America*, 1901: Payne in *Cambr. Mod. Hist.* I, 18, 66. Madariaga, *Christ. Columbus*, 1939, pp. 80–1. Wonder, Sen. *N.Q.* VII, 25, 5 and 30–1. Yet S.'s view of progress has curious limitations, J. B. Bury, *Idea of Progress*, 1921, pp. 13–14.

fair wind! How small to the philosopher is his earthly domicile! *Quantum enim est quod ab ultimis litoribus Hispaniae usque ad Indos iacet? Paucissimorum dierum spatium, si navem suus ferat ventus, implebit.* This remark needs a large discount in its context, but it was to have important effects. Roger Bacon noted it as 'repeating Aristotle's ideas of the nearness of Spain and India', which were in fact, he thought, much nearer across the sea than Ptolemy supposed. Columbus himself was impressed, and particularly, it seems, by the 'fair wind': he got one by starting from the Canaries, so fair that his men began to doubt if they would ever get back. (The return was on another line, to the Azores with west winds and easterly currents; these had been observed beforehand, Nunn argues, but Madariaga says that Columbus did not know so much and was very lucky on the first voyage.)[1] Such was the fortune of Seneca's book; throughout the Middle Ages it was a chief authority on its kind of science, and they might have had a much worse. The note of belief in progress woke little response, it is true, and Seneca himself was far from Francis Bacon, for whom 'the true and lawful goal of science is that human life be endowed with new powers and inventions'.

Vitruvius, architect and engineer, likes to air a half-baked learning. His profession should know something of most things, he opines, including medicine in relation to *inclinationes caeli, quae Graeci climata dicunt*, and the healthiness of the airs and waters and places (the wording seems to recall the old Hippocratic treatise). Apropos of various forms of sun-dial and their supposed inventors he gives a queer sketch of the 'almost superhuman science' of the stars; he does not question their influence, though he leaves horoscopes to the professionals. Canopus does not appear to the southward traveller first in south Egypt as he says, but already at Rhodes. He makes a show of having studied the famous measurement of the globe by the use of shadows. A discussion of climate and its effects depends on Posidonius. (Providence has placed Rome, he thinks, in a fine and temperate region to win the empire of the world.) He talks of some wonderful waters, and has a notion that south winds bring rain to northern mountains, so that the biggest rivers rise there and most seem to flow south, including the Nile from the Atlas![2] Among his machines are a hodometer with wheels to register distances travelled by land—we hear of one later on a carriage of

---

1 Op. cit. pp. 88, 201-2, cp. Nunn, *Geogr. Conceptions of Columbus*, 1924, pp. 36-7, 45-8, denied also by A. P. Newton, *Great Age of Discovery*, 1932, p. 93. Sen. *N.Q.* I, prol. 13. Bacon, copied by D'Ailly read by Columbus, Taylor in Jane, *Documents*, II, p. lxxix (see p. 339, n. 1): Woodruff, *Roger Bacon*, 1938, pp. 126, 133, and see p. 119, n. 2.

2 Vitr. VIII, 2, 6: waters, VIII, 3, 16-25: Nile, see p. 267, n. 2. Climate, Vitr. VI, 1 (see p. 109, n. 1). Globe, I, 6-9. Stars, ibid. IX, influence, IX, 6, 2: Canopus, IX, 5, 4, cp. Gem. 3, 15, Cleom. I, 10, Plin. II, 178 (Rhodes). Climata, Vitr. I, 1, 10.

the Emperor Commodus—and an adaptation as a sea-log, but there is little evidence that either was seriously used.

Some try to make poetry of science, like the prince Germanicus, who translates Aratus. The best is Manilius, who is inspired by a real enthusiasm for astrology. He gives various proofs of the globe, and explains how an eclipse is seen earlier from some parts than from others, how as we travel some stars disappear behind the earth's convexity, and how the day lengthens northward till it becomes six months at the Pole. In the south temperate zone are Antipodes, unknown peoples in unknown realms, where the shadows fall in the reverse direction. From the fact that tides are caused by the moon and sun he takes the usual false step to the influence of the stars. Those presiding at a man's birth decide his character and vocation, and each sign of the zodiac has a particular effect on certain lands and their climates and peoples. Here he gives a rapid survey of the known earth, which is an island with gulfs from the Ocean, including the Caspian.[1] Much of this, good or bad, belongs to the Stoic doctrine as developed by Posidonius. The old notion of climatic influence was long to be muddled with this other kind, of which there are still traces to-day, as when we call people jovial or saturnine, martial or mercurial. There is a poem on Etna, written before the great eruption of Vesuvius; it scorns silly myths about Vulcan's forge or a buried giant, and expounds rather obscurely the usual theory that air gathers inside the earth and catches fire. Notable are some lines glorifying scientific research: the author is surprised that people should travel far to see temples or works of art or ruined towns and not to see this volcano, *artificis Naturae ingens opus*. Ovid puts a lecture on geology in the mouth of Pythagoras, explaining why sea-shells are found far inland, and so on. The science seems taken from some popular manual (it had the fortune to make a curiously strong impression on the musings of Shakespeare's *Sonnets*). Elsewhere he describes the globe hanging in the middle 'poised by its own weight'. It has five zones determined by the heavenly, only two being habitable, and so say several others, ignoring any modification about the 'torrid'.[2] Lucan, Seneca's nephew, parades his knowledge

---

[1] Manilius, IV, 585–817; tides, ibid. II, 89–92: Antipodes, I, 238–45 (with some confusion, see Housman) and 377–483. Days, III, 301–84. Stars disappear, I, 215–20 (see Housman). Eclipses, ibid. 221–9. J. van Wageningen, *R.E.* XIV, 1114–33. Monceaux, *Les Africains*, 1894, pp. 135–84. R. B. Steele, *Amer. J. Phil.* 1932, pp. 339–40. Carruccio in *Archeion*, 1936, pp. 330–49. On tides cp. Silius, III, 58–60. Hodometer, X, 14: Hist. Aug., *Pertinax*, 8: Humboldt, *Cosmos*, II, 632 (a much better described by Hero, *Dioptra*).

[2] Ovid, *Met.* I, 45–51, Horace, *Odes*, I, 22, 17–22, Pseudo-Tibullus, IV, 1, 152–69. Globe, Ovid, *Met.* I, 12–35, *Fasti*, VI, 269: Lucan, V, 94, IX, 537, Silius, XI, 453, Statius, *Theb.* VIII, 31. Lecture, Ovid, *Met.* XV, 66–71, 262–356: St-Denis, *Rev. Ét. Lat.* 1940, pp. 113–25: sonnets, Sir S. Lee, *Quart. Rev.* 1909, p. 465. *Aetna*, ed. Sudhaus, 1898, R. Ellis, 1901, Vessereau, 1905: J. W. and A. M. Duff, *Minor Latin Poets*, Loeb, 1935. Research, verses 233–49: Vesuvius extinct, 431–2.

on things like tides and the Nile problem and the Antipodes ('if there are any'); he can say that there is never sun at the Pole, and he was censured even in ancient times for the blunder that a place at the tropic never casts shadows, but this charge depends on a false text, *umbras nunquam flectente Syene*, for *nusquam*, casting shadows in no direction (at the solstice).[1] Some slip easily into talk of the setting sun hissing in the western Ocean and such old-fashioned phrases, even some who mention the globe, so that these lapses need not be taken too seriously. Even a vulgar upstart in a realistic novel is supposed to know that the earth is round (as round as an egg, he says, but this embellishment may be ignored). It is startling, therefore, to find so important a writer as Tacitus giving no hint of the globe, in trying to explain the short northern nights, and speaking as if the sun came close to the edges of a flat or convex disk. Yet he comments on the ignorance of science of some soldiers who made a blare of horns and trumpets during an eclipse. His doubts about astrology do little good to his geography. A few voices were still raised against that false science, but by now it had generally prevailed.[2]

Of Greek writers on geography Ptolemy must be reserved for special consideration. On a far lower level is the verse primer of Dionysius 'Periegetes'. For the outlines of the known earth it follows in general Eratosthenes and Posidonius, perhaps mostly through an earlier versification of the same brand (by Alexander Lychnus?). The description is often absurdly out of date, and has many disproportions, oddities, and old weeds like the Amazons. He wants his readers to understand their poets and to score among the unlettered, as he naïvely says, by knowing that Homer's Erembi were the Red Sea cave-dwellers. Special interests of his are precious stones and places with supposed rites of Dionysus, from an island off the Loire to the two pillars set up by the god near the eastern Ocean and the Ganges.[3] Of science there is hardly a feeble reflection: Ceylon is under blazing Cancer, and at Thule the midsummer sun is visible 'both days and nights'

---

1 Pole, Lucan, IV, 107 (as Ps.-Tibullus, IV, 1, 154): shadow, Lucan, II, 587, censured by Macrobius, II, 7, 16, but cp. Housman. Tides, Lucan, I, 409–17 (see p. 323, n. 2). Antipodes, ibid. VIII, 160. Nile, see p. 273, n. 1. On L.'s geography, Pinter, 1902, Baümer, 1902, Pucci, 1938: A. Bourgery, *Rev. de Phil.* 1928, pp. 25–40 (on his loose use of place-names).

2 Cumont, *Oriental Religions in R. Paganism*, 1911, pp. 162–82. Boll-Bezold, *Sternglaube und Sterndeutung*, ed. Gundel, 1926. Voices, Columella, *Res Rustica*, XI, 1, 31, Favorinus ap. Gell. XIV, 1, Tac. *Ann.* IV, 58, VI, 22: Duhem, *Système du Monde*, II, 297. Sun, Tac. *Agr.* 12, *Germ.* 45: Anderson, ad locos. Eclipse, Tac. *Ann.* I, 28. Hissing, Juv. XIV, 280, Statius, *Silvae*, II, 7, 27: phrases, ibid. III, 1, 183, Silius, VI, 1, even Lucan, IX, 625: Florus, I, 33 (II, 17): Calp. Flaccus, *Declam.* II, 14. Cp. Juv. II, 160, *minima contentos nocte Britannos*.

3 Dion. Per. 620–6, island, 570–9 (cp. Pos. ap. Str. 198). Stones, Dion. Per. 1118–23, etc. Score, ibid. 172, Erembi, ibid. 963: weeds, see p. 229, n. 1. Lychnus, see p. 215, n. 3.

(elsewhere the sun is said to warm first the eastern Ocean); tides are briefly mentioned, at the Syrtes.[1] In view of the sources used the author presumably knew of the globe, but he says nothing direct about it. Just for its neglect of science this poor stuff was later popular as a handy school-book: it was translated by Avienus in the fourth century and Priscian in the sixth, and much commented on down to a big book by Archbishop Eustathius in 1175.

Among more general writings the best is Plutarch's debate on the markings of the moon; it has been praised by Duhem as a work of genius. The argument runs thus. They are not an optical illusion, nor do they reflect our inhabited earth and its surrounding Ocean. Nor are they a ripple or darkening of the air over a ball of fiery ether. The moon is not made of that: there is no such special fifth element, as the Stoics and Aristotle suppose, with a 'natural place' (up) and a 'natural motion' (in a circle). If the moon were a star, it would be a feeble thing, slow and tepid and passive. In fact it is an earth, as some older philosophers thought. That is why the sun leaves half of it in shadow. As an earth it is beautiful, and its place and motion may be left to Providence. Since its air diffuses the sun's rays, it may quite well sustain life, plants able to do without rain, like the Arabian, and even men of some sort, very different from us, slender and eating little.[2] The markings are deep ravines containing water or air which the sunlight does not penetrate; these need not be huge to cast a shadow visible to us. After all the moon is very near, say about twenty times nearer than the sun, to believe Aristarchus. Thus it has an affinity to the earth, and its nature, moist and feminine, softens various things and affects the growth of plants and some animals; also by its action on the water-masses of the earth it causes tides. (So much Plutarch admits, but he has little anywhere on astrology, and he condemns those ignorant enough to fear an eclipse, like the old general Nicias.)[3] The moon is far smaller than the earth, its diameter being slightly more or less than a third. The earth is a globe, and its round shadow is seen on the moon at eclipses. If it rests at the centre of the universe —has infinite space a centre?—it does not do so because that is its 'natural place', and he notes casually a clever speculation of Aristarchus that it is not there at all but goes round the sun. The size is as measured by

1 Dion. Per. 107, 201–3. Sun, ibid. 587, 1115. Thule, ibid. 580–6, Ceylon, 592–608.

2 Plut. *de Facie in Orbe Lunae*, 24–5, as Anaxagoras (not Xenophanes as stated by Cic. *Acad. Pr.* II, 122). On earth, 16, 18, as Heraclides ap. Stob. 1, 26. Genius, Duhem, op. cit. II, 360: praised also by Humboldt, *Cosmos*, 1868, IV, 488. Ed. Raingeard, 1935. On its geogr. indications a book by Ebner, 1906: on sources, Adler, 1910. Transl. Prickard, *P. Select Essays*, II, 1918.

3 Plut. *Nicias*, 23: Thorndike, op. cit. pp. 209–11. Moist, *de Facie*, 25, affinity, ibid. 19: near, 8, 10. Ravines, ibid. 21–2. Various theories on moon, Aet. II, 23–31. Its influence, p. 212, n. 1. Its mountains, Anax. ap. Plut. *Nicias*, 42, and see p. 100, n. 2.

Eratosthenes (the figure of Posidonius is ignored, very rightly). One debater sneers at Antipodes clinging like caterpillars or lizards upside down. The known earth is an island with gulfs from the Ocean, including the Caspian, and it is reduced for practical use by cold or hot deserts. Beyond the Atlantic there is room for another continent, and he borrows Plato's for a story in the same 'mythical' manner.[1]

Theon of Smyrna, who himself observed the stars and left his material to Ptolemy, writes on the astronomy 'useful for reading Plato'. He gives the usual proofs for the globe, at rest in the middle of the universe. For the size he accepts the figure of Eratosthenes.[2] About then (or early first century A.D.?) is the pleasing essay of Pseudo-Aristotle *On the Universe*. Plenty of the doctrine is from Aristotle, the dry and moist exhalations from the earth, the wind and fire produced within it, and the harmony of the divine stars. The author admires the great organism and the Providence which ordains even earthquakes and eruptions. Much of this is in a Stoic spirit, and especially that of Posidonius, it is held. But he denies the latter's periodic conflagration, and has a different order of the planets, and many contacts with Philo suggest free borrowing from a Neo-Pythagorean source.[3] The length of the known earth, 70,000 stades, is not necessarily from Posidonius, and the breadth, less than 40,000, hardly agrees. He thinks that there may well be several other continents or vast islands, some smaller, some even larger than ours: this is aimed against any attempt at symmetry on the lines of Crates, and also quite unlike Aristotle, who has one inhabited world stretching far round and leaving a narrow Atlantic between west Africa and India. There is a free Latin version of the essay by Apuleius, about A.D. 140, though sometimes suspected as later. A fancy island Loxe is a bad misunderstanding of the original, where Ceylon lies oblique (*loxe*) to the continent. In his novel the same writer talks of a southern 'opposite land' of Antichthones, who are accessible at least to witches.[4] About now too is probably Cleomedes, who professes to borrow most from Posidonius, and

---

1 *De Facie*, 26–9. Deserts, ibid. 25. Island, 4, 29 (Caspian also, Plut. *Alex.* 44). Antipodes, *de Facie*, 7. Size, ibid. 10. On the myth, see p. 238, n. 1.

2 Ed. Hiller, 1878, pp. 120–8, including the ship proof.

3 Maguire, *Yale Class. Studies*, 1939, pp. 111–67 (and Goodenough, ibid. 1932, pp. 153–8) against Capelle, *Neue Jahrb.* 1905, pp. 529–68. Ed. Lorimer, 1933: transl. Forster, 1924, in Oxford Aristotle. Element, *de Mundo*, 392, wind, 395 b, exhalations, 394 a (cp. Pos. ap. Sen. *N.Q.* II, 54).

4 *Golden Ass*, I, 8. J. Hoffmann, *de Pseudo-Apul. libro de Mundo*, 1880: but it is Apul., Lorimer, op. cit. p. 18: S. Müller, *Philologus*, Suppl. 1939 (A. meant a parallel work rather than paraphrase). Loxe, ch. 7. Several, Ps.-Arist. 392b: 'many', also Str. 65, 810: Berger, *Erat.* 89, and see p. 213, n. 2. Length, 393 b much as Artem. and Hipp. ap. Str. 113, Pos. ap. Str. 102. (On the unreal geography of N. Greece in A.'s novel, Mahaffy, *Greek World under Roman Sway*, 1890, pp. 295–7, but cp. Dill, op. cit. pp. 551–2.)

explains both his bad measurement of the globe and the good one which it travestied.

Maps are mentioned fairly often as in practical use. There was known the type of the old soldier who likes to draw his battles in red wine on a marble table (*in mensa pingere castra mero*); he had been doing it, according to a poet, since the Trojan War. Campaigning maps (*situs depicti*) were sent home from Armenia, and the Nile scouts brought back one, *Aethiopiae formam*. There is an inscription about a legionary employed on mapping work (χωρογραφήσας) in Nubia in A.D. 33, unless this was some humbler kind of land surveying. We hear of people who *terrarum situs pingunt*. Evidently generals already had, as a later military writer recommends, both detailed descriptions of routes, *itineraria perscripta*, and maps, *itineraria provinciarum non tantum adnotata sed etiam picta*.[1] There were also general maps. A lovesick girl cons a 'painted world' for her soldier's camp on the eastern frontier and

> What lands are stiff with frost or cracked with heat,
> And what fair wind blows sails to Italy.

A senator who had a map of the world seemed to betray secret thoughts of ruling it and was put to death by a suspicious Emperor. Some regarded such maps as unduly ambitious in other ways, and smiled at their way of filling the outer blanks with wild beasts, or deserts or swamps, or frozen lands or seas.[2]

Rome could show one map remarkable at least for the eminence of its authors. Agrippa, long second only to Augustus, had meant to build a portico and paint on the walls *orbem terrarum urbi spectandum*. When he died in 12 B.C., the Emperor himself carried out the map *ex destinatione et commentariis M. Agrippae*, which mean no doubt the papers containing the material. He published these as a companion-text, it is natural to suppose, and from it come the figures which are preserved.[3] Oddly Strabo does not mention the work, unless it is 'the chorography' or 'the chorographer' cited several times as a well-known authority, though only for Italy and the islands near. Pliny tells how the map was set up, as above; he praises it as careful and quotes its distances very often, generally with respect. The figures, many

---

1 Vegetius, III, 6. Pingunt, Florus, *praef.* 3: world maps, Vitr. VIII, 2, 6. Scouts, Plin. XII, 14 (and VI, 181): Armenia, ibid. VI, 40. Wine, Ovid, *Her.* I, 31, Tibullus, I, 6, 19, I, 10, 29–32. On Cleom. see p. 215, n. 2. Legionary, *O.G.I.S.* 205.

2 Plut. *Theseus*, 1. Emperor, Suet. *Domitian*, 10, Dio, LXVII, 12. Girl, Propertius, V, 3, 35. Kubitschek, *R.E.* Karten, x, 2022–2149 (1919).

3 Plin. III, 17. Fragments now best by Klotz, *Klio*, 1931, pp. 38–58, 386–466 (cp. his *Quaest. Plin. Geogr.* 1906, pp. 13–16). Riese, *Geogr. Lat. Minores*, 1878, pp. 1–8. Vast bibliography in Schanz-Hosius, *Gesch. der röm. Lit.* 1925, II, 329–35. F. A. Wright, *Marcus Agrippa*, 1937, p. 134 is brief.

corrupted, reappear in two late texts, used probably to explain school maps, a *Divisio Orbis* and a *Dimensuratio Provinciarum* (about A.D. 400). As late as 825 the Irish monk Dicuil was still copying the first and repeating its statement that *terrarum orbem...divus Augustus primus omnium per chorographiam ostendit*. About 400, too, there begins a story that four wise Greeks spent many years in measuring the four quarters of the earth for Caesar and Augustus. Older writers have nothing like it, unless the sending east of Isidorus before an expected Parthian war. Agrippa's map must, indeed, have had the benefit of official matter, including some new measurements and the census statistics of provincial towns which Pliny uses, but this does not amount to a geographical survey. Some strangely deny the companion-text and argue that the figures and even longish legends (as about the rocky coast of the Caspian) were entered on the map itself and taken down from it in short texts written to explain hand-copies of the map, such as were known already to Strabo and Pliny.[1]

The map included the outer edges of the known earth, Ireland, the Vistula and the supposed northern Ocean, and the Silkmen to their eastern Ocean. Its figures for such parts could not have any advantage from official information, as Pliny sees, and they are of very dubious value (those for India are quite inexplicable).[2] What did the whole look like? Ptolemy censures some world-maps which 'give most of the room to Europe, because the names to be got in are thicker there, while they leave small space lengthwise for Asia or breadthwise for Africa'. The only extant specimen, the Peutinger, derived from a late Roman, stretches the world out lengthwise and leaves small space breadthwise for anything. But there is no good reason to assume that Agrippa began either this very wild type or another crude later pattern, the round maps. The fragments indicate rather something vaguely after Eratosthenes in outline and in many details, an oval island of similar length, though greatly reduced in breadth (from 38,000 to 24,000 stades) according to the prevalent tendency to reject Pytheas. Within the Empire there may have been a Roman reliance on practical road and sea measurements; yet even here some distances are shown to be Greek estimates. The execution need not have been primitive: it is not proved that figures were added on the map to supply the absence of a fixed

---

1 Detlefsen, *Ursprung...der Erdkarte Agrippas*, 1906, and *Geogr. Bücher des Plinius*, 1909, pp. 11–16: statistics, ibid. pp. 26–34. Legends, Plin. VI, 39: so Kubitschek, *R.E.* Karten, § 60. Survey possible, he thinks, *R.E.* x, 627: Müllenhoff, *D.A.* III, 300 denies. *Div.* and *Dim.* in *G.L.M.* pp. 8–20: survey, ibid. 21, 72. Isid. ap. Plin. VI, 141. Chorography, Str. 224–5, 261, 266, 277, 285: not same, Dubois, *Géogr. de Strabon*, p. 330: 'the map' of Str. 120 seems too vague, despite Wright, loc. cit.

2 Plin. VI, 57, Klotz, op. cit. p. 436, Herrmann, *Land der Seide*, p. 46. Ireland, Plin. IV, 102: north, ibid. 81, 91, 98. Seric Ocean ap. Plin. VI, 37, *Divisio*, 24.

scale.[1] He is not quoted as discussing any matter of science, like astronomical determinations, but he need not have ignored these entirely, and has now been defended as forming a link between Hipparchus and Ptolemy. The evidence is slight and obscure, and after a vast discussion (mostly German) the map remains ghostly. Many presume that, being Roman, it was quite unscientific, a mere diagram of the imperial road system, displayed by way of patriotic propaganda.[2] Agrippa himself had planned the network of roads in Gaul, and the Romans were to relapse more and more into a milestone kind of geography, but this great early show-piece may not have been so bad.

Marinus is known solely through Ptolemy's free use of his 'Correction of the Map'. This work, which was twice revised, made a brave effort to apply recent expansions of knowledge, especially southward and eastward. He is diligent, Ptolemy admits, and not always uncritical, as he distrusts merchants on the size of Ireland, but he is not nearly drastic enough in handling such travel data, and thus badly overestimates the length and breadth of the inhabited world.[3] Yet, with a carelessness shocking in an astronomer, Ptolemy passes over his basic error, and himself adopts the disreputable figure of Posidonius for the globe, 180,000 stades: it is 'in accord with the generally received measurements', he remarks quite casually, though in fact it seems to have enjoyed little respect hitherto, and he had ignored it in his own earlier work. So, against the 700 stades of Eratosthenes, he gets a degree of 500 stades on a great circle, and it becomes 400 on the main parallel of Rhodes. Naturally very bad mistakes result when travel distances are translated into such faulty gradation. Thus the Mediterranean, already overstretched as 24,800 stades, is expressed as 62° on that parallel, as against about 42 of our degrees. The exaggeration affects everything to eastward, and the world as known to China becomes 180°, even after severe reductions of Marinus, who had got 228°. Again there is the bother about the value of the stade. Many defend him as meaning 180,000 of a long 'royal' stade of 210 metres now used in the Roman East;

---

[1] As think Detlefsen, *Erdkarte Agrippas*, p. 99 (map oblong, p. 106), and Uhden, *Klio*, 1933, p. 275 (map round, as many like K. Miller, *Mappaemundi*, 1898, IV, 10, VI, 143–7). Not round, Philippi, *Zur Reconstr. der Weltkarte des A.* 1880. Oval and at least the two main lines of Erat., Müllenhoff, *Hermes*, IX, 182. Greek figures, e.g. ap. Plin. VI, 3 (south Black Sea) as Erat. ap. Str. 91. Censures, Ptol. VIII, 1, 2.

[2] S. N. Miller in *Eur. Civ.* ed. Eyre, II, 510: G. H. Stevenson in *Legacy of Rome*, 1923, p. 159. Link, Schnabel, *Philologus*, 1935, pp. 405–40 (editing *Div.* and *Dim.*), approved by Herrmann, loc. cit., against Klotz, op. cit. pp. 463, 466 (map ignored astr. determinations). Schnabel notes Plin. VI, 219, where *sequentium diligentissimi* improve on a parallel of Hipparchus (Don, 16 hours, not 17).

[3] Ptol. I, 6–20. Revised, I, 7, 4: I, 17. Merchants (through Philemon), ibid. I, 11, 7. Admits, I, 6, 1: I, 19. Bibliography on M., p. 229, n. 3.

this would equal 240,000 of the short stade assumed for Eratosthenes (the alternative total given by Posidonius), and it gives 37,800 km. as compared with the real figure of 40,000. At the other extreme Berthelot takes him as using the short stade and meaning 28,350 km., which makes the underestimate very bad indeed.[1] On the ordinary stade the result is about 32,000.

Before turning to geography Ptolemy had written his *System of Astronomy*, embodying the work of Hipparchus and any done since, while he himself could add observations and reckonings and develop the theory with various improvements. Here he gives the usual proofs of the globe. He accepts it as at rest in the middle of the universe; that it may go round the sun, as Aristarchus had suggested, is not even considered, and axis-rotation is dismissed as absurd, for very poor reasons, though he admits that it would allow a much simpler explanation of the appearances. In Book II he describes how the known earth lies on the globe, stretching half-way round the north temperate zone, while its breadth fills that zone and overlaps southward over the tropic. The equator may be habitable, he thinks, as the sun does not stay long at the zenith there, but whether it is actually inhabited is not yet known from credible reports (he finds plenty to hand by the time of the *Geography*).[2] He explains how 'climates' or parallels are determined by their longest day and by the dial shadows at solstices and equinoxes. The underlying theory is worked out in detail for Rhodes ($14\frac{1}{2}$ hours, latitude 36°), the mean of seven climates from Meroe, 13 hours, to the north coast of the Black Sea, 16 hours. He promises to deal with the subject again in a *Geography*, where he will fix the positions of the chief towns in all countries. But already he gives an elaborate table of 33 latitudes up to the arctic circle, each except the last three being named after a place upon it (see the diagram p. 341). Similar data in his minor astronomical works, like the list of famous cities in the Hand Tables, are also older than the *Geography*.[3]

He was not above writing a defence of astrology. The moon does more than cause tides: it is moist and softening, as being near the earth and its vapours. The sun—supposed a planet—has familiar effects. Why should not

---

[1] Berthelot, *Rev. Ét. Anc.* 1933, p. 294, and *L'Asie...d'après Ptol.* pp. 120–56. Royal, Hultsch, *Metrol.* p. 64: Dreyer, *Hist. of Planetary Systems*, 1906, p. 178: Viedebantt, *Klio*, 1920, pp. 94–108 (and on Pos. see p. 213, n. 1): Duhem, op. cit. II, 7: Heath, *Aristarchus*, p. 346. Shocking, Berger, *Erdkunde*, p. 592: Thalamas, *Érat.* p. 130. Ignored, *Almag.* II, 6. 22,500 m. (=37,800 km.), Kimble, *Geogr. in Middle Ages*, 1938, p. 9.

[2] *Almag.* II, 13, p. 188, Heiberg. Known earth, ibid. II, 1, pp. 87 f. Rotation, I, 7, p. 21. His system in W. M. Smart, *The Sun, the Stars and the Universe*, 1928, p. 27: Dreyer, op. cit. pp. 108–9, 164–5, 193–200 (on planets): Tollinton, *Alexandrine Teaching on the Universe*, 1932, p. 104: Tannery, *Mém. Scient.* III, 343.

[3] Schnabel, *Text u. Karten des Ptol.* 1938, pp. 74–5. Table, *Almag.* II, 6 (also 7–8, calculations for ten basic parallels, and 9). Day, II, 3: shadows, ibid. 5.

other planets and the stars have their influences? Here he is mainly concerned with the planets and their apparent path, the circle of the twelve zodiacal signs. They are hot and moist or cold and dry, and affect not only persons but whole regions and the physical and moral character of their inhabitants. There is some sense amid a deal of rubbish. The countries on the globe differ in their heavenly phenomena and may be divided into seven climates. The peoples differ according to these: a vertical sun makes the Ethiopians what they are, while the Scythians are their opposites in most respects, and only the races of temperate lands between are capable of civilization. All this is the ordinary climatic ethnology and taken mainly from Posidonius. But the peoples differ also according to longitude: the eastern have more of the sun's nature, the western more of the moon's. Further, the inhabited world can be divided into four sections or triangles answering to those of the zodiac: the north-western or European people are ruled by three signs and two planets, and are all high-spirited, but some are more intelligent than others, so especially the Greeks, who come partly under the influence of an adjoining triangle. It is notable that meanwhile Ptolemy is content with a rough kind of geography, with no detail of recent discovery except rather surprising mentions of Fezzan and the Zanzibar coast. There is already a sort of meridian from the sea of Azov to the Red Sea.[1]

The *Geography*, or rather 'Instruction in Map-drawing', is concerned solely with the task of scientific mapping, as it professes. It scorns 'chatter about the ways of peoples' and all the descriptive and historical matter which makes works like Strabo's readable. Very rarely natural products are mentioned, as those of Ceylon, diamonds and beryls at two places in India, and bearded cocks and white parrots Burma way; still rarer are such notes as on the long hair of the men in Ceylon and the physique of a tribe in Assam.[2] The plan is as follows. Book I discusses principles and methods. A map should be based, it insists, on positions astronomically fixed, though few such are in fact available and for most places we must just estimate from travel reports (chs. 3–5). In using these we must allow far more than Marinus does for the overstatements of traders, for halts and irregular rates of travel, and divergences from a parallel (6–20). He then explains how to make a globe with its proper network of parallels and meridians, and how to place the known earth on its surface (22–3), also how to draw a map on a plane

[1] Cp. Pos. ap. Str. 105. *Tetrabiblos* now ed. Robbins, Loeb, 1940 (with Manetho, ed. Waddell). The geography esp. in II, 2–4. Uhden, *Philologus*, 1933, pp. 302–25, *G.Z.* 1933, p. 287. Thorndike, op. cit. I, pp. 110–16. Boll in *Jahrb. f. klass. Phil. Suppl.* 1894, pp. 181–238: Boll-Bezold, op. cit. p. 65.

[2] Ptol. VII, 2, 15: hair, VII, 4, 1: Burma, VII, 2, 23: India, VII, 1, 65, 86. Chatter, II, 1, 5. Books on Ptol. see p. 230, n. 1.

by various methods of projection (21, 24, resumed in the mapping directions of the final books). Dividing the continents into many regions, he takes each region in turn and gives its boundaries, mountains and rivers, tribes and towns, and islands if any—a long list of names, most with their figures of longitude and latitude. (Altogether there are some 8000 so placed.) In this way he treats Europe, beginning with the two British islands, describing Spain in three provinces, Gaul in four, and so on (II–III); then he covers Africa from Morocco eastwards and southwards (IV), and Asia from the west to the Sinae (V–VII, 4). From these lists the reader can draw for himself regional maps on various suitable scales, and even a general map of the world. Only one map need be made for Gaul or Spain, though each has been described in several sections. Thus there will be drawn 10 maps for Europe, 4 for Africa, and 12 for Asia, apart from the world-map. (It is also possible to take each section as described and make a set of 63 maps, such as accompany some of the manuscripts, but he gives no sign that he meant this to be done.) As a further help he adds, as promised in the *Astronomy*, a list of notable cities, some 360 of them, each with its longest day or other datum of latitude, and its longitude as expressed in hours from the meridian of Alexandria (VIII, 3–28); this seems to be an older collection of material, which he tacks on without troubling to reconcile its data with those in the body of the work.[1] There longitudes are translated in terms of a prime meridian running through some of the still vaguely known Fortunate Islands (the Canaries), and Alexandria itself is $60\frac{1}{2}°$ (we count it only $48°$ from the same line, or $30°$ from that of Greenwich, which replaced it only in the last century).

Unhappily he adopted a bad figure for the globe, and so a false degree of 400 stades on the parallel of Rhodes, the time-honoured line for measuring the length of the known earth. How this line appears in his map is shown in the next diagram (Fig. 59). The prime meridian itself is very wrongly placed $7\frac{1}{2}°$ west of Gibraltar, instead of our $12\frac{1}{2}°$ (if taken as through Ferro, the outermost of the Canary Islands). For the Mediterranean he accepts the 24,800 stades of Marinus, still far too much, though an improvement on previous estimates, and he counts it as $62°$, as compared with the real $42°$. There are 1000 stades or $2\frac{1}{2}°$ thence to the Euphrates bend. From here along the silk-road to Stone Tower he reduces Marinus only mildly, from 26,250 stades or $65\frac{1}{2}°$ to 24,000 stades or $60°$; this is still grossly in excess (for about 34 modern degrees). For the final stretch to Sera, said to be seven months' journey, he reduces by half to 18,100 stades or $45\frac{1}{4}°$. By way

---

[1] As a control of these, Forbiger, *Alte Geogr.* II, 417, but no, Bunbury, II, 576. Berger, *Erdkunde*, p. 644, Kubitschek, *R.E.* x, 2061. Sestos (on the Dardanelles) is $15\frac{1}{2}$ hours' day = $45°$, as cp. $41° 15'$ in III, 11, 9.

of check he starts from Cape Cory, opposite Ceylon, accepted as 125° 10′, and takes the sea-distances thence to the Golden Chersonese and on to the port of the Sinae, again nearly halving the figures of Marinus. So he reaches a grand total of 177¼° to Sera or 180° (72,000 stades) to the last meridian with the capital of the Sinae, while Marinus had got 228° or roundly 225° or 90,000 stades.[1] (The real figure in modern degrees is 126, if Sera is taken as Si-an, or at best only a little more.) Thus Ptolemy's known earth reached exactly half round the globe on that parallel, and even at the end of his overstretched Asia there was not Ocean but 'unknown land'.

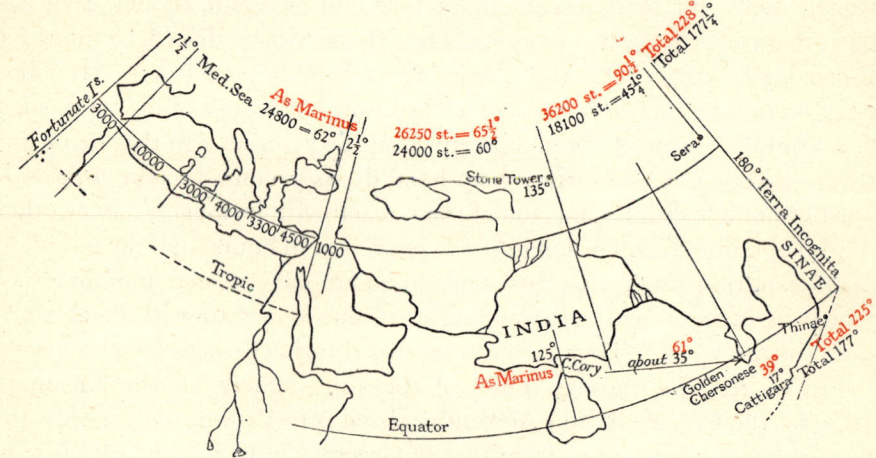

Fig. 59. Ptolemy: length-line.

It is familiar, of course, that this overstretching was important for Columbus, though there is still vast debate about his exact conceptions and intentions. After the great medieval travellers like Marco Polo there was a substantial China with Cipango and other islands well beyond. A globe of 1492 added 60° of mainland to Ptolemy's, and Toscanelli in his letter and map of 1474 (if genuine) thought that Marinus had been nearer the truth than his corrector. So did Columbus himself. Besides he made the globe a quarter smaller than it is. (He used a degree measured by the astronomers of the Caliph Al-Mamun as 56⅔ miles, but he misread it in Italian miles, which were about 500 metres shorter.) The unexplored remainder of the globe was therefore only 78° of about 50 miles on that parallel, or 3900 miles. But he also believed from a text of Esdras that no

[1] I, 11–14. Beyond C. Cory M. had 61°+39°, Ptol. about 35°+17°. Med., cp. Erat. 26,500, Bunbury, I, 635, II, 234. Length, Marinus, Berger, pp. 602–4, Ptol. ibid. 620–2. For the long tradition of this prime meridian, Raisz, *General Cartography*, 1938, p. 79, Jervis, *World in Maps*, 1938, p. 31, Fordham, *Maps*, 1921, pp. 42–5.

more than a seventh of the world was sea, and so he fully expected islands after some 2500 miles, and gave his men a strong hint of this confidence.[1] (*Septima pars, ubi erat aqua congregata....Leviathan autem dedisti septimam humidam*—was there ever a queerer scientific authority?) There were, too, plenty of legendary islands, a ghost of Atlantis and others said to have been sought by St Brandan from Ireland in the sixth century or seven bishops fleeing from the Moorish conquerors of Spain in the eighth; the rumours were enough to take Bristol merchants out looking for islands by 1480, and various Portuguese for thirty years or so before them. Some have tried to prove that he lied about himself, and that his first idée fixe was not Asia but such a phantom Antilia, shown on a map of 1436 and the globe just mentioned (Martin Behaim's). But most deny this, or admit at best that he thought of islands as well as of Asia.[2] Las Casas says that he 'intended to come upon lands of India, and the great island of Cipango and the kingdoms of the Grand Khan', for whom he carried a letter. He had stayed at Porto Santo and heard evidence of western land, such as a piece of carved wood and big reeds washed up there, and pines and two broad-faced corpses cast on the Azores; but all this has been doubted, like an alleged visit to Thule or Iceland in 1477 (if he went, he may well have heard, as probably did the Bristol fishermen there, of the old Norse voyages to Greenland and beyond). His authority from the Spanish sovereigns was 'to discover and gain certain islands and mainland in the Ocean sea', and they took him as going '*ad partes Indie*', including perhaps some islands on the way. But he was a self-educated man with an untutored imagination and a strong sense of a divine mission, and Jane holds that he meant something more than to open a shorter route to a known far east and had a vague conception of a big land worth finding in the unknown south. Anyhow with his three small ships he sailed from the Canaries resolutely west, and in 34 days, after a 'miracle of...daring, skill and luck', he reached —an islet of the Bahamas. He found his Cipango in Cuba, and presently in Haiti, while Cuba now seemed part of the mainland itself, near Cathay, and he sent off the letter to the Khan, but the bearers returned in a few

---

[1] Madariaga, op. cit. pp. 100, 201: Nunn, op. cit. p. 11. Degree, ibid. p. 13: old world 283°, ibid. pp. 29, 61. T. letter genuine (despite Vignaud), Madariaga, pp. 76, 439: A. P. Newton, *Great Age of Discovery*, 1932, p. 82 is sceptical. II Esdras vi. 50–2, ed. Oesterley. J. Johnstone, *Study of the Oceans*, 1926, p. 72. J. H. Rose, *Man and the Sea*, 1935, pp. 85–94. C. Jane, *Select Documents illustrating the Four Voyages of C*. 1930–3 (Hakluyt Soc.).

[2] As Madariaga, pp. 76, 115, 447, Jane, I, p. cvi: deny, Nunn, op. cit. pp. 25, 32, 41, against Vignaud (and M. André's book, 1927, pp. 70, 89). Against V. also S. E. Morison, *Christ. Columbus*, 1943, pp. 54–8. On the islands Babcock, *Legendary Islands of the Atlantic*, 1922. Bristol, J. A. Williamson, *The Ocean in English History*, 1941, p. 13. Portuguese, Newton, op. cit. p. 83.

days after seeing a village. On his third voyage he struck South America, and was impressed by the volume of the Orinoco, which seemed to require a continental basin, presumably part of Asia, and he had a hallucination that it came down from the earthly Paradise, a swelling on the earth like a nipple or the thin end of a pear! On a last voyage he coasted south to Panama and failed to find any strait to the Indian Ocean, but the place had gold mines and seemed only some nineteen days or less from the Ganges; he thought of Ophir, which Josephus had put in the Golden Chersonese, and still believed himself to have reached Asia. To the end he never understood that he had not found islands '*en la parte de las Indias*' or any part of the 'Indian' continent.[1] Thus the most important thing in ancient geography was an error which caused the unconscious discovery of America. What had been actually discovered was soon realized, among others, by Amerigo Vespucci, who never commanded in any voyage: he spoke of 'those new regions which we have found and which we may call a new world'. So he won from a German teacher of geography in 1507 the extravagant honour of giving his name to two new continents, which should have been Columbia and Cabotia. (At first 'America' was meant only for the southern, but about 1519 Rastall, brother-in-law of the author of *Utopia*, seems already to use it for both.) John Cabot had led the Bristol men in 1497 to discover a mainland (North America) which he too misunderstood as Asia, but just after his disappearance in the next year Portuguese and English seem to have somehow become conscious of the mistake and started probing for a north-west passage. Doubts had soon sprung up among the Spaniards themselves: already in 1496 a friend told Columbus that the real Asia was still 1200 leagues west. In fact the truth about a new continent slipped in almost unawares. As for the western way to the Indies, it was revealed only in 1520 when Magellan passed through his strait, just inside Cape Horn, and the route proved vastly longer than had been supposed. The royal commission of Salamanca had been quite right in thinking that Columbus absurdly underestimated the distance to India; only he happened to hit on something else.

The breadth of the known world appears in Ptolemy as in the diagram (Fig. 60). Marinus, it seems, drew only eight parallels north of the equator

[1] As usual view, confirmed by Nunn, pp. 54–90, despite Lives of C. by Winsor, 1891, Harrisse, 1892, Thacher, 1903–4. Golden Chersonese, Nunn, pp. 74–5, E. G. R. Taylor in Jane, op. cit. II, p. lxxx (but not Jane's 'terra australis', I, p. cxxi): Mangi next Cathay, Newton, op. cit. p. 115. Ophir, Madariaga, p. 379. Nipple, ibid. pp. 323–7 Cipango, ibid. pp. 220, 223: luck, p. 193: Khan, p. 111. Pines, etc., ibid. p. 89, Nunn, pp. 38–9: doubted by J. H. Rose, op. cit. p. 85. Case for Iceland, Stefansson, *Ultima Thule*, 1942, pp. 61–149. Newton, p. 78 rejects. Norse, denied by Winsor, p. 135: no evidence, Jane, I, p. xiv: possibly in I. and heard vaguely, Beazley, *Enc. Brit.* ed. 14, Columbus. Bristol, Williamson, op. cit. p. 12.

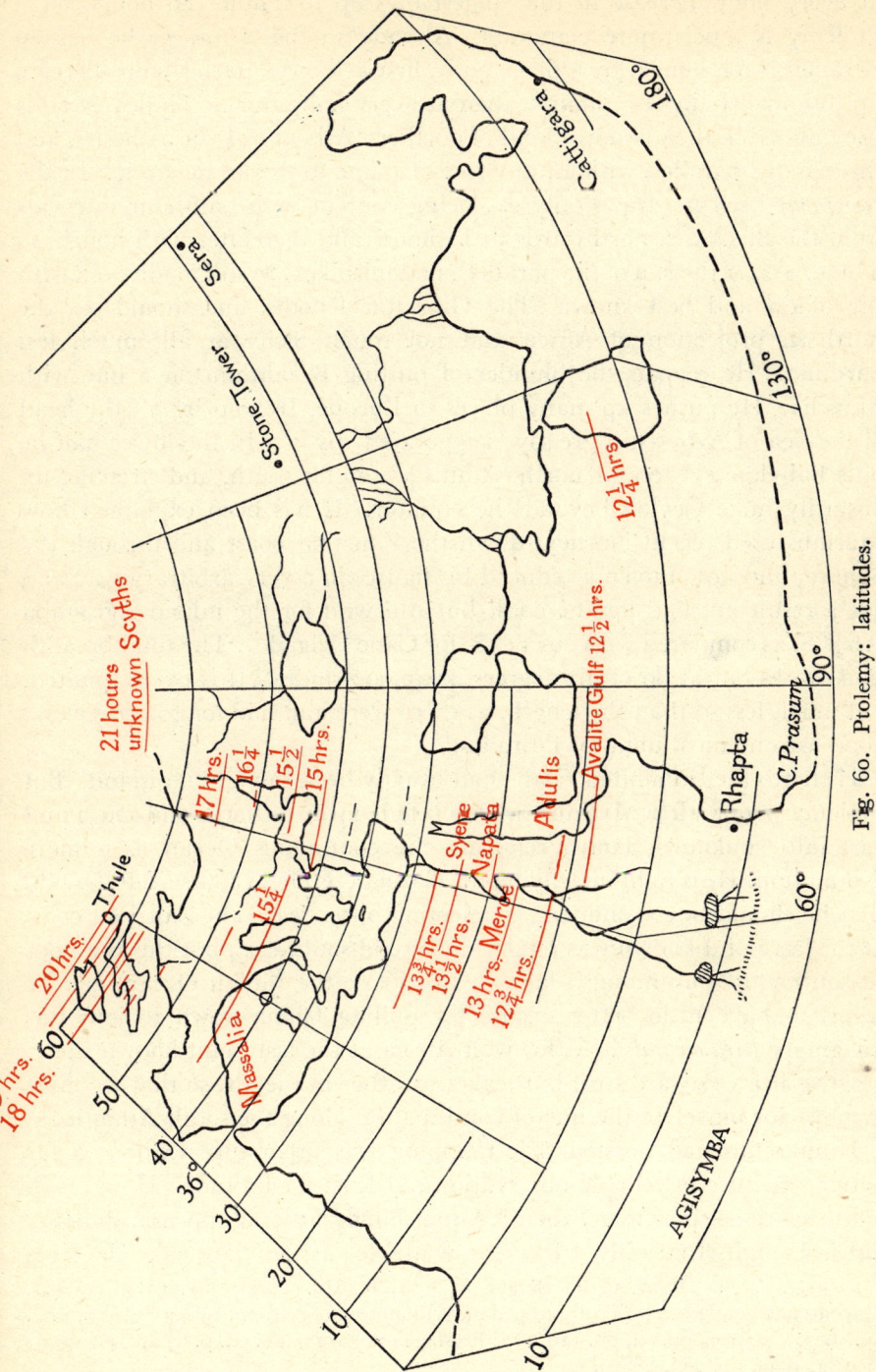

Fig. 60. Ptolemy: latitudes.

at every hour increase in the longest day up to Thule (20 hours, 63°). Ptolemy is much more elaborate. Already in the *Astronomy* he has 29 parallels, each named by a place on it, first at every quarter-hour increase up to mid-Britain (17½ hours), then at every half-hour to Thule; he adds 'Scythians' in the unknown land of northern Asia at 64½° or 21 hours, and three more parallels without any sort of name to the arctic circle. In the *Geography* itself he draws only 21, being content with half-hour intervals from the Black Sea northwards to 18 hours and thereafter with hourly to Thule. As for the run of the parallels, bad mistakes are still made even with the oldest and best known. The Gibraltar–Rhodes line should cut the northern projection of Africa and not touch Sicily at all, much less Sardinia. He repeats the blunder of putting Byzantium on a line with Massilia. He pushes up many places in Europe, Ireland by 5°, the head of the Sea of Azov (still greatly exaggerated) by 7°. In the lower half he puts Babylon 2½° too far north, Adulis 3° too far south, and stretches an absurdly huge Ceylon beyond the equator. It has been explained how Marinus used recent journeys down the Zanzibar coast and through the Sahara, and how Ptolemy reduced his figures in a very arbitrary way and got a result not bad for the coast but still wild for the inland Agisymba (16¼° S. as compared with our 11° S. for Cape Delgado). The total breadth thus works out at 80 of his degrees or 40,000 stades. It is overestimated, but much less so than the length, as there were and had long been several good astronomical data for latitudes.[1]

Hitherto the 'inhabited earth' had usually been thought an island. But Ptolemy (again after Marinus) makes it fade away in north and south and east into 'unknown land', rejecting the continuous Ocean as a mere assumption. He is right in denying the Caspian 'gulf', of course, but it is odd that he should be so confident in rejecting outer seas. The Zanzibar coast at the last point known was reported to trend south-east, but this is a poor reason for his continuing it far east to enclose the Indian Ocean, and he seems to have little better excuse for pulling China down to join this imaginary *terra australis*. As for west Africa at the last point known there, he gives it a westward turn but leaves it rather in the air, so that we must imagine for ourselves the line of continuation along the south Atlantic.

Hipparchus had insisted that mapping was premature without a far better structure of reliable observations, at least for latitude. How much had been done since to get them? Astonishingly little, it appears: Ptolemy himself admits that only a few are available 'as foundations'. He gives

[1] *Geogr.* I, 23. *Almag.* II, 6. Berger, pp. 594–8, 619. Tozer, *Anc. Geogr.* p. 341. Marinus had got 63°+24°. Truth slipped in, Williamson, op. cit. pp. 19–27 (Rastall, ibid. pp. 56–7): Newton, op. cit. pp. 110, 127: Prestage in Newton, op. cit. p. 62 and *Portuguese Pioneers*, 1933, pp. 283, 288–9.

THEORY IN THE SAME PERIOD 343

thousands of names, indeed, with their supposed co-ordinates of longitude and latitude, but these positions are merely read off his own maps, and the vast bulk are not observed at all but computed by the ground distance from some better-known place, itself often badly fixed.[1] Each map is thus largely a compilation from routes with their usual errors about distances and bearings (lack of the compass made the best itineraries very uncertain). There was still no practical method for getting longitudes, nor was there to be until good time-pieces were invented in the eighteenth century: even after the voyages of Columbus the Azores could be put on the same meridian as Cape Verde. (On his way back he argued with his lieutenant whether they were near Madeira or the Azores, their reckonings of longitude thus differing by 600 miles!) Hipparchus had suggested a means from the observing of an eclipse on the Tigris and at Carthage at times said to differ by three hours or 45°, a gross excess for the real 33°. Ptolemy finds the figure tolerable, as he overstretches the Mediterranean badly anyhow, but he does not seem to know of any other usable observation of the kind. His longitudes are rough reckonings, and often very wrong indeed. He chooses to draw his meridians at every 5°, instead of every hour or 15° as Marinus.

How serious are his mistakes in outline and detail will be obvious from any of the sketch-maps in the previous chapters. There are amazing distortions even of the most familiar countries, as of the direction of the Italian boot and the coasts of Sicily. Evidently Marinus was uncritical in many ways, and so is Ptolemy. The working material is rarely set before us, as it is for the silk-road, but it was very various in time and quality. The geographer should seek the newest reports, he says, but he carries this out very unequally: clearly many maps do not represent the best knowledge of his time, for instance about Roman roads and frontiers, and there are queer mistakes and omissions about so well-trodden a province as Gaul. Often he fails to combine the route data, and gets the same place twice far apart, and he can falsely double the island of Elba under two names, Greek and Latin.[2] He fills blanks with Amazons and Hyperborean mountains and other things which are none the less fables because they figure on what looks like a sober map.

As regards projection Marinus spaced out his points along the main parallel of Rhodes as on Fig. 61. Then he drew straight meridians through

---

[1] E.g. from Milan, 1° 13′ wrong, or Boulogne, 2° 46′ wrong, Cuntz, op. cit. p. 119. Berger, p. 642. Foundations, Ptol. I, 4, 2. Hipp. and eclipses, see p. 208, n. 1. On longitudes from eclipses, Prestage, *Portuguese Pioneers*, p. 323: E. G. R. Taylor, *Tudor Geography*, 1930, p. 26.

[2] Ptol. III, 1, 78, cp. Megara and Hybla in Sicily, III, 4, 14, Beroea and Chalybon in Syria, V, 15, 13 and 17: Bactra-Z., see p. 294, n. 1. Columbus, Fiske, *Discovery of America*, 1920, I, 440, and see pp. 315, 416.

them to cut straight parallels at right angles! He knew that this meant bad distortions, the degree on the equator becoming one-fifth too small and that on the Thule parallel four-fifths too big; but apparently he thought that it did not matter much, as the outer parts were so poorly known anyhow. He might at least have kept the converging meridians. Ptolemy duly finds fault, but allows straight lines for mapping small areas.[1] For each area he calculates an average value of the degree of longitude according to what seems right for its middle parallel: so in Britain one of 275 stades, $\frac{11}{20}$ of the degree of latitude (constant at 500 stades), and in Italy one of $\frac{3}{4}$. (The fraction for Britain is in fact very nearly right.) Each of the regional maps is thus drawn on its own suitable scale, and they cannot be fitted together.

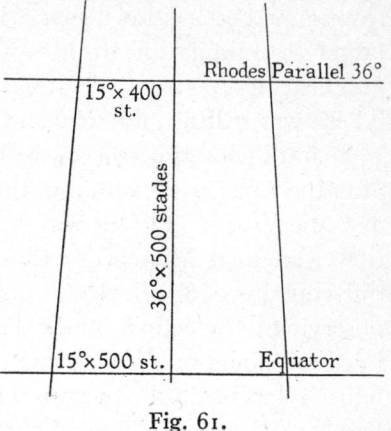

Fig. 61.

Otherwise he recommends more scientific methods. The first, probably that of Hipparchus, has curved parallels, to be drawn from A with radii

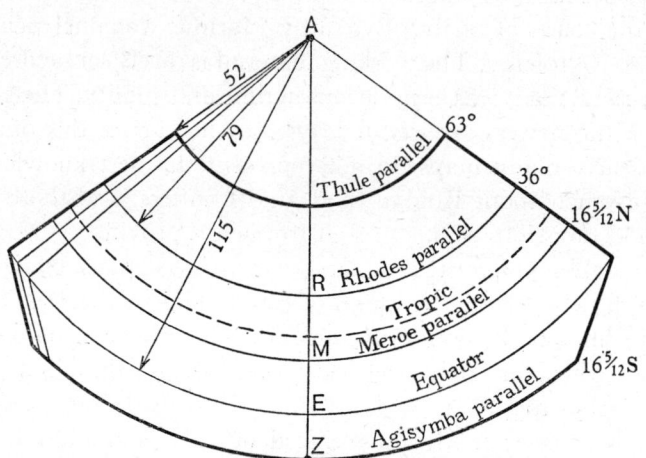

Fig. 62. Ptolemy's first projection.

of the length indicated. Then along the Rhodes parallel from R space out, four units apart, 18 points westwards and as many eastwards, and through these draw the meridians from A. EZ is $16\frac{5}{12}$ units like EM; the southern-

[1] II, 1, 10, VIII, 2, 6. Bunbury, II, 577. On Marinus, Ptol. I, 20, 4–5, Bunbury, II, 543: Berger, pp. 609–10. T. Schöne, *Die Gradnetze des Ptol.* 1909 (on Ptol. I, 21–4).

most parallel is to be divided into parts of the same value as those of the Meroe parallel, and the meridians then slant back from the equator as shown (a crude device). The thick lines are the framework of the known world. This is a simple conical projection with one standard parallel.

The second shows as curved not only the parallels but also the meridians (except one). The radii are from H, and the points on HZ are so spaced that EZ and EM are each $16\frac{5}{12}$ units, ER is 36 and ET is 63 units. The same number of meridians are drawn as before, and they are spaced $2\frac{1}{4}$ units

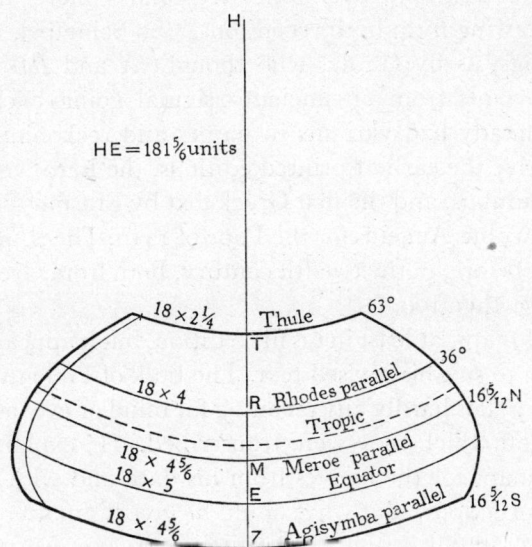

Fig. 63. Ptolemy's second projection.

apart on the parallel of Thule, 4 units apart on that of Rhodes, 5 apart on the equator, and $4\frac{5}{6}$ apart on the parallels of Meroe and Agisymba. This projection is an obvious improvement (it may be compared with Bonne's, the distortion being the greater the farther we go from the central meridian). But the other projection was to be generally used as more convenient, and he apparently foresaw that it would be. A third is mentioned, on a plane inside an armillary sphere, but he hardly pretends to have used it, and no map on it is preserved.[1]

Such a book, with masses of numbers and obscure names was peculiarly liable to corruptions in transmission. A slight change in figures can mean a bad displacement in mapping, and the maps which we draw off his texts

[1] Ptol. VII, 6–7, drawn in Nobbe's ed. II, 188: probably decorative, Rylands, *Geogr. of Ptol. Elucidated*, 1893, p. 23: but P. preferred it, Schnabel, op. cit. p. 91. Foresaw, Ptol. I, 24, Bunbury, II, 577. Second, Ptol. I, 24, 9–20: first, ibid. 1–8. Forbiger, op. cit. I, 406–9: Berger, pp. 632–9: J. Ball, *Egypt in Classical Geographers*, 1942, pp. 89–95.

may often saddle him with the blunders of copyists, when he has quite enough of his own. None of the manuscripts is older than 1200 or so. They seem traceable to two ancient recensions, which already showed many alterations and interpolations. One is represented purely only by X (Vaticanus graecus 191, without maps), generally accepted as having the best tradition. The other, which split into four groups at Constantinople by the sixth century, includes several with maps like Urbinas graecus 82, now sumptuously edited by Fischer: it is really a fine copy of an indifferent original, and he seems to overvalue it. Besides there are some mixed manuscripts drawing from both recensions. (So Schnabel, revising several earlier groupings, as by Cuntz, who thought X and RW diverged by a selection of variants from an ancient original going back to Ptolemy's copy, which already had variants in names and reckonings.)[1] From the mixed type derive the earliest printed editions, the Latin versions from the life time of Columbus, and the first Greek text by Erasmus in 1533; the first Latin was by Jacobus Angelus for the Pope of 1410. The *Astronomy* had been translated long before, in the twelfth century, both from Greek and Arabic, and the *Astrology* then too.

Marinus had maps, at least in his first edition, but it appears that he failed to correct them to suit his revised text. The bulk of Ptolemy's book, a long series of positions, has hardly any meaning for mind or eye until retranslated into the maps off which they were transcribed. He explains that readers can make the maps for themselves from his data and with the help of his preliminary instructions. But why should he give his matter in so laborious a form and not simply in maps? Because maps are apt to be gradually deformed by copiers, he knows, and the text seems a better preservative (and it did act as a check against corruptions of the outlines, in so far as it was not corrupted itself). Many conclude that he did not publish his maps with his text.[2] But more deny that this inference is justified.[3] It seems likely that he would expect few readers with such bowels of brass that they would sit down to make their own atlas. So he would give his own; if he added the mass of figures, this was presumably a check and also to furnish some 'instruction in map-drawing', as his title indicates.

It is another question whether the maps attached to several manuscripts preserve any genuine tradition of Ptolemy's own or at least of ancient copies made from a better text than survives. He himself recommends the drawing

---

1 Schnabel, op. cit. cp. groupings also of C. Müller, Renou and Fischer. K, Const. Seraglio gr. 57, found in 1927, is a poor copy of a valuable original.

2 As St Martin, *Hist. de la Géogr.* 1873, p. 209: Berger, p. 639: Gisinger, *R.E.* Geogr. § 44: Kubitschek, *R.E.* Karten, §§ 40, 82.

3 So Bunbury, II, 578, curtly: Fischer, Cuntz, Schnabel, Tudeer, *J.H.S.* 1917, pp. 62–76, Mieli-Brunet, op. cit. p. 769, Ball, op. cit. p. 99.

of 26 land-groups, while he describes them in subdivisions, from which a set of 63 can be drawn. In fact K, U, R have or had 26 maps, and a few of the mixed manuscripts, O and its scions, draw the long set. This practice seems to have begun quite early, but is generally recognized as a secondary development: only Fischer oddly derives the long set from a first edition of Ptolemy himself and the short from a second. For a map tradition of independent value it is argued that the maps are often not by the writers of the manuscripts to which they belong, though interpolated and corrected according to their recension, and that they may therefore contain older matter, even going back ultimately to Ptolemy.[1]

Some manuscripts have at the end a notice that one 'Agathodaemon of Alexandria, a draughtsman, drew the whole world from Ptolemy's eight books', whether this refers to the whole set or only the world-map, as many take it. Nothing else is known about him, and he has been guessed as anywhere between Ptolemy and the sixth century. He made a new set to replace maps deformed by copyists, thought St Martin, or a calligraphic copy of Ptolemy's (Nordenskjöld). Several make him perhaps even an assistant or pupil working under the master's eye. If so, two world-maps in the manuscripts (U and O) can hardly go back to him, as they are on the first projection, which Ptolemy does not recommend. Another, K's, is on the second, but cannot be proved to have any special authority either.[2]

Various general writers have a few things touching on geography. Curtius foolishly remarks that the seasons are reversed in India, which is unbearably hot when other lands are frozen and is snowy when they are roasted by the sun, and he cannot explain why. He is fond of the commonplace that a wild country produces wild men: '*ingenia hominum... situs format*' —'*locorum asperitas hominum quoque ingenia duraverat*'—'*ipsa solitudo natura quoque immitia efferavit ingenia.*' Lucian, besides his parody of travel tales, has some cheap scoffs at science, which pretends to measure the circuit of the earth, the depth of the sea, the height of the air, and the sizes and distances of the moon and sun, and which says that the moon is inhabited and the sun a fiery stone; all this in a skit where his hero flies up to the moon to look down on the tiny earth, with Greece four fingers long, and laugh at the ambitions and wars of men. A defence of astrology under his name is not his, but he

---

[1] Schnabel, op. cit. pp. 2, 95 (the 26 set). Back to redactions not before 4th century, Tudeer, loc. cit. Medieval mappers could not have drawn them so well off MSS., Dinse, *Zt. Ges. Erdk. Berl.* 1912, pp. 745–70. None P.'s or early Empire, Berthelot, *Rev. Ét. Anc.* 1933, p. 246.

[2] Schnabel, p. 92, A.'s world-map (before the two recensions) lost like P.'s own, against Fischer. Nordenskjöld, *Facsimile-Atlas to the Early Hist. of Cartography*, 1889, p. 6. St Martin, op. cit. p. 209. Assistant, Forbiger, I, 411, Bunbury, II, 579.

strangely fails to mock that pseudo-science.[1] Pausanias has some digressions on distant parts like the northern sea and the Silkmen; he knows that the sun while in Cancer casts no shadow at Aswan, and he dwells on earthquakes, the signs of their coming and the kinds of shock, but piously leaves the causes to the gods.[2] Some could still make useful summaries of older opinions in science, like Aetius, through whom comes a good deal of our evidence, but often they seem to collect such things without being able to judge their relative value. There are a few fragments of a 'Meteorology' by Arrian. The Sceptic Sextus Empiricus examines postulates like the fifth element with its 'natural' circular motion; he at least mentions the view of Aristarchus that the earth revolves, while the heaven does not, and he attacks astrology.[3] Galen, though a great doctor, with a respect for observed fact, is not free from that superstition. He likes to display his general philosophy, and various remarks concern geography, as when he refers to the old treatise *On Airs* or echoes Aristotle about the fierce men of the cold north: he even knows the original essay on the famous measurement of the globe. But much of the writing of the time is trivial chatter or a very empty kind of rhetoric, with hardly any intelligent interest in science: take for instance the scholars' talk in Gellius about the Bear and its name, and the showy discourse of Aristides on the problem of the Nile flood, dismissing the more reasonable theories in favour of some mysterious working of God. The papyri seem to have yielded hardly anything of value for geography.[4]

The spirit of inquiry was flagging badly in a jaded civilization. The world craved for faith and revelation, and several religions were in the field. By 200 Christianity was making considerable headway, though still fitfully persecuted. It should not be blamed for the decline of science: that had

[1] Ed. Jacobitz, II, 187–95: Thorndike, op. cit. I, 282. Scoffs, *Icaromenippus*, esp. 6: they pain M. Croiset, *Essai sur...Lucien*, 1882, p. 90. Parody, Rohde, *Griech. Roman*[2], pp. 204–5: see p. 238, n. 1. India, Curt. VIII, 3, 6 (Plin. VI, 58 is more sober): wild, Curt. VIII, 9, 20, VIII, 3, 6, IX, 10, 9.

[2] Paus. VII, 24, 6–13. (Hot springs, ibid. II, 34, VIII, 29.) Aswan, VIII, 38, 6. Sea, p. 253, n. 2, Seres, p. 318, n. 1: western Nile, p. 267, n. 2, animals, p. 274, n. 1. Digressions, Frazer, *P.'s Descr. of Greece*, 1913, I, pp. xl–xli.

[3] *Adv. Math.* v ed. Bekker, pp. 729–48: Schmekel, *Phil. der mittleren Stoa*, pp. 155–8. Revolves, *Adv. Physicos*, II, 174: element, ibid. p. 316. Ed. R. G. Bury, Loeb, 1936. Arrian, ed. Roos, II, p. xxv: Brinkmann, *Rh. Mus.* 1924, pp. 373–401, 1925, pp. 25–63 (not an A. of 150 B.C. as Capelle, *Hermes*, 1905, pp. 614–35). Aet. *Plac.* pp. 273–444 in Diels, *Doxographi*.

[4] Scraps like Oxyrh. Pap. II, 218, IV, 681 hardly count. Schubart, *Einführung in die Papyruskunde*, 1918, p. 167. Aristides, *Or.* 36 K. (48 D.). Gell. II, 21. Globe, Galen, *Inst. logica*, 12. Airs, XVI, 393, Kühn, XVIIB, 398. Fierce, *de Temperamentis* (I, 627). Tides and moon, XIX, 189. Ps.-Galen, π. φιλοσόφου ἱστορίας, with opinions on earth ch. 21 (XIX, 293) is a late compilation, *c.* 500. G.'s astrology, Duhem, op. cit. II, 366, Thorndike, op. cit. pp. 178–80, Singer, *Short Hist. of Science*, p. 92.

begun before, and most pagans were as credulous as Christians.¹ But undeniably it could do science no good when it defended texts on the flat earth and the six days of Creation as revealed truth. Much of the argument goes back to the Jews, especially Philo of Alexandria (A.D. 40). He liked to suggest that the best in Greek wisdom was anticipated by Moses, or even derived from him, a debt which Christian writers assert crudely and ad nauseam.² This notion, with much perverse allegory, left him free to borrow what he pleased, Plato's Ideas, the Stoic 'sympathy' pervading the universe, and the Pythagorean number-mysticism. So he makes great play with seven, as for the seven planets, including the sun, supposed to go round the earth, and the seven zones of heaven, made up by including the zodiac and the Milky Way. The stars by their motions give signs, he thinks, according to a text of Genesis, but are not first causes. The Christians also firmly rejected astrology on the same lines, and as being against their doctrine of free will (often they knew much less about the stars than believers in that false science).³ There were various attitudes to pagan 'wisdom'. At first it was suspect: the vulgar still fear it, admits Clement of Alexandria, and most would reject it wholesale for their one book. But 'apologists' had soon begun to defend their creed against educated men like Celsus as fit not merely for cobblers and fullers and not irreconcilable with the best in philosophy. Clement himself welcomes especially the 'almost inspired' Plato as a preparation for truth, and has much of the desultory and uncritical learning of the time. So has Tertullian, but he is less weighed down by it, and has fits of scorn for a science which has compromised with the falsehood of polytheism; Scripture must be accepted as a higher authority, and contains all the knowledge permitted to man, and Christians have no need of vain curiosity about things which God meant to keep hidden.⁴ Despite this tone he has some notions of science. He complains that Christians are

---

1 Farrington, *Science and Politics in Anc. World*, 1939, p. 53: Halliday, *Pagan Background of Chr.* 1925, p. 10: H. O. Taylor, *Medieval Mind*, 1911, p. 74: Thorndike, op. cit. pp. 481–93: C. Dawson, *Medieval Religion*, 1935, pp. 61–3.

2 Justin Martyr, *Apol.* I, 59: Tatian, *Or.* 36–41: Tert. *Apol.* 19 and 47, *de Anima*, 28: Clem. *Strom.* I, 105, V, 90–107, and later Eus. *H.E.* IV, 29, *P.E.* XIII, 1–3, etc.: Aug. *C.D.* VIII, 11 has some doubts. Philo, *de Opificio Mundi*, 54–5. On him, Thorndike, op. cit. pp. 348–59: Bréhier, *Idées de Philon*², 1925: transl. Colson and Whitaker, 10 vols. Loeb, 1929–41: Wolfson, *Philo*, I, 1947.

3 Duhem, op. cit. II, 402–7, 454–60. Philo, *Opif.* 19. Seven, ibid. 112–13: sympathy, ibid. Cumont, *Oriental Religions in R. Paganism*, 1911, p. 167.

4 *De praescr. Haer.* 7, *Apol.* 46, *de Spect.* 18, *de Testimonio Animae* 1 and 5. P. de Labriolle, *Hist. de la Litt. lat. chrétienne*, 1920, pp. 25, 82. Vulgar, Clem. *Strom.* VI, 80, 5, VI, 11, 89, VII, 1, Labriolle, op. cit. p. 23. Tollinton, *Clement of Alex.* 1914, I, 166, 225, 234: uses Philo freely, ibid. p. 165: McGiffert, *Hist. of Chr. Thought*, 1932, I, ch. 10. Glover, *Conflict of Religions in the early R.E.*⁸ 1919, ch. 9. Burkitt, *C.A.H.* XII, 479–81. E. Bevan, *Christianity*, 1932, pp. 74–5.

talked of as if they were outlandish people, Shadow-feet or *aliqui de subterraneo Antipodes*. He mentions the rather obscure Utopia of Theopompus with its Transatlantic land. He knows of many changes on the face of the earth: shells prove that even mountains were once covered by the waters—does he mean Noah's Flood?—and lands have been torn off like Sicily or engulfed like Atlantis (so too were the wicked cities by the Dead Sea).[1] As for what lies beyond the Ocean, God alone knows surely, said Irenaeus, with excuse enough then, though Clement of Rome had spoken boldly of 'worlds' beyond an impassable Ocean. Most efforts of science seemed to matter little for salvation, at a time when Christians 'should be...looking for and earnestly desiring the coming of the day of God'. For serious clashes with the texts allegory was more and more used. The method had been invented long before, to explain away things which seemed offensive in Homer, and Plato had refused nevertheless to allow the use of poets in education, as the young could not distinguish what was allegory or not. Now the four rivers of Eden were turned into cardinal virtues, and so on, and Celsus might well attack the 'matchless folly' of such interpretations.[2] Yet he and others later, like Porphyry, who attacked the Christians in this matter, themselves used allegory freely enough when they chose.[3]

[1] Tert. *de Pallio*, 2, *Apol.* 40. Antipodes, *ad Nat.* I, 8: Utopia, *adv. Hermog.* 25. On him Glover, op. cit. ch. 10: H. Moss, *Birth of the Middle Ages*, 1935, p. 261: Cochrane, *Christianity and Classical Culture*, 1940, pp. 222–7.

[2] C. in Origen, *c. Celsum*, IV, 52. Poets, Plato, *Rep.* II, 378d. Rivers, p. 40, n. 1. Irenaeus, *Haer.* II, 28 (41) 2. Clem. Rom. *Ep. ad Cor.* 20 ed. Lightfoot, 1890 (quoted by Clem. Alex. *Strom.* v, 12, Origen, *de Princ.* II, 6, etc.). F. Strunz in *Scienta*, LXVI, pp. 64–5 (1939).

[3] Origen, op. cit. III, 18: P. de Labriolle, *La Réaction païenne*, 1934, pp. 160–1, 263–4: H. Chadwick, *J. Theol. Studies*, 1947, p. 43.

CHAPTER XII

THE DECLINE

IN the third century the Empire came near to utter breakdown. The legions, never too many for the long frontiers and increasingly barbarized by local recruiting, lost their sense of mutual cohesion and failed to check stronger attacks. Dozens of Emperors rose and fell. One was killed by the Goths, another taken by the Persians (A.D. 251, 260). At last the frontiers were re-established at the cost of sacrificing untenable outworks like Dacia; some invaders were left inside to fend off worse, a kind of infiltration allowed quite early but now threatening to pass beyond control.[1] Diocletian ended the military anarchy by subdividing the provinces and pulling them together under a more absolute Caesarism. But it was a restoration at a much lower level of power. There had been an irretrievable worsening of economic conditions: a declining population with a ruined middle class was overtaxed to maintain an oppressive bureaucracy and army, and society sank into a peculiar structure of hereditary castes with each man tied to his place and calling. Presently Constantine, having accepted Christianity as a new principle of union, transferred the centre of gravity to his new city, Constantinople (330). Even from these close quarters the Danube line was not always safely held, and another Emperor, Valens, was killed by the Goths in 378, a terrible shock from which Gibbon begins the Fall. The Empire was now divided into two (395). Early in the next century the Western was flooded with barbarians, Rome itself being sacked by the Goths in 410; in 476 its last puppet Caesar was set aside by his German king-maker. The Eastern Empire held firm, though Justinian (526–65) strained its resources to reconquer Italy and other parts of the lost west; by this effort and in other ways he is 'less a Byzantine than the last of Roman Emperors'.[2]

It is usual to begin the Middle Ages from Constantine, but paganism was tolerated almost until the division of the Empire (395). Some would begin with that event and the great figure of Augustine. But the tradition of pagan

---

[1] H. A. L. Fisher, *Hist. of Europe*, I, 88, 110. Albertini, *L'Empire romain*, 1929, pp. 131, 304. Early, see p. 240, n. 2, p. 248, n. 2. S. N. Miller in *Eur. Civ.* ed. Eyre, 1935, II, 373.

[2] Diehl in *C.M.H.* II, 4 (though it begins from Constantine): 'plausibly', Baynes, *Byz. Empire*, 1923, p. 8: Toynbee, *Study of History*, IV, 321. On the econ. regression, Lot, *La Fin du Monde antique*, 1927 (Engl. 1931), ch. 4. Miller, op. cit. pp. 181, 432. Fisher, op. cit. p. 100. C. Singer, *From Magic to Science*, 1928, p. 61 counts the Middle Ages for science as 400–1543. Augustine, Coulton, *Studies in Med. Thought*, 1940, p. 24.

literature and science continued much longer, at least until Justinian closed the school of Athens. It is hard to say at what point ancient geography became medieval, and no apology is needed for tracing this curious transition some little way.

Just before his disaster Valens is praised for not exterminating the enemy 'because they too are in a sense a part of your dominion and a complementary section of mankind'. His successors are still described as 'lords of the earth under the sun'. Just before the Gothic sack of Rome a poet could glorify her imperial mission and speak as if it would last for ever. Just after the sack another could write thus:

> Wide as the ambient Ocean is thy sway,
> And broad thy Empire as the realms of day;
> Still on thy bounds the sun's great march attends,
> With thee his course begins, with thee it ends.
> Thy strong advance nor Afric's burning sand
> Nor frozen horrors of the Pole withstand;
> Thy valour, far as kindly Nature's bound
> Is fixed for man, its dauntless way has found.

Really, of course, these were times of calamitous invasion or at best of anxious defence. Any expansion of the horizon could hardly be expected; on the contrary the outer lands were bound to recede from view. Trade narrowed its range and was content to get distant luxuries through middlemen, though at the end there were again direct touch with India and good hearsay of China. For exploration there was no heart left, if there had ever been much. By war and diplomacy a good deal was learnt of the various barbarians who flung themselves on the frontiers, some coming from afar like the Huns, but this passive kind of information was not well used or of much benefit to geography: the Romans did not care to know much about the background from which the movements started, or about any foreign people except perhaps the Persians, the only one in contact which could be regarded as a civilized power. Among the writers were still a few good historians, Ammianus Marcellinus in the fourth century and Procopius in the sixth; but even their accounts suffer from a sort of literary atavism, garbling the new reports with old and still talking of Scythians and even of Amazons.[1] The set descriptions of the known world are in general feeble

---

[1] K. Dieterich, *Byz. Quellen zur Länder- und Völkerkunde*, 1912, I, p. xvii. Care, Albertini, op. cit. pp. 271, 276. On Amm. Marc. see Mackail, *Classical Studies*, 1925, pp. 159–87: H. A. L. Fisher, *Studies in Hist. and Politics*, 1920, pp. 7–26: Glover, *Life and Letters in the Fourth Century*, 1901, pp. 20–46. Poets, Claudian, *de Cons. Stil.* 150–60: Rutilius Namatianus, 55–62 (transl. A. J. Church). Lords, Dessau, *Inscr. Lat. Sel.* 5809, cp. 'dominus totius orbis', *C.I.L.* III, 247. Praised, Themistius, *Or.* x, *de Pace*, cited by Hodgkin, *Italy and her Invaders*[2], 1892, I, 169: Bury, *Hell. Age*, 1925, 29.

compilations, sometimes from Ptolemy, far oftener from Pliny, himself a bad compiler. For theory there was at best some more or less intelligent repetition; usually it was neglected even in drawing maps, except some copies of Ptolemy's, and the ignorance was such that many Christians could deny the globe as inconsistent with Scripture. The tradition of science never quite died away, and the Greek mind retained its subtlety, but this was mainly devoted to theology or a philosophy which was almost theology.

In the north we hear plenty of the Germans. It is the Germany of Tacitus on the move, with some new and formidable names. The Alamanni, 'all men', are first mentioned as beaten on the Main (A.D. 213, 235), and lower down are the Franks (first in an inscription of 231); they were leagues formed from the debris of the old warring tribes. They made terrible inroads, the Franks far into Gaul and even Spain, the Alamanni over the Raetian frontier and thrice into Italy (261, 268, 271). They were repelled, and the Rhine was fortified again, but the salient beyond was gone, though Probus in 277 'was fully convinced that nothing could reconcile the minds of these barbarians to peace unless they experienced in their own country the calamities of war', and he even 'entertained some thoughts of compelling the Germans to relinquish the exercise of arms'. Several of their tribes once comfortably distant like Vandals and Burgundians were now drifting close up. The Goths had migrated from the Baltic to pass the lower Danube and kill an Emperor in 251, while their left wing crossed the Black Sea to ravage in Asia Minor and Greece. Heroic efforts threw them back over the river, but the bastion of Dacia was wisely abandoned (271); by another curious piece of face-saving, as with 'Germany', the name was transferred to the Roman bank, to two provinces carved out there between the two Moesias. (The Rumanians claim descent from some Latin-speakers who are thought to have held on throughout in Dacia.) Even much later Roman armies could still attack the Alamanni at home (357, 368), but they could not prevent deep invasions, while Saxon pirates harried Gaul and Britain. The Goths became dangerous again when jostled from behind by the Huns entering Europe from the Caspian steppes. They killed Valens and shook the Empire in 378. They had to be permitted south of the Danube as allies: how forcible-feeble sound the courtly phrases about Theodosius, that the lands sundered by continual winter live in dread of him![1] Alaric was

---

[1] Pacatus, *Paneg.* 38, cp. Claudian, *in Rufinum*, II, 40, *Cons. Stil.* I, 94. Dacia Ripensis and Mediterranea, *Vita Aur.* 39, Albertini, op. cit. p. 298: *C.A.H.* XII, 151. Oros. I, 2, 52, Dacia, ubi et Gothia, between Alania and Germany. Alamanni = 'mixed men', Annius Quadratus in Agathias, I, 6. Franks, *C.A.H.* XII, 157. Bury, *Invasion of Europe by the Barbarians*, 1928, p. 10: Dacia virtually lost in 256, ibid. p. 23. Rumanians, Pârvan, *Dacia*, 1928, p. 201.

adroitly diverted against the Western Empire and sacked Rome itself in 410; his successor withdrew to found a Visigoth kingdom round Toulouse. A host of Sueves and Vandals and Alans had just burst over Gaul and into Spain, and the Vandals, who have left their name in Andalusia, if hardly any other trace, passed on to conquer 'Africa'. Some of these invaders were not incapable of feeling the spell of the old civilization which they pillaged. More terrible enemies were the mounted nomads, the Huns. After blackmailing the Eastern Empire they turned west, but were stopped in Gaul by allied Romans and Germans (451), and soon rolled back to the Ural steppes; among the few good travel records of the times is that of Priscus, who attended an envoy to Attila's camp-capital somewhere in the old Dacia. In 455 Rome was again sacked, by Vandals from Africa, and in 476 the last feeble western Caesar was deposed and Italy became a German kingdom. The Franks had advanced to the Loire, and Clovis began to found France. The Eastern Empire should have fought its hardest to check its own bad neighbours on the Danube, Slavs who had filtered down from their marshes and forests, Hunnish Bulgars who had swept over them from the Volga (485), and Avars who overran both, having emerged apparently from inner Asia (558) like the Huns before them.[1] Instead Justinian played them off with subsidies, like the Lombards on the upper river, while he wasted his strength in recovering parts of the west, a ruined Italy and 'Africa' and south-east Spain, none of them long tenable. Yet the city of Constantine was to endure for many centuries to come, a watch-tower looking over a seething barbarian world, and its story is no longer called, as by Gibbon, 'a tedious and uniform tale of weakness and misery'.

Many of the writers are poor scribblers, absurdly meagre and inadequate for such events. The best show little fresh curiosity on the outer geography, and tend to give undigested slabs of old matter going back to Herodotus and even to Homer's Abii or mare-milkers. There was seldom now any temptation to idealize the Germans, the 'most treacherous people in the world', though one writer (Salvian, about 450) harps on their moral superiority to explain their victory as a judgment on a sinful society. A little later Sidonius, bishop of Auvergne, has good sketches of his barbarian masters and neighbours, disliking even the mild Burgundians, who grease their hair with rancid butter and eat ravenously. Characteristic of the time

---

[1] Theophyl. VII, 8 (see p. 365, n. 3): Bury, *Later R. Empire*, 1923, II, 314–16. On Slavs, ibid. pp. 293–8: Peisker, *C.M.H.* II, 426: Moss, *Birth of Middle Ages*, 1935, p. 182: Kluchevsky, *Hist. of Russia*, 1911, I, 33–4: Vernadsky, *Anc. Russia*, 1943, pp. 103–9, 167: Chadwick, *Nationalities of Europe*, 1945, pp. 55, 62–8. Marshes (Pripet), Jordanes, 35. Huns, Priscus, ibid. 178: Hodgkin, op. cit. II, 60–91. Jordanes, ed. Mommsen, 1882: transl. and comm. Mierow, Princeton, 1915: Hodgkin, op. cit. I, 24–9.

is his list of Attila's host with its hubbub of barbaric names, at least two of them quite obsolete:

> subito cum rupta tumultu
> barbaries totas in te transfuderat Arctos,
> Gallia; pugnacem Rugum comitante Gelono
> Gepida trux sequitur; Scirum Burgundio cogit,
> Chunus, Bellonotus, Neurus, Bastarna, Toringus,
> Bructerus, ulvosa vel quem Nicer alluit unda
> prorumpit Francus.

Vivid with knowledge and hate are the descriptions of the Huns, stunted and beardless, bandy-legged from living on horseback, and almost incredibly uncouth and savage; but their origin is left vague, with a puzzling remark that they were slightly known before, beyond the Azov and near the icy Ocean, meaning apparently in the narrow space between Azov and Baltic like Ptolemy's Chuni (no hint here of their coming from far east, and most Byzantines trace them only to the Azov–Caucasus region).[1] Latterly the old Crimean foothold was recovered, and one set of Huns was played off against another across the Don. The accounts of the hinterland are as bad as ever, with Alans jostling obsolete Geloni and the like, a mere rehash of Pliny and Ptolemy, full of stale unrealities including the old Rhipaean mountains. It is 'a damned part of the world, drowned by the nature of things in endless darkness', says Solinus; it is full of gold and gems, but *grypes tenent universa, alites ferocissimi*. There are golden mountains, says Jerome, which no man can approach *propter gryphas et dracones et immensorum corporum monstra*. Towards the end some new and genuine things are heard from the traditions of the victorious Goths about their old home in the Scandinavian 'island'. Procopius describes it as Thule, ten times the size of Britain and far from it towards the north; most is desolate but the inhabited part has thirteen large tribes, one of the largest being the Gauti. Only the Scrithifinni are wild hunters in the forests and mountains, with no tillage (apparently 'skiing Finns' or Lapps); the others live much like the rest of men, but worship many gods and demons and sacrifice prisoners of war as the noblest victims. He tells of some far-wandering Heruli or Goths who drifted back from the Danube past all the nations of Sclaveni

---

1 Amm. Marc. XXXI, 2, 1–12 (Alans, 12–25), Priscus ap. Jord. 123–8, Proc. *B.G.* IV, 5, Agathias, V, 11. Chuni, so Kiessling, *R.E.* VII, 2583, 2592. Huns, also Sid. *Carm.* II, 243–71, imitating Claudian, *in Ruf.* I, 323–31. Bury, *Invasion of Europe*, pp. 132–8: Diehl and Marçais, *Hist. du moyen Âge*, 1936, III, 16–18: Vernadsky, op. cit. ch. 4. Crimea and Huns, Bury, *L.R.E.* II, 298–304, 310–14. Treacherous, Proc. *B.G.* II, 25, Amm. Marc. XVII, 6, 1, etc., Seeck, *Gesch. des Untergangs der ant. Welt*, 1895, I, 477. Superiority, Salvian, *de Gubern. Dei*, IV, 61–2, but cp. 67, VII, 64: Dill, *Roman Society in Last Century of Western Empire*, 1899, pp. 301, 318–23. Sketches, Sid. XII, 6, VII, 236, 369: Dill, pp. 323–7. The verses quoted are Sid. *Pan. Aviti*, 319–25.

and a barren stretch (between Oder and Elbe?) and Varni and Danes to settle near the Gauti. The other source is a history of the Goths by Cassiodorus, as abridged soon after by Jordanes (551). For him Scandza is an ample island, a 'forge of nations', the hive from which the Goths swarmed. He still knows the description of Ptolemy, but can tell much more: among the names are brave Gautigoth, Suehans with fine horses and trading some sort of furs, and Screrefennae, who live on wild beasts and birds' eggs, and mild and peaceful Finni. The Sclaveni or Slavs referred to above are the old Venedi, but widely extended in the Carpathians, with an eastern section down the Dniester and Dnieper, both rivers now mentioned with new names like the modern.[1]

Britain was fairly often in the news till it was lost. The warlike Septimius Severus came himself, and rebuilt the main Wall, apparently wrecked when a rival usurper had withdrawn its garrison to the continent. He is credited with punitive raids (A.D. 208–11) through the Maeatae 'near the Wall which bisects the island' and the Caledonians 'to the end of the island'; there is vague talk of bogs and forests and barren mountains, and of 'unspeakable hardships' and the loss of 50,000 men, which is quite incredible. These people still use war-chariots, we hear, like the Britons in Caesar's day, and they are wild brigands and shepherds and hunters, naked and unshod, and hold their wives in common (an echo of a rumour from Caesar). Evidence of the Emperor's route is very slight, but at a guess he may have gone by sea to the Forth and marched on possibly to Aberdeen or beyond even to the Moray Firth.[2] When he died at York, nothing was kept beyond the Wall or its Cheviot outposts, and he himself had not meant to re-establish the weak Scottish wall. An interesting usurper, Carausius, seized the island with the 'British fleet' given to him to check Frank and Saxon pirates from his base at Boulogne (286–93); a coin shows Britannia welcoming him with a tag from Virgil, *expectate veni* (Plate II E). When he and a successor had been removed, Constantine's father drove out and punished the northern tribes before dying at York. There now appears a

---

[1] Jord. 34–5, 119: Proc. op. cit. III, 14. Heruli, ibid. II, 15: Schütte, *Our Forefathers*, 1929, I, 505: Nansen, *In Northern Mists*, 1911, pp. 139–50: Chadwick, op. cit. pp. 59–60. Hive, Jord. 9: forge, etc., ibid. pp. 16–25: Nansen, pp. 129–38. Jerome, *Ep.* 125, cp. Solinus, 15, 20–2. Rhip., ibid. 17: 38, 12: Sid. II, 243: Basil, *Hex.* III, 6 (and even Aristotle's Danube from Pyrenees!): Proc. *B.G.* IV, 6, 5 (some say): Amm. Marc. XXII, 8, 38. Amazons, ibid. 18–19: Geloni, ibid. 31: Abii, XXIII, 6, 53. Geloni also, Oros. I, 2, 23, 28, Claudian, *in Ruf.* I, 310, Sid. *Ep.* IV, 1. Finns, see p. 244, n. 2.

[2] Miller in *C.A.H.* XII, 36–42: Collingwood and Myres, *R. Britain and the English Settlements*[2], 1937, p. 159. Sir G. Macdonald, *R. Wall in Scotland*[2], 1934, pp. 13–19 is reserved. Dio, LXXVI, 11–13, Maeatae also LXXV, 5: Herodian, III, 47–8. Beyond Forfar, Haverfield and Macdonald, *R. Occupation of Britain*, 1924, p. 123. Over Dee to Moray Firth, C. S. Terry, *Hist. of Scotland*, 1920, p. 8.

THE DECLINE

new general name, Picti. It seems simply the 'painted' or 'tattooed' people, but may rather be a form of a native name, like the Pictones and Pictavi of Gaul. Once they are described as in two nations, the Vecturiones or Verturiones, perhaps the Forth-Tay kingdom of Fortrenn, and the Dicalydones (Ptolemy had a Duocaledonicus Oceanus). Scots raided from Mevania (Man) and from Ireland, whence came also fierce Attacotti, alleged by Jerome to be cannibals, but this may be only an echo of antique hearsay about the Irish and a way of expressing the saint's dislike of a British-born theologian. In 368 a general, Theodosius, repelled many foes and counter-attacked, but the province he called Valentia was not between the walls, and some phrase-making about soaking the Orkneys and Thule with Saxon and Pictish blood need not be taken too seriously. Nor need phrases about Stilicho's men who would at his command explore the icy sea and drive their reluctant oars through the sluggish Cronian waters.[1] In fact he had to recall troops for a Gothic war; others were withdrawn more than once to fight for usurpers, and the Britons, appealing for help, were told to look to themselves (410). So the island was left a prey to the Saxons and their old neighbours the Angles and Jutes. After an obscure interval their raiding began to change to settlement about 450. Meanwhile the Church had won some new ground in Ireland with Patrick, who went first as a captive and returned later as bishop; it flourished there, sheltered from invasion, so that its missionaries could help to bring back the faith and civilization to Britain.

The descriptions of Britain extant are slight and borrowed mostly from Mela and Pliny, with a few new details. Solinus makes Thanet and Ireland snakeless, mentions jet as well as pearls, and brings Ulysses all the way to Caledonia past Lisbon, supposed to be named after him (a poet made him invoke the ghosts somewhere about Boulogne, and some before Tacitus had already brought him to the Rhine). There is still strangely no word of Cornish tin, though it was now worked a good deal. Ireland can still be described as lying between Britain and Spain.[2] There is a remark that the

---

[1] Claudian, *Cons. Stil.* I, 174–80: phrase-making, ibid. IV, *Cons. Hon.* 31–3. Valentia Wales, Collingwood-Myres, p. 286. Amm. Marc. XXVIII, 3, 7, XXVII, 8, 4–6, Scots, XX, 1, 1 (his excursus on Britain lost). Picts, Eum. *Pan. Constantino Aug.* 7. Man, Oros. I, 2, 28. Cannibals, Jerome, *Ep.* IX, *Contra Jovin.* II, 7: hearsay, see p. 144, n. 2. Pict question, Childe, *Prehistory of Scotland*, 1935, p. 261: painted, Collingwood-Myres, pp. 31, 282, but cp. J. Fraser, *History and Ethnology* (Oxf. lecture), 1923, p. 8: A. M. Mackenzie, *Foundations of Scotland*, 1938, p. 26: W. C. Mackenzie, *Scottish Place-Names*, 1931, p. 275 (he denies Fortrenn and connects Di-calydones with Welsh de = 'south', p. 222). Fortrenn, Rhys: W. J. Watson, *Celtic Place-Names of Scotland*, 1926, p. 68: ruling race Celts, and he compares 'Pictones', as Quiggin, *Enc. Brit.* Celtic Lit.

[2] Oros. I, 2, 80. Solinus, 22: Ulysses, ibid. cp. Claudian, *in Ruf.* I, 124: some ap. Tac. *Germ.* 3. Tin, Collingwood in *C.A.H.* XII, 289: T. R. Holmes, *Anc. Britain*, 1907, p. 499.

lack of sun is compensated by the warmth of the seas flowing round Britain; this sounds like an idea of the Gulf Stream, but only embroiders Caesar's statement that the island is milder than the continent. On Thule and the *pigrum et concretum mare* beyond there are various echoes of Pliny. Jordanes, who still quotes Tacitus on the short bright nights of north Britain, has Thule apart from Scandza, north of which is an 'unsailable' Ocean. Procopius fixes the name Thule in Scandinavia, rightly according to many. Yet for him Britain itself has become fabulous. 'One hundred and fifty years after the reign of Honorius, the gravest historian of the times describes the wonders of a remote isle, whose eastern and western parts are divided by an antique wall, the boundary of life and death, or more properly of truth and fiction. The east is a fair country, inhabited by a civilized people; the air is healthy, the waters are pure and plentiful, and the earth yields her regular and fruitful increase. In the west, beyond the wall, the air is infectious and mortal: the ground is covered with serpents, and this dreary solitude is the region of departed spirits, who are transported from the opposite shores in substantial boats and by living rowers. Some families of fishermen, the subjects of the Franks, are excused from tribute in consideration of the mysterious office which is performed by these Charons of the ocean. Each in his turn is summoned, at the hour of midnight, to hear the voices and even the names of the ghosts: he is sensible of their weight; and he feels himself impelled by an unknown but irresistible power. After this dream of fancy we read with astonishment that the name of this island is Brittia, that it lies in the ocean over against the mouth of the Rhine and less than thirty miles from the continent, and that it is possessed by three nations, the Frisians, the Angles, and the Britons.' Thus in a shrinking world, as Oman says, the old western spirit-land has become localized in Britain, and apparently in Wales and Cornwall. It should be added that Procopius has a Britannia as well, but it is Ireland, 'west almost in a line with the end of Spain'.[1] About the same time Gildas, writing in Brittany, if not in the west of Britain itself, can suppose that the Wall was built only in the last days of the province!

'Africa' reached its zenith of Romanization in the third century. But we seek in vain any notice of a campaign going remarkably deep like that of Suetonius over the Atlas, or of explorations far over the desert like those used by Ptolemy. Of various wars with Moors only a few are told with some detail, and the hinterland remains rather vague. At the eastern end

---

[1] Proc. *B.G.* IV, 20: Gibbon on it: Sir C. Oman, *Col. Despard and Other Studies*, 1922, pp. 215–16. Jord. 8 and 17: Britain, ibid. 13. Thule, Solinus, 22 and 17–18: Oros. loc. cit.: Claudian, *Cons. Stil.* I, 176, *in Ruf.* II, 240. Warmth, Minucius Felix, *Oct.* 18 (of third rather than second century?).

THE DECLINE

there were detachments at Ghadames, behind Tripoli, and beyond the Aurès the outposts penetrated to the desert, but this and other wild blocks of the Atlas, even when crossed or flanked by roads, obstinately resisted the civilizing process. The strong Emperor Septimius Severus, himself an African, fully developed the system of roads and posts here and probably all along, towards the high plateau of the salt-lakes and far west between Rabat and Fez (Morocco was still usually little connected with the rest and attached rather to Spain).[1] Later with native risings (253–60, 289–98, etc.) and bitter sectarian strife the provinces had their full share of the miseries of the times. A local chief turned rebel and usurper (372–5) was dealt with by the general Theodosius, who is extravagantly said to be feared by the peoples beyond the torrid zone, *quas aeternis ardoribus inaccessas...natura disterminat*. Another usurper (394–8) roused all the Moors under the Atlas, we hear, and south as far as that zone, where Stilicho would pursue him if necessary. The old province itself did not escape the fate of becoming a barbarian kingdom, when the Vandals attacked from Spain (Augustine died during their siege of his bishopric in 430). From them it was retaken in ruinous wars by Justinian's generals; one of them, John, is lauded in a special epic, with much sound and fury of barbaric names, *saevis Naffur in armis Silcadenitque ferus...et accitus longis convenit ab oris Astrices, Anucatasur*, and so on. Mauretania, behind some coast towns, was practically independent.[2] None could foretell, of course, the conquest which was to sweep along from distant Arabia and wrench all these lands from Europe for 1200 years.

The few formal descriptions surviving are meagre and bad. For Solinus vaguely behind the known fringe are *barbarorum variae nationes et solitudo inaccessa*, or Garamantes and tribes of Ethiopians 'to the Ethiopian Ocean'. Orosius has some novel names like a mons Astrixis. There is no record of any long journey down the Ocean coast, where the last outpost was just beyond Sala (Rabat). Here Solinus talks of a snowy Atlas rising from the desert, with many wild beasts, and fires by night and the music of satyrs, all echoes of Pliny's garblings of still older things; there are too the burning mountain and Hanno's hairy women. The Fortunate Isles have become remote again.

---

1 Albertini, op. cit. pp. 303, 330 (connecting road not long used): also pp. 248, 272. Morocco to past Sala, Itin. Ant. 3–8. Ghadames, see p. 265, n. 1: *C.I.L.* VIII, 10,990: Cidama, Proc. Aed. VI, 3, 9.

2 Proc. *Bell. Vand.* II, 10, cp. Aed. VI, 3. Epic by Corippus, ed. Petschenig, 1886: Skutsch, *R.E.* Corippus and *Byz. Zt.* IX, 152 (on Berber names). J.'s wars, Bury, op. cit. II, 124–50: F. R. Rodd, *People of the Veil*, 1926, pp. 327–8. Rebel Firmus, Amm. Marc. XXVII, 5: torrid, Pacatus, *Pan. Theod.* 22. Pursue, Claudian, *Cons. Stil.* I, 248–50, 333–8, *Bell. Gild.* 319: Oros. VII, 26.

Eastwards we hear of *iter quod limitem Tripolitanum...ducit*, and of brigand tribes raiding down that way and to Cyrene, where a vigorous bishop raised local troops to fight them. Towards the end there are still forts there and at Ghadames, under Justinian. But we hear no word of anyone going far inland on these unalluring tracks. There are more echoes of Pliny, with a desert full of snakes, a series of oases, and a spring at its coldest at noon (now misplaced among the Garamantes). For the coast from near Carthage to Alexandria we have a very minute account, the *Stadiasmus Maris Magni* (probably of the late third century), with accurate details of roadsteads and other conditions important for seamen to know—see the maps in the *Geographici Graeci Minores*, with insets of Derna and Tobruk![1]

Alexandria was punished for backing several usurpers in the evil third century, and Egypt decayed under an oppressive fiscal policy. For Christians it became a land of new wonders as the first home of hermits or 'desertmen' and of monks: some visitors had no interest in anything else, and a history of the monks could dismiss the pyramids as 'granaries of the kings'. The frontier, withdrawn to Aswan, was not safe from the raids of the Blemmyes, even when they were paid to keep off (about the end the Nobades were converted and employed to check them). Some writers talk of headless Blemmyes, with eyes and mouth in the breast, and of other monstrous tribes vaguely hereabouts, such as men with elastic legs, besides long-lived Ethiopians and the old Dog-milkers, Locust-eaters and the like. Animals from these parts were still shown in the arena, as the giraffe and rhinoceros and even two kinds of zebra, described as 'tiger-horses' or horses with tiger-like stripes: it would be interesting to know from what islands in the Red Sea a centurion stole some zebras sacred to the sun. The desert roads are still mentioned as used, and shipping was active down the Red Sea, if seldom far beyond. By this way missionaries reached Abyssinia. A Syrian boy Frumentius, the story goes, was stranded at a port, probably Adulis, where his guardian was killed; he was taken up to Axum and became a royal tutor and then minister. Having returned to Alexandria to report, he was sent back as bishop (fourth century, but the main work of conversion seems to have been done in the next). Closer relations developed with these parts, now sometimes referred to as India Minor or simply Indi (et Barbari)

---

1 *G.G.M.* II, 487–514 and Tabulae, XIX–XXIII: Bunbury, *Anc. Geogr.* II, 665–7: J. Ball, *Egypt in Classical Geographers*, 1942, pp. 130–8. Bishop Synesius in 407–13: Albertini, op. cit. pp. 381, 415. Iter, Itin. Ant. 72. Forts, Proc. *Aed.* VI, 2, 4–20 (on Syrtes, VI, 3, 1–8). Spring, Solinus, 29, Aug. *C.D.* XXI, 5, 1. Names, Oros. I, 2, 90–4. Echoes, Solinus, 31 oases, 27 solitudo, 24, 9–10 Atlas, 14 burning, 56 women, 53 isles. Athen. 83*b* refers briefly to Hanno. Basil, *Hex.* III, 6 copies the Chremetes from Aristotle.

—a confusing habit.¹ Cosmas, arriving as a trader about 522, found many Christians. Adulis was still a great port for ivory. Here he copied two Greek inscriptions, one of a Ptolemy, the other of a native king who had made conquests towards the Nile and the Incense Coast and even in Arabia. Every year armed caravans, he heard, were sent up through Agau (the Lake Tana country) to do a dumb barter for gold nuggets, returning before the heavy rains which flush the Nile (the Blue Nile). He describes fairly well strange animals like the giraffe and rhinoceros, and is honest about not seeing the unicorn. He knows the Incense Coast of Barbaria and the mouth of the Ocean which they call Zingium (the sea of Zenj, as 'Zanzibar' means). He tells with a strong flavour of the Ancient Mariner, how once big birds followed the ship, showing the Ocean to be near, and the crew, frightened lest the current should sweep them into it, cried to the pilot to steer left.² Presently an envoy of Justinian, going up to Axum, saw vast herds of elephants. Other things said of distant parts are less real. Stilicho's men would at his order go to the springs of the Nile. A fantastic novel by Heliodorus about an Ethiopian princess borrows the Mountains of the Moon and adds obviously invented details of the headwaters and the great lakes. Various discussions of the Nile only repeat old ones, more or less intelligently, including the view that it may come from a south temperate zone, *flumina profundens alieni conscia caeli*. There are frequent echoes of Juba's queer theory of a Saharan river as the upper course, and one historian goes out of his way to give this as if it were a triumph of Roman discovery. The mysterious sage Apollonius is made to travel some way up the Nile, to places haunted by demons and satyrs, and there is some vague rubbish about Cannibals and Pygmies and Shadow-feet to the Ethiopian Ocean, into which none sails unless driven against his will. Most assumed that Ocean on the old lines, it seems, and knew or cared nothing about Ptolemy's idea of the continent as ending southwards in unknown land. But there are queer renewals of the antique comparison of the Nile with the Indus as having crocodiles, and Biblical texts help to revive the wild suggestion that it may be the same

---

1 *Expositio totius mundi*, 18, 35: see p. 368, n. 1. F. story, Rufinus, *Hist. Eccl.* x, 9, Theophanes, v, 13: Hennig, *Terrae Incognitae*, II, 4–17: A. H. M. Jones and E. Monroe, *Hist. of Abyssinia*, 1935, pp. 26–9: Albertini, op. cit. p. 394: W. Walker, *Hist. of Chr. Church*, 1922, p. 158: Budge, *Hist. of Ethiopia*, 1928, I, 147–52: Zeiller, *L'Empire rom. et l'Église*, 1928, p. 110: Latourette, op. cit. p. 236. Roads, Itin. Ant. 172: Xen. *Eph.* IV, 1: Proc. *Aed.* VI, 2: Ball, op. cit. pp. 139, 146 (and p. 153 Tab. Peut.). Headless, etc., Solinus, 31, 4: 30, cp. Mela, III, 103. Blemmyes, *Vita Probi*, 10, *Vita Aur.* 33. Proc. *B.P.* I, 19, 27–36. Nobades, ibid. 28–9, Bury, *L.R.E.* II, 328. Giraffe, Oppian, *Cyn.* III, 461–81: *Vita Aur.* loc. cit.: *Vita Gord.* 33. Zebras, Dio, 75, 14: Sir D'Arcy Thompson, *C.R.* 1943, p. 103.

2 Cosmas, ed. Winstedt, Cambridge, 1909, 88 BC. Animals, ibid. 440 B, 441 D, unicorn, 444 B. Caravans, 100 B–101 A. Inscription, ibid. 101 B–108 C. Christians, 169 C.

river, *Nilus in Paradiso oriens et universam Aethiopiam circumiens.*[1] As for the 'torrid' zone, the old ideas prevail again. Whatever we think of Ptolemy's geography here in detail, he had some information at least to the equator, which he knew to be habitable. But this was now forgotten by western writers, who put the Ethiopian Ocean just beyond the Garamantes or began uninhabitable heat at or soon after the tropic; so Macrobius counts 4600 stades to the Cinnamon Coast, beyond which *inaccessum est propter nimium solis ardorem.*

The eastern frontier was unsatisfactory as before, and from 227 there was a strongly national and aggressive Persian dynasty to be reckoned with, the Sassanids. Several wars swayed forwards and backwards over the Mesopotamian road. Once an Emperor was carried away captive, and a relief near Persepolis shows him kneeling before the victor (260). The caravan city of Palmyra played a notable part in avenging this defeat, but presumed on her service and was destroyed by Aurelian (273). By the end of the century the frontier was brilliantly restored, with some gains towards Lake Van and an acknowledged protectorate in Armenia, where Christianity began to be introduced just after. But the endless quarrel started again. For some years it is well told by Ammianus Marcellinus, who took part himself (353–78). His hero Julian moved down the Euphrates and against Ctesiphon, but had to withdraw up the Tigris and was killed (363), and a retreat was bought by ceding everything so long disputed. In 387 a quarter of Armenia was regained, but it is pompous nonsense of a courtly poet to say that a suppliant 'Parthia' bought peace and Rome was dreaded as far as the Ganges.[2] In the fifth century the frontier was quiet, as Persia was threatened from behind, on the Oxus. Procopius tells the long and exhausting wars of the sixth, which were to make easy the conquests of Islam at the expense of both empires. Each had a client state on the fringe of Arabia, and it was remarked that the 'Saracens' were mischievous either as friends or foes; something was heard of idols and a place with a black stone visited

---

[1] Jerome, *de Loc. Hebr.* 124, 11. See p. 388, n. 2. Nile out of India, Proc. *Aed.* VI, 1, 6. Philostr. *Apoll.* VI, 25. Ocean also Oros. I, 2, 90, 92. Echoes, Solinus, 27, 5: 32, 2–6 after Plin. V, 51: Amm. Marc. XXII, 5, 3–13: Oros. I, 2, 18 blunderingly, see Bunbury, II, 692: Tab. Peut.: Joh. Lyd. *de Mens.* IV, 107: and see p. 270, n. 2. Historian, Dio, 75, 13, 3–5. S. temperate, Claudian, *Carm. Minora*, 28, 14: Proclus in Plat. *Tim.* p. 120 Diehl: see p. 118, n. 1. Hel. *Aeth.* IV, 38. Springs, Claudian, *Cons. Stil.* I, 174–80. Envoy, Nonnosus ap. Phot. cod. 3: *F.H.G.* IV, 178: Freese, *Library of Photius*, 1920, pp. 17–20: Dieterich, *Byz. Quellen*, I, 75, II, 19: Beazley, *Dawn of Mod. Geogr.* p. 208. Torrid, Macr. *S.S.* II, 8, 3: J. K. Wright, *Geogr. Lore of the Time of the Crusades*, 1925, p. 41.

[2] Claudian, *Epithal. Hon.* 295, *in Ruf.* I, 273, 374. Julian's march detailed in Amm. Marc. XXIII–XXV, Zosimus, III, 12–31, Bunbury, II, 650–2. Earlier Persian wars, *C.A.H.* XII, 126–37, etc.: relief, *C.A.H.* Plates V, p. 149. On Palmyra, Besnier, *Bas Empire*, 1937, pp. 212–23, 236–40.

THE DECLINE 363

during a holy truce, but none could foresee the power which was to emerge from the desert and overwhelm both Syria and Persia and much more.[1]

The writers could not, of course, add anything but minor detail about such old ground. Some bad mistakes were still repeated: the Persian Gulf is said to be perfectly round and the Tigris to flow through or under Lake Van. There is a curious little work, *Expositio totius mundi et gentium*, probably shortened from a Greek original of about 350 (with part of a later recension, *Totius orbis descriptio*). It deserves mention for its unusual attention to economic matters, like the 'civitates industriosae' of Syria and their exports.[2] The *Stadiasmus of the Great Sea*, so accurate for the Libyan coast, continues in a less detailed form round to Cyprus and Ionia. It is Orosius who first speaks of 'Asia Minor'. For the north coast there are an anonymous periplus, compiled from Arrian and such usual sources, and part of one by Marcianus of Heraclea.[3] A so-called *Route of Alexander*, once accompanied by a similar account of Trajan, was written for Constantius when setting out for his long Persian wars (about 340). It is a feeble compilation, mainly from Arrian, but using also the recent version by Julius Valerius of the nameless text known as Pseudo-Callisthenes.[4] This popular romance of Alexander, growing ever more luxuriant, was to be among the favourite reading of the Middle Ages, with its medley of fantastic geography, and its monstrous peoples and other wonders in the more distant parts (the beginnings of this degeneration can be traced back far, if not to the hero's own lifetime).

The situation at the Caucasus corner was much as before, and this flank was watched now at closer quarters from Constantinople. Control was kept of Lazica after war with the Persians. Amid old matter about the Phasis are fresh details of the peoples and of trade down the river in skins and slaves.[5] (It is noteworthy that Procopius goes back to the very antique

---

1 Truce, Proc. *B.P.* II, 17: Kiernan, *Unveiling of Arabia*, 1937, p. 38. Stone, Arnobius, VI, 11. Clients, Proc. I, 17, 47, II, 1, 6; mischievous, I, 19, 10, cp. Amm. Marc. XIV, 4, 6, *nos vidimus*: province, ibid. XIV, 8, 13: Scenitae, ibid. XXII, 15: the general description in XXIII, 6, 45–7 is quite unreal.

2 *G.G.M.* II, pp. xliv–li and 513–28 (and *Descr.* in *G.L.M.* pp. 104–26): ed. Lumbroso, 1903. Sinko and Wölfflin question a Greek original, *Arch. f. lat. Lexik.* 1904, pp. 531, 573. Mistakes, Amm. Marc. XXIII, 6, 11, 15.

3 Bunbury, II, 663–4. Arrian, ed. Roos, II. Name Asia Minor in Oros. I, 2, 14. *Stad.* 129–296 (and C. and Crete, 297–335) and Tab. XXIV–XXVII: see p. 360, n. 1.

4 *Itin. Alex.* with Arrian, Didot ed. 1846, 1879: Bunbury, II, 649: Kubitschek, *R.E.* IX, 2363–6. Thorndike, *Hist. of Magic and Exper. Science*, I, 197–203: on Alex. romance, ibid. ch. 24: Kroll, *R.E.* Kallisthenes: J. K. Wright, *Geogr. Lore of...the Crusades*, 1925, pp. 73–4, 381.

5 Proc. *B.P.* II, 15, 17, 29: *B.G.* IV, 3, 12–21 (Abasgi), *Aed.* III, 6 (Tzani). Gibbon, ch. 42. Bury, op. cit. II, 113–20: Moss, op. cit. p. 118. Crimea also held, *Aed.* III, 7, 10. See also W. E. D. Allen, *Hist. of the Georgian People*, 1932, pp. 49–56, 76–8.

notion of the Phasis as the boundary between Europe and Asia; old writers chose that river and the isthmus, remarks another, while the newer favour the Don-Azov.) Roman influence reached the inner kingdoms, helped by the spread of Christianity, but the Persians were stronger there. There was also a certain common interest, and we hear even of a subsidy paid them to defend the main pass, which was still often miscalled the Caspian Gates, against the northern barbarians, Alans and presently Huns.[1] The Huns more than once raided deep by this way, first in 395. Many Christians saw in them the Gog and Magog predicted to 'come out of the uttermost parts of the north' and now breaking through the barriers supposed to have been built by Alexander against them, *ubi Caucasi rupibus feras gentes Alexandri claustra cohibent*. The mountains could easily be taken as the other or Indian Caucasus, and the legend was to have queer ramifications; inevitably the gates were to be moved on far north-east and east, till they got confused with the Great Wall of China, the excluded peoples becoming Turks and finally Mongols.[2] Gog and Magog were still to figure on early modern maps.

Sometimes Persian kings are mentioned as turning away to deal with enemies appearing in their rear, including various Huns. There is no account of travel in Iran, but there were at least missionaries there: despite persecution they made some headway, especially after adopting the unofficial doctrine of Nestorius (431), and churches were founded as far as Herat, Merv, and Samarcand. But the western writers are content to repeat and garble old accounts. Thus Ammianus Marcellinus gives a feeble rehash here, and there is no reason to credit him with a notion of the Aral sea when he is merely overstating Ptolemy's Oxus lake. What is worse, most take a step back to the obstinate error of a Caspian gulf: so Solinus, among his bad echoes of Pliny, and so too some who should have learnt better from Ptolemy.[3] Cosmas has heard of churches even among the Huns of the upper Indus, and has fresh knowledge of the really far east; yet he also lapses into this old blunder. Macrobius knows that some deny the gulf, and Basil has a queer echo of Aristotle: some think, he says, that the Hyrcanian and Caspian seas

---

1 Priscus, fr. 8, *F.H.G.* IV, 90 a. Proc. *B.P.* I, 16, 4, II, 15, 3, 35. *C.M.H.* I, 469, 481, II, 28. Chapot, *Frontière de l'Euphrate*, p. 369. Gibbon, ed. Bury, IV, 260. Vernadsky, op. cit. p. 194. Spread, Zeiller, op. cit. p. 108, Latourette, I, 105–6. Boundary, Proc. *B.G.* IV, 2, 29, IV, 6, 1–8, cp. *Aed.* VI, 1, 7: Agathemerus, I, 3: Marcianus as Ptolemy.

2 Anderson, op. cit. (see p. 291, n. 1): Hennig, op. cit. II, 162–5: Marinelli, *Scritti Minori*, 1908, pp. 387–438: Oman, *On the Writing of History*, 1939, pp. 268–9: Olschki, *Marco Polo's Successors*, 1943, pp. 2, 62. Huns, Claudian, *in Ruf.* II, 28, Jerome, *Ep.* 60, 16, 77, 8 (Gog, ibid.), and later in 441, 502. A.'s gates also Proc. *B.P.* I, 10, 9.

3 As Agathemerus, I, 13. Solinus, 15, 18: 54. Amm. Marc. XXIII, ch. 6: Arius to Caspian, ibid. 69: lake, ibid. 59, Aral, thinks Barthold, *Aral-See*, 1910, p. 8: see p. 294, n. 1. Enemies, Amm. Marc. XVI, 9, 4 (Chionites), XVII, 5, 1, etc.

THE DECLINE

are closed, but geographers make them communicate with each other and both discharge into the Ocean, and he also repeats a river Araxes sending a branch, the Tanais, to the Azov. Orosius has the gulf, and for the rest is very sketchy.[1]

The Huns who shook the western world broke in about 370 from the Caspian-Aral steppes, where they may have been for many generations. No ancient writer states that they had come from the far east, but this has long been generally assumed, though the exact connection over longish gaps of space and time is still not very clear. The best link seems a notice of the Wei Annals that the Hiung-nu conquered the old Alan land.[2] After the collapse of the Han dynasty China had a bad period of 'three kingdoms' fighting each other; then the Tsin restored unity for a short time, only to lose the whole north to the Hiung-nu and kindred tribes pressing behind them. Various barbarian kingdoms contended there until one of them, the Wei, became Chinese enough to defend civilization against further attacks (from 386). They checked the new masters of Mongolia, the Juan-Juan. It was the rise of this nomad empire which may have started the movement among the Caspian Huns. The same power jostled and drove away the Ephthalite or White Huns, who began to invade the Persians about 428 and even killed a king of theirs in 484. They are described as having some settled life and as not bestial like other Huns. The Chinese thought these Ye-t'a a branch of the old Yue-chi, probably wrongly, and at least one traveller visited them in north India, which they entered about 510. The Juan-Juan themselves were overcome about 552 by the Tou-kiue or Turks, hitherto their vassals and smiths in the Altai, and were either destroyed or, as many suppose, driven west to appear on the Volga as the Avars.[3] The Turks presently split into Eastern and Western, and the latter extended rapidly west to crush the White Huns and face the Persians across the Oxus.

[1] Oros. I, 2, 14 f.: gulf, ibid. 24, 48. Macr. *S.S.* II, 9, 7. Basil, *Hex.* IV, 2: III, 6. Cosmas, 88A. Churches, ibid. 169B, 449A: Zeiller, op. cit. p. 102: Grousset, *Hist. de l'extrême Orient*, 1929, I, 353: Latourette, op. cit. I, 103–5: Yule-Cordier, *Cathay and the Way Thither*, 1915, I, 101–3, J. Stewart, *Nestorian Missionary Enterprise*, 1928. For books on Cosmas, see p. 369, n. 2.

[2] Kiessling, *R.E.* VIII, 2585 after Hirth, and see p. 355, n. 1, p. 252, n. 3. *C.A.H.* XII, 105. *C.M.H.* I, 215. Doubts in Cordier, *Hist. de la Chine*, 1920, I, 292: Bury on Gibbon, ch. 26 (III, App. 6), *L.R.E.* I, 101 (despite E. H. Parker, *A Thousand Years of the Tartars*, 1895, pp. 131–2): but 'almost certain', *Invasion of Eur.* 1928, p. 49: Halphen, *Les Barbares*, 1926, p. 11.

[3] Theophyl. VII, 7: Yule-Cordier, 29, Cordier, op. cit. p. 347: more doubtfully, Grousset, p. 253: Vernadsky, op. cit. p. 179. But destroyed, Parker, op. cit. p. 159, Hirth, *Anc. Hist. of China*, p. 123, Bury on Gibbon, ch. 42 (IV, App. 16). Bestial, Proc. *B.P.* I, 3, 4. Yue-chi, Parker, p. 131, Bury, Yule-Cordier, p. 205: more likely akin to H., Cordier, p. 391, Grousset, p. 254, II, 94: Vernadsky, p. 127. Visited by Sung Yun in 518.

Throughout these centuries China failed to regain control of the Tarim corridor, and only a few rulers were strong enough to draw respectful envoys. Yet the people there had an interest in conveying silk, and the Annals describe the roads as still active.[1] Along the roads there is further evidence of the trade and the overlapping of cultures which it had brought about. Indian colonies were strong at first on the south road, with their Buddhism and its traces of Greek art. More surprising are paintings of cherubs and girls which might be expected rather in a villa of the Roman East, or even of Pompeii; one is signed in Indian characters by a Tita whom the discoverer takes as a Eurasian Titus.[2] There are impressions of classical sealings, as before, and others showing the influence of Persian designs. At Lou-lan was found a bale of silk, evidently of a regulation width, dropped by a trader on its way westwards. By A.D. 300 many of the southern oases were abandoned owing to increasing desiccation, and this road became impossible for ordinary travellers. Trade continued along the northern road, and here too there were remarkable fusions of cultures: the evidence chiefly concerns a later period, but a red-haired and blue-eyed type in the frescoes has been equated with the old Tochari and Yue-chi.[3] Buddhist missionaries now reached China itself and had their successes even with Emperors, and Fa-hien in 399 began a long counter-stream of stout-hearted pilgrims to the holy places of the faith in India. We hear of several embassies to China from the Possu or Persians, but not of any in return, still less of caravans going all the way to the Persian capital or to a Mesopotamian fair to sell their silk, as some have supposed.[4] A few new things are said about Ta-ts'in—some word of the road to Antioch and of Alexandria apparently and more details of wares—but the hearsay is little better than before, and the notion of western geography remains very nebulous. At the very end the name begins to be replaced by another, Fu-lin, which has been variously explained as from 'Bethlehem' (so Hirth)

---

[1] Hirth, *China and R. Orient*, pp. 13, 67. Homage to Tsin in 285, Wei in 435, Grousset, op. cit. pp. 222, 251, Cordier, pp. 302, 333.

[2] Frescoes at Miran near Charklik, Sir M. A. Stein, *Ruins of Desert Cathay*, 1912, I, chs. 40–4, esp. p. 492: *Serindia*, 1921, I, ch. 13, esp. p. 530 (Tita), IV, plates 40–1: *On Anc. Central-Asian Tracks*, 1933, pp. 118–26, figs. 54, 56. Halphen in *C.A.H.* XII, 98 (accepts Titus). Grousset, op. cit. I, 307–8.

[3] Von le Coq, *Auf Hellas Spuren in Alt-Turkistan*, 1926 (Engl. as *Buried Treasures of Chin. Turkestan*, 1926). Grousset, op. cit. pp. 309–15. Bale, Stein, *Desert Cathay*, I, 381, other pieces, ibid. and II, 126 (one made about A.D. 100). Sealings, *Anc. Khotan*, plates 49, 89. See p. 311, n. 2. Desiccation, Huntington, *Mainsprings of Civ.* 1945, pp. 548–51.

[4] As Warmington, *Commerce between R.E. and India*, p. 138, from Amm. Marc. XIV, 3, 3: to Ctesiphon, Christensen, *C.A.H.* XII, 117. Embassies, Yule-Cordier, p. 95. Missionaries in 3rd–4th centuries, Grousset, pp. 246, 256. Pilgrims, Cordier, op. cit. I, ch. 25: H. A. Giles, *Hist. of Chin. Lit.* 1901, pp. 111–16.

or from πόλιν or 'Rome', both meaning Constantinople.¹ Christianity did not reach China in this period, but a Nestorian mission arrived in 635, and the famous inscription of Si-an in 781 describes the coming of the 'brilliant teaching' of Ta-ts'in, where a sage had been born of a virgin; the name seems to stand here for Syria in particular, though the missionaries were probably Iranian.

The silk-trade was real enough, even in the wretched third century. The tittle-tattle on Emperors has quite a lot about silk: one was the first to wear pure silk, Aurelian forbade it to his wife as it was worth its weight in gold, and so on. An edict on prices mentions various kinds and their values. Presently it came more freely, but a statement that it reached 'even the lowest' seems wild, as it was always dear owing to the long transport and the Persian tolls. To reduce these exactions the government took over a monopoly, buying the silk at frontier markets and reselling what little the court factories did not need. The wrong idea of silk as a down from leaves still prevailed. The trade was very indirect, and the writers could learn little. They echo Pliny on a shy people doing dumb barter at a certain river (one gives it a name, Campulinus, otherwise unknown). Or at best they combine this with Ptolemy's account of the long road past Stone Tower. So Ammianus Marcellinus, who uses that writer probably indirectly, through some manual of geography little older than himself; a mention of *celsorum aggerum summitates* may be only a flourish for mountains and not a first rumour of the Great Wall, as some believe.² Various odd assertions seem merely Utopian, as that this people have no idols or no gods, and no harlots and murderers, or that the men adorn themselves while the women do all the work.³

About India the western writers for long have hardly a scrap of fresh information. On the contrary, after having been 'brought nearer', India

---

1 'Rome', Hudson, *Eur. and China*, p. 128, Grousset, p. 241: discussion in Yule-Cordier, pp. 44–5: Pelliot, *J. As.* 1914, 1, 498–9 ('Rome' = R. East through an Iranian form), *T'oung Pao*, 1914, p. 625. Road, Hirth, op. cit. p. 49 (Antioch as An-tu), pp. 184, 218. Alex., ibid. p. 180, Hudson, pp. 84, 97. Wares, Hirth, op. cit. p. 73, *Chin. Stud.* pp. 14, 63. On oldest map of west, Herrmann in *Festschrift Hirth*, 1920, p. 191, *Land der Seide*, p. 5, cp. Soothill, *Geogr. J.* 1927, p. 534. Mission, Yule-Cordier, p. 105, Cordier, p. 486, Hirth, p. 323: Moule, *Christians in China*, 1930, ch. 2.

2 As Herrmann, *R.E.* Seres, *Land der Seide*, p. 35. Amm. Marc. XXIII, 6, 14 and 60–8. Echo, Solinus, 50: river named, Aelian, *N.A.* III, 4. Down, Sol., Amm. Marc., Aus. *Id.* 12, Jerome, *Ep.* 107, 10, etc. Monopoly, Hudson, p. 118. Lowest, Amm. Marc. loc. cit. (67). Emperors (see *Vitae*), Elagabalus, 26, Aur. 48 (and Alex. Sev. 40, Tac. 16). On the (rare) R. and Byz. silks from the cemetery of Achmim (in Egypt) R. Forrer, 1891: R. Cox, *Les Soieries d'Art*, 1914, ch. 3.

3 Epiphanius, III, 1: rest in Origen, *c. Celsum*, 7, 63, Arnobius, II, 12, Ps.-Bardesanes (see p. 384, n. 3) ap. Ps.-Clem. *Recogn.* IX, 17 and 19–29 (and Eus. *H.E.* VI, 10): Thorndike, op. cit. I, 373–6, 412–13: Moule, op. cit. p. 23. Oros. I, 2, 13, 64–7 is bad.

was now allowed to recede into a hazy distance: the monsoon trade was lost almost entirely, it seems, to middlemen of Axum and Yemen, and shipping from Egypt hardly went beyond these parts, which were themselves often vaguely called 'India'.[1] (Yet Indian wares did come, and as late as 410 Alaric could demand 3000 pounds of pepper in the ransom of Rome.) A few Indian embassies are mentioned. From one met in Syria about 218 something was heard of cave-temples and of certain devotees, evidently Buddhist monks. Another, to Aurelian, seems as dubious as his alleged envoys from the Silkmen.[2] Others came to Constantine and to Julian, in his case from as far as the Serendivi (the first half of the name is a Persian form of the same which survives as 'Ceylon'). We hear of no one sent in return, and little faith can be put in a few notices of supposed travellers, like one said to have gone from Adulis to Muziris.[3] It does not seem likely that the missionary Theophilus went beyond Socotra and Aden (356). It is possible that Christianity reached India by 300, but its origin there is quite obscure: there is no good evidence for it much before the sixth century, when we hear of churches with bishops from Persia in most of the western ports and Ceylon, if not farther. The wise and happy Brahmans were popular as a pattern of the philosophic or monastic life, though some disliked the comparison: so Tertullian denies that Christians are 'Brahmans, exiles from life, or Indian Gymnosophists dwelling in forests'. A common feature of the Alexander legend was a supposed correspondence with an Indian king about his pure and simple Brahmans. There were new Utopianisms, like a pious and long-lived people who do no work and live on honey and manna: the *Expositio* has this in a strange brew of obscure names including the Havilah of Genesis, with various unintelligible figures. It knows, however, that sericum comes from India Major.[4] Of other accounts Solinus echoes Pliny as usual, and ignores Ptolemy's extension of the map to the Sinae Marcianus copies Ptolemy all

1 Ships to 'India', *Vita Firmi*, 3: *C.A.H.* XII, 277. Middlemen, Hudson, op. cit. pp. 103, 108. Vaguely, p. 361, n. 1: Bury, *L.R.E.* II, 318: Kimble, op. cit. p. 128: Sir E. D. Ross in Newton, op. cit. p. 34.

2 *Vita Aur.* 33, cp. 41, though Warmington, op. cit. p. 138 believes, as does Oertel, *C.A.H.* XII, 271. Syria, Bardesanes ap. Porph. *de Abstinentia*, IV, 17–18, Stobaeus, *Ecl. Phys.* I, 56: H. G. Rawlinson, *Intercourse between Western World and India*, 1916, pp. 142–6 and in *Legacy of India*, 1937, p. 18, cp. Thomas, ibid. p. 216: Tollinton, *Clement of Alex.* 1914, I, 139 f.: Bidez, *C.A.H.* XII, 614.

3 In Ps.-Palladius, believed by Beazley, op. cit. I, 190 but not Winstedt, *Cosmas*, p. 11. Eus. *Vita Const.* IV, 7, 50. J. in Amm. Marc. XXII, 7, 9, cp. 'Diva gens', *Expos. G.L.M.* p. 107. Lies of Metrodorus, Amm. Marc. XVIII, 6, 75: Milman, *Hist. of Latin Christianity*, 1867, II, 401.

4 *Expos.* 16. Eviltae, ibid. 9. Who are the Camarini of 8 and 12? Tert. *Apol.* 42. Churches, Cosmas, 169A. Obscure, Latourette, I, 107–8. Theoph., Hitti, *Hist. of Arabia*, p. 61: Winstedt, op. cit. p. 348 (to Yemen): where?, Hennig, op. cit. II, 16.

the way, adding only a still grosser exaggeration of Ceylon. Nearly everything said at this time is of interest only for the taste shown in the selection from obsolete matter: there is a good deal especially on animals, with a more and more medieval flavour, as on the unicorn, *monoceros monstrum mugitu horrido*. (New for the elephant is a queer statement that he has a sweet breath from eating a 'black rose', which has been guessed to be the clove.) A wild epic by Nonnos on the god Dionysus and his conquest of India hardly comes into question, as it makes little attempt at plausible local colour. Avienus has a Chryse, but only as an echo of old fable. A late map, the Peutinger, has no Golden Chersonese or Sinae, and shows no sign of any good recent knowledge, despite a supposed 'Temple of Augustus' near the pepper mart of Muziris. It is odd that the information should have been so meagre and stale, as India was now enjoying a brilliant period under the Gupta dynasty (320–535), and some elements of its science and art were derived from Greek, as obviously in astrology and astronomy, including an earth-globe, of which the old fabulous Mount Meru has now become the axis. Possibly there was some influence in the reverse direction, as traces of Hindu mysticism have been seen in Plotinus.[1]

At last comes a report of a different order, comparable in its way with the old Periplus. It is strangely embedded in one of the most cranky of books, a 'Christian Topography', written about 547 to disprove the pagan notion that the earth is a globe. There were illustrations, from which those of the manuscripts probably derive. When not bemused by his texts and theories, the author has good things to say, and he is veracious enough, despite the sharp remarks of Photius, who quotes him three centuries later. He is described as Cosmas, a monk, no doubt of Alexandria. In his younger days, he tells us, he had himself traded in the Red Sea and beyond, and gathered accurate information from other traders and from natives.[2] What he says of Africa has already been mentioned. Closely connected with Axum were the Homerites of south Arabia, and he knows of many

1 Albertini, op. cit. 269: Nock, *Conversion*, 1933, p. 47 is sceptical. Guptas, V. Smith, *Oxf. Hist. of India*[2], 1923, p. 160. Science, W. E. Clark in *Legacy of India*, 1937, pp. 348–51. Avienus, 769. Solinus, 52–3 (unicorn 52, 39). Animals, Aelian, *N.A.* XVI, 2–23 (early 3rd cent.). Nonnos, no Ind. tradition, Lassen, *Ind. Alt.* III, 443–51: transl. Rouse, Loeb, 1940. Marcianus, Bunbury, II, 661: map in *G.G.M.* Tab. XXX: Yule-Cordier, p. 13: Lassen, op. cit. III, 287 praises. Agathem. II, 6 has Salice. Oros. I, 2, 19 is queer. Clove, Achilles Tatius, IV, 5, ed. Gaselee, 1917.

2 88B. Cosmas Indicopleustes, ed. Winstedt, Cambridge, 1909. Transl. and comm. McCrindle, 1897. Yule-Cordier, op. cit. pp. 25–8, 212–31: Beazley, *Dawn of Mod. Geogr.* 1897, I, 191–6 and (theory) 273–303: Dalton, *Byz. Art and Arch.* 1911, pp. 460–2, 481: Dieterich, *Byz. Quellen*, p. 79: Gibbon, ch. 40, Bury, ad loc. and *L.R.E.* II, 319–21: Kaeppel, *Off the Beaten Track in the Classics*, 1936, pp. 21–3: Wecker, *R.E.* XI, 1487–90 (1912). On the miniatures Stornajolo, 1908. First ed. Montfaucon, 1706. Vol. 88 of Migne, *Patrol. Graeca*, 1864.

Christians there and in Socotra, where descendants of old colonists still spoke Greek. He expressly claims to have sailed in the Persian Gulf, and gives much about India, though some deny that this need be from direct personal knowledge.[1] Book XI on Indian animals and trees and on Ceylon may have originally belonged to another work of his, perhaps a description of the earth. He names with their wares a port on the Indus, three Bombay way, five on the Pepper Coast of 'Male', and two round the corner to the Cauvery. He knows of local churches. He knows of the pepper vine, and can give native words for the coconut and its milk. He tells a remarkable anecdote as heard from one Sopatros, who sailed from Adulis (in a local ship?) to Sielediba or Ceylon, about 512. This man, being brought before the king, displayed a fine gold coin far outshining the silver of his rival, a Persian trader, and so proved the superiority of his nation, and had an elephant-ride round the town with drums beating. (The coin motif is as old as Pliny, and some like the most recent editor doubt the story.) The island is still absurdly overestimated. One king is said to have the port and chief mart, the other the gem country; over a temple flashes a great red gem (presently to be seen by Chinese and Arabs and later by Marco Polo). Round about are very many islets with coconuts. Being central, Ceylon is a great place of trade, receiving ships from all India and Persia and sending out its own. It also receives and forwards wares, aloeswood and sandalwood, cloves and silk, from the regions beyond as far as the silk country of Tzinista. After that there is no sailing or habitation; it lies on the Ocean far up to the left from the Indian, and so the overland route is much shorter, and plenty of silk always goes that way to the borders of Persia, though the road is long enough (the distance is exaggerated as 150 stages, apparently at least 4500 Roman miles). All this is still more explicit than the Periplus, and plainly refers to China, with a name coming through a Persian form, Chinistan, despite a few who have seen here only a dim notion of something in Malaya or Indo-China.[2] But at best it is hearsay picked up in Ceylon, and there is no hint of any western trader going on himself like the Skipper Alexander or the 'envoys' of An-tun.

Yet the Chinese Annals have two notices of 'envoys' from Ta-ts'in, in 226 and 284. They have been taken in both cases as again only merchants

[1] Deny, Lassen, op. cit. II, 773 (heard from Sopatros), Tennent, *Ceylon*, 1860, I, 542, Hudson, *Eur. and China*, p. 110, Laistner in A. P. Newton, *Travel and Travellers of Middle Ages*, 1926, pp. 34–6, against Yule-Cordier, p. 25, Beazley, Winstedt, p. 3, Hennig, *T.I.* II, 96. Gulf, Cosmas, 88 B. Christians, ibid. 169 B.C.

[2] As Beazley, I, 197, citing Walckenaer, 1832 (only Tenasserim!): Winstedt, p. 335. China, Yule-Cordier, pp. 25, 28. Silk-road, Cosmas, 96D–97B: cloves, 445D, silk, 448B. Doubt story, Winstedt, Rawlinson, op. cit. p. 150. Cp. Plin. VI, 24 (see p. 299, n. 1). Ports, Cosmas, 448A–B: Caber, cp. Ptolemy's Chaberis. On Ceylon Tennent, op. cit. pp. 565–70.

from Egypt or Syria, though some believe in real envoys seeking to reopen trade relations.[1] Either way they seem hard to accept for such dates in the doldrums of the Empire, and we may wonder if the country's name is used with any accuracy. There are frequent mentions of India and Ceylon as sending envoys and other travellers like Buddhist missionaries.[2] Probably most of the traffic in these far eastern waters was by the Indians, who had continued to found flourishing colonies on many coasts and islands on the way to China. It was by sea that the pilgrim Fa-hien came from the Ganges port to Ceylon, and later across the open to Java, from which he reached home after hard adventures in 414. But it does not seem clear that his ship from Ceylon was Chinese, or that many such ships ventured yet to that 'hospitable island', as Gibbon imagined.[3]

The overland silk came through the Persians, and latterly they had got more and more hold of the sea-route also. When Justinian encouraged the Red Sea kingdoms—both then under Axumite rule as sometimes before—to fetch him silk from India, they found the supply there bought up. When he tried to dictate a maximum price, the Persians refused to sell, and the silk-workers of Syria were ruined (part of the blame is put on a profiteering controller). At last about 552 certain monks offered to solve the problem: they had lived long in Serinda, a country 'above' India or 'of Indians' (the text is dubious), and heard that silk was made by caterpillars. With the Emperor's consent they returned 'to India' and brought back some eggs; the caterpillars, hatched out by warming, were fed on mulberry leaves, and so henceforth silk could be produced on Roman soil. In a variant it was 'a certain Persian' who smuggled out the eggs in a hollow cane and 'from the Seres'.[4] The country has been understood most often as Khotan, which had silkworms, it appears, since a Chinese princess had brought eggs hidden in her hat, when she came to marry the local king (her date is doubtful and her story is first told by a Buddhist pilgrim of the

1 Envoys, Halphen in *C.A.H.* XII, 105, Yule-Cordier, p. 54, Beazley, I, 180, Hennig, *T.I.* I, 369 (the second). Cp. Hirth, *China and Roman Orient*, pp. 45, 48, 306, Grousset, I, 243.

2 Tennent, op. cit. pp. 387, 590, Yule-Cordier, p. 67, Hennig, op. cit. II, 24, 31, Grousset, pp. 246, 260, II, 155–6, V. Smith, op. cit. p. 162.

3 And Lassen, II, 543, Beazley, p. 191. Few, Hirth, p. 173, Hudson, p. 115: W. G. Holmes, *Age of Justinian*, 1905, I, 186. For F. see H. A. Giles, *Travels of F.* 1923: Hennig, op. cit. II, 28–32. Ship Chinese, Wales, *Towards Angkor*, 1937, pp. 31–2, Richthofen, *China*, I, 568. Colonies (mainly 200–600), Hudson, p. 109, see p. 314, n. 1: Wales, op. cit. pp. 26, 82–5, 147.

4 Theophanes, fr. 3 ap. Phot. in *F.H.G.* IV, 276: monks, Proc. *B.G.* IV, 17: Gibbon, ch. 40, ed. Bury, IV, 233: Yule-Cordier, pp. 203–5. Beazley, p. 189: Dieterich, *Byz. Quellen*, p. 22: Baynes, *Byz. Empire*, 1923, pp. 208–10: Vernadsky, op. cit. p. 183. Controller, Proc. *Anecd.* 25. Axumites and Homerites, Proc. *B.P.* I, 20, 9, Bury, *L.R.E.* II, 322–7, Beazley, pp. 184–6, Dalton, op. cit. p. 584, Dieterich, p. 19. An envoy, see p. 362, n. 1.

seventh century and in a fresco found by Stein at a place east of Khotan). It seems unlikely that the strange mission of monks went on to China itself, as Gibbon supposed. Some have thought of another mixture of Seres and Indians in Indo-China, reached by sea, and some suppose that the name does not mean any such mixture but is the same as the Serendib of the Persians, the Sielediba of Cosmas, which is Ceylon.[1]

Till the rising industry could meet the demand, silk had still to be got through the Persians, and from the Turks, who now ruled westwards to the Oxus. There were stoppages due to Persian caprice, and a Sogdian vassal suggested to the Western Turks the using of a direct route round the Caspian Sea. As their envoy he was well received in Constantinople, though unpleasantly surprised to find silkworms in operation there (568). Meanwhile some import was needed, and an envoy Zemarchus accompanied him back to the Khan's luxurious camp, apparently somewhere in the western Tien-shan. He returned round a big lake to the Volga. Thus the Sea of Aral came distinctly into view for the first time.[2] Also the Caspian was confirmed as a lake; yet the mistake about a gulf was still to be long repeated.

Such is what these times have to say of distant parts, very little of it both new and accurate. For the scientific side of geography they have still less: with most of the writers the only question is how poorly they understand the work already done, an important question, however, because some of them were to have great influence throughout the Middle Ages.

The line of progress was to improve on Ptolemy by getting a better structure of observed points and by criticizing his methods, especially the bad assumption for the size of the globe. Of any such effort we hear practically nothing. An Emperor marching about Scotland had observations taken of the sun's position, it is said, and the length of the days and nights; if so, there is no word of the results being used. There were still respectable commentators on the *System of Astronomy* as Pappus and Theon, both of Alexandria, about 320 and 380, and even much later. The first also wrote a description of the earth, apparently read off Ptolemy's text or maps (it is known only as having been used by an Armenian historian). The extant transcribers of the *Geography* are feeble enough. Marcianus (about 400?)

1 So Herrmann, *R.E.* Serinda, Winstedt, p. 352, Grousset, p. 213 (possibly). Indo-China, Bury, op. cit. II, 332. China, perhaps Nanking, Gibbon, ch. 40: N. China, Dalton, Beazley. Khotan, Yule-Cordier, pp. 24, 203–5 (or perhaps China): Richthofen, op. cit. pp. 529, 550: Stein, *Anc. Khotan*, I, 134 (and *Serindia*). Princess, ibid. ch. 9, *On Anc. C.-Asian Tracks*, p. 63: towards fourth century?, Rémusat, cited by Cox, *Les Soieries d'Art*, 1914, p. 7, not B.C. as Sykes, *Quest for Cathay*, 1936, p. 25.

2 Menander, *Exc. de Legationibus*, pp. 7–8: *F.H.G.* IV, 225: Dieterich, op. cit. II, 14. Bury, Gibbon, ch. 42, App. 16, and *L.R.E.* II, 96: Hudson, op. cit. p. 124: Hennig, II, 62–73: Yule-Cordier, pp. 205–7: Beazley, pp. 186–8: Barthold, *Aral-See*, 1910, p. 20. Camp near Kucha, Grousset, p. 254: in Altai, Vernadsky, op. cit. p. 183.

THE DECLINE

in a periplus of the Ocean coasts followed the 'most divine and wise' Ptolemy, or rather an obscure person who had already recast him in this form; for the inner sea he abridged a much older authority, Artemidorus.[1] A 'sketch of geography' under the name of Agathemerus, of uncertain date, is really made up of inconsistent pieces using different sources, here Ptolemy's figure for the globe, his series of 23 parallels with lengthening days, and his horizon east to the Sinae, elsewhere older figures for the breadth and the length of a known earth reaching only to the Ganges. There survive also two nameless epitomes of Ptolemy, perhaps by school-masters and both incompetent.[2] Later his astronomy was to be reflected through an Arab medium and the *Almagest* was translated in 1160–75, but his mapping was almost forgotten in the west, and not fully recovered till the fifteenth century; it was then that it had its greatest days, and a strong influence on the work of exploration, especially by inspiring (as well as misleading) Columbus.

Several writers may be grouped as copiers of Pliny. Solinus (early third century?) collects for each country 'remarkable facts' on animals, plants, gems, and wonders of Nature like the Nile, and strange races and customs; except something from Mela he borrows the rest wholesale and unacknowledged from Pliny, perhaps partly at second hand through some compilation. He seems never to have heard of Ptolemy or any recent extensions of the horizon. In theory he has hardly any interest. Thule has no night at the summer solstice, he says, and no day at the winter one, and he oddly associates the six months' night with happy Hyperboreans. Tides are a sort of breathing of the Ocean, if not caused by the moon, and he vaguely connects the theory of the Black Sea filling up and bursting out. Incidentally he remarks that tides reach some 'mediterranea maria' (he does not use the singular as a name). He is so beautifully credulous that he is quite entertaining reading, but he would hardly deserve so much notice if he had not been extravagantly respected in the Middle Ages as *Polyhistor seu de mirabilibus mundi*: for them his fairy tales were facts.[3] Ammianus Marcellinus, after a good old fashion of historians, gives liberal digressions on geography, but his are diffuse and uncritical, cluttered with obsolete stuff about

---

1 *G.G.M.* I, 515–73. Schoff, 1927. Bunbury, II, 660–4. Pappus in Moses of Chorene, J. Fischer, *Zt. Ges. Erdk. Barl.* 1919, pp. 336–58. Scotland, Dio, LXXVI, 13.

2 *G.G.M.* II, 489–509. Agath. ibid. pp. xli–xliii, 471–87: Berger, *R.E.* I, 742: Bunbury, II, 667–8. Agath. I, 6 as Artem. ap. Plin. II, 242: II, 1 as Erat.: parallels, I, 7–8, figure, II, 13.

3 Ed. Mommsen, 1864, 1895. Thule, Sol. 22: Hyp., ibid. 16, 2: maria, 18, tides, 18 and 23, 20–2. Direct from Pliny, Rabenald, *Quaest. Solin.* 1907 (Columba, *Quest. Solin.* 1920 thinks of a common source of P. and S.). Bunbury, II, pp. 675–7: Tozer, *Anc. Geogr.* pp. 364–6: Beazley, op. cit. I, 247–73: Thorndike, op. cit. pp. 326–31: Kaeppel, op. cit. pp. 9–25. 'Med. Sea' first in Isid. *Etym.* XIII, 16 (7th cent.). S. uses only the first third of Pliny.

Amazons and the like; mainly they are a bad writing-up of Pliny and Solinus, with additions from Ptolemy, used perhaps indirectly (and something from a copy of the imperial wall-map?). He likes to display a half-baked learning on such matters as earthquakes, eclipses and tides; odd remarks betray little understanding, as on the shadows at Aswan and Meroe. He does not reprove the astrology of his hero Julian.[1] Martianus Capella (about 400?) frames in a foolish allegory a dull summary of the subject-matter of each of the seven liberal arts, including geometry and astronomy. He made much use of Varro's *Disciplinae*. There is hardly a trace of astrology, and he still mentions the view that the earth, like Mercury and Venus, may go round the sun, though his own cosmology is Neoplatonic. A section on geography refers to Ptolemy on the width of the north temperate zone, but uses Pliny and Solinus with added garblings. The south temperate is the only other habitable zone, and is in fact inhabited both by dwellers opposite and Antipodes, who do not see the north star visible to us; they have summer when we have ours, but with short days, whereas ours are short in winter. On Thule he repeats both of Pliny's statements, the right and the wrong (see p. 324). The known earth is an island, for Pliny's bad reasons, including the supposed voyage from the Caspian 'gulf' to India. Hyperboreans and other fables are duly copied.[2] The book was highly popular in the Middle Ages, and deserves some credit for keeping the idea of the globe alive then.

Orosius, a Spanish priest, was encouraged by Augustine, just after the Goths had sacked Rome in 410, to write a general history in defence of Christianity: he seeks to prove that the world had suffered even worse before than after Christ from wars, plagues, and natural disasters. He shows no deep research, but makes an unscrupulous selection of facts from a very limited range of Latin writers. The introduction on the known earth is neither like Ptolemy nor obviously borrowed from Pliny; perhaps he used some manual based on old sources including a world-map on the pattern of Agrippa's. Some praise the sketch as clear and intelligent, but the choice of details is rather odd, with many obscure names, and some blunders seem confusions of his own, as on the upper Nile. With science he has hardly any

---

1 XXII, 12, 8, XXIII, 1, 7. Shadows, XXII, 15, 31. Earthquakes, etc., XVII, 7, 9–14, XX, 3, 1, XXVII, 8, 4. Seres with towns from Ptolemy, XXIII, 6, 66–7. Digressions on Black Sea, XXII, 8, Egypt, ibid. 15, Gaul, XV, 9–12, Syria and Cilicia, XIV, 8, Persian provinces (and eastward), XXIII, 6. A diss. on his sources, Gardthausen, 1873: I have not seen others by Schieffner, 1877, Christophe, 1879. Wall-map, K. Miller, *Mappaemundi*, VI, 83–9.

2 VI, 664: island, 619–22: Thule, 609, 666: zones, 602–7. Section, VI, 596–703. Sun, VIII, 857 (as Macr. II, 4). Erat. and Archimedes on circuit of earth, ibid. 858. Thorndike, op. cit. p. 545: H. Osborn Taylor, *The Medieval Mind*, 1911, I, 71–2. Date, Wessner, *R.E.* (1928) though Dick's ed. 1925, thinks 284–330. Kimble, *Geogr. in Middle Ages*, 1938, pp. 9–12. Dill, op. cit. pp. 412–15. Sandys, *Hist. of Class. Scholarship*, 1906, pp. 241–2 (date 410–27).

concern. Some who never heard of Noah have inferred a flood, he says, from 'stones rough with shells' found on remote mountains. (Augustine mentions a huge tooth picked up on the African shore and thinks it proves giants before the Flood.)[1] Our King Alfred translated Orosius on geography, but left out much, and put in instead an account of some interesting voyages of his own time to the Baltic and White Seas.

A few notes in a commonplace book by Ampelius (third century?) mention the earth as an island, with its gulfs including the Caspian and with Antichthones and Antipodes in the other habitable zone. Hardly worth mentioning is a booklet (fifth century?) under the name Vibius Sequester, explaining the geographical names in some Roman poets. Two feeble versifiers, Avienus (about 370) and Priscian (about 512), thought it worth while to translate the still popular primer of Dionysius Periegetes, with various slight omissions and insertions but hardly any attempt to correct the obsolete geography, except on the sources of the Rhine and Danube. The second adds some matter about gems and the like, mostly from Solinus, and a notion that shells found inland on mountains prove the extent of the Flood. The first also paraphrased Aratus on the stars, and wrote a verse periplus, *Ora Maritima*, which makes a virtue of using recondite sources. The extant part preserves important data, though ill arranged and often obscure, for very antique voyages to Spain and the tin marts; probably he used a Greek original which had already conflated old peripli in this confusing way. Another book valuable for the old matter it saves, especially from Hecataeus, is a dictionary of geographical names (those mentioned in literature) by Stephanus of Byzantium, surviving mostly in a slightly later abridgment (sixth century). Various general writers have occasional remarks of interest, like the poet Claudian on northern seas and the Nile and the torrid zone (of the universe he has an idea like Cicero's). Servius, commenting on Virgil, notes that at Ceylon there are really two summers a year, geometers say, and at Thule there is continuous day when the sun is in Cancer; they say that the earth is surrounded on all sides by sky and air, and infer Antipodes by reasoning, these being in the south temperate zone, *ad quos torrente zona ire prohibetur*, but he mentions, without condemning, some philosophers who deny that the sun lights up any such people and talk of perpetual darkness 'there'—a curious uncertainty reflecting the poet's own. An imitation of the same lines merely asserts two habitable zones and a torrid zone between, *rubro obsessam fervore*, while the earth 'hangs' as usual

---

[1] Giants, Aug. *C.D.* xv, 9 (but so Paus. III, 22, 5, VIII, 32, 5, and see p. 103, n. 1). Oros. I, 3, 3. Nile, see p. 362, n. 1. Sources, Zangemeister's ed. 1889, p. vi, Schanz-Hosius, *Röm. Lit.* IV², 493. Praise, Bunbury, II, 691–2: Kimble, op. cit. pp. 10, 20–3. K. Miller, *Mappaemundi*, 1898, VI, 61–8 and Tafel 3 (O. mainly used a world-map). On O.'s history Dill, op. cit. pp. 66–70, 312–15.

376 HISTORY OF ANCIENT GEOGRAPHY

in the centre of the universe. A curious book owing much to Varro talks of the length of life as varying in different regions, *prout in singulis sit caeli ad circulum finitorem inclinatio, quod vocatur clima*; for this it cites some *astrologos, qui in stellarum signorumque ratione verum scrutantur.* (We are hardly concerned here with minor topographical details such as are found in a poem on the Moselle, another on a journey from Rome towards Gaul, and a list of garrisons along the British Wall.)[1]

A lowly kind of geography is that of the road-books, which do not bother about the fact that the earth is a globe. A general, says Vegetius, should have *itineraria adnotata*, with details of roads and paths, distances, hills and rivers, though none quite answering this description happens to remain. A soldier who starts on a journey, says Ambrose, receives an itinerarium from his commander. There was a vast amount of travelling by officials and others, who needed a list of stations and distances, with or without a few notes about things of interest on the way, and we have some late specimens of such guides. We have also something more comprehensive, which the manuscripts call *Itinerarium Provinciarum Antonini Augusti*. It includes many roads (nearly 53,000 miles of them, somebody counts) as far as the frontiers and the last outposts, like those just beyond the British Wall. It has the distances generally in Roman miles, but for Gaul in the native leuga. It has too many clumsy repetitions and arbitrary deviations to be either an official publication or a practical road-book giving the shortest and best routes. Possibly much of the matter was transcribed from a copy of a general map drawn under one of the Antonines, Caracalla (211–17), supplemented perhaps by various minor road-maps.[2] But the present edition, as several names show, is not before Diocletian (280); a still later mention of 'Byzantium which is also Constantinople', in an inferior manuscript, may be dismissed as an interpolation. The whole is of interest for topography, and conveys a sense of the greatness of the Empire, but it has no bearings or indication how the lie of the land was conceived.

---

1 Notitia Dignitatum: Rutilius Namatianus: Ausonius (Moselle). Servius ad Virg. *Georg.* 1, 48, 60, 235–43, *Aen.* VI, 127. Ceylon, after Plin. VI, 81. Claudian, p. 357, n. 1, p. 362, n. 1: Semple in *C.Q.* 1937, p. 161. Imitation, Claud. *Rapt. Pros.* 1, 257–63. Clima, Censorinus, *de Die Natali*, 17, 4 (A.D. 238). Steph. Byz., Sandys, op. cit. 1, 379: Bunbury, II, 669. Avienus, *O.M.* ed. Schulten, 1922, Berthelot, 1934 (see p. 53, n. 2). *Descriptio*, *G.G.M.* II, 177–89 (Priscian, ibid. 190–9): Bunbury, II, 683–9: Schanz, *Röm. Lit.* IV, 1[2], 14–21: Marx, *R.E.* II, 2386. Rhine, Av. 433–40. Flood, Priscian, 432–8. Ampelius 6 and 7, ed. Wölfflin, 1879. Vibius, Schanz, op. cit. IV, 2, 120.

2 So Kubitschek, *R.E.* Itineraria, IX, 2320–44 and Karten, §§ 68, 71. *Itin. Romana* of K. Miller, 1916, pp. liv–lxvii, and Cuntz, I, 1929. Bunbury, II, 694–6. Tozer, op. cit. pp. 306–9 (with a map of R. roads, 298). G. H. Stevenson in *Legacy of Rome*, ed. Bailey, 1923, p. 159. Veg. III, 6. For Egypt most of errors are probably its own, not due to copyists, Ball, op. cit. pp. 138–51. Ambrose, Migne, XV, 125.

Attached is a short *itinerarium maritimum* giving a few sea-routes, with some figures in stades, and a queer list of islands; this is copied from a map so ignorantly that Mount Parnassus is misread as an island.

Akin to the road-book is some matter found elsewhere, as on a few of the more elaborate milestones. One in Belgium details the stations on roads to the Rhine and the Channel and other places. Another at Cadiz had the 106 stages or 1041 miles to Rome, and it was copied with these particulars in four silver cups dedicated by travellers near the journey's end at Vicarello. A Palmyrene archer garrisoned at Dura on the Euphrates, probably before 235, had the fancy to paint on his shield a memento of his service. It is a list of stages and distances (in miles) from Byzantium past the Danube mouths to Olbia on his way to the Crimea, whence he returned by sea to Trapezus and on past Artaxata in Armenia; there are a blue sea with ships, and blue streaks for rivers, and the whole is something between a list of names and a crude pictorial map.[1]

With the victory of Christianity there began a new motive for travel, an urge to visit the scenes of the Bible story and also the Egyptian desert and other places recently made famous by their hermits and monks. Already in 333 a nameless pilgrim of Bordeaux details the long series of halts and rests all the way (by Milan and Belgrade) to Constantinople, and thence by the usual military road across Asia Minor to Antioch and so to Jerusalem. There are only a few odd notes en route but rather more in the Holy Land, such as 'Aser ubi fuit villa Job' and a remark that the Dead Sea has no fish and its water is heavy enough to turn a swimmer over. The homeward journey is by Brindisi and Rome. Next, from the same district or somewhere near (north Spain?), comes an important and determined lady, whose name is now guessed as Aetheria, probably about 395 (the finder of her work thought her the grim St Silvia of Aquitaine). She describes for her reverend sisters the holy city and the ritual there. We find her, with her Book of Exodus in hand, climbing Mount Sinai and tracing the route of the Israelites through Goshen (she seems to have 'done' Egypt before). From Jerusalem she makes an excursion over the Jordan; she rides a donkey up Mount Nebo to view the Promised Land and visits Job's tomb, but admits she did not see the pillar of salt that was Lot's wife. From Antioch she goes to the Euphrates, which reminds her of the Rhône, and she crosses to visit Edessa, with the tomb of St Thomas, and Harran, being stopped only by the Persian frontier. In the next few centuries there are

---

1 Cumont in *Syria*, 1925, pp. 1–15: Rostovtzeff, *Soc. and Econ. Hist. of Hell. World*, II, 1038. Cups, *C.I.L.* IV, 3281–4, Kubitschek, *R.E.* IX, 2318, Miller, op. cit. p. lxxi. Tongres milestone, *C.I.L.* III, 9158, Dessau, *Inscr. Lat. Sel.* 5839, Kubitschek, op. cit. p. 2314, Miller, p. lxxii.

various similar writings, all intent on the goal and incurious about everything else.[1] A late papyrus has a list of places from Asia Minor to Egypt of some interest when compared with such itineraries.

Maps are not very often mentioned. The orator Eumenius pleads in 297 for his native Autun and the restoration of its schools, destroyed by a Gallic usurper some thirty years before; he hopes they will have in a public place a map of the world (*orbem depictum*), so that the young can study it proudly 'now at last when we see nothing that is not ours'—a pitiful jingoism for such a time. He seems to be thinking of a copy of Agrippa's map, and perhaps other provincial towns had already set up copies in their porticoes. He is not ignorant of the globe, as he refers to the old orb (of Crates), *orbis quadrifariam duplici discretus Oceano*. Tantalizing is a letter of Julian thanking a friend, who was or had been governor of Britain, for a 'geography' and (or?) a 'map', which 'has drawings better than any yet made'. The poet Ausonius in 379 talks vaguely of world-maps which make no sacrifice of truth despite the small scale: this would imply an excellent projection, but it is doubtful if he means anything so scientific. A general should have *itineraria picta* besides written ones (*adnotata*), says Vegetius, though his wording suggests that they were not quite a matter of course, and those he means were no doubt mere road-maps taking no notice of the globe.[2] Maps were probably attached sometimes to discussions of Scriptural place-names like that of Eusebius and the free version of it by Jerome. There survives under a church at Madeba in Moab part of a mosaic map of about 550; it shows Palestine and also, foreshortened and pulled out of direction, the adjoining coast of Egypt. It has legends like 'the desert of Sin where were sent down manna and quails', and there are little pictures in the medieval fashion, ships on the Dead or Salt Sea, a gazelle and palms, and vignettes of the chief towns, especially Jerusalem, with the Church of the Holy Sepulchre.[3]

---

[1] Ed. Geyer, *Itin. Hierosolymitana*, 1898. Aeth., ed. Heraeus[3], 1929: finder, Gamurrini, 1887. Beazley, I, 72–81: Labriolle, *Hist. de la Litt. lat. chrét.* 1920, pp. 502–8. Dorothy Brooke, *Pilgrims Were They All*, 1937, pp. 91–139: Glover, *Life and Letters in the Fourth Century*, 1901, pp. 125–47: A. P. Newton, ed. *Travel and Travellers of Middle Ages*, 1926, ch. 3. *Itin. Burdigalense*, Miller, op. cit. pp. lxviii–lxx, Cuntz, op. cit., Beazley, pp. 57–67, Kubitschek, *R.E.* IX, 2352–63: in Palestine Pilgrims' Text Soc. I, 1897 (A. Stewart). 'Silvia', ibid. (J. H. Bernard): some later pilgrims, vol. II. A Gallic monk's travels described in Sulp. Sev. *Dial.* I, Dill, op. cit. pp. 183–4.

[2] Veg. III, 6 (probably *c.* 400). Aus. *Grat. Actio pro Consulatu*, 2, 9. Eum. *pro inst. Scholis*, 20–1. Jullian, *Hist. de la Gaule*, 1926, VIII, 285, 'cartes informes'. On the circumstances, Van Sickle, *Amer. J. Phil.* 1934, pp. 236–43. Orb, see p. 203, n. 1. *Letter* 7 to Alypius, Julian, transl. W. C. Wright (Loeb), 1923, III, 19. Papyrus, Noordegraaf, *Mnemosyne*, 1939, pp. 273–310.

[3] Dalton, *Byz. Art and Arch.* 1911, p. 422, figs. 248–9. K. Miller, *Mappaemundi*, 1898, VI, 148–54, figs. 57–8. Sarton, *Introd. to Hist. of Science*, I, 432. Jerome, Miller, op. cit. III, 1–21, Tafel 12: Kubitschek, *R.E. Karten*, § 14.

One world-map has claims to be at least derived from an ancient. It is now at Vienna, and named after a certain Peutinger, who acquired it in 1508. Only the westernmost corner is missing, including most of Britain. Some take this to be the map mentioned as drawn on twelve parchment leaves by a monk of Colmar in 1265, though the script has been thought a century older. Anyhow it is a copy of something far more antique. The copier seems to have been careful, but he omits or corrupts names and makes false drawings, often where he could not decipher his faded original. The form is very peculiar, a parchment roll over 21 ft. long by only 1 ft. wide. As a geographical map this ribbon is absurd, of course, the outer lands in north and south being squeezed almost out of existence. Yet it does not pretend to be such a map, but only to give the roads with their stations; the distances are added in figures, so that no need is felt even of a uniform scale. Little room can be wasted on seas and roadless lands, which are therefore narrowed to a mere indication. Instead of directions there are only left and right, and there is little concern for meridians, though Rome is placed opposite Carthage. So the crazy-looking construction has a principle of a sort. The details are curious, with vignettes for ranges and forests, temples and even lighthouses, and towns of various status, marts, forts, spas, colonies, and Imperial residences (Rome, Constantinople, and Antioch —a pointer to the date of the early matter). There are some Christian things, 'Constantinople' itself, St Peter's, and legends like 'the desert where the Israelites wandered forty years'. Miller attempts to fix the original as of 365 and by one Castorius. He presumes that the Geographer of Ravenna, about 670, who often cites this person, is really transcribing his map wholesale; but the Geographer is more than suspect of inventing spurious authorities. If the Christian features just mentioned are set aside as later additions, one ultimate source—as also of Ravennas—may be a copy of the same road-map of Caracalla's time which was used by the Antonine Itinerary.[1] Owing to the queer shape it is hard to give any reproduction of reasonable size, but the sketches of the end sections will convey some idea (they exaggerate the relative width in order to find space for legible names, and they give only a few of the roads, in red, and mark only those towns which have special vignettes). In the first the Mediterranean

---

[1] This and 'some world-map', Kubitschek, op. cit. §§ 71, 78–95, against K. Miller, *Weltkarte des Castorius*, 1887, *Peutingersche Tafel*, 1916 and *Itin. Romana*, pp. xiii–lxii. Large bibliography, Schanz, *Röm. Lit.* II, 333, IV, 103–5, 363–6. Now *R.E.* Peutingeriana, 1938, Gisinger. A Dutch 'Introduction to an Edition' by Wartena, 1927. Dept, *Rev. Belge Phil.* 1931, pp. 997–1011 (neither in form nor names derived from a recension of Agrippa's map). Another section in *Enc. Brit.* ed. 14, 'Map'. J. Ball, *Egypt in Classical Geographers*, 1942, pp. 151–60 and plate IV (Egypt–Asia Minor–Black Sea). Gaul in Jullian, *Rev. Ét. Anc.* 1912, p. 60.

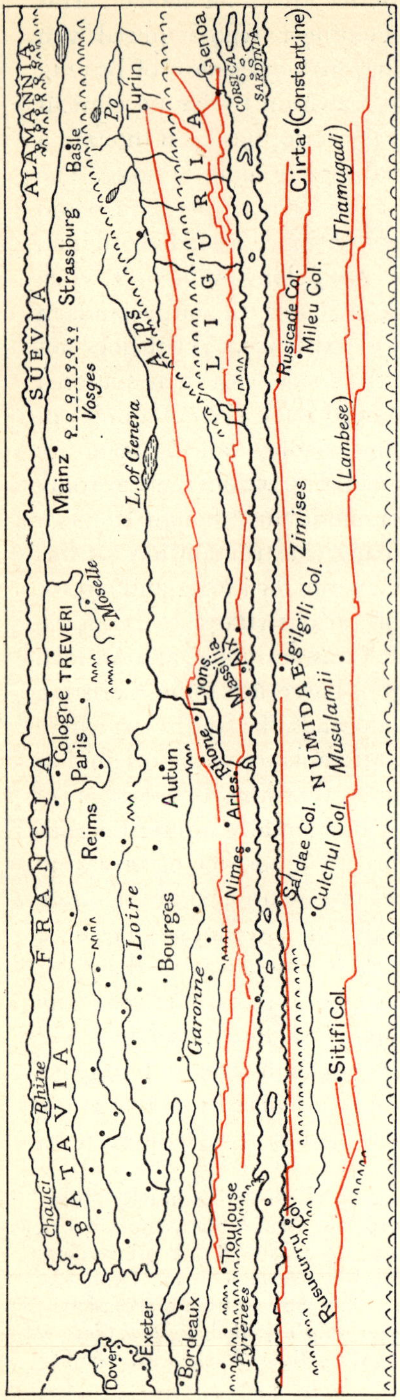

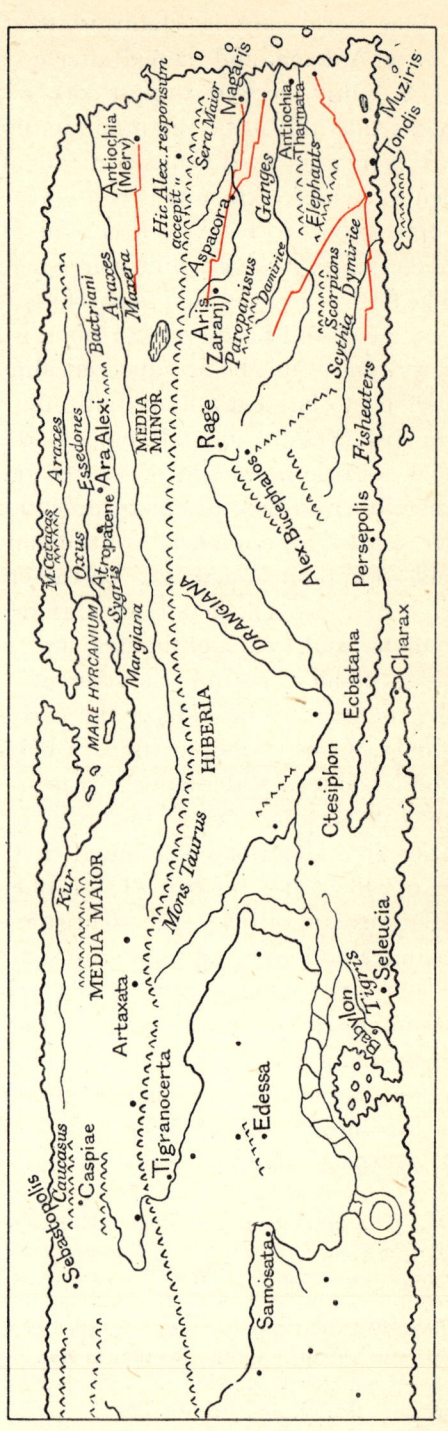

Fig. 64. Peutinger map: west section of Europe and North Africa (many names modernized).

Fig. 65. The same: east section of Asia.

has become a mere strip, as has all northern barbariandom including 'Alamannia'; the Rhine seems to flow west, and the shape of Gaul is quite unrecognizable. The second has a similar strip north of the Caucasus and all along past the Caspian 'gulf'. An Araxes flows from Armenia past the south of this sea, as in Herodotus, but it is carried into the eastern Ocean at a point above Merv! Hereabouts are two altars where the reply was received 'How far Alexander?'—presumably near his last city on the Jaxartes, but that river is not named. The great central range of Taurus-Imaus still halves Asia, and near its eastern end is Sera Maior, queerly near the altars. India has some fairly recent details like the pepper ports, but the shape is old-fashioned and the ports beyond the Ganges are ignored. The Ganges is run into the Tigris from the false copying of the faded original. There is a strange Persian Gulf without Arabia, fantastic things are done with its rivers, and many towns are grossly misplaced, as Seleucia far from Ctesiphon and Rhagae (Rage) far from its own doublet Europus (an attempt to see behind this mess to a Seleucid itinerary seems very precarious).[1] In Africa the Nile is drawn flowing from west to east, partly because it could not be got in otherwise in the narrow strip allowed to the continent, but partly no doubt from a reminiscence of the old theory of an upper course through the Sahara (on or near the river are the name Girin and the legend *hoc flumen quidam Grin vocant alii Nilum appellant dicitur enim sub terra Etyopum in Nylum ire lacum*).

Two short lists, a *Divisio Orbis* and a *Dimensuratio Provinciarum*, about 400, give countries with their boundaries and figures of length and breadth; they imply a map from which they were read, and it was apparently in the tradition of Agrippa's. An Irish monk Dicuil uses the first as late as 825, in a book *de Mensura Orbis Terrarum*, and he connects it with a map drawn for Theodosius (II, who reigned 408–30); he supposes that the map was the result of a new imperial survey, but this is no doubt a misunderstanding of some verses which he quotes.[2] A sixth-century manuscript has 'excerpts' professedly taken down from a 'learned master' Julius Honorius, with an injunction that they should not be separated from the 'sphaera', meaning a school-map, it seems, but not probably a globe. We hear elsewhere of a *libellus Julii oratoris*, describing the world in a certain order, the same as our text's. Cassiodorus, about 540, recommends it along with 'the map of Dionysius', evidently one drawn to illustrate that old verse primer; this is in the darkness of Gothic Italy, when he wants his monks to learn a little

[1] Tarn, *Greeks in Bactria*, p. 55 and *J.H.S.* 1940, p. 90, after Tomaschek, 1883. Names, Herrmann, *Land der Seide*, pp. 47–51 (suspects 'Sera'). Still Homer's Abii (Scythae)!

[2] Dicuil, 5. Lists in *G.L.M.* pp. 8–20 and Schnabel, see p. 333, n. 1, p. 334, n. 2: K. Miller, *Mappaemundi*, vi, 108–10. Dicuil on Thule, see p. 148, n. 3: Nansen, *In Northern Mists*, pp. 162–4.

geography, enough to recognize the places of Scripture. He himself seems to have used it, perhaps in a fuller form than the one now known, for his Gothic history, which was followed by Jordanes (the latter, for instance, gives a string of islands of the Indian Ocean in the same order as our text). This text is a worthless list of names, often very corrupt and copied from a map with such desperate ignorance that Thule is misread as a sea, the Syrtes as islands, and the Pyramids and the British Wall as mountains. There are two other recensions, and they have the statement that certain Greeks (named) carried out a prolonged survey in the various directions for Caesar and Augustus. The third adds a slightly altered version of the geographical chapter of Orosius, and the combination has often been confused with a quite different text; this is in manuscripts from the eighth century on and passes under the name of an imaginary traveller, Aethicus (meaning apparently 'the philosopher'), who is supposed to be translated by a presbyter Hieronymus and to have seen Griffins and other marvels in many lands between Thule and the earthly Paradise.[1] The author wrote probably in France and not before the seventh century, and he no doubt intended that the great Jerome should be thought to authorize his absurdities.

Thus many who dealt with geography simply ignored the fact of the earth-globe, as did general writers who glibly repeated old phrases about Indians close to the sun, or the sun hissing in the western Ocean or going to bed, *si quid est cubile solis*, as one says, while another echoes Tacitus and his queer attempt to explain the short northern nights. Yet the globe was familiar enough to some of these probably and certainly to plenty of others. There were translators of Aratus as late as Avienus, and many intelligent commentators like Achilles (probably third century); these explain the zones, for instance, and remark that, against 'the old' writers, some like Panaetius think the torrid zone inhabited (there is no doubt of Antoikoi and Antipodes beyond). The Emperor Julian understands well enough about shadows in the torrid zone, whatever else he says in a queer hymn to the sun. Chalcidius (early fourth century?), in a commentary on Plato's *Timaeus*, has a section on astronomy, using Theon; he gives the usual proofs of the globe, and explains things like the summer and winter tropics, though he takes the torrid zone as uninhabitable. His translation included the story of Atlantis, which was to be much read in this form, when Plato was little known otherwise, and so to keep alive the notion that an unknown

[1] Ed. D'Avezac, 1852: Wuttke, 1853 (H. really is Jerome!). Beazley, op. cit. I, 355–63: Thorndike, op. cit. pp. 600–3: M. R. James in *C.M.H.* 1922, III, 500. Text of J.H. in Riese, *G.L.M.* pp. 24–55, with B below, and C pp. 71–90. Kubitschek, *R.E.* x, 614–28. Miller, op. cit. VI, 69–82 and Tafel 4. 'Map of D.' ibid. pp. 95–101. Cassiodorus, *Inst. Div. Litt.* 25. Islands, Jord. 6: see Mierow's ed. p. 37.

THE DECLINE

western continent might exist.[1] Macrobius, probably about 400, is also full of similar Neoplatonic matter, though he writes round Cicero's little show-piece, the *Dream of Scipio*, with its vision of the musical spheres: the commentary is a queer medley, far longer than the original which it preserved. He explains by a diagram how the earth's zones lie under the heaven's. He accepts the measurement of Eratosthenes as 'unquestionable', but strangely diverges on the width of the north temperate zone, which he takes as $\frac{5}{60}$ instead of $\frac{7}{60}$ of the circumference. The torrid is uninhabitable, at least beyond the Cinnamon Coast, and cuts us off from all intercourse, but the south temperate may be assumed as inhabited: there are both dwellers opposite (*transversi*) and Antipodes (*obliqui*), who cannot fall into the sky, as nothing can fall upward. He approves the orb-like arrangement of four inhabited worlds separated by Oceans. This revival of the obsolete fancy of Crates was undesirable, but in general the book was not the worst of guides for the Middle Ages, which liked it enormously. Many others write of the music of the spheres, of which the earth-globe at the centre is a sort of sounding-board, as a pupil of Augustine says.[2] Neoplatonism flourished long after its greatest personality, Plotinus, who came to Rome in 244. When violently suppressed at Alexandria in 415 it found a last retreat at Athens, till the intolerance of Justinian closed the school in 529. Its spirit was not, indeed, very favourable to science: aspiring to rise by intuition and ecstasy to the mind of the Creator, it was impatient of observation, like Plato himself. In the last phase it paid more attention to Aristotle. He too had assumed uniform and circular movements, which were contradicted, as was early noticed, by Ptolemy's astronomy. Proclus, head of the school in 450–85, wrote an introduction to this, accepting it in general, but some attempted a defence of the old, and this high debate went on to the end. It was a last flicker of a dying tradition. In Gothic Italy then the tradition was almost dead, but there was still Boethius. Of the earth he says that it is a mere point relatively to the heaven sphere, and our known earth is about a quarter of it, as Ptolemy teaches—he has in mind rather Pliny and the *Dream of Scipio*—and much is desert or marsh or sea or

---

1 See p. 92, n. 1. Torrid, Chalc. 66: globe, ibid. 59–61: section, 58–90. Mullach, *Fr. Phil. Gr.* 1887, II, 181 f. Kroll, *R.E.* VI, 2042–3. Duhem, *Système du Monde*, II, 417–26. *Pan. Constantini*, 9 echoes Tac. *Agr.* 12 (see p. 329, n. 2). Hissing, Aus. *Ep.* 19, echoing Juv. XIV, 280: bed, *Pan. Theod.* 22. *Comm. in Aratum Reliquiae*, ed. Maass, 1898: Achilles, ibid. 25–85: zones, 62–5 and Anon. ibid. 96–7. Panaetius, see p. 210, n. 1. Julian, *Or.* IV, 147 C. Theon of Smyrna is meant, see p. 331.

2 Favonius Eulogius, ed. Holder, p. 12: also Plotinus, IV, 4, 8, Chalc. 72, Macr. II, 3, 7. Boethius, *de Musica*, I, 1–2, 27. Orb, Macr. *S.S.* II, 5, 29, II, 9. Antipodes, etc., II, 5, 17, 23, 25, 33. Torrid, II, 8, 3. Erat., ibid. I, 20, 20. Temperate, II, 6. Diagram, II, 5, 13. On M.'s science Pickman, *Mind of Latin Christendom*, 1937, pp. 207–10: Dill, op. cit. pp. 106–12: Stahl, *Trans. Amer. Phil. Ass.* 1942, pp. 232–58.

not reached by the fame of Rome.[1] His translation of Aristotle unfortunately did not go beyond the logic, which was alone to survive in the west for some seven centuries, when a little of the science would have done far more good.

Astrology was widespread, though condemned by Christians, and its believers at least had some intelligent ideas on astronomy and geography. It was a commonplace that some peoples were savage or dull or fickle or sly owing to the *natura climatum*, but Firmicus Maternus dislikes such generalizing: all Ethiopians are black from their climate, he admits, but individuals among them differ according to their stars. He describes the torrid zone as uninhabitable, a carelessness which had long become usual. Plotinus accepted the stars only as signs, not causes, but Proclus justified astrology from Plato himself and commented on Ptolemy's book about it.[2] Nearly all Christians abhorred it, as before; they did not question a demonic power in the stars, indeed, but believed that this could be overcome by man's free will and God's grace. Augustine was attracted in youth, and later shrank from going deeply into astronomy, lest he should relapse into the false science so often associated with the true. Remarkable is a Syriac dialogue, the *Book of the Laws of the Countries*, by a disciple of Bardesanes, who died about 222: here it is sensibly argued that peoples in like climates are not always like and may keep their old customs after migration.[3] Hippolytus (about 235) attacks astrology in a *Refutation of All Heresies*, a book much used later and with good matter on the opinions of old philosophers; it mentions that Ecphantus made the earth rotate in the centre of the universe, and gives the figure of Eratosthenes for the globe.

The decline of science had set in before the Christians became strong. In fact the attitude of pagans to science was now often curiously like theirs: to learn the movements of the heavenly bodies, the measurement of the earth, and the depth of the sea is desirable, says one, only if it leads us to adore God's wisdom, and mischievous if it turns our thoughts away from that to lower things. But the Christians did do much towards the demise of any really objective study of Nature. For all of them their doctrine is a

---

[1] *Cons. Phil.* II, 7, going back to Macr. II, 10, 3 and Cicero. Debate, Simplicius, John Philoponus, Duhem, op. cit. II, 61–2, 108, 202.

[2] Ed. Manitius, 1909. Duhem, II, 321–6, 336. Plotinus, IV, 4, 34, III, 1 and ap. Firm. Mat. I, 7, 18: Duhem, II, 309: Thorndike, pp. 303–6. Natura climatum, Serv. ad Virg. *Aen.* VI, 724: Firm. Mat. I, 3, 3. Torrid, ibid. I, 104–5. Ethiopians, ibid. 6–11, I, 21–2, I, 5–6. Thorndike, pp. 525–37. Boll, *R.E.* XII, 2365–79.

[3] See p. 367, n. 3: Thorndike, op. cit. pp. 373–6: Tollinton, *Clement of Alex.* p. 149: Rehm, *Philologus*, 1938, pp. 218–47: on Bard. Burkitt, *C.A.H.* XII, 496–8. Aug. *Civ. Dei*, V, 7, cp. *Confess.* V, 3, VII, 6: Thorndike, p. 521. Abhorred, Hippol. *Ref.* IV, 27, 50, Lact. II, 17, Basil, *Hex.* VI, 4–7 (only signs), etc. Duhem, II, 402–7, 454–60: Boll-Bezold, op. cit. p. 32. Hippolytus in *Dox.* pp. 144–56: much repeated later by Epiphanius A.D. 403 and Theodoret A.D. 428.

revelation to be received by faith, with Scripture as the inspired word of God. 'Crede ut intellegas'—one must start with belief, and intelligence comes only from grace. God created the universe, and the ultimate cause of everything is simply His will, which is unsearchable. Some like Basil and his friends wish to retain from the pagans what is proper and will help to understand the wonderful works of God. If the texts leave the case open, they are ready to adopt the usual science, as on earthquakes and volcanoes and the dependence of the tides on the moon.[1] But all are aware of the free philosophizing tradition of 'the Greeks' as a rival power, and they handle this science with a more or less jaunty uneasiness. They like to point out the contradictions of the 'physici', and do not feel obliged to go into the details of the many false systems, which cancel each other out (some knew them poorly and at second-hand). 'Secular wisdom' has its uses, they admit, but only as a help and when duly purged of its pride and other corrupting elements: astronomers have discovered much, so much that they can even predict eclipses exactly, but they fail to seek or find the Creator. Often the note becomes more crudely hostile. If Christians think little of these matters, it is not from ignorance but from contempt of such useless labour. 'Qui naturalia, quae sciri ab homine non possunt, scire se putant, furiosi dementesque iudicandi.' Christians have more serious things to do than this vain prying into the secrets of Nature. The music of the spheres is an ingenious frivolity. Why worry about the sizes and distances of the heavenly bodies? Why inquire whether the sun is larger than the earth or a foot broad, and trouble about things so remote, when the learned cannot save their own souls? We cannot know the hidden causes of natural phenomena, and we should not be happier if we could: blessed are the simple, and the perfect wisdom is to know that one God made the universe. Anyhow Scripture is to be accepted as higher than any human reason: in a sense it makes all other books superfluous. 'Nam quicquid homo extra didicerit, si noxium est, ibi damnatur; si utile est, ibi invenitur.'[2] An unhealthy atmosphere for the judgment of pagan science!

1 Basil, *Hex.* VI, 11, Ambrose, *Hex.* IV, 7, 29, Aug. *C.D.* V, 6: Duhem, II, 460–2. Kimble, *Geogr. in Middle Ages*, 1938, pp. 146–8, 168, 171. For the Fathers on meteorology, J. Hoffmann, 1907, on phys. geography, K. Kretschmer, 1889, J. K. Wright, *Geogr. Lore of...the Crusades*, 1925 (much on earlier periods). Globe, Hippol. IV, 8. Rotate, ibid. I, 13. Pagan attitude, *Hermetica*, I, 311, ed. W. Scott, 1924, who compares Clem. *Strom.* VI, 79–83.

2 Aug. *de Doctr. Christ.* II, 42, *de Genesi ad Litteram*, II, 5, II, 14, 7. Contempt, Eus. *P.E.* XV, 61. Simple, Lact. *Div. Inst.* III, 6: furiosi, ibid. 4. Sun, Arnobius, II, 59. Music, Basil, *Hex.* III, 3: foolish wisdom, ibid. IX, 1: cancel, I, 2. Prying, Ambrose, *Hex.* VI, 2, 8, Aug. *Conf.* X, 35, *Gen.* II, 16. Not obliged, ibid. 10, *C.D.* XVIII, 41. Labriolle, op. cit. pp. 278, 281, etc.: Dreyer, *Hist. of Planetary Systems*, 1906, ch. 10. On Christian attitudes see also p. 42, n. 1, p. 349, n. 4: Pickman, op. cit. pp. 108–17: Kimble, op. cit. pp. 14–16.

So much the worse for the earth, among other things. The earth of the texts is obviously a flat disk, established above the waters and under the firmament, though once 'He hangeth the earth upon nothing'. The Fathers take every way except the right one, namely to admit that these expressions are not revealed truth but only old Jewish notions, most as obsolete as Homer's.[1] One resort is allegory or the 'deeper sense', which all use more or less freely and perversely when it seems necessary to remove 'snares' or 'scandals' from the holy writings. So Origen has little embarrassment in giving the globe with a Platonic sort of cosmology. Basil, though 'not ashamed' of the literal Gospel, seems to accept much from Aristotle and the astronomers, objecting only that they omit due praise to the Creator. If the earth hangs upon nothing, according to the one promising text, the will of God appears reason enough, not that the nature and position of the earth matter for the future life. There is an increasing reluctance to make any unambiguous avowal of the globe.[2] Special reasons are produced against Antipodes, though this does not in itself imply a rejection of the globe. Augustine speaks of parts where the sun rises when it sets for us; if land is there, and not merely water, it cannot be inhabited, as Scripture says nothing of Adam's descendants there and none could have reached it across the torrid zone and an immense Ocean, nor did the Apostles go there, though bidden to preach the Gospel to all the earth. This pronouncement was to make a heresy of Antipodes or any people beyond the Equator. Already Lactantius had denied the globe itself outright, alleging that it is not necessitated by a spherical heaven. He scoffs at Antipodes as a marvellous fiction, and wonders that any can still be tasteless enough to believe that men can stand head downward (the reason given, that heavy bodies tend to the centre, seems to him silly). It should be said, however, that this argument does not spring wholly from preoccupation with Scripture, but echoes old ridicule from Epicureans like Lucretius. Many Fathers, especially the eastern, insist rightly that the texts mean a flat earth, and wrongly that this must be accepted as revelation. Such were the various attitudes, all boding little good to science. Even Basil, while aware that some have measured the globe as 180,000 stades, can talk as if this shape were still disputable, because Moses did not mention it nor say how the shadow on the moon produces eclipses nor bother with things

[1] For their geography, Marinelli, *Scritti Minori*, 1908, 1, 283–342: Duhem, op. cit. pp. 393–501: Wright, op. cit. ch. 2: Mieli-Brunet, *Hist. des Sciences: Antiquité*, ch. 48: Thorndike, op. cit. esp. ch. xxi: H. O. Taylor, *Medieval Mind*, 1911, 1, ch. 4: Kimble, op. cit. Much in A. D. White, *Warfare of Science and Theology*, 1, 1896.

[2] Wright, op. cit. pp. 54, 384, Kimble, pp. 36, 163. Most against globe, Marinelli, op. cit. 325, Beazley, 1, 275–6 after Peschel. Hangs, Basil, *Hex.* 1, 9, Ambrose, *Hex.* 1, 6, 22: Taylor, op. cit. 1, 72.

unimportant for us to know. He can defend the upper 'waters' as placed where they are to keep the firmament cool.[1]

Some of the naïve literalists, like Diodorus of Tarsus and his disciple Theodore (died 428) and Severian, develop very crude notions of the earth as the bottom of a box or trunk. Through them we come to the same Cosmas who as a trader saw or heard so much about distant lands, even China. As a monk he is the slave of his texts, and writes 'a Christian topography of the world, established by proofs from Scripture, of which it is not lawful for a Christian to doubt': he will show that the pagans were all wrong and Moses a 'great cosmographer'. The Antipodes are an old wives' tale: it is against all reason that men should stand head down, and the Apostles,

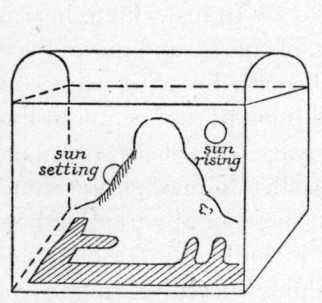 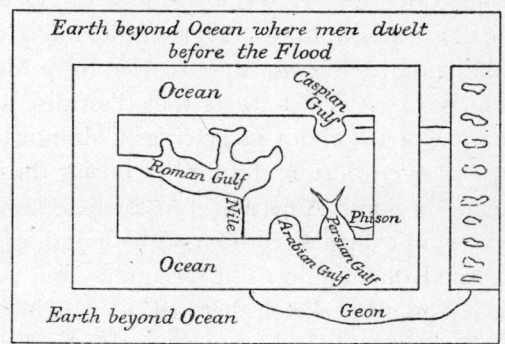

Fig. 66. Notions of Cosmas.

who went everywhere, did not go there. The earth is 'God's foot stool' and has 'foundations' and 'four corners' and men live 'on the face of the earth', not on several faces, and how could a globe have appeared from the waters at Creation or been covered by Noah's Flood? The earth is in fact the oblong floor of a box or room, and on the walls is glued a rounded lid or firmament—he actually compares the vaulted roof of a bathroom. The stars are moved along from the lower side of the firmament by angels (this is what has come of giving the stars divine souls). The sun is quite near and small, much smaller than the earth, and disappears nightly behind the high northern parts of the earth, in fact behind a huge conical mountain there; it passes round the top or the base at various seasons, which explains why the days differ in length. The fancy recalls the old Greek one of the northern range hiding the sun, but he is reviving something older still, the

---

[1] Basil, *Hex.* IX, 1, globe: waters, Wright, op. cit. pp. 58–9: see p. 42, n. 1. Echoes, Rand, *Founders of Middle Ages*, 1929, p. 58: Lact. III, 24. Aug. *C.D.* XVI, 8–9. Not imply, Thorndike, p. 274, Kimble, p. 36, Wright, pp. 55–7. On all this, J. T. Simpson, *Landmarks in the Struggle between Science and Religion*, 1925, ch. 5: McGiffert, *Hist. of Chr. Thought*, 1933, II, 121–3. White, op. cit. pp. 102–5.

Babylonian earth-mountain towering from the Ocean. He adds a tenet of the eastern Fathers mentioned, a strange elaboration of an allegory begun some two centuries before. The tabernacle of Moses is supposed by its shape and furniture to give, according to an obscure text, a pattern of the world.[1] The inhabited earth is an oblong, and of the dimensions two by one, as many pagan geographers said, but not for their reasons, rather because the table of shewbread was 'in length two cubits and in breadth one'. As there was a 'waved moulding' round the table, so there is an Ocean round the known earth; as there was a garniture of gold round the moulding, so there is round the Ocean itself an outer earth. Here men dwelt before Noah floated away to the Armenian mountains. Paradise is in its eastern part, from which four rivers flow under the Ocean to emerge in our inhabited earth as the Euphrates, Tigris, Nile, and Ganges (or Indus). Plato had an inkling of this lost world, borrowed from Moses, of course, and mislaid it in the west. (A few Fathers took Paradise as allegory, like Augustine, but many worried about its placing; Columbus still thought that he might find it, and even that he did find it, on his third voyage, or at least some land near—in South America!) As for the known earth, Cosmas has got somewhere an exaggerated idea of the length as 400 stages or apparently about 12,000 Roman miles. The Ocean has four gulfs, including the Caspian, and he is content to sketch them with a roughness almost incredible in one who had sailed in the Indian Ocean and heard something of the long way round to China. For the flat earth he quotes not only Scripture but some of the Greeks themselves, Pytheas (who in fact knew better), Ephorus, and old Xenophanes.[2] Thus by strange paths geography was brought back to its Ionian beginnings, and even behind them to crude eastern fancies. This 'crotchety monk' can hardly be treated as a mere curiosity, as he quotes bishops galore for his opinions, though these were unknown to the West. It is strange that with so wide a horizon to Zanzibar and China he should be so blindly hostile to the earth-globe. About the same time two writers know something of northern Scandinavia. There at midsummer, it is said, the sun never sets for forty days and nights, and at midwinter never rises for forty, so that the people send scouts up the mountains to watch for its

---

1 Hebrews ix. 23. Tabernacle, Exod. xxvi–xxvii. Sun, Cosmas, 89 C D. Bab., Dalton, *Byz. Art and Arch.* 1911, fig. 268. Beazley, op. cit. I, 273–303, Marinelli, op. cit. pp. 335–42. Theodore refuted by John Philoponus, *in Mos. Mundi Creat.* III, 9, Winstedt, 7. Beckers, *Kosmol. Kuriosa...*, *Klio*, 1913, pp. 105–18. Moss, *Birth of Middle Ages*, p. 90. Dreyer, op. cit. pp. 211–18. Simpson, op. cit. pp. 44–8. Lecky, *Rationalism in Europe*, 1865, ch. 3. White, op. cit. pp. 93–5. And see p. 369, n. 2.

2 Cosmas, 116B–117A. Length, 97B. An echo of the old Indus–Nile?, 117A, 452A, cp. p. 362, n. 1. Madariaga, *Columbus*, pp. 96, 323–6. Aug. *C.D.* XIII, 21: few, Marinelli, p. 304: see p. 40, n. 1. Atlantis, Cosmas, 453B, 456C. Moulding, 160D. Angels, 128D. On the eastern Paradise, Sir C. Oman, *Col. Despard and Other Studies*, 1922, pp. 216–22.

return, because 'they always become afraid, I imagine, that it may fail them some time'. Thus Procopius, who says nothing of scientific theory, while Jordanes talks of the sun returning to the east along the rim of the horizon and is ignorant of what Pytheas could explain some nine centuries before.[1]

The offence of Cosmas is rank: he roundly denies the best things in ancient science, like the globe itself. But at least he knows something about them, and his very vehemence implies that some still believed them. In the west there was falling a worse darkness, in which men pored over old books often without seeing what they meant. So presently in the seventh century does Isidore, bishop of a Gothic Seville, compiling mainly from Pliny an encyclopaedia which was vastly used throughout the Middle Ages; he quotes ancient writers on the globe, for instance, but he fails to understand that they are talking of a globe and not a circle, and he misconceives the zones as circles on a flat earth. The geographer of Ravenna cites 'philosophers' for mighty mountains placed by God in the north to screen the sun. A bishop Arculf makes Jerusalem the centre of the earth not only because of the usual text but because he had seen a column there which cast no shadow at noon at the summer solstice!

Medieval geography is a fascinating mixture. It seldom represents the full amount of contemporary knowledge, but is largely made up of traditional elements, Christian and classical, blended in various proportions. The first comes from a literal reading of Scripture. Hence the reversion to primitive-looking maps of a flat earth disk, 'stretched out above the waters', having the Holy City in the centre and Paradise with its four queer rivers in the far east (drawn at the top where we put the north). Hence, too, legends like Gog and Magog, the barbarians hourly expected to invade across Alexander's wall. The second main element is classical learning, taken not from the best sources but chiefly from Pliny and even less critical compilers. There is a persistent copying of the old clichés like the mountains of the north wind, the Caspian 'gulf', the western Nile, gold ants, gold-guarding Griffins, monstrous peoples in distant parts, such as men with tails, Shadow-feet and what not, and all sorts of unnatural natural history. But there is also a copying of the good things. Anyone who assumes from a few monkish maps that everybody then thought the earth flat will be disconcerted to find how many of the writers from Bede on talk quite intelligently about the globe and its zones; they include Dante and even the popular author of *Mandeville's Travels*, who knows that the earth must be a globe because the pole star is not seen in the south. Most went astray, indeed, about the zones, believing

[1] Proc. *B.G.* II, 15, 6–15. Jord. 19–20. But later Dicuil, VII, 2, 6 understood, Dreyer, op. cit. p. 225.

an ancient opinion (not the best) that the torrid is uninhabitably hot; the south temperate might in theory be peopled by Antipodes, but against them was the argument that neither the sons of Adam nor the Apostles could have crossed the equatorial belt. Yet Albertus Magnus, about 1260, says that the whole torrid zone is habitable, as proved by known peoples in Ethiopia and India, and that 'the lower hemisphere antipodal to ours is in great part inhabited, and, if they do not come to us, it is because of vast seas between'.

The Arabs were translating and copying Ptolemy when he was almost entirely lost to Europe; they based some original work on his astronomy and made their own attempt to measure the globe. It was only in the twelfth century that his *Astrology* and *Astronomy* were translated from the Arabic at Toledo and Palermo; his *Geography* had to wait much longer, though it had some slight influence through maps like Al-Idrisi's.

Not all medieval maps are of the crude monkish type. There are also portolans or 'compass charts', in which the outlines of the Mediterranean are quite startling in their accuracy: Ptolemy's bad lengthening of that sea is duly corrected, as it was already by the Arabs.

The Middle Ages can show remarkable travels, though some were little known at the time. By 758 there were so many Arab traders at Canton that they could sack the place. Till 1245 few Europeans had passed Baghdad, but then quite suddenly a friar (John of Plano Carpini) went 3000 miles east to the camp of the Grand Khan at Karakorum; soon there followed William of Rubruck, who was not the last of such envoys inspired by the vain hope of winning this mighty ally against Islam (the legendary Prester John was sometimes found in these parts). After William came traders, the father and uncle of Marco Polo, and Marco himself, the prince of all travellers, who covered vast stretches in Asia, including a large proportion of new ground and populous islands like Java and Sumatra in a torrid zone supposed uninhabitable. Yet these wonderful journeys had long hardly any influence on geography, so that the Caspian 'gulf', for instance, corrected already by William and indeed by Al-Idrisi, was repeated long afterwards. The final effect was to increase an Asia already overstretched by Ptolemy, and to place beyond it a hearsay island of Cipango, and so to make the western Ocean seem shorter for Columbus.

In Africa exploration hardly went beyond ancient limits. The Arabs knew the east coast only to the Mozambique channel, but were inclined to reject Ptolemy's closed Indian Ocean basin. From the north they learnt something of lands beyond the desert and of the Niger, but they were confused by Ptolemy's queer mapping and by still older fancies of a western Nile. Others rediscovered the Canary Islands and Madeira, and perhaps visited the Azores. Little seems to have been known of the west coast past Cape Bojador. When Henry of Portugal began his work, the sea beyond and the torrid zone were dreaded as impassable. At his death in 1460, his men had reached only Sierra Leone or thereabouts, but the impetus had been given: there was a pause of disappointment when the Guinea coast was seen to turn sharply south, but in 1487–8 the Cape was rounded and ten years later Vasco da Gama sailed up the east coast and on to India.

It was only now that Ptolemy's *Geography* became known, in poor versions from about 1410 but more especially after the fine edition of 1478 (a Greek one came in 1533). The effect was great and not too healthy. The Renaissance, less interested in furthering science than in recovering classics, was minded to force new knowledge into his framework and to uphold errors like the exaggerated length of the Mediterranean. In the latter sixteenth century the first really modern geographers, Mercator and Ortelius, shook off most of this influence, but it has been indicated in the previous chapters how traces of it are still visible on mapping down to the eighteenth century and sometimes even the nineteenth, as in the matters of the great southern continent, the Niger, and the sources of the Nile.

NOTE ON BOOKS AND ABBREVIATIONS

Books are mentioned where they are used, but a short list may be added here. Of formal histories of ancient geography Sir E. H. Bunbury's (^{2}1883) remains indispensable, supplemented by H. Berger's *Geschichte der wissenschaftlichen Erdkunde der Griechen* (Pts. I–IV, 1887–93, ^{2}1903), which deals, as it professes, mostly with the development of mapping based on the earth-globe (it is often hard reading). Good matter can still be quarried out of Forbiger's tomes (1842–8, ^{2}1877). Introductions are Tozer's (1897, reprinted with a few notes by Cary, 1935) and H. E. Burton's *Discovery of the Ancient World*, 1932, only 130 pages but a neat summary with good references to sources. See also Cary and Warmington, *The Ancient Explorers*, 1929, better in some parts than in others. Important for theory is Heidel's *Frame of the Ancient Greek Maps*, 1937. A lot of the best recent work has gone into the articles of Pauly-Wissowa-Kroll, *Realencyklopädie*, often cited as *R.E.*, as on Oikumene (1937) and on Geography itself (Suppl. IV, 521–685, 1924), both by Gisinger, on Maps (X, 2022–2149, 1919) and Earth-measurement (Suppl. VI, 31–54, 1935), both by Kubitschek, on authorities like Eratosthenes (Knaack, 1906), Marinus and Strabo (both Honigmann, 1931), on peoples and places from Britain to China, and on all sorts of things more or less concerned, amber and tin and silk, the Ocean, meteorology, the Nile-flood, and countless others; the various writers do not always agree, of course, and the difficulty is to get an intelligent survey of what matters in this vast mass of scattered detail. An article 'Geographia' by Rainaud in Daremberg and Saglio's *Dictionnaire des Antiquités*, 1896, is good chiefly for physical geography. For the sources there are useful collections, *Geographici Graeci Minores* (*G.G.M.*, ed. C. Müller, 2 vols. and one of maps, 1855–61, 1882) and *G. Latini Minores* (*G.L.M.*, ed. Riese, 1878). Parts of *Fragmente der griech. Historiker* (*F.G.H.*, ed. Jacoby, 1923–43) are of great value. *F.H.G.* means the old *Fragmenta Historicorum Graecorum*, ed. C. Müller, 1848–74. A series of original passages translated with commentary is given by Hennig, *Terrae Incognitae*, I, 1936, II (A.D. 200–1200), 1937, and a selection of such in Warmington, *Greek Geography*, 1934. A basic work is H. Berger's *Fragmente des Eratosthenes*, 1880. Some writers have been much edited like Herodotus, but others, including the most important, Strabo and Ptolemy, are not nearly so familiar or so fully explained. For all these the best books are cited at the proper places. Some particularly useful books deal with ancient knowledge of certain regions, such as Yule's *Cathay and the Way Thither*, I, 1866, revised by Cordier, 1915, and Berthelot's *L'Afrique saharienne et soudanaise: ce qu'en ont connu les Anciens*, 1927, and his *L'Asie ancienne centrale et sud-orientale d'après Ptolémée*, 1930. Kiepert's *Lehrbuch*, 1878 (English, 1881), is a description of ancient lands with a very brief preliminary sketch on the development of geography.

Greek science was only slowly disengaged from the philosophy in which it began, and the usual histories of philosophy are partly relevant, though most pay too little attention to the matters in question, for instance the earth-globe, how it was first conceived and presently applied to geography. Such things are handled more for their own sake elsewhere, as in O. Gilbert's *Meteorologische Theorien des griech. Altertums*, 1907, Sir T. L. Heath's *Aristarchus of Samos, the ancient Copernicus*, 1913 (including a history of Greek astronomy), also his *Greek Astronomy*, 1932, a selection of original passages, Duhem's *Système du Monde de Platon à Copernic*, 5 vols. 1913–17, Dreyer's *History of Planetary Systems from Thales to Kepler*, 1906, and Tannery's *Pour l'Histoire de la Science hellène*, 1887, rev. Diès, 1920, and his other studies reprinted in *Mémoires Scientifiques*, 1912–31. Farrington's *Science in Antiquity*, 1936, is an illuminating survey. The section by Rehm and Vogel on exact sciences in Gercke-Norden's *Einleitung in die Altertumswissenschaft*, II, 2^4, 1933, is often cited as Rehm-Vogel. Geography receives some space in Mieli and Brunet, *Histoire des Sciences: Antiquité*, 1935, very little in Reymond's *Science in Graeco-Roman Antiquity*, 1927 (French, 1924). See also Heiberg's short *Math. and Physical Science in Classical Antiquity*, 1922 (German, 1912). A great source-book for the opinions of Greek philosophers is Diels, *Doxographi Graeci* (1879, ed. iterata, 1929) often cited as *Dox*.

Ancient geography is sometimes handled as part of general histories of geography of various sizes, like Peschel's 1865 (revised by Ruge, 1877), Vivien de St Martin's, 1873, S. Günther's, 1904 (pp. 3–39), and Dickinson and Howarth's short outline, *The Making of Geography*, 1933, where it receives 45 pages out of 264. Or it may be treated, without the theory, as part of histories of exploration, as briefly by J. N. L. Baker, 1931, and Sir P. Sykes, 1934. Such accounts have their uses for perspective, if carefully done, but the more popular writing in this kind abounds with dubious or wrong statements. In general histories of all science the subject is often too slightly and sometimes uncritically handled, but C. Singer gives it fair value, *Short History of Science*, 1941 (as elsewhere in the *Legacy of Rome*, ed. C. Bailey, 1923): see also parts of Dampier (Dampier-Whetham), *Hist. of Science*, 1929, (^{3}1942), Sarton, *Introd. to Hist. of Science*, I, 1927, and others cited especially for points important for theory.

It is hard to say where ancient geography ends, and the last chapter overlaps with books on medieval geography, like K. Miller's *Mappae mundi, die ältesten Weltkarten*, 1895–8, and Sir C. R. Beazley's *Dawn of Modern Geography* (A.D. 300–1420), I, 1897. Of great interest are Kimble's *Geography in the Middle Ages*, 1938, Laistner's chapter on the decline in A. P. Newton's *Travel and Travellers of the Middle Ages*, 1926, and J. K. Wright's *Geogr. Lore of the Time of the Crusades*, 1925, which has much on far older times, and also, less directly, Lynn Thorndike's *History of Magic and Experimental Science during the first thirteen Centuries*, 1^2, 1929. See also W. W. Jervis, *The World in Maps, a Study in Map Evolution*^{2}, 1938.

All good histories of the ancient world are relevant, of course, especially when they deal in some detail with those wars or efforts of trade or colonization which brought gains of geographical knowledge. But often they become rather casual or nebulous about the remote parts which interest us most in this connection, and it is strange how seldom they think of giving a contemporary map or description (if they did, they would sometimes be less ready to assume distant trade and trade-routes). Of particular value are the special histories of the regions concerned like the *Cambridge History of India* (*C.H.I.*), 1, 1922, and Gsell's *Hist. anc. de l'Afrique du Nord*, 1913–28, and many others cited in the notes. There is much bearing on trade and travel in economic histories such as Heichelheim's, 1938, Rostovtzeff's (*Roman Empire*, 1926, *Hellenistic World*, 1941) and the *Economic Survey* edited by Tenney Frank (II, *Roman Egypt*, 1936, and other volumes), and in Charlesworth's *Trade-Routes and Commerce of the Roman Empire*^{2}, 1926. There is an interesting summary in the early chapters of Oakeshott's *Commerce and Society, a Short History of Trade and its Effects on Civilization*, 1936. General histories often cited are the *Cambridge Ancient* and *Medieval* (*C.A.H.*, *C.M.H.*) and *European Civilization*, ed. Eyre, 1935.

L.G. means the *Legacy of Greece* by various writers, 1922, and the same Oxford series has *Legacies* of Rome, Egypt, Israel, India (also Islam and the Middle Ages). Periodicals used are the *Classical Quarterly* and *Review*, *C.Q.*; *C.R.*, and the *Journals* of Hellenic and Roman Studies, *J.H.S.*, *J.R.S.*, of *Egyptian Archaeology*, *J.E.A.*, of the Royal Asiatic and Geographical Societies, *J.R.A.S.*, *J.R.G.S.*, the *Journal Asiatique*, *J.As.*, the *Geogr. Journal* and *Zeitschrift*, *G.J.*, *G.Z.*, and *Petermanns Mitteilungen*, *Pet. Mitt.* Many others are indicated by shortenings which are probably not too short to explain themselves.

Among recent writings noticed in the Addenda are Ninck, *Die Entdeckung von Europa durch die Griechen*, 1945, Carcopino, *Le Maroc antique*, 1943 (for Hanno etc.), and W. W. Hyde, *Ancient Greek Mariners*, 1947.

A good atlas is necessary, of course, like Kiepert's *Atlas Antiquus*^{2}, 1902: really beautiful, with coloured relief, are the maps in Murray's *Small Classical Atlas*^{2}, ed. Grundy, 1917, and his separate *Handy Classical Maps* of the Eastern Empires, the Roman Empire, Gallia, Hispania, etc. See also Sieglin's *Schulatlas zur Gesch. des Altertums* and Philips' *Atlas of Anc. and Classical History*, ed. Muir and Philip, 1938.

ADDENDA

Chapter I

P. 4. B. Hrozný, *Die älteste Geschichte Vorderasiens und Indiens*², 1946, pp. 59, 62 finds the cradle of mankind in Central Asia, and looks in that direction for the original homes of the Hamito-Semites and the Sumerians, not far from that of the Indo-Europeans.

The primitive (food-gathering) peoples existing to-day are in remote parts, obviously last refuges to which they were driven: the geographical distribution suggests shadowy movements, as does that of the various primary and secondary cultures, all lower than the earliest civilizations, W. Schmidt, *Origin and Growth of Religion*, Engl. tr. 1931, pp. 238–41, 252–3, citing Graebner, *Methode der Ethnologie*, 1911, etc. Mankind began probably in Asia, ibid. p. 234.

P. 5, n. 1. Dynasty I is now put lower, about 3000 B.C., Hrozný, op. cit. p. 19.

P. 6, n. 1. Little is now heard of a theory (Sir G. Elliot Smith, W. J. Perry) that 'civilization', i.e. a certain complex of supposed beliefs and practices, was spread by 'Children of the Sun' from Egypt of the Old Kingdom. For early attacks see Peet, *J.E.A.* 1924, pp. 63–9, Crawford, *Edin. Rev.* 1924, I, 101–16, Kendrick, *The Axe Age*, 1925, ch. 4: also Marett in *Frazer Lectures*, ed. W. R. Dawson, 1932, pp. 172–89. It is not proved even that the idea of 'megalithic' tombs spread from Egypt, and, if it were, it would not prove distant Egyptian travels.

P. 6, n. 2. Egyptian sea-going ships were steadily improved, within certain limits, Faulkner, *J.E.A.* 1940, pp. 3–9, Hornell, *Water Transport: Origins and early Evolution*, 1946, pp. 48–51, 213–29.

P. 7, n. 1. A predynastic ivory shows strangers with strange boats invading, from Sinai way some think: from Punt (and ultimately from Elam), Sir Flinders Petrie, *The Making of Egypt*, 1939, pp. 65, 77: Peet, *C.A.H.* 1923, I, 252–6 is reserved, as still Drioton and Vandier, *L'Égypte*, 1938, p. 3. Petrie ibid. brings the Phoenicians too from Punt, like Lieblein's old book on Egyptian Red Sea trade, 1886. The Greeks had a notion of Phoenicians from the 'Red Sea', Hdt. I, 1, VII, 89, Str. 766, and see p. 24, n. 1 and p. 133.

P. 9, n. 2. The ships did go round Arabia, Montet, *La Vie quotidienne en Égypte au temps des Ramsès*, 1946, pp. 185–7. Certain envoys, really to the Hittites, it seems (Breasted, *A.R.E.* III, 188–94) are strangely sent by Montet to Bactria, and by way of the Indus! The evidence (chiefly an obscure name B.kht.n) is obviously flimsy.

P. 12, n. 1. Some speak of Egyptian influences passing to west Africa, even Guinea, as Sir H. H. Johnston, *Hist. of the Colonization of Africa*², 1913, p. 19, and C. de la Roncière, *La Découverte de la Terre*, 1938, p. 4. Meshwesh = Maxyes, and the Libyan tribes included immigrant Aegean elements, J. Bérard, *Rev. Ét. gr.* 1944, pp. 73–84.

P. 13, n. 1. Doubts on Etruscan immigration still in Altheim, *Hist. of Roman Religion*, 1938, pp. 46–50, *Italien und Rom*, 1941, I, 90–101, but most accept it, as Hrozný, op. cit. p. 172. A bold theory seeks to trace the Philistines (via Crete) to Illyria (cp. a Palaeste in Epirus), Bonfante, *Am. J. Arch.* 1946, pp. 251–62.

P. 15, n. 1. Many writers in *Hirt-Festschrift*, 1936, still argue confidently for a German (or W. Baltic) home. Some are now again for Asia (E. of Caspian), Sir A. Keith in *Frazer Lectures*, 1932, pp. 289–304, McGovern, *Early Empires of Central Asia*, 1939, pp. 30–1, and see Hrozný, op. cit. p. 59. Linguists like Meillet care little for speculation about original homes, *Introd. à l'Étude comp. des Langues indo-eur.*⁶, 1924, pp. 55–6.

P. 16, n. 1. Sargon probably to Cyprus and even Crete and perhaps Greece, Hrozný, op. cit. p. 83. He puts Sargon about 2400 and Hammurabi 1791–1749 B.C. On Bab. chronology Cavaignac, *Hist. gén. de l'Antiquité*, 1946, pp. 10–19, 551–3. Sargon to Lydia, Dussaud, *Babyloniaca*, 1930, p. 84.

ADDENDA

One should say rather that Hdt. I, 194 describes the round ferry-boats and wrongly makes them come downstream, as the skin-rafts did, Ravn, *Herodotus' Description of Babylon*, 1942, p. 88, Hornell, op. cit. pp. 28–9.

P. 17, n. 2. E. Mackay, *Further Excavations at Mohenjo-Daro*, 1938: S. Piggott, *Some Ancient Cities of India*, 1945, pp. 13–17. Now dated 2400–2000 B.C., Hrozný, op. cit. pp. 184–230, who claims to decipher the language as Idg. of a type nearest Hittite: the people had in fact come from N. Mesopotamia. The contacts are of 2500–2000 and perhaps some centuries later, R. E. M. Wheeler in *Ancient India*, 1947, pp. 78–85.

P. 17, n. 3. On the languages several writers in *Hirt-Festschrift*, 1936, I, 233–9, II, 30–6, 216–17: Hrozný, op. cit. pp. 126–36 (Hittites came by the Caucasus, ibid. p. 145). On the geography of Asia Minor Schachermeyr, *Hethiter und Achäer*, 1935, pp. 57–69, Götze, *Kizzuwatna and the Problem of Hittite Geography*, 1940, who puts K. in Cilicia (E. Cilicia and Cataonia, Hrozný, op. cit. p. 129). Forrer finds it and its ironworkers in Pontus, like the Chalybes of Greek tradition: so Gurney inclines, *Liverpool Annals*, 1940, p. 13. On geography also Cavaignac, op. cit. pp. 56–7.

P. 18, n. 2. Forrer is now partly justified by Schachermeyr, op. cit. pp. 20–30, and Hrozný, op. cit. pp. 154–9. Cavaignac, op. cit. pp. 70, 79. Troy 7a, after Blegen, *Am. J. Arch.* 1935, pp. 550–1. The place was destroyed by Thracian invaders, not Greeks, Rhys Carpenter, *Folk Tale, Fiction and Saga in the Homeric Epics*, 1946, p. 67.

P. 19, n. 1. Hrozný, op. cit. pp. 231–6 claims to be deciphering Cretan as partly Idg. (Indo-Eur.) of a type akin to Hittite.

P. 20, n. 1. The *Iliad* is at best of the 8th century B.C. (with rhapsodic accretions of the 7th): the *Odyssey* is late 7th, and both were written down in the 6th, Carpenter, op. cit. p. 180. The poets had very little genuine tradition about the Mycenaean age, and invented freely, ibid. pp. 27–31, 89. They give us, with some older elements, the Ionian society of the 9th and 8th centuries B.C., Cavaignac, op. cit. pp. 174–7.

P. 21, n. 1. Carpenter, op. cit. ch. 3 shares Vellay's doubts of Hissarlik as the site of Troy: Homer thinks of Troy as a larger place and farther inland, as did Demetrius of Scepsis. As for the Catalogue, it reflects early classical conditions, ibid. p. 178.

P. 21, n. 2. Carpenter, op. cit. p. 168 thinks that an earlier setting in Corfu (betrayed in *Od.* IX, 25–6) has been incompletely adapted to Thiaki. A discussion in W. W. Hyde, *Ancient Greek Mariners*, 1947, pp. 93–6.

P. 21, n. 3. It is odd that only the Carians are expressly called 'barbarian', Jüthner, *Hellenen und Barbaren*, 1923, p. 2. As for 'Hellenes', it was not yet a national name, as Thucydides I, 3, 3 observes.

Early Phoenician texts now known describe the god El as a bull, united to a seagoddess, and establishing his seat in Crete, Schaeffer, *Cuneiform Texts of Ras Shamra-Ugarit*, 1939, p. 60, Dussaud, *Découvertes de Ras Shamra*², 1941, pp. 95, 112, who connect him with Europa. But Ninck, *Die Entdeckung von Europa durch die Griechen*, 1945, pp. 15–23 insists that the name Europa belongs to Greece (north and central): in *Iliad*, XIV, 321 her father is merely Phoenix, not yet the Phoenician Agenor. Probably a Greek name for the Cretan earth-goddess, Farnell, *Cults of Greek States*, 1896, II, pp. 479, 632. Greek, and means 'widely extended', Hyde, op. cit. p. 74 (after Fick). Hrozný, op. cit. p. 12 still derives it from Sem.-Bab. erêbu, set (of sun).

P. 22, n. 1. Some explain the Hyperboreans as originally the people beyond the bora or mountains (Bora mons in Macedonia, Livy, XLV, 29), Grace Macurdy, *C.R.* 1916, pp. 180–3, 1920, pp. 137–41, cp. Daebritz, *R.E.* Hyperboreer, 1916, p. 260.

P. 22, n. 2. Homer's Amazons seem to come from Thermodon way, but, after the colonists had failed to find them there, later epic brought them from Thrace, Severyns, *Musée Belge*, 1926, pp. 5–16. Eur. *Or.* 409 has them about the Azov. In art they appear sometimes in Scythian dress.

P. 23, n. 1. Gold in fleeces, so still J. S. Gregory, *Land of the Soviets*, 1946, p. 171, and even Hyde, op. cit. p. 63, who cites Gibbon and J. Scott, *Class. Journal*, 1927, p. 541.

ADDENDA

The goal was not localized in Colchis much before 650 B.C., Carpenter, op. cit. p. 59. A long article by Jessen, *R.E.* Argonautai, 1896, pp. 743-87 (sceptical on the fleeces, 786). Carian rovers or colonists, Cary-Warmington, *Ancient Explorers*, 1929, p. 27, Hyde, op. cit. pp. 50-2. In the first phase of the Argo story the Black Sea is thought of as open, and the return is either by the S. Ocean or by the N. Ocean (to an Adriatic open from the north), Wilamowitz-Moellendorff, *Hell. Dichtung*..., 1924, II, 322: the *Odyssey* has Laestrygones at Cyzicus after an Argo epic, as Meuli proves, ibid. p. 236.

P. 24, n. 1. Pharos was in fact one day off—from the Rosetta mouth: the knowledge shown is of about 630 B.C. thinks Carpenter, op. cit. pp. 95-102.

P. 25, n. 1. 7th cent. B.C. also Carpenter, p. 91.

P. 26, n. 1. Temese and the Taphians are just humorous inventions of Homer, L. Deroy in *L'Ant. classique*, 1947, pp. 227-39. Phaeacians are Naples way: other things about the west are Phoenician lies, Cavaignac, op. cit. p. 177.

P. 27, n. 1. The lotus is the date, in Tripoli, the Cyclopes are cave-dwellers in the Atlas opposite Jerba, and the isle of the winds is Pantelleria, Carpenter, op. cit. pp. 103-5. These western Cimmerians—probably not in the original text—have nothing to do with the Crimean ones, ibid. p. 109. He finds the harbour of the Laestrygones in S. Corsica, p. 107. The L. are northern trolls on a fjord, W. P. Ker, *Collected Essays*, 1925, II, 131. Meuli, *R.E.* Laistrygonen, 1931 questions any reference to the north. Hesiod, *Theog.* 748-51 applies similar phrases about night and day to the far west. For ancient localizations of the adventures, Hyde, op. cit. pp. 76-86, modern ones, pp. 86-96, and most fully Wüst in *R.E.* Odysseus, 1937, §§ 42-3, 47-71. All places after the Lotus-eaters are vague and probably fanciful, thinks Hyde, though rumours had come of the north with its sunless winters and short summer nights.

P. 28, n. 2. On the Table also Benzinger, *Hebr. Archaologie*[2], 1907, p. 162.

P. 29, n. 2. J. W. Jack, *Ras Shamra Tablets*, 1935, pp. 42-3 thinks that the Phoenicians had been at Akabah long before, and had already sent ships to 'Ophir and probably India' for gold. Dussaud, op. cit. p. 22.

P. 30, n. 2. The notorious Carl Peters, *Eldorado of the Ancients*, 1902, p. 395 took Hatshepsut's fleet as far as Quelimane (the same, he thinks, as the Rhapta of Greek writers).

P. 32, n. 1. Chinese race indigenous, but probably some impulses to civilization come across C. Asia, McGovern, *Early Empires of Central Asia*, 1939, pp. 28-30. Some early influences that way, whether by migration or trade or both, Latourette, *The Chinese*[2], 1941, pp. 33-7.

P. 33, n. 1. Huns, McGovern, op. cit. pp. 88-96.

P. 34, n. 1. Tiamat, Jean in *Eur. Civ.* ed Eyre, 1935, I, pp. 271-3: Astley, *Biblical Anthropology*, 1929, pp. 91-3. On Egyptian cosmogonies Vandier, *La Religion égyptienne*, 1944, pp. 32-4. Egg, ibid. p. 34: W. M. Müller, *Egyptian Mythology*, 1923, pp. 42, 71. The monster fought by the Creator is ignored in Genesis but reappears in other Biblical texts, S. Reinach, *Cultes, Mythes et Religions*, II[3], 387-95 (1928). Like a shell-fish, Dhorme, *Les Religions de Bab. et d'Assyrie*, 1945, p. 306, Contenau, *Le Déluge babylonien*, 1941, p. 33: Langdon, *Semitic Mythology*, 1931, p. 303 hints that the 'Red Sea' was possibly named from Tiamat's blood.

P. 35, n. 2. Pillars, Petrie, *Religion of Ancient Egypt*, 1908, p. 68: Müller, op. cit. pp. 37, 55. Shu, ibid. fig. 39. Rain-clouds are seen to gather at the horizon, as if from some vast reservoir there, Navarre in Daremberg-Saglio, *Dict. des Antiquités*, s.v. Oceanus, citing Ploix, *Rev. Arch.* 1877, p. 50.

P. 36, n. 1. For Egyptian ideas of the sun's nightly passage Petrie, op. cit. p. 69, Müller, op. cit. p. 27, Vandier, op. cit. pp. 101-3. Primitive men did not speculate much about the heavenly bodies, Lord Raglan, *The Hero*, 1936, pp. 125-8, Kelsen, *Society and Nature*, 1946, p. 3. They took night and day for granted, and did not fear that the sun might not return (Lucretius, V, 973-81 is right and Manilius, I, 66-72 wrong).

ADDENDA

On the Bab. earth-mountain E. Burrows in *The Labyrinth*, ed. S. H. Hooke, 1935, pp. 54, 60. On Bab. astrology Dhorme, op. cit. pp. 79–81, 282–9.

P. 37, n. 1. On Egyptian astronomy Müller, op. cit. pp. 54–9. On Babylonian see Armitage, *Copernicus*, 1938, pp. 15–19. The rudiments of the science came as part of the common sense of agriculture (astrology only later), Carveth Read, *Man and his Superstitions*[2], 1925, p. 265: Grahame Clark, *From Savagery to Civilization*, 1946, p. 73. Pleiades associated with rain and agriculture, Frazer, *Golden Bough*, VII, pp. 307–19: Hesiod, *Op.* 383, ed. Sinclair, 1932. Even the Indians of British Columbia observe the solstices, the days when the rising or setting sun reaches its most N. and S. points, F. Boas, *General Anthropology*, 1938, p. 274. Savages have much common-sense knowledge, which is either distorted into magic or slowly corrected into science, Read, op. cit. p. 257 (modifying Frazer's view of a progress from magic to science).

P. 38, n. 1. Mountains are represented in the same childish fashion on an Assyrian bas-relief, *Syria*, 1941, p. 149.

P. 39, n. 2. The map *is* old (I Bab. Dyn.), Langdon, op. cit. pp. 216–18: the west, with the place where the sun sets, is at the top: the text mentions Sargon as crossing the sea of death like Utnapishtim (the Bab. Noah). So Contenau, op. cit. p. 75.

P. 41, n. 1. Elysium, Jack, *Ras Shamra Tablets*, 1935, p. 14, as Schaeffer. But to the Greeks the name suggested 'coming', the place to which the pious come, and many moderns have accepted this derivation, see Waser, *R.E.* Elysion, 1905. On the El bull and Crete, Dussaud in Dhorme, op. cit. p. 361: 'field of El', Dornseiff in *L'Ant. classique*, 1937, p. 239. Name Elysium perhaps Minoan and idea probably from Egypt via Crete, J. G. Griffiths in *Greece and Rome*, 1947, pp. 122–6 (and Hesperides another version). Brugmann explained Oceanus as akin to Skt. âçayana, 'lying round', so Eisler, *Weltenmantel und Himmelszelt*, 1910, p. 202, but this is now mostly given up, says Gisinger, *R.E.* Okeanos, 1937, who is for Phoenician origin: but probably Aegean, Herter, ibid. From Sumerian uginna, thought Hommel, as Ogenos in Pherecydes: Ogenos is, Eisler in *L'Ant. classique*, 1939, pp. 55–6. Navel, Ninck, op. cit. p. 31. Eagles also Claudian, XVI, 11–16.

Chapter II

P. 46, n. 1. Rarely over 18 tons, but some up to 360, Cloché, *Les Classes, les Métiers, le Trafic*, 1931, p. 88.

P. 50, n. 1. On native towns J. Perret, *Siris*, 1941, p. 205. Calf (L. vitulus), J. D. Craig, *C.R.* 1929, p. 207: Itali were the young bulls of the bull-god Mars, Altheim, *Hist. of Roman Religion*, 1938, pp. 65–7.

P. 51, n. 1. For early Greek traders and wares in Italy from 9th century B.C., Blakeway, *Brit. Sch. Athens*, 1932–3, pp. 170–208, *J.R.S.* 1935, pp. 129–49: Ninck, op. cit. p. 157. J. Bérard, *Rev. Ét. gr.* 1944, pp. 71–2. First Greek mentions of Rome, Jüthner, *Hellenen und Barbaren*, 1923, pp. 72–3.

P. 52, n. 1. Celts to Spain even before 500 B.C., G. Kraft in *Antiquity*, 1929, pp. 33–44: Chadwick, *Nationalities of Europe*, 1945, p. 152. Some read in Hesiod, loc. cit. not 'Ligyes' (Ligurians) but 'Libyes', as *Ox. Pap.* 1358: Ninck, op. cit. p. 271.

P. 52, n. 3. Basques pre-Iberian, Uhlenbeck in *Lingua*, I, 60–1 (1948).

P. 54, n. 1. Probably 'white' from cliffs, W. J. Watson, *Hist. of Celtic Place-Names of Scotland*, 1926, p. 10, as Holder, *Altkelt. Sprachschatz*, 1896. But pre-Celtic (like Hierni), S. Casson, *Greece and Britain*, 1943, p. 16, Hyde, op. cit. p. 122. Possibly not Celtic: meaning utterly unknown, J. Rhys, *Celtic Britain*, 1882, p. 203. On the strange scepticism of Herodotus about these parts L. Pearson, *Trans. Amer. Phil. Ass.* 1941, p. 345.

P. 55, n. 1. Not Sargasso also Hyde, op. cit. p. 123, against Elton and Tozer.

P. 55, n. 2. Midacritus, about 500 B.C., reached Britain, Casson, op. cit. N.W. Spain or Brittany, Hyde, op. cit. p. 120. Midacritus only a misreading of Midas Phryx, cp. Hyginus, *Fab.* 274, S. Reinach, *Cultes, Mythes et Religions*, III, 322–37 (1908).

ADDENDA

P. 56, n. 1. The invaders of Britain about 1000 and 600 B.C. were both Celts, Chadwick, op. cit. p. 150 (and some bring Celts there already about 1800). Linguists think no Celtic name in Britain before 700 B.C., E. Plant, *Man's Unwritten Past*, 1942, p. 250. Goidels or Q Celts about 800, Brythonic or P Celts 400–300 B.C., Hyde, op. cit. p. 123.

P. 56, n. 2. On the siting of the colonies up to the Danube, G. A. Short, *Liverpool Annals*, 1937, pp. 41–55. For the site of Byzantium, D. G. Hogarth, *The Nearer East*, 1920, pp. 240 1.

P. 57, n. 1. Pârvan, *Dacia*, 1928, p. 43 puts the Sigynnae about the Save: they were Scythians already absorbed by native subjects: so were the Agathyrsi, of whom Herodotus heard at Olbia by a northern Scythian trade-route, pp. 39, 53: of the Danube he would have learnt more at Istria, p. 88. The notion of early promiscuity (Bachofen, 1861, MacLennan, 1865, L. H. Morgan, 1877) was attacked by Andrew Lang and Westermarck, and is now almost abandoned, Malinowski, *A Scientific Theory of Culture*, 1944, p. 26: R. Firth, *Human Types*, 1938, p. 107.

P. 58, n. 1. Axeinos from Askanios, Ninck, op. cit. p. 83: from an Iranian word for 'dark', Hyde, op. cit. p. 29., W. S. Allen in *Class. Quart.* 1947, pp. 86–8. The mountains of both coasts *are* sometimes visible from mid-sea, J. G. C. Anderson in *Anatolian Studies...to W. H. Buckler*, 1939, p. 2.

P. 59, n. 1. On the tribes of the Caucasus coast, Namitok, *Origines des Circassiens*, 1939, pp. 50–6. Mossynoeci, ibid. pp. 83–6.

P. 59, n. 2. But the boundary of Hecataeus was rather the Kuban, as the fragments assign some places N. of the Caucasus to Asia, Ninck, op. cit. p. 39, after Jacoby: someone (Hec.?) ap. Str. 107 makes the Don flow from that range.

P. 60, n. 1. Also Ebert in his *Reallex.* s.v. Südrussland, 1929, pp. 55–98: K. Kretschmer in *R.E.* Scythae, Scythia, 1923. Hdt. is wrong on the summer, which is hot, cp. Arist. *Probl.* 938a, Theophr. *H.P.* IV, 5, 3, Ninck, op. cit. p. 95. The steppe is really in three zones, B. H. Sumner, *Survey of Russian History*, 1944, pp. 20–1.

P. 60, n. 2. Ninck, op. cit. p. 91, attempts to map Hdt. A few types in art suggest a Mongol mixture, ibid. p. 98. The expedition of Darius was imagined partly from tumuli being represented by travellers as his forts, P. E. Legrand, *Rev. Ét. anc.* 1940, pp. 219–26.

P. 61, n. 1. Where the Slavs were then is uncertain, Entwistle, *Trans. Phil. Soc.* 1944, p. 40, citing Niederle, *Manuel de l'Antiquité slave*, 1923, who sees them in the Neuri, Ploughmen Scythians, and Budini. The Iranians when in Russia gave to Slavonic the element danu, water (in Danube, Dniester, Dnieper, Don), and other words, ibid. p. 35. On Niederle also Reche in Ebert's *Reallex.* Slaven, 1928: the least doubtfully Slav are the Neuri: the Budini are mostly thought Finnish.

P. 62, n. 1. Aristeas a real pioneer and early (7th cent. B.C.), Ninck, op. cit. p. 130: Issedones as Ptolemy's in C. Asia, a far-ranging trading people, p. 125. But Ptolemy transfers them there wrongly, Kretschmer, op. cit.: the Iurcae, and Urgi of Str. 306, are ancestors of the Magyars (Jugra), he thinks. Ninck, pp. 126–8 finds Gelonus near Stalingrad, and takes a line towards the S. Urals.

P. 64, n. 2. On the wanderings of Io in Aesch. *P.V.* 707–869, Sir J. L. Myres, *C.R.* 1946, pp. 2–4: the sea of 792 is the Caspian, which for Aesch. perhaps extends far north.

P. 65, n. 1. For Herodotus and later Greeks on Egypt see J. Vogt in *Genethliakon W. Schmid*, 1929, pp. 97–137.

P. 66, n. 1. On theories of the Nile flood Hyde, op. cit. p. 275: Kathleen Freeman, *The Pre-Socratic Philosophers*, 1946, p. 271: Gigon, *Der Ursprung der griech. Philosophie*, 1945, pp. 48–50.

P. 67, n. 1. H. Last in *Class. Quart.* 1923, pp. 35–6 suggests that Macrobii meant originally 'with long bows', though already misunderstood by Hdt. as 'long-lived'.

ADDENDA

P. 68, n. 1. On silphium, Forster, *C.R.* 1942, p. 60: not surely identified, Romanelli, *La Cirenaica Romana*, 1943, p. 30. The material being weighed on the vase looks more like wool, thinks Cloché, op. cit. plate XL.

P. 71, n. 1. The Nasamones went perhaps along the S. side of the Ahaggar via Air to the basin of our Niger, Windberg, *R.E.* Niger, 1936, p. 199.

P. 72, n. 1. An epic by Sir Edwin Arnold, 1901, names the leader Ithobal and takes him all the way round, after raising a crop at the Pungwe and making a trip inland to found Zimbabwe. Two forged scarabs bring the leader, Peduneit, 'to the horn of the earth', *J.R.G.S.* 1908, II, pp. 480–5, 1909, I, p. 214 (I owe the refs. to Mr A. M. Woodward). The ships anyhow reached the S. temperate zone, where the sun is always in the N. sky at noon, Sir H. H. Johnston, *Colonization of Africa*^{2}, 1913, pp. 33–5. The story is fantastic, though based on some observations of the sun south of the tropic, Mieli, *I Prearistotelici*, 1916, I, p. 71. Hyde, op. cit. pp. 234–40 accepts, though he admits that the sun datum could have been deduced. Another doubter Hassinger, *Geogr. Grundlagen der Geschichte*, 1931, p. 212, cited by Hyde.

P. 74, n. 1. Marcy, *Hesperis*, 1935, pp. 21–62: Carcopino, *Le Maroc antique*, pp. 73–155 (the Punic original had deliberate omissions and obscurities): Hyde, op. cit. pp. 141–8.

P. 74, n. 2. Carcopino, op. cit., is novel in denying Lixus=Draa: Hanno turned *back*, he reads, half a day eastwards at Cape Soloeis (Cantin), and settled five colonies *north* of it. Marcy, *J. As.* 1943–5, pp. 1–57 rejects this.

P. 76, n. 1. Carcopino finds Cerne at Rio de Oro: Arrian's 35 days are to Cape Palmas, including 22 from Cerne: the rivers are two arms of the Senegal. Marcy places Cerne like Gsell.

P. 77, n. 1. Cameroon in eruption, C. de la Roncière, *La Découverte de la Terre*, 1938, p. 14 (the final island is Fernando Po, where there are still gorillas). Johnston, *Liberia*, 1906, I, pp. 18–21 and op. cit. p. 35 has Cerne at Herne (Rio de Oro): the first reconnaissance is to the Senegal, the second to Sherbro: the fires are bush-fires, and the wild men, if not human, probably chimpanzees. Cameroon and negrilloes of Gaboon, not apes, Carcopino, op. cit. pp. 78, 152. Perhaps chimpanzees or baboons, Hyde, loc. cit., who ends at Sherbro or Macaulay Island. Not probably gorillas, Ashley Montagu in *Isis*, 1940, pp. 70–3.

P. 77, n. 2. Euthymenes *c.* 320 B.C. and not beyond Senegal, Carcopino, op. cit. p. 61. Silver Mountains=Atlas and Chremetes=Draa, ibid. p. 53. Senegal, Hyde, op. cit. p. 140.

P. 78, n. 1. Sargasso: wild also is de la Roncière, op. cit. p. 137. Coins accepted by Hyde, op. cit. p. 155.

P. 79, n. 2. Calder is right, Erik Gren, *Kleinasien und der Ostbalkan in...der röm. Kaiserzeit*, 1941, p. 41: the real highway was the one used later, as described by Artem. ap. Str. 663 (see p. 171, n. 2, p. 287, n. 3).

P. 85, n. 1. For Assyrian and Mede history Ctesias did not invent but repeated what was told him by the Persians, G. Goossens in *L'Ant. classique*, 1940, pp. 25–45.

P. 85, n. 2. Ephorus, like Hecataeus, had two continents and gave a book to each, but he put the boundary at the Don, Ninck, op. cit. p. 137.

P. 87, n. 2. Ephorus' description is partly influenced by the Cynics, who glorified the 'natural' life of wild peoples, Jüthner, *Hellenen und Barbaren*, 1923, p. 58.

P. 89, n. 1. On these Nile theories, K. Freeman, op. cit. pp. 216, 281, 306.

P. 90, n. 2. But Aristotle means only the S. sea off E. and W. Africa within our zone: he had not an equatorial Ocean, but made Africa stretch into the S. temperate zone, like Eudoxus, thinks P. Friedländer, *Jahrb. D. Arch. Inst.* 1914, p. 116.

ADDENDA

Chapter III

P. 94, n. 1. The Greeks did not experiment enough, and thought that mathematics and pure reasoning, aided by everyday knowledge of fact, would provide all they needed, A. D. Ritchie, *Civilization, Science and Religion*, 1945, pp. 37–47: see also D. W. Hill, *Impact and Value of Science*, 1944, p. 13, F. S. Taylor, *Science Past and Present*, 1945, p. 16, R. Latham, *In Quest of Civilization*, 1946, pp. 253–4. H. Kelsen, *Society and Nature*, 1946, stresses the influence of pre-scientific concepts on early Greek philosophy, pp. 233, 245. Science would never have been started (or sustained) by simple observation of facts, even with experiments, G. C. Field, *Studies in Philosophy*, 1935, pp. 93, 101.

P. 96, n. 1. Convex, see also Mondolfo in *Archeion*, 1936, p. 8, but not so, Ninck, *Die Entdeckung von Europa durch die Griechen*, 1945, pp. 51, 254: it rests on a doubtful text, Diels, *Vorsokr.* 2, 11, and one would expect Anaximander's earth-disk to be concave like that of other Ionians. So Gigon, *Der Ursprung der griech. Philosophie*, 1945, p. 88. North parts higher, ibid. pp. 90, 110: Capelle, *Die Vorsokratiker*, 1935, pp. 91–2.

P. 96, n. 2. Add Gisinger, *R.E.* Oikumene, 1937, § 3: Kathleen Freeman, *Pre-Socratic Philosophers*, 1946, pp. 71 (Anaximenes), 270, 276, 282, 305 (still Democritus).

P. 96, n. 3. For Ionian notions of the sun see diagram in Ninck, op. cit. p. 27: Gigon, op. cit. pp. 168–70: Capelle, op. cit. p. 117. Xenophanes, Freeman, op. cit. p. 101.

P. 97, n. 1. Anaximander may already have used the term 'the inhabited earth', Gisinger, loc. cit. It appears in Hdt. III, 106, cp. 114. Anaximander may be credited with the basic scheme of Hecataeus' map, and is the founder of scientific geography, W. Jaeger, *Paideia*, Engl. tr. 1939, I, 155–6.

P. 101, n. 1. Custom, Hdt. III, 38: a theme often repeated later, with stock examples of barbarian practices, H. Chadwick, *Journ. Theol. Studies*, 1947, p. 35. Plato did not despise knowledge of the sensible world but only those who were content with such knowledge alone, Field, op. cit. pp. 222–5.

P. 103, n. 1. A fuller and better case could be made for ancient geology than in F. D. Adams, *Birth and Dev. of the Geol. Sciences*, 1938, esp. ch. 2. On fossils, Mieli, *I Prearistotelici*, 1916, I, pp. 54, 390–4: K. Freeman, op. cit. pp. 89, 102: Gigon, op. cit. p. 167: Capelle, op. cit. p. 119.

P. 104, n. 1. On silting, Hogarth, *The Nearer East*, 1902, pp. 6–7: Ephesus now five miles inland.

P. 105, n. 1. And still Claudian, *de Raptu Pros.* I, 169–76. Burnt Country, Hogarth, op. cit. p. 34.

P. 106, n. 1. Also Trüdinger, *Studien zur Gesch. der griech.-röm. Ethnographie*, 1918, pp. 37–43, F. Heinimann, *Nomos und Physis*, 1945, pp. 13–23, 170–80.

P. 107, n. 1. Ch. 2 suits Anaximander's disk and does not imply the globe or Antipodes, Mondolfo, op. cit. pp. 7–17.

P. 108, n. 1. The Arcadians insisted on musical education to counteract the harshness produced by a harsh country, Polybius, IV, 20, Mahaffy, *Rambles and Studies in Greece*, 1907, p. 291 (cp. the false notion of Arcady). On the inconsequence of Aristotle, Jüthner, *Hellenen und Barbaren*, 1923, p. 27.

P. 109, n. 1. Now Huntington, *Mainsprings of Civilization*, 1945, esp. chs. 20 and 29, on the 'geographical optima' of civilization. On Buckle's 'laborious endeavour to degrade the history of mankind', Lord Acton, *Hist. Essays and Studies*, 1907, pp. 305–43: an analysis in Gauld, *Man, Nature and Time*, 1946, pp. 113–18. See also Teggart, *Processes of History*, 1918, ch. 2: Brunhes and Vallaux, *La Géographie de l'Histoire*, 1921, pp. 282–3: R. G. Collingwood, *Idea of History*, 1946, p. 78. Much of interest, after Bodin, etc., in R. Burton, *Anatomy of Melancholy*, 1621, Everyman ed. I, pp. 237–41, II, pp. 43–6, 61. A medical Professor, C. A. Mills, *Climate makes the Man*, 1944, finds the influences of climate very far-reaching.

ADDENDA

P. 110, n. 1. Among later writers the killing of the aged is ascribed to the Sarmatian Iazyges, Val. Flaccus, *Argon.* VI, 123–8, 288–9, the Heruli Goths, Procopius, *B.G.* II, 14, 2, and the Huns, Claudian, *in Ruf.* I, 328 (repeating a stock charge? Maenchen-Helfen in *Byzantion*, 1945, p. 237). The aged are in fact often killed or helped to die, L. W. Simmons, *The Rôle of the Aged in Primitive Society*, 1945, pp. 225–40: Dumézil, *Mythes et Dieux des Germains*, 1939, pp. 66–8.

P. 111, n. 1. On Philolaus, Mieli, op. cit. pp. 295–303, Freeman, op. cit. pp. 225–7.

P. 116, n. 2. The figure is E.'s, Gisinger, *R.E.* Oikumene, § 8.

P. 117, n. 3. Probably length 100,000 stades, breadth 50,000, as Geminus 15, 4, thinks Gisinger, op. cit. § 7.

P. 118, n. 1. Nicagoras (also Schol. Apoll. Rhod. IV, 269 and cp. Geminus 16, 1) was probably before Plato and already had zones, thinks Gisinger, op. cit. § 6. He brought the Nile from far south, and Eudoxus expressed this, in terms of the zone theory, as from Antoikoi in the S. temperate zone, Friedländer, op. cit. p. 117. Aristotle also stretched Africa south to this zone, Gisinger, § 9.

P. 119, n. 2. All this, including the elephants, is no doubt after Eudoxus, Gisinger, *R.E.* Perioikoi, p. 837, and see Friedländer, op. cit. pp. 114–19. J. H. Bridges, *Life and Work of Roger Bacon*, 1914, pp. 36, 135.

Chapter IV

P. 123, n. 1. By conquering so large a part of it Alexander made 'the inhabited earth' something more than a geographical expression, R. G. Collingwood, *Idea of History*, 1946, p. 32.

P. 127, n. 4. Alexander at Samarcand received envoys 'from the Scythians called Abii, whom Homer praised as most just of men...and from the Scythians of Europe', Arrian, IV, 1, 1, Curtius, VII, 6, 11–12.

P. 133, n. 1. Sir A. T. Wilson, *Persian Gulf*, 1928, pp. 36–43 (uses W. Vincent, *Voyage of Nearchus*, 1809). Hyde, op. cit. pp. 178–86. I have not seen Berthelot in *Mélanges...Navarre*, 1935, on Greek accounts of the south coast of Iran.

P. 136, n. 2. On Alexander's plans, Arr. *Anab.* IV, 15, 5–6, V, 26, 1–2, cp. Diod. XVIII, 4, C. A. Robinson, *Amer. J. Phil.* 1940, pp. 402–12, Hyde, op. cit. pp. 186–8.

P. 137, n. 1. Inscriptions on elephant-hunts also O.G.I.S. no. 82, H. R. Hall, *C.R.* 1898, pp. 274–80 (one in Egyptian talks of netting elephants, Naville, *Store-City of Pithom*, 1885, p. 18, and has an echo of Punt), Budge, *Hist. of Ethiopia*, 1928, I, pp. 53–4. Householder, *Trans. Amer. Phil. Ass.* 1945, pp. 108–16 gives a new inscription, with further references for elephant-hunting. Wainwright in *Man*, 1947, p. 145.

P. 138, n. 3. Nile from S. sea through torrid region, as p. 118, n. 1, thinks Wehrli, *Dikaiarchos*, 1944, p. 79.

P. 139, n. 1. The poets have old stories about the Argonauts in Lake Tritonis and the founding of Cyrene, Ap. Rhod. IV, 1230 ff., Callimachus, himself of Cyrene, *Hymn*, II, 65–96 (elsewhere he mentions the Nasamones and a place in Tripoli, Mair's edition, pp. 309, 317).

P. 140, n. 1. Celts, Pârvan, *Dacia*, 1928, pp. 111–13. Alexander's Celts are generally thought to come from N. Italy, Chadwick, *Nationalities of Europe*, 1945, p. 156. The Dacian princes used and copied Macedonian and Thasian coins, Pârvan, p. 135.

P. 140, n. 2. Pompey, who used the Genèvre, is said to have opened a route different from Hannibal's, but this refers only to a shorter route west from that pass, Marindin, *C.R.* 1899, pp. 235–49.

P. 143, n. 2. Add Ninck, *Die Entdeckung von Europa*, 1945, pp. 218–25 (Pytheas about 330 B.C. and unequalled among ancient explorers): Hyde, *Ancient Greek Mariners*, 1947, pp. 124–34.

P. 144, n. 2. 'Orcas' shows Celtic speakers there already. W. J. Watson, *Hist. of Celtic Place-Names of Scotland*, 1926, p. 28: Royal Commission on Anc. Monuments of

ADDENDA

Scotland, *Orkney and Shetland*, 1946, I, p. 7. Welsh Prydain points to Pretani as the most correct of many classical spellings, Watson, op. cit. p. 12. Celts invaded about 750 B.C. and more about 450, Jacquetta Hawkes, *Early Britain*, 1945, pp. 26, 29.

P. 146, n. 1. St Michael's, Casson, *Greece and Britain*, 1943, p. 30, Hyde, op. cit. p. 127. Off Land's End at entrance of 'Ictian Sea' of Adamnan, Ninck, op. cit. p. 275.

P. 146, n. 3. Berrice is Pomona (Orkneys) and Dumna is Stroma in the Pentland Firth, Ninck, op. cit. p. 220. But D. is Lewis (or all the outer Hebrides), Watson, op. cit. p. 40.

P. 147, n. 1. Metuonis means meadow or marsh-land: 6000 is a gross exaggeration for the stretch Scheld-Esbjerg, Ninck, op. cit. p. 224. The Abalus of Plin. IV, 94 is the same as Glaesaria (from a Teutonic word for amber) of 97, though Pliny himself does not realize it: Abalus is from the old Celtic word for apple, and, if not Heligoland, may be Appelland or Habel off Schleswig, A. H. Krappe in *Speculum*, 1943, pp. 303–22. The Celts, Ap. Rhod. IV, 609–16 knows, say that amber is the tears wept by 'Apollo', when banished to the Hyperboreans, i.e. they thought amber was exuded by apple-trees (so Rendel Harris, *J.H.S.* 1925, pp. 229–42). To a sacred island with such trees Krappe traces the idea of an island paradise Avallon. P. meant the Elbe and Heligoland, Hyde, op. cit. p. 133.

P. 147, n. 2. Vistula also Elton, *Origins of English History*[2], 1890, p. 39.

P. 149, n. 1. Hearsay, Berger; no, P. himself observed the very short night, Ninck, op. cit. pp. 222, 275, who leaves the case open between Iceland and Norway, as does Royal Commission, op. cit. p. 8. Thule hearsay and most think Norway, Hyde, op. cit. p. 130.

P. 149, n. 2. A clammy Arctic sea-fog, as Hergt: perhaps Aurora borealis in Tac. *Germ.* 45, from P. via Timaeus, thinks Hyde, p. 131. Perhaps spongy ice, Elton, op. cit., who takes P. from Jutland up Norway to see the midnight sun and thence to Orkney.

P. 150, n. 2. Krappe, op. cit. pp. 312–16 Heligoland (after Rendel Harris, *Bull. Rylands Library*, 1925, p. 372), the same as Abalus, the paradise of the Celtic 'Apollo', really an island of the dead, cp. the island with the apples of the Hesperides. The name Helixoia seems suggested by Helice, the Bear, Grace Macurdy, *C.R.* 1920, pp. 137–41, who compares one detail with Plin. VI, 34, a river Carambucis (the Eider, thinks Pape, *Wörterbuch der griech. Eigennamen*, but Pliny places it much farther east, the Dvina of the White Sea, suggests K. Freeman, op. cit. pp. 333–4: she takes the name H. as 'Twisted' Island). H. is Albion, Kiessling, *R.E.* Hyperboreios Okeanos, 1916. Old things on the Hyperboreans repeated in Callimachus, *Hymn* IV, 281–94.

CHAPTER V

P. 152, n. 1. Armitage, *Copernicus*, 1938, pp. 70, 88 (C. does refer to Philolaus, and a scored-out passage in the manuscript adds that some say that Aristarchus was of the same opinion): Hyde, op. cit. p. 11. On Hicetas and Ecphantus Kathleen Freeman, *The Pre-Socratic Philosophers*, 1946, pp. 227, 241: H. apparently got rid of the counter-earth by transferring the name to the moon. Copernicus was chagrined to find himself anticipated in a complete heliocentric theory and deleted a reference to Aristarchus, Stahl, *Trans. Amer. Phil. Ass.* 1945, pp. 322–3.

P. 152, n. 3. Hicetas a fictitious person as Tannery, Bidez, *Volume offert à Jean Capart*, 1935, p. 82. Certainly real like Ecphantus and before 400 B.C., Capelle, *Vorsokratiker*, 1935, pp. 472, 486.

P. 153, n. 1. Pytheas knew the truth, as cp. Aristotle's movable arctic circle, Ninck, op. cit. p. 56, and that the height of the pole star above the horizon corresponds to geogr. latitude, p. 190.

P. 154, n. 1. Gisinger, *R.E.* Oikumene, 1937, § 9 doubts: Ninck, op. cit. pp. 58–9 does not name the author: if really his, Wehrli, *Die Schule des Aristoteles, I, Dikaiarchos*, 1944, p. 77.

P. 154, n. 2. Probably Dicaearchus thought of Antoikoi like Eudoxus and Aristotle, Gisinger, loc. cit.: Wehrli, op. cit. p. 79.

P. 155, n. 1. A short itinerary from Athens with remarks on climate, people, etc., Ninck, op. cit. pp. 142–51, who compares Horace, *Satires*, 1, 5 (on his journey to Brindisi). D. on mountains, Wehrli, op. cit. pp. 75–6.

P. 156, n. 1. Strato thought of currents in straits as due to different sea-levels, and so did Eratosthenes, though he connected the Atlantic and 'Red' Seas, which, as Hipparchus pointed out, implied one level. That the seas were connected and at one level was proved by the work of Archimedes on floating bodies, Ninck, op. cit. p. 255. Aratus was no astronomer, Wilamowitz-Moellendorff, *Hell. Dichtung*, 1924, II, 200–5.

P. 158, n. 1. Apollonius ap. Ptol. XII, 1 knew systems both of movable eccentrics and of epicycles: the latter were eventually preferred, Armitage, op. cit. pp. 31, 50.

P. 158, n. 2. For Berossus also Bidez, op. cit. pp. 48–52. Absence of parallax (as objected by Tycho Brahe against Copernicus), D. Stimson, *The Gradual Acceptance of the Copernican Theory*, 1917, p. 35, Stahl, op. cit. pp. 328–9, Mees, *The Path of Science*, 1946, pp. 90–1.

P. 161, n. 2. Lehmann-Haupt, *R.E.* Stadion, 1927, followed by Ninck, op. cit. p. 13, gives Eratosthenes a very short stade of 148·8 metres ($\frac{1}{40}$ schoenus or $\frac{1}{10}$ Roman mile), 'though he also naturally referred to other stades'. Hultsch, op. cit. p. 57 had ascribed this low figure to Herodotus, Eudoxus and Timaeus. Hyde, op. cit. p. 16 adopts Dörpfeld's stade of 177·4 metres (the Olympic stade of 192·3 was exceptional and never used as a road measure). No secure datum for the value attached by each writer to the stade, says C. Errera, *L'Epoca delle Grandi Scoperte Geografiche*[2], 1910, p. 267.

P. 162, n. 1. F. S. Taylor, *Science Past and Present*, 1945, p. 34 as Heath.

P. 162, n. 2. On the above super-short stade the result is about 37,500 km. (about 7 % too little), Ninck, op. cit. pp. 59–61. Hyde, op. cit. p. 15 gets 27,557 miles as cp. the real (meridional) 24,860. Laurand, *Manuel des Études grecques et latines*, 1934, III, § 45 gives 39,000–41,000 km. according to the stade used (no word of the method, and he dismisses ancient mapping in a page!). Cavaignac, *Hist. de l'Antiquité*, 1914, III, 227 gives 51,000 km. (about 32,000 miles) and refers to Nissen, op. cit. For Newton, see Taylor, loc. cit., Mees, op. cit. p. 92.

P. 163, n. 2. Much in the cosmology of the poem is from Plato's *Timaeus* (and *Rep.* 617b, harmony of the spheres), but Erat. adds the five earth-zones, Solmsen, *Trans. Amer. Phil. Ass.* 1942, pp. 192–213.

P. 164, n. 1. Erat. shifted Thule to this meridian for the sake of simplicity, Ninck, op. cit. p. 65: the 8400 stades S. of Aswan are a handy figure ($\frac{2}{60}$ of the meridian).

P. 165, n. 1. Old texts caused much trouble by a false reading, 'through Thinae' for 'through Athens', in Strabo, 68, 79, etc.

P. 166, n. 2. Gisinger, *R.E.* Perioikoi, 1937, p. 835: Erat. apparently had no Perioikoi, though in a poem he had mentioned Antipodes.

CHAPTER VI

P. 171, n. 1. For a moment, as governed by Cicero in 51 B.C., Cilicia included a large district protecting the old province of 'Asia', Syme in *Anatolian Studies...to W. H. Buckler*, 1939, pp. 299–306: on Cicero's journey to Cilicia, L. W. Hunter, *J.R.S.* 1913, pp. 73–97.

P. 171, n. 2. There is in Plut. *Caes.* 58 a wild fancy that Caesar meant, after conquering Parthia, to return by the Caucasus and round the Black Sea to Germany, and so to 'complete the circle of an empire bounded on all sides by the Ocean'. Strabo's Mantiana and 'Spauta' (a corruption of Kapauta) are both Lake Urmia: Thospitis

ADDENDA

is Van (Pliny's Aretissa and Ptolemy's Arsissa are really its N. bay): there *is* a Tigris tunnel, rediscovered by Lehmann-Haupt, but it is at a headstream of the *western* Tigris, Weissbach, *R.E.* Thospitis, and Honigmann, ibid. Tigris (1936).

P. 172, n. 1. Also Plut. *Pompey*, 34–6, various reports whether the Aras joins the Kur or not: Amazons said to have fought for the Albanians, but no Amazon corpse found: P. near the Caspian turned back owing to the host of venomous serpents.

P. 172, n. 2. On the name Syria F. M. Abel, *Géogr. de la Palestine*², 1933–8, I, 310: on divisions in the Hell. period, ibid. II, ch. 6.

P. 173, n. 1. From Apollodorus Strabo has a river Ochus and some distances. Sound and fury in Lucan, III, 246, 266–8, on wild tribes of Iran roused in Pompey's cause, and in Pseudo-Tibullus, IV, 1, 137–41 (Messalla could, if he liked, conquer the Araxes, etc. and even the cannibal Padaei of India). Dubs (see p. 318, n. 3) suggests that some of Crassus' men, escaping from the Parthians, fought for a western Hun king against the Chinese. On this king, according to Hirth an ancestor of Attila, see McGovern, *Early Empires of Central Asia*, 1939, pp. 187–96, 439. See also p. 252, n. 3.

P. 174, n. 1. On the '*Questions of Milinda*' Goblet d'Alviella, *Ce que l'Inde doit à la Grèce*, 1926, pp. 23–7.

P. 174, n. 3. The Phauni can hardly be Hiung-nu of Mongolia, or *these* Seres Chinese, Maenchen-Helfen in *Byzantion*, 1945, pp. 248–50.

P. 175, n. 2. Wainwright in *Man*, 1947, p. 144 mentions a coin of Ptolemy X (about 100 B.C.) found near Dar es Salaam (Ingrams, ibid. 1925, p. 140), and a Jewish coin of about 140 B.C. found near Durban, Otto and Stratman in *Anthropos*, 1909, p. 168, noted also by H. Breuil, *Comptes Rendus Acad. Inscr.* 1947, pp. 101–6 (on early influences which possibly reached South Africa).

P. 177, n. 2. The farce is late Ptolemaic or early Empire, though the papyrus itself is 2nd century A.D., Barber, in Bury, *Hellenistic Age*, 1925, pp. 61–3.

P. 177, n. 3. Now *History of the Former Han Dynasty*, ed. Dubs, 1938–44.

P. 178, n. 1. McGovern, op. cit. pp. 126–8, 473–83: Yue-chi = Tochari (with a ruling clan of Asiani), and spoke an Idg. language (E. Iranian) but not the misnamed 'Tocharic' of Kucha-Turfan. See also Feist in *Ostas. Zt.* 1919–20, pp. 74–84, Konow, ibid. pp. 232–7.

P. 178, n. 2. McGovern, op. cit. pp. 131–5, 146.

P. 180, n. 2. Alans, McGovern, op. cit. p. 247.

P. 181, n. 2. On Cato's route Romanelli, *La Cirenaica Romana*, 1943, pp. 60–2 (Lucan seems to misplace Ammon). Laserpiciferis...Cyrenis, Catullus, 7, 4. The spring of Ammon, cool at noon and warm at night (Hdt. IV, 181), was a commonplace now and later, Lucr. VI, 848–9, Plin. II, 228 (cp. another in V, 36), Solinus 7 and 29, Aug. *C.D.* XXI, 5, 1.

P. 183, n. 2. Holroyd, *J.R.S.* 1928, pp. 1–20.

P. 184, n. 1. Polybius himself not as far as the Draa, and misled by Lixite pilots regarding Cerne, Carcopino, *Le Maroc antique*, 1943, p. 159. Hyde, op. cit. is confused: P. to Senegal, p. 148, or to Cape Nun, p. 237.

P. 184, n. 2. The Cadiz seamen were not trying to sail round to 'Aethiopia' = Somaliland, as Hyde, op. cit. p. 245 wildly suggests. Madeira, Schulten, *Sertorius*, 1926, pp. 48–50.

P. 185, n. 1. Carcopino, op. cit. pp. 156–8: the figure-head business is absurd, but there is some truth in the story: the island was probably Cerne, at Rio de Oro. For E. also Hyde, op. cit. pp. 200–1, 245–9.

P. 188, n. 1. For Posidonius on Spain Capelle, *Neue Jahrb.* 1920, p. 322, Ninck, op. cit. pp. 198–205. The ancient writers vary in the extension they give to tribal names, Albertini, *Les Divisions admin. de l'Espagne romaine*, 1923, p. 107.

P. 188, n. 2. Polybius badly lengthens W. Spain, and has mistakes even about Saguntum and New Carthage, Jung, *Geogr. und pol. Gesch. des klass. Alt.* 1889, p. 514. A. Melón, *Geogr. Hist. Española*, 1928, I, p. 36.

P. 189, n. 1. Polybius on N. Italy, Ninck, op. cit. pp. 171–8.

P. 189, n. 2. Then and later, before the making of dykes, these coasts *were* intermittently inundated, Brunhes-Vallaux, *La Géogr. de l'Histoire*, 1921, p. 227.

P. 190, n. 2. Posidonius on the Gauls, Ninck, op. cit. pp. 232–41.

P. 192, n. 2. The Arduenna Silva was, even then, 300 m.p. long at most, not 500 as Caes. VI, 29: Str. 194 notes the exaggeration. The names Ausci (in Aquitania) and Vascones (in Navarre) show the same root as Euskara, the native name of Basque, Lacombe and Lafon in *Hirt-Festschrift*, 1936, II, pp. 117–18.

P. 193, n. 1. Caesar played up Ocean in his dispatches, cp. Lucan, II, 571, Plut. *Caes.* 23: C. E. Stevens, *Antiquity*, March 1947, p. 5. Caesar does not mention certain Britanni in Gaul, but Plin. IV, 106 has them near the Morini (about Boulogne).

P. 194, n. 1. Tacitus certainly knew the suspect chapters because he steadily contradicts them in his dislike of Caesar, Couissin, *Rev. de Phil.* 1932, pp. 97–117. The attempt to prove interpolations in Caesar has largely failed, Fabre, *Rev. Ét. Lat.* 1943, pp. 221–2.

P. 195, n. 2. Crassus of 95 B.C., and Strabo's islands are Scilly, Hyde, op. cit. p. 134.

P. 196, n. 1. But all ancient frontiers were marches left empty by tacit accord, Brunhes-Vallaux, op. cit. p. 341, after Ratzel. Caesar is copied by Mela, III, 27, 'ut circa ipsos quae iacent vasta sint'.

P. 196, n. 2. On the name also R. Much in *Hirt-Festschrift*, II, pp. 506–31. It is not proved Germanic, says Chadwick, *Nationalities of Europe*, 1945, pp. 147–9, and its use as a general name for Teutonic peoples was due to a Roman misunderstanding.

P. 197, n. 1. Caesar gives hearsay, and is biased, Dopsch, *Econ. and Social Foundations of Europe*, 1937, pp. 22, 33–4: agriculture had long been important.

P. 198, n. 1. Many Italian traders in Dacia, Pârvan, *Dacia*, 1928, pp. 139, 154. Bastarnae, ibid. p. 111 (with Celts driving behind): Ninck, op. cit. p. 265. Dardanians very wild and dirty, Str. 316.

P. 198, n. 2. 'Russia' is probably derived from Ruotsi, a Finnish name for the Swedes, apparently a corruption of a Swedish word for 'rowers', *Enc. Brit.* Russia.

P. 200, n. 2. Plenty of traders far ahead, Pârvan insists, loc. cit. Some in Caes. *B.G.* VII, 3. Via Egnatia, Pol. ap. Str. 322–3, 'paced by miles and milestoned, 535 m. to the river Hebrus'. It ran quite against the grain of the country, where the natural roads are from the north, Brunhes-Vallaux, op. cit. p. 574, W. Fitzgerald, *The New Europe*, 1945, p. 50. We should be glad of a few itineraries like Horace, *Satires*, I, 5 (Rome–Brindisi, imitating one of Lucilius Rome–strait of Messina). On Roman roads H. Stuart Jones, *Companion to Roman History*, 1912, pp. 40–9, Nilsson, *Imperial Rome*, 1926, pp. 211–22. On Via Egnatia also Erik Gren, *Kleinasien und der Ostbalkan in der wirtsch. Entwicklung der röm. Kaiserzeit*, 1941, pp. 31–2.

P. 200, n. 3. Lucr. V, 1006, 'improba navigii [naucleri?] ratio', is serious enough, Rand, *Founders of the Middle Ages*, 1929, p. 97, if Horace, *Odes*, I, 3 is genial banter: no, it is more, and the Romans really detested the sea, Nilsson, op. cit. p. 209.

Chapter VII

P. 203, n. 1. His is the first earth-globe we hear of, but Eudoxus had probably made one, Gisinger, *R.E.* Oikumene, § 13.

P. 204, n. 1. The ornament of the orb is not from C.'s globe but from a celestial globe, Schlachter, op. cit. p. 69, Gisinger, *R.E.* Perioikoi, 1937. But the globe on coins *is* often the earth-globe, when not distinguished by stars and two bands or the zodiac, J. Vogt, *Orbis Romanus*, 1929, p. 14, and he cites a statue of Caesar as a demi-god 'mounted on a likeness of the inhabited world', Dio, XLIII, 14, cp. Athen. XII, 536a on Demetrius Poliorcetes painted in Athens 'riding on the inhabited world'. Mattingly, *Coins of the Roman Empire*, IV, 1940 gives coins of Pius with two Capricorns above a globe (Plate 33, 8), Britannia seated on a globe, and Italia seated on a globe with zones and stars (Plate 39,

ADDENDA

10 and 11). The globe means the ruler's cosmic power, a Hellenistic notion from eastern solar theology, Lambrechts in *L'Ant. classique*, 1938, pp. 218–20: Cumont, *L'Égypte des Astrologues*, 1937, p. 27.

P. 204, n. 4. For Seleucus also Bidez in *Volume offert à Jean Capart*, 1935, pp. 81–2.

P. 208, n. 1. Pliny says two hours Arbela-Sicily, Ptolemy wrongly somehow three Arbela-Carthage, Ninck, op. cit. p. 70, n. 1.

P. 209, n. 1. For Polybius the Romans held 'almost all the inhabited earth', I, 1, 5, whereas the Macedonians hardly knew the warlike West, I, 2, 5, Gisinger, *R.E.* Oikumene, § 29.

P. 210, n. 1. He has not an equatorial Ocean like Strabo, but stretches Africa S. into a S. temperate zone like Eudoxus, says Gisinger, op. cit. § 19.

P. 213, n. 1. One figure expressed in different stades, Hultsch, *Metrologie*, 1882 (198·4 and 148·8 metres): Mžik, *Mitt. Geogr. Ges. Wien*, 1915, p. 175: A. Diller, *Klio*, 1934, pp. 258–9. No, Drabkin, *Isis*, 1942–3, pp. 509–12, but he questions also Berger's explanation, and suggests that P. estimated 300 stades, the arc over which the sun at the zenith casts no shadow (Erat. ap. Cleom.), as $\frac{1}{600}$ of the circumference. Ninck, op. cit. pp. 61–2 gets 180,000 stades of 178·6 metres, total 32,148 km., which is much worse than Eratosthenes. J. Ball, *Egypt in Classical Geographers*, 1942, p. 96, with a stade of 185·3 metres, gets 33,354 km., much too small, as he says (with no hint of P.'s bad procedure). Hyde, op. cit. p. 16 gets about 19,842 miles (31,936 km.).

P. 213, n. 2. India, if Seneca, *N.Q.* praef. 13 goes back to Posidonius, Gisinger, *R.E.* Perioikoi, 1937, p. 835.

P. 216, n. 1. Witchcraft, see also Statius, *Theb.* VI, 685–7, Claudian, *Bell. Get.* 233–4. Lawrence of Arabia heard Turks 'firing rifles and clanging copper pots to rescue their threatened satellite', *Revolt in the Desert*, 1927, p. 157.

P. 217, n. 1. 'Nearly two-thirds' of the space under heaven is made uninhabitable by heat and cold, and some of the rest by mountains, forests and sea, Lucr. V, 200–5. He denies the globe, yet seems to be thinking here of zones. Some remarks about the effects on complexion and health of climates from Britain to the sun-baked blacks, VI, 1102–11: 1107 (cp. Virgil, *Georg.* I, 240) seems the old theory of the earth-disk tilted to the north, see Ernout-Robin and C. Bailey ad loc.

P. 217, n. 3. The *Dream* goes back in essential features to the poem of Eratosthenes, Solmsen, op. cit. p. 213 (see above, p. 163, n. 2). On the sources Boyancé, *Études sur le Songe de Scipion*, 1936.

P. 218, n. 2. Varro Atacinus has the usual five zones, two of them habitable, *Fragm. Poet. Lat.* (ed. Morel, 1927), p. 97.

P. 219, n. 1. Triumphs, Ovid, *A.A.* I, 220–4, 'quae loca, qui montes, quaeve feruntur aquae': *Ep. ex Ponto*, II, 1, 37–9. But Livy, loc. cit. does mean a map of Sardinia, T. Birt, *Rhein. Mus.* 1920–4, pp. 306–23, who also detects a map of 129 B.C. in Plin. III, 129: 'Tuditanus, qui domuit Histros, in tabula [*not* statua] sua ibi inscripsit ab Aquileia ad Titium flumen stadia M.' Ulysses maps on the sand an old exploit for Calypso, 'in spisso litore pingit opus', Ovid, *A.A.* II, 132, and the old soldier type likes 'pingere castra mero', Tibullus, I, 10, 29: see p. 332, n. 1.

P. 219, n. 2. Peculiar is the pushing of the boundary of Asia well west of the Nile, Sallust, *Jug.* 17, 4, 19, 3 (so Mela, I, 40 and 49), Gisinger, *R.E.* Oikumene, § 34. Sallust is copied in part of Isid. XIV, 5, 17, but not probably his are the fabled Antipodes in a continent inaccessible for heat beyond the equatorial Ocean.

P. 219, n. 3. Virgil, *Aen.* VII, 233–7 imagines that the news of the Trojan war has in its own generation reached the S. temperate zone and the farthest land in Ocean (Britain or Thule).

P. 220, n. 1. Virgil bringing the Nile *ab Indis* means only Ethiopians, say editors (Conington with some hesitation). Editors are little troubled by 'Armenian tigresses', Virgil, *Ecl.* V, 29, Ovid, *Am.* II, 11, 35 and *Met.* XV, 86, Prop. I, 9, 19, Tib. III, 6, 15, but see Préchac, *Rev. Ét. lat.* 1936, pp. 105–9, Aymard, *Rev. de Phil.* 1943, pp. 80–3. Roman poets like geogr. names but use them very loosely, W. Kroll, *Studien zum Verständnis der röm. Lit.* 1924, pp. 278–9, 294–9.

Chapter VIII

P. 223, n. 1. 'Mari Oceano aut amnibus longinquis saeptum imperium', Tac. *Ann.* I, 9. Ovid, *Fasti*, II, 685, 'Romanae spatium est urbis et orbis idem': *Am.* I, 15, 26, 'Roma triumphati dum caput orbis erit': *A.A.* I, 177, 'ecce parat Caesar domito quod defuit orbi addere. nunc, Oriens ultime, noster eris.' But cp. 'orbis qua Romanus erat', Lucan, VIII, 211, and on the development of 'orbis' see p. 201, n. 4.

P. 224, n. 1. The speed records of Plin. XIX, 3 were due to the invention of the top-sail, C. de la Roncière, *Rev. Arch.* 1941, pp. 121–38. Pliny's speeds abnormal, H. S. Jones, *Companion to Roman History*, 1912, pp. 50–1: Plin. II, 128, 'prolatis pedibus', shows that ships *could* sail with the wind before the beam. Rome failed to develop adequate shipping and seamanship, Nilsson, *Imperial Rome*, 1926, pp. 207–11. Trading-ships of 500–1000 tons, Oertel, *C.A.H.* X, pp. 413–14, but probably most under 100, Lefebvre des Noettes, *De la Marine antique à la Marine moderne*, 1935, p. 70, Walbank, *Decline of the Roman Empire in the West*, 1946, p. 16.

Owing to the blight of slavery technique stagnated and there was no wide internal market as a basis for industrialization, ibid. pp. 22–7.

P. 225, n. 1. On the date J. G. C. Anderson in *Anatolian Studies...to Sir W. M. Ramsay*, 1923, pp. 1–13 (like Pais). Strabo is scrimpy on remote lands and reluctant to give lists of barbarian names, as for Spain 155, Arabia 177, Dubois, op. cit. pp. 320, 327.

P. 226, n. 1. Mela too dislikes giving barbaric names, III, 15 and 20.

P. 228, n. 1. Schoff at first dated A.D. 60, but 70–89 in *J.R.A.S.* 1917, p. 830. J. A. B. Palmer in *C.Q.* 1947, pp. 137–40 dates the Indian political conditions of Peripl. 41, 51–3 as A.D. 110–15, and hints that it may be a compilation from different sources, not the record of one voyager.

P. 230, n. 1. On Schnabel's book Diller, *Class. Phil.* 1940, pp. 333–6, Hyde, *Amer. J. Phil.* 1941, pp. 244–6. Marinus floruit not after 120, Mžik on Ptol. I, 6.

P. 231, n. 1. Martial, with the snobbish smirk of an urbanized provincial, gives 'uncouth' names of places near his native Bilbilis, I, 50, IV, 55, XII, 18. Albertini, *Les Divisions admin. de l'Espagne romaine*, 1923. Melón, op. cit.

P. 234, n. 1. On Lucan's curious mistakes Bourgery, *Rev. de Phil.* 1928, pp. 31–3 (L. used a verse description, perhaps by Varro of Atax?). S. Reinach, *Cultes, Mythes et Religions*, 1908, I, 311–14. For a map after Ptolemy see Desjardins, *Géogr. hist. et admin. de la Gaule*, III, 1875.

P. 235, n. 2. The fleet went round, hence the good description of the west coast, thinks Tarn, *C.R.* 1942, p. 126. For Tacitus on Caesar see above, p. 194, n. 1.

P. 237, n. 1. For Ptolemy's drawing of the S. coast of England, H. Bradley, *J. Brit. Arch. Ass.* 1881, pp. 269–78. P.'s names and placings deserve great respect, W. J. Watson, *Celtic Place-Names of Scotland*, 1926, pp. 8–71, though the 'towns' are mostly guess-work: he denies Lossie, p. 39: Scetis and Dumna are Skye and Lewis misplaced, Malaios (Maleos) is Mull: P.'s Thule is Shetland, p. 42: the Camp has been thought Burghead, p. 31 ('Winged' merely means fortified in a certain way). Morecambe a bogus name, *Victoria County Hist. of County of Lancaster*, 1914, VIII, p. 65. For other Celtic scholars on P.'s northern names see (Sir) J. Rhys, *Celtic Britain*, 1882, pp. 158–62, 214–22, E. W. B. Nicholson, *Goidelic Studies*, 1904, pp. 28–31 (both accept Lossie). P. mislays the Caledonian Forest because he twists Scotland round, Rhys, p. 222. P. ignores Hadrian's Wall and uses information of the time between Agricola and its building, Sir G. Macdonald, *J.R.S.* 1919, pp. 136–8, 1939, pp. 21–2. See p. 234, n. 2. The Wroxeter inscription spells Cornovii.

ADDENDA

P. 237, n. 2. For 'Roman material in Ireland' found since Haverfield's paper see Ó Ríordáin, *Proc. R. Irish. Acad.* 1947, pp. 35–82 (kindly sent me by Prof. Bodkin).

P. 238, n. 1. A touch of real Celtic legend, Krappe, *Science of Folklore*, 1930, p. 90, and in *Speculum*, 1943, pp. 312–13, he connects with the island paradise which he traces back to the Abalus of Pytheas. I. A. Richmond, *Antiquity*, 1940, pp. 193–5 sees in Plut. *de Def. Orac.* 18 a real exploration in Agricola's time to the western isles of Scotland: so Soury, *La Démonologie de Plut.* 1942, p. 43 (but P. says little real).

P. 241, n. 2. Scadinavia means 'shady island' (as wooded), Karsten in *Hirt-Festschrift*, 1936, II, 489: so Gutenbrunner, ibid. p. 466 (and 'sinus Scadanus', dark sea?).

P. 241, n. 3. Sir J. Rhys, *Studies in Arthurian Legend*, 1891, p. 359 thinks the 'dead sea' meant the sea crossed by the dead.

P. 242, n. 1. The Germans liked Roman coins—and current ones—well enough, Dopsch, *Econ. and Soc. Foundations of Eur. Civ.* 1937, pp. 345, 359: rotation farming, pp. 35–7.

P. 244, n. 2. 'Suebian river' = Viadua = Oder, Gutenbrunner, op. cit. II, 460. The Veneti were originally Illyrian, and the name passed to the Slavs, thinks Karsten, ibid. p. 571. Aestii were Germans mixed with Balts, Karsten, ibid. p. 477. Fenni, Finni, a Germanic name ('finders' or 'gatherers') given to the primitive aborigines, and passed later to the Lapps and the present Finns, ibid. p. 482. Kvaen name originally Finnish (Kainulaiset), ibid. pp. 480–1: A. S. C. Ross, *The Terfinnas and Beormas of Ohthere*, 1940, p. 24. Finns in Estonia by first century A.D., later in Finland, thinks J. H. Jackson, *Estonia*, 1941, p. 38, *Finland*, 1940, p. 23. The Finns were then only beginning to cross the Gulf of Finland northwards (leaving some to take their neighbours' name as Esths); they were not the degraded savages of Tacitus, whose description is merely fantastic, Burnham, *Who are the Finns?*, 1946, pp. 80, 85.

P. 246, n. 1. There were tribal centres and in the west a good deal of trade, Dopsch, op. cit. pp. 57, 315–16, citing various writers on Ptolemy's 'towns'. Several names like Kalisia are Illyrian in origin, thinks Krahe, op. cit. II, p. 572.

P. 248, n. 2. On the development of the frontier from Augustus Pârvan, *Dacia*, 1928, pp. 158–60, 179–83.

P. 249, n. 1. On the N. frontier and on forts east of the Aluta H. S. Jones, op. cit. pp. 248–50. Daicoviciu, *Siebenbürgen im Altertum*, 1943, argues that a considerable Dacian population survived (even after Trajan's drastic conquest) to be soon and thoroughly Romanized, and many remained (even after Aurelian's drastic evacuation) to become the Rumanians there: against this thesis of continuity Alföldi, *Zu den Schicksalen Siebenbürgens im Altertum*, 1944. On the frontier, ibid. p. 72.

P. 250, n. 2. On Dacian towns Pârvan, op. cit. p. 195: some elements Celtic, p. 113. Ptolemy often used strangely out of date accounts, as here, Kubitschek, loc. cit., and cp. Müllenhoff, *Deutsche Alt.* IV, 51 on Germany, and his silence on Hadrian's Wall, Macdonald, loc. cit.

P. 251, n. 1. The plain to the Dniester was pacified under client kingdoms, and Olbia and Chersonesus accepted protection (Plautius), Pârvan, op. cit. pp. 180–1. In a curious romance, Lucian's *Toxaris*, a Bosporan king gives his daughter to a king of the Machlyes, and, with Alans and Sarmatians, helps him against a Scythian rival. Plautius probably only sent ships to the Crimea, Halkin in *L'Ant. classique*, 1934, p. 146. On Arrian's *Periplus*, Patsch, *Klio*, 1904, pp. 68–75 (defends against Brandis: all is well if 17–25 is transposed before 12–16): Chapot, *Rev. Ét. gr.* 1921, pp. 129–54.

P. 252, n. 2. Ptolemy's map of Sarmatia is almost worthless, Reche in Ebert's *Reallex*. Slaven, 1928, against Niederle's overestimate.

P. 252, n. 3. No word of these Chuni coming from the far east, though Hirth and Kiessling derive them from a Hiung-nu kingdom near the Jaxartes, beaten by the Chinese in 36 B.C., Maenchen-Helfen in *Byzantion*, 1945, pp. 231–3: Dion. Per. wrote 'Uitii', ibid. p. 250. An early Attila thus prevented, Cavaignac, *Hist. gén. de l'Antiquité*, 1946, p. 424.

ADDENDA

P. 253, n. 1. Amazons often in Mela, I, 13 and 116, III, 34 and 39.

P. 255, n. 1. Brunhes-Vallaux, *La Géographie de l'Histoire*, 1921, pp. 150–4, 293: Huntington, *Civ. and Climate*[3], 1924, ch. 20. Some hint of the value of a tidal estuary (Garonne) in Mela, III, 21, cp. Claudian, *in Ruf.* II, 113–14 and Ausonius, *Ordo Nobilium Urbium*, on Bordeaux. Plin. III, 45, VI, 143 is far more correct on the direction of the Italian boot than Ptolemy.

P. 255, n. 2. Climatic pulsations, Huntington, *Mainsprings of Civilization*, 1945, pp. 528–40: Brunhes-Vallaux, op. cit. p. 227 doubt if nomad migrations are often to be explained by such pulsations (or by gradual desiccation in inner Asia), but cp. Toynbee, *Study of History*, 1934, III, pp. 395–454.

Chapter IX

P. 256, n. 2. For the Jedi frontier Guey in *Mél. d'Arch. et d'Hist.* 1939, pp. 178–248.

P. 258, n. 2. But the Taza corridor *was* used, and by A.D. 200 there was a sort of outer Limes over the high plateau Tlemcen–Aumale, Carcopino, *Le Maroc antique*, 1943, pp. 237–42.

P. 259, n. 1. Suetonius crossed the Atlas E. of Tamghent, with the snowy Aiashi on the right, to the Ghir, Carcopino, op. cit. p. 37, after F. de la Chapelle, *Hesperis*, 1934, pp. 107–24.

P. 262, n. 1. Draa from Kaphas = Atlas, Carcopino, op. cit. p. 53.

P. 262, n. 2. As Gsell also Carcopino, op. cit. pp. 33, 172.

P. 264, n. 1. Cyrenaica began to decline after the Jewish rising, Romanelli, *La Cirenaica Romana*, 1943, pp. 116–18. The stretch east of Derna was apparently annexed to Egypt, Ptol. IV, 4, 1, IV, 5, 1, Romanelli, p. 119. A papyrus giving names here, ibid. pp. 124–8.

P. 268, n. 1. The Nigris 'qui Africam ab Aethiopia dirimit,' Plin. V, 30, is the Jedi, Guey, op. cit. p. 230.

P. 271, n. 2. Isthmus the frontier, not the Nile, which would 'split' Egypt, say Str. 32, Ptol. II, 1, 6, against old views ap. Hdt. II, 15–17 (not Hdt. himself).

P. 272, n. 1. Virgil, *Aen.* VI, 794–7 perhaps refers to Petronius, as some editors say.

P. 273, n. 1. Tacitus implies more than curiosity in Nero, Eva M. Sanford, *Harvard Studies*, 1937, p. 91, despite B. W. Henderson, *Nero*, 1903, p. 223.

P. 275, n. 2. The lakes are 'a long way inland', Ptol. I, 17, 6, and Diogenes is one of a list of skippers. Hyde, *Ancient Greek Mariners*, 1947, pp. 285–7 makes him reach the Lakes, passing within sight of Kilimanjaro and mistaking it for a range. On the process of modern exploration here, ibid. pp. 288–95.

P. 278, n. 1. The dream of a Terra Australis was ended by Cook, C. Lloyd, *Pacific Horizons*, 1946, pp. 26–7: he oddly traces the notion to Theopompus.

P. 280, n. 1. For Herodotus on the Nile see pp. 41, 66, 70–1. 'The learned Job Ludolphus' in *A new History of Ethiopia*, 1684, pp. 37–9 has a wonderful muddle including a real Blue Nile and a false western Nile flowing *west* through 'the country of the Nigrites' to the Ocean.

Chapter X

P. 284, n. 2. Indian or Arabian wares coming by way of Syria are often called by poets Syrian (or Assyrian), Tib. III, 6, 63, Hor. *Odes*, II, 7, 8, II, 11, 16 etc.

P. 285, n. 1. Southern guard-posts of Roman Arabia about Medain-Saleh, Seyrig, *Syria*, 1941, pp. 218–23.

P. 285, n. 2. It now appears that Palmyra was already annexed by Tiberius, Seyrig, op. cit. p. 170. Some of its traders went on to 'Scythia', i.e. Indoscythia, ibid. pp. 259–63.

P. 285, n. 3. For Roman times Abel, *Géogr. de la Palestine*, 1938, II, chs. 7–8.

ADDENDA

P. 287, n. 1. Possibly there is, or was, a subterranean outflow from Lake Van to the Bitlis river and so to the Tigris, D. G. Hogarth, *The Nearer East*, 1902, p. 39. Milton makes Satan hide in the Tigris tunnel, *Paradise Lost*, IX, 68–72. For the real tunnel of the *western* Tigris see above, p. 171, n. 2.

P. 287, n. 3. Erik Gren, *Kleinasien und der Ostbalkan in der wirtsch. Entwicklung der röm. Kaiserzeit*, 1941.

P. 290, n. 4. Eva M. Sanford, *Harvard Studies*, 1937, pp. 94–8 says Nero thought more of rivalling Alexander than of trade (as cp. Schur); he meant by the 'Caspian Gates' the Dariel (against the Alans), not Derbend (against the Albanians, as Tacitus).

P. 291, n. 2. A poetic commonplace is the fierce Hyrcanian tigress, Virgil, *Aen.* IV, 367, and how the hunter, to delay her swift pursuit, jettisons her cubs one by one, Lucan V, 405, Martial, III, 44, 6, Claudian, *in Ruf.* I, 227, as Mela, III, 43, Plin. VIII, 66.

P. 294, n. 1. But Oxian lake a first hint of the Aral, thinks Kretschmer, *R.E.* Scythia, 1923.

P. 295, n. 1. Cape Tabis in Mela, III, 60 is well north of his Tamus, the end-cape of the 'Taurus' range, off which is an island Chryse, ibid. and 68 and 70. See p. 313, n. 1. R. Burton, *Anatomy of Melancholy*, 1621 (Everyman ed. II, p. 35) still wonders 'whether... there be any probability to pass by the straits of Anian to China, by the promontory of Tabin'. For Mercator see Hakluyt, Everyman ed. II, p. 224, cp. p. 364: Oechardes, ibid. p. 213 (though Ptolemy had not sea but 'terra incognita' in the north).

P. 299, n. 2. The Scythian envoys mentioned with Indian in Suet. *Aug.* 21, Hor. *C.S.* 55, and the traders in Dio Chrys. *Or.* 32. 413, were Indoscythians, thinks Seyrig, *Syria*, 1941, p. 259 (very questionably). The Alexandrian glass found by Hackin at Begram (Afghanistan) came up the Indus, ibid. p. 262.

P. 300, n. 1. The *Memoirs* of Apollonius' disciple, Damis, which Philostratus professes to use, are a swindle, and the India of I, 18–III, 58 is as real as Laputa, P. de Labriolle, *La Réaction païenne*, 1934, pp. 175–88. Christian propaganda may quite well have reached the Indian ports early: if Thomas did not come, the legend shows knowledge of India, Gondophares and Mazdi=Vasudeva, Goblet d'Alviella, *Ce que l'Inde doit à la Grèce*, 1926, p. 134. V. Pisani in *Scientia*, 1939, I, p. 227.

P. 300, n. 2. For the drain, Walbank, *Decline of the Roman Empire in the West*, 1946, pp. 18, 43. On the bullionist argument against the East India Company, G. M. Trevelyan, *English Social History*, 1946, pp. 218, 323: Heckscher, *Mercantilism*, 1935, II, pp. 233, 253.

P. 301, n. 1. A list of the coin-finds by R. E. M. Wheeler in *Ancient India*, July 1946, pp. 116–21. Tamil mentions of 'Yavana' ships at Muziris, wines, mercenaries, etc., ibid. p. 21, citing books on the ancient Tamils by Pillai and Iyengar, Madras, 1929.

P. 304, n. 2. Wheeler and others, op. cit. pp. 17–124 report finds of Italian pottery of A.D. 20–50—but no coins—at 'an Indo-Roman trading-station' close to Pondicherry, which may be the ancient Poduce.

P. 306, n. 1. The diamond was certainly known to Pliny etc., Laufer, *The Diamond, a Study in Chinese and Hellenistic Folk-Lore*, 1915, p. 43.

P. 308, n. 1. Darautkurgan also Mžik in notes on Ptol. I, 11, 3, 1, 12, 8: K. Kretschmer, *R.E.* Scythia, 1923, who relies here mainly on Herrmann.

P. 311, n. 1. H. S. Jones, *Comp. to Roman History*, 1912, p. 320 thought Issedon Scythia was Kashgar and I. Serica Khotan.

P. 312, n. 1. Hyde, op. cit. p. 231 wrongly makes Kan Ying reach Syria.

P. 312, n. 2. 'Envoys', Goodrich, *Short Hist. of the Chinese People*, 1943, p. 73. Latourette, *The Chinese*², 1941, p. 130 finds An-tun himself 'somewhat dubious': so too some jugglers supposed to come from Ta-ts'in via Burma in A.D. 120, but cp. Goodrich, pp. 54, 73.

P. 315, n. 3. Marinus misunderstood Alexander's wording, and 20 days from Tacola (on gulf of Martaban) to Zabae hardly take one beyond Singapore Mžik, op. cit., notes on Ptol. I, 13, 8 and I, 14, 1.

P. 317, n. 3. Chinese envoys to Indian Ocean and perhaps across it, Goodrich, op. cit. pp. 38, 73.

P. 318, n. 1. Possibly from An-tun's 'envoys', also H. S. Jones, op. cit. p. 319 (he puts Cattigara in Tongking).

Chapter XI

P. 320, n. 1. Cp. Ovid, *Am.* II, 16, 19, 'si premerem ventosas horridus Alpes'.

P. 323, n. 2. S. temperate zone cut off from us by the torrid, Mela, I, 4 (as Plin. II, 172). In part of India 'neuter septentrio' appears, and the shadows fall southward, III, 61. On the rising sun seen from Mt. Ida, I, 94–5, cp. Diod. XVII, 7, 6. Black and Adriatic seas visible from the Haemus, II, 18 (see pp. 49, 220). Usual fable about the Crau plain of stones, II, 78 (see p. 41, n. 3). Shells in Numidia show sea once inland, I, 32: cp. Apul. *Apol.* 41, fossil fish in inland mountains of Gaetulia owing to Deucalion's Flood, noted by R. Eisler, *Isis*, 1942–3, p. 363.

P. 326, n. 3. 'This prophecy was fulfilled by my father', wrote Ferdinand Columbus in the margin of Seneca, Sir J. Sandys, *Harvard Lectures on the Revival of Learning*, 1905, p. 54.

P. 328, n. 2. Ancient views on volcanoes in Sudhaus, op. cit. pp. 51–9. The *Aetna* is Epicurean in its principles, P. de Lacy, *Trans. Amer. Phil. Ass.* 1943, pp. 169–78.

P. 329, n. 2. A poet knows that, when a ship recedes from land, the mast is the last part to disappear from sight, Val. Flaccus, *Argon.* I, 496.

P. 334, n. 2. Bilinski in *Eos*, 1946, p. 155 suspects some connection with Isidorus.

P. 335, n. 2. Two systems in Ptolemy, if *Hypotheses of the Planets* (later adopted by the Arabs) is his, McColley in *Studies and Essays...offered to George Sarton*, 1946, p. 331.

P. 336, n. 1. Eisler, *Royal Art of Astrology*, 1946, pp. 224–6.

P. 339, n. 1. Columbus knew his Marco Polo only after 1485, and was long not educated enough to appreciate Ptolemy, though a note on Agisymba in his copy of D'Ailly is before 1492, C. E. Nowell in *Univ. of Michigan Hist. Essays*, 1937, pp. 25–44.

P. 339, n. 2. On Vignaud's case J. N. L. Baker, *Hist. of Geogr. Discovery and Exploration*, 1931, pp. 76–8. On the latest views R. Almagià in *Scientia*, 1948, pp. 51–9.

P. 340, n. 1. Even Amerigo did not conceive the 'New World' in the modern sense, but still as a projection from Asia, thinks C. Errera, *L'Epoca delle Grandi Scoperte Geografiche*², 1910, pp. 337–41, as Fiske, *Discovery of America*, 1892, reprint 1920, II, 177.

P. 344, n. 1. The projection suggested by Marinus is the germ of Mercator's, Delevsky, *Isis*, 1942–3, p. 113.

P. 345, n. 1. On Ptolemy's projections Hopfner in Mžik, op. cit. pp. 104–5: Ninck, *Die Entdeckung von Europa*, 1945, pp. 74–7.

P. 348, n. 1. A philosopher quizzes a 'natural scientist' about his topsy-turvy Antipodes by showing him his reflection in a well, Lucian, *Demonax*, 22.

P. 348, n. 4. Galen (Kühn, IV, 798–805) closely follows the essay on *Airs*, E. C. Evans, *Trans. Amer. Phil. Ass.* 1945, pp. 296–7.

Chapter XII

P. 351, n. 1. On the causes of decline Walbank, *Decline of the Roman Empire in the West*, 1946.

P. 352, n. 1. Even the outermost peoples like the Scythians and Lice-eaters (apparently the old Budini) and Mouse-eaters (where?) are not cannibals, like the Christians with their communion, says Porphyry, *Gegen die Christen*, ed. Harnack, 1916, fr. 69 (about A.D. 270). Now E. A. Thompson, *The Hist. Work of Amm. Marc.* 1947 (on geogr. disquisitions, pp. 117–19).

P. 353, n. 1. The very names of German tribes are barbarous and warlike, 'bellicum strepunt nomina', Nazarius, *Paneg. ad Const.* 18.

P. 357, n. 1. Theodosius, who hardly passed London, *Amm. Marc.* XXVII, 8, is said to pitch his camp in Caledonian forests, Claudian, *IV Cons. Hon.* 27: S. Reinach, *Cultes, Mythes et Religions*, 1908, I, 258–64. Dicalidonae, meaning two groups of Caledonians, C. proper and Maeatae, thought Rhys, *Celtic Britain*, 1882, pp. 93, 164.

ADDENDA

P. 360, n. 1. Silphium was now a mere rarity, Synesius, *Ep.* 106, Romanelli, *La Cirenaica Romana*, 1943, p. 158: on Syn. ibid. pp. 140–1.

P. 362, n. 1. Among remote peoples, who are at least not cannibals, are the long-lived Ethiopians, Root-eaters, and Reptile-eaters, says Porphyry (passage quoted above). A Roman coin of A.D. 270 and beads of fifth-century R. Empire types are reported (rather doubtfully) as found in S. Rhodesia (and a coin of Constantine in Madagascar), Wainwright in *Man*, 1947, p. 145. The Pygmies-cranes commonplace is repeated by Claudian, XL, 13–14.

P. 363, n. 4. The Alexander romance becomes indifferent to facts of time and space, M. Braun, *History and Romance in Graeco-Oriental Lit.* 1938, pp. 31–43.

P. 365, n. 2. Cp. Maenchen-Helfen in *Byzantion*, 1945, pp. 222–51: *Wei Annals*, ch. 102, relied on by Hirth, etc., is a later interpolation and refers not to Hiung-nu but to White Huns taking Sogdiana (some time in A.D. 370–435): there were Huns near the Black Sea already in 150, Ptolemy's Chuni: some things in the descriptions of the Huns are unlike the Hiung-nu, and archaeological arguments are against the identification.

P. 367, n. 1. On the Chinese map of A.D. 267, Goodrich, op. cit. p. 75. Fu-lin first mentioned about A.D. 520, Laufer, *The Diamond*, 1915, pp. 7–8: a story how diamonds are got there is like one in Epiphanius, IV, 190 (and cp. Sindbad's Rokh and the cinnamon birds of Hdt. III, 111).

P. 368, n. 4. A few scraps of a travel romance by one Hierocles (of A.D. 400–50 ?) mention wise Brahmans but also Ear-sleepers and Shadow-feet and Hyperboreans, Müller, *F.H.G.* IV, 430, Jacoby, *R.E.* Hierokles (1913).

P. 371, n. 3. Fa-hien back in a foreign ship, Goodrich, op. cit. p. 86: the Chinese lagged as sea-farers for some time, ibid. p. 74. The sea route from China to Ceylon was opened about A.D. 320, Hornell, *Water Transport*, 1946, p. 231.

P. 372, n. 1. Sericulture reached Khotan early in 5th century, Latourette, *The Chinese*, 1941, p. 168.

P. 372, n. 2. Marinelli, op. cit. I, 287–9.

P. 376, n. 1. Censorinus, 13, 2 refers to the figure of Eratosthenes for the earth.

P. 376, n. 2. Itin. Ant. certainly derived from maps, H. S. Jones, *Comp. to Roman History*, 1912, p. 49.

P. 383, n. 1. Claudian (about 400) knows the real cause of eclipses, *Bell. Get.* 235–6, and is intelligent on tides, XVII, 107, and volcanoes, *R.P.* I, 171–6 (besides the conventional buried giants, ibid. 153, III, 183–7, and Neptune letting out the Thessalian lake, ibid. II, 179–83). He has the old geographical commonplaces, like the Eridanus, Panchaea, the Pygmies: cp. also Indians next the sun, *Phoenix*, 2–3. For C. on the Nile see p. 270, n. 2, on north p. 357, n. 1, on zones p. 362, n. 1, p. 376, n. 1.

P. 383, n. 2. The cosmology of Macrobius is Platonic, with Venus and Mercury above the sun (not going round the sun as Dreyer and Heath read him), Stahl, op. cit. p. 238: the figure $\frac{5}{60}$ is as Geminus 5, 45–6 and 16, 7–8, ibid. p. 253: M. dishonestly ascribes Greek things in astronomy to the Egyptians, ibid. p. 245.

P. 385, n. 2. Also W. W. Hyde, *Paganism to Christianity in the Roman Empire*, 1946, pp. 198–9. For Basil's *Hex.* see Courtonne, *St Basile et l'Hellénisme*, 1934: Bidez in *L'Ant. classique*, 1938, pp. 19–21. Marrou, *St Aug. et la Fin de la Culture antique*, 1938: Courcelle, *Les Lettres grecques en Occident de Macrobe à Cassiodore*, 1943.

P. 386, n. 2. Remarkable is a phrase of John Chrysostom about 'the islands outside this one', Migne, *Patr. Gr.* XLVII, p. 459, cited by Gisinger, *R.E.* Oikumene, § 26. See also p. 350, n. 2.

P. 389, n. 1. For an intelligent German cleric of 1069 on these things see Kohlmann, *Adam von Bremen*, 1908, pp. 40–50.

P. 389. The medieval universe is a strange complex of incompatible Aristotelian and Ptolemaic and Biblical elements, G. McColley in *Studies and Essays...offered to George Sarton*, 1946, pp. 324, 333–4. For medieval geography see Note on Books.

INDEX

This Index refers to the text: further details will often be found in the maps, notes and Addenda

Abalus, 147
Abyssinia, 10, 272, 278; *and see* Axum, Ethiopians
Achaeans, 13, 15, 18–21
   of Caucasus, 58
Achilles (writer), 382
Aden, 175, 296, 368
Adriatic, 19, 48–9, 87–8, 141–2, 249
Adulis, 136, 273, 361, 368
Aea, 22, 289
Aegean, 19–21
Aeolis, 20
Aeolus, Aeolian Islands (Lipari), 25–6, 104
Aeschylus, 59, 66, 82
Aestii, 244
Aetheria (Silvia ?), 377
Aethicus, 382
Aetius, 348
'Africa' (Roman province), 139, 181, 256, 358
Africa, general, 23, 64–78, 89–90, 136–9, 256–81, 358–62
   few inlets, 254, 278, 322
Agatharchides, 136, 175, 182, 210
Agathemerus, 373
Agathodaemon, island, 317
   mapper, 347
Agathyrsi, 57
Agisymba, 266–7, 270, 275, 281, 345
Agricola, 234, 237
Agrippa, map, 332–4, 374, 378, 381; *also* 184, 194
   roads, 233, 334
   Vistula, 241
Ahaggar, 70, 268
Alamanni, 353
Alans, 180, 229, 251, 290, 354
Alashia, 12
Albania (Caucasus), 171, 290
Albertus, 390
Albion, 54, 144, 194
Alcmaeon, 111
Alexander Lychnus, 215, 218, 329
   Polyhistor, 173, 218
   skipper, 314–15
Alexander the Great, 86, 123–36
   his altars, 381
   his columns, 252
   his gates, 291, 364
   itinerary of, 363
   on Nile, 82, 136
   popular romance of, 363

Alexandria (Egypt), 125, 138, 271
Alexandrian science, 156
Alfred, 375
Al-Idrisi, 389
allegory, 42, 350, 386, 388
Almagest, 335
Alpis, 49
Alps, 49, 140, 188, 233, 321
Altai, 63, 365
Alybe, 22
Amalcian sea, 150
Amazons, 22, 62, 103, 127, 141, 171, 186, 226, 229, 252, 329, 343, 352, 374
amber, 5, 13, 18–19, 24, 26, 49, 52–3, 147, 150, 241, 244
Amerigo Vespucci, 208, 340
Ammianus Marcellinus, 352, 362, 364, 373
Ammon (Siwa) oasis, 70, 89, 125, 139, 264
Ampelius, 375
Anartii, 239
Anaxagoras, 100–1, 105, 113
Anaximander, 47, 96–7, 102, 110, 122
Anaximenes, 96
Andaman Islands, 317
Andhra, 301
Angles, 243, 246, 357
An-si, 180, 312
ant-gold, 80, 301, 389
Antichthones, 323, 331, 375
Antilia, 339
Antioch, 172, 285
   as An-tu, 312
Antiochus III, 130, 169
   IV, 170, 173
Antiphanes, 151
Antipodes, 115, 122, 163, 167, 214, 216–17, 219, 324, 328–9, 331, 374–5, 383, 386, 390
Antoikoi (dwellers opposite), 203, 214, 323, 382
Antonius Diogenes, 238
Antony, 170, 173, 285
An-tun, 312, 317
Aorsi, 180, 251, 290
Apollodorus of Artemita, 173
   of Athens, 20, 204
Apollodotus, 173
Apollonius of Perga, 158
   of Rhodes, 141
   of Tyana, 299, 361
Apuleius, 331
Aquitania, 191, 233

INDEX

Arabia, 7, 9, 15, 17, 27
  Greeks on, 81–2, 133
  mapping, 297–8
  Ophir, 29
  Romans and, 172, 284, 286, 295–6, 362
Arabs, in E. Africa, 274
  on western Nile, 278, 390
Aral, 80, 85, 128, 180, 294, 364
Aratus, 117, 156, 205, 218, 375, 382
Araxes, 79, 85, 172, 290, 365, 381
Archelaus, 100
Archimedes, 114, 157–8
Archytas, 114
Arctic, 112, 116, 147, 209, 213–14, *and see* zones
Arculf, 389
Argaeus, 288
Argippaei, 62
Argonauts, 22, 58, 66, 84, 141, 148, 289–90
Argyra, 313, 317
Aria, 126, 292
Arimaspi, 62, 229, 294
Ariovistus, 190, 196
Aristarchus, 152, 157–8, 205, 330, 335, 348
Aristeas, 62
Aristides, 348
Aristotle, 35, 77, 86–90, 105, 107, 118–21, 153, 155, 211, 214, 348, 383, 386
Armenia, 28, 169, 222, 282–3, 289–90, 362
Arminius, 239–40
Aromata (Cape of Perfumes), 137, 274, 281
Arrian, 251, 286, 289–90, 348, 363
Artemidorus, 182, 188–9, 210, 225, 373
Arverni, 189, 191
Aryans, 14, 16–17, 31
'Asia' (province), 170, 287
Asia, general; name, 21
  boundaries, 66, 254, 271, 364
Asia Minor, descriptions, 171, 288–90
  early, 11, 17
  name, 171, 287, 363
  neck, 79, 87, 171, 288
  Romans in, 169–71, 282–3
Asii, 174, 178
Asoka, 130–1, 174
Assyria, 15, 19, 27–8, 47
  Roman province, 284
astrology, 36–7, 158, 167, 212, 217–18, 221, 323, 328–30, 335–6 (Ptolemy's), 347
  Christians on, 349, 384
astronomy, 36–7, 42
  Hipparchus and, 205
  Ptolemy and, 335
Asy, 12
Athens, 45
  dislike of physics, 101
  empire, 78, 87
Atlantic, 47, 91
  legendary islands, 92, 339

Atlantis, 26, 54, 90–3, 105, 115, 155, 214, 238, 339, 350, 382
Atlas, myth, 25, 35
  mapping, 259–61, 268, 359
  mountains, 70, 74, 139, 183
  Romans cross, 258
Atropatene, 173
Attacori, 131
  (Ottorocorrae, 310); *and see* Hyperboreans, Indian
Attacotti, 357
Attila, 355
Augila, 69, 264
Augustine, 42, 359, 374, 384, 386
Augustus, 222, 230, 232, 234, 238, 247
Aurelian, 362, 368
Aurès, 256, 265, 359
Ausones, 50
Ausonius, 378
Australia, 278, 318
Avallon, 238
Avars, 354, 365
Avienus, 53, 330, 369, 375, 382
Axum, 272, 300, 360–1, 368, 371
Azania, 274
Azores, 78, 184, 339, 391
Azov, sea of, 59, 87, 103, 129, 198, 209, 252

Babylonia: its horizon, 15–17
  canals, 133
  Greek debt to, 95
  Greeks on, 79, 135, 286–7
  later science, 158
  notions, 34–5, 39, 388
Bacon, Francis, 91, 93
  Roger, 119, 327
Bactra (Balkh), 126, 294
Bactria, kingdom, 126, 130, 173–4
  Chinese on, 178–81
  silk-road, 291–2
Badakshan, 16
Baetica, Baetis, 231
Bagradas, 260, 269
Bahrein, 133
Baker, Sir Samuel, 272, 276
Balbus (in Fezzan), 264
Balcia, 147
Balearic Islands, 228
Bali, 177
Balkan mountains (Haemus), 49, 56, 220, 249
Baltic, 226, 241, 246
Barbaria, 276, 361
Barbarians, 47, 123
Bardesanes, 384
Barygaza, 173, 298, 302
Basil, 364, 385–6
Basilia, 147
Basques, 52

Bastarnae, 198, 247
Batavians, 240
Bautae, 310
Bear, constellation, 31, 33, 37, 134, 210
bear, white, 200
Behaim globe, 339
Belgae, Belgica, 190, 193, 233
Bérard on Homer, 20, 24, 26
Berbers, 12
Berenice, 136, 273
   (Benghazi), 68
Berossus, 123, 158
Berrice, 146
beryls, 300, 303, 306
Bhils, 306
Biscay, 187, 230
Bithynia, 171
Black Sea, 11, 18, 20, 22–3, 45, 56–60, 141, 289, 373
   Arrian and the, 251
   overflow theory, 155, 293
Blemmyes, 360
Blest, Isles of, 78, 184, 238; *and see* Fortunate Isles
Boeotians, 107
Boethius, 383
Boii, 189, 239
Borneo, 317–18
Bosporus, anaplus of, 255
Brahmans, 177, 299, 368
Brandan, Saint, 339, 358
breadth-line of world, 163–4, 207, 210, 340–2
Breton language, 233
Brigantes, 234–5
Britain, 13, 55–6
   Caesar and, 193–5, 201, 207, 218, 222, 234–7, 356–8
   Pytheas and, 144–6, 149
Brittany, 54, 144, 192, 233
Brittia, 358
Bruce on Blue Nile, 280
Brutus (Spain), 186
Brythons, 144
Buckle, 108
Buddhism, 131, 174, 293, 300, 371
   art (Gandhara), 293, 311, 366
   pilgrims from China, 366, 371
Budini, 62
Bulgars, 354
Burgundians, 245, 353–4
Burma, 313–15
Byblos, 10
Byzantium, 45, 56
   mapping, 207, 342
   site, 209

Cabot, 340
Cadiz, *see* Gades
Caesar, Caius, 296
Caesar, Julius, 173, 187, 190–8, 218
Caledonians, 235, 356
Callippus, 119
Callisthenes, 153
   Pseudo-, 363
Calypso, 25–6
camel, 70, 266
Cameroon, 76
Canary Islands, 77–8, 184, 262, 323
Canidius, 170
cannibals, 61, 87, 145, 275, 357
Canopus (star), 116, 212, 327
Canton, 316, 390
Carausius, 356
Carians, 22
Carmania, 132
Carneades, 218
Carpathians, 197, 249–50, 356
Carthage, 30, 47, 50–1, 54, 68, 71, 76, 87–8, 136, 139–40, 142–3, 181, 256
Caspian Gates, 125, 206–7
   (Caucasus), 290–1, 364
Caspian Sea, 16, 28, 62, 66, 79–80, 85–6, 172, 293–4, 372
   as 'gulf', 124, 127–9, 163, 199, 209, 218, 226, 228, 252, 294, 328, 331, 364, 375, 387, 390
cassia, 81, 274, 297
Cassiodorus, 356, 381
Cassiterides, *see* Tin Islands
castes, Indian, 130
Castorius, 379
Cathay, 339
Cato, elder, 216
Cato, younger, African march, 181
Cattigara, 315–16
Caucasus, 16, 58, 86, 119, 170–1, 253–4, 290, 363–4
Caucasus, Indian, *see* Paropanisus
Cauvery, 304–5, 370
Celsus, 350
Celtiberians, 186
Celtoscyths, 189
Celts, 15, 51–2, 56, 87–9, 124, 139, 144–7, 233
Cerne, 74–6, 90, 184, 261, 321
Ceylon, 131, 134, 208, 300, 302–3, 306, 329, 342, 370–1
Chad, lake, 266, 267, 270, 281
Chalcidius, 382
Chalybes, 18, 22, 58, 60, 84, 289
Chang K'ien, 178–81
Charax, 286
Chariot of the Gods, 75–6, 261, 270
Charybdis, 25, 27
Chatti, 196, 239
Chera, 301, 307
cherry brought, 228
Cherusci, 196, 239
China, name, 313
   Great Wall of, 178, 364, 367

INDEX

China, Roman coins in, 311
Chinese horizon, 32–3, 178–81, 311–12, 366–7
  notions, 42–3
Chinese in western writers, *see* Seres, silk, Sinae, Thina, Tzinista
Chinese Turkestan, *see* Tarim
Chorasmia, 127
Chremetes (= Chretes ?), 74, 89
Christianity, 285, 364, 368
  attitude to earth-globe, 386–9
  attitudes to pagan science, 42, 123, 349–50, 384–5
Chryse, 313–15, 369
Chuni, 252
Cicero, 193, 217, 383
Cilicia, 17, 28, 47, 170, 287
  Gates, 82
Cimbri, 26, 189, 196, 239, 241
Cimmerians, 25–6, 28, 60, 190, 202
cinnamon, 81, 297, 303
Cinnamon coast, 137, 273
Cipango, 338–9, 390
Circe, 25
Clapperton, 269, 280
Clashing Rocks, 22, 25
Claudian, 375
Claudius, 299, 362
Cleanthes, 157
Clement of Alexandria, 300, 349
  of Rome, 350
Cleomedes, 148, 215, 331
Cleopatra, 182
climate, maritime, 122, 151, 153
  Mediterranean, 44, 222
'climates', 116, 122
  the seven, 221, 335–6
climatic changes, 80, 132, 183, 255, 285
  influence, 106–9, 188, 209, 214, 322, 327, 347, 384
Coan, *see* silk
Codanovia, 241
Codanus, Sinus, 241
Colaeus, 46, 53
Colchis, 22, 39, 58; *and see* Lazica, Phasis
Columbus, 3, 30, 91, 119, 282, 326–7, 338–40, 343, 373
Comedae, 308–9
comets, 120, 326
Commagene, 282
Comorin, 304–5
compass, 317
Confucius, 32
Constantine, 351
Constantinople, 351, 354
Constantius, 363
continental drift, 93
continents, boundaries, 10, 59, 66, 209, 254, 271, 290, 364
  names, 21, 41

Cook, 37, 278
Copernicus, 121, 152, 158
Corbulo, 283
Corinth, 45
Cornwall, 13, 55, 144–5, 151, 193, 357
Coromandel, 304
Corsica, 51, 140
Cosmas, 36, 43, 361, 364, 369
  theory, 386–9
cosmogony, 34
counter-earth, 111, 152
Crassus, M. (Danube), 247
Crassus, P. (East), 173, 283
Crassus and Tin Islands, 195
Craterus, 129, 132
Crates, 26, 202–3, 217, 322, 331, 378, 383
Crete, 12–13, 16, 19, 21, 23
Crimea, 26, 59, 87, 170, 198, 250, 355
Cronian sea, 148, 357
Cronos, 237
Ctesias, 86, 102, 137
Cumae, 50
Curtius, 286, 291, 293, 347
Cyclopes, 25
Cymry, 190
Cynetes, 52
Cyprus, 12–13, 16, 20, 28, 78, 103
Cyrene, 67–8, 139, 181, 263, 360
Cyrus, elder, 28, 44, 84, 126
Cyrus, younger, 82
Cyrus, river (Kur), 171, 290

Dacia(ns), 198, 222, 248–50, 353–4
Dahae, 127, 181
Dalmatia, 197, 239, 247
Damascus, 11, 27, 172
Damastes, 82, 102
Danes, 356
Danish islands, 241, 246
Danube, 18, 22, 48, 52, 56, 88, 238
  branch to Adriatic, 48, 141, 197, 226, 250
  Roman frontier, 197–8, 247–50, 351, 353–5
  symmetry with Nile, 98
Daradus, 261, 269
Dardanians, 197, 249
Dariel, 290
Darius, 60, 81
Dead Sea, 104, 172, 285
Deccan, 301
Deimachus, 130
Delgado, 275, 277
Delos, 170
Delphi, 201; *and see* navel
Demetrius of Bactria, 173
  of Callatis, 105
  of Scepsis, 21, 105, 204
Democedes, 79
Democritus, 65–70, 89, 100, 113, 167
Demodamas, 127

TH

denudation, 103, 153
Derbend, 290
Deserters (Sennar), 66, 138
diamonds, 300, 306
diaphragm (central parallel), 98, 134, 141, 153, 164
Dicaearchus, 124, 134, 138, 142, 153–5, 164, 204
Dicalydones, 357
Dicuil, 333, 381
diffusionists, 6
Dimensuratio Provinciarum, 333, 381
Diocletian, 351
Diodorus Siculus, 123, 186, 215
  of Tarsus, 387
Diogenes of Apollonia, 89, 101
  skipper, 275
Dionysius of Byzantium, 255
  of Periegetes, 228–9, 235, 252, 302, 304, 329, 375, 381
  of Syracuse, 87
Dioscoros, skipper, 275
Dioscurias, 58, 171, 289
dip of earth, southward, 96
Divisio orbis, 333, 381
Dog-heads, 69, 325
Don, *see* Tanais
Dorians, 20
Draa, 74, 184, 269
drain of specie, 300–1
Druids, 190, 192, 218
Drusus, 238
dumb barter, 5, 73, 307, 315, 361, 367
Dumna, 237, 247
Dura, 285
Durdus, 261
Dyrin, 184, 261

Ear-sleepers, 130, 147, 325
earth, flat, 35, 42, 94–101; *and see* dip, north
earth-globe, *see* globe
earthquakes, 41, 91, 102, 105–6, 214, 288, 322, 325, 385
Ebudae, *see* Hebrides
eclipses, 36, 41, 95, 101–2, 325
  for longitude, 207–8, 343
Ecphantus, 152, 384
Eden (Paradise), 40, 340, 382, 388–9
Egypt, Greeks in, 64–5, 91, 122, 170, 270–1, 360
  horizon, 5–15, 19, 23
  map, 38–9
  notions, 34–9
Elam, 17, 28
Elba, 50
Elbe, 56, 146, 189, 222, 239
elephants, 17, 24, 69, 136–7, 183, 369
elevations and subsidences, 120, 214
elks, 197, 253

Elysium, 40, 78
Eneti, 22, 49
Ephorus, 87, 89, 97, 102, 388
Ephthalites, *see* Huns (White)
Epicureans, 167, 216
epicycles, 158, 205
equator, habitable, 163, 177, 209, 213, 215, 321, 335
Eratosthenes, 124, 134–5, 138, 143, 146, 154, 158–66, 205, 210, 228, 273, 321, 324, 331
Erembi, 23, 202, 329
Eridanus, 49, 52–3, 56, 141, 150
Eryth(e)ia, 81, 261
Erythraean, *see* Red Sea
Esdras, 338–9
etesian winds, 12, 89
Etheria, *see* Aetheria
Ethiopians, 9–10, 23, 36, 66, 80, 90
  compared with India, 107, 138, 166, 206; *and see* Abyssinia, Agisymba, Axum
  Ptolemies and, 137
  Romans and, 272, 359–61
ethnographical clichés, 64, 110, 242
Etna, 104
  poem, 328
Etruscans, 13, 19, 26, 47, 50–1
Euclid, 156
Eucratides of Bactria, 174
Euctemon, 88, 102
Eudemus, 153
Eudorus, 213
Eudoxus of Cnidus, 88, 115–17, 122, 143, 154, 156, 205, 272
  of Cyzicus, 176, 185–6, 213, 262, 277
  of Rhodes, 117
Euhemerus, 133
Eumenius, 378
Euphrates, 9, 15, 82, 286
  frontier, 173, 282, 364
Europe, name and boundaries, *see* continents
  superiority of, 107–9, 255, 322
Eusebius, 378
Eustathius, 330
Euthydemus, 174
Euthymenes, 77
Euxine, name, 57; *and see* Black Sea
evolution, 103
Exodus, 11
Expositio totius mundi, 363, 368
Ezekiel, 31, 33

Fa-hien, 366, 371
Fathers, *see* Christianity
Fenni, Finns, Gulf of Finland, 61, 244, 247, 355–6
Fezzan, 69, 264, 336
firmament, 33, 42
Firmicus Maternus, 384

INDEX

Fish-eaters (Makran), 132, 135
  elsewhere, 262, 318
fisheries, 59
Flaccus, Septimius, 266
  another F. (?), 263
  Valerius, on Argo, 290
Flavians, 222
Fleece, Golden, 22
Flood, 91, 120, 350, 375, 387
Fortunate Isles, 184, 262, 337, 359
fossils, bones, 103
  sea-shells inland, 43, 103, 350, 375
Frankincense Coast, 137, 296
  terraces, 7
Franks, 353–5
Frisian islands, 240
Frumentius, 360
Fu-lin, 366–7

Gades, 53, 88, 185, 187, 211, 231
Gaetuli, 183, 258–9
Galatians, 124, 170, 282
Galen, 348
Galileo, 158
Gallus, Aelius, 271, 295
  Sulpicius, 216
Gandhara art, *see* Buddhism
Ganges, 129–31, 217, 304, 306, 313, 388
Garamantes, 69, 183, 256, 264–5, 270, 359, 362
Gaul(s), 140, 188–92, 232–4
Gauti, 355
Geir, 269
Gelonus, Geloni, 62, 355
Geminus, 148, 214
Genesis, 28, 31
geology, Greek, 103–6
geometry, 38, 95
Ger, 258, 268–9
Germanicus, 239, 271, 328
Germans, Germany, 146, 189–90, 196–9, 238–47, 353–4
  name, 196
Gerrha (Gerra), 133, 175
Getae, 56, 198, 249
Ghadames, 264, 359–60
Ghats, 85, 305
Ghir, 259
Giants, 41, 103, 328, 375
Gibraltar, 26, 46, 88, 155
  reef, 102, 155
Gildas, 358
ginger, 303
Gir, 270
giraffe, 10, 138, 182, 212, 361
globe, earth, 43, 110–22, 167, 203, 321, 323–4, 326, 328, 330, 334, 382–3, 389
  Fathers on, 386–9
  measurement, 154, 159–62, 205, 212–13, 321, 324, 334

globe, revolves, *see* Aristarchus,
  rotates, 115, 326, 384
gnomon, 195
Gog and Magog, 28, 127, 291, 364, 389
Goidels, 144
Golden Chersonese, 315, 340
Gomer, 28
Gonds, 306
'Gorgons', 261
Gorillas, 75–6, 281
Goths, Gotones, Gut(h)ones, 147, 239, 241–4, 249, 353–6
Gutae, 246
Greece poor, 44
  colonial movement, 44–7
Greeks, coming of, 14; *see* Achaeans, Dorians
Greek wisdom from East, 95, 123
Griffins, 62, 226, 294, 355, 382, 389
Guinea, 73, 391
Guiones, 147
Gulf Stream, 151, 255, 358
Guptas, 369
Gymnosophists, 130
Gyzantes, 69

Habiru, 11
Hadhramaut, 296; *and see* Arabia, Frankincense
Hadrian, 222, 234, 284, 289
Haemus, *see* Balkan
Halizones, 22
Halys, 79
Hammurabi, 15
Han, 177
Hannibal, 140
Hanno, 54, 73–6, 90, 183, 261–2, 270, 324, 359
Hanoi, 316
Harkhuf, 10
Hatshepsut, 7
Hauran, 284
Havilah, 368
Hebrews, 11, 27, 39
Hebrides, (H)aemodae, Haebudes, Ebudae, 146, 235–6
Hecataeus of Abdera, 123, 133, 150, 238
  of Miletus, 47, 49–69 *passim*, 79–82, 85, 102, 107
  map, 97–9
Heligoland, 147, 150, 240
Heliodorus, 361
Helixoia, 150
Helvetii, 189–90
Hemodus, *see* Himalaya
Henry of Portugal, 76, 186, 278, 391
Henu, 7
Heraclides, officer of Alexander, 127
  Ponticus, 90, 152
Heraclitus, 96
Hercules, 41, 46

27-2

420 INDEX

Hercules, Pillars of, *see* Gibraltar
Hercynian Forest, 87, 197, 239–40, 242, 246, 249
hermits and monks, 360, 377
Herodotus, 48, 78–9, 49–82 *passim*, 103, 107
 map, 97–100, 107
Heruli, 355
Hesiod, 21, 24, 26, 34, 41, 238
Hesperides, 36, 261
Hicetas, 152
Himalaya, Hemodus, Imaus, 131, 134, 307–8
Himilco, 54–5, 74
Hippalus, 176, 298
Hipparchus, 117, 124, 143, 147, 155, 159, 166, 205–8, 320–1, 323–5, 334, 342
Hippocrates on *Airs*, 106, 348
Hippolytus, 384
hippopotamus, 65, 75, 182, 323
Hittites, 11, 16–19
Hiung-nu, 32, 178; *and see* Huns
hodometer, 327
Holland, 239
Holy Land, 377; *and see* Palestine
Homer, 20–7, 34–6, 40–1, 156, 159, 202, 204, 209, 225, 288, 321
Homerites, 296, 369
Honorius, Julius, 381
Horace, 219
Huns, 63, 174, 252, 318, 355, 365; *and see* Hiung-nu
Huns, White, 365
Hwang-ti, 32
Hyksos, 11
Hyperboreans, 21, 36, 57, 63, 98, 102, 150–1, 252, 323, 343
 Indian, 36, 131
Hyrcania, 80, 125–6, 291

Iabadiu, *see* Jabadiu
Iambulus, 176, 215
Iazyges, 248
Iberians of Caucasus, 171, 290
 of Spain, 52, 231
Iceland, 149–50, 339
Ictis, 145
Ierne, *see* Ireland
Ili, 174, 178
Illyrians, Illyricum, 48, 88, 141, 197
Imaus, *see* Himalaya
incense, 7, 9, 133; *see* Frankincense
'India', loosely used, 300, 360, 368
India, early, 9, 17, 28–30, 36
 Chinese knowledge, 180
 Greek knowledge and mapping, 80–1, 129–31, 134, 165, 173–7, 207
 Indus-Nile, 82, 124, 361–2
 Roman knowledge and mapping, 298–306, 368–70
Indian Ocean, closed, 277–8, 318, 390

Indo-China, 315–16, 318, 370, 372
Indo-Europeans, *see* Aryans: in Tarim, 178
Indoscythians, 174, 229, 293, 301
inhabited worlds, other, 166, 213, 322, 331, 350, 383
Ionian Sea, 48
Ionians, 20, 28, 78, 95
Iran, 14, 16, 80, 125–6, 135, 291–4, 364; *and see* Parthia, etc.
Ireland, 54, 144, 194, 235, 237, 334, 357–8
Irenaeus, 350
iron, 18, 197
Isidore of Seville, 389
Isidorus, 286, 291
Islam, 362, 390
Issedones, 62–4, 294, 310
Ister, *see* Danube
Istria, 48
Istros, 56
Italics, 15
Italy, 19
 advantages, 209, 254
 Greeks in, 49–51
 name, 50
Ithaca, 21
Itineraries, 332, 376–7
 Alexandri, 363
 Antonine, 376, 379
 Christian, 377–8
ivory, 7, 9, 24, 274

Jabadiu, Java, 281, 316, 371, 390
jade, 18, 33
Javan, 28, 31
Jaxartes, 85, 127–8
Jerome, 357, 378, 382
Jews on Greek wisdom, 123
 and Romans, 172, 284; *and see* Hebrews
Jonah, 31
Jordanes, 356, 358, 382, 389
Juan-Juan, 365
Juba I, 181
Juba II, 181, 258, 262, 296
 theory of Nile, 70, 267–8, 323, 361
Jugurtha, 181
Julian, 362, 368, 374, 378, 382
Justin (Trogus ap.), 173
Justinian, 351, 354, 360–1, 371
Jutes, 246, 357
Jutland, 13, 148, 196, 240–1

Kandahar, 126, 291
Kan Ying, 312
Karun, 133
Kashgar, 174, 180, 310
Kassites, 15–16
Kattegat, 241
Keftiu, 12
Kenya, 275

INDEX

Kepler, 115, 158
Kharga, 69
Khotan, 180, 309, 371
Khyber, 129
Kiao-chi, 316
Kidinnu, 205
Kur river, *see* Cyrus
Kush, 9
Kushans, 292, 301

Lactantius, 386
Laestrygones, 25
Langobardi, 239, 354
lapis lazuli, 16
Lapps, 244, 355
Latinus, 26
latitude, 116, 122, 134, 342
  how observed, 143, 147, 153, 207
Lazi, Lazica, 289, 363; *and see* Colchis
Lebanon, 6, 9
Lemnos, 22, 104
length-line of world, 119, 164–6, 210, 331
Leptis, 265
Leucas, 21
Leuce, 56
Leuce Come, 284
Leucippus, 100
Leviathan, 27, 34
Libya(ns), 12, 23, 67–8
Libyan depression, 103, 153; *and see* Ammon
lighthouses, 226, 271
Ligurians, 51
Lipari, *see* Aeolian Islands
Lisbon, 231, 357
Livy, 140, 221
Lixus, 74
Lizas, 74
Locust-eaters, 138, 360
Lombards, *see* Langobardi
London, 235
longitude, 165, 207, 343
Lotus-eaters, 25, 68–9
Lou-lan, 180
Lucan, 263, 272, 328
Lucian, 238, 347
Lucretius, 216
Lucullus, 170, 173, 228
Lugians (Vandals), 244, 246
Lusitania, 186, 231
Lycia, 12, 25, 287
Lydia, 19, 28, 44

Macedonia(ns), 56, 86, 139, 141, 169–70, 197–8
Macrobius, 203, 217, 383
Madagascar, 274, 281
Madeba map, 378
Madeira, 26, 78, 92, 184, 262
Maeatae, 356

Maeotis, *see* Azov
Maes, 291, 294, 307, 309, 311
Magan, 17
Magellan, 340
magnetic islands, 317
Mago, 71
Mainace, 53
Malaya, 30, 315
Male (Malabar), 370; *and see* pepper
Man, Isle of, 194, 357
Mandeville, 389
Manetho, 123
Manilius, 328
maps, early, 37–9
  in Lyceum, 153
  Ionian, 97–102, 119
  Roman, 219, 332–4, 378–81; *and see* Eratosthenes, Hipparchus, Ptolemy, etc.
Marcianus, 363, 368, 372–3
Marcomanni, 196, 239
Marcus Aurelius, 222, 249, 284, 312, 325
mare-milkers, 21, 355
Marib, 295
Marinus, 229, 265–6, 291, 294, 307, 309, 315–16, 334
Marmaridae, 263
Martianus Capella, 374
Massagetae, 62, 64, 80
Massalia, Massilia, Marseilles, 51, 143, 145, 189
  placing, 207, 321, 342
Maternus, 266
Matieni, 79
Mauretania, 182, 222, 258–9, 359
Maxyes, 12, 69
Medes, Media, 28, 125, 173, 290, 292
medieval geography, 389–91
Mediterranean, 44, 97
  length, 142, 334, 337
  name, 373
megaliths, 13
Megarians, 44
Megasthenes, 130, 134, 301–2
Mela, 218, 225–6, 323
  on various parts, 231, 235, 241, 267, 313
  used later, 357, 373
Menander (King), 174
Menelaus, 23, 202
Menippus, 289
Menuthias, 274
meridians, early attempts, 98
mermaids, 132, 240
Meroe, 10, 66, 134, 138, 266, 271, 273
Meropis, 155
Meru, Mount, 36, 369
Merv, 126, 173, 364
Meshech, 31
Mesopotamia, 16, 172
  (name), 284, 287

Messina, 26, 106, 121, 140, 165, 207
meteorites, 120, 325
meteors, 325
Meton, 102
Metuonis, 146
Mexican maps, 37
Mictis, see Ictis
Midacritus, 55
midnight sun, 150
milestones, 221, 334, 377
Miletus, 45, 47, 57, 78
Minoans, 12, 19, 27, 40
Minos, 19, 21
Mitanni, 11, 17
Mithridates, 170
Modura, 302, 306
Moesia, 247-8
Mona, 194, 234
Mongolia, 318; and see Hiung-nu, Huns
monsoons, 175, 224, 228, 296, 298, 302; see Hippalus
monstrous peoples, 130, 273, 325, 360, 389
Montesquieu, 108
moon, 100, 211, 330, 335; and see tides
Moses, 123, 172, 388
Mossynocci, 58, 84
mountains, ancients on, 320
  heights of, 119, 154, 220
Mountains of the Moon, 89, 275, 361
Mozambique current, 71, 277
Mulucha, 183, 259
Muscat, 274
music of the spheres, 111, 167, 383
Muza, 296
Muziris, 301-2, 368
Mycenae, 13, 18
Myoshormos, 136, 273
Myrrh Coast, 137
mythical geography, 33-43, 97; see Ocean, Eden

Nabataean Arabs, 172, 284
Nagas, 315
Nanking, 316
Napata, 10, 271
Naples, 50
Narbonensis, 189
nard, 300
Nasamones, 70, 263, 266
Nature, love of, 320
Naucratis, 64
navel of the earth, 40, 98, 201
Nearchus, 132-3
Necho, 71-2, 98, 163, 277
Nelcynda, 301-2
Neoplatonism, 383
Neopythagoreans, 218, 324, 331
Nepos, 199, 201, 324
Nervii, 189

Nestorian missions, 364, 367
Neuri, 61
Newton, 162
Nicagoras, 117
Nicias, 101, 209
Nicobars, 317
Nicolaus of Damascus, 173
Nigeir, 269
Niger, 70, 266, 268-70, 280, 390-1
Nigidius, 217
Nigris, 259, 267, 269
Nigritae, 183, 268
Nile, abysses, 41, 271
  canal, 9, 71, 81, 136, 273
  delta, 103
  exploration, 10, 66, 136, 138, 272, 275;
    modern, 272, 275-6
  from India, 82, 124, 361-2
  from Ocean, 41, 66, 77, 138
  from South Zone, 117, 272, 323, 361
  from west, 70-1, 77, 89, 138, 267-8, 278, 323, 327, 389-90
  mapping, 138, 275-6
  marshes or lakes, 89, 138, 275
  other theories, 65-6, 89, 272, 323, 329, 348, 374
  rains, 65, 89, 130, 138, 182, 209, 272
Nineveh, 28, 44
Niphates, 171
Nobades, 360
noble savage, 21, 198, 242
Nonnos, 369
Noricum, 197, 238
north part of earth higher, 96, 387; and see Rhipaean
North Sea, 240
Norway, 149-50, 241, 246
Nuba, lake, 270
Nubia, 9, 64, 137
Numantia, 257
number-mysticism, 115, 218, 349
Numidia(ns), 139, 181, 256
Nun, cape, 186

oases of Sahara, 69, 264
obliquity of ecliptic, 96, 153, 163
Ocean, continuous, 97-9, 119, 163, 185, 208-9, 213, 324, 361
  equatorial, 168, 202, 213, 322, 324
  mythical, 24, 27, 34-5, 39-41, 62, 64, 97-9
  not continuous, 90, 208, 277, 342
  outer sea, northern, 87, 213, 252
  southern, 90
Ochus, king, 82
Odysseus, Odyssey, 23-7, 240, 357
Oechardes, 295, 309
Oenopides, 89, 113, 153
Oestrymnis, 54, 144

INDEX

Ogygia, 25, 237
Olbia, 59, 198, 207, 251
Onesicritus, 132
onyx, 85, 301
Ophellas, 139
Ophir, 29, 30, 313, 340
Oporto, 231
orb, 203, 378, 383; *and see* Crates
orbis terrarum, 201, 222
Orcades, Orkneys, 146, 195, 234
Origen, 385
Ormuz, 132, 175
Orosius, 359, 363, 365, 374, 382
Ottorocorrae, *see* Attacori
Ovid, 247, 328
Oxus, 80, 85, 126–8, 172, 294, 362
Ozene, *see* Ujjain

pacers, 124
Palestine, 11; *and see* Hebrews, Holy Land, Jews
Palmyra, 285, 362, 377
Pamirs, 308
Panaetius, 211, 213
Panchaea, 133
Pan Ch'ao, 311–12
Pandya, 299, 301
Pannonia, 239, 247, 249
Panticapaeum, 59
Paphlagonia, 22
Pappus, 372
papyri, 280, 348, 378
Paradise, *see* Eden
parallax, 158
parallel, central, *see* diaphragm
parasang, 62
Park, Mungo, 76, 280
Parmenides, 112–13, 122, 321
Paropanisus, 85, 126
Parthia(ns), 28, 127, 173, 222, 282–4, 286
 as An-si, 180, 312
Patna, 131, 174, 176
Patrick, St, 357
Patrocles, 127–9, 163, 199, 324
Paul, 224
Pausanias, 204, 253, 281, 317–18, 348
peacocks, 29
pearls, 292, 300
Peneus, 105
pepper, Pepper Coast, 300–2, 369, 381
Perfumes, Cape of, *see* Aromata
Pergamum, 124, 170
Pericles, 102
Perimulic gulf, 316
Perioikoi, 166; *and see* inhabited worlds, Transatlantic
Periplus Maris Erythraei, 228, 274, 292, 297, 301–4
Persian empire, 28, 44, 78
 in Chinese notices, 366

Persian empire, Sassanid, 362
 gulf, 17, 23, 28, 30, 81, 86, 136, 292, 298, 363, 370
Persis, 125, 132
Petra, 285
Petronius, 271
Peutinger map, 333, 369, 379–81
Phaeacians, 25, 91
Pharusians, 183
Phasis, 58–9, 84, 106, 113, 289, 363–4
Phauni, Phryni, 174
Phileas, 102
Philemon, 235, 241
Philip of Macedon, 86
Philistines, 11
Philistus, 88
Philo Judaeus, 331, 349
Philo, officer of Ptolemy, 138, 160
Philolaus, 111, 114
Phlegraean fields, 104
Phocaeans, 44, 46, 51
Phoenicians, 3, 10, 12, 23–4, 30–1, 40, 50–3, 133
 in Britain ?, 55, 195 (Tin Islands), 285; *and see* Carthage, Sidon, Tyre
Phrygia(ns), 18, 28, 44
Picts, 357
Pillars, horizon, 35
 of Hercules, *see* Gibraltar
Pius, Antoninus, 234
Plato, 90, 103–4, 112–15, 211
Plautius, 248
Pliny, 226–8, 323–5
 copiers of, 355, 373–4
 on Africa, 259, 261–3, 267, 272–3
 on Asia, 285–9, 290, 294, 297–8, 302, 313
 on Europe *passim*, 231–5, 241–3, 252
Plotinus, 369, 383–4
Plutarch, 238, 330–1
Polemo, 204
Polo, Marco, 278, 338, 370, 390
Polybius, 74, 170, 216
 on Africa, 183–4, 225
 on theory, 209
 on W. Europe, 186–90
Polynesians, 281
Pompey, 170, 172
Pontus, 170, 282, 288
population, 45, 223
porphyry, 350
portolans, 390
Porto Santo, 184, 339
Portugal, *see* Lusitania
Portuguese, 76, 186, 278
Posidonius, 172
 equator habitable, 163
 in later writers, 214–15, 324, 327, 331, 334, 336
 on Africa, 182, 185, 267
 on climate, 107
 on earth measurement, 212–13

Posidonius, on theory, 211–14
　on W. Europe, 188–9, 192, 195–6
Prasum, 275, 277, 281
precession of equinoxes, 205
Prester John, 186, 278, 390
Priscian, 375
Priscus, 354
Probus, 353
Proclus, 383–4
Procopius, 352, 358, 362, 389
projection, 166, 208, 322, 344–5
Promathos of Samos, 77
Pseudo-Aristotle *on Universe*, 121, 331
　Flood of the Nile, 121
　Wonderful Stories, 121
Pseudo-Callisthenes, 363
Pseudo-Scylax, 88
Pseudo-Scymnus, 210
Psylli, 68, 181, 263
Ptolemais of the Hunts, 136–7
Ptolemies, 123, 136–7
Ptolemy (Claudius), 229–30
　astrology, 335–6
　astronomy, 335
　geography, 335–45
　his copiers, 372–3, 389
　on Africa, 259, 261–5, 269–71, 273, 275–7
　on Asia, 286–7, 289–90, 292, 294, 298, 302–10, 313–17
　on Europe, *passim*, 232–4, 236–7, 245–7, 250–2
　text and maps, 345–7
Punt, 7, 9
Purple Islands, 262
Pygmies, 10, 24, 273, 277, 281
Pyrenees, 52, 88, 188, 231–2
Pyrrhus, 139
Pythagoras, Pythagoreans, 64, 79, 111–14, 118, 120, 122
Pytheas, 143–51, 153, 193–4, 201, 206, 209–10, 215, 240, 321, 388

rabbits, 228
Raetia, 238
rains, in India, 130; *and see* Nile
Ratzel, 108
Ravenna Geographer (Ravennas), 379, 389
Red Sea, name, 7, 81
　voyages, 7, 9, 81, 136–7, 273, 295, 360, 368
reindeer, 52
Rhapta, Rhaptum, 274–5, 281
Rhegium, 105
Rhine, 52, 190, 222
rhinoceros, 138, 266, 272, 361
Rhipaean mountains, 21–2, 61–2, 87, 141, 150, 199, 227, 241, 252, 355
Rhodes, 19, 170; *and see* diaphragm
rivers, 103–4, 119
Road, Royal, 79

roads, Roman, 200, 221, 223, 233
　desert, 136, 273
Romans, incurious in science, 200, 216, 320, 325
　wild geography, 220
Roman writers on geography, 225–8, 323–9, 373–6, 381–3; *and see* maps
Rome, early mentions, 50–1, 88
　site, 221
rotation, *see* globe
Roxolani, 198, 252
Rumanians, 353
Russian history, 253–4
Ruwenzori, 276

Sabaeans, 29, 133, 175, 295–6
Sabana, 315
Sacae, 80, 178
Sacarauli, 174
Sacastene (Seistan), 174, 291, 293
Saevo, Mons, 241
Sahara, oases, 69, 264
　rivers, 70, 267–70
　Roman expeditions to, 258, 264–7
Salice, *see* Ceylon
Sallust, 183, 219, 226
Salvian, 354
Samarcand, 126, 294, 364
Saracens, 286, 362
Sardinia, 13, 19, 26, 51, 88, 140
Sargasso Sea, 55, 78
Sarmatia(ns), 198, 248, 251–3
Sargon, 15–16
Sassanids, *see* Persian empire
Sataspes, 73
Satyrs, 281, 317
Saxons, 242, 246, 353, 356
Scandia, 246
Sca(n)dinavia, 149–50, 241, 355, 358, 388
Scandza, 356
Sceptics, 168, 348
Schine, 318
Scipio, 141, 146, 186, 193
Sciri, 198
Scordisci, 197
Scotti, 357
Screrefennae, Scrithifinni, 356
Scylax, 80–1, 96, 132; cp. Pseudo-Scylax
Scylla, 25
Scymnus, 210; cp. Pseudo-Scymnus
Scythians, 22, 60, 87, 294, 309–10
sea, depth of, 119, 155
　curdled or dead or sluggish, 148, 241, 244, 253, 358; *and see* Cronian
　outer, *see* Ocean
　unsailable, 9, 73, 91, 213, 253
　why salt, 102
Sebosus, Statius, 262
Seleucia (on Tigris), 173, 284
Seleucids, 123, 126

INDEX

Seleucus (King), 127, 130
  (scientist), 157, 204, 208, 211
Sembritae, 138, 273; *and see* Deserters
Semiramis, 28
Semites, 15
Semnones, 239, 244
Seneca, 271, 301, 325–7
Senegal, 73, 76, 184, 261, 278
Serapio, 207
Serendivi, Serendib, 368, 372 (Ceylon)
Seres or Silkmen, 132, 174–5, 282, 309, 371
serica, silk, 174, 300, 366–7
  Chinese notices, 177–81, 311–12, 366, 368, 370–1
  silk-roads, in Iran, 291–3
  Stone Tower to Sera, 307–11
Seric iron, 311
Serinda, 371
Sertorius, 184, 187
Serus, 318
Servius, 375
Sesostris, 9, 11, 39
Severian, 387
Severus, Septimius, 284, 356
  in Scotland, 372
Sextus Empiricus, 348
Shadow-feet, 85, 361, 389
Sheba, 29; *and see* Sabaeans
shells inland, *see* fossils
ships, 6, 12, 23, 31, 46, 140, 224
Si-an, 309, 316, 367
Siberia, 63, 174, 294
Sicans, 50
Sicels, 50
Sicily, 19, 21, 26, 30, 50, 87–8, 105, 140
Sidon, 24
Sidonius, 354
Sielediba, 372
Sierra Leone, 73, 76, 391
Sigynnae, 57
Silingae (Vandals), 244
silk, Chinese, notions of, 307
  Coan, 86, 306
  wearing of, 174, 367; *and see* Seres, serica
silkworms, introduction of, 371
silphium (Cyrene), 67, 263
silting, 103, 287, 322
Silver Mountains, 77, 89
Silvia, *see* Aetheria
Sinae, 315–16, 338
Singapore, 315
Sinim, 33
Sinope, 57, 288
Siraci, 250
Sirbonian bog, 172
Sirens, 25–6
slavery, 45, 170, 224
Slavs, Sclaveni, 354–6; *and see* Neuri, Venedi
Snefru, 6

Sobat, 272
Socotra, 134, 274, 297, 368
Socrates, 101
Sodom, 104
Sofala, 30
Sogdians, 126, 294
Solinus, 355–7, 359, 364, 368
Soloeis, 73
Solomon, 29–30
Solomon Islands, 313
Solon, 90
Somaliland, *see* Cinnamon, Myrrh, Punt
Sopatros, 370
Sophists, 101
Southern Horn, 75
Spain, 16, 19, 52–3, 88, 139–40
  Roman, 186–8, 230–2
  Vandals, 354
Spain west to India, 119, 166, 213, 322, 326–7, 338–40
Sparta, 78, 105
stade, value of, 161–2, 213, 334
Stadiasmus Maris Magni, 363
stars, divine, 114, 121, 167
  angels push, 387
Stein, Sir Aurel, 178, 311
Stephanus of Byzantium, 375
Stilicho, 357, 359
Stoics, 121, 157, 167, 211, 217
Stone Ages, 4–5, 14, 33
Stone Tower, 307–9, 337, 367; *and see* serica, silk
Stonehenge, 5, 150
Strabo, 169, 224–5, 321–3
  follows Polybius, 209
  on Africa, 182–6, 259
  on Asia, 171, 286, 288–9, 301, 304
  on climatic influence, 107, 322
  on Europe, 122, 188, 192, 194–5, 198
  on Homer, 21, 26
  preserves Eratosthenes and Hipparchus, 124, 159, 205
Strato, 57, 155–6
Stromboli, 104; *and see* Aeolian Islands
Sudan, 9, 268
sudd, 10, 272
Suebi, 196, 242–4, 354
Suetonius Paulinus, 258
Suez, 7, 136
Sugambri, 196
sugar, 300
Suiones, 244, 246
Sumatra, 313
Sumerians, 15–16
sun, notions of, 36, 97–8, 168, 329, 388–9
  hissing in sea, 329, 382
  large in Spain, 210
survey of Empire, 332, 381–2
Sweden, *see* Suiones
Switzerland, 189–90, 238

INDEX

Sybaris, 49
symmetry, notion of, 98, 100, 278
  of worlds, 202-3, 331
sympathy in universe, 211, 348
Syracuse, 50-1, 87, 125
Syria, 11-12, 16-17, 19, 27, 79, 124
  Romans in, 172, 284-5
Syrtes, 68, 263

Tabis, Tabin, 131, 295
table of nations, 28, 39
Tacitus, 198, 234, 242-4, 329, 358, 382
Tahia, 178, 181
Tamarus, Tamus, 131, 313
Tamil, 302
Tanais, 59, 141, 146
  boundary of Europe, 59, 254, 290
  false connection with Jaxartes, 85, 127, 172, 293
Taprobane, see Ceylon
Tarim basin, 180, 308-11
  classical art in, 311, 366; and see Buddhism, Seres, serica
Tarshish, 29
Tartessus, 29, 53-5, 89, 92
Ta-ts'in, 312, 367, 370
Taurus, 16, 28, 134, 171, 207
Ta-wan, 178, 180
Taxila, 129, 174
Temala(s), 131, 314 (map)
Temese, 26
Teneriffe, 26, 262
terra australis, 277-8, 318, 323, 342
Tertullian, 349
Teutons, 15, 147, 189
Thales, 64, 77, 95, 110
Theodore of Mopsuestia, 387
Theodosius (writer), 215
Theon Ochema, see Chariot of the Gods
Theon of Alexandria, 372, 382
  of Smyrna, 331
Theophrastus, 153
Theopompus, 88, 151
Thera (Santorin), 104
Thin(a), 315
Thinae, 316
Thomas, St, 299
Thrace, 21, 56, 198, 248
Thrasyalces, 65
Thrinacie, 25-6
Thucydides, 102
Thule, 145-51, 201, 235-8, 323, 326, 339, 355, 358, 373-5
Tiao-chi, 180, 312
Tibareni, 58
Tiberius, 239, 247, 300
Tibesti, 69, 266, 281
Tibet, 310, 313
tidal waves, 91, 105

tides, 27, 89, 120, 189, 193
  due to moon, 146, 204, 211, 330, 335, 385
  theories, 120, 155, 202, 322-3, 325, 328, 330, 335, 373
  uniform in outer seas, 163, 208, 213
Tigris-Van mistake, 171, 286, 290, 363
Timaeus, historian, 140, 143, 145
  Plato's, 115, 211
Timbuctoo, 268, 280
Timosthenes, 137
tin in Britain, 13, 26, 56, 143, 145, 193-5, 235, 357
  in Spain, 16, 55, 89, 195, 231
Tingis, Tingitana, 258
Tin Islands, 55, 195, 232
Tochari, 174, 178, 293, 366
Tongking, 33, 317
Toynbee, 108
trade and industry, scale of, 45, 223
Trajan, 222, 248, 289, 299
Transatlantic continent, 91, 151, 166; and see Perioikoi, inhabited worlds
Trapezus (Trebizond), 57, 84, 282, 288-9
Tripoli(s), 68, 181, 264, 359
Tritonis, lake, 68, 260-1, 263
Trog(l)odytes, 280
Trogus, 173
tropic line, 117, 138, 271
  desert belt, 213
Troy, 11, 13, 18, 20-2, 204, 288
Ts'in, 177, 313
Tubal, 31
Tunisia, 12, 69
  projection misconceived, 139, 342; and see 'Africa'
tunny, 56
Turks, Western, 365, 372
Tursha, 13
Tyrannio, 217
Tyre, 11, 28-9, 124
Tzinista, 370

Ubii, 196, 240
Ujjain, 174, 301
Ulysses, see Odysseus
unicorn, 85, 361, 369
unsailable, see sea
Ur, 16
Urals, 59, 63, 253-4, 294
Ushant, 144
Utopias, 92, 110, 133, 138, 151

Valerius, Julius, 363
Van, lake, 82, 283, 362; and see Tigris-Van
Vandals, 243-4, 246, 249, 353-4, 359
Varro (Atacinus), 218
  M. Terentius, 169, 218, 226, 374, 376
Vasco da Gama, 2, 277, 391
Vegetius, 376, 378

INDEX

Venedae, Venedi, 199, 244, 356
Veneti of Gaul, 144, 190
  of Italy, 49, 57
Verde, cape, 76
Vespasian, 290
Vesuvius, 104, 226, 326, 328
Vibius Sequester, 375
Vicarello cups, 377
Virgil, 218-19, 375
Visigoths, 354; *and see* Goths
Vistula, 241, 246
Vitruvius, 267, 327
Vivaldi, 186
volcanoes, 41, 104, 214, 288, 322, 328, 385
Volga, 61-2, 79, 252, 294, 318, 372

waters, 33-5, 42, 95, 386-7
Western Horn, 75, 261
White Sea, 375
Wight, Isle of, 143
Wild-beast country, 69
winds, *see* etesian

women, communism of, 57, 87, 110, 176
world-egg, 34, 42
Wu-sun, 178

Xenophanes, 96, 103, 113, 388
Xenophon, 82, 102, 141, 170, 289
  of Lampsacus, 147
Xerxes, 78

Yangtse, 318
Yellow River, 32, 318
Yü, 32
Yue-chi, 178, 292, 366

Zabae, 315
Zagros, 16, 291
Zanzibar coast, 229, 274, 277, 361
Zemarchus, 372
Zimbabwe, 30
zones, 116-117, 122, 154, 163, 214, 217, 321, 323-4, 328, 335, 359, 375, 382-4, 390-1
Zuyder Zee, 239

LIBRARY
STATE TEACHERS COLLEGE
WAYNE, NEBRASKA